The Law of Athens

Vol. I

The Law of Athens

Volume I

The Family and Property

A.R.W. Harrison

New Edition

Foreword and Bibliography by
D.M. MacDowell

Published in the U.K. by
Gerald Duckworth & Co. Ltd
London

Published in North America by
Hackett Publishing Company, Inc.
Indianapolis/Cambridge

To M.E.H.

Cover illustration: from busts of Aischines and Demosthenes

First published in 1968 by Oxford University Press
This edition published, with permission, in 1998 by
Bristol Classical Press
an imprint of
Gerald Duckworth & Co. Ltd
The Old Piano Factory
48 Hoxton Square, London N1 6PB
and by
Hackett Publishing Company, Inc.
P.O. Box 44937
Indianapolis, Indiana 46244-0937

U.K. edition:
ISBN 1-85399-570-3

U.S. edition:
ISBN 0-87220-410-3 paperback
ISBN 0-87220-411-1 cloth
ISBN 0-87220-414-6 paperback set (Vols. I and II)
ISBN 0-87220-415-4 cloth set (Vols. I and II)
LC number 98-13464

A CIP Catalogue record for this book is available from the British Library

The paper used in this publication meets the minimum requirements of American National Standard for Information Sciences - Permanence of Paper for Printed Library Materials, ANSI Z39.48-1984

Printed in the United States of America

FOREWORD

THE law of classical Athens is a subject which straddles two academic professions, law and classics. For historians of law its special interest is that it is almost the only developed but pre-Roman system of which a fairly full reconstruction is possible, thanks to the survival of about a hundred forensic speeches of the Attic orators and a substantial quantity of Athenian inscriptions on stone. For classical scholars Athenian law is an essential part of Athenian life, revealing much of politics, religion, and moral beliefs. These two approaches have often been divided by geography. In continental Europe, especially Germany, Athenian law has been studied mainly by academic lawyers, who see it as a remote ancestor of their own civil law systems. In anglophone countries, on the other hand, it has received little attention from lawyers, but more from classicists having a historical and literary background.

A.R.W. Harrison struck a happy medium. He was an ancient historian by profession, but he had a sound knowledge of Roman law, and, as the preface to his first volume shows, he saw himself as a successor to the great European writers on Athenian law, especially Beauchet and Lipsius. His first volume does in fact largely supersede their works as far as the family and property are concerned. His second volume remained incomplete (as explained in its preface), so that for the topics omitted from it Lipsius remains indispensable.

In the years since Harrison's death no one else has attempted to produce a detailed study of the entire field. I have myself offered a shorter account of the whole subject in *The Law in Classical Athens*, and more recently Todd has produced another, *The Shape of Athenian Law*, concentrating more on the law's social implications. At a more specialized level European legal historians have continued to produce good studies of particular problems: Thür's *Beweisführung vor den Schwurgerichtshöfen Athens* is an outstanding example. On procedural and constitutional topics there are several important books by Hansen. Britain has been the principal location for editions of the relevant Greek texts, including a new edition of *Inscriptiones Graecae*, vol. i, by the late David Lewis, a commentary by Rhodes on the Aristotelian *Athenaion Politeia*, and commentaries by myself and others on several of the forensic speeches. In America the early history of Athenian law (mainly before Harrison's period) has been elucidated in Gagarin's *Drakon and Early Athenian Homicide Law* and *Early Greek Law*. Court procedures and buildings are discussed in Edward E. Cohen's *Ancient Athenian Maritime Courts* and in Boegehold's *The Lawcourts at Athens*. At the sociological end of the subject there are two important books by David Cohen: *Law, Sexuality, and Society*; and *Law, Violence, and Community in Classical Athens*.

These books and others of the last three decades are listed in the selective bibliography which I have compiled for this reissue of Harrison's work (pp xxi-xxiii in vol I; pp xvi-xviii in vol II). They exemplify a wide diversity of approaches to Athenian law—still, it seems, with a geographical basis: head west if you want sociology, east if you want jurisprudence. But it would not be right to imply that there is a schism among the scholars in this field. The contrary is the case; and this is due in large part to an initiative taken by the late H.J. Wolff. A German scholar who had spent the period of the Second World War in America, he inaugurated in 1971 a series of colloquia on ancient Greek law which has continued at intervals of two or three years until the present time. These meetings bring together scholars from many different countries, and their papers are published together in the volumes entitled *Symposion*, which give a good impression of the range of work in progress. Harrison died too soon to participate in these colloquia. He worked largely alone, and thus it is the more remarkable that he produced the best work of the last half-century on Athenian law.

June 1997 D.M. MacDowell

PREFACE

THIS volume aims at providing a systematic account of the law of Athens concerning the family and concerning property. It will be followed by a second volume dealing with the law of obligations and of procedure. The scope of the inquiry is deliberately restricted to Athens during the period of the orators.

Though much may have been gained for the Roman and the comparative lawyer by the wide horizons, spatial and temporal, over which many recent writers on Greek law have cast their gaze, much has been lost for those who are more concerned to get a keenly focused picture of the law of the one Greek city state for which, at this one period of its history, a considerable mass of detailed evidence is available than to reconstruct a somewhat hypothetical system of 'Greek' law. It has been a mistake to think that a study of the papyri could contribute much to the elucidation of Athenian law of the fourth century, though it may be that rules well-authenticated for that law can help to elucidate rules which seem to be operative in the papyri. This is strikingly illustrated by F. Pringsheim's learned work, *The Greek Law of Sale* (Weimar, 1950). Useful as that book must be for those whose primary interest is the law of the Roman empire, and valuable as are many of the discussions of individual problems proper to classical Athenian law, it presents to the student of this latter law a frustratingly blurred and indeterminate picture.

Any work in this field must owe much to the two most recent comprehensive treatises on the law of Athens, those of Beauchet and of Lipsius. Each of them raises important issues of principle as to the proper selection and disposition of material.

The most important issue raised by Beauchet is his restriction of his subject to private law. He explains briefly what he understands by this on pp. xlviii ff. of his preface. It leads him to exclude in principle such topics as the rules concerning the acquisition and loss of citizenship, everything relating to criminal law (he does not, incidentally, define criminal law), including topics which have a clear connexion with private law, such as penal actions designed to protect property or the facts giving rise to delictual obligations, and in general procedural law, which governed the sanctions for the rules of private law which are his primary concern. This programme has serious defects, and indeed Beauchet by no means adhered to it. Of course the legal historian must carve up his subject in order to make a meal of it, and all such dismemberments are bound to have an element of the arbitrary in them. But it is doubtful whether for Athenian law the division into private and other law is fruitful. It may not perhaps be conclusive against it that a contemporary Athenian would probably not have seen the significance of it; but its inadequacy is amply proved by Beauchet's own failure to follow it out systematically. Thus he devotes about sixty pages to the so-called civil actions protecting property, among them seventeen to the δίκη ἐξούλης, which by a rather face-saving understatement he admits to have had 'in certain respects' the character of a penal action. In truth it is impossible to arrive at any idea of what in Athenian law corresponded to our own concept of property without a full discussion of the remedies. Again Beauchet has about forty pages on the actions concerned with guardianship, actions which were for the most part markedly penal in character, but an understanding of which is indispensable for the understanding of the institution as a whole. As a principle of exclusion therefore the concept of private law does not work, and I have disregarded it.

Another, and even more questionable, principle followed, albeit tacitly, by Beauchet is to fill out gaps in the structure due to lack of direct evidence by drawing not only on rules ascertainable for other contemporary or roughly contemporary Greek states but on the rules of Roman law. I have attempted to be much more strict in this respect.

Methodologically Lipsius's book stands at the opposite extreme to Beauchet's. It is in form an account of Athenian legal procedure—naturally, since it grew out of Meier and Schömann's *Der attische Process* though in practice it includes discussion of the rules of substantive law which the procedural law was designed to protect. Thus it is more embracing than

Beauchet's book. Its three books deal with (I) the machinery for the administration of justice, (II) the various legal remedies open to litigants, (III) the course of procedure (*Prozessgang*). Even here there is something left out, namely what we should now call the rules of constitutional law (except those which were concerned with the administration of justice). This is in accordance with modern conceptions, though here too it is not entirely clear what the exclusion would have meant to an Athenian. Almost certainly the 'laws' dealing with constitutional matters would not have been neatly segregated in the Athenian code. However that may be, this degree of exclusion seems more defensible than Beauchet's. What is more open to criticism is Lipsius's principle of arrangement of his material. Briefly this is to stick closely throughout to procedural remedies. Thus his second book subsumes the substantive rules under the various actions. These are segregated first into *γραφαί* and *δίκαι*, and within these two categories the actions are grouped under the magistrates responsible for each. This method has its inconveniences. In particular the treatment of *γραφαί* and *δίκαι* in two separate sections instead of bringing together *γραφαί* and *δίκαι* which dealt with the same subject-matter is sometimes confusing.

The method followed in the present works is a compromise between those of Beauchet and Lipsius. I have started with a dichotomy between procedural and substantive law. This is not absolute, and in some topics—the law of property is the most striking example—the two threads are inextricably interwoven. Nevertheless there is a large body of rules which are simply procedural. The discussion of these is reserved for a succeeding volume.

In treating of the substantive law I follow the plan of Beauchet, adhering to his threefold division into the law of the family, the law of property, and the law of obligations (this last reserved for the succeeding volume), save that I take the law of succession under the law of the family rather than under the law of property.

In referring to the orators I give the name of the orator, the number of the speech, the short title of the speech, and the number of the section, in that order. In citations I make no distinction between genuine and spurious speeches, though occasionally I call attention to the distinction where it affects the value of the citation as evidence.

My debts are too numerous for individual acknowledgement, but I must make specific mention of my colleagues in the sub-faculty of ancient history at Oxford, to my own college, Merton, and its former Warden, John Miles, to Miss E. A. Livingstone, who compiled the index of sources, and to the staff of the Clarendon Press.

A. R. W. HARRISON

May 1967

CONTENTS

LIST OF ABBREVIATIONS xv

BIBLIOGRAPHY xx

PART I · LAW OF THE FAMILY

I. MARRIAGE

§ 1. Introduction 1

§ 2. ἐγγύη 3

§ 3. ἐπιδικασία 9

§ 4. Less formal unions 13

§ 5. Polygamy 15

§ 6. Forms 17

§ 7. Legal bars to marriage 21

§ 8. ἐπιγαμία 29

§ 9. Relations between husband and wife

(i) κυριεία 30

(ii) Marital fidelity 32

(iii) Offences allied to adultery 36

§ 10. Dissolution of marriage

(i) By death or statutory regulation 38

(ii) Dissolution at the instance of either or both spouses 39

(iii) Children of parents whose marriage was dissolved 44

§ 11. Dowry

(i) Introduction 45

(ii) Bestowal of dowry 48

(iii) Dowry during marriage 52

(iv) Dowry after dissolution of marriage 55

(v) δίκη προικός, δίκη σίτου 57

II. CHILDREN
§ 1. νόθοι 61
§ 2. Legitimation 68
§ 3. Parental authority 70
§ 4. Rights of children 78

III. ADOPTION
§ 1. Introduction 82
§ 2. Qualifications for adopter and adoptee 84
§ 3. Procedure 89
§ 4. Effects 93

IV. GUARDIANSHIP
§ 1. Introduction 97
§ 2. Males
(i) Appointment 99
(ii) Functions of guardians 104
§ 3. Females
(i) Introduction 108
(ii) Appointment 109
(iii) Functions of guardians 111
§ 4. Actions
(i) φάσις 115
(ii) εἰσαγγελία 117
(iii) δίκη ἐπιτροπῆς and δίκη σίτου 119

V. SUCCESSION
§ 1. Introduction 122
§ 2. The estate 124
§ 3. Intestate succession: order of succession
(i) Sons 130
(ii) Heiresses 132
(iii) Ascendants 138
(iv) Collaterals 143
§ 4. Wills
(i) Introduction 149
(ii) Capacity 151

(iii) Form 153
§ 5. Entry
(i) Immediate 156
(ii) ἐπιδικασία 158

VI. SLAVERY
§ 1. Introduction 163
§ 2. Origin of status 164
§ 3. Legal status
(i) *Vis-à-vis* the state 166
(ii) *Vis-à-vis* masters 171
(iii) *Vis-à-vis* third parties 176
§ 4. Public slaves 177
§ 5. Actions 178

VII. FREEDMEN
§ 1. Introduction 181
§ 2. Origin of status 182
§ 3. Characteristics of status 184

VIII. METICS
§ 1. Terminology 187
§ 2. Characteristics of status 189

PART II · LAW OF PROPERTY

I. OWNERSHIP AND POSSESSION
§ 1. Introduction 200
§ 2. Ownership 201
§ 3. Possession 204

II. PROCEDURAL PROTECTION
§ 1. Introduction 206
§ 2. Movables: ἀπαγωγή, ἐφήγησις 206
§ 3. δίκη εἰς ἐμφανῶν κατάστασιν 207
§ 4. Formal seizure, warranty, summons 210
§ 5. διαδικασία 214
§ 6. δίκη ἐξούλης, δίκη ἐξαιρέσεως 217
§ 7. δίκαι οὐσίας, καρποῦ, ἐνοικίου 222

III. KINDS OF THING
§ 1. Land and chattels 228
§ 2. Visible and invisible 230
§ 3. Productive and unproductive 232
§ 4. Ancestral and acquired 233
§ 5. Public, sacred 234

IV. CAPACITY TO OWN 236

V. JOINT OWNERSHIP 239

VI. MODES OF ACQUISITION 244

VII. EASEMENTS 249

VIII. REAL SECURITIES
§ 1. Introduction 253
§ 2. Types 258
§ 3. Pledge 260
§ 4. Hypothec 262
§ 5. Sale with right of redemption 271
§ 6. Rules in pledge, hypothec, and sale with right of redemption 280
§ 7. *ἀποτίμημα*
(i) Pupillary 293
(ii) Dotal 296
(iii) Miscellaneous 303
§ 8. Security in maritime loans 303

IX. PUBLIC NOTICE 305

APPENDIX A. Judicial dissolution of marriage of *ἐπίκληρος* 309

APPENDIX B. *δίκη ἐξούλης* 311

APPENDIX C. *ἐξαγωγή* 313

APPENDIX D. Mineral rights 315

APPENDIX E. U. E. Paoli on types of real security 316

ADDENDA 319

INDEX OF SOURCES 321

GENERAL INDEX 339

LIST OF ABBREVIATIONS

(*See also Bibliography*)

AAW — *Anzeiger der Akademie der Wissenschaften*. Philosophisch-historische Klasse (Vienna).

AEG — *Annuaire des études grecques.*

AG — *Archivio giuridico.*

AHDO — *Archives d'histoire du Droit oriental.*

AJA — *American Journal of Archaeology.*

AJP — *American Journal of Philology.*

An. Bekk. — A. E. Bekker, *Anecdota Graeca* (Berlin, 1814–21).

AP — *Archiv für Papyrusforschung und verwandte Gebiete.*

ATL — B. D. Meritt, H. T. Wade-Gery, M. F. McGregor, *The Athenian Tribute Lists* (Princeton: i, 1939; ii, 1949; iii, 1950).

Beauch. — L. Beauchet, *L'Histoire du Droit privé de la République athénienne* (Paris, 1897).

Becker, *Plat.* — W. G. Becker, 'Platons Gesetze und das griechische Familienrecht' (*Münchener Beiträge zur Papyrusforschung und antiken Rechtsgeschichte*, 1932).

BIDR — *Bullettino dell'Istituto di Diritto Romano.*

Boeckh, *Staatsh.* — A. Boeckh, *Die Staatshaushaltung der Athener* (3. Auflage, Berlin, 1886).

Bo. Sm. — R. J. Bonner (with G. Smith), *The Administration of Justice from Homer to Aristotle* (Chicago: i, 1930; ii, 1938).

BPW — *Berliner Philologische Wochenschrift.*

Bruck, *Schenkung* — E. F. Bruck, 'Die Schenkung auf den Todesfall im griechischen Recht' (*Studien zur Erläuterung d. bürgerlichen Rechts*, Hft. 31, Breslau, 1909).

BSGW — *Berichte der Sächsischen Gesellschaft der Wissenschaften.* Philologisch-historische Klasse.

Bu. Sw. — G. Busolt (with H. Swoboda), *Griechische Staatskunde* (Mueller, *Handbuch der klassischen Altertumswissenschaft*, 4. Abt., 1. Teil, 1. Bd., München, 1920, 1926).

Caillemer, *Succession*	E. Caillemer, *Le Droit de succession légitime à Athènes* (Paris, 1879).
Dareste, *Dem.*	R. Dareste, *Plaidoyers civils de Démosthène, traduit en français avec arguments et notes*, 2 vols. (Paris, 1879).
Demisch, *Schuldenerb.*	E. Demisch, *Die Schuldenerbfolge im attischen Recht* (Borna–Leipzig, 1910).
DS	C. V. Daremberg (with E. Saglio), *Dictionnaire des Antiquités* (Paris, 1877–1919).
Erdmann, *Ehe*	W. Erdmann, 'Die Ehe im alten Griechenland' (*Münchener Beiträge zur Papyrusforschung und antiken Rechtsgeschichte*, 1934).
F.Gr.H.	F. Jacoby, *Die Fragmente der griechischen Historiker* (Berlin, Leiden, 1923 onwards).
FHG	C. Müller, *Fragmenta Historicorum Graecorum* (Paris, 1841–70).
Fine, *Horoi*	J. V. A. Fine, 'Horoi: studies in mortgage, real security and land tenure in ancient Athens' (*Hesperia*, Suppl. 9, Baltimore, 1951).
Finley, *Land*	M. I. Finley, *Studies in Land and Credit in Ancient Athens 500–200 B.C. The Horos Inscriptions* (New Brunswick, 1951).
Gernet, *Dem.*	L. Gernet, *Démosthène, plaidoyers civils*, 4 vols. (Paris, 1954, 1957, 1959, 1960).
Gernet, *DSGA*	L. Gernet, *Droit et Société dans la Grèce ancienne* (Paris, 1955).
Gernet, *Lys.*	L. Gernet (with M. Bizos), *Lysias, discours I–XV, XVI–XXXV et fragments* (Paris, 1924, 1926).
Gernet, *Plat.*	L. Gernet, *Platon. Œuvres complètes, tome XI. Les Lois* (Paris, 1951).
GGA	*Göttingische Gelehrte Anzeigen.*
Glotz, *Solidarité*	G. Glotz, *La Solidarité de la famille dans le droit criminel en Grèce* (Paris, 1904).
Guiraud, *Prop. fonc.*	P. Guiraud, *La Propriété foncière en Grèce jusqu'à la conquête romaine* (Paris, 1893).
HAC	C. Hignett, *A History of the Athenian Constitution* (Oxford, 1952).
Hafter, *Erbtochter*	E. Hafter, *Die Erbtochter nach attischem Recht* (Leipzig, 1887).
Hitz.	H. F. Hitzig, *Das griechische Pfandrecht* (München, 1895).
Hruza, *Beitr.*	E. Hruza, *Beiträge zur Geschichte des griechischen und römischen Familienrechtes. I, Die Ehebegründung nach*

	attischem Rechte. II, *Polygamie und Pellikat nach griechischem Rechte* (Erlangen, Leipzig, 1892, 1894).
IJ	R. Dareste (with B. Haussoulier and T. Reinach), *Recueil des inscriptions juridiques grecques* (Paris, 1891).
Jones, *LLTG*	J. W. Jones, *The Law and Legal Theory of the Greeks* (Oxford, 1956).
JNES	*Journal of Near Eastern Studies.*
Kahrstedt, *Mag.*	U. Kahrstedt, *Untersuchungen zur Magistratur in Athen* (Stuttgart, Berlin, 1936).
Kahrstedt, *Staatsg.*	U. Kahrstedt, *Staatsgebiet und Staatsangehörige in Athen* (Stuttgart, Berlin, 1934).
Kaser	M. Kaser, 'Der altgriechische Eigentumschutz' (*Z* 64, 1944, 134–205).
Kränzlein, *Eig. und Bes.*	A. Kränzlein, *Eigentum und Besitz im griechischen Recht des fünften und vierten Jahrhunderts v. Chr.* (Berlin, 1963).
KVGR	*Kritische Vierteljahrschrift für Gesetzgebung und Rechtswissenschaft.*
Lauffer, *Bergwerkssklaven*	S. Lauffer, *Die Bergwerkssklaven von Laureion*, Teil i, ii (Wiesbaden, 1956, 1957).
Ledl, *Stud.*	A. Ledl, 'Studien zum attischen Epiklerenrechte', I, II (*Jahresbericht I. Staatsgymnasium*, Graz, 1907, 1908).
Leist, *Att. Eig.*	G. A. Leist, *Der attische Eigentumsstreit im System der Diadikasien* (Jena, 1886).
Lipsius, *AR*	J. H. Lipsius, *Das attische Recht und Rechtsverfahren* (Leipzig, 1905–15).
MacDowell, *Homicide*	D. M. MacDowell, *Athenian Homicide Law in the Age of the Orators* (Manchester, 1963).
Mitteis, *RV*	L. Mitteis, *Reichsrecht und Volksrecht in den östlichen Provinzen des römischen Kaiserreichs* (Leipzig, 1891).
Morrow, *Slavery*	G. R. Morrow, 'Plato's law of slavery in its relation to Greek law' (*Illinois Studies in Language and Literature* 25, 3, 1939).
MSL	M. H. E. Meier (with G. F. Schömann, neu bearbeitet von J. H. Lipsius), *Der attische Process* (Berlin, 1883).
NJ	*Neue Jahrbücher für klassische Philologie* (Leipzig).
Paoli, *St. Dir.*	U. E. Paoli, *Studi di diritto attico* (Firenze, 1930).
Paoli, *St. Proc.*	U. E. Paoli, *Studi sul processo attico* (Padova, 1933).

Papp.	D. P. Pappoulias, Ἡ ἐμπράγματος ἀσφάλεια κατὰ τὸ ἑλληνικὸν καὶ τὸ ῥωμαϊκὸν δίκαιον (Leipzig, 1909).
Partsch, *GB*	J. Partsch, *Griechisches Bürgschaftsrecht* (Leipzig, 1909).
Pringsheim, *GLS*	F. Pringsheim, *The Greek Law of Sale* (Weimar, 1950).
RE	*Realenzyklopaedie* von Pauly–Wissowa–Kroll–Mittelhaus.
RÉG	*Revue des Études grecques.*
RHD	*Revue historique de droit français et étranger.*
RIDA	*Revue internationale des Droits de l'Antiquité.*
RM	*Rheinisches Museum für Philologie.*
RP	*Revue de Philologie.*
Schodorf, *Beiträge*	K. Schodorf, *Beiträge zur genaueren Kenntnis der attischen Gerichtssprache aus den 10 Rednern* (Würzburg, 1904).
Schömann, *Isai.*	G. F. Schömann, *Isaei orationes xi* (Greifswald, 1831).
Schulin, *Gr. Test.*	F. Schulin, *Das griechische Testament verglichen mit dem römischen* (Basel, 1882).
Schulthess, *VAR*	O. Schulthess, *Vormundschaft nach attischem Recht* (Freiburg, 1886).
Schulz, *CRL*	F. Schulz, *Classical Roman Law* (Oxford, 1951).
SDHI	*Studia et Documenta Historiae et Iuris.*
SEG	*Supplementum Epigraphicum Graecum.*
SIFC	*Studi italiani di filologia classica.*
SIG	W. Dittenberger, *Sylloge Inscriptionum Graecarum* (3rd ed., Leipzig, 1915).
SbB	*Sitzungsberichte der Bayerischen Akademie der Wissenschaften.* Philosophisch-philologische und historische Klasse.
TAPA	*Transactions of the American Philological Association.*
Thalheim, *RA*	T. Thalheim, *Lehrbuch den griechischen Rechtsalterthümern* II 1 (Leipzig, 1895).
Tod, *GHI*	M. N. Tod, *Greek Historical Inscriptions* (Oxford: i, 1946; ii, 1948).
TR	*Tijdschrift voor Rechtsgeschiedenis.*
Vinogradoff, *HJ*	P. Vinogradoff, *Outlines of Historical Jurisprudence.* II, *The Jurisprudence of the Greek City* (Oxford, 1920–2).
Wade-Gery, *EGH*	H. T. Wade-Gery, *Essays in Greek History* (Oxford, 1958).

Weiss, *GP*	E. Weiss, *Griechisches Privatrecht auf rechtsvergleichender Grundlage* (Leipzig, 1923).
Weiss, *Pfand.*	E. Weiss, *Pfandrechtliche Untersuchungen*, Bd. i (Weimar, 1909).
Wilamowitz, *A. und A.*	U. von Wilamowitz-Moellendorf, *Aristoteles und Athen* (Berlin, 1893).
Wolff, *Beitr.*	H. J. Wolff, *Beiträge zur Rechtsgeschichte Altgriechenlands und des hellenistisch-römischen Ägypten* (Weimar, 1961).
WS	*Wiener Studien.*
Wyse, *Isai.*	W. Wyse, *The Speeches of Isaeus* (Cambridge, 1904).
Z	*Zeitschrift der Savigny-Stiftung für Rechtsgeschichte* (Romanistische Abteilung).

BIBLIOGRAPHY

(*See also List of Abbreviations*)

A. Albertoni, *L'apokeryxis: contributo alla storia della famiglia* (Bologna, 1923).

C. K. J. Bunsen, *De iure hereditario Atheniensium* (Göttingen, 1813).

E. Caillemer, 'Le droit de tester à Athènes' (*AEG* 4, 1870, 19 ff.).

——, *La Prescription à Athènes* (*Études sur les antiquités juridiques d'Athènes* 7, Paris, 1869).

A. Calderini, *La manomissione e la condizione dei liberti in Grecia* (Milan, 1908).

M. Clerc, *Les Métèques athéniens* (Paris, 1893).

A. H. G. P. van den Es, *De iure familiarum apud Athenienses libri tres* (Leiden, 1864).

G. Foucart, *De libertorum conditione apud Athenienses* (Paris, 1896).

L. Gernet, *Recherches sur le développement de la pensée juridique et morale en Grèce* (Paris, 1917).

J. Korver, *De Terminologie van het Creditwesen in het Griekschk* (Amsterdam, 1934).

H. Meyer-Laurin, *Gesetz und Billigkeit im attischen Prozess* (Weimar, 1965).

U. E. Paoli, 'L'ἀγχιστεία nel diritto successorio attico' (*SDHI* 1, 1936, 92 ff.).

——, 'L'ἐπίκληρος attica nella palliata Romana' (*Atene e Roma* 45, 1943, 19 ff.).

——, 'La legittima aferesi della ἐπίκληρος nel diritto attico' (*Studi e Testi* 125, 1946, 529 ff.).

——, *Comici latini e diritto attico* (Milan, 1962).

E. Platner, *Der Process und die Klagen bei den Attikern* (Darmstadt, 1824–5).

E. Pringsheim, *Der Kauf mit fremdem Geld* (Leipzig, 1916).

E. Rabel, 'Elterliche Teilung' (*Festschrift zur 49. Versammlung deutschen Philologen in Basel* 1907, 528 ff.).

——, *Die Verfügungsbeschränkungen des Verpfänders* (Leipzig, 1909).

P. Roussel, *Isée, discours* (Paris, 1922).

V. Thumser, ''Ἐγγύησις, γαμηλία, ἐπιδικασία' (*Serta Harteliana*, Vienna, 1896, 189 ff.).

H. A. Wallon, *Histoire de l'Esclavage dans l'Antiquité* (2nd ed., Paris, 1879).

W. L. Westermann, *The Slave Systems of Greek and Roman Antiquity* (Philadephia, 1955).

SELECT BIBLIOGRAPHY, 1967-97

Bauman, R.A., *Political Trials in Ancient Greece* (London, 1990).

Behrend, D., *Attische Pachturkunden* (Munich, 1970).

Biscardi, A. *Diritto greco antico* (Milan, 1982).

Boegehold, A.L., *The Lawcourts at Athens* (The Athenian Agora, vol. xxviii; Princeton, 1995).

Cantarella, E., *Studi sull'omicidio in diritto greco e romano* (Milan, 1976).

Carey, C., *Lysias: Selected Speeches* (Cambridge, 1989).

——, *Trials from Classical Athens* (London, 1997).

Carey, C. and Reid, R.A., *Demosthenes: Selected Private Speeches* (Cambridge, 1985).

Cartledge, P., Millett, P. and Todd, S. (editors), *Nomos: Essays in Athenian Law, Politics, and Society* (Cambridge, 1990).

Cohen, D., *Law, Sexuality, and Society* (Cambridge, 1991).

——, *Law, Violence, and Community in Classical Athens* (Cambridge, 1995).

——, *Theft in Athenian Law* (Munich, 1983).

Cohen, E.E., *Ancient Athenian Maritime Courts* (Princeton, 1973).

——, *Athenian Economy and Society* (Princeton, 1992).

Dimakis, P.D., Αττικό δίκαιο (Athens, 1986).

Fisher, N.R.E., *Hybris* (Warminster, 1992).

Foxhall, L. and Lewis, A.D.E. (editors), *Greek Law in its Political Setting* (Oxford, 1996).

Gagarin, M., *Antiphon: The Speeches* (Cambridge, 1997).

——, *Drakon and Early Athenian Homicide Law* (New Haven, 1981).

——, *Early Greek Law* (Berkeley, 1986).

Garner, R., *Law and Society in Classical Athens* (London, 1987).

Gauthier, P., *Symbola: les étrangers et la justice dans les cités grecques* (Nancy, 1972).

Hansen, M.H., *Apagoge, Endeixis and Ephegesis against Kakourgoi, Atimoi and Pheugontes* (Odense, 1976).

——, *The Athenian Democracy in the Age of Demosthenes* (Oxford, 1991).

——, *Eisangelia: the Sovereignty of the People's Court in Athens in the Fourth Century* BC *and the Impeachment of Generals and Politicians* (Odense, 1975).

——, *The Sovereignty of the People's Court in Athens in the Fourth Century* BC *and the Public Action against Unconstitutional Proposals* (Odense, 1974).

Hillgruber, M., *Die zehnte Rede des Lysias* (Berlin, 1988).

Hunter, V. J., *Policing Athens: Social Control in the Attic Lawsuits, 420-320* BC (Princeton, 1994).

Isager, S. and Hansen, M.H., *Aspects of Athenian Society in the Fourth Century* BC (Odense, 1975).

Just, R., *Women in Athenian Law and Life* (London, 1989).

Koch, C., *Volksbeschlüsse in Seebundangelegenheiten: das Verfahrensrecht Athens im Ersten attischen Seebund* (Frankfurt, 1991).

Lambert, S.D., *The Phratries of Attica* (Ann Arbor, 1993).

Lewis, D.M., *Inscriptiones Graecae,* vol. i, editio tertia, fasc. 1 et 2 (Berlin, 1981, 1994).

MacDowell, D.M., *Demosthenes: Against Meidias* (Oxford, 1990).

——, *The Law in Classical Athens* (London, 1978).

Manville, P.B., *The Origins of Citizenship in Ancient Athens* (Princeton, 1990).

Millett, P., *Lending and Borrowing in Ancient Athens* (Cambridge, 1991).

Ogden, D., *Greek Bastardy* (Oxford, 1996).

Osborne, M.J., *Naturalization in Athens,* vols. i, ii, iii-iv (Brussels, 1981, 1982, 1983).

Osborne, R. and Hornblower, S., *Ritual, Finance, Politics: Athenian Democratic Accounts presented to David Lewis* (Oxford, 1994).

Ostwald, M., *From Popular Sovereignty to the Sovereignty of Law* (Berkeley, 1986).

——, *Nomos and the Beginnings of Athenian Democracy* (Oxford, 1969).

Patterson, C., *Pericles' Citizenship Law of 451-50* BC (New York, 1981).

Pomeroy, S.B., *Families in Classical and Hellenistic Greece* (Oxford, 1997).

Quass, F., *Nomos und Psephisma* (Munich, 1971).

Rhodes, P.J., *The Athenian Boule* (Oxford, 1972).

——, *A Commentary on the Aristotelian* Athenaion Politeia (Oxford, 1981).

Rhodes, P.J. and Lewis, D.M., *The Decrees of the Greek States* (Oxford, 1997).

Roberts, J.T., *Accountability in Athenian Government* (Madison, 1982).

Rubinstein, L., *Adoption in IV. Century Athens* (Copenhagen, 1993).

Ruschenbusch, E., *Untersuchungen zur Geschichte des athenischen Strafrechts* (Cologne, 1968).

Schaps, D.M., *Economic Rights of Women in Ancient Greece* (Edinburgh, 1979).

Sealey, R., *The Justice of the Greeks* (Ann Arbor, 1994).

——, *Women and Law in Classical Greece* (Chapel Hill, 1990).

Spina, L., *Il cittadino alla tribuna: diritto e libertà di parola nell' Atene democratica* (Naples, 1986).

Stroud, R.S., *Drakon's Law on Homicide* (Berkeley, 1968).

Thompson, W.E., *De Hagniae hereditate* (Leiden, 1976).

Thür, G., *Beweisführung vor den Schwurgerichtshöfen Athens* (Vienna, 1977).

Todd, S.C., *The Shape of Athenian Law* (Oxford, 1993).

Tulin, A., *Dike phonou: the Right of Prosecution and Attic Homicide Procedure* (Stuttgart, 1996).

Wallace, R.W., *The Areopagos Council* (Baltimore, 1989).

Wankel, H., *Demosthenes: Rede für Ktesiphon über den Kranz* (Heidelberg, 1976).

Whitehead, D., *The Demes of Attica* (Princeton, 1986).

——, *The Ideology of the Athenian Metic* (Cambridge, 1977).

Wolff, H.J., *'Normenkontrolle' und Gesetzesbegriff in der attischen Demokratie* (Heidelberg, 1970).

Worthington, I., *A Historical Commentary on Dinarchus* (Ann Arbor, 1992).

The *Akten der Gesellschaft für griechische und hellenistische Rechtsgeschichte* are published by Böhlau at Cologne as follows:

Symposion 1971, edited by H.J. Wolff (1975).
Symposion 1974, edited by A. Biscardi (1979).
Symposion 1977, edited by J. Modrzejewski and D. Liebs (1982).
Symposion 1979, edited by P.D. Dimakis (1983).
Symposion 1982, edited by F.J. Fernandez Nieto (1989).
Symposion 1985, edited by G. Thür (1989).
Symposion 1988, edited by G. Nenci and G. Thür (1990).
Symposion 1990, edited by M. Gagarin (1991).
Symposion 1993, edited by G. Thür (1994).
Symposion 1995, edited by G. Thür and J. Velissaropoulos-Karakostas (1997).

PART I

LAW OF THE FAMILY

I · MARRIAGE

§ 1. *Introduction*

IN very general terms we can say that marriage was essential for the preservation of the 'houses' or *οἶκοι* which were the constituent elements of the Athenian city state or for the formation of new 'houses'.[1] Unfortunately, when we come to examine the details of the institution, we find many unresolved doubts as to some of its most important features.

The first and most serious difficulty is to determine what constituted a valid marriage. We are confronted at once with a semantic problem. For there is no single Greek word which can be taken to stand for 'marriage'. Nor are there words which normally stand for 'husband' and 'wife'; where this relationship has to be described the usual words are *ἀνήρ* and *γυνή*, the latter sometimes with a qualifying epithet.[2] We have first then to examine the principal terms used in connexion with the institution.

The two most important words are *ἐγγύη* and *γάμος* and their

[1] Besides the exhaustive treatments in Beauchet i. 32–535 and Lipsius, *AR* 468–88, the Athenian law of marriage has been minutely studied by W. G. Becker in 'Platons Gesetze und das griechische Familienrecht' and W. Erdmann in 'Die Ehe im alten Griechenland', each with a full bibliography. Cf. also Bu. Sw. 239 f. Since then the most important studies have been H. J. Wolff, 'Marriage Laws and Family Organisation in Ancient Athens', *Traditio* 2 (1944), 43 ff., id., 'Grundlagen des gr. Eherechts', *TR* 20 (1952), 1 ff., id., *RE* s.v. *προίξ* (1957), O. Schulthess, *RE* s.v. *φερνή* (1938). For the significance of the *οἶκος* in the city state and the importance attached to its continuance see below, pp. 92, 123.

[2] For *δάμαρ*, obsolete in prose in the classical period, see L. Gernet, *Ann. Inst. Phil. Hist. Or. Slav.* 5 (1937), 393.

derivatives. *ἐγγυᾶν* seems etymologically to mean 'to put into the hand'. It is the word used for giving a pledge. When used in the context of marriage the bride's father *ἐγγυᾷ τινι τὴν θυγατέρα*, the bridegroom *ἐγγυᾶταί τινα*, and the bride is either *ἐγγυωμένη* or *ἐγγυητή*. The *ἐγγύη*, or as it is called in only one passage in the classical authors the *ἐγγύησις*, is then a transaction between the bride's father and the bridegroom of which the bride is the object, and we may guess that in its earliest form the transaction involved a putting of something into the hand.[1]

Γάμος as a word had the basic sense of 'pairing' and was used of the physically consummated marriage. The active verb *γαμεῖν* is normally used of the man in a fully solemnized union, as opposed, for instance, to what is called an adulterous union, *μοιχεύειν*. So a 'married' woman is sometimes called *γαμετή* as opposed to a 'concubine', *παλλακή*.[2]

Ἐκδιδόναι is used of the father who gives his daughter in marriage, the act is *ἔκδοσις*, and the daughter so given is *ἔκδοτος*.[3]

Finally, the word *συνοικεῖν* is used of the factual cohabitation of a man and woman, and there is one passage in the Demosthenic corpus which suggests that it became the accepted term for living together in a legitimate union, though there is some doubt as to how much weight should be put on this particular passage.[4]

[1] Dem. 41 *Spoud.* 6 *ἠγγύα μοι Πολύευκτος τὴν θυγατέρ' ἐπὶ τετταράκοντα μναῖς*, Isai. 3 *Pyrrh.* 70 *ὁ ἀδελφιδοῦς ὑμῶν ἠγγυᾶτο τὴν μητέρα τὴν ταύτης κατὰ ⟨τοὺς⟩ νόμους ἕξειν γυναῖκα*, id. 8 *Kir.* 19 *ὀμόσας κατὰ τοὺς νόμους τοὺς κειμένους ἦ μὴν ἐξ ἀστῆς καὶ ἐγγυητῆς γυναικὸς εἰσάγειν*, ibid. 29 *θυγατέρα . . . δὶς ἐκδοθεῖσαν, δὶς ἐγγυηθεῖσαν*. On the etymology of the word see V. Thumser, *Serta Harteliana* (Wien, 1896), 191, Partsch, *GB* 48, L. Gernet, *RÉG* 23 (1910), 375, Weiss, *GP* 222 ff., Becker, *Plat.* 44, Erdmann, *Ehe* 231, Wolff, *Traditio* 2 (1944), 52. See Isai. 3 *Pyrrh.* 53 for the sole classical use of *ἐγγύησις*, but cf. *IG* ii². 10 (Tod, *GHI* 100), l. 10.

[2] There is no need to quote passages for the straightforward uses of *γάμος* and its derivatives; but note Lykourg., fr. 91 (Blass) *εἴ τις . . . καλὸς ὢν μοιχεύειν μᾶλλον ἢ γαμεῖν προῄρηται οὗτος τῶν ἀπὸ τῆς φύσεως ἀγαθῶν ὑπαρξάντων προδότης ἐστίν*, Lys. 1 *Killing of Erat.* 31 *καὶ οὕτω σφόδρα ὁ νομοθέτης ἐπὶ ταῖς γαμεταῖς γυναιξὶ δίκαια ταῦτα ἡγήσατο εἶναι, ὥστε καὶ ἐπὶ ταῖς παλλακαῖς ταῖς ἐλλάττονος ἀξίαις τὴν αὐτὴν δίκην ἐπέθηκε*. In Dem. 59 *Neair.* 93 the phrase *οἱ τὸν αὐτὸν τρόπον τούτῳ γεγαμηκότες καὶ παιδοποιούμενοι* is used of those who have formed what the speaker is arguing to be an illegitimate union, but this exception proves the rule, for the word *γεγαμηκότες* might almost be in inverted commas.

[3] Isai. 8 *Kir.* 8 *ἐπεὶ συνοικεῖν εἶχεν ἡλικίαν ἐκδίδωσιν αὐτὴν Ναυσιμένει Χολαργεῖ*, id. 3 *Pyrrh.* 8 *ἐπιθυμῶ . . . πυθέσθαι, ἥντινά ποτε προῖκά φησιν ἐπιδοὺς ἐκδοῦναι τὴν ἀδελφὴν ὁ μεμαρτυρηκὼς τῷ τὸν τριτάλαντον οἶκον κεκτημένῳ*, Dem. 40 *Boiot.* ii. 61 *πολὺ δικαιότερόν ἐστι τὴν τῆς ἐμῆς μητρὸς προῖκα τῇ ἐμῇ θυγατρὶ εἰς ἔκδοσιν ὑμᾶς ψηφίσασθαι*, and id. 59 *Neair.* 8 where *ἀνέκδοτος* is used for a girl who is *ἄπροικος*.

[4] Isai. 8 *Kir.* 8 (n. 3), Dem. 59 *Neair.* 122 *τὸ γὰρ συνοικεῖν τοῦτ' ἔστιν, ὃς ἂν*

§ 2. ἐγγύη

Our first and most difficult task is to determine the precise significance of the word ἐγγύη in connexion with marriage. Examination of the meaning of the word will merge into examination of the institution. The earliest appearance of the word is in Homer (*Od.* 8. 351). Hephaistos holds Aphrodite and Ares bound. Free them, says Poseidon (347), ἐγὼ δέ τοι αὐτὸν ὑπίσχομαι ὡς σὺ κελεύεις / τίσειν αἴσιμα πάντα μετ' ἀθανάτοισιν θεοῖσι. Not so, says Hephaistos, δειλαί τοι δειλῶν γε καὶ ἐγγύαι ἐγγυάασθαι. / πῶς ἂν ἐγώ σε δέοιμι μετ' ἀθανάτοισι θεοῖσιν, / εἴ κεν Ἄρης οἴχοιτο χρέος καὶ δεσμὸν ἀλύξας; To which Poseidon Ἥφαιστ', εἴ περ γάρ κεν Ἄρης χρεῖος ὑπαλύξας / οἴχηται φεύγων, αὐτός τοι ἐγὼ τάδε τίσω. In response to this second promise Hephaistos releases the lovers and Ares does in fact take himself off to Thrace. There has been much controversy on this passage. Partsch in his book on the Greek law of surety argues that Poseidon is offering himself as a personal hostage or security for the debt which Ares has incurred by his adultery. The 'hand' element in the word ἐγγύη is the joining of right hands to signify agreement between the guarantor (Poseidon) and him who accepts the guarantee (Hephaistos). The common factor between the later use of ἐγγύη as surety and its use in connexion with marriage will then be simply that in both cases there is assumed to have been a formal hand-shake by the two parties to the agreement. There are two objections to this view. First, it only provides a very external link between the two uses of the word in later times. Why should a word implying hand-shake be found in connexion with only these two kinds of agreement? And, more seriously, this theory fails to explain the vital line 351 δειλαί τοι κτλ. It takes the meaning to be 'powerless are the sureties which are given to the powerless'. Hephaistos is δειλός ('a poor thing'), and therefore the 'surety' he has so far been asked to accept, ἐγγυάασθαι, is a poor thing too. This 'surety' is Poseidon's undertaking that *Ares* will pay up. Poseidon then alters the form of his undertaking: he promises that he will pay himself if Ares goes off and

παιδοποιῆται καὶ εἰσάγῃ εἴς τε τοὺς φράτερας καὶ δημότας τοὺς υἱεῖς, καὶ τὰς θυγατέρας ἐκδιδῷ ὡς αὐτοῦ οὔσας τοῖς ἀνδράσιν, Isai. 6 *Philokt.* 14, Erdmann, *Ehe* 174. On marriage terminology, Schodorf, *Beitr.* 66 (interpretations to be used with caution), U. E. Paoli, *Studi e Testi* 125 (Vatican, 1946), 524.

evades his debt. The weakness of this interpretation is that it does not suggest how Hephaistos' δειλία is in any way helped by the altered form of Poseidon's undertaking. In fact to serve Partsch's purpose the word ἐγγύη should apply only to the second undertaking. It was *this* undertaking that cured Hephaistos' weakness. Otherwise we are still at the stage where might is right, and it is the primary aim of Partsch's elaborate examination of the passage to show that we have here the first known step in Greece towards a *legal* concept, moving away from the world of brute force. A much more convincing interpretation has been worked out by L. Gernet, developing a thesis first put forward by Esmein and accepted by Glotz. By this theory ἐγγύη means originally a solemn promise, ratified by shaking hands. In the scene in the *Odyssey*, under Poseidon's first undertaking the ἐγγύη would have been between Hephaistos and *Ares*; but Ares, taken as an individual, is weak, δειλός, and the promises that the weak undertake are themselves weak. Poseidon's second undertaking is equivalent to the acceptance of family solidarity for what is due, and the ἐγγύη in *this* case is a solemn pact by which a debtor is freed through an act of family solidarity. A similar pact, Gernet suggests, may have operated at this stage of legal development when a father betrothed his daughter, though we do not as a matter of fact find the word ἐγγύη used in Homer in this connexion. This theory, of which more will have to be said in dealing with the law on suretyship, does at least suggest how the word ἐγγύη and its derivatives might have come to be used exclusively in two such apparently disparate fields as marriage and suretyship.[1]

[1] Partsch, *GB* 9 ff. and especially 46–54 for the marriage terminology. On p. 76 he gives the following hypothetical definition of the earliest ἐγγύη: 'eine verträgliche — zunächst vielleicht körperliche, Hand in Hand erfolgende — Selbsthingabe einer freien Person zur Haftung für den Fall, daß ein garantierte Erfolg ausfiel'. (Gernet, incidentally, does well to point out that in the *Odyssey* scene nothing of the kind in fact takes place.) A· Esmein, *Mélanges de Rome* 8 (1888), 426–36. Glotz, *Solidarité*, 131. Gernet first sketched his view in a paper reported in *RÉG* 23 (1910), 375, and Lips., *AR* 706, n. 109, characterized it as 'ein sonderbarer Gedanke'. But he subsequently worked it out in a brilliant article in *RÉG* 30 (1917), 249 ff., and this statement of it received the commendation of Vinogradoff in *HJ* 235. In the context of suretyship 'l'ἐγγύη est le nom du contrat interfamilial qui fonde une obligation *ex delicto* et dont l'élément capital est la promesse faite au nom de la famille du délinquant'; while in the context of marriage it is the promise of the bride's family group to give her in marriage into another group. See also Gernet, *Ann. Sociol.* (1948–9), 112 f. Wolff, *Traditio* 2 (1944), 51 ff. (*Beitr.* 170 ff.), sees the common ground in the fact that in both kinds of ἐγγύη a free person is

It must, however, be candidly admitted that not a great deal of light can be shed forward from the *Odyssey* passage on to the character of ἐγγύη in the classical period, whether it be in connexion with suretyship or marriage.[1] Another comparatively early appearance of the word is more helpful. Herodotos (6. 130) at the end of his account of the famous wooing of Agariste puts the following words into the mouth of her father, Kleisthenes of Sikyon: *τῷ δὲ Ἀλκμέωνος Μεγακλέϊ ἐγγυῶ παῖδα τὴν ἐμὴν Ἀγαρίστην νόμοισι τοῖσι Ἀθηναίων*. And Herodotos adds *φαμένου δὲ ἐγγυᾶσθαι Μεγακλέος ἐκεκύρωτο ὁ γάμος Κλεισθένεϊ*. This may not be very good evidence for Athenian practice in the sixth century, when the marriage of Agariste actually took place; but it is good evidence for Athenian practice in the middle of the fifth century, the latest date at which one can imagine the story Herodotos is using first became current.

One other passage where the word can be assigned confidently to a fairly early date is in a law cited in a speech in the Demosthenic corpus where the word *δάμαρ*, obsolete in prose in the classical period, vouches for the antiquity of the law.[2]

We can then conclude that from an early date ἐγγύη was an essential element in some, if not in all, such permanent unions between a free man and a free woman as we should now call marriages. If Greek marriage of the classical period developed out of marriage by purchase (some scholars find traces of marriage by purchase in Homer),[3] the ἐγγύη will have been in origin a kind of contract of sale between the father of the bride or other authorized person and the bridegroom, the 'hand' element being either the physical handing over of the bride or the hand-shake

handed over to another not finally and absolutely, but for a specific purpose, and he who hands over retains a right in the person handed over.

[1] Bortolucci has a detailed discussion of the passage in *St. Bonfante* i (1930), 589 ff., but comes to much the same negative conclusion.

[2] Dem. 46 *Steph*. ii. 18 *ἣν ἂν ἐγγυήσῃ ἐπὶ δικαίοις δάμαρτα εἶναι ἢ πατὴρ ἢ ἀδελφὸς ὁμοπάτωρ ἢ πάππος ὁ πρὸς πατρός, ἐκ ταύτης εἶναι παῖδας γνησίους*. Cf. Dem. 44 *Leoch*. 49, Hyper. 5 *Athenog*. 16, Lips., *AR* 471, n. 9.

[3] See, for example, *Il*. 11. 243 ff., 16. 190, 22. 472, *Od*. 11. 117, 282, where the *ἕδνα* seem to represent a purchase price: so Erdmann, *Ehe* 204 ff.; but E. Hruza, *Ehebegründung* 10 ff., regards the *ἕδνα* not as a purchase price, but as a kind of *douceurs* to secure the goodwill of the bride's father. Cf. also Ar., *Pol*. 1268^{b} *τοὺς γὰρ ἀρχαίους νόμους λίαν ἁπλοῦς εἶναι καὶ βαρβαρικούς. ἐσιδηροφοροῦντό τε γὰρ οἱ Ἕλληνες καὶ τὰς γυναῖκας ἐωνοῦντο παρ' ἀλλήλων*. For a wholly different view see M. I. Finley, *Seminar* 12 (1954), 7 ff.: at marriage there is an exchange of gifts and *ἕδνα* is sometimes used of the gift of the bride's father to the groom; nothing suggests sale.

which sealed the agreement. When we come to consider what this procedure purported in the classical period we are met with an unresolved controversy. To some scholars it has seemed to be nothing more than a betrothal of the bride by her father to the bridegroom, a necessary step towards a full marriage, but certainly not constituting a marriage in and by itself. For this there was needed the consummation, *γάμος*, which converted an *ἐγγυητή* into a *γαμετή* or *ἐκδεδομένη*. The principal support for this view is the action of Demosthenes' father with regard to his wife and daughter. While still alive he 'contracts' (*ἐγγυᾷ*) his wife to Aphobos and his daughter to Demophon, but clearly his wife could not actually marry Aphobos till he himself was dead, nor did she immediately after his death, and Demosthenes tells us that Demophon, though he was to receive two talents as dowry at once, was not to receive the daughter till she reached maturity in ten years' time.[1] These two excellently attested cases seem conclusive against the alternative view, which would see in the *ἐγγύη* marriage itself and not merely betrothal. It is in vain that Erdmann, *Ehe* 233, quotes passages from the orators where *ἐγγυᾶν* and *ἐκδιδόναι*, occurring in close conjunction, describe, in his words, 'two phases of the same act'. It goes without saying that often, perhaps normally, *ἐγγύη* and the completion of the marriage, whether we call it *γάμος* or *ἔκδοσις*, were virtually simultaneous acts between which there was no particular reason to distinguish. But this would in no way dispose of the argument, based on the action of Demosthenes' father, that the acts were in principle distinct.[2]

But it is one thing to recognize a distinction between *ἐγγύη* and completed marriage and quite another to determine what the legal significance of this distinction was. In the first place it is surprising that we find no evidence for any legal action to enforce upon either party the carrying out of the *ἐγγύη*, though indeed it might be equally surprising if there had been such an

[1] Dem. 28 *Aphob.* ii. 15 f., 29 *Aphob.* iii. 43.

[2] These are the passages: Isai. 3 *Pyrrh.* 70 *ὅτε δὲ ἠγγύα καὶ ἐξεδίδου ὁ Ἔνδιος τὴν γυναῖκα, ἐπετρέπετε ὑμεῖς οἱ θεῖοι τὴν τοῦ ἀδελφιδοῦ τοῦ ὑμετέρου αὐτῶν ὡς ἐξ ἑταίρας οὖσαν ἐκείνῳ ἐγγυᾶσθαι*, id. 8 *Kir.* 14 *τίνας δ' εἰδέναι τὰ περὶ τὴν ἔκδοσιν τῆς μητρὸς ἀνάγκη; τοὺς ἐγγυησαμένους καὶ τοὺς ἐκείνοις παρόντας ὅτε ἠγγυῶντο.* Erdmann also cites Dem. 59 *Neair.* 52, 53, id. 57 *Eubul.* 41. The phrase in Isai. 8 *Kir.* 29, *θυγατέρα δὶς ἐκδοθεῖσαν, δὶς ἐγγυηθεῖσαν*, a passage which he also refers to, seems to tell strongly against him.

action in view of the extreme ease with which a marriage could be dissolved by either party.[1] Nor is it easy to define the further step which was needed to convert ἐγγύη into full marriage. In fact Lipsius, one of the main proponents of this view, admits that no further legal act was needed. Presumably we are to suppose that it was the factual living together of the pair as man and wife which produced the required change, *γάμος* being simply *copula carnalis*. Certainly the *γαμηλία*, whatever its precise nature, was not a legal act required to make a marriage valid.[2]

There are two directions in which we might look for legal changes effected by an ἐγγύη before it has become a full marriage. It might affect the tutelage of the girl who was the object of the transaction. It is virtually certain, as we shall find later, that on the completion of a marriage she passed from the tutelage of her father—to assume for the moment that he was still alive—to the tutelage of her husband. What was the position when there was an interval of time between ἐγγύη and *γάμος*? All that we have to go upon is the case of Demosthenes' mother and sister already mentioned. His father's disposal of their hands in marriage, although it took place *inter vivos*, was *mortis causa* and thus also incorporated in a testament, *διαθήκη*. We need not therefore consider the position of the women during his lifetime, since it could be held that even the ἐγγύη did not become operative until his death. As soon as he died Aphobos should have married his wife, but in fact he did not. And Demophon could not marry his

[1] In Roman comedy the seducer of a girl could be forced to marry her, but it is hard to say whether this represents Athenian law. See p. 19, n. 2, below.

[2] Lips., *AR* 469, Weiss, *GP* 222. For the *γαμηλία*: Dem. 57 *Eubul.* 43 *κάλει . . . τῶν φρατέρων τοὺς οἰκείους, οἷς τὴν γαμηλίαν εἰσήνεγκεν ὑπὲρ τῆς μητρὸς ὁ πατήρ*, Isai. 3 *Pyrrh.* 76 *οὔτε γαμηλίαν εἰσήνεγκεν ὁ θεῖος ἡμῶν οὔτε τὴν θυγατέρα, ἣν φασι γνησίαν αὐτοῦ εἶναι οὗτοι, εἰσαγαγεῖν εἰς τοὺς φράτερας ἠξίωσε*, id. 8 *Kir.* 18 *ὅτε γὰρ ὁ πατὴρ αὐτὴν ἐλάμβανε, γάμους εἱστίασε . . . τοῖς τε φράτερσι γαμηλίαν εἰσήνεγκε κατὰ τοὺς ἐκείνων νόμους*, Harpokr. s.v. *γαμηλία· Δημοσθένης ἐν τῇ πρὸς Εὐβουλίδην ἐφέσει καὶ Ἰσαῖος καὶ Δίδυμος ὁ γραμματικὸς ἐν μὲν τοῖς Ἰσαίου ὑπομνήμασί φησιν εἶναι γαμηλίαν τὴν τοῖς φράτορσιν ἐπὶ γάμοις διδομένην, παρατιθέμενος λέξιν Φανοδήμου, ἐν ᾗ οὐδὲν τοιοῦτον γέγραπται, ἐν δὲ τοῖς εἰς Δημοσθένην ὁ αὐτὸς πάλιν γαμηλίαν φησὶν εἶναι τὴν εἰς τοὺς φράτορας εἰσαγωγὴν τῶν γυναικῶν, οὐδεμίαν ἀπόδειξιν τῆς ἐξηγήσεως παραθέμενος*. Cf. Phanodemos, *F.Gr.H.* 325 F 17 with Jacoby's commentary. From these passages it seems that the *γαμηλία* was an offering accompanied by a feast to phratry members which was customary, and even in some phratries laid down by their law, on the occasion of a marriage and the giving of which was therefore often used as one means of establishing the existence of the marriage; but there is nothing to suggest that without it a marriage would have been invalid.

daughter, as she was only five years old. Though Demosthenes' language is not absolutely clear it suggests that in the interim the two women were to be under the tutelage of three guardians, Aphobos, Demophon, and Therippides.[1] We must assume, though Demosthenes does not enlighten us on the point, that in view of Aphobos' and Demophon's unwillingness to complete their respective ἐγγύαι it would have been in the power, and was probably the duty, of these three to effect other marriages for the two women.

The other sphere in which an unfulfilled ἐγγύη might have important legal consequences was the dowry. The general topic of the dowry will be dealt with later. The relevant point here is that a dowry, though not an essential, was a normal accompaniment to an ἐγγύη. It was paid down to the prospective husband, and all the legal effects which might attach to a dowry began to run from the moment it was paid. Thus the prospective husband had to provide out of it for the sustenance (σῖτος) of the woman, and presumably the bestower of the dowry enjoyed all the rights protected by the δίκη προικός. It is worth noting that Demosthenes criticizes Aphobos not so much for failing to marry his mother as for refusing both to provide her σῖτος while the possibility of the marriage was still open and to return the dowry when the marriage was off.[2]

The best conclusion seems to be that in the perhaps rather rare cases where the ἐγγύη took place an appreciable time before the marriage was completed the tutelage of the woman was unaffected by it, but that important legal relationships would arise if there were a dowry.[3]

[1] 27 *Aphob.* i. 4 οὑμὸς πατὴρ κατέλιπεν οὐσίαν μὲν σχεδὸν τεττάρων καὶ δέκα ταλάντων, ἐμὲ δ' ἔπτ' ἐτῶν ὄντα καὶ τὴν ἀδελφὴν πέντε, ἔτι δὲ τὴν ἡμετέραν μητέρα πεντήκοντα μνᾶς εἰς τὸν οἶκον εἰσηνεγμένην. βουλευσάμενος δὲ περὶ ἡμῶν, ὅτ' ἔμελλε τελευτᾶν, ἅπαντα ταῦτ' ἐνεχείρισεν Ἀφόβῳ τε τουτῳὶ καὶ Δημοφῶντι . . . ἔτι δὲ Θηριππίδῃ. When he says in the next paragraph Δημοφῶντι δὲ τὴν ἐμὴν ἀδελφὴν καὶ δύο τάλαντ' εὐθὺς ἔδωκεν ἔχειν we must take εὐθύς with δύο τάλαντα alone. On this case see Bruck, *Schenkung* 99 ff., 122 ff., Gernet, *Dem.* i. 28. It is interesting to speculate whether in principle it would have been open to Demophon, without dissolving the ἐγγύη, to contract another marriage during the ten years which had to elapse before he could actually marry Demosthenes' sister, provided of course that he continued to pay for her sustenance (σῖτος), with the intention of dissolving it as soon as she reached maturity.

[2] 27 *Aphob.* i. 17 μὴ γήμαντος αὐτοῦ τὴν μητέρα τὴν ἐμήν, ὁ νόμος κελεύει τὴν προῖκ' ὀφείλειν ἐπ' ἐννέ' ὀβολοῖς, ibid. 15 οὐ διδόντος τούτου σῖτον τῇ μητρί.

[3] E. Hruza was the first to challenge the view that ἐγγύη was in essence betrothal

However, although we cannot regard ἐγγύη as in itself constituting a marriage, 'betrothal' is too weak a word to translate it, since it formed an essential element in certain types of marriage at least. That this is so is proved by the law already cited (p. 5, n. 2, above) from Dem. 46 *Steph.* ii. 18. Thus one requirement for γνησιότης, whatever that may mean, was being born of a union mediated by an ἐγγύη.[1]

§ 3. ἐπιδικασία

There were other types of more or less permanent union between a man and a woman than those we have hitherto considered. The

and not full marriage, in *Beitr.* i. 35 ff. He was followed by Beauchet i. 123, Thumser, *Serta Harteliana* 190, A. Albertoni, *L'apokeryxis* 15 ff., and Erdmann, *Ehe* 232 ff., among others. The contrary view is held by Kübler, *Z* 15 (1894), 395, Lipsius, *AR* 469, Wyse, *Isai.* 289 ff. (a good summing-up at the bottom of 292), Partsch, *GB* 48, n. 4, Gernet, *RÉG* 30 (1917), 278 ff., Becker, *Plat.* 41 ff. with good bibliography (he sums up on p. 48 thus: 'Engyesis ist der zwischen Gewalthaber und Werber geschlossene obligatorische Vertrag auf Hingabe einer Frau. Gamos ist der dingliche Hingabevertrag, wobei der Werber die ihm obliegende Besitzergreifung ausdrücklich oder stillschweigend durch Willenserklärung vollzieht und durch die Tathandlung der copula carnalis deklariert'). Cf. H. J. Wolff in *Written and Unwritten Marriages in Hellenistic and Post-classical Roman Law* (Haverford, 1939) 78: 'the *engyesis* was a contract to create the marriage and not a mere engagement; but marriage definitely ensued only on completion by *ekdosis*.' Cf. P. Koschaker, 'Die Eheformen bei den Indogermanen', *Deutsche Landesref. II Intern. Kongr. f. Rechtsvergl.* (Haag, 1937), 92, 98. A rather unsatisfactory compromise view, based on the two senses of ἐγγυᾶν, was first stated by E. Gans, *Das Erbrecht* i (Berlin, 1824), 295, adopted by the editors of *IJ* i. 52 and developed at length by P. S. Photiades in *Athena* 32 (1920), 100 ff. On this view the ἐγγύη was nothing more than a guarantee given by the father of the bride that she had been born in wedlock and was an Athenian, a guarantee to the bridegroom, that is, that she would bear him Athenian children. More will have to be said on this in dealing with legitimacy. Even less convincing is the suggestion of Schodorf, *Beitr.* 66, that the ἐγγύη was the guarantee given to the father for the return of the dowry.

[1] Wolff, *Traditio* 2 (1944), 75 (*Beitr.* 207) and *TR* 20 (1952) 4, maintains that the law here is defining, not marriage, but γνησιότης, a point discounted by A. Ledl, *WS* 30 (1908), 30 f. In Dem. 44 *Leoch.* 49 the words from the law are quoted in the text of the speech. In Dem. 59 *Neair.* 60 in order to establish his son's legitimacy a man is required to swear ἦ μὴν νομίζειν εἶναι αὑτοῦ υἱὸν ἐξ ἀστῆς γυναικὸς καὶ ἐγγυητῆς κατὰ τὸν νόμον: ibid. 92, 106, Dem., 57 *Eubul.* 54, Isai. 8 *Kir.* 19, Hyper. 5 *Athenog.* 16 οἱ ἐκ τῶν ἐγγυητῶν γυναικῶν παῖδες, οὗτοι γνήσιοί εἰσ[ι]ν. ἀλ[λὰ] μ[ὴ̣ν̣ ο̣ὐκ ἀπ̣]έ̣[χρ]ησε τῶι νομοθ[έτηι] τὸ ἐγγ[υηθῆ]ναι τὴν γυναῖκα ὑπὸ [τοῦ πατ]ρὸς [ἢ̣ τοῦ ἀδ]ελφοῦ, ἀλλ' ἔγραψε δι[α̣ρρή]δην ἐν [τῶι νόμ]ωι· [ἣ̣ν̣] ἂν ἐγγυήσηι τ[ις ἐπὶ δικαίοις δάμαρτα], ἐκ ταύτης εἶνα̣[ι παῖδας γνησίους, καὶ οὐ]κ̣· ἐάν τις ψευσ̣[άμενος ὡς θυγατέρα ἐγ]γυήσηι ἄλ[λην τινά. ἀλλὰ τὰς μὲν δι]καίας ἐγγύας κ̣[υρίας, τὰς δὲ μὴ δικαίας ἀκύρους̣] καθίστη[σιν.

most important of these was the marriage of an 'heiress' or ἐπίκληρος. The topic of ἐπίκληροι will have to be dealt with at length under the law of succession (see below, pp. 132 ff.). Here we are only concerned with the procedure by which they were married. If a citizen died leaving no other issue but a daughter (ignoring for the moment the possibility of more than one daughter), and if he had not taken the course which was open to him of adopting a son and marrying the daughter to him by ἐγγύη (he probably could not adopt a son without doing this), then the daughter became an ἐπίκληρος. The right to her hand passed to the nearest male relative in a prescribed order. But a legal procedure was necessary to ensure that she went to the duly qualified man. This procedure was called ἐπιδικασία, and, until it was completed, she was called ἐπίδικος.[1] The procedure was as follows. Any man who wished to lay claim to her hand by virtue of relationship to her father made a declaration to the appropriate magistrate (the eponymous archon if her father had been a citizen, the polemarch if he had been a metic), stating in writing the grounds of his claim, λῆξιν λαγχάνειν τῆς ἐπικλήρου.[2] The archon then published the λῆξις, and on the next fixed meeting of the assembly these λήξεις were read out. As Aristotle (*Ath. Pol.* 43. 4) puts it, δεῖ . . . ἀναγιγνώσκειν καὶ τὰς λήξεις τῶν κλήρων καὶ τῶν ἐπικλήρων, ὅπως μηδένα λάθῃ μηδὲν ἔρημον γενόμενον. At some point in the procedure—it is impossible to say exactly when—further publicity was given to the matter by a herald's inviting anyone who wished to put in a claim. If as a result of this publicity no more than one claimant appeared the archon adjudged the heiress to him and their marriage followed.[3]

[1] For modern literature on ἐπίκληροι see below, p. 132, n. 2. The general rule is put succinctly in Dem. 46 *Steph.* ii. 22 τὸν νόμον . . . ὃς κελεύει ἐπιδικασίαν εἶναι τῶν ἐπικλήρων ἁπασῶν, καὶ ξένων καὶ ἀστῶν, καὶ περὶ μὲν τῶν πολιτῶν τὸν ἄρχοντα εἰσάγειν καὶ ἐπιμελεῖσθαι, περὶ δὲ τῶν μετοίκων τὸν πολέμαρχον, καὶ ἀνεπίδικον μὴ ἐξεῖναι ἔχειν μήτε κλῆρον μήτε ἐπίκληρον. ΝΟΜΟΣ. Κληροῦν δὲ τὸν ἄρχοντα κλήρων καὶ ἐπικλήρων, ὅσοι εἰσὶ μῆνες, πλὴν τοῦ σκιροφοριῶνος. ἀνεπίδικον δὲ κλῆρον μὴ ἔχειν.

[2] Dem. 46 *Steph.* ii. 23 αὐτόν . . . λαχεῖν ἔδει τῆς ἐπικλήρου εἴτε κατὰ δόσιν αὐτῷ προσῆκεν εἴτε κατὰ γένος. Isai. 3 *Pyrrh.* 30, 4 *Nikostr.* 2, for the fact that λῆξις was in writing. Paoli, *Studi e Testi* 125 (1946) 529, suggests that if she was already married her husband was required to notify the archon of her becoming an ἐπίκληρος: he argues from Pollux 8. 53 Δημοσθένης ἐν τῷ κατὰ Μέδοντος καὶ κατὰ τῶν μὴ προσηκόντων (codd: προσηκόντως Meier) τῇ ἐπικλήρῳ συνοικούντων γίνεσθαι τὰς εἰσαγγελίας λέγει, retaining the MS. reading; but see p. 32, n. 5.

[3] According to Wolff, *Traditio* 4 (1946), 70 ff. (*Beitr.* 65 ff.), who is followed by Kränzlein, *Eig. und Bes.* 94, this was an administrative act of the archon based on

If, on the other hand, there was more than one claimant, the issue was decided by a *διαδικασία* before a dicastery sitting under the archon as president. In either of these cases the heiress is said to have been adjudged, *ἐπιδεδικασμένη*. Even when an heiress had been adjudged, a rival claimant to her hand could still come forward and, after duly summoning the previous claimant, could have the matter reopened. What, if any, statute of limitations obtained here we do not know. It has been plausibly suggested that such a claim was at least barred if there had been male issue of the original union; for in that case one of the main purposes of the institution, the maintenance of the 'house' of the deceased father, would have been achieved.[1]

If a woman who was already married became an *ἐπίκληρος* her nearest male relative could claim her hand and force the dissolution of her existing marriage. If we are to believe a statement in one of Isaios' speeches this often actually happened.[2] Here again it has been argued that the next of kin could not claim if the heiress had already borne a son to, or some would hold even if she was pregnant by, her existing husband. The case of the *ἐγγυητή* is not quite on all fours with that of the *ἐπιδεδικασμένη* referred to at the end of the previous paragraph. The husband

his coercive power, not in any sense a judgement. For a different view see Lips., *AR* 581, Gernet, *AHDO* 1 (1937), 125, n. 1, 127 (*DSGA* 69, n. 3, 70), and p. 159, n. 5, below.

[1] For the herald's announcement see Dem. 43 *Makart.* 5 *τοῦ κήρυκος κηρύττοντος, εἴ τις ἀμφισβητεῖν ἢ παρακαταβάλλειν βούλεται τοῦ κλήρου τοῦ Ἁγνίου ἢ κατὰ γένος ἢ κατὰ διαθήκας*. Weiss, *GP* 283 ff. The law on *ἐπιδικασία* is quoted ibid. 16: *ἐὰν δ' ἐπιδεδικασμένου ἀμφισβητῇ τοῦ κλήρου ἢ τῆς ἐπικλήρου, προσκαλείσθω τὸν ἐπιδεδικασμένον πρὸς τὸν ἄρχοντα, καθάπερ ἐπὶ τῶν ἄλλων δικῶν· παρακαταβολὰς δ' εἶναι τῷ ἀμφισβητοῦντι. ἐὰν δὲ μὴ προσκαλεσάμενος ἐπιδικάσηται, ἀτελὴς ἔσται ἡ ἐπιδικασία τοῦ κλήρου. ἐὰν δὲ μὴ ζῇ ὁ ἐπιδικασάμενος τοῦ κλήρου, προσκαλείσθω κατὰ ταὐτά, ᾧ ⟨ἂν⟩ ἡ προθεσμία μήπω ἐξήκῃ. τὴν δ' ἀμφισβήτησιν εἶναι τῷ ἔχοντι, καθότι ἐπεδικάσατο οὗ ἂν ἔχῃ τὰ χρήματα*. The active of *ἐπιδικάζειν* is used of the archon (Dem. 48 *Olymp.* 26) or of the court which decided the case (Isai. 11 *Hagn.* 26); the passive of the property or the heiress (Isai. 6 *Philokt.* 14). In the middle the sense differs with different tenses; it can either be 'to put forward a claim' or 'to have one's claim confirmed (by archon or court)'; in the present, imperfect, and future tense only the former meaning is found, in the perfect only the latter, while in the aorist both meanings occur. See Wyse, *Isai.* 323 f. Caillemer, *Succession* 43, argues for prescription after the birth of a son, Hruza, *Beitr.* i. 111, against. Lips., *AR* 585, follows Caillemer, so too Paoli, *Studi e Testi* 125 (1946), 530.

[2] Isai. 3 *Pyrrh.* 64 *τὰς μὲν ὑπὸ τῶν πατέρων ἐκδοθείσας καὶ συνοικούσας ἀνδράσι γυναῖκας (περὶ ὧν τίς ἂν ἄμεινον ἢ ὁ πατὴρ βουλεύσαιτο;) καὶ τὰς οὕτω δοθείσας, ἂν ὁ πατὴρ αὐτῶν τελευτήσῃ μὴ καταλιπὼν αὐταῖς γνησίους ἀδελφούς, τοῖς ἐγγύτατα γένους ἐπιδίκους ὁ νόμος εἶναι κελεύει, καὶ πολλοὶ συνοικοῦντες ἤδη ἀφῄρηνται τὰς ἑαυτῶν γυναῖκας*.

of the latter was at least of the kin, if not next of kin, and had been so adjudged by an archon. The husband of the former might be a complete stranger. The state might well have been prepared to uphold the marriage within the kin, but not the other. The evidence is far from conclusive, but on the whole seems to justify the view that, where a son had been born, the next of kin could not force the dissolution of the marriage. In this case the property of course remained with the heiress to pass into the hands of the son as soon as he came of age. The wide statement in Isaios (3 *Pyrrh.* 64) will then have to be narrowed down to cover only those marriages which had produced no male issue.[1]

It is puzzling that in the law on legitimacy quoted above (p. 5, n. 2) nothing is said of children born of a woman married by ἐπιδικασία. Probably the lawgiver thought their inclusion too obvious to need special mention. We certainly need not suppose that, in these cases, the archon performed some kind of ἐγγύη.[2]

There is one important feature which is common to the two types of formal union hitherto considered. In both of them the bride is purely passive. In ἐπιδικασία, subject to the possible provisos mentioned above, the next of kin has an absolute right to her hand, and we find no hint that any revulsion to the match on her part would have influenced the archon or the dikastery in disposing of her. In ἐγγύη the contract was between the groom and the woman's κύριος. Here she at least had the chance of trying to play on the latter's feelings if she found the proposed match distasteful. But if she failed there seems no doubt that her κύριος could make a valid contract without her consent.

[1] See Appendix A.

[2] Isai. 6 *Philokt.* 14 προσῆκε τὴν Καλλίππην . . . πάνυ πάλαι συνοικεῖν, ἢ ἐγγυηθεῖσαν κατὰ τὸν νόμον ἢ ἐπιδικασθεῖσαν puts the two formal types of union clearly side by side. See Wyse ad loc., Lips., *AR* 473, n. 15. F. Bozza, *Ann. della R. Univ. di Catania* 1 (1934), 352 ff., *Scr. Jovene* (Naples, 1954), 487 ff., argues that ἐγγύη as a formal contract of marriage owed its origin to a definite act of legislation, possibly that of Solon. This would explain why in that law there is no reference to marriage by ἐπιδικασία. That one form of oath to certify the legitimacy of a son was εἶναι ἐξ ἀστῆς καὶ ἐγγυητῆς γυναικός may spring from the fact that marriage by ἐπιδικασία involved a public procedure which marriage by ἐγγύη did not. It was therefore more easily susceptible of proof by later issue of the marriage and there would have been less likelihood of the father's being required to certify the existence of the marriage by oath. Note that the oath prescribed in line 110 of the Demotionid inscription (*IG* ii². 1237 = *SIG* 921) is ὑὸν εἶναι . . . γήσιον ἐγ γαμετῆς and compare Ar., *Ath. Pol.* 4. 2, Isai. 12 *Euphil.* 9.

§ 4. *Less formal unions*

There can be no doubt that occasionally an Athenian would form a union with a woman which was based neither on an ἐγγύη nor on an ἐπιδικασία, but which was none the less more than purely casual. We have to determine what forms these unions might take, and whether they had any legal characteristics other than the negative one of not being based on ἐγγύη or ἐπιδικασία.

There are two particularly important texts bearing on this question. The first is from Drakon's homicide law quoted in Dem. 23 *Aristokr.* 53: Ἐάν τις ἀποκτείνῃ ἐν ἄθλοις ἄκων, ἢ ἐν ὁδῷ καθελὼν ἢ ἐν πολέμῳ ἀγνοήσας, ἢ ἐπὶ δάμαρτι ἢ ἐπὶ μητρὶ ἢ ἐπ' ἀδελφῇ ἢ ἐπὶ θυγατρί, ἢ ἐπὶ παλλακῇ ἣν ἂν ἐπ' ἐλευθέροις παισὶν ἔχῃ, τούτων ἕνεκα μὴ φεύγειν κτείναντα. The second text is from Isai. 3 *Pyrrh.* 39: Δοκεῖ ἂν ὑμῖν οὕτως ὀλιγώρως ἔχειν χρημάτων Νικόδημος ὥστε, εἰ ἦν ἀληθὲς τὸ πρᾶγμα, οὐκ ἂν σφόδρα διακριβώσασθαι περὶ τῶν ἑαυτῷ συμφερόντων; ναὶ μὰ Δία, ὥς ἔγωγ' οἶμαι, ἐπεὶ καὶ οἱ ἐπὶ παλλακίᾳ διδόντες τὰς ἑαυτῶν πάντες πρότερον διομολογοῦνται περὶ τῶν δοθησομένων ταῖς παλλακαῖς. Drakon's law included among those women whose seduction justified the immediate killing of the seducer without trial a παλλακή ('concubine')[1] whom a man had taken to himself with the purpose of breeding free children from her.[2] It may well be that in the early period when this rule was first framed such women would often be captives of war who were socially on the same level as their captors, women like Chryseis, Kassandra, or Andromache in the heroic sagas. These women would be the slaves of their captors, but in Homer at least the status of their offspring, though these were called νόθοι, could, if the father so willed, be much the same as that of his legitimate children.[3] In the aristocratic society of the middle seventh century B.C. the law was prepared to regard

[1] Some such word must be used, but we must not import into it anything like the same degree of moral censure as it now bears. παλλακαί were certainly socially inferior to married women; cf., for example, Lysias 1 *Killing of Erat.* 30 f. ἐπὶ ταῖς γαμεταῖς γυναιξί contrasted with ἐπὶ ταῖς παλλακαῖς ταῖς ἐλάττονος ἀξίαις. But they were not social outcasts and still less were the men who were their partners.

[2] For the status of the children see below, p. 164.

[3] For example, Agamemnon gives Teuker, the νόθος of Telamon, the patronymic (Τελαμώνιε, κοίρανε λαῶν) *Il.* 8. 281, and Odysseus, in his feigned character, says to Eumaios: ἐμὲ δ' ὠνητὴ τέκε μήτηρ / παλλακίς, ἀλλά με ἶσον ἰθαγενέεσσιν ἐτίμα / Κάστωρ, *Od.* 14. 202. Cf. Hruza, *Beitr.* ii. 71.

the seducer of such a woman as an adulterer, for the purposes of homicide rules at least, provided that her master was intending to breed free children from her.[1] Without such an intention on his part of course the children would have been slaves. Now it is true that with the passage of time and the disappearance of aristocracy this type of παλλακή became rarer or perhaps vanished altogether. Hence some scholars have taken the view that this clause in the law is an archaic survival and that there were no such unions in the classical period.[2] But Lysias (in the passage cited on p. 2, n. 2, above) does not seem to regard the clause as a dead letter, and the passage from Isai. 3 *Pyrrh.* 39, though its interpretation is controversial, tends in the same direction. The speaker is trying to impugn the contention of Nikodemos that he had married his sister by ἐγγύη to Pyrrhos. He suggests that, Pyrrhos being rich and Nikodemos poor, the natural thing would have been to fix up a fictitious dowry provided ostensibly by Nikodemos but really by Pyrrhos. This dowry would be forfeit to Nikodemos if the marriage were dissolved. He then argues, *a fortiori*, that even those who give their women-folk to men as *concubines* (καὶ οἱ ἐπὶ παλλακίᾳ διδόντες τὰς ἑαυτῶν) make some contract of this kind in advance to safeguard the position of the woman.[3] This passage suggests that there was a category of women whose fathers or brothers had established them as concubines in more or less permanent unions by means of arrangements similar to the ἐγγύη and dowry of a legitimate marriage, though without the legal backing which attached to those

[1] Not, as some would maintain, 'had already bred free children from her'. The Greek could not mean this, though it must be admitted that the mere intention of a master to treat a particular concubine in this way would have been difficult to prove. Lips., *AR* 480, n. 32.

[2] Hruza, *Beitr.* ii. 74 ff., Beauchet i. 105, Becker, *Plat.* 91, Erdmann, *Ehe* 108.

[3] To Hruza, *Beitr.* ii. 83 ff., and Beauch. i. 100 ff., it seemed impossible that τὰς ἑαυτῶν could refer to the daughters or sisters of the men who gave them as concubines. They argued that it would not merely have been socially degrading for a man to give his daughter as a concubine, but might even have rendered him liable to a prosecution for procuring, προαγωγεία (for which see Aischin. 1 *Timarch.* 14 and 184). They would therefore understand after τὰς ἑαυτῶν either δούλας or θεραπαίνας rather than θυγατέρας or ἀδελφάς. Erdmann, *Ehe* 111, takes the same view. But this argument is a *petitio principii*. Free Athenian women certainly became ἑταῖραι (see, e.g., Antiphanes, fr. 212 K.); it needs to be proved that no self-respecting father would commit his daughter to the more permanent union of παλλακία, and there is absolutely no evidence that such an act could lay him open to a charge of προαγωγεία. See Wyse, *Isai.* 318 f., Lips., *AR* 480. For the terms ἑταίρα and παλλακή see Wolff, *Traditio* 2 (1944), 74 (*Beitr.* 205), Bu. Sw. 941, n. 3.

institutions. Such παλλακαί would have fallen within, though they would not have exhausted, the category of παλλακαί covered by the homicide law. For within the latter would also have been included free women who formed these unions on their own initiative and without the intervention of any male relative, and also slave women on whom their masters had conferred this status. The basic difference between the free concubine and the married woman was that the former was not, like the latter, introduced into the husband's οἶκος and her children were not of the ἀγχιστεία. Whether they enjoyed any of the rights of a full citizen will be discussed in the chapter dealing with legitimacy.[1]

§ 5. *Polygamy*

There can be no doubt that the Athenians were, like other Greeks, generally speaking monogamous.[2] It does not necessarily follow, however, that there was a rule of law enforcing monogamy, and in fact some scholars have argued that there was not. They base their view on two different kinds of argument of very unequal weight. In the first place there is no direct evidence of a law which prohibited the contracting by married persons of subsequent marriages without the dissolution of the first. And yet, had there been such a law, one would have expected to find some reference either to a δίκη brought by an aggrieved consort or to a γραφή brought by some third party against a bigamist or polygamist; but nothing of the kind occurs. This argument carries great weight considering the comparative wealth of our information on Athenian litigation. Less convincing are the arguments drawn from supposed cases of actual bigamy at Athens. The details of the story of Mantias, round which Demosthenes' two speeches against Boiotos revolve, cannot be completely unravelled; but there is absolutely nothing which compels us to believe that he

[1] For the full significance of the transfer of the wife to the husband's οἶκος see below, pp. 30 ff. Wolff, *Traditio* 2 (1944), 43 ff., especially 69 ff. (*Beitr.* 196 ff.), has elaborated the distinction between what he calls 'solemn' marriage, originated by ἐγγύη or ἐπιδικασία, and less-formal unions. The theory comes, in effect, very near to H. Buermann's theory of a 'legitimate' concubinage put forward in *NJ*, Suppl. 9 (1877–8), 567 ff., though many of Buermann's arguments are misconceived.

[2] Hdt. 2. 92 of Egyptians γυναικὶ μιῇ ἕκαστος αὐτῶν συνοικέει κατάπερ Ἕλληνες. Klearchos *ap.* Athen. xiii. 2. 555 D ἐν Ἀθήναις πρῶτος Κέκροψ μίαν ἑνὶ ἔζευξεν. Erdmann, *Ehe* 87, Becker, *Plat.* 82 ff., Beauch. i. 39 ff., Lips., *AR* 478.

was married *simultaneously* to Plangon and to the mother of Demosthenes' client. Similarly, in connexion with Isaios' speech on the estate of Philoktemon, we are asked by those who rely on this case as evidence to suppose that at all material times Euktemon was married to the mother of Philoktemon, and that therefore when a subsequent marriage is alleged and the speaker, who wishes to discredit it, does not object that Euktemon was already married, this can only be because the first marriage was in law no bar to the second. But, though it is clear from the speech that Philoktemon's mother survived Euktemon, there is nothing to prove that their marriage had not been dissolved, and it would certainly not have been in the speaker's interest to draw attention to a divorce if it had taken place.[1] No weight should be attached to the expressions used by Andokides in his bitter attack on Kallias in his speech on the Mysteries, which, taken strictly, imply that Kallias was married both to the daughter of Ischomachos and to her mother simultaneously, nor to the second marriage which an Athenian contracts under a false name in Lemnos in Terence's *Phormio*, based on the *'Επιδικαζόμενος* of Menander.[2] Finally there are the stories that Sokrates was married both to Xanthippe and to Myrto, a granddaughter of Aristides, at the same time, and that Euripides had two wives at the same time. The former story occurs in Diogenes Laertios, where it is given on the authority of Aristotle. There is no hint of it in Plato or Xenophon. The latter is from Aulus Gellius.[3] These

[1] Isai. 6 *Philokt.* 10–16 and 39–40 with Wyse ad loc. The objection in the text above also applies to using yet another marriage—or perhaps merely projected marriage—of Euktemon, to a sister of Demokrates, as evidence of bigamy, ibid. 22.

[2] Andok. 1 *Myst.* 124 *γαμεῖ μὲν 'Ισχομάχου θυγατέρα· ταύτῃ δὲ συνοικήσας οὐδ' ἐνιαυτὸν τὴν μητέρα αὐτῆς ἔλαβε, καὶ συνῴκει ὁ πάντων σχετλιώτατος ἀνθρώπων τῇ μητρὶ καὶ τῇ θυγατρὶ . . . καὶ εἶχεν ἐν τῇ οἰκίᾳ ἀμφοτέρας . . .* (128) *ἐπέγημε τῇ θυγατρὶ τὴν μητέρα*. Lips., *AR* 479, n. 29, plausibly suggests that Kallias may well have taken the mother on as a concubine during his marriage with the daughter and only married the former after he had divorced the latter. Terence, *Phorm.* 114; later in the play, 958, 972, 1009, Chremes' conduct is strongly criticized. Cf. O. Müller, *NJ*, Suppl. 25 (1899), 707 ff., and Lips., loc. cit.

[3] D.L. 2. 26 *φησὶ δ' Ἀριστοτέλης δύο γυναῖκας αὐτὸν ἀγαγέσθαι, προτέραν μὲν Ξανθίππην, . . . δευτέραν δὲ Μυρτώ . . . οἱ δὲ προτέραν γῆμαι τὴν Μυρτώ φασιν· ἔνιοι δὲ καὶ ἀμφοτέρας σχεῖν ὁμοῦ, ὧν ἐστι Σάτυρός τε καὶ 'Ιερώνυμος ὁ 'Ρόδιος . . . φασὶ γὰρ βουληθέντας Ἀθηναίους διὰ τὸ λιπανδρεῖν συναυξῆσαι τὸ πλῆθος, ψηφίσασθαι γαμεῖν μὲν ἀστὴν μίαν, παιδοποιεῖσθαι δὲ καὶ ἐξ ἑτέρας· ὅθεν τοῦτο ποιῆσαι καὶ Σωκράτην.* Athen. xiii. 2. 556 adds Demetrios of Phaleron, Kallisthenes, and Aristoxenos to the witnesses and says that they were drawing on Aristotle's *Περὶ Εὐγενείας*. He goes on *εἰ μὴ ἄρα συγκεχωρημένον κατὰ ψήφισμα τοῦτο ἐγένετο τότε διὰ σπάνιν ἀνθρώπων,*

stories, based on late authority, may well be apocryphal in themselves. Their interest lies in their connexion with an alleged decree of the Athenians that allowed a man who was married to one woman to produce children from another (*γαμεῖν μὲν ἀστὴν μίαν, παιδοποιῆσαι δὲ καὶ ἐξ ἑτέρας*). The supposed purpose of the decree was to check a fall in the population, and it may well have been passed during the stress of the Peloponnesian war. Its effect would be that the children of the second union would have all the public rights and duties of full citizens, but what their position would have been in regard to family law and rights of succession we cannot say. From the fact that their mother was not a *γυνὴ γαμετή* we can probably conclude that they would at least have been at a disadvantage over against the children of the 'married' woman, otherwise why did not the decree simply say 'a man may marry a second wife'? On the other hand, if we are to believe Herakleides Pontikos (Plut., *Sol.* 22), they were excused from the duty of maintaining their parents in old age. Even assuming, as we probably should, that this decree was in fact passed, it does not prove that, even for this temporary emergency, Athenian law recognized bigamy. What it did was to give a more formal status to those informal unions between citizens described in the preceding paragraph.[1]

§ 6. *Forms*

There seem to have been few, if any, formal requirements to secure the validity of a solemn marriage. No doubt where there

ὥστ' ἐξεῖναι δύο ἔχειν γυναῖκας τὸν βουλόμενον . . . παρέθετο δὲ περὶ τῶν γυναικῶν ψήφισμα Ἱερώνυμος ὁ Ῥόδιος . . . ἀντεῖπε δὲ τοῖς λέγουσι περὶ τῶν Σωκράτους γυναικῶν Παναίτιος ὁ Ῥόδιος. His statement that Hieronymos actually quoted the decree counteracts the doubt cast on Aristotle's testimony from the fact that the *Περὶ Εὐγενείας* was probably not his work. Cf. Plut., *Aristeid.* 27, Aul. Gell., *N.A.* 15. 20 'sive quod (Euripides) duas simul uxores habuerat, cum id decreto ab Atheniensibus facto ius esset', Lips., *AR* 480, n. 31. Note that if Diogenes is following at all closely the wording of the decree the second partner is expressly not a *γυνὴ γαμετή*. On the decree see O. Müller, op. cit. 744 ff., 786 ff., Wyse, *Isai.* 279 f., Wolff, *Traditio* 2 (1944), 85 ff. (*Beitr.* 223 ff.), Bu. Sw. 940, Hignett, *HAC* 343 f.

[1] Hruza, *Beitr.* ii. 31 ff., is the main exponent of the view that polygamy, though neither expressly forbidden nor expressly allowed by law, was in fact practised at Athens; see his critical examination of the decree at op. cit. 53. He is followed by O. Damsté, *Mnemos.* 55 (1927), 365, and, hesitantly, by Wolff, *Traditio* 2 (1944), 81 (*Beitr.* 217), who refers especially to Dem. 39 *Boiot.* i. 26; but on this see p. 15, above.

was *ἐπιδικασία* the decision of the archon or the dikastery was formally recorded. As for *ἐγγύη*, the solemn statement of Kleisthenes of Sikyon and Megakles' words of acceptance, as recorded by Herodotos (p. 5, above), have a formal ring; and a similar exchange of words between the bride's father and the groom occurs in Menander, *Περικειρομένη* 435 (K.).[1] While some such expressions of intention by the two parties to the contract must have been necessary, there is no evidence that any particular form of words was needed. Similarly, while it was customary for both parties to bring their own witnesses to the transaction, this was not because witnesses were needed to give validity to the act, but because, in the absence of any form of registration, it was in the interest of both parties to be able to establish by witnesses that the *ἐγγύη* had taken place.[2]

There is equally little evidence that the completion of marriage by *ἔκδοσις* or *γάμος* required any special formality.[3]

As an *ἐγγύη* was a contract both parties to it naturally had to be of age, that is, to have reached the end of their seventeenth (or conceivably their eighteenth) year.[4] Once he had reached that age it seems that a man could marry (or for that matter refrain from marrying) without the consent of his father.[5] Nor

[1] *(Παταικός) ταύτην γνησίων / παίδων ἐπ' ἀρότῳ σοι δίδωμι. (Πολέμων) λαμβάνω. / (Πατ.) καὶ προῖκα τρία τάλαντα. (Πολ.) καὶ κάλως τόδε.* Cf. fr. 220 K. The bridegroom's intention to produce children from the union was probably considered a normal factor in an *ἐγγύη*, though we cannot assume that it was indispensable. Not too much stress should be laid on Isai. 3 *Pyrrh.* 70 *ὁ ἀδελφιδοῦς ὑμῶν ἠγγυᾶτο τὴν μητέρα τὴν ταύτης κατὰ τοὺς νόμους ἕξειν γυναῖκα.* It has been inferred from this that the groom bound himself, like a surety, to keep the woman as his lawful wife in the future. But the form of words here is unusual; normally the middle, *ἐγγυᾶσθαι*, has the woman as direct object, which leads Wyse ad loc. to read *ἔχειν* for *ἕξειν*. See, however, Lips., *AR* 469, n. 3, Partsch, *GB* 49.

[2] Dem. 30 *Onet.* i. 21 speaks as though witnesses were necessary rather for the purpose of proving than of validating a marriage: *μὴ γὰρ ὅτι πρὸς τοῦτον τοιοῦτον ὄντα, ἀλλ' οὐδὲ πρὸς ἄλλον οὐδ' ἂν εἷς οὐδένα τοιοῦτον συνάλλαγμα ποιούμενος ἀμαρτύρως ἂν ἔπραξεν· ἀλλὰ τῶν τοιούτων ἕνεκα καὶ γάμους ποιοῦμεν καὶ τοὺς ἀναγκαιοτάτους παρακαλοῦμεν, ὅτι οὐ πάρεργον, ἀλλ' ἀδελφῶν καὶ θυγατέρων βίους ἐγχειρίζομεν, ὑπὲρ ὧν τὰς ἀσφαλείας μάλιστα σκοποῦμεν.* Cf. Isai. 3 *Pyrrh.* 18 ff., 29, 8 *Kir.* 14, Dem. 57 *Eubul.* 41, and Beauch. i. 140, Becker, *Plat.* 55, Erdmann, *Ehe* 242. Lack of form characterized Athenian contracts generally.

[3] See p. 7, with n. 2, above.

[4] See p. 74 with n. 3, below.

[5] Lysias, fr. 24 Th., Dem. 40 *Boiot.* ii. 4 *συνέβη γάρ μοι δεηθέντος τοῦ πατρὸς ὀκτωκαιδεκέτη γῆμαι.* The words imply that the father could urge, but not command. According to Ar., *Ath. Pol.* 42. 5, one of the limited number of lawsuits in which an *ephebos* was permitted to become engaged during his two years of military duty on reaching eighteen years of age was a suit for the hand of an heiress.

did the Athenian state, as did some others (notably Sparta), penalize celibacy. It is unlikely that there was at Athens a γραφὴ ἀγαμίου.[1] There is some evidence that an unmarried man who had raped or seduced a girl could in certain circumstances be forced to marry her; possibly the rule was that if he was caught *flagrante delicto* in the girl's house (and thereby technically a μοῖχος) he could escape the death penalty at the hands of the girl's father by marrying her without dowry provided his own father consented. The evidence, however, is almost entirely from Roman comedy and writers on rhetoric of the Roman period.[2]

Those who were competent to make the contract on the woman's side are given in the law in Dem. 46 *Steph.* ii. 18 (p. 5, n. 2, above). They were, in the following order, her father, brother by the same father, paternal grandfather. If none of these were alive she might be technically an ἐπίκληρος. In that case, the law says, 'her master is to have her' (τὸν κύριον ἔχειν). This must surely mean that the ἐπιδικασία determined who was her κύριος, but that this κύριος, unlike all others, could not dispose

[1] Ariston *ap.* Stob., *Flor.* 67. 16 Σπαρτιατῶν νόμος τάττει τὴν μὲν πρώτην ἀγαμίου, τὴν δευτέραν ὀψιγαμίου, τὴν τρίτην καὶ μεγίστην κακογαμίου. Pollux 3. 48 ἦσαν δὲ ἀγαμίου δίκαι πολλαχοῦ. Plut., *Lys.* 30, *Lyk.* 15, Klearch. *ap.* Athen. xiii. 2. There is no trace of anything similar at Athens. Even the statement of Dinarchos, *Dem.* 71, that to be a *rhetor* or a general at Athens you had to have children, which would have been a mild discouragement of celibacy, is unlikely to be true. Kahrstedt, *Mag.* 23. Cf. Lips., *AR* 341, 481, Erdmann, *Ehe* 113 ff., who makes the conclusive point that if there had been a γραφὴ ἀγαμίου at Athens it must have been mentioned in Dem. 44 *Leoch.*, where the speaker is trying to establish the fact that Archiades died unmarried.

[2] Plaut., *Aul.* 793 ff. 'ut mi ignoscas eamque uxorem mihi des, ut leges iubent: ego me iniuriam fecisse filiae fateor tuae', Ter., *Andr.* 780 f. 'coactus legibus eam uxorem ducet'. Hermogenes π. στασ. 10, p. 87 Rabe, δύο τις κατὰ ταὐτὸν ἐβιάσατο κόρας, καὶ ἡ μὲν γάμον, ἡ δὲ θάνατον αἱρεῖται τοῦ βιασαμένου, gives the injured girl the choice between marrying the man and requiring his death. According to Plut., *Sol.* 23, on the other hand, a law of Solon made the penalty for rape 100 drachmai. It is difficult to disentangle fourth-century Athenian law out of this evidence. MSL 509 thought the passages from Roman comedy conclusive, as did Beauch. i. 139, Glotz, *Solidarité* 356, n. 1, O. Fredershausen, *Herm.* 47 (1912), 212, Lips., *AR* 482. Erdmann, *Ehe* 116, n. 20, argues against on the ground, first, of the alleged Solonian law and, second, that Menander's *Arbitr.*, which concerns a girl who has been seduced, makes no mention of such a rule. MSL, loc. cit., supposed that there was a special suit to enforce marriage, Lips., loc. cit., that a γραφὴ ὕβρεως or δίκη βιαίων would have sufficed to compel the seducer to marry if the girl's relatives so desired. Paoli, *RIDA* 1 (1952), 267 deduces the rule as stated in the text from Seneca, *Contr.* ii. 3, Quintilian, *Decl.* 349, *Inst. Or.* 9. 2. 90. Men., *Fab. Inc.* 30, confirms that the man's father must ἐπιβεβαιοῦν.

of her hand at his discretion, but had to marry her himself.[1] She might, however, not be an ἐπίκληρος. For example, she might have a nephew by a brother who was dead; the nephew would then be heir. The provision of the law for this case is unfortunately obscure. Three different meanings have been suggested for the first three words of the relevant sentence ὅτῳ ἂν ἐπιτρέψῃ, τοῦτον κύριον εἶναι: either 'he to whom she has committed herself' or 'he to whom the archon has committed her' or 'he to whom her father has committed her' shall be her master. As the text stands the woman herself seems to be the only possible subject for the verb ἐπιτρέψῃ.[2] But it is difficult to believe that a woman would have been allowed to choose her own κύριος, particularly in view of the early age at which girls were often married at Athens. It is probably better therefore to assume that either ὁ ἄρχων or ὁ πατήρ has fallen out before ἐπιτρέψῃ: the latter conjecture is slightly preferable, and the rule will then be that, where a woman was not an ἐπίκληρος, her father could appoint a κύριος for her by will.[3]

[1] Dem. 46 *Steph.* ii. 18, after the words quoted in p. 5, n. 2, ἐὰν δὲ μηδεὶς ᾖ τούτων, ἐὰν μὲν ἐπίκληρός τις ᾖ, τὸν κύριον ἔχειν,' ἐὰν δὲ μὴ ᾖ, ὅτῳ ἂν ἐπιτρέψῃ, τοῦτον κύριον εἶναι. When there was more than one brother they acted together, Isai. 2 *Menekl.* 3 ff.; Dem. 40 *Boiot.* ii. 7, 44 *Leoch.* 9, 17. For this purpose an adoptive brother was apparently in the same position as a blood brother; in Isai. 3 *Pyrrh.* 45 Endios, the adopted son of Pyrrhos, gives his daughter in marriage to Xenokles; this is not quite a straight case, however, since the legitimacy of the daughter was in question. In Isai. 7 *Apollod.* 9 Apollodoros makes a will devising his property to his stepsister by the same mother and giving her in marriage to Lakratides; as he was not the woman's ἀδελφὸς ὁμοπάτωρ he could presumably only act thus as her adoptive father (cf. Wyse ad loc., Hruza, *Beitr.* i. 56, n. 21, Lips., *AR* 471, n. 9). It appears from Lys. 32 *Diogeit.* 1–9 that Diogeiton had given the daughter of his brother (who was also his son-in-law) in marriage to the speaker of the speech. His relationship to the woman (uncle and maternal grandfather) would not have entitled him to act. He will have acted either as guardian of the woman herself (so Lips., *AR* 472, n. 9) or as guardian of her brother, who was not of age at the time of the marriage (so Hruza, *Beitr.* i. 59, n. 24, Erdmann, *Ehe* 229, n. 10). When in Isai. 9 *Astyph.* 29 a man gives his stepdaughter in marriage though she has a brother ὁμοπάτωρ who is of age, he does it with the consent of that brother. Gernet, *RÉG* 34 (1921), 340, doubts whether the order—father, brother, grandfather—is strictly hierarchic; Plato, *Laws* 774 e, puts the grandfather before the brothers. He quotes (ibid. 353) Andok. 1 *Myst.* 119 to show that at that date it was felt that the next of kin had a moral duty to marry an ἐπίκληρος; he believes that at an earlier date this would have been a legally binding duty. If an ἐπίκληρος belonged to the lowest of the four Solonian census classes her next of kin was bound to marry her or to provide her with a dowry of a specified amount related to the census class to which *he* belonged. Dem. 43 *Makart.* 54, Wyse, *Isai.* 285, p. 136, below.

[2] So Wolff, *TR* 20 (1952), 25, n. 70.

[3] The law makes no provision for the father's having omitted to do so; probably

In some circumstances at least a husband could bestow his wife on another man. The case of Demosthenes' father has already been mentioned (p. 6 and cf. p. 30, below). In the same way Pasion bestowed his wife on Phormion by will (Dem. 36 *For Phorm.* 8), and other instances are given later in the same speech (28, 29), one of them of a man who lived on after the second marriage and on the death of the woman married off his daughter to the same man (though this was in Aigina). According to Plutarch (*Per.* 24), Perikles bestowed his wife, with her consent, on another man (*ἑτέρῳ βουλομένην συνεξέδωκεν*: the last word could be taken to mean that her former *κύριος* consented also).

The bride was the passive object of the contract; her consent to it was not necessary, and in *ἐγγύαι* during the classical period at least even her presence was not required. Similarly for *ἐγγύη* no minimum age was laid down; the hand of Demosthenes' sister was thus disposed of when she was only five (p. 6, above). The completion of marriage by *ἔκδοσις* naturally depended on her reaching maturity, which happened about the age of fourteen. But there is no trace of any minimum age laid down by law.[1]

§ 7. *Legal bars to marriage*

As we have seen above (pp. 15 ff.), it is doubtful whether the fact that one or other spouse (or indeed both) was already married would have invalidated a second marriage. Owing, however, to the extreme ease with which either spouse could dissolve a marriage it is not likely that the situation often arose.

Blood relationship between the man and wife might be a bar to marriage, but the degree of affinity which created a bar was not nearly so remote as that in modern systems based on the canon law. In principle the Athenian system was endogamic, as

in such cases the archon was called in. For *ὁ πατὴρ* before *ἐπιτρέψῃ* see Gernet, *Dem.* ii. 191, n. 2. He has rightly there abandoned the view he put forward in *RÉG* 31 (1918), 193 that *ὅτῳ ἂν ἐπιτρέψῃ κτλ.* means 'he to whom her father has *wedded* her (sc. by *ἐγγύη*) shall be her master'. Cf. C. Gatti, *Acme* 10 (1957), 57 ff. For earlier views on this passage see Lips., *AR* 536, n. 77.

[1] Demosthenes' sister was five at his father's death (27 *Aphob.* i. 4) and was due to marry Demophon in nine years' time on reaching maturity. The archon ceased to be responsible for an heiress's property when she reached the age of fourteen, Ar., *Ath. Pol.* 56. 7, Lips., *AR* 481.

can be seen very clearly in the rules relating to ἐπίκληροι.[1] Marriage between ascendants and descendants was repugnant to Greek morality and contrary to that unwritten law which in some matters was regarded as equally binding with the written law.[2] Marriage between brothers and sisters by the same mother was forbidden, and therefore by implication that of full brothers and sisters. But marriage between brothers and sisters by the same father but a different mother was allowed. This rule has been doubted, but not only is it specifically vouched for by Nepos, Philo Judaeus, and a scholiast to Aristophanes (rather late authorities, it is true); in at least two instances of a marriage between brother and sister (one drawn from a fourth-century source) it is emphasized that they were not of the same mother. The inference from this must be that they were of the same father only and that this sanctioned their marriage.[3] No satisfactory

[1] E. Weiss, 'Endogamie und Exogamie', *Z* 29 (1908), 340 ff., Becker, *Plat.* 62 ff., Erdmann, *Ehe* 179 ff. (with further references on p. 179, n. 1).

[2] Plato, *Laws* 838 b, *Rep.* 461 b, Xen., *Mem.* 4. 4. 20, Eur., *Andr.* 173 ff.

[3] Nepos, *Cim.* 1, 2 'habebat in matrimonio sororem suam germanam nomine Elpinicen non magis amore quam patrio more ductus: nam Atheniensibus licet eodem patre natas uxores ducere', where 'germana' must stand for ὁμοπάτριος (cf. Festus, p. 95 'germen—unde et germani quasi eadem stirpe geniti'). Philo, *de spec. leg.* iii. 4, p. 303 M. ὁ μὲν οὖν Ἀθηναῖος Σόλων ὁμοπατρίους ἐφεὶς ἄγεσθαι τὰς ὁμομητρίους ἐκώλυσεν. ὁ δὲ Λακεδαιμονίων νομοθέτης ἔμπαλιν τὸν ἐπὶ ταῖς ὁμογαστρίοις γάμον ἐπιτρέψας τὸν πρὸς ὁμοπατρίους ἀπεῖπεν. Schol. Aristoph., *Cl.* 1371 ἐπεὶ δὲ παρ' Ἀθηναίοις ἔξεστι γαμεῖν τὰς ἐκ πατέρων ἀδελφάς, εἰς αὔξησιν τοῦ ἀδικήματος προσέθηκε τὴν ὁμομητρίαν. Dem. 57 *Eubul.* 20 ἀδελφὴν γὰρ ὁ πάππος οὑμὸς ἔγημεν οὐχ ὁμομητρίαν. In Plut., *Them.* 32, one of Themistokles' daughters is married by her brother οὐκ ὢν ὁμομήτριος. Hruza, *Beitr.* ii. 165, vainly tries to discount this evidence, which runs counter to his view that even marriage or extramarital intercourse between parent and child, though impious and morally reprobated, was not forbidden or punishable by law, nor was such a marriage treated as null; *a fortiori* there can have been no distinction in law between marriages of ὁμοπάτριοι and ὁμομήτριοι. Hruza uses two arguments of unequal cogency to support his view. In the most famous instance of an incestuous marriage, that of Oidipous and Jokasta, the discovery of the incest does not make the marriage void, nor are the children legally incapacitated by it. But, even if we can accept the outline of the legend as valid evidence for the rules of historical Athens, we should at least take the version of the legend as it appears in Sophokles. In *O.T.* 1214, 1256 the marriage is ἄγαμον γάμον and Jokasta is γυναῖκα οὐ γυναῖκα. Further, in Sophokles the status of the children *is* affected; thus in *O.C.* 367 ff. Eteokles and Polyneikes are represented as criminal usurpers of the royal power which had belonged to Oidipous, and ibid. 830–3 Kreon claims to be κύριος of Antigone, which means that she is regarded as the illegitimate daughter of Jokasta and falls under the power of her mother's nearest male relative, her brother; cf. Glotz, DS s.v. *incestum* 450. A more plausible argument is that we hear of no action at law which either was or could be brought against those guilty of incest, and in fact there is in Greek no technical term for incest. But, as Glotz (loc. cit.) points out, there were indirect sanctions which could

rationale for this rule has been advanced. The rule at Sparta was the exact opposite (see Philo, loc. cit.), and this rule was more consonant with the concept put into the mouth of Apollo in Aisch., *Eum.* 657 ff. and recurring elsewhere that the mother is nothing more than the nurse of the father's seed and as such is not strictly related to the child: ἡ δ' ἅπερ ξένῳ ξένη / ἔσωσεν ἔρνος.[1]

Since a brother could marry his half-sister we are not surprised to find that an uncle could, and often did, marry his niece, whether she were the daughter of his brother or of his sister. In fact her father's brother had the first claim to the hand of an ἐπίκληρος.[2]

Adoptive relationships were no bar to marriage. In fact a man who had only daughters would often adopt a son or sons, at the same time marrying them to the daughters; he probably could not adopt a son without so marrying him (see below on adoption,

be brought to bear on those who offended against the unwritten law, if indeed this was an unwritten law. For example, ἐγγύη ἐπὶ δικαίοις would have been impossible in such cases, the ceremonies in connexion with the γαμηλία could have been interdicted, the guilty parties might have been excluded from all religious rites, as were women taken in adultery (Dem. 59 *Neair.* 85). Cf. Glotz's formulation (loc. cit. 455): 'l'inceste, interdit par la θέμις, entravé par le droit public, n'était punissable que s'il lésait un tiers.' Hruza, op. cit. 170, relies much too heavily on Minucius Felix, *Oct.* 31. 3 'Aegyptiis et Atheniensibus cum sororibus legitima matrimonia', to show that marriage between full brother and sister was permitted. It would be equally wrong to deduce from Menander *Arbitr.* 165 ff. (K.), that marriage between ὁμοπάτριοι was prohibited. In general statements such as these the necessary qualifying words were often quite naturally omitted. Becker, *Plat.* 66, deduces from Plut., *Kim.* 4, that the only penal offence was extramarital intercourse between brother and sister, and that the offence was the abuse of the brother's position as κύριος of his sister. Cf. also Lips., *AR* 476, O. Fredershausen, *Herm.* 47 (1912), 202 ff.

[1] Cf. for the same sentiment Eur., *Or.* 552. E. Weiss, *Z* 29 (1908), 341 ff. Glotz, loc. cit., sees nothing but social and economic reasons for the two different rules at Athens and Sparta. The Athenian made provision for an undowered girl by allowing a brother by the same father to marry her; there is here no fusion of οἶκοι or properties. On the other hand, if the common parent was the mother and *if the daughter was an ἐπίκληρος and the son an only son* a marriage between them would fuse the houses and properties, and this was contrary to the spirit of Athenian law since the time of Solon at least. But the effects described only follow if the condition in the italicized clause applies. If, for example, Neaira has a son and daughter by Aristonikos and another son and daughter by Euboulos, marriages between the two pairs of children will have precisely the same economic effect as if the children had had different mothers as well as different fathers (except that there might have been extra property available from the dowry of the second mother). The legislator would have achieved the purpose suggested by Glotz more simply by forbidding an ἐπίκληρος to marry a brother by the same mother unless there were another brother to remain in the father's house.

[2] Dem. 44 *Leoch.* 10, 59 *Neair.* 2, 22, Lys. 32 *Diogeit.* 4, Isai. 10 *Aristarch.* 5.

pp. 84 ff.). A law, purporting to be Solon's, banning the marriage of a guardian either to his ward or to his ward's mother and the marriage of his son to his ward is either wholly apocryphal or had fallen into disuse by the fourth century.[1]

The status of the parties might be a bar to their marriage. It may be taken as certain, though there is no direct evidence on the point, that marriage by ἐγγύη or ἐπιδικασία could not take place between a slave and a free person. For a slave woman could not by any circumstance become an ἐπίκληρος and could therefore never be ἐπίδικος. While as for ἐγγύη, if the man were the slave we should have to suppose that in this instance alone a slave was deemed capable of making a contract, and if the woman were the slave that her κύριος could somehow convey her to the groom by a contract which was distinct from that of sale; of course if she was already the property of the groom there could be no ἐγγύη. It is probable that an informal union (as described on pp. 13 ff., above) could be formed between a free man and a slave woman, but not of course between a free woman and a slave man.[2]

Where one of the parties was Athenian and the other a foreigner or metic, the rule differed at different periods.[3] In the heroic period marriages between foreigners were common enough, at least in the heroic class. Helen, for example, is the wife of Paris, and Penelope's suitors come from all over the Greek world. Specific examples prove that the same was true of Athens in the sixth and early fifth centuries B.C. The Alkmaeonid Megakles married Agariste, daughter of Kleisthenes of Sikyon (see above, p. 5). The great Miltiades married Hegesipyle, daughter of

[1] D.L. 1. 56 κάλλιστον κἀκεῖνο, τὸν ἐπίτροπον τῇ τῶν ὀρφάνων μητρὶ μὴ συνοικεῖν. Syrianus on Hermog. 2. 72 Rabe. νόμος τὴν ἐπιτροπευομένην γυναῖκα μήτε τὸν ἐπίτροπον μήτε τὸν παῖδα αὐτοῦ γαμεῖν. Demosthenes' father intended that after his death his wife should marry Demosthenes' guardian, 27 *Aphob.* i. 5. Phormion marries Pasion's widow and becomes guardian of his son, 36 *For Phorm.* 8. In Isai. 9 *Astyph.* 27 Theophrastos marries the widow of Euthykrates and seems to be acting as guardian of their son, Astyphilos. In Isai. 6 *Philokt.* 13 a woman is alleged to have borne two sons to her guardian. The speaker is trying to throw doubt on the parentage of these sons, and if it had been against the law for a guardian to marry his ward he must surely have made the point. Beauch. i. 177 ff., Lips., *AR* 477, Erdmann, *Ehe* 188.

[2] Becker, *Plat.* 70, Erdmann, *Ehe* 195.

[3] Lips., *AR* 417 ff., 473 ff., Paoli, *St. Dir.* 258 ff., Becker, *Plat.* 74, Bu. Sw. 939 ff., Erdmann, *Ehe* 167 ff. (bibliography, ibid., n. 1). O. Fredershausen, *Herm.* 47 (1912), 205 ff., for the evidence which can be drawn from Roman comedy.

Oloros, a Thracian prince, and Kimon was their son. Themistokles' mother was a Thracian or Carian. The only hint that any of these was not a true marriage is Plutarch's story that Themistokles had, as a bastard (*νόθος*), to exercise in the gymnasium of Kynosarges. But, as Themistokles was almost certainly archon in 493/492, it is highly improbable that he was a *νόθος*.[1]

A change was made in 451/450 when a law, proposed by Perikles, enacted that only he whose parents were both Athenians should enjoy citizen rights; as Aristotle puts it in *Ath. Pol.* 26. 4, *ἐπὶ Ἀντιδότου διὰ τὸ πλῆθος τῶν πολιτῶν, Περικλέους εἰπόντος, ἔγνωσαν μὴ μετέχειν τῆς πόλεως ὃς ἂν μὴ ἐξ ἀμφοῖν ἀστοῖν ᾖ γεγονώς*, or, as Plut. *Per.* 37, *Π. νόμον ἔγραψε μόνους Ἀθηναίους εἶναι τοὺς ἐκ δυεῖν Ἀθηναίων γεγονότας*. It seems probable that in one sense this law was not, and that in another sense it was, retrospective. We can hardly believe that all existing children of mixed marriages were disfranchised by it. To go no further, Kimon was such a one, and he was still a strategos when he died late in 450 or early in 449. On the other hand, it would seem likely that children of mixed marriages born after the passing of the law would not have been citizens, and that therefore, if one mark of a marriage is that it should guarantee the citizenship of the children, the law annulled existing mixed marriages.[2] This law was still in force in 414, for in that year Aristophanes (in *Birds* 1649 ff.) makes Peisthetairos explain that Herakles is excluded from rights of succession as a *νόθος* and he is a *νόθος* because his mother was a foreigner. This must be based on the Athenian law of the time (and indeed the law is attributed by Peisthetairos to Solon). During the next decade, however, partly perhaps because of the manpower problem which led to the rule legitimizing the offspring of informal unions (p. 17, above), the law must have fallen into disuse, for in 403/402 a decree was passed

[1] For Megakles, Hdt. 6. 126; for Miltiades, Hdt. 6. 39, Plut., *Kim.* 4; for Themistokles, Plut., *Them.* 1, Nepos, *Them.* 1, and Hruza, *Beitr.* ii. 111 and 120, n. 29, Ledl, *WS* 30 (1908), 188 ff. See further below on *νόθοι*, pp. 61 ff.

[2] Or perhaps better 'fundamentally altered their character'. If there were no desire to have more children the marriage could go on. For a full discussion of this law see Appendix X in Hignett, *HAC* 343 ff. He aptly points out that, unless the law was retrospective as regards the children, the motive given by Aristotle (to contain the citizen population) must be wrong except on the assumption that Athenian men who would before have married foreign women would now not marry at all. The more probable motive was a desire to preserve the racial purity of the citizen stock.

in the same terms as the law of 451/450, but with the proviso that children of mixed marriages born before 403/402 should retain their citizenship. The famous Timotheos, son of Konon, was the child of a mixed marriage; his mother was a Thracian.[1] Probably at some later date, but certainly before the date of Demosthenes 59 *Neaira* (*c.* 340), a further step was taken. Hitherto mixed marriages had been discouraged indirectly by the disabilities falling on the children; now the parties to any such marriage are to be subject to heavy penalties if convicted in a *γραφή* before the court of the thesmothetai. Two laws were passed. By the first a foreign man who was convicted of living with an Athenian woman as her husband was to be sold into slavery, his goods confiscated, and one-third of the proceeds given to his accuser; a foreign woman convicted of living with an Athenian man as his wife was liable to the same penalty, and in addition the man had to pay a fine of 1,000 drachmai. By the second law anyone ('any Athenian' must be meant) who was convicted of giving a foreign woman in marriage to an Athenian man representing her as related to him (viz., related in such a way as entitled him to give her in marriage) is to suffer *ἀτιμία*, his goods are to be confiscated, and a third of the proceeds to be paid to his accuser.[2] This second law is carelessly drafted; it would have been clearer if *ὡς ἄστην* had stood for *ὡς ἑαυτῷ προσήκουσαν*, since it would

[1] Eumelos, *F.Gr.H.* 77 F 2 *Εὔμηλος ὁ περιπατητικὸς ἐν τῷ γ' περὶ τῆς ἀρχαίας κωμῳδίας φησὶ Νικομένη τινὰ ψήφισμα θέσθαι μηδένα τῶν μετ' Εὐκλείδην ἄρχοντα μετέχειν τῆς πόλεως, ἂν μὴ ἄμφω τοὺς γονέας ἀστοὺς δείξηται, τοὺς δὲ πρὸ Εὐκλείδου ἀνεξετάστους ἀφεῖσθαι.* In Karystios, fr. 11 Müller, *F.Gr.H.* iv. 358, the law is attributed to Aristophon. Possibly Aristophon's law made the rule retrospective and Nikomenes' decree simply reversed this particular clause: A. Schäfer, *Dem. und seiner Zeit*[2] (Leipzig, 1885), 139. Dem. 57 *Eubul.* 30 *τοῖς χρόνοις τοίνυν οὕτω φαίνεται γεγονὼς (ὁ πατὴρ) ὥστε εἰ καὶ κατὰ θάτερα ἀστὸς ἦν, εἶναι πολίτην προσήκειν αὐτόν· γέγονε γὰρ πρὸ Εὐκλείδου.* Isai. 6 *Philokt.* 47, 8 *Kir.* 43. Lips., *AR* 414, n. 146, points out that Demosthenes' wording implies that the proviso covered mixed marriages where *either* the mother *or* the father was Athenian and that this is slightly confirmed by a decree recorded by Krateros, *F.Gr.H.* 342 F 4, *ἐὰν δέ τις ἐξ ἀμφοῖν ξένοιν γεγονὼς φρατρίζῃ, διώκειν εἶναι τῷ βουλομένῳ Ἀθηναίων.* See Jacoby's commentary ad loc. and further discussion below in connexion with *νόθοι*, pp. 61 ff. For Timotheos' parentage Athen. xiii. 38, 577, Erdmann, *Ehe* 171.

[2] Dem. 59 *Neair.* 16 *'Εὰν δὲ ξένος ἀστῇ συνοικῇ τέχνῃ ἢ μηχανῇ ᾑτινιοῦν, γραφέσθω πρὸς τοὺς θεσμοθέτας Ἀθηναίων ὁ βουλόμενος οἷς ἔξεστιν. ἐὰν δὲ ἁλῷ, πεπράσθω καὶ αὐτὸς καὶ ἡ οὐσία αὐτοῦ, καὶ τὸ τρίτον μέρος ἔστω τοῦ ἑλόντος· ἔστω δὲ καὶ ἐὰν ἡ ξένη τῷ ἀστῷ συνοικῇ κατὰ ταὐτά, καὶ ὁ συνοικῶν τῇ ξένῃ τῇ ἁλούσῃ ὀφειλέτω χιλίας δραχμάς.* Ibid. 52 *'Εὰν δέ τις ἐκδῷ ξένην γυναῖκα ἀνδρὶ Ἀθηναίῳ ὡς ἑαυτῷ προσήκουσαν, ἄτιμος ἔστω, καὶ ἡ οὐσία αὐτοῦ δημοσία ἔστω, καὶ τοῦ ἑλόντος τὸ τρίτον μέρος. γραφέσθων δὲ πρὸς τοὺς θεσμοθέτας οἷς ἔξεστιν, καθάπερ τῆς ξενίας.*

have been a nice point whether an Athenian who had had a daughter by a foreign woman, a daughter who was thus a *ξένη*, would have been liable under the law if he gave this daughter in marriage *ὡς ἑαυτῷ προσήκουσαν*. But the two laws should probably be read together. We may conjecture that under the first law the Athenian man who married a foreign woman was liable to a fine only if he had known her true status when he married (or persisted in the marriage on coming to know it); the second law meets the case where he has been deceived, by punishing the deceiver. Symmetry would require that some penalty should fall on the *κύριος* of an Athenian woman who knowingly married her to a foreigner, for the woman, not being a free agent, could not be punished; but there is no evidence for this.[1] A very different view of the force of the first law has been taken, based partly on the fact that the law does not declare these marriages void, partly on the supposed need to import into the phrase *τέχνῃ ἢ μηχανῇ ᾑτινιοῦν* the idea of deceit. On this view what this law is punishing is not the mixed marriage itself, but fraud used to procure a mixed marriage. The fine is imposed on the Athenian husband only if he continues to cohabit with the woman between the time the charge was brought and her conviction as a foreigner.[2] But there was no reason for the legislator to declare these marriages null explicitly. They were in fact already null in the sense that they could not produce legitimate children; but it is one thing to say that the offspring of a union shall be treated as though the union did not exist and quite another to inflict drastic penalties on those who entered upon the union. Nor is it plausible to suppose that, where an Athenian man had married a woman in good faith, supposing her to be Athenian too, he should have been made liable to a heavy fine simply for persisting in

[1] Unless we believe in a *δίκη* or *γραφὴ ἐξαγωγῆς* available against such a person on the evidence of Dem. 25 *Aristogeit.* i. 55 (*ἀδελφὴν ἐπ' ἐξαγωγῇ ἀπέδοτο, ὥς φησι τὸ ἔγκλημα τῆς δίκης*) and id. 24 *Timokr.* 203 (*τὴν μὲν ἀδελφὴν ἐπ' ἐξαγωγῇ, φησὶ μὲν ἐκδοῦναι, πέπρακε δὲ τῷ ἔργῳ*). But, even if the first speech against Aristogeiton were better evidence than it is for Athenian law—and on this see Lips., *AR* 420, *Leipz. Stud.* 6 (1883), 317 ff.—the charge seems to have been selling rather than giving in marriage, and the wording of the other passage is too vague to support the existence of a suit *ἐξαγωγῆς*.

[2] Hruza, *Beitr.* ii. 135 ff., Beauch. i. 203 ff. criticized by Ledl, *WS* 30 (1908), 7. Erdmann, *Ehe* 173 f. Wolff, *Traditio* 2 (1944), 66 ff., is ambiguous: he takes *τέχνῃ ἢ μηχανῇ* to indicate fraud, but oscillates between regarding the fraud as practised by one spouse on the other and as practised by both on the world at large.

cohabitation after a charge was brought; manifestly such a penalty would only have been equitable if he had persisted after the wife's conviction, and this would have involved in effect two quite separate *γραφαί*.

On the other, and preferable, view of these two laws, the Athenian husband had alternative defences. He could join with the wife in pleading that she was not in fact a foreigner; if there was a conviction he would then be liable to the fine. Or he could plead good faith; but if he did not then himself bring a *γραφή* against his wife's *κύριος* the prosecution could make considerable play with his failure to do so.

The foreign man's offence in such a case will have consisted in entering into a permanent union with an Athenian woman, whether by *ἐγγύη*, which would have involved his falsely representing himself as a citizen, or in a less formal union, which, though not necessarily based on deception of his wife, may have been intended to impose on the outside world. Purely casual relationships would not have come under the statute, though it would clearly have been difficult in specific cases to determine whether the union was sufficiently settled to be described as *συνοικεῖν*.[1]

[1] On the view favoured above *τέχνῃ ἢ μηχανῇ ἡτινιοῦν* means 'in whatsoever manner'. The question arises whether, when joined to *συνοικεῖν*, these words made the penalty apply to any kind of union, whether marital or not. P. S. Photiades, *Athena* 32 (1921), 146 f., argued that they did. Against him Erdmann, *Ehe* 174, relying principally on two passages (they could be multiplied) where *συνοικεῖν* is used as the technical legal term for 'marry', Isai., locc. citt. (p. 2, n. 4, above). But it is doubtful whether we should press these and other instances of the use of the word to describe solemn marriage to the point of arguing that it could never be used to describe those less formal unions which, for some purposes, the law seems to have recognized (see p. 13). Assuming that such unions were recognized, there seems no *a priori* reason why the legislator should have been any less concerned to prevent *them* between Athenian and foreigner than he was to prevent solemn marriages, and, if *συνοικεῖν* has here this wider meaning, point is given to the otherwise somewhat otiose phrase *τέχνῃ ἢ μηχανῇ ἡτινιοῦν*. Gernet, *Dem.* iv. 67, 107; on the latter page he asserts that *συνοικεῖν* could be used of concubinage. Kahrstedt, *Staatsg.* 65, n. 2, rejects as absurd the view that a foreign man could have been punished simply for forming a permanent union with an Athenian woman and he cites Dem. 34 *Ag. Phorm.* 37 for a recorded instance of such a union. What was punishable, Kahrstedt thinks, was passing oneself off as a citizen if one was a foreigner, and he implies that the deception punished was of the bride or her *κύριος*, not of the public at large. But the recorded instance is weak, for the speaker simply says that Phormion, who was a foreigner, was living in Athens and had a wife and children there; but his aim is to establish that Athens was Phormion's permanent home, and it was not necessary for his argument that the wife should have been Athenian: *οἰκῶν μὲν*

We may perhaps assume, though there seems to be no direct evidence on the point, that in this context metics, whether male or female, were regarded as *ξένοι*.

§ 8. *ἐπιγαμία*

Exceptionally the right to contract marriages with Athenians (men or women, we must suppose) was conferred on the whole citizen body of some other state by what was known as *ἐπιγαμία*. By the time of Aristotle it must have been quite common for one city to confer such a right on the citizens of another, since he is at pains in the *Politics* to point out that, when this happened, it did not make the two cities one. There is good evidence that Athens had conferred this right on certain cities in Euboia towards the end of the fifth century, and in 401/400, while honouring some of the metics who had helped in the liberation of 403 with full citizenship, she conferred on others what was the equivalent of *ἐπιγαμία*, even if the word was possibly not used. Other instances cited are questionable.[1] When Plutarch (*Thes.* 13) says that there was no *ἐπιγαμία* between the demes of Pallene and Hagnous we should not imagine that a marriage between members of these two demes would have been invalid, but only that in practice such marriages had been avoided.

Ἀθήνησιν, οὔσης δ' αὐτῷ γυναικὸς ἐνθάδε καὶ παίδων. For one definition of *συνοικεῖν* see Dem. 59 *Neair.* 122, quoted p. 2, n. 4.

[1] Ar., *Pol.* 1280^b, Lys. 34 *Patr. Pol.* 3 *ὅτε τὰ τείχη καὶ τὰς ναῦς καὶ χρήματα καὶ συμμάχους ἐκτησάμεθα, οὐχ ὅπως τινὰ Ἀθηναῖον ἀπώσομεν διενοούμεθα, ἀλλὰ καὶ Εὐβοεῦσιν ἐπιγαμίαν ἐποιούμεθα*. On this see *ATL* iii. 295 ('the klerouchs in Chalkis and Eretria were to marry Euboian women in order to produce sons to add to the roll of Athenian citizens'). Hruza, *Beitr.* ii. 144, would explain this not as the conferment of a continuing right of intermarriage, but as a once-for-all act recognizing as Athenian citizens existing children of mixed marriages. He is followed in this strained and improbable interpretation by Beauch. i. 210 f. and Kahrstedt, *Staatsg.* 70; against him are Lips., *AR* 418, Bu. Sw. 223, n. 2, Becker, *Plat.* 75, Paoli, *St. Dir.* 292, Erdmann, *Ehe* 175 (with further bibl. 167, n. 1), Thalheim, *RE* s.v. *ἐπιγαμία*. When Isok. 14 *Plat.* 51 says *διὰ γὰρ τὰς ἐπιγαμίας τὰς δοθείσας ἐκ πολιτίδων ὑμετέρων γεγόναμεν* he is using the term in a non-technical sense; for the Plataians had received Athenian citizenship, which naturally included the right to contract marriages. The concession of the privilege by Athens to Thebes and by Byzantion to Athens is vouched for only in spurious decrees in Dem. 18 *Crown* 187, 91. Kahrstedt, loc. cit., denies that *ἐπιγαμία* should be restored in the decree honouring metics in 403, *IG* ii^2. 10 (*SEG* iii. 70, *GHI* 100), [*τούτοις εἶναι ἰσοτέλειαν οἰκοῦσι Ἀθήνησιν καὶ ἐπιγαμίαν καὶ ἐ*]*γγύησιν καθάπε*[*ρ Ἀ*]*θηναίοις*. Certainly there the *word ἐπιγαμίαν* seems otiose, but only because the substance of it is contained in *ἐγγύησιν*.

§ 9. *Relations between husband and wife*

(i) κυριεία

If, as is probable, Athenian marriage developed out of marriage by purchase, we should expect to find that the husband became 'master' (κύριος) of his wife, whether he had acquired her by ἐγγύη or by ἐπιδικασία. And certainly in some cases we can see the husband acting as the wife's κύριος. Thus in Isai. 3 *Pyrrh.* 2, 3 Xenokles, the husband of Phile, puts in a claim to the estate of Pyrrhos on her behalf acting as her κύριος. We have already seen (p. 21, above) that there were cases where a husband disposed of the hand of his wife, either *inter vivos* or by will; this he could only do as her κύριος.[1] The difficult question to decide is how far, if at all, the original κύριος of a woman, whether her father or another, retained any rights over her after her marriage. The cases cited above give no help here, since we know nothing about the previous κύριοι of the respective wives.

We must steer here between two extreme views. On the one hand it has been held that marriage extinguished the rights of the woman's original κύριος by transferring them entire to her husband. At the other extreme is the view that the original κύριος retained all his powers save those that he explicitly transferred to the husband, and that even the woman's legal domicile would be with the former unless there were provision to the contrary.[2] Our answer to the problem depends largely on whether we think that a woman's original κύριος had, or had not, the right to dissolve the marriage, the right of ἀφαίρεσις. Those who took the second view believed that he had. They relied mainly on a not very satisfactory piece of evidence from Dem. 41 *Spoud.* 4. Polyeuktos, we are there told, had no sons, but two daughters; he therefore adopted his wife's brother, Leokrates, and married his younger daughter to him; the elder he gave in marriage to the

[1] But it does not necessarily follow that he was κύριος by virtue of being her husband. Thus Gernet, *RÉG* 31 (1918), 191 f., maintains that Kleoboule's father had by a special disposition over and above the ἐγγύη made Demosthenes' father her sole κύριος and that it was in virtue of this disposition and under the law ὅτῳ ἂν ⟨ὁ πατὴρ⟩ (*coni.* Gernet) ἐπιτρέψῃ, τοῦτον κύριον εἶναι that Demosthenes' father was acting. But on this see pp. 19, 20, n. 3, above.

[2] For the second view see Hruza, *Beitr.* i. 70 ff., Beauch. i. 214 ff., Mitteis, *RV* 66, W. A. Goligher, *Hermath.* 14 (1906), 190 ff., Lips., *AR* 483, Erdmann, *Ehe* 271, F. Bozza, *Scr. Jovene* iii (Naples, 1954), 508, Jones, *LLTG* 182; Gernet, *Dem.* ii. 53 is doubtful.

plaintiff against Spoudias with a dowry of forty minai. He then fell out with Leokrates, took his daughter away from him (*ἀφελόμενος . . . τὴν θυγατέρα*), and gave her to Spoudias. Leokrates did not acquiesce in this, but sued Polyeuktos and Spoudias. Eventually a reconciliation was effected. Leokrates was to recover what property he had put into the estate (*κομισάμενον ἅπερ ἦν εἰς τὴν οὐσίαν εἰσενηνεγμένος*), and all claims on either side were to be dropped. But the details of this transaction are far too confused to allow us to press the word *ἀφελόμενος* as evidence of a right reserved to Polyeuktos; apart from the fact that besides the marriage there was an adoption, Leokrates had certainly challenged in some way the legality of the proceeding. Much more conclusive is the evidence which has come to light in the fragments of Menander's *Arbitrants*. In that play Smikrines wishes to dissolve his daughter's marriage, being fearful that her husband is dissipating the dowry. He says of himself *ἀλλ' ἴσως ἐγὼ / πολυπραγμονῶ πλείω τε πράττω τῶν ἐμῶν / κατὰ λόγον ἐξὸν ἀπιέναι τὴν θυγατέρα / λαβόντα* (480 K.). Later the daughter protests *ἀλλ' εἴ με σῴζων τοῦτο μὴ πείσαις ἐμὲ / οὐκέτι πατὴρ κρίνοι' ἂν ἀλλὰ δεσπότης* (510 K.). Both the general situation and the actual words used demand the hypothesis that Smikrines had the *legal* right to remove his daughter. Certainly the daughter says that he ought to persuade her first if he did not wish to be thought a tyrant rather than a father; but she is simply underlining the difference between a moral and a legal right, as against her father, who is suggesting that his undoubted legal right is also moral.[1]

We can then accept the view that a woman's original *κύριος* retained, or at least might retain, the right to dissolve her marriage; where this happened it was a limitation, and a very serious limitation, on the *κυριεία* of the husband, but it is perfectly

[1] E. Levy, *Gedächtnisschr. Seckel* (Berlin, 1927), 152 ff., and Erdmann, *Ehe* 272 ff., misunderstand the situation; the latter, for example, says 'wollte der Vater sie zur Scheidung zwingen, so würde er sein Recht überschreiten'; but how could the father compel her save by exercising a legal right? So too in the Didot papyrus (*Herm.* 61 (1926), 134 ff.) 34 ff. the passionate plea of the daughter makes no sense unless the father had the *legal* power. Ar., *Rhet.* 1401^b, where it is denied that Helen could have had the authority to marry Paris from her father, since his authority came to an end on her first marriage, cannot weigh in the scales against this evidence: R. Taubenschlag, *Z* 46 (1926), 75, C. Gatti, *Acme* 10 (1957), 61 ff. Paoli, *Aeg.* 32 (1952), 284, denies the father's right if the woman had borne a son to her husband.

possible to suppose that in all other matters than the disposal of her hand the husband was her κύριος.[1] Perhaps the most important of these would be to represent her in court when she was a party to a δίκη or a διαδικασία.[2] If a woman was killed and the husband declined to take proceedings—or indeed if he had killed her himself—we may conjecture that her original κύριος could act, but it is nothing more than conjecture.[3]

(ii) *Marital fidelity*[4]

The husband owed no duty of fidelity to the wife, though he was liable in various ways for misconduct with the wife or recognized concubine of another man.[5] The wife, on the contrary, did owe a duty, for her misconduct might introduce an adulterine bastard into the family.[6] The aggrieved husband's remedy depended on the circumstances. If the adulterer was caught *in flagrante delicto* the husband had the right to put him to death at

[1] For the κυριεία of the ἐπίκληρος see below, pp. 109 ff. Even in marriage by ἐγγύη it may have been possible for a father to transfer his right to dispose of his daughter's hand to her husband, cf. p. 30, n. 1, above; but this would not normally have happened, and there is much to be said for the suggestion of Wolff, *Traditio* 2 (1944), 51 ff., that in origin the word ἐγγύη (marriage), like ἐγγύη (surety), implied transference with a reserved right with the transferor, and that this is also the implication of the use of the word ἐκδιδόναι rather than ἀποδιδόναι of the bride's κύριος. He developed the thesis in *TR* 20 (1952), 1 ff. (especially 9 ff.), emphasizing the distinction between the husband's 'hausgewalt' or day-to-day control of his wife with the right to dispose of her hand (W. rather confusingly uses κυριεία of this latter only, but surely in so far as he used 'hausgewalt' the husband was acting as κύριος). See Beseler, *St. Bonfante* ii (1930), 55, for the continuing κυριεία of the father as solely the right to dissolve the marriage. Further treatment of the topic in connexion with the law of divorce, pp. 40 ff., below, parental authority, pp. 73 f., law of guardianship, pp. 109 ff., below.

[2] Schol. Aristoph., *Kn.* 965 οὕτω γὰρ προσκαλεῖσθαι εἰώθασιν ἐν τῷ δικαστηρίῳ· ἡ δεῖνα καὶ ὁ κύριος, τουτέστιν ὁ ἀνήρ.

[3] Throughout the above section the phrase 'original κύριος' has been assumed to cover, in a case where the original κύριος was dead, the man who would have been her κύριος had she still been single at the relative date. This again is simply an assumption.

[4] Becker, *Plat.* 97, Caillemer, DS s.v. *adulterium*, Erdmann, *Ehe* 286 ff. (with bibl. 286, n. 1), Beauch. i. 232 ff., Bu. Sw. 535, Lips., *AR* 429 ff., Paoli, *SDHI* 16 (1950), 123 ff.

[5] The husband of an ἐπίκληρος, however, was under a special duty to consummate the marriage, Plut., *Sol.* 20 τρὶς ἑκάστου μηνὸς ἐντυγχάνειν πάντως τῇ ἐπικλήρῳ τὸν λαβόντα. Probably failure to comply rendered him liable to an εἰσαγγελία κακώσεως ἐπικλήρων. This would be confirmed by Pollux 8. 53, if Meier's conjecture σπροηκόντως for προσηκόντων is accepted, as it is by Lips. 349, n. 34; but see p. 10, n. 2.

[6] Lys. 1 *Killing of Erat.* 33 τοὺς παῖδας ἀδήλους εἶναι ὁποτέρων τυγχάνουσιν ὄντες, τῶν ἀνδρῶν ἢ τῶν μοιχῶν.

once; Drakon's homicide law classed such a killing as justifiable, and Lysias' first speech, on the *Killing of Eratosthenes*, was delivered by a defendant in a homicide case who put up this plea.[1] Alternatively, the husband could inflict on the adulterer various bodily humiliations, or he could accept compensation from him, holding him a prisoner until he could provide sureties for the payment of the sum agreed.[2] The man so imprisoned (or *ὁ βουλόμενος* acting on his behalf) could, if he wished to rebut the charge of adultery, bring a *γραφὴ ἀδίκως εἱρχθῆναι ὡς μοιχόν* in the court of the thesmothetai against the husband; if he won, he and his sureties were released from all further liability, though no mention is made of a penalty falling on the husband; if he lost, his sureties had to hand him over to the husband, who could do with him what he would in the presence of the court, short of wounding with the sword.[3] It was a condition of the husband's right to redress that he should not have enticed the adulterer to the act.[4]

This primitive right of self-help laid the man who used it open to serious risks, as is shown by the case of Euphiletos in Lysias' first speech, though if he only resorted to holding the alleged adulterer to ransom and was subsequently judged by a court to

[1] Law cited in Dem. 23 *Aristokr.* 53; the terms of the law are repeated by Demosthenes at 55: *ΝΟΜΟΣ. 'Εάν τις ἀποκτείνῃ . . . ἢ ἐπὶ δάμαρτι ἢ ἐπὶ μητρὶ ἢ ἐπ' ἀδελφῇ ἢ ἐπὶ θυγατρί, ἢ ἐπὶ παλλακῇ ἣν ἂν ἐπ' ἐλευθέροις παισὶν ἔχῃ, τούτων ἕνεκα μὴ φεύγειν κτείναντα.* The law is attributed, probably wrongly, to Solon in Plut., *Sol.* 23 (p. 34 below). Lucian, *Eunuch.* 10 *καὶ μοιχὸς ἑάλω ποτὲ ὡς ὁ ἄξων φησίν· ἄρθρα ἐν ἄρθροις. Dig.* 48. 5. 24 *pr.* hoc est, quod Solo et Draco dicunt: *ἐν ἔργῳ.* Paoli, loc. cit. 143, adds that the act had to be in the house of the husband or in the woman's own home; but the evidence is hardly conclusive.

[2] Lys., op. cit. 49 *ὑπὸ τῶν νόμων . . . οἳ κελεύουσι μέν, ἐάν τις μοιχὸν λάβῃ, ὅ τι ἂν βούληται χρῆσθαι.* Schol. Aristoph., *Cl.* 1083 *ῥαφανιδωθῇ· οὕτω γὰρ τοὺς ἁλόντας μοιχοὺς ᾔκιζον· ῥαφανῖδας λαμβάνοντες καθίεσαν εἰς τοὺς πρωκτοὺς αὐτῶν, καὶ παρατίλλοντες αὐτοὺς τέφραν θερμὴν ἐπέπασσον.* Lys., op. cit. 25 *κἀκεῖνος ἀδικεῖν μὲν ὡμολόγει, ἠντεβόλει δὲ καὶ ἱκέτευε μὴ ἀποκτεῖναι ἀλλ' ἀργύριον πράξασθαι.* Dem. 59 *Neair.* 64 *'Επαίνετον . . . Στέφανος . . . λαμβάνει μοιχὸν ἐπὶ τῇ θυγατρὶ τῇ Νεαίρας ταυτησί, καὶ εἰς φόβον καταστήσας πράττεται μνᾶς τριάκοντα, καὶ λαβὼν ἐγγυήτας τούτων . . ., ἀφίησιν ὡς ἀποδώσοντα αὐτῷ τὸ ἀργύριον.*

[3] Dem. 59 *Neair.* 66 *κατὰ τὸν νόμον ὃς κελεύει, ἐάν τις ἀδίκως εἵρξῃ ὡς μοιχόν, γράψασθαι πρὸς τοὺς θεσμοθέτας ἀδίκως εἱρχθῆναι, καὶ ἐὰν μὲν ἕλῃ τὸν εἵρξαντα καὶ δόξῃ ἀδίκως ἐπιβεβουλεῦσθαι, ἀθῷον εἶναι αὐτὸν καὶ τοὺς ἐγγυήτας ἀπηλλάχθαι τῆς ἐγγύης· ἐὰν δὲ δόξῃ μοιχὸς εἶναι, παραδοῦναι αὐτὸν κελεύει τοὺς ἐγγυήτας τῷ ἑλόντι, ἐπὶ δὲ τοῦ δικαστηρίου ἄνευ ἐγχειριδίου χρῆσθαι ὅ τι ἂν βουληθῇ, ὡς μοιχῷ ὄντι.* Paoli, *SDHI* 16 (1950), 149, supposes that *ἄνευ ἐγχειριδίου* simply excluded bloodshed, not killing by other means.

[4] Lys. 1 *Killing of Erat.* 37.

have acted wrongfully he appears to have suffered no penalty. If he could not catch the adulterer in the act, or if having done so he did not wish to run the risks of self-help, the husband could resort either to the court of the thesmothetai by way of a *γραφὴ μοιχείας* or a *γραφὴ ὕβρεως* or to the court of the Forty by way of a *δίκη βιαίων*.[1] It has been argued from Plut., *Solon* 23 (*μοιχὸν μὲν γὰρ ἀνελεῖν τῷ λαβόντι δέδωκεν· ἐὰν δ' ἁρπάσῃ τις ἐλευθέραν γυναῖκα καὶ βιάσηται, ζημίαν ἑκατὸν δραχμὰς ἔταξε*) and Lys. 1 *Killing of Erat.* 32 (*ὁ νόμος κελεύει, ἐάν τις ἄνθρωπον* [codd.: *ἄνδρα* Dobree] *ἐλεύθερον ἢ παῖδα αἰσχύνῃ βίᾳ, διπλῆν τὴν βλάβην ὀφείλειν· ἐὰν δὲ γυναῖκα, ἐφ' αἷσπερ ἀποκτείνειν ἔξεστιν, ἐν τοῖς αὐτοῖς ἐνέχεσθαι· οὕτως, ὦ ἄνδρες, τοὺς βιαζομένους ἐλάττονος ζημίας ἀξίους ἡγήσατο εἶναι ἢ τοὺς πείθοντας*) that the penalty for rape was less than that for seduction and that, whereas for the latter a *γραφὴ μοιχείας* would lie with the possibility of the death penalty, for the former one of the other suits had to be employed and the penalty was at one stage 100 drachmai, later twice the assessed damage. While we can accept the broad point that, paradoxically, seduction was more severely dealt with than rape, we cannot be certain of the details; for, taken strictly, Lysias' words imply that, even when the adulterer was caught *in flagrante delicto*, he could be killed with impunity only if he had seduced, not if he had raped the woman. But not only is this not what the law says; it would clearly have been in practice impossible for the husband exercising his right of immediate self-help to establish to his own satisfaction and in such a way as to be able to prove it subsequently that his wife had been seduced, not raped; whereas to establish this by argument and witnesses in a legal process would have been perfectly possible.[2] We may take it

[1] Ar., *Ath. Pol.* 59. 3, assigns a *γραφὴ μοιχείας* to the thesmothetai. Lysias' lost speech against Autokrates was in a suit *μοιχείας* (frs. 18–21 Th.), but the fragments shed no light on the nature of the suit.

[2] The Lysias passage may be paraphrased thus: 'the law lays down that if a man forcibly violates a free adult or boy, he shall be liable to a penalty of double the estimated loss suffered by his victim; if he forcibly violates a woman in one of the categories set out in the homicide law (a wife, mother, daughter, sister, or recognized concubine of a free Athenian citizen), he shall be liable to the same penalty.' There is here a twofold difficulty. In Plutarch the penalty for rape is fixed at 100 drachmai; in Lysias, if this paraphrase is right, the penalty depends on the assessment of damage by the court. Lips., *AR* 639, sought to evade this difficulty by supposing that between the time of Solon and Lysias this suit from being an *ἀτίμητος* had become a *τιμητὸς ἀγών*. But there is the further difficulty of understanding what it could mean to assess the loss suffered in such a case and then

then that where the husband caught the adulterer in the act he could proceed to immediate execution without being required subsequently to show that his wife had been seduced, not raped. If he decided not to take immediate action, or if he had not caught the adulterer in the act, three actions were available: a *γραφὴ μοιχείας*, which required that he should prove seduction and in which the penalty, if he succeeded, would be death, a *γραφὴ ὕβρεως*, or a *δίκη βιαίων*, which required that he should prove rape and in which the penalty was either a sum of money laid down by law or one arrived at by *τίμησις*, but in any case something less than death. Alternatively, the husband could reach a composition with the adulterer. There is no reason to suppose that either of the *γραφαί* were an exception to the rule that *ὁ βουλόμενος* could prosecute in a *γραφή*. In fact the rule would have been a salutary safeguard against the complaisant husband. In our ignorance of the details we cannot say what motives would have influenced the husband in choosing between the *δίκη βιαίων* and the *γραφὴ ὕβρεως*.[1]

The law forbade the husband who had taken his wife in adultery to continue to cohabit with her on pain of *ἀτιμία*. The

double the figure; such a procedure suits a material loss either of money itself or of goods readily expressed in terms of money (cf. Din. 1 *Dem.* 60 *οἱ νόμοι περὶ μὲν τῶν ἄλλων ἀδικημάτων τῶν εἰς ἀργυρίου λόγον ἀνηκόντων διπλῆν τὴν βλάβην ὀφείλειν κελεύουσι*); but hardly a moral injury such as violation of a person's chastity. One would rather have expected in this context the formula *ὅ τι ἂν τὸ δικαστήριον τιμήσῃ, παθεῖν ἢ ἀποτεῖσαι*: cf., for example, Dem. 24 *Timokr.* 118. Hence the suggestion of Glotz, *Solidarité* 393, that the paraphrase should run 'a penalty of double that for which he would have been liable if he had forcibly violated a slave', has much to recommend it. Cf. also Platner ii. 207 ff., Beauch. i. 234 ff. When Lys. 13 *Agorat.* 66 says *ἐλήφθη μοιχός· καὶ τούτου θάνατος ἡ ζημία ἐστίν* he is referring simply to the right of the husband to kill when he caught the offender in the act. From Hyper. 2 *Lyk.* 20 we learn that Lykophron, who was charged with adultery, would if convicted have been condemned to death and not allowed burial. But his case was being dealt with by the exceptional procedure of *εἰσαγγελία*.

[1] It is very unfortunate that we have not got the speech for the prosecution for the killing of Eratosthenes. There is something very suspicious about the reasoning of Lysias' speech at 32 ff. The precise terms of the provision that the husband must not have enticed the adulterer into the house do not survive, and the dividing line between doing that and allowing an intrigue of which you were aware to develop until you could catch the adulterer in the act would necessarily have been narrow. That seduction should have entailed severer punishment than rape seemed paradoxical to Lysias, as it does to us. But looked at exclusively from the husband's point of view there is a sense in which the seduction of his wife is a graver injury to him than her rape. Cf. p. 19 above. Paoli, *SDHI* 16 (1950), 152, holds on rather slender evidence that a *μοιχός* was a *κακοῦργος* and as such subject to the procedure of *ἀπαγωγή*.

woman was forbidden to take part in any public cult ceremonies. If she did, she could be subjected to any indignity short of death.[1] It is significant of the general disability under which women laboured in the face of the law that, so far as we know at least, no action at law had to be, or could be, taken against an alleged adulteress. No doubt if a woman was insulted as an adulteress and wished to assert her innocence she could, through her *κύριος* or other well-disposed person, have her insulter tried by a *γραφὴ ὕβρεως*. But this was not the same thing as having the right to be heard in the first instance. Moreover, it would seem that the victim of rape was liable to just the same treatment as she who had been a willing co-operator in the adultery.

(iii) *Offences allied to adultery*

It seems likely that originally the word *μοιχός* and its derivatives referred to the violation of the marriage tie, and that it was only by an extension that it was applied to the rape or seduction of an unmarried or widowed free woman or of a concubine from whom her lord intended to rear free children.[2] However, the extension had taken place by Drakon's time, for in his homicide law the women whose violators (whether by rape or seduction) were liable to summary execution by their nearest men-folk included mothers, sisters, daughters, and concubines, besides wives, and it is clear that what was said in the previous section of the actions *γραφὴ ὕβρεως*, *γραφὴ μοιχείας*, and *δίκη βιαίων* as applying to married women applied, *mutatis mutandis*, to these

[1] Dem. 59 *Neair.* 87 *ΝΟΜΟΣ ΜΟΙΧΕΙΑΣ. Ἐπειδὰν δὲ ἕλῃ τὸν μοιχόν, μὴ ἐξέστω τῷ ἑλόντι συνοικεῖν τῇ γυναικί· ἐὰν δὲ συνοικῇ, ἄτιμος ἔστω. μηδὲ τῇ γυναικὶ ἐξέστω εἰσιέναι εἰς τὰ ἱερὰ τὰ δημοτελῆ, ἐφ' ᾗ ἂν μοιχὸς ἁλῷ· ἐὰν δ' εἰσίῃ, νηποινεὶ πασχέτω ὅ τι ἂν πάσχῃ, πλὴν θανάτου.* As Gernet, *Dem.* iv. 97, n. 2, points out, in the classical period *ἕλῃ* would primarily suggest 'procure the conviction of', whereas in the original Solonian law it would rather have meant 'take in the act'. We should assume that in the classical period the woman was treated alike in both cases. Aischin. 1 *Timarch.* 183 adds that the woman had to forgo all ornament, attributes the law to Solon, and gives as his motive the desire to dishonour such women and make their life intolerable. Paoli, loc. cit. 159, holds that the adulterer too was barred from sacred places, even though no action at law had been taken against him, but there is no direct evidence for this.

[2] Lips., *AR* 429. Erdmann, *Ehe* 286 ff., on the other hand, takes the view that from the first there had been no distinction in principle between the violation of a married woman and that of a woman in the other categories. Paoli, *SDHI* 16 (1953), 123 ff., regards the essential and unifying feature of the concept of *μοιχεία* as the fact that it was an attack upon the *οἶκος*. The matter will need further discussion in connexion with other uses of the *γραφὴ ὕβρεως*.

other categories.[1] Women who served in brothels or who openly offered themselves for hire were excluded from these categories.[2]

If we could rely on a law quoted in Aischin. 1 *Timarch.* 12, violation of a free boy (φθορὰ ἐλευθέρου) would have rendered a man liable to prosecution by γραφή; but this is probably not a genuine citation.[3] On the other hand, the orator's own words vouch for an action against procuring (προαγωγεία) of a free boy or woman for immoral purposes with the penalty of death. According to Plutarch, Solon had imposed a penalty of twenty drachmai for this offence. We cannot say when the savage increase was introduced.[4]

Several rules aimed at the discouragement of male prostitution of free citizens. A man who had prostituted himself for reward, whether monetary or other, was subject to total ἀτιμία; he could not hold office, speak in the assembly or council, appear in court in his own person, act as priest, herald, or ambassador. If he did any of these things, but only then, he was liable to a γραφὴ ἑταιρήσεως.[5] The penalty again was death. On the other hand, a γραφὴ ἑταιρήσεως could be brought immediately against anyone who let out on hire a male citizen as a prostitute or anyone who hired one, and the action lay whether the prostitute was a minor or of age. One who had thus been hired out as a minor lost the right of addressing the assembly. On the other hand, if

[1] For the possible avoidance of the death penalty by the seducer of an unmarried woman see p. 19, above.

[2] Dem. 59 *Neair.* 67 τὸν νόμον . . . ὃς οὐκ ἐᾷ ἐπὶ ταύτῃσι μοιχὸν λαβεῖν ὁπόσαι ἂν ἐπ' ἐργαστηρίου καθῶνται ἢ πωλῶνται ἀποπεφασμένως (codd.: ἢ ἐν τῇ ἀγορᾷ πωλῶσί τι, Harpokr. s.v. ἀποπεφασμένως and πωλῶσι, Lys. 10 *Theomn.* 19 quoting a law of Solon ὅσαι δὲ πεφασμένως πολοῦνται (πωλοῦνται OX)), Plut., *Sol.* 23 κἂν προαγωγεύῃ, δραχμὰς εἴκοσι, πλὴν ὅσαι πεφασμένως πωλοῦνται. Despite the confusion in the manuscripts of Demosthenes the general sense of the law is plain. Cf. Lips., *AR* 430, n. 43.

[3] E. Drerup, *NJ*, Suppl. 24 (1897), 305 f., Lips., *AR* 435, n. 57.

[4] Aischin. 1 *Timarch.* 14 τὸν τῆς προαγωγείας (νόμον ἔθηκε), τὰ μέγιστα ἐπιτίμια ἐπιγράψας ἐάν τις ἐλεύθερον παῖδα ἢ γυναῖκα προαγωγεύῃ. Ibid. 184 καὶ τὰς προαγωγοὺς καὶ τοὺς προαγωγοὺς γράφεσθαι κελεύει, κἂν ἁλῶσι, θανάτῳ ζημιοῦν. Plut., loc. cit. n. 2, above.

[5] Aischin. 1 *Timarch.* 19 ἄν τις Ἀθηναίων, φησίν (ὁ νομοθέτης), ἑταιρήσῃ, μὴ ἐξέστω αὐτῷ τῶν ἐννέα ἀρχόντων γενέσθαι . . . ἐὰν δέ τις παρὰ ταῦτα πράττῃ, γραφὰς ἑταιρήσεως πεποίηκε καὶ τὰ μέγιστα ἐπιτίμια ἐπέθηκεν. The law cited ibid. 21 should be ignored; see n. 3 above. Andok. 1 *Myst.* 100 οὗτος ἑτέρων τολμᾷ κατηγορεῖν, ᾧ κατὰ τοὺς νόμους τοὺς ὑμετέρους οὐδ' αὐτῷ ὑπὲρ αὑτοῦ ἔστιν ἀπολογεῖσθαι. Aischin., op. cit. 87 προκειμένης ἑκατέρῳ ζημίας ἐκ τοῦ νόμου θανάτου, ὥσπερ ἐνθάδε, ἐάν τις μισθώσηταί τινα Ἀθηναίων ἐφ' ὕβρει, καὶ πάλιν ἐάν τις Ἀθηναίων ἐπὶ τῇ τοῦ σώματος αἰσχύνῃ ἑκὼν μισθαρνῇ.

his father had let him out on hire he was freed from all obligations towards his father save that of burial.[1]

Two features of these rules concerned with sexual behaviour especially strike us. First, the woman and her chastity are hardly protected in their own right, but only because she is the humble but necessary vehicle for carrying on the *οἶκος*. Second, sexual acts of males outside matrimony are only punished if committed with free-born Athenians; it was not the acts themselves, but the involvement of two citizens in them which made them sufficiently abhorrent to entail legal punishment.

§ 10. *Dissolution of marriage*

(i) *By death or statutory regulation*

Death dissolved marriage, and there is no trace of any rule at Athens prohibiting or imposing delay on the remarriage of widows. Demosthenes indeed gives one instance of the immediate remarriage of a divorced woman. *A fortiori* a widow could remarry at once.[2] If she had had sons by her dead husband she probably had the choice between remaining in his house or returning to her father's. If she remained she was under the tutelage of her sons, if they were of age; of their *κύριοι*, if they were minors. The same choice was open to her if she claimed to be with child by her husband. In that case she was under the special care of the eponymous archon, who could fine up to the level of his competence anyone who treated her unlawfully or, if the offence seemed to him too grave for that remedy, could bring the offender before a court with a proposal for the penalty he deemed proper. A pregnant woman was also probably protected

[1] Aischin., op. cit. 13 *διαρρήδην λέγει ὁ νόμος, ἐάν τινα ἐκμισθώσῃ ἑταιρεῖν πατὴρ ἢ ἀδελφὸς ἢ θεῖος ἢ ἐπίτροπος ἢ ὅλως τῶν κυρίων τις, κατ' αὐτοῦ μὲν τοῦ παιδὸς οὐκ ἐᾷ γραφὴν εἶναι, κατὰ δὲ τοῦ μισθώσαντος καὶ τοῦ μισθωσαμένου . . . καὶ ἴσα τὰ ἐπιτίμια ἑκατέρῳ πεποίηκε, καὶ μὴ ἐπάναγκες εἶναι τῷ παιδὶ ἡβήσαντι τρέφειν τὸν πατέρα μηδὲ οἴκησιν παρέχειν, ὃς ἂν ἐκμισθωθῇ ἑταιρεῖν· ἀποθανόντα δὲ θαπτέτω . . . ζῶντος μὲν αὐτοῦ ἀφαιρεῖται τὴν ὄνησιν τῆς παιδοποιίας, ὥσπερ ἐκεῖνος ἐκείνου τὴν παρρησίαν*. Ibid. 195, *τοὺς δὲ τῶν νέων, ὅσοι ῥᾳδίως ἁλίσκονται, θηρευτὰς ὄντας εἰς τοὺς ξένους καὶ τοὺς μετοίκους τρέπεσθαι κελεύετε*, shows that it was no offence to procure or violate a metic or a foreigner.

[2] Dem. 30 *Onet.* i. 33 *αὕτη ἡ γυνή . . . μίαν ἡμέραν οὐκ ἐχήρευσεν* (note the use of this word for a divorced woman). Beauch. i. 373 suggests that the rule cited in Dem. 59 *Neair.* 75 that the wife of the basileus must only have been once married may go back to a time when remarriage was prohibited. Cf. Paus. 2. 21. 7.

by the *εἰσαγγελία κακώσεως ὀρφανῶν*. We do not know what happened if she had borne only daughters.[1] On the other hand, if she was childless and not pregnant she would naturally fall again under the power of her original *κύριος* or his heir.[2] (See also the section on guardianship, pp. 109 ff., below.)

Other causes than death might impose the dissolution of a marriage. As we have seen (pp. 26 f.), a man who learnt after marriage that his wife was a foreigner was bound to divorce her (at least in the fourth century), as was the man who had taken his wife in adultery (p. 35). Again, in certain circumstances the marriage of a woman who became an *ἐπίκληρος* after she had married could be dissolved by the decision of a court (p. 11). But there is no reason to believe that any other change of status would automatically have dissolved a marriage. Since the time of Solon slavery for debt had disappeared from Athens; but a man might still fall into temporary bondage if he had been ransomed from the enemy by a fellow citizen and did not refund the money.[3] There is, however, nothing to suggest that this would entail the dissolution of his marriage, and the same applies to cases where a man had been punished by partial or total *ἀτιμία*.

(ii) *Dissolution at the instance of either or both spouses*

Voluntary dissolution of marriage might arise from agreement to separate between the husband and wife. Isaios' second speech contains a pretty story of such an agreement between an

[1] Isai. 3 *Pyrrh.* 9, 78 suggest that she would have been expected to return to the *οἶκος* of her father.

[2] Dem. 43 *Makart.* 75 *ΝΟΜΟΣ. Ὁ ἄρχων ἐπιμελείσθω τῶν ὀρφανῶν καὶ τῶν ἐπικλήρων καὶ τῶν οἴκων ἐξερημουμένων καὶ τῶν γυναικῶν, ὅσαι μένουσιν ἐν τοῖς οἴκοις τῶν ἀνδρῶν τῶν τεθνηκότων φάσκουσαι κυεῖν. τούτων ἐπιμελείσθω καὶ μὴ ἐάτω ὑβρίζειν μηδένα περὶ τούτους. ἐὰν δέ τις ὑβρίζῃ ἢ ποιῇ τι παράνομον, κύριος ἔστω ἐπιβάλλειν κατὰ τὸ τέλος. ἐὰν δὲ μείζονος ζημίας δοκῇ ἄξιος εἶναι, προσκαλεσάμενος πρόπεμπτα καὶ τίμημα ἐπιγραψάμενος, ὅ τι ἂν δοκῇ αὐτῷ, εἰσαγέτω εἰς τὴν ἡλιαίαν. ἐὰν δ' ἁλῷ, τιμάτω ἡ ἡλιαία περὶ τοῦ ἁλόντος, ὅ τι χρὴ αὐτὸν παθεῖν ἢ ἀποτεῖσαι.* Lips., *AR* 486, seems to imply that the pregnant widow always remained in her husband's house, and this is what we should expect *a priori*. But the words *ὅσαι μένουσιν* suggest that there might be women who did not so remain, and Lipsius himself later (495, n. 96) follows A. H. G. P. van den Es, *De iure familiarum apud Athenienses* (Leiden, 1864), 59, in denying that the pregnant woman was bound to remain in her dead husband's house. But see p. 44. The other rules referred to in the above paragraph are surmises from evidence primarily concerned with the dowry, and this evidence will be examined later in connexion with that institution. Cf. Isai. 8 *Kir.* 8 and Dem. 40 *Boiot.* ii. 6.

[3] Dem. 53 *Nikostr.* 11.

old husband and a young wife, and we are told by Plutarch that Perikles and his wife parted by mutual consent.[1] Alternatively, one or other of the spouses might act alone. When the husband did so the terms used were *ἀποπέμπειν*, *ἐκπέμπειν*, *ἐκβάλλειν*, when the wife did so it was *ἀπολείπειν*.[2]

When the husband divorced he seems to have been required to do nothing further than dismiss the wife from his house. It is true that Hipponikos summoned witnesses to his action (Lys., loc. cit. in n. 2), declaring to them his reasons for it. But there is no suggestion there or elsewhere that witnesses were necessary to make the act valid.

There is considerable difference of opinion as to what was required when the divorce proceeded from the wife. We have three cases to go on. The first is that of Hipparete, wife of Alkibiades. According to Plutarch, owing to Alkibiades' wanton behaviour with courtesans, she had left his house for that of her brother; when Alkibiades persisted in his ways she was driven to present in person to the archon a plea of divorce, but her action was frustrated by Alkibiades, who seized her by force and carried her home quite illegally.[3] If we can accept the detail of this story it suggests that Hipparete's leaving her husband's house did not in itself dissolve the marriage. To effect this she was forced to leave the protection of her brother's house and appear in person before the archon, and this gave Alkibiades the opportunity to bring her back forcibly to the marital home. Although Alkibiades' dissolute behaviour is given as the cause of Hipparete's action, there is nothing in the story as it is told either in Plutarch

[1] Isai. 2 *Menekl.* 7 ff., Plut., *Per.* 24 (cf. p. 21, above).

[2] Of the husband *An. Bekk.* 421 (*Συν. Λέξ. Χρησ.*) *Ἀπέλιπεν: ἀπέλιπε μὲν ἡ γυνὴ τὸν ἄνδρα λέγεται· ἀπέπεμψε δὲ ὁ ἀνὴρ τὴν γυναῖκα. οὕτω Μένανδρος.* Suda s.v. *σίτου.* Lys. 14 *Alk.* i. 28 *Ἱππόνικος δὲ πολλοὺς παρακαλέσας ἐξέπεμψε τὴν αὑτοῦ γυναῖκα, φάσκων τοῦτον οὐχ ὡς ἀδελφὸν ἀλλ' ὡς ἄνδρα ἐκείνης εἰς τὴν οἰκίαν εἰσιέναι τὴν αὑτοῦ.* Dem. 59 *Neair.* 51 *ἐκβάλλει τὴν ἄνθρωπον ὡς ἐνιαυτὸν συνοικήσας αὐτῇ, κυοῦσαν, καὶ τὴν προῖκα οὐκ ἀποδίδωσιν.* Thomas Magister s.v. *ἀπολείπει* (29, l. 13 Ritschl). Of the wife *An. Bekk.* 201 (*Λέξ. Ῥητ.*) *Ἀπόλειψις: σημαίνει μὲν ἁπλῶς τὸ ἀπολείπειν· ἰδίως δὲ καὶ ὅταν γαμετὴ τὸν ἄνδρα ἀπολείπῃ καὶ χρηματίζῃ πρὸς ἄνδρα ἀπόλειψιν.* Isai. 3 *Pyrrh.* 8 *πότερον ἡ ἐγγυητὴ γυνὴ ἀπέλιπε τὸν ἄνδρα ζῶντα ἢ τελευτήσαντος τὸν οἶκον αὐτοῦ.* Ibid. 78 *πρὸς ὁποῖον ἄρχοντα ἡ ἐγγυητὴ γυνὴ ἀπέλιπε τὸν ἄνδρα ἢ τὸν οἶκον αὐτοῦ.* For further references Weiss, *GP* 309 ff., Wyse, *Isai.* 295.

[3] Plut., *Alk.* 8. *ἡ Ἱππαρέτη . . . ἐκ τῆς οἰκίας ἀπιοῦσα πρὸς τὸν ἀδελφὸν ᾤχετο. τοῦ δ' Ἀλκιβιάδου μὴ φροντίζοντος . . . ἔδει τὸ τῆς ἀπολείψεως γράμμα παρὰ τῷ ἄρχοντι θέσθαι, μὴ δι' ἑτέρων, ἀλλ' αὐτὴν παροῦσαν. ὡς οὖν παρῆν τοῦτο πράξουσα κατὰ τὸν νόμον, ἐπελθὼν ὁ Ἀλκιβιάδης καὶ συναρπάσας αὐτὴν ἀπῆλθε δι' ἀγορᾶς οἴκαδε κομίζων.* Cf. Andok. 4 *Alk.* 14.

or in Ps.-Andokides 4 *Alk.* to suggest that she would have had to convince the archon that her grievances against him justified her leaving him. The story leaves one interesting question unanswered, namely by what legal act Alkibiades could, if he had so wanted, have converted his wife's desertion of the marital home into *ἀπόπεμψις* by himself, which seems to have been what Hipparete was hoping for. Our second case is that of Onetor's sister who was married to Demosthenes' guardian, Aphobos (see p. 285). The facts as stated by Demosthenes in 30 *Onet.* i were that Aphobos, among other devices to defraud Demosthenes of the ten talents awarded to him in his guardianship case, had pretended that a certain farm valued at one talent had been hypothecated by him to Onetor as security for the dowry paid to him when he married Onetor's sister; Onetor had registered with the archon the divorce of his sister from Aphobos and had entered upon the land allegedly hypothecated for the return of the dowry. Demosthenes contended that, first, no dowry had in fact been paid to Aphobos and the hypothecation was a fraud, and, second, that the divorce was a sham; though her relatives had registered an *ἀπόλειψις* with the archon, the woman had not genuinely left him, but was still cohabiting (*συνοικεῖν*). Here there is no mention of the personal appearance of the woman before the archon, but the point was not material to Demosthenes; the plural is used of those who made the plea, but we may suppose that in effect it was put in by Onetor. The fact that Demosthenes makes no mention of any ground for the divorce as being advanced before the archon is strong evidence that no such ground was required, for any such ground would have been material to his argument that the whole business was a collusive fraud. Again an interesting question is left unanswered. Assuming that Demosthenes' facts are right, what was the exact legal status of Onetor's sister when she had gone through the form of *ἀπόλειψις* from Aphobos, but was still cohabiting with him?[1] Our third case is that of Phile's mother as set out in the third speech of Isaios, on the estate of Pyrrhos. One of the points at issue in that case was whether there had ever been a marriage between that lady and

[1] Dem. 30 *Onet.* i. 17 *ὕστερον δ' ᾗ ἐγὼ τὴν δίκην ἔλαχον τὴν ἀπόλειψιν οὗτοι πρὸς τὸν ἄρχοντα ἀπεγράψαντο.* Ibid. 26 *μετὰ τὸ γεγράφθαι παρὰ τῷ ἄρχοντι ταύτην τὴν γυναῖκ' ἀπολελοιπυῖαν.* Ibid. 31 *αὐτὸς ἔδειξεν 'Ονήτωρ, ὅτι οὐκ ἀληθινὴν ἐποιήσατο τὴν ἀπόλειψιν.*

Pyrrhos and whether therefore Phile herself was Pyrrhos' legitimate daughter. One argument on which the speaker relies to discredit her legitimacy is that at some point of time after Phile's birth her mother had ceased to be in the *οἶκος* of Pyrrhos; this she might have done by *ἀπόλειψις*, but, if she had, the fact would have been notified to the archon; yet his opponents had not been able to point to such a notification. The argument is specious, since the woman might either have been divorced by Pyrrhos or have left his house after his death, and in either of these cases the archon would not have been involved. The language used of the hypothetical divorce (see the two quotations from Isaios in n. 2 on p. 40) sheds no light on the question whether she would have been present herself before the archon, or on the part in the procedure played by her brother, Nikodemos, who had acted as her *κύριος* in her alleged *ἐγγύη* to Pyrrhos.

It is manifest from this evidence that a divorce proceeding from a woman was only valid if it had been reported in writing to the archon and in spite of the doubt expressed by Weiss (*GP* 311, n. 224) it must surely have been the eponymous archon. It is not so self-evident whether this was merely a report, intended to give publicity to the act, or whether the archon had to approve and, as a corollary of that, the woman had to show cause. There is not the slightest suggestion in the three cases examined above, or anywhere else, that the archon or his court had any power of decision in the matter, and, in view of the considerable body of evidence we have from the orators and lexicographers on marital matters, we might certainly have expected to find some reference to argument before the archon or to an adverse decision on his part if he had possessed this power. On the other hand, it is not easy to see why notification was required of the wife and not of the husband. We may perhaps conjecture that, whereas the husband who had dismissed his wife had nothing more to fear from her, since she had never exercised any power over him,[1] the woman would necessarily be deemed to be in her husband's power in default of clear evidence that she had ceased to be his wife. This would be particularly damaging to her in cases where the desire for divorce proceeded from her and not her husband. If this conjecture be correct, the rule, although arising out of the

[1] The child of a woman born after her divorce would have had no rights as against the father: see p. 71.

inferior status of woman, is a somewhat half-hearted attempt to ameliorate that inferiority. The case of Alkibiades' wife will be a neat exception to prove the rule.[1] Faint traces of a δίκη ἀποπέμψεως and a δίκη ἀπολείψεως, the former referred to, according to Pollux, in a speech by Lysias, might seem to indicate that divorce might be a matter of court proceedings. It has, however, been plausibly suggested that the former may have been a suit, not for restitution of the marriage, but for damage suffered by the wife as a result of divorce. The latter, only vouched for by a late *rhetor*, may be simply his invention to pair with the former.[2]

We can be pretty sure *a priori* that the wife would have needed the co-operation of some male citizen to go through the proceedings before the archon. Looking at the three cases above it seems clear that Phile's mother's brother (Nikodemos) and the brother of Aphobos' wife (Onetor) acted for their sisters, and both had been responsible for the ἐγγύη of their sisters; probably the same is true in the case of Alkibiades' wife. As it happens, in all these cases the wife's father would seem to have been dead, and we have no evidence for ἀπόλειψις mediated through the father. It is possible that the father's intervention on his daughter's behalf was always known technically as ἀφαίρεσις; and—a much more speculative hypothesis—that this difference in terminology indicated that only the father had the right to dissolve the marriage against the wishes of the wife.[3] It might of course happen that the next of kin to whom an aggrieved wife

[1] Beauch. i. 381 ff., Caillemer, DS s.v. *divortium*, Schoemann–Lips., *Gr. Alt.* (1897), 561, give the power of decision to the archon; so also apparently Lips., *AR* 59, 487; Becker, *Plat.*, gives contradictory views on pp. 146 and 147; Weiss, *GP* 309 ff. (with full bibliography) regards the archon's function here as purely declaratory; so too Erdmann, *Ehe* 391 ff., who makes two further points: (1) that very probably the intervention of the archon in the matter arose out of the part he had to play when an ἐπίκληρος had to be separated from her husband and that there it might happen that cause had to be shown, which of course took the form of διαδικασία before a court, (2) that if, as seems certain (see below), the wife had to be represented either by her former κύριος or other relative or, if none such was available, possibly by ὁ βουλόμενος in a γραφή, then some grounds for her action, even if they did not amount to legally defined grounds, would have had to be put forward by her.

[2] Poll. 8. 31 καὶ ἰδιωτικὰ μὲν δικῶν ὀνόματα . . . ἀποπομπῆς καὶ ὡς Λυσίας ἀποπέμψεως. Kyros 8, p. 393 (Waltz), Erdmann, *Ehe* 398, Jones, *LLTG* 182, n. 3. The law of Gortyn, ii. 46 ff., imposed a penalty on the husband who divorced his wife wrongfully.

[3] Gatti, *Acme* 10 (1957), 63. On ἀφαίρεσις see p. 30, above.

would look to represent her for the purpose of *ἀπόλειψις* was also her husband. One would have expected a case of this kind to be covered by a *γραφή*. In many cases, though not necessarily in all, such wives would have been *ἐπίκληροι*, and for their protection an *εἰσαγγελία κακώσεως* was available against their husbands. But whether one of the things the court could do was to dissolve their marriage we are not told; still less can we assume that the scope of this action was widened to embrace wives of this category who were not *ἐπίκληροι*.[1]

(iii) *Children of parents whose marriage was dissolved*

When a marriage was dissolved by the death of the husband, the children, as one would expect, remained in their father's house, while their mother could either remain or return to her own father (p. 38). It is, for example, clear that the children of Kleomedon mentioned in Dem. 40 *Boiot.* ii. 6 remained in his house when he died, while his wife left it with her dowry and was married to Mantias. Similarly Lys. 32 *Diogeit.* 5–14 shows that after his death and the remarriage of his widow the sons of Diodotos remained under the tutelage of Diodotos' brother, Diogeiton, who was also their maternal grandfather. What happened to a posthumous child whose mother had elected to return to her father's house (p. 39, n. 2, above) we cannot say; we should have expected that it would have been maintained in its father's house, particularly if it were the only child; but that is difficult to square with the mother's freedom of choice.

The rules affecting the children of divorced parents are obscure from lack of evidence. In Dem. 57 *Eubul.* 40 ff. the children of Protomachos remain with him after his divorce from Euxitheos' mother; he gives the daughter away in marriage; but this was a divorce by consent, and we should like to know the rule in cases of *ἀπόπεμψις* and *ἀπόλειψις*. Only a fitful gleam is provided by Andok. 1 *Myst.* 125 ff. (see p. 16 with n. 2, above). Kallias, so runs Andokides' story, had been cohabiting simultaneously with a woman and her daughter. The mother drove

[1] Ar., *Ath. Pol.* 56. 6, *γραφαὶ δὲ καὶ δίκαι λαγχάνονται πρὸς αὐτόν (τὸν ἄρχοντα) . . . ἐπικλήρου κακώσε[ως . . . αὗτ]αι δ' εἰσὶ κατὰ τῶν ἐπιτρόπων καὶ τῶν συνοικούντων.* Cf. Isai. 3 *Pyrrh.* 46, Poll. 8. 31, 89, Suda, Harpokr. s.v. *κακώσεως*. These latter speak of the suit as a *δίκη*, but they are certainly using the word in its wider sense. The very nature of this action, which probably took the form of an *εἰσαγγελία* (Lips., *AR* 351), demanded the intervention of *ὁ βουλόμενος*.

the daughter out, and later Kallias threw out the mother in her turn. She claimed to be pregnant by him and bore a son. Kallias disclaimed paternity, and when the woman's relatives tried at the Apaturia to father the child on him he took a solemn oath that the only son he had ever had was Hipponikos. A good deal later he became reconciled to the woman and acknowledged the boy.[1] This is unsatisfactory evidence, as it is not certain that the woman was, properly speaking, Kallias' wife. Assuming, however, that she was, and that ἐξέβαλε is used in the technical sense of 'divorce', then it appears that the relatives of a pregnant woman divorced by her husband could bring pressure on him to accept paternity, which he could avoid only by means of a solemn oath.[2]

§ 11. *Dowry*

(i) *Introduction*

Important as were the relations between husband and wife dealt with in the preceding sections, perhaps the most important relation—certainly the one which figures most largely in the evidence which has come down to us—is that set up by the dowry.[3]

The early history of this institution in Athens is obscure. Some have traced it back to the exchange of gifts which took place in the heroic age between the bride's father and the groom, itself supposed to be a development from marriage by purchase. In Homer the ἕδνα, given to the bride's father by the groom and representing the original purchase price, are requited by gifts (μείλια, but sometimes also ἕδνα) from the bride's father to the groom. But in fact these latter gifts have little in common with the προίξ of Athenian law in the classical period. They were in essence gifts to the groom, whereas the Athenian dowry of the fourth century is rather a fund or an estate created by the bride's relatives to give her as it were a stake in the οἶκος to which she is by the marriage transferred. And just as the ἐγγύη is a

[1] Andok., loc. cit. ταύτης δ' αὖ διαπεπλησμένος ἐξέβαλε καὶ ταύτην. ἡ δ' ἔφη κυεῖν ἐξ αὐτοῦ· καὶ ἐπειδὴ ἔτεκεν υἱόν, ἔξαρνος ἦν μὴ εἶναι ἐξ αὐτοῦ τὸ παιδίον.

[2] Beauch. i. 394 ff., Becker, *Plat.* 152, but see p. 42, n. 1.

[3] See works cited above, p. 1, n. 1, especially Wolff, *RE* s.v. προίξ (1957), whose account has been followed closely. This article is cited in this section simply as Wolff, *RE*, with the number of the column. See also E. Gerner, *Beiträge zum R. der Paropherna* (*Münch. Beitr.*, Hft. 38 (1954), 39 ff.).

conditional transfer of the bride herself, which can be revoked, if he think fit, by the transferor, so it is with the *προίξ* which goes with her.[1]

The first point to make about the dowry is that by the classical period it was the subject of a number of statutory rules. To what date these go back we cannot say. The law dealing with the obligation of the next of kin of a girl of the thetic class to dower her if he did not wish to marry her (on which see below, pp. 135 ff.) is attributed by some sources to Solon and, in one case at least, in words which suggest reference to an *axon*.[2] This, if accepted, would mean that as an institution recognized by the state the dowry went back at least as far as Solon; but we certainly could not be sure that other statutory provisions, as to which we have absolutely no chronological evidence, were equally early. One rule at least, that which lays down an obligatory rate of interest payable on a dowry which is due to be, but has not yet been, returned, could only have emerged at a time when it was normal to lend out money at generally recognized rates, and Solon's time seems too early for that.

Before examining the rules themselves we have to determine what, for the purposes of the rules, a dowry (*προίξ*) was. It was property of any kind, whether money, chattels, land, or claims, made over by a woman's *κύριος* to a man in contemplation of their marriage by *ἐγγύη*. The property was valued when it was handed over, and its value was in certain circumstances returnable by the husband to the woman's *κύριος*. An analogous transaction may have been fairly common when a less formal union than marriage by *ἐγγύη* was being entered into, but property handed over in such a case was probably not a *προίξ* for the purposes of the law.[3] It is clear that a wife's trousseau,

[1] This does not mean of course that the *προίξ* could be recovered without taking back the woman. Nor is it likely that the woman's rights as such were being protected; rather, her rights as a possible vehicle for perpetuating her father's *οἶκος*. Her potentialities in this respect would have vanished if she had been completely swallowed up in the *οἶκος* of her husband. Wolff, *RE* 164. If M. I. Finley, *Seminar* 12 (1954), 7 ff., is right about the institution of marriage in Homer there is even less reason to see any foreshadowing of the *προίξ* in Homeric society (p. 5, n. 3, above). But cf. Beauch. i. 118.

[2] Law quoted in Dem. 43 *Makart.* 54 (for text see p. 135, n. 2); Aristoph. Byz., *Λέξεις*, fr. 39 N., referring to the law says *ὡς ἔταξε Σόλων*, and D.S. 12. 18 uses a formula which suggests quotation from an *axon*, *ὁ καὶ παρὰ Σόλωνι κείμενος* (*νόμος*).

[3] It is probably by design that Isai. 3 *Pyrrh.* 39 avoids the use of the word

jewels, and so forth were only part of the dowry proper if expressly declared to be so. In Pasion's will there is a clear distinction between the dowry (consisting of two claims to one talent each and a tenement house) and a gift to his wife of slave women, golden ornaments, and household goods. So too in Isai. 2 *Menekl.* 9 Menekles, after the agreed dissolution of his marriage, duly handed over (ἀποδίδωσι or, as the manuscripts read, ἐπιδίδωσι) his wife's dowry to her new husband and made a gift (δίδωσι) to her of the trousseau and jewels she had brought with her.[1] On this point we must insist: *legally*, whatever popular usage might be, that only was προίξ which was included in the valuation. This is stated expressly in a passage in Isaios and is the only view compatible with the evidence as a whole. How else, for example, could there be an enforceable rate of interest on the dowry to which the husband became liable if he did not return it at the proper time?[2]

προίξ in describing the money given with a concubine; οἱ ἐπὶ παλλακίᾳ διδόντες τὰς ἑαυτῶν πάντες πρότερον διομολογοῦνται περὶ τῶν δοθησομένων ταῖς παλλακαῖς. That money was the most natural form for a dowry to take appears from Dem. 30 *Onet.* i. 11, and this point needs no further evidence. Chattels ἐν τῇ προικὶ τετιμημένα in Dem. 47 *Euerg.* 57. Real property in the dowry provided for his wife in Pasion's will, Dem. 45 *Steph.* i. 28 (see next note). Claims to money, ibid. The Mykonos register of dowries of the early second century B.C. (*IJ* vi) provides parallels for all types, permissible evidence as Mykonos was once within the Athenian sphere.

[1] Lys. 32 *Diogeit.* 6 ἐπέσκηψε . . . τάλαντον ἐπιδοῦναι τῇ γυναικὶ καὶ τὰ ἐν τῷ δωματίῳ δοῦναι. Dem. 45 *Steph.* i. 28 δίδωμι τὴν ἐμαυτοῦ γυναῖκα Ἀρχίππην Φορμίωνι, καὶ προῖκα ἐπιδίδωμι Ἀρχίππῃ τάλαντον μὲν τὸ ἐκ Πεπαρήθου, τάλαντον δὲ τὸ αὐτόθεν, συνοικίαν ἑκατὸν μνῶν, θεραπαίνας καὶ τὰ χρυσία, καὶ τἄλλα ὅσα ἐστὶν αὐτῇ ἔνδον, ἅπαντα ταῦτα Ἀρχίππῃ δίδωμι. Isai. 2 *Menekl.* 9 ἐκδίδομεν αὐτὴν Ἠλείῳ Σφηττίῳ, καὶ ὁ Μενεκλῆς τήν τε προῖκα ἀποδίδωσιν (Jenicke, ἐπιδίδωσιν codd.) αὐτῷ . . . καὶ τὰ ἱμάτια, ἃ ἦλθεν ἔχουσα παρ' ἐκεῖνον, καὶ τὰ χρυσίδια, ἃ ἦν, δίδωσιν αὐτῇ. Whichever reading we adopt in the latter passage, Wolff, *RE* 138, is surely right to insist that the difference here between the simple and the compound verb is significant; Finley argued in *Land* 243, n. 53 that there was no distinction, but withdrew and accepted Wolff's interpretation in *Seminar*, (loc. cit. p. 46, n. 1, above), p. 23, n. 58.

[2] Isai. 3 *Pyrrh.* 35 ἐάν τίς τι ἀτίμητον δῷ, ἕνεκα τοῦ νόμου, ἐὰν ἀπολίπῃ ἡ γυνὴ τὸν ἄνδρα ἢ ἐὰν ὁ ἀνὴρ ἐκπέμψῃ τὴν γυναῖκα, οὐκ ἔξεστι πράξασθαι τῷ δόντι ὃ μὴ ἐν προικὶ τιμήσας ἔδωκεν. Dem. 59 *Neair.* 52 κατὰ τὸν νόμον ὃς κελεύει, ἐὰν ἀποπέμπῃ τὴν γυναῖκα, ἀποδιδόναι τὴν προῖκα, ἐὰν δὲ μή, ἐπ' ἐννέ' ὀβολοῖς τοκοφορεῖν. Dem. 27 *Aphob.* i. 17 μὴ γήμαντος δ' αὐτοῦ τὴν μητέρα τὴν ἐμήν, ὁ μὲν νόμος κελεύει τὴν προῖκ' ὀφείλειν ἐπ' ἐννέ' ὀβολοῖς. There is no need to tinker with the words ἕνεκα τοῦ νόμου in the Isaios passage, which precisely underline the distinction between the legal and the popular usage. Wolff confuses the issue when he says in *RE* 137 that valuation was not an essential mark of the προίξ, but had only procedural significance. If, for example, a farm was given as part of a dowry and was at the same time made into an ἀποτίμημα, it would none the less have been necessary to put a value on it, if only for the effective working of the rule on interest. See further p. 299, n. 2.

(ii) *Bestowal of dowry*

Normally the grantor of the dowry was the woman's *κύριος*, he who had also given her in marriage. It might, and did, happen that a third party provided, or contributed to, the dowry. There is no evidence to suggest that such a contributor was entitled, as of law, to the return of his contribution if the marriage was dissolved, and the language used in one or two recorded cases suggests the contrary. In default of direct evidence we must conjecture that, if the case arose for the obligatory return of a dowry thus composed, these contributions would revert to the woman's *κύριος*.[1] There are several cases of a husband providing by will for a dowry for his widow.[2]

Although social convention had made it usual by the fourth century for a middle- or upper-class girl to be provided with a dowry she had no legal claim to one, either from her father in his lifetime or from her brothers on his death if he had made no provision for it in his will. If she had no brothers she was an *ἐπίκληρος* and her father's estate took the place of a dowry. It is true that if she belonged to the thetic class her next of kin could be made by the archon to provide a dowry for her proportionate to his property census, if he was not willing to marry her himself. But this is really an exception which proves the rule; for it is fairly clear that the aim of this provision was not to protect the interests of the girl as such, but to guard against the extinction of the *οἶκος*; the archon was by statute charged with the care of *οἶκοι ἐξερημούμενοι*.[3] Equally strong is the evidence against the

[1] Lys. 19 *Prop. Arist.* 59 *ἰδίᾳ τισὶ τῶν πολιτῶν ἀποροῦσι συνεξέδωκε θυγατέρας καὶ ἀδελφάς*. Dem. 59 *Neair.* 70 *πείθουσι τὸν Ἐπαίνετον χιλίας δραχμὰς εἰσενεγκεῖν εἰς τὴν ἔκδοσιν τῇ θυγατρὶ τῇ Νεαίρας*. *SIG* 496. 19 (Athenian inscription of 229/228 B.C. honouring Timosthenes) *διδόναι δὲ καὶ θυγ[ατ]έρω[ν] ε[ἰ]ς ἔγ[δοσ]ιν τὸν [δῆ]μον π[ροῖ]κα [ὅ]σην ἂν βούλ[η]τ[α]ι*.

[2] Dem. 27 *Aphob.* i. 5, 29 *Aphob.* iii. 43, 45, *Steph.* i. 28. Cf. p. 21, above.

[3] Apart from the misleading analogy from the thetic *ἐπίκληρος* the most serious piece of evidence in favour of a compulsory dowry is from Dem. 40 *Boiot.* ii. 19 *ἡ μήτηρ μου τάλαντον ἐπενεγκαμένη προῖκα, ἐκδοθεῖσα ὑπὸ τῶν ἀδελφῶν τῶν αὑτῆς, ὥσπερ οἱ νόμοι κελεύουσιν, συνῴκησεν τῷ πατρί*, quoted by Lips., *AR* 543, n. 13, to prove compulsory dowering, though he himself (489, n. 66) had pointed out that the words *ὥσπερ οἱ νόμοι κελεύουσιν* refer to the giving in marriage, not to the bestowal of the dowry. Cf. Erdmann, *Ehe* 305. Harpokr. s.v. *ἐπίδικος· ἐπίκληρος μέν ἐστιν ἡ ἐπὶ παντὶ τῷ κλήρῳ ὀρφανὴ καταλελειμμένη μὴ ὄντος αὐτῇ ἀδελφοῦ. ἐπίπροικος δὲ ἡ ἐπὶ μέρει τινὶ τοῦ κλήρου ὥστε προῖκα ἔχειν ἀδελφῶν αὐτῇ ὄντων* taken by itself postulates a class of *ἐπίπροικοι*, women entitled to a dowry from the estate left by their father. Cf. *An. Bekk.* (*Λέξ. Ῥητ.*) 256. But in view of the total silence of the orators on such a class we may perhaps assume that the grammarians

view that a dowry was an essential ingredient of a valid marriage. The passages from Isaios which have been advanced to prove this have been misunderstood, and there are other remarks in the orators which amply substantiate the possibility of dowerless brides.[1]

The quasi-technical word for bestowing a dowry was ἐπιδιδόναι. It is frequently followed by the bride in the dative. The fact that we also find phrases like προῖκα ἐπ' αὐτῇ δίδωσι (Dem. 59 *Neair.* 50) and ἔλαβεν ἐπὶ τῇ ἀδελφῇ προῖκα (Isai. 2 *Menekl.* 5) suggests that in this context the force of the dative is rather 'for the woman' than 'to the woman'.[2]

The natural moment for the bestowal of the dowry would have been when the ἐγγύη took place, and there are texts which confirm that this was usually what happened. For instance, the somewhat twisted argument in Isai. 3 *Pyrrh.* 29 and 35 assumes that normally the same witnesses would have attested to the ἐγγύη and the bestowal of a dowry, and this actually happened at the ἐγγύη of Polyeuktos' daughter (Dem. 41 *Spoud.* 6 μάρτυρας παρέξομαι τοὺς παραγενομένους ὅτ' ἠγγύα μοι Πολύευκτος τὴν θυγατέρ' ἐπὶ τετταράκοντα μναῖς). The Mykonos register suggests a similar position there. There was, however, a complication arising from the fact that a considerable interval might separate the ἐγγύη from the consummation of the marriage by ἔκδοσις

wrongly attributed to a factual word, 'a dowered woman', a legal sense, 'one entitled to a dowry'. Dem. 41 *Spoud.* 26 shows that the father was perfectly free to give two daughters dowries of different amounts. The suggestion of A. Biscardi, *SIFC* 11 (1934), 70, that a father could be forced to dower a daughter by threat of an εἰσαγγελία κακώσεως is unsupported by evidence and in itself improbable.

[1] A. Biscardi, loc. cit. 57 ff. In Isai. 2 *Menekl.* 5 the speaker's opponent is not being made to argue 'no dowry, therefore no ἐγγύη'. He is rather trying to suggest that the alleged failure to provide a dowry for his sister showed that the speaker was a man of no substance who had foisted himself on Menekles for mercenary reasons. Again in Isai. 3 *Pyrrh.* 8–9, 28–29, 35–39, 78 the argument is not that no woman could be validly married ἄπροικος, but that no one would have given in marriage *such a woman as Phile's mother was alleged to be ἄπροικος*; cf. especially 29 οἱ δὲ θεῖοι τῷ ἀδελφιδῷ ἄπροικον τὴν τοιαύτην ἐγγυωμένῳ μεμαρτυρήκασι παραγενέσθαι. For possible or actual dowerless brides see Lys. 19 *Prop. Arist.* 15 τὰς ἐμὰς ἀδελφὰς ἐθελόντων τινῶν λαβεῖν ἀπροίκους πάνυ πλουσίων. Ibid. 14 τὴν ἐμὴν μητέρα ἔλαβεν οὐδὲν ἐπιφερομένην. Dem. 40 *Boiot.* ii. 25 οὔτε τὸν ἐκείνου προσῆκεν υἱὸν ἄπροικον αὐτὴν γῆμαι. Cf. Bruck, *Schenkung* 94.

[2] Lys. 19 *Prop. Arist.* 17 αὐτός τε ἄνευ χρημάτων ἔγημε τοῖν τε θυγατέροιν πολὺ ἀργύριον ἐπέδωκε τῷ τε ὑεῖ ὀλίγην προῖκα ἔλαβε, a father provides large dowries for his two daughters and, exceptionally if not uniquely, receives a small one for his son. For other instances of προῖκα ἐπιδιδόναι with the woman in the dative Dem. 41 *Spoud.* 26, 45 *Steph.* i. 28, Lys. 16 *Mantith.* 10, Isai. 2 *Menekl.* 5.

(see above, pp. 7 f.). The case of Demosthenes' sister shows clearly that the actual bestowal of a dowry (and not merely the promise to bestow) could be contemporaneous with an ἐγγύη necessarily far removed in time from the ἔκδοσις. There is, on the other hand, no reason to doubt either that a dowry could be bestowed after the ἐγγύη or that an original dowry could be increased, though we have no instance of the one or the other. In short, we can say that until there was an ἐγγύη there could be no προίξ, but that once there was an ἐγγύη a προίξ could be bestowed at any time.[1]

As with ἐγγύη itself and many other juristic acts, there does not seem to have been any set, legal form which had to be followed in bestowing a dowry, except that it had to be valued (see p. 46, above). The exchanges in Menander's *Περικειρομένη* (p. 18, above) very likely picture the normal procedure. Witnesses would be present for purposes of providing proof rather than giving validity.[2] There is no evidence to suggest that any kind of public registration of property, whether chattels or land, bestowed as dowry was required in Athens, as it was, for example, in Tenos in the third century B.C.[3]

Sometimes a dowry was agreed upon at the ἐγγύη, but was not handed over at the time or was only handed over in part.[4] What means a husband or prospective husband had of enforcing payment if it was withheld is a matter of dispute. Some have thought that the δίκη προικός was available for this purpose. Aristotle (*Ath. Pol.* 52. 2), listing the suits in the competence of the eisagogeis, begins εἰσὶ δ' ἔμμηνοι προικός, ἐάν τις ὀφείλων μὴ ἀποδῷ. These words certainly could cover a dowry promised but not paid as well as a dowry due to be returned, but they need not necessarily do so and are not in themselves sufficient to prove

[1] Wolff's formulation of the problem of time, *RE* 142. 3 (a), is not clear. There was a story that Alkibiades, having received ten talents as Hipparete's dowry, claimed and was paid a further ten talents on the birth of a child, alleging an agreement to that effect. This, if genuine, is the only recorded case of such an agreement. Andok. 4 *Alk.* 13, Plut., *Alk.* 8.

[2] Demosthenes tries to throw doubt on the genuineness of a dowry from the fact that there had been no witnesses at its actual handing over; 30 *Onet.* i. 19 f. *τῷ τοῦθ' ὑμῶν πιστόν, ὡς ταλάντου τῆς προικὸς οὔσης ἄνευ μαρτύρων 'Ονήτωρ καὶ Τιμοκράτης Ἀφόβῳ τοσοῦτον ἀργύριον ἐνεχείρισαν;*

[3] The heading of *IJ* vii reads [*Κατὰ τάδε πράσεις ἐγέ*]*νοντο χωρίων* [*καὶ οἰ*]*κιῶν καὶ προι*[*κῶν*] *δόσεις*.

[4] Dem., loc. cit. n. 2, 41 *Spoud.* 5 (p. 51, n. 2, below).

that the suit served this dual purpose. Demosthenes' speech 41 *Spoud.* bears the title *Πρὸς Σπουδίαν ὑπὲρ προικός*, and it is concerned in part with the speaker's claim to collect the rent on a house which he alleges to have been made an *ἀποτίμημα* by the will of his father-in-law for the balance of the dowry not paid up at the time of his marriage; Spoudias had been preventing him from collecting this rent (see p. 298, n. 1). But it is very questionable whether we should press this title as proof that in fact this case was a *δίκη προικός*, for in the first place the title would more naturally have been simply *προικός* and in the second the suit concerns not only the dowry but other matters connected with the inheritance. And if there is no direct proof that this suit was available for this purpose, there is an *a priori* reason against it. We shall find that there was a rationale behind the use of a special suit for the return of the dowry, but there is no similar rationale for a special suit to enable the husband to enforce the promise of a dowry.[1] It must on, the other side, be admitted that we cannot say what suit was available for this purpose if it was not the *δίκη προικός*. One would gladly accept the conjecture that it was the *δίκη παραβάσεως συμβολαίων* but for the fact that the very existence of such a suit is doubtful. Wolff (loc. cit., n. 1), argues that a promise to provide a dowry was only enforceable when accompanied by an express *ὁμολογία*, analogous to the agreement on which Spoudias' opponent relied to secure the unpaid balance of his wife's dowry out of the estate of her father when he died.[2] But, having rejected the *δίκη παραβάσεως συμβολαίων*, Wolff suggests no alternative suit. We must then either suppose that there was a suit whose name has not come

[1] The following have argued that the suit was available for the husband: Lips., *AR* 496 f., Harrell, *Arbitration* 38 (followed by Bo. Sm. ii. 116), who states that the suit referred to in Dem. 40 *Boiot.* ii. 16–17, 41 *Spoud. passim* is to be distinguished from that in *Ath. Pol.* 52. 2, but does not say how (except procedurally, the latter being monthly, the former not); Fine, *Horoi* 136 ff., Pringsheim, *GLS* 49, Gernet, *RÉG* 51 (1938), 8 (*DSGA* 177). Against, Wolff, *RE* 144 ff.; but his main reason, that the Athenians did not name their suits after the economic end at which they aimed ('das mit ihnen erstrebte wirtschaftliche Ziel'), is very weak; no one questions that the suit was available for the recovery of the dowry, surely just as much 'an economic end' as the original getting of it. Erdmann, *Ehe* 317, is also against.

[2] Dem. 41 *Spoud.* 5 *τὴν προῖκ' οὐ κομισάμενος ἅπασαν, ἀλλ' ὑπολειφθεισῶν χιλίων δραχμῶν καὶ ὁμολογηθεισῶν ἀπολαβεῖν ὅταν Πολύευκτος ἀποθάνῃ, ἕως μὲν ὁ Λεωκράτης ἦν κληρονόμος τῶν Πολυεύκτου, πρὸς ἐκεῖνον ἦν μοι τὸ συμβόλαιον.* Note that in this case the agreement (called *συμβόλαιον*) is with the (then) heir presumptive of the bride's father.

down to us dealing with this particular kind of breach of contract, or accept the δίκη προικός, which having been invented for the purpose of recovering the dowry might have been later extended to cover the case of a dowry promised but not paid. This latter solution would be more acceptable if we could be certain that the same sort of thing had happened with regard to dotal ἀποτίμημα (on which see p. 298 and n. 1).[1]

(iii) *Dowry during marriage*

In view of the extremely fluid concept of ownership in Greek thought (see pp. 201 ff.), to ask who owned the things making up a dowry while the marriage lasted is perhaps to ask the wrong question. It is true that Demosthenes in two places uses expressions which suggest that the dowry was the wife's.[2] But we should not lean too heavily on such phrases for a juristic meaning; at the most they are reflections of the undoubted fact that the husband had not an absolute right of disposal, since if the wife died during the marriage without having given birth to a child the dowry reverted to her family.[3] In fact it is difficult to see what the wife's ownership could mean in respect of dowries consisting wholly or partly in money; such sums were clearly intended to be used as capital, and the woman, being legally incapacitated from doing any business beyond the trivialities of housekeeping, could not herself use them as productive investment; nor is there adequate evidence that the husband, who, if he were prudent, would wish to do this himself, had to obtain the consent of his wife.[4] Further, the whole business of valuing the

[1] For the unsolved problem of the type of suit in which Dem. 41 *Spoud.* was delivered see Lips., *AR* 653, n. 61, Gernet, *Dem.* ii. 59. The latter rejects the δίκη προικός. A δίκη βλάβης is conceivable; in that case the speech should have been described not as πρὸς Σπουδίαν, but as κατὰ Σπουδίου; but it is described as κατὰ Σ. in Harpokr. s.v. νεμέσεια. Gernet rightly, however, points out the difficulty of founding the pleas of the speaker on the notion of damage and he suggests a contamination of the suits ἐνοικίου (for the house) and ἀργυρίου (for the sums borrowed by Spoudias).

[2] In Dem. 30 *Onet.* i. 12 a man paying a dowry with a bride is described as τἀκείνης ἀποδούς, and in 40 *Boiot.* ii. 25 for brothers not to provide a dowry for a second marriage of their widowed sister, who had had a dowry with her first, is ἀποστερῆσαι τὴν ἀδελφήν. Erdmann, *Ehe.* 323, Wolff, *RE* 147.

[3] Isai. 3 *Pyrrh.* 36 (see further below, p. 56), Wolff, *RE* 148.

[4] Evidence has been sought (cf. Lips., *AR* 492 f., Erdmann, *Ehe* 325 f.) in three third-century inscriptions from Amorgos. In *IG* xii. 7. 57 (Finley, *Land*, no. 155) houses and orchards which had been 'valued for Nikesarete into her dowry' (on this phrase see p. 299, n. 2) are dedicated *mortis causa* to Urania Aphrodite ὑπὸ

dowry and making the *δίκη προικός* an action *in personam* against the husband for a sum of money necessarily implies that he was *κύριος* of the dowry while the marriage lasted. Doubt only remains as to the rule which applied when the dowry contained chattels or land. Evidence here is inconclusive, but the most probable view seems to be that any non-fungible thing that was made an *ἀποτίμημα* in a dowry was strictly inalienable by the husband, just as land which he had made *ἀποτίμημα* for the return of the dowry must have been.[1] On the other hand, real property which had not been made into an *ἀποτίμημα* could be alienated, the husband of course still remaining liable for the return of its value. Thus in Isai. 5 *Dikaiog.* 27 a husband alienates a house which he has acquired *ἀντὶ τῆς προικός*; we can conjecture that this house had not been made an *ἀποτίμημα*.[2] As to chattels, the evidence derived from Dem. 47 *Euerg.* 57 is inconclusive: in that case a very brutal judgement execution is being carried out, and the wife protests against the seizure of objects *αὐτῆς . . . ἐν τῇ προικὶ τετιμημένα*: but it is not clear whether we can rule out the possibility that these objects had been made an *ἀποτίμημα*, and, even if we can, whether the speaker implies the illegality, as distinct from the brutality, of the act.

Two other pieces of evidence have been held to support the view that the husband was *κύριος* of the dowry during the

Νικησαρέτης τῆς γυναικὸς τῆς Ναυκράτους καὶ κυρίου Ναυκράτους. But the fact that this is a testamentary disposition, and that, on the assumption that there were no children, by Athenian law at least the dowry on her death would have reverted to the woman's kin, robs this case of evidential value. In *IG* xii. 7. 58 (Finley, *Land*, no. 8) a man hypothecates some real property with the concurrence (*συνεπιχωρούσης*) of his wife and of her *κύριος* (a third party); the property may have been part of her dowry, but it is not so described. In *IG* xii. 7. 55 (Finley, *Land*, no. 102) *ἀπέδοτο Νικήρατος καὶ Ἡγεκράτη καὶ ὁ κύριο[ς] Τελένικος Κτησιφῶντι Πυθίππου τὰ χωρία κτλ.*; but the property in question was explicitly not part of a dowry or *ἀποτίμημα* for a dowry, nor is it even certain that Hegekrate was wife of Nikeratos. On these three texts see Finley, *Land* 265, n. 22, Wolff, *Traditio* 2 (1944), 59 ff. (*Beitr.* 180 ff.)

[1] This assumes that land which formed part of a dowry could be, and normally was, an *ἀποτίμημα*; on this see p. 301 and below on the *δίκη προικός*.

[2] Wolff, *RE* 148 f. (also *Traditio* 2 (1944), 58, *Beitr.* 180) criticizes Beauch. i. 304, Lips., *AR* 492, n. 82, Erdmann, *Ehe* 325, who, in the interest of their view that the dowry belonged to the wife, argue that this house was a *datio in solutum* for a monetary dowry; but in effect that is surely what Wolff's view makes it. He misses the real point, that the husband's power of alienation compels us to assume that in this case, exceptionally, a piece of real property forming part of a dowry was not made an *ἀποτίμημα*. Wolff is right to discount the evidence from the law of Gortyn (vi. 9 ff.); the position of women *vis-à-vis* property and inheritance is so different in Gortyn from that in Athens that the parallel is valueless.

marriage. It seems likely that the dowry of Demosthenes' mother (fifty minai) was included in the assessment of the value of his estate during his minority, for according to the figures he gives in 27 *Aphob.* i. 4–9 his father left fourteen talents while the assessment for εἰσφόρα was fifteen talents.[1] But this case is inconclusive, for it is possible that Demosthenes' father was sole κύριος of Kleoboule by a special disposition (p. 30, n. 1, above); this would mean that her father had renounced any rights in the dowry, and it would naturally therefore fall to be assessed in the οἶκος of Demosthenes. More cogent is a passage in Dem. 42 *Phain.* 27 which, properly read, seems to imply that for the purposes of challenge to exchange of property known as ἀντίδοσις the dowry of a widow who had chosen to remain in her husband's house on his death was reckoned in with the property of her son.[2] On the other hand, the rule which applied when a man's goods were confiscated by the state, so far as it can be elicited from the evidence, seems to tend in the other direction. A lexicographical article says that by a procedure described by the word ἐνεπισκήψασθαι a wife could, if her husband's goods were being confiscated, have her dowry excepted from the confiscated property, as ordinary creditors could their debts, and we have an actual instance of a creditor doing this very thing in the poletai records for 367/366 B.C. (see pp. 270 f.). Whether this concession applied only to secured debts, and by analogy only to an ἀποτίμημα in the case of a dowry, is here irrelevant. The point is that, for this purpose at least, a dowry, or part of a dowry, was in certain circumstances treated as not belonging to the husband. When Wolff (*RE* 150) would discount this evidence on the ground that, according to the lexicographer as confirmed by the poletai records, this concession was shared by all the man's creditors, he seems to miss the point, which is precisely whether the dowry was, or was not, to be counted as a debt. This is clear from the words used by the speaker in Dem. 42 *Phain.* 27 οὐκ ἀπογράφω τὴν προῖκα χρέως αὐτῇ (τῇ μητρί). There was perhaps no compelling reason why the rule for ἀντίδοσις and for confiscation should be the same; but it is idle to maintain that the rule was, on this evidence, not different.[3]

[1] The inclusion of the dowry would roughly account for the difference.

[2] So Wolff, *RE* 148 against Lips., *AR* 493, Erdmann, *Ehe* 324, n. 10.

[3] *An. Bekk.* (Λέξ. Ῥητ.) 250 Ἐνεπίσκημμα καὶ ἐνεπισκήψασθαι· προφώνησις

(iv) *Dowry after dissolution of marriage*

There is ample evidence to show that by a statutory rule a dowry was repayable by the husband on the dissolution of the marriage.[1] This was the general principle. We must now try to determine whether there were exceptional cases which excused repayment and what were the precise rules in various particular circumstances.

The dowry was repayable on a divorce irrespective of which spouse had initiated the divorce and almost certainly irrespective of the grounds on which they had acted. Isai. 3 *Pyrrh.* 35 necessarily entails the former rule. The latter has been questioned on two insufficient grounds. It has been suggested that in the case of Mantitheos against Boiotos (Dem. 40 *Boiot.* ii) Plangon, mother of Boiotos, having married Mantias, the father of Mantitheos, with a dowry (loc. cit. 20), had been divorced by him for adultery, and that this entitled Mantias to retain the dowry. But it is pure conjecture that there had been a divorce for this reason, and, if this was indeed why Mantias had retained the dowry, why did not Mantitheos say so? Even less cogent is a possible analogy from the law of Ephesos in the early third century B.C.[2] We have no direct evidence for Athens as to what happened to the dowry of a woman divorced for adultery. On the other hand, we can deduce with some certainty from Dem. 59 *Neair.* 52 that the law which required a man who had divorced his wife to return her dowry or pay interest on it did not except the case where a foreign woman had been fraudulently given in marriage by her *κύριος* as being of citizen birth; for, if it had, the speaker would surely have said so, and would not have implied, as he does, that Phrastor, who had been sued for the interest on Phano's dowry, could not simply plead that it was not returnable, but had to

γυναικὸς καὶ δανειστοῦ, δημευομένης οὐσίας, περὶ προικὸς καὶ χρέους, ὀφειλόντων αὐτὰ ἐξ αὐτῆς λαμβάνειν. Cf. Pollux 8. 61 *ἐνεπισκήψασθαι δ' ἦν, ὁπότε τις ἐν τοῖς δημευθεῖσιν ἑαυτῷ τι ὀφείλεσθαι ἢ προσήκειν λέγοι*. Dem. 53 *Nikostr.* 28.

[1] See the passages from Isaios and Demosthenes quoted on p. 47, n.2, and add Dem. 40 *Boiot.* ii. 59 *περὶ προικός, ἣν ἐνεγκαμένης τῆς μητρὸς οἱ νόμοι κελεύουσιν ἐμὲ κομίζεσθαι* and 42 *Phain.* 27 *ταύτῃ χρέως φησὶν ὀφείλεσθαι Φαίνιππος τὴν προῖκα, ἧς οἱ νόμοι κύριον τοῦτον ποιοῦσιν*.

[2] O. Müller, *NJ* Suppl. 25 (1899), 697, Lips., *AR* 494, n. 92. The law of Ephesos as given by Achilles Tatius 8. 8.13: *τὴν μὲν κατὰ τὸν νόμον ἀφεῖσθαι τῆς προικός φημι δεῖν ἐμοί*. *SIG* 364. 59 *ὅσοι . . . γήμαντες καὶ διαλυθέντες μὴ ἀποδεδώκασι τὰς φερνὰς οὔσας ἀποδότους κατὰ τὸν νόμον* confirms that some dowries were not returnable in Ephesos in the early third century.

have recourse to a γραφή against Phano's κύριος for having given her in marriage to him though she was a foreigner. But if by law the dowry was returnable to a κύριος who had acted fraudulently, it was surely *a fortiori* returnable to the innocent κύριος of a woman who had committed adultery.[1]

This firm statutory provision for the return of the dowry in all cases without exception was undoubtedly a protection of the woman and was generally so regarded. The point is well put by the speaker in Isai. 3 *Pyrrh.* 36—τί γὰρ ἔμελλεν ὄφελος εἶναι αὐτῷ τῆς ἐγγύης, εἰ ἐπὶ τῷ ἐγγυησαμένῳ ἐκπέμψαι ὁπότε βούλοιτο τὴν γυναῖκα ἦν; ἦν δ' ἂν ἐπ' ἐκείνῳ, δῆλον ὅτι, εἰ μηδεμίαν προῖκα διωμολογήσατο ἕξειν ἐπ' αὐτῇ—and the same speaker seems to suggest that where a poor girl was marrying a rich man the position of the girl could be safeguarded by the husband's providing a fictitious dowry which would be forfeit if he divorced the girl (ibid. 28 .).[2]

If a marriage ended by the death of the wife without children the dowry was repayable to the κύριος who had given her in marriage. This is expressly stated in Isai. 3 *Pyrrh.* 36 τῆς ὁμολογηθείσης προικὸς ἐκ τῶν νόμων γιγνομένης εἰς αὐτόν, εἴ τι ἔπαθεν ἡ γυνὴ πρὶν γενέσθαι παῖδας αὐτῇ, where αὐτόν is a brother who had given the woman in marriage. We may be pretty sure, though there is no direct evidence, that the same thing happened when a husband died leaving a childless widow. Isai. 3 *Pyrrh.* 9, 78 suggests that the dowry was returnable when a widow was left with a daughter, for in that case the speaker's opponents alleged that there was a legitimate daughter of the widow and the speaker argues the non-existence of a dowry from the fact that the widow's brother had not claimed its return. We have no evidence for the case of a widower with a daughter only; but as she might become an ἐπίκληρος and in that case her sons, if any, would succeed to the estate of her father, it is conceivable that her sons' claims might have extended to the dowry of her mother.[3]

When a widow was left with sons and she chose to return to

[1] Beauch. i. 319, Erdmann, *Ehe* 330, Wolff, *RE* 152, id., *Traditio* 2 (1944), 61, 95 (*Beitr.* 184, 241).

[2] E. Rabel, *Z* 28 (1907), 332.

[3] This is a conjecture of Wolff, *RE* 153. He does not suggest what might seem even more likely *a priori*, that the mother's dowry might have been used to dower the daughter.

her own family she took her dowry with her (p. 44, above). If she remained in her husband's house her sons were κύριοι of the dowry, being charged with her maintenance out of it (Dem. 42 *Phain.* 27 quoted p. 55, n. 1, above). Probably this control over the dowry by the sons did not become absolute when she made her choice, but was conditional on their mother's remaining in their house; thus the speaker in Dem., loc. cit., when explaining that he has not excluded his mother's dowry from the valuation of his property, stresses that she is still living with him.[1]

If the wife died while still in the οἶκος of her husband, leaving sons, the dowry was not returnable. But it was not simply assimilated into the husband's estate; one thing at least seems clear in the confused case of Dem. 40 *Boiot.* ii, namely that sons by different wives were entitled by law to take their mothers' dowries out of the father's estate first and the remainder was then divided equally (see especially 14 f.).

(v) δίκη προικός, δίκη σίτου

These rules for the repayment of a dowry were enforced by two special suits, the δίκη προικός, which has to be considered in some detail in discussing the dotal ἀποτίμημα (p. 298; cf. also p. 50, above), and the δίκη σίτου. On the former nothing further need be said except to point out that it was for the value of the whole dowry and to add that though Dem. 40 *Boiot.* ii. 50 shows that a son might expect to receive maintenance from the interest on his mother's dowry during his minority, we do not know how this was enforced; nor is there anything in this passage or elsewhere to suggest that on reaching his majority he could make his father pay him the capital.

The δίκη σίτου, on the other hand, was for interest at the statutory rate of 18 per cent. on the capital value of the dowry. This interest began to run from the moment the marriage was dissolved, for whatever reason, and continued to be payable till the capital value was refunded. Its basic object was to provide for the maintenance of the woman. The suit was heard in the Odeion, probably in the archon's court.[2] It seems probable that

[1] So Wolff, *RE* 153, *Traditio* 2 (1944), 61 (*Beitr.* 185), arguing against Beauch. i. 312.

[2] See Dem. 59 *Neair.* 52, quoted p. 47, n. 2; the passage continues καὶ σίτου εἰς Ὠιδεῖον εἶναι δικάσασθαι ὑπὲρ τῆς γυναικὸς τῷ κυρίῳ. Dem. 27 *Aphob.* i. 17 (ibid.);

in origin the suit was related to dowries due to be returned and the high rate of interest (18 per cent. as against the normal 12 per cent.) had a certain penal element in it. It has, however, been held that its use was extended to cover two other contingencies: first, where the prospective husband held the dowry between the *ἐγγύη* and the consummation of the marriage, in which case, it is suggested, he had to provide for his future wife's maintenance and could be compelled by this suit to do so (though not necessarily at the rate of 18 per cent. on the dowry); second, where the marriage had been consummated, but the wife's *κύριος* had failed to pay up the dowry, in which case the husband could use the suit against the *κύριος* (though again not necessarily being entitled to a rate of 18 per cent.). The second suggestion stands or falls with our acceptance or rejection of the view that the *δίκη προικός* was available to the husband in these circumstances; if it was, then the *δίκη σίτου* must surely have been available also. As to the first, the only direct evidence we have is the case of Aphobos and Demosthenes' mother, and this must be used with some caution. It is true that he argues in 27 *Aphob.* i. 17 (quoted p. 47, n. 2) that by law Aphobos owed interest on the dowry he had received under Demosthenes' father's will at the rate of 18 per cent. But it might be contended that the phrase *μὴ γήμαντος αὐτοῦ τὴν μητέρα* implies that this law could only be invoked because Aphobos never in fact married the woman, or in other words that this was a dissolved marriage rather than an *ἐγγύη* waiting to be consummated. Possibly Demosthenes was not sure of his ground here and that was one

Isai. 3 *Pyrrh.* 78 *ἢ εἰ ἀπαιτῶν μὴ ἐδύνατο κομίσασθαι ἐν εἴκοσιν ἔτεσιν, ὁποίαν δίκην σίτου ἢ τῆς προικὸς αὐτῆς ὑπὲρ τῆς ἐγγυητῆς γυναικὸς ἐδικάσατο τῷ ἔχοντι τὸν Πύρρου κλῆρον οὗτος;* Although the first passage refers only to a case of *ἀποπομπή*, and the second to a case where the *ἐγγύη* with which the dowry had been connected had never been completed by a *γάμος*, they probably all go back to a single provision covering all cases where a woman still alive (or her *κύριος* on her behalf: note the phrase *ὑπὲρ τῆς γυναικός*) was entitled to the repayment of the dowry, Wolff, *RE* 154. Harpokr. s.v. *σῖτος*: *καλεῖται ἡ διδομένη πρόσοδος εἰς τροφὴν ταῖς γυναιξὶν ἢ τοῖς ὀρφανοῖς, ὡς ἐξ ἄλλων μαθεῖν ἔστι καὶ ἐκ τοῦ Σόλωνος α΄ ἄξονος καὶ ἐκ τῆς Ἀριστοτέλους Ἀθηναίων πολιτείας. Τιμαχίδας δὲ ἡγεῖται παρὰ τοῖς Ἀττικοῖς σῖτον λέγεσθαι τὸν τόκον, ἀγνοεῖ δὲ ὅτι ἓν ἀνθ' ἑνὸς οὐδέποτε παρ' αὐτοῖς ὁ τόκος σῖτος καλεῖται.* It is very probable that Solon's first *axon* contained the archon's laws: cf. A. R. W. Harrison, *CQ* 11 (1961), 4. It is doubtful whether we should infer from the fact that on one occasion grain was distributed in the Odeion (Dem. 34 *Ag. Phorm.* 37) that originally this suit was for the delivery of maintenance in kind and that that was the reason for its being heard in the Odeion (Lips., *AR* 498, n. 104).

reason why he actually reckoned the interest at only 12 per cent. Another slight indication in the same direction is that in 29 *Aphob.* iii. 33 Demosthenes seems to describe a formal agreement by Aphobos that, as holder of the dowry, he would provide for Kleoboule's maintenance: *οἱ παρόντες ἐμαρτύρησαν σῖτον τῇ μητρὶ δώσειν ὁμολογεῖν τοῦτον ὡς ἔχοντα τὴν προῖκα.* If *ὁμολογεῖν* means something more than merely 'said that he would', then what need was there for a formal agreement to perform what was a statutory duty?[1] On the whole it would seem more probable that the *δίκη σίτου* was not available in this case, in other words that there was no statutory duty on the prospective husband to provide maintenance for his prospective wife between *ἐγγύη* and *γάμος* at the rate of 18 per cent.; for after all at that stage, in normal circumstances, both parties to the agreement were, so far as we can see, completely free to withdraw, and neither party stood to lose much in the material sense by cancelling the agreement, on the assumption that the woman's father had taken the elementary precaution of exacting adequate security for the return of the dowry. In a sense Demosthenes' case is the exception which proves the rule; for his mother's *κύριος*, until her marriage with Aphobos should be consummated, was either Aphobos himself or he together with the other two guardians appointed by the elder Demosthenes' will. In other words she had no effective representative to compel either the return of the dowry or the provision of an income out of it adequate for her maintenance.[2]

We know that the son of an *ἐπίκληρος* two years after he came of age took over control of the estate, but had to provide out of it for his mother's maintenance. We can infer from this, though it is only an inference, that where a widow who was not an *ἐπίκληρος* had chosen to remain in her husband's house on his death a son of the marriage would have had the like duty. It is improbable, however, that in either case the woman would have had to rely on a *δίκη σίτου* to enforce this duty, for the son himself might well be his mother's *κύριος* in these circumstances. It is more likely,

[1] But this speech may well be spurious, and evidence from it is therefore weak: see below, p. 105, n. 5.

[2] Beauch. i. 314, Lips., *AR* 497, Erdmann, *Ehe* 337 ff., Fine, *Horoi* 138, Wolff, *RE* 154, id., *Traditio* 2 (1944), 62 (*Beitr.* 186). We should do well to stick to the simple hypothesis that the law provided for a rate of 18 per cent. in all cases where the *δίκη σίτου* was available.

therefore, that she would have had to depend on some third party to bring a *γραφὴ κακώσεως γονέων*.[1]

If we ask why a plaintiff should ever have chosen to sue for the interest on the dowry by a *δίκη σίτου* rather than for the dowry itself by a *δίκη προικός*, the answer may perhaps be that the procedural costs in case of an unfavourable verdict would have been less, since court fees were in proportion to the value of the claim, whereas if he won his case the chances were, considering the high rate of interest, that the defendant would prefer to pay up the capital.

[1] Dem. 46 *Steph.* ii. 20 *ΝΟΜΟΣ. Καὶ ἐὰν ἐξ ἐπικλήρου τις γένηται καὶ ἅμα ἡβήσῃ ἐπὶ δίετες, κρατεῖν τῶν χρημάτων, τὸν δὲ σῖτον μετρεῖν τῇ μητρί.* Lips., *AR* 495, and others write as though this law expressly covered property forming the dowry of women who were not *ἐπίκληροι*. For the *γραφὴ κακώσεως γονέων* see Isai. 8 *Kir.* 32. Pollux 3. 47 puts the suits *κακώσεως*, *προικός*, and *σίτου* together; *δίκη* is there used in the generic sense which includes *γραφή*.

II · CHILDREN

§ 1. νόθοι

THOUGH it may sometimes have been used loosely, the term νόθος must have denoted a strictly identifiable class of persons, certainly in the classical period and possibly as far back as the time of Solon, since there was at least one law, attributed to Solon, defining or limiting the rights of such persons. The contrary term to νόθος was γνήσιος. Pollux 3. 21 gives the following definition of the two terms: γνήσιος μὲν ὁ ἐκ γυναικὸς ἀστῆς καὶ γαμετῆς—ὁ δὲ αὐτὸς καὶ ἰθαγενής—νόθος ὁ ἐκ ξένης ἢ παλλακίδος· ὑπ' ἐνίων δὲ καλεῖται μητρόξενος. τὰ δὲ χρήματα τὰ τοῖς νόθοις διδόμενα Ἀριστοφάνης νοθεῖα καλεῖ. This is an unsatisfactory definition, but it does draw attention to the confusion which may arise from ignoring changes in the law of citizenship effected in the middle and again towards the end of the fifth century (above, pp. 24 ff.). Certainly after Perikles' citizenship law of 451/450 no child of a marriage between a foreign man and Athenian woman or Athenian man and foreign woman was Athenian, and this rule, which was relaxed during the Peloponnesian War, was re-enacted in 403/402 and held throughout the classical period thereafter. But it does not follow, as the Pollux passage seems to imply, that children of marriages of mixed nationality exhausted the class of νόθοι. There might be children whose parents, though both Athenian, had not been married either by ἐγγύη or by ἐπιδικασία. That such children were νόθοι is implied by the definition of γνήσιοι given in a law in Dem. 46 *Steph.* ii. 18 cited above (p. 5); and, as is there suggested, the antiquity of that law is guaranteed by the use of the word δάμαρ.[1] It seems

[1] On νόθοι in general see Beauch. i. 488–535, C. A. Savage, *The Athenian Family* (Baltimore, 1907), 107, ff., Glotz, *Solidarité*, 340 ff., Bu. Sw. 940, Lips., *AR* 473 ff., Paoli, *St. Dir.* 272 ff., Becker, *Plat.* 194 ff., Erdmann, *Ehe* 363 ff., K. Latte, *RE* s.v. (1936), Kahrstedt, *Staatsg.* 66 ff., Wolff, *Traditio* 2 (1944), 75 ff. (*Beitr.* 207 ff.). The use of the word γνήσιοι in a highly probable restoration of line 22 of the decree of Themistokles at Troizen (*Hesp.* 29 (1960), 200) should certainly not be taken as

highly probable that at least the first sentence of the law quoted in Aristoph., *Birds* 1660 ff. is equally old. Peisthetairos is there disabusing Herakles of the idea that he will inherit anything from his father, Zeus. He says *ἐρῶ δὲ δὴ καὶ τὸν Σόλωνός σοι νόμον· Νόθῳ δὲ μὴ εἶναι ἀγχιστείαν παίδων ὄντων γνησίων· ἐὰν δὲ μὴ ὦσι γνήσιοι, τοῖς ἐγγυτάτω γένους μετεῖναι τῶν χρημάτων.* We probably have here part of Solon's law on intestate succession. It was re-enacted in the archonship of Eukleides, as we know from Dem. 43 *Makart.* 51, and the last clause there quoted runs *νόθῳ δὲ μηδὲ νόθῃ μὴ εἶναι ἀγχιστείαν μήθ' ἱερῶν μήθ' ὁσίων ἀπ' Εὐκλείδου ἄρχοντος.* The wording is confirmed in Isai. 6 *Philokt.* 47.[1] This evidence justifies the view that from an early period, probably from the time of Solon at the latest, there was a legal distinction between *γνήσιοι* and *νόθοι* and that this distinction rested on whether the parents had or had not been married either by *ἐγγύη* or by *ἐπιδικασία*. Until the passing of Perikles' law the children of an Athenian man and a foreign woman would have been *γνήσιοι* if their parents had been properly married; Themistokles and Kimon are notable instances. Nor is there any reason to suppose that the same was not true of children of an Athenian woman and a foreign man, though this would have happened much more rarely and there is no known instance of it. The precise effect of Perikles' law on the law of marriage is not clear (see above, p. 25); but it seems reasonable to hold that either explicitly or by implication it ruled out marriage either by *ἐγγύη* or by *ἐπιδικασία* between an Athenian of either sex and a foreigner. At least, since the children of such unions were in future not to be Athenian citizens, it is difficult to see what possible advantage they could have gained by their parents' *ἐγγύη* or, lacking some gain to *them*, what their parents would have gained by it. To put the matter in another way, we are probably justified in saying that even after the law of Perikles a sufficient definition of *νόθος* was 'child of a marriage not initiated by either *ἐγγύη* or *ἐπιδικασία*'. The difference made by Perikles' law was that *ἐγγύη* was no longer possible between an Athenian and a foreigner. As a result there were from that time

ruling out an early fifth-century date for the original of this decree. The distinction between *γνήσιος* and *νόθος* would by then have been long embedded in Athenian law.

[1] For a clause of the same law dealing with *νόθοι* whose parents were not both Athenians see schol., Aischin. 1 *Timarch.* 39 (Eumelos, *F.Gr.H.* 77 F 2) quoted on p. 26, n. 1.

onwards two categories of νόθοι, those who had one foreign parent and who were thereby excluded from the citizenship, and those whose parents, though not united by ἐγγύη or ἐπιδικασία, were both Athenian.

This brings us to the vexed question whether those in the latter category were, equally with the children of mixed marriages, excluded from all citizen rights.[1] Those who hold that they were excluded base themselves partly on the very general, and perhaps in the end circular, argument that the Athenian state was built up essentially of οἶκοι, and that all νόθοι were explicitly excluded from ἀγχιστεία ἱερῶν καὶ ὁσίων. Not being members of the οἶκος, therefore, neither could they be members of the πόλις.[2] More specifically, they rely on arguments used in three speeches in the Demosthenic corpus, 39 and 40 *Boiot.* i, ii and 57 *Eubul.* In the case of Mantitheos and Boiotos it is clear that in some sense or other the citizenship of Boiotos was confirmed by his proving that he was the son of Mantias and Plangon. Thus in 39 *Boiot.* i. 31 the speaker says οὐκοῦν δεινὸν εἰ τῆς μὲν πόλεως καὶ τῶν ὑπ' ἐκείνου καταλειφθέντων διὰ τοὔνομα τοῦτο μέτεστί σοι, ibid. 34 ἀγάπα δ' ὅτι σοι πόλις, οὐσία, πάτηρ γέγονεν, ibid. 2 ἐδικάζετο (Βοιωτὸς) φάσκων . . . τῆς πατρίδος ἀποστερεῖσθαι, and in 40 *Boiot.* ii. 10, as part of the abortive compact whereby Plangon was to refuse to swear that Boiotos was the son of Mantias, the difficulty of his citizenship was to be got round by his being adopted by Plangon's brothers, τούτων γὰρ γενομένων οὔτε τούτους ἀποστερήσεσθαι τῆς πόλεως. Undoubtedly the simpler hypothesis here is that both Boiotos' right to be a citizen and his right to a share in Mantias' inheritance depended on his being a legitimate son of Mantias, and this is the hypothesis adopted by those who hold that all νόθοι were excluded from the citizenship. On the other side it has been argued that, when Boiotos links his claim to the citizenship with his claim to be a legitimate son of Mantias, he does so because, once Mantias' paternity was denied, he would find it extremely difficult to prove that his father was an Athenian. This is certainly a possible, if a less simple, hypothesis.[3] Equally inconclusive is the argument from

[1] Wolff, op. cit., n. 147, lists those who argue for and against this proposition. Add to those for, W. A. Goligher, *Hermath.* 32 (1906), 187 ff.; to those against, Latte, op. cit. 1071, Hignett, *HAC* 343, A. Kränzlein, *Z* 79 (1962), 359.

[2] This is a constant theme with A. Ledl, *WS* 30 (1908), 173 ff.

[3] Wolff's reasons for rejecting this hypothesis, op. cit. 77 (211), are inconclusive.

57 *Eubul.* There Euxitheos is attempting to establish his right to the citizenship. He certainly emphasizes in 46 that he was introduced into the phratry (*οὐ μὴν ἀλλὰ καὶ τὰ προσήκοντα πάντ' ἐπιδείξω μάρτυρας παρεχόμενος, ὡς εἰσήχθην εἰς τοὺς φράτερας κτλ.*), and in 40–43 he is at pains to show that his father married his mother. But here again his action is certainly explicable on the assumption that all he had to prove was first that both his mother and his father were Athenian and second that he was indeed their son. The fact that his mother had been *married* by *ἐγγύη* to his father, as she had been previously to another Athenian citizen, Protomachos, was important contributory evidence that she was a *πολῖτις*, and it is this point which Euxitheos stresses, for example, in 43, *φαίνεται τοίνυν οὐχ ὁ ἐμὸς πατὴρ πρῶτος λαβὼν τὴν ἐμὴν μητέρα, ἀλλ' ὁ Πρωτόμαχος, καὶ παῖδας ποιησάμενος καὶ θυγατέρ' ἐκδούς· ὃς καὶ τετελευτηκὼς ὅμως μαρτυρεῖ τοῖς ἔργοις ἀστήν τ' αὐτὴν καὶ πολῖτιν εἶναι.* Here as in other cases confusion has been caused by failure to understand the significance of phratry membership in claims to citizenship. It seems probable that in the classical period membership of a phratry was not an indispensable condition for citizenship.[1] Why

It may be, as he says, that Boiotos was more concerned with the question of citizenship than with that of the inheritance, though there is no evidence for this. But we cannot say that the only explanation of his anxiety to get enrolled on the phratry list was that this was the only way to prove his legitimacy and to be a citizen he had to prove his legitimacy. He undoubtedly had a very strong economic motive for proving his legitimacy; for, if we are to believe Mantitheos, the recognition of it secured him two-thirds of Mantias' patrimony, 40 *Boiot.* ii. 2 *διὰ τοῦτο τὰ δύο μέρη τῶν πατρῴων ἀπεστερήθην.*

[1] So Wilamowitz, *A. und A.* ii. 276, A. Korte, *Herm.* 37 (1902), 587, H. Francotte, *La Polis grecque* (Paderborn, 1907), 82, W. S. Ferguson, *CP* 5 (1910), 264, Lips., *AR* 505, n. 25, Wolff, op. cit. 78 (211). The strongest argument is that Ar., *Ath. Pol.* 42. 1, which gives in some detail the qualifications for entry on the deme register, does not list membership of a phratry. Kahrstedt, *Staatsg.* 231, takes the opposite view; but the passages he cites ibid., n. 2 (his reference to Plut., *Per.* 22 should read 37) only prove that membership of a phratry was the normal thing, not that it was indispensable. He fails to mention the most important piece of evidence, namely the provision in Drakon's homicide law, apparently confirmed in 409/408, that in default of certain prescribed relatives of the dead man action should be taken by ten of his fellow phratry members (*IG* i². 115. 18, Tod, *GHI* 87; the restoration is controlled by Dem. 43 *Makart.* 57). This implies that every man is in a phratry. It would be an anomaly if some citizens had no fellow phratry members, but hardly an inconceivable anomaly; such citizens would in any case be comparatively few in number, and the possibility that one of them should be killed and should also lack any near relative might have been considered sufficiently remote to render an amendment of Drakon's provision unnecessary. A. Andrewes in *JHS* 81 (1961), 1 ff. shows grounds for thinking that in Philoch., *F.Gr.H.* 328 F 35a and

then, ask those who would deny citizenship to all νόθοι, do claimants to citizenship make such a point of their membership of a phratry? It can only be because membership of a phratry was restricted to those born in wedlock and this was the simplest way of proving that you possessed this necessary qualification. But this ignores the fact that in any case the great majority of citizens would have been members of phratries and that the simplest way of proving that your parents were both Athenian would be to prove that you were a phratry member. Not to be one, though it would not disqualify you, would inevitably give rise to suspicions which unscrupulous advocates would be ready to make the most of.[1]

On the other side of the case there seem to be two very strong arguments. First, if illegitimacy was at all times a disqualification for citizenship, why did Perikles' law take the form it did? Why did it not simply say that from then on the children of mixed marriages were to be νόθοι? Second, and more decisive, what could have been the conceivable object of Solon's law on νόθοι or of its re-enactment in 403/402 if all νόθοι were excluded from the citizenship? At the later date at least it would surely have been unthinkable, and therefore needless specifically to forbid that a non-citizen should come within the ἀγχιστεία.[2]

Krateros 342 F 4, we have traces of a law, possibly to be dated to the middle 430s, dealing generally with admission to the phratries and particularly with μητρόξενοι. Any of these who had been born just before Perikles' law of 451/450 would be coming of age and qualifying for enrolment on the deme lists just about that time. The state would be concerned with regularizing admission to the phratry because to prove membership of a phratry was certainly one way, and probably the easiest way, to prove citizen birth.

[1] Cf. especially Isai. 3 *Pyrrh.* 73–76. It is vital to bear constantly in mind that there was at Athens no state register of citizens. The deme registers contained the names of all male citizens of age. Males who were minors would mostly get on to phratry registers, though there was no prescribed age at which they were entered. Females were not registered at all. See Paoli, *St. Dir.* 258 ff.

[2] Some slight confirmation of this view comes from three other pieces of evidence. At one time, though no longer in Demosthenes' day (Dem. 23 *Aristokr.* 213), a special gymnasium in Kynosarges was made available for νόθοι. A probably apocryphal story in Plut., *Them.* 1, implies the existence of this institution in the time of Themistokles; according to Polemon *ap.* Athen. vi. 26 a decree of Alkibiades (probably the famous Alkibiades) does the same. Cf. also Suda s.v. *Κυνόσαργες*: ἐπειδὴ οὖν καὶ ὁ Ἡρακλῆς δοκεῖ νόθος εἶναι, διὰ τοῦτο ἐκεῖ οἱ νόθοι ἐγυμνάζοντο, οἱ μήτε πρὸς πατρὸς μήτε πρὸς μητρὸς πολῖται. *An. Bekk.* (Λέξ. Ῥητ.) 274 *Κυνόσαργες*: γυμνάσιόν τι Ἀθήνησιν καλούμενον εἰς ὃ ἐνεγράφοντο καὶ οἱ νόθοι ἐκ τοῦ ἑτέρου μέρους ἀστοί. Secondly, Lysias' speech against Theozotides (*Hib. Pap.* 1, no. 14) shows that at the time illegitimate orphans of citizens killed in war were

Assuming then that νόθοι whose parents were both Athenians were full citizens, we have to ask what were the precise disabilities from which they suffered. The case of Phile in Isai. 3 *Pyrrh.* 45 ff. proves that the illegitimate daughter of Athenian parents could be given in marriage by ἐγγύη. We may perhaps conclude from analogy that an illegitimate son of Athenian parents could himself marry by ἐγγύη.[1] It is somewhat surprising that this should have been the rule in view of the fact that νόθοι were excluded from the ἀγχιστεία ἱερῶν καὶ ὁσίων and could not therefore in their own persons be full participators in their fathers' οἶκος. We can only suppose that to some legislator, possibly to Solon, the need to maintain the number of οἶκοι was felt to outweigh the anomaly of perpetuating an οἶκος by means of one who had not been a full member of it. It is much more difficult to be sure what rights of succession νόθοι possessed at different periods. If we take the words of Solon's law as quoted by Aristophanes quite strictly, and if we ignore their context, they seem to imply that, if there were legitimate children, a νόθος was completely excluded, while if there were no legitimate children a νόθος would share with the next of kin. This does not fit the context, which demands that Herakles, as a νόθος, be totally excluded. Perhaps, however, we should not take the context of the quotation too seriously. It is worth noting that on Peisthetairos' showing Athene was the ἐπίκληρος of Zeus, and he is now quoting the law as a counter to Herakles' argument that Zeus would leave him his property as νοθεῖα. If we are to take Peisthetairos seriously he argues that Athene was Zeus' ἐπίκληρος and that Poseidon would get the property—by marrying Athene presumably, though Peisthetairos does not say this.[2] The law quoted should go to prove that in such circumstances as this a father could not by will adopt a natural son and make him his heir by having him marry the ἐπίκληρος. The law certainly does not say this directly, and in fact it is much more likely that it is referring to intestate succession. But for the purposes of a joke its force is sufficiently close to that

brought up at the state's expense. It seems unlikely that the beneficiaries of this provision of a gymnasium and of state education should have been non-citizens. Thirdly, if all νόθοι were ξένοι the speaker in Dem. 57 *Eubul.* 53 would not naturally have said εἰ νόθος ἢ ξένος ἦν ἐγώ.

[1] Paoli, *St. Dir.* 272 ff., Wolff, op. cit. 82 ff. (219 ff.); but doubted by Kränzlein, *Z* 79 (1962), 359.

[2] Ledl, *WS* 30 (1908), 175.

which it ought to have if it is to support Peisthetairos' argument. We may then perhaps ignore the context and concentrate on the words. The joke would be utterly pointless unless these gave the gist of the law as it stood in Aristophanes' time. The most economic hypothesis is to suppose that this is a clause of the law of intestate succession, laying down that where there were legitimate children *νόθοι* were excluded, where there were no legitimate children *νόθοι* had the first claim in default of any kin within the *ἀγχιστεία* (since the law in Dem. 43 *Makart.* 51 ends with the words quoted on p. 62, which expressly exclude them from the *ἀγχιστεία*).[1] Some scholars appear to think that this was also the position laid down in the Aristophanes passage; but in the first place this is to do violence to the phrase *τοῖς ἐγγυτάτω γένους μετεῖναι τῶν χρημάτων*, which would have to mean not 'the next of kin are to share in the property' but 'the next of kin are to have the property'. And in the second place the phrase *παίδων ὄντων γνησίων* would be otiose. The only way out of this difficulty is to suppose that in the archonship of Eukleides a change was made by which the position of the *νόθοι* was worsened. It is just conceivable that this change was indicated by the addition of the words *μήθ' ἱερῶν μήθ' ὁσίων* to *ἀγχιστεία*.[2]

In one other respect the law seems to have recognized a private right of *νόθοι*. Even where there were *γνήσιοι* a father was permitted to bequeath legacies to *νόθοι*. The maximum which could be thus bequeathed was according to some grammarians 1,000 drachmai, according to others 500; it is not clear whether these maxima were for each individual *νόθος* or for the whole estate of the testator. The grammarians suggest that this limitation was often evaded by gifts *inter vivos*. The phraseology used by the Suda makes it plain that such legacies were only permissive and were entirely within the discretion of the father.[3]

We may, very tentatively, then posit the following historical changes in the status and composition of the class. At the earliest

[1] See p. 148, below.

[2] Some scholars cut this knot by excising the words *παίδων ὄντων γνησίων* from the text of Aristophanes; Latte, op. cit. 1070.

[3] Beauch. i. 498 f., Gernet *RÉG* 33 (1920), 265, n. 2 (*DSGA* 143, n. 5), Erdmann, *Ehe* 369 f., Harpokr. s.v. *νοθεῖα: τὰ τοῖς νόθοις ἐκ τῶν πατρῴων διδόμενα οὕτω καλεῖται, ἦν δὲ μέχρι χιλίων δραχμῶν· Λυσίας ἐν τῷ πρὸς Καλλιφάνη ξενίας, εἰ γνήσιος, Ἰσαῖος πρὸς Λυσίβιον περὶ ἐπικλήρου.* Suda s.v. *ἐπίκληρος: . . . ἐπειδὴ δὲ οὐκ ἐξῆν τοῖς νόθοις κληρονομεῖν, τἀργύριον διὰ χειρὸς ἐδίδοσαν. νόμος δὲ ἦν Ἀττικὸς τοῖς νόθοις μέχρι ε΄ μνῶν καταλιμπάνειν.* Schol., Aristoph., *Birds* 1655.

stage we can trace, perhaps as early as Solon or even before, *νόθοι* were the children of parents who had not been married by *ἐγγύη*. One parent, but one only, would have had to be Athenian, and probably, though not certainly, that parent would have had to be the father. The father would have had to be a free man. In all other respects save that of *ἀγχιστεία*, *νόθοι* were on the same footing as *γνήσιοι*. For purposes of inheritance, however, they were completely excluded by the latter. But if there were no *γνήσιοι*, male *νόθοι* shared, perhaps *per capita*, with those who came next in the prescribed order of kinship. About females we can say nothing, except that it is extremely unlikely that they could in any circumstances become *ἐπίκληροι*. The law of 451/450 excluded from the citizenship anyone who had a foreign parent. This was not a law primarily about *γνησιότης*, but its effect would have been to put future offspring of mixed unions in a position inferior to that of the existing *νόθοι*, since as non-citizens they would not only lack the political rights which we have supposed these latter enjoyed, but they must surely also have been deprived of any right of intestate succession even in the absence of *γνήσιοι*, nor would they have been eligible for adoption or for marriage by *ἐγγύη*. At some time during the Peloponnesian War, either by tacit agreement or more probably by specific legislation, the Periklean rule was relaxed, and the position was thus restored to what it had been before 451. In 402/401 the law of Perikles was re-enacted, and at the same time the position of *νόθοι* whose parents were both Athenian was worsened in that they were now entirely excluded from the succession *ab intestato* even if there were no *γνήσιοι*. They continued, however, to enjoy political rights (and of course to be subject to political duties), and there is no good reason to believe that they were ineligible for adoption, by which means they could, if occasion arose, be brought back into the stream, as it were, of full life in an *οἶκος*. This they could also do, whether they were male or female, by entering into a marriage by *ἐγγύη*.

§ 2. *Legitimation*

There has been some controversy as to whether a father was permitted to legitimate a bastard child. The alleged instances of this do not stand up to examination. When Mantias is finally driven to introduce Boiotos and his brother into his phratry (Dem. 40 *Boiot.* ii. 11) he is not being compelled to legitimate acknowledged bastards. On the contrary by Plangon's acceptance of the oath that he was the father of the children he is being compelled to acknowledge that they had all along been legitimate. The abortive agreement under which the boys were to be adopted into the family of their mother's brothers might have amounted to a *de facto* legitimation; but it would not have made them legitimate sons of *Mantias*, and it looks more like a device to evade the strict law.[1] Again, when Kallias induced the Kerukes to enrol as his son a boy whose paternity he had previously repudiated he does so by swearing that the boy was indeed his (Andok. 1 *Myst.* 127). Either this or his previous oath that the boy was not his was perjury. Naturally it was possible to get an illegitimate son made legitimate by such a method as this; a man could do so today by giving false information to a Registrar. But this is not the same as an acknowledged right of the father to remedy by a simple declaration a defect in his child's birth qualifications. Equally unconvincing is the instance sometimes adduced from Isai. 6 *Philokt.* 19 ff. The speaker there alleges that Euktemon, having fallen under the influence of a prostitute, Alke, wished to introduce one of her sons by a freedman into his phratry. His son, Philoktemon, procured the postponement of the admission by the phratry members, but Euktemon countered by threatening to marry again and produce more children. Philoktemon then did a deal with Euktemon under which he promised to withdraw opposition to the enrolment of Alke's son provided that the latter's share in Euktemon's estate was limited to one farm. The enrolment then went through. Although the speaker uses the rather vague phrase ἐπείσθη . . . τὸν πρεσβύτερον . . . εἰσαγαγεῖν εἰς τοὺς φράτερας ἐπὶ τῷ αὑτοῦ ὀνόματι to describe the enrolment, there is not much doubt that Euktemon would have had to swear the usual oath ἦ μὴν ἐξ ἀστῆς καὶ ἐγγυητῆς γυναικὸς εἰσάγειν (cf. Isai. 8 *Kir.* 19). Here

[1] Beauch. i. 525 ff., Lips., *AR* 508, n. 27, Erdmann, *Ehe* 375 ff., Wolff, *Traditio* 2 (1944), 79 (*Beitr.* 214), Gernet, *Dem.* ii. 8, 36, n. 1. Paoli, *St. Dir.* 274 f., holds that legitimation of a son (but not of a daughter) was possible and that, when it occurred, the father in introducing the son to the phratry simply omitted from the oath the words which guaranteed that his mother was ἐγγυητή or γαμετή. But there is no evidence for the latter conjecture and it is difficult to see why the words should ever have been included in the oath if they could be omitted at will.

again we have a factual legitimation procured by an open evasion of the law; if legitimation had been permissible the whole story as recounted by the speaker would have been utterly pointless.[1] It is important to note, however, that in all these instances there were, or had been, *γνήσιοι* in existence. They cannot help us therefore to answer the question whether, in the absence of *γνήσιοι*, *νόθοι* were eligible for adoption, which was tentatively answered in the affirmative on p. 68, above.[2]

§ 3. *Parental authority*

Some scholars depict the parental power of the father in Athenian law as a very attenuated survival of what had originally been a power closely analogous to the Roman *patria potestas*. Erdmann, for example, heads his treatment of this topic with the words 'Charakter der griechischen patria potestas'. This is probably a mistake, and the better view is that in its origins parental authority in Greece belonged to a wholly different pattern of family life from the Roman.[3] It is true that at its birth a child in Athens was so completely in its father's power that it rested with him whether or not he admitted it to membership of the family. He openly signified his intention to do this at the ceremony of the *ἀμφιδρόμια*, which took place on the fifth, seventh, or tenth

[1] Although strictly speaking the law which prescribed the form of oath to be taken when the boy was presented to the phratry was the law of the phratry, we are probably justified in assuming that in such an important respect as this the requirements would have been the same for all phratries.

[2] In Menand., *Arbitr.* 381 ff. K., Onesimos guesses that if the foundling proves to be Charisios' son and the mother (who is not known at that point to be Charisios' wife) proves to be a free woman he will divorce his wife and marry the child's mother. This suggests the power to legitimate a child born out of wedlock by a subsequent marriage. At an earlier stage Onesimos has suggested that if Charisios believes it is his child by a slave woman he would buy the slave woman and free her; again presumably in order to legitimate the child. But in either case there is nothing to rule out the hypothesis of a false declaration by the father.

[3] Beauch. ii. 74 ff., Lips., *AR* 499 ff., Erdmann, *Ehe* 342 ff., lean to the view that the Athenian father's parental authority was basically similar to the Roman *patria potestas*. Van den Es, on the other hand, wrote in *De iure fam. ap. Ath.* 101 'patria potestas apud Athenienses magis est tutela quam potestas, ideoque quam maxime ab eodem instituto apud Romanos abhorret'; he is quoted with approval by Becker, *Plat.* 198, n. 3, A. Albertoni, *L'apokeryxis* (Bologna, 1923), 25. Gaius seems to have had much the same opinion, for in i. 55 he says 'fere nulli alii sunt homines qui talem in filios suos habent potestatem qualem nos habemus'. Cf. D.H., *Ant. Rom.* 2. 26, Mitteis, *RV* 66.

day after birth.[1] At this ceremony the child was also named. But the father had no duty, even towards a legitimate child, to take this step. He could, either of himself or by the agency of some other person, a slave for example, expose the child, that is, abandon it in some place where there was a chance of its being found and nurtured by another person. There seems no reason to doubt that the father had this absolute discretion and that the right of exposure was more than a purely formal one. Plato's oblique reference to the practice in the *Theaitetos* and the frequency with which the *motif* of the exposed child recurs in the New Comedy show that it was neither a rare occurrence nor morally, let alone legally, taboo.[2] We must realize, however, that the act of exposure was legally negative in character. The legal tie between the exposed child, whether it was a legitimate son or daughter or a slave, and the father or master who exposed it remained and could be revived if the child later reappeared, either by the procedure *ἄγειν εἰς δουλείαν* or by *ἀφαιρεῖσθαι εἰς ἐλευθερίαν*. The finder of an exposed child might at his discretion treat it as slave or free; but he acquired no rights over it and he could not even adopt it, since adoption of a minor was a reciprocal transaction between the adopter and the adopted child's father or his representative.[3]

[1] Articles on *ἀμφιδρόμια* in Harpokr., Suda, Et. Mag., and by Saglio in DS., Harpokr. s.v. *ἑβδομενομένου*, Suda s.v. *δεκάτην ἑστιᾶσαι*, Hesych. s.v. *δεκάτην θύομεν*, Aristoph., *Birds* 494, 922. In Isai. 3 *Pyrrh.* 30, 70, Dem. 39 *Boiot.* i. 22, 40 *Boiot.* ii. 28 the father's celebration of the *δεκάτη* is evidence of the child's legitimacy. Beauch. i. 341, Lips., *AR* 501, Erdmann, *Ehe* 436 ff., E. Samter, *Familienfeste der Gr. u. R.* (Berlin, 1901), 59 ff.

[2] Plato, *Theait.* 160 e, speaking metaphorically of a new-born argúment, *μετὰ δὲ τὸν τόκον τὰ ἀμφιδρόμια αὐτοῦ ὡς ἀληθῶς ἐν κύκλῳ περιθρεκτέον τῷ λόγῳ, σκοπουμένους μὴ λάθῃ ἡμᾶς οὐκ ἄξιον ὂν τροφῆς τὸ γιγνόμενον . . . ἢ σὺ οἴει πάντως δεῖν τό γε σὸν τρέφειν καὶ μὴ ἀποτιθέναι;* Schol. ad loc., Plaut., *Casina* 41, *Cistell.* 124, Ter., *Heaut.* 625, Poseidip., F 11 Kock, Suda s.v. *ἐγχυτρίστριαι*, Hesych. s.v. *ἐγχυτρίζειν*. Glotz in DS s.v. *expositio*, Lips., *AR* 500, E. Weiss, *RE* s.v. *kinderaussetzung*, Erdmann, *Ehe* 343 ff. The articles of L. Van Hook, *TAPA* 51 (1920), 134 ff., and H. Bolkestein, *CP* 17 (1922), 222 ff., are more concerned to challenge Glotz's view of the prevalence of the practice than with legal technicalities. There seems general agreement that there was probably no explicit enactment conferring the right to expose and that *a fortiori* there was no right to put to death. We can confidently reject such statements as that of Sext. Emp., *Hypot. Pyrrh.* 3. 211 *ὁ Σόλων Ἀθηναῖος τὸν περὶ τῶν ἀκρίτων νόμον ἔθετο καθ' ὃν φονεύειν ἑκάστῳ τὸν ἑαύτου παῖδα ἐπέτρεψεν.*

[3] For these procedures see Dem. 59 *Neair.* 40, 58 *Theokr.* 19, Lys. 23 *Pankl.* 12, Isok. 17 *Trapez.* 14, none of them admittedly referring to foundlings. The whole plot of Menand., *Arbitr.*, assumes the father's right to claim a foundling, but in that case the father had not himself exposed the child; cf. above, p. 70, n. 2 and

What were the father's rights *vis-à-vis* an unborn child depends to some extent on the interpretation to be put on a speech against Antigenes attributed to Lysias. In this speech Lysias inquired, according to Theon, *Progymn.* 2 (Sp. ii. 69. 9), *εἰ τὸ ἔτι ἐγκυούμενον ἄνθρωπός ἐστι καὶ εἰ ἀνεύθυνα τὰ τῶν ἀμβλώσεων ταῖς γυναιξί.* Cf. Sopater, *Rh. Mus.* 64 (1909), 576: *Λυσίᾳ . . . περὶ ἀμβλωθριδίου ἐν ᾧ Ἀντιγένης κατηγορεῖ τῆς ἑαυτοῦ γυναικὸς φόνου* (l. *φόνον*) *ἀμβλωσάσης ἑκουσίως, φάσκων ὡς ἐξήμβλωκε καὶ κεκώλυκεν αὐτὸν πατέρα κληθῆναι παιδός.* One important fragment of this speech survives (F 8 Th.): *σκέψασθε δὲ καὶ ὡς Ἀντιγένης πεποίηκεν οὑτοσί· γραψάμενος τὴν μητέρα ἡμῶν ἀξιοῖ λαβεῖν τὴν ἀδελφὴν καὶ ἀγωνίσασθαι μέν, ἵνα μὴ ἀποτείσῃ τὰς χιλίας δραχμὰς ἃς δεῖ ἀποτίνειν ἐὰν μέν τις μὴ ἐπεξέλθῃ γραψάμενος.* L. Gernet (*Lys.* ii. 239) is probably right in his conjecture that the speech should properly be entitled *πρὸς Ἀντιγένη* and not as in Lex. Cant. 669. 20 *κατὰ Ἀντιγένους*; a widow is being accused of abortion by Antigenes; the speech is for the defence and is delivered by sons by a former marriage; Antigenes is a relative of her last husband and as such is claiming the hand of a daughter of the accused; the suit is a *γραφή*, since the accuser cannot abandon it without incurring the fine of 1,000 drachmai laid down for such a dereliction. Although abortion might sometimes have been a private wrong against the father, whose interests could have been protected by a *δίκη* to be initiated by him and him alone as the injured party, the fact that a *γραφή* was available might suggest that abortion was regarded as a public wrong also and as such open to prosecution by *ὁ βουλόμενος*. If we accept this we should have to suppose that the father had no right to procure an abortion, though he had no duty to nurture the child when born. This line of reasoning is, however, not completely watertight. As will be argued elsewhere, the original function of *ὁ βουλόμενος* was probably not so much to secure redress of a public wrong as to step in where for one reason or another the wronged party would under a system confined to *δίκαι* have found difficulty in getting his case before a court. With abortion the wronged party might have been considered to be the embryo itself, in which case we should have to suppose that a father could be charged under the *γραφή*. But we cannot rule out the possi-

R. Taubenschlag, *Z* 46 (1926), 71 ff. On the rights in the matter of adoption see below, p. 89.

bility that it was only the embryo *qua heir to his father* that was thought of as wronged and that the *γραφή* only lay in cases such as the present seems to be, where the father is dead and where it might be very much in the interest of the embryo's next of kin to procure an abortion. If we accept this possibility the existence of the *γραφή* does not entail the view that a father was liable to a penalty for procuring an abortion.[1]

In addition to his right to expose his child, perhaps better expressed as the absence of a duty to introduce it into the family, the Athenian father had enjoyed, up to the time of Solon, the right to sell his children and therefore presumably also to pledge them against a debt. Solon limited this right to cases where a father (or a brother) had caught his daughter (or sister) in the act of fornication.[2]

As we shall see later, a father had a right to transfer his son while a minor into another family by way of adoption (*ἐκποιεῖσθαι*), as also to provide a guardian for him in case he should die before the son came of age (pp. 84 ff., 99 ff., below).

Until a son came of age his father represented him in every kind of legal transaction, whether procedurally before a court or in matters of contract, since a minor was incapacitated from entering into any contract.[3] This would have meant that the

[1] Glotz, *Solidarité* 351 ff., argued that there was no *γραφὴ ἀμβλώσεως*, but that abortion was treated on all fours with homicide, with the proviso that the father could not be prosecuted for it; thus when Galen 19. 177 Kuehn attributes a law to Solon imposing penalties for abortion these are to be thought of merely as securing the rights of the father; equally we must suppose that it was concern for his rights which dictated the phrase in the Hippocratic oath *οὐδὲ γυναικὶ πεσσὸν φθόριον δώσω*. Glotz, however, mistakenly followed Sauppe in supposing that Antigenes was defendant in the Lysias case and that the case was a *δίκη φόνου*; he must presumably have taken the last part of F 8 to refer to some other suit, which is very improbable. Glotz was followed by Lips., *AR* 608 f. The strong point in their case, despite their misunderstanding of Lysias, is that, reading F 8a Th. (*ὥσπερ οἱ ἰατροὶ καὶ αἱ μαῖαι ἀπεφήναντο*) with Ar., *Pol.* 1335^{b} (*πρὶν αἴσθησιν ἐγγένεσθαι καὶ ζωήν, ἐμποιεῖσθαι δεῖ τὴν ἄμβλωσιν*), one would infer that the charge only lay if the embryo was viable; this would suggest that it was its rights rather than the father's which were at issue.

[2] Plut., *Sol.* 13 *πολλοὶ δὲ καὶ τοὺς παῖδας ἰδίους ἠναγκάζοντο πωλεῖν· οὐδεὶς γὰρ νόμος ἐκώλυε.* 23 *ἔτι δὲ οὔτε θυγατέρας πωλεῖν οὔτ' ἀδελφὰς δίδωσι πλὴν ἂν μὴ λάβῃ παρθένον ἀνδρὶ συγγεγενημένην.* The statement in the former quotation may be nothing more than an inference from the law which forms the basis for the latter. But there is no reason to doubt the existence of the law or its Solonian origin, and the inference may therefore stand.

[3] Isai. 10 *Aristarch.* 10 *παιδὸς γὰρ οὐκ ἔξεστι διαθήκην γενέσθαι· ὁ γὰρ νόμος διαρρήδην κωλύει παιδὶ μὴ ἐξεῖναι συμβάλλειν μηδὲ γυναικὶ πέρα μεδίμνου κριθῶν.*

father would have control of any property accruing to the son through his mother until the son's majority.[1]

Lastly, a father had the right to give his daughter in marriage at any age and in all probability the right, in certain circumstances at least, to annul her marriage (see pp. 19, 30 ff.).

On the other hand, the Athenian father never in historical times enjoyed a power remotely resembling the Roman father's *ius vitae ac necis*.[2] There is not a trace of anything comparable with the Roman father's emancipation of his son, without which the latter could not himself become a *paterfamilias* during his father's lifetime. An Athenian male child seems to have been almost wholly free from parental control as soon as he reached the end of his seventeenth (conceivably eighteenth) year.[3] At that point he was presented by his father or guardian to his demesmen, and, after passing an examination into his qualifications to be a citizen by them and by the boule, he was enrolled among the demesmen (ἐγγράφονται δ' εἰς τοὺς δημότας ὀκτωκαίδεκα ἔτη γεγονότες Ar. *Ath. Pol.* 42. 1). Here we are only concerned with

There is a strong *a priori* presumption that the last three words qualify γυναικί only. This was the interpretation of Dio Chr. 74. 9, though not of Harpokr. s.v. ὅτι παιδί. Wyse, *Isai.* ad loc., is doubtful; Lips., *AR* 502, n. 12; see also Aischin. 1 *Timarch.* 18 (p. 98, n. 3, below).

[1] It is conceivable that the father of sons by an ἐπίκληρος had less absolute power over these sons while minors than did the fathers of other sons; for if he had the same right of exposure he could secure the continuance of his own control of the property. But there is no direct evidence for this difference, and he could secure the same end by practising birth control like Peisistratos. Cf. Beauchet i. 464 for a general treatment of the sons of ἐπίκληροι.

[2] As is suggested above, p. 73, the right to expose should perhaps be thought of as the absence of a duty to rear, and we need not suppose that this right was ever expressly stated. If abortion by a father was punishable, we might distinguish it from exposure by the fact that the latter could have been regarded rather as the omission of an act than as an act. We need not perhaps take too seriously the fable of Hippomenes' barbarous execution of his daughter for fornication, even though Aischines did in 1 *Timarch.* 182; still less the statements of such late authorities as Sextus Empiricus (p. 71, n. 2, above) or Hermogenes, *De Inventione* 1. 1, that there was a law (of Solon, according to the former), described as ὁ περὶ τῶν ἀκρίτων νόμος, allowing a father to execute his son. As Beauch. ii. 84 points out, such a law would have been wholly inconsistent with the liberal tendency of Solon's legislation already noted by D.H. 2. 26. Cf. Erdmann, *Ehe* 350.

[3] The passage quoted from *Ath. Pol.* states unequivocally that it was after the lad reached the age of eighteen. R. Sealey, *CR* 7 (1957), 195 ff., shows from the evidence in Demosthenes 27 *Aphob.* i that Demosthenes was almost certainly enrolled in his deme register and ceased to be under tutelage when he was still seventeen. The evidence of Demosthenes is to be preferred, but from the legal point of view the issue is not of vital importance.

the effects of this coming of age on the son's relation to his father. It is reasonably certain that it meant release from all legal control except in one important respect, though it must be admitted that on this precise point evidence is lacking.[1] The exception is the father's continuing right, as head of his house, to remove the son from the house (ἀποκηρύττειν), with which was perhaps connected the right to take away his name.[2] This would affect the son in three main ways. It would cut him off from the family worship. We should do wrong to make light of this deprivation. Secondly, as we saw above (pp. 63 f.), although it is not likely that in itself it could invalidate the son's claim to citizenship, it might, as a repudiation of the father's paternity, make it difficult for the son to defend his citizenship against attack. But, most important of all, perhaps, it would exclude the son from his share in the inheritance of his father's property, an exclusion which the father could not bring about by testamentary means.[3] It is surprising that we can point to very few, if any, actual instances of

[1] There is evidence that on enrolment in the deme a man who had been in tutelage entered into control of his property, which his guardian had then to hand over and account for, that he could at once sue in court at least for an inheritance or for the hand of an heiress (for other procedural rights he might have to wait till he had completed two years as an ephebe), that he was punishable for his wrongs, liable for liturgies and military service, and permitted to vote in the ekklesia. This evidence (collected in Kahrstedt, *Staatsg.* 76) will have to be examined in various other contexts. Unfortunately, at the points vital to us here it always relates to men whose fathers were already dead. Late, but more specific evidence comes from D.H. 2. 26 οἱ μὲν γὰρ τὰς Ἑλληνικὰς καταστησάμενοι πολιτείας βραχύν τινα κομιδῇ χρόνον ἔταξαν ἄρχεσθαι τοὺς παῖδας ὑπὸ τῶν πατέρων, οἱ μὲν ἕως δεύτερον (Bücheler, τρίτον codd.) ἐκπληρώσωσιν ἀφ' ἥβης ἔτος, οἱ δὲ ὅσον ἂν χρόνον ἠίθεοι μένωσιν, οἱ δὲ μέχρι τῆς εἰς τὰ ἀρχεῖα τὰ δημόσια ἐγγραφῆς, ὡς ἐκ τῆς Σόλωνος νομοθεσίας καὶ Πιττακοῦ καὶ Χαρώνδου ἔμαθον.

[2] Dem. 39 *Boiot.* i. 39 ὁ νόμος . . . τοὺς γονέας ποιεῖ κυρίους οὐ μόνον θέσθαι τοὔνομα ἐξ ἀρχῆς, ἀλλὰ κἂν πάλιν ἐξαλεῖψαι βούλωνται καὶ ἀποκηρῦξαι. It is true that the main issue in this case (on which see above, p. 63) was the right to a name, but the deprivation of this right meant more than the mere inconvenience of having to use another name (see p. 63, n. 3).

[3] For ἀποκήρυξις in general van den Es, *de iur. fam. ap. Ath.* 128 ff., Beauch. ii. 128 ff., Thalheim, *RE* s.v., Lips., *AR* 502 ff., Weiss, *GP* 315 f., A. Albertoni, *L'apokeryxis* 1 ff., S. Luria, *Aeg.* 7 (1926), 243 ff., Becker, *Plat.* 217 ff., Gernet, *Plat.* clxiii. See p. 151, below (law on wills), for the absolute bar on disinheriting sons by will. If he had sons the most a father could do was to make testamentary dispositions which would take effect only if the sons died before reaching majority, Dem. 46 *Steph.* ii. 24 *ΝΟΜΟΣ.* ὅ τι ἂν γνησίων ὄντων υἱέων ὁ πατὴρ διαθῆται ἐὰν ἀποθάνωσιν οἱ υἱεῖς πρὶν ἐπὶ δίετες ἡβᾶν, τὴν τοῦ πατρὸς διαθήκην κυρίαν εἶναι. By implication this meant the right of a son to make a will on coming of age provided he himself had no son, since at that point any will made by his father became invalid. Beauch. ii. 30.

a son's being thus cast out. There is a story mentioned by Plutarch that it happened to Themistokles, but he was probably right to reject it; nor need we suppose that either the threatened proclamation of Alkibiades when he ran away from his guardian's house or the expulsion from his home of Glaukippos by his father, Hyperides, was a technical ἀποκήρυξις.[1] This has led some scholars to follow van den Es (op. cit., pp. 130 ff.) in denying that an Athenian father had this power. But the passage from 39 *Boiot.* i. 39 quoted on p. 75, n. 2, above, is best interpreted as implying a statutory right of a father to revoke the act whereby at the ἀμφιδρόμια he had formally taken the child into the family.[2] This scrap of contemporary evidence is supported by the passage from D.H. 2. 26 quoted on p. 75, n. 1, above, which continues τιμωρίας τε κατὰ τῶν παίδων ἔταξαν ἐὰν ἀπειθῶσι τοῖς πατράσιν, οὐ βαρείας, ἐξελάσαι τῆς οἰκίας ἐπιτρέψαντες αὐτοὺς καὶ χρήματα μὴ καταλιπεῖν, περαιτέρω δὲ οὐδέν. And a large number of references to the institution in the grammarians and lexicographers, though they indicate some confusion as to its exact nature, would be hard to explain if it had never existed. We cannot say why this power was not widely used, if indeed we are entitled from the paucity of our evidence to conclude that this was so. It is not enough to say that a father's major concern was to perpetuate his family, and that this would make him reluctant to disinherit a natural son. Our evidence shows that adoption was a readily available device to enable a disgruntled father to cut off his son without extinguishing his own house. Possibly the religious consequences of ἀποκήρυξις were felt to be so severe that public sentiment would have condemned its use except in extreme cases.

It would appear that public sentiment was the only bar to an arbitrary use of this power. There is nowhere any suggestion that before exercising it a father was either legally or morally bound to consult any council of members of the family, nor is it likely, in spite of evidence to that effect in Lucian and Thomas Magister, either that a father had to submit a case for expulsion to a court for its sanction or that an expelled son had a right of appeal to

[1] For the Themistokles story Plut., *Them.* 2, Ael. *V.H.* 2. 12, Val. Max. 6. 9, *ext.* 2, Nep., *Them.* 1; for Alkibiades, Plut., *Alk.* 3; for Glaukippos, Athen. xiii. 58. 590c, Plut., *Mor.* 849 d. On these cf. Lips., *AR* 503, n. 16.

[2] Gernet, *Dem.* ii. 10, puts his finger on the essential point.

a court. It is surely not too bold an argument from silence to suppose that, had either of these rules obtained, cases would have come before the courts and have left some trace in the pages of the lexicographers, who were obviously on the look-out for information about the institution.[1] If this view is right, the question whether there were any strictly legal grounds needed to justify a father in thus treating a son does not arise, though this would not mean that some doctrine of sufficient cause did not acquire the sanction of custom. The passage from Dem. 39 *Boiot.* i. 39 referred to on p. 75, n. 2, above, suggests that a father might use this power where he had come to doubt the paternity of a son already acknowledged and not only, as the lexicographical passages rather imply, in the case of his son's misconduct.

A father, in common with other ascendants both male and female, had a right in his old age to be fed and housed by his son or sons, and this right was protected by a *γραφὴ γονέων κακώσεως*. This action also protected him from physical violence and from neglect of the rites due to him after death. A *γραφή* was peculiarly apt for the protection of these rights; a person of advanced years might have found difficulty in setting a *δίκη* on foot, whereas to secure redress by *γραφή* he had only to obtain the goodwill of some third party who was competent to sue (*ὁ βουλόμενος*), and a dead man's rights had to be left to a similar well-wisher. This sanction was fortified by the fact that a prosecutor in such a suit was liable to no penalty (Ar., *Ath. Pol.* 56. 6, listing suits in which the eponymous archon conducted the *anakrisis*, *γονέων κακώσεως —αὗται δ' εἰσὶν ἀζήμιοι τῷ βουλομένῳ διώκειν*), in the event, that

[1] Van den Es and Albertoni, locc. citt. on p. 75, n. 3, above, quote much of this evidence in full. A recurring theme is the distinction between *ἐκποίησις* and *ἀποκήρυξις*, the point of similarity being that both involved complete severance from the original *οἶκος*. Note, for example, Suda s.v. *ἐκποίητον γενέσθαι: ἀποκηρυχθῆναι τοῦ γένους. οἱ δέ φασι διαφέρειν ἐκποίητον ἀποκηρύκτου, ὅτι ὁ μὲν ἀποκήρυκτος ἐπὶ κολάσει ἐκβάλλεται, ὁ δὲ ἐκποίητος ὑπὸ τοῦ φύσει πατρὸς εἰς ἕτερον οἶκον δίδοται τῇ προθέσει*. Cf. *An. Bekk.* (*Λέξ. Ῥητ.*) 215 s.v. *ἀποκήρυκτος*, 247 Et. Mag. s.v. *ἐκποίητον γενέσθαι*; Hesych., s.v. *ἀποκήρυκτος*; Pollux 4. 93 (*ἀποκηρῦξαι υἱὸν καὶ υἱωνόν. τὸ μέντοι ὄνομα, ὁ ἀποκήρυκτος, οὐκ ἔστιν ἐν χρήσει τῇ παλαιᾷ, Θεόπομπος δ' αὐτῷ κέχρηται ὁ συγγραφεύς*); Thom. Mag. 37 *ἀποκήρυκτος ὁ ἐπὶ ἀδικήματι ἐκβληθεὶς τῆς οἰκίας παρὰ τοῦ πατρὸς μετὰ ψήφου δικαστικῆς*; Lucian, *Abd.* 8 (*ὁ νομοθέτης*) *οὐκ ἐλευθέραν ἐφῆκε γίγνεσθαι οὐδὲ ἄκριτον τὴν τιμωρίαν, ἀλλ' ἐς δικαστήριον ἐκάλεσε καὶ δοκιμαστὰς ἐκάθισε τοὺς μήτε πρὸς ὀργὴν μήτε πρὸς διαβολὴν τὸ δίκαιον κρινοῦντας*. The passage in Plato, *Laws* 928 d, which deals with this matter does not help much, as we cannot tell what, if any, part of it would have been applicable to the law of Athens.

is, of his either withdrawing the case or his not securing at least one-fifth of the votes. Moreover, he was free from the limitations of the water-clock.[1]

The penalty on conviction in such cases was total *ἀτιμία*, that is, exclusion from the agora and temples and from acts of public worship, the loss of public rights, in particular the right to address the assembly, and incapacity to plead in defence of private rights. This *ἀτιμία* lasted for life unless it was specifically repealed. It did not include banishment from the city, loss of juridical personality, or loss of private rights as distinct from the right to plead in their defence. Any transgression against these bans rendered the culprit liable to the summary procedure of *ἀπαγωγή*; this involved imprisonment by the Eleven, who then brought him before a heliastic court; the prosecution was conducted by any duly qualified citizen and in case of conviction the court could impose what penalty it pleased. If it imposed a money fine the accused remained in custody till he paid.[2]

§ 4. *Rights of children*

As we have seen, a child had no right on birth to be nurtured by its father; but once the father had admitted it to the family at the *ἀμφιδρόμια* the child became the subject of rights, though the sanctions against breach of these rights might be weak. Thus according to Plutarch a law of Solon enacted that a father who failed to teach his son a trade could not claim maintenance from him in old age.[3] Again, although the precise details are obscure,

[1] Isai. 8 *Kir.* 32 (*ὁ περὶ τῆς κακώσεως νόμος*) *κελεύει τρέφειν τοὺς γονέας· γονεῖς δ' εἰσὶ μήτηρ καὶ πατὴρ καὶ πάππος καὶ τήθη καὶ τούτων μήτηρ καὶ πατήρ, ἐὰν ἔτι ζῶσιν.* The law is attributed to Solon in Dem. 24 *Timokr.* 103 and D.L. 1. 55, rightly if we can deduce from Aristoph., *Birds* 1354, that it stood on an *axon.* Lys. 13 *Agorat.* 91, Aischin. 1 *Timarch.* 28 show that it covered physical violence, Xen. *Mem.* 2. 2. 13, Dem. 24 *Timokr.* 107 that it covered neglect of posthumous honours. Harpokr. s.v. *κακώσεως· ἦν δὲ καὶ ἄνευ ὕδατος.*

[2] Aischin. 1 *Timarch.* 28 "*δοκιμασία*", *φησί* (*ὁ νομοθέτης*), "*ῥητόρων· ἐάν τις λέγῃ ἐν τῷ δήμῳ τὸν πατέρα τύπτων ἢ τὴν μητέρα, ἢ μὴ τρέφων, ἢ μὴ παρέχων οἴκησιν·*" *τοῦτον οὐκ ἐᾷ λέγειν.* Dem. 24 *Timokr.* 60, 103, 105 *ἐὰν δέ τις ἀπαχθῇ, τῶν γονέων κακώσεως ἑαλωκὼς ἢ ἀστρατείας ἢ προειρημένον αὐτῷ τῶν νόμων* (codd. *νομίμων* Salmasius) *εἴργεσθαι, εἰσιὼν ὅποι μὴ χρή, δησάντων αὐτὸν οἱ ἕνδεκα καὶ εἰσαγόντων εἰς τὴν ἡλιαίαν, κατηγορείτω δὲ ὁ βουλόμενος οἷς ἔξεστιν. ἐὰν δ' ἁλῷ, τιμάτω ἡ ἡλιαία ὅ τι χρὴ παθεῖν αὐτὸν ἢ ἀποτεῖσαι. ἐὰν δ' ἀργυρίου τιμηθῇ, δεδέσθω τέως ἂν ἐκτείσῃ.* Lips., *AR* 330, Paoli, *St. Dir.* 316 ff., Kahrstedt, *Staatsg.* 110 ff.

[3] Plut., *Sol.* 22 *νόμον ἔγραψεν, υἱῷ τρέφειν πατέρα μὴ διδαξάμενον τέχνην ἐπάναγκες μὴ εἶναι.* It may have been a free interpretation of this law which led Plato to say in

the Mantias case, round which Dem. 39 and 40 *Boiot.* i, ii revolve, seems at least to show that a son once recognized could bring an action to compel his father to enrol him as his son in his phratry and, on his coming of age, in his deme. Unfortunately, we cannot say what this suit was called. The suit would come in the first instance before an arbitrator, and the mother's word as to the paternity of the child, confirmed, if she was challenged, by an oath, was conclusive.[1]

The interest of children—and indeed of remoter heirs—in preserving the family property from dissipation was protected by two actions, that against idleness (ἀργία) and that against mental incapacity (παρανοία). We know little of the detail of either action. Lysias wrote two speeches for γραφαὶ ἀργίας; in one of these he alleged that Drakon had laid down the death penalty for it, for which Solon had substituted 1,000 drachmai for the first conviction and ἀτιμία for the third.[2] A reference in Dem. 57 *Eubul.* 32 (about 345 B.C.) shows that the law governing this action was still in force at that date. That this action fell under

Krit. 50 d οἱ νόμοι παραγγέλλοντες τῷ πατρὶ τῷ σῷ σε ἐν μουσικῇ καὶ γυμναστικῇ παιδεύειν. It is hardly necessary with Lips., *AR* 505, n. 23, to hold that Plutarch deliberately altered the terms of the law to point a contrast between Solon and Lykourgos.

[1] See especially 39 *Boiot.* i. 2 λαχὼν δίκην τῷ πατρὶ τῷ ἐμῷ. . . . ἐδικάζεθ' υἱὸς εἶναι φάσκων ἐκ τῆς Παμφίλου θυγατρὸς καὶ δεινὰ πάσχειν καὶ τῆς πατρίδος ἀποστερεῖσθαι. Cf. 40 *Boiot.* ii. 9 ff. Mantias challenged Plangon, the mother of Boiotos, before an arbitrator to swear that he was indeed Mantias' son. Plangon, contrary to an agreement she was alleged to have entered into with Mantias, took the oath, and this had the effect of compelling Mantias to introduce Boiotos into the phratry. It is not necessary to suppose, as does Gernet, *Dem.* ii. 10, that Mantias had actually pronounced an ἀποκήρυξις against Boiotos and his brother, though he may have done so. His failure to introduce them into the phratry would probably have had the same effect. Bo. Sm. ii. 108 argue, on insufficient grounds, that Boiotos' suit against Mantias was a δίκη βλάβης. It is hardly conclusive that the phrase δεινὰ πάσχειν above corresponds with the phrase ἕτερα πολλὰ καὶ μεγάλα βλάπτεσθαι used of a δίκη βλάβης in Dem. 41 *Spoud.* 12; nor is it certain that the suit of Mantitheos against Boiotos to which Dem. 39 *Boiot.* i. relates was a δίκη βλάβης—Gernet, *Dem.* ii. 14, doubts this on the ground that 40 *Boiot.* ii. 35 shows that that suit was not for compensation in money—but even if it had been, this affords no presumption that the suit of Boiotos against Mantias was a δίκη βλάβης. It is most misleading to say 'there is practically no difference between the suits'.

[2] D.L. 1. 55 δοκεῖ δὲ (Σόλων) καὶ κάλλιστα νομοθετῆσαι . . . ὁ ἀργὸς ὑπεύθυνος ἔστω παντὶ τῷ βουλομένῳ γράφεσθαι. Λυσίας δ' ἐν τῷ κατὰ Νικίδου Δράκοντά φησι γεγραφέναι τὸν νόμον, Σόλωνα δὲ τεθεικέναι. Lex. Cant. 665. 20 Λυσίας ἐν τῷ κατὰ Ἀρίστωνός φησιν ὅτι Δράκων ἦν ὁ θεὶς τὸν νόμον, αὖθις δὲ καὶ Σόλων ἐχρήσατο, θάνατον οὐχ ὁρίσας ὥσπερ ἐκεῖνος, ἀλλ' ἀτιμίαν, ἐὰν τρὶς ἁλῷ τις, ἐὰν δ' ἅπαξ, ζημιοῦσθαι δραχμαῖς ἑκατόν. The speech against Nikides was at one time in the Codex Palatinus.

the competence of the archon suggests that its main *raison d'être* was protection of the rights of the family.[1] Since it was a γραφή the rights of children could be protected while they were still minors. The action παρανοίας was also almost certainly a γραφή; so at least the wording of the reference to it in Ar., *Ath. Pol.* 56. 6, seems to imply (γραφαὶ δ[ὲ καὶ] δίκαι λαγχάνονται πρὸς αὐτόν (viz. τὸν ἄρχοντα) . . . παρανοίας, ἐάν τις αἰτιᾶταί τινα παρανοοῦντα τὰ [ὑπάρχοντα ἀ]πολλύν[αι]).[2] We have no instance of such a case, but we can conjecture that the action would have lain against a man who was not mentally fit to manage his own affairs and that its main purpose would have been to prevent the dissipation of his estate. As with ἀργία, it was reasonable to protect the rights of minors by allowing ὁ βουλόμενος to prosecute.[3] It was in the

[1] *An. Bekk.* (Λέξ. Ῥητ.) 310. 1 πρὸς τὸν ἄρχοντα κακώσεως ἐλαγχάνοντο γραφαὶ καὶ τῶν γονέων . . . καὶ τῶν ὀρφανῶν· ἔτι δὲ παρανοίας καὶ ἀργίας ἐπιδικασίαι καὶ (? καὶ ἐπιδικασίαι) ἐπικλήρων γυναικῶν. It must be noted, however, that this delict, or something closely resembling it, figured with some others, such as κάκωσις γονέων, among those which in the law on the δοκιμασία ῥητόρων disabled a man from addressing the assembly; according to Aischin. 1 *Timarch.* 30 the words of the law were τὰ πατρῷα κατεδηδοκώς, ἢ ὧν ἂν κληρονόμος γένηται. As the speeches on either side of the speech against Nikides in the Codex Palatinus (Lysias 25 and 26) were probably both concerned with δοκιμάσιαι it is likely that the speech against Nikides was also. Cf. Gernet in *Lys.* ii. 240, Lips., *AR* 340, 353. Plut., *Sol.* 22, asserts that under Solon this action was before the Areopagus; this would have meant that it was not the concern of the archon, so that we must either suppose that a change had taken place between the time of Solon and the classical period or, preferably, reject Plutarch on this point. The account in Hdt. 2. 177 of the origin of this action is apocryphal. There is a difference concerning the penalties in Poll. 8. 42, τῆς δὲ ἀργίας ἐπὶ μὲν Δράκοντος ἀτιμία ἦν τὸ τίμημα, ἐπὶ δὲ Σόλωνος εἰ τρίς τις ἁλοίη, ἠτιμοῦτο.

[2] All the preceding actions listed in this passage are γραφαί, all that come after are δίκαι. The passage from Λέξ. Ῥητ. cited in n. 1, above, also suggests that both ἀργία and παρανοία were dealt with by γραφή. Aristoph., *Cl.* 844 ff., though assuming an action παρανοίας available to a son against his father, does not reveal whether it was a γραφή or a δίκη. Beauch. ii. 382 f. argues for a δίκη, Lips., *AR* 340, 355 f. for a γραφή. The latter also holds that we should not deduce from Xen. *Mem.* 1. 2. 49 φάσκων κατὰ νόμον ἐξεῖναι παρανοίας ἑλόντι καὶ τὸν πατέρα δῆσαι that a further object of the action was to prevent a lunatic doing general damage by being at large; his relatives would have had a duty to restrain him without any need to apply to a court.

[3] Plato, *Laws* 929 d–e, allows the son of a father who has been rendered by old age, sickness, or difficulty of temperament ἔκφρων διαφερόντως τῶν πολλῶν to proceed against him by γραφή after first consulting with a body of nomophylakes; in such a case the father ὀφλὼν τοῦ λοιποῦ χρόνου ἄκυρος ἔστω τῶν αὐτοῦ καὶ τὸ σμικρότατον διατίθεσθαι, καθάπερ παῖς δὲ οἰκείτω τὸν ἐπίλοιπον βίον. Cf. Aischin. 3 *Ktes.* 251 ὁ δὲ δῆμος . . . ὥσπερ παραγεγηρακὼς ἢ παρανοίας ἑαλωκὼς αὐτὸ μόνον τοὔνομα τῆς δημοκρατίας περιποιεῖται, τῶν δ' ἔργων ἑτέροις παρακεχώρηκεν. If this action is rightly classified as a γραφή this would be one more argument against assimilating

same context of ideas that those who were mentally unfit were disqualified from making wills.[1] In either case the decision as to what constituted mental unfitness was with a dikastery.[2]

For a minor's incapacity to make contracts see p. 73, above, and for the question whether this incapacity extended to making a will see below, p. 151.

γραφαί to criminal prosecutions. The object here is not to punish the defendant, but to protect the rights of the prosecutor or of those whom he represents.

[1] See below, p. 151.

[2] Little can be gained from the story in *Vita Sophocl.* 13 (cf. Plut., *Mor.* 785 a, Cic., *de sen.* 7. 22) that Iophon brought a case *παρανοίας* against his father Sophokles; in particular we may ignore the mention of the phratry in this connexion.

III · ADOPTION

§ 1. *Introduction*

METHODOLOGICALLY it is not easy to decide where to treat of adoption. At first sight it would seem to fall naturally into place in the consideration of relations between parents and children. But owing to certain peculiarities of the Athenian—and indeed of the Greek—outlook on adoption the subject is very closely tied up with that of the making of wills. Although, therefore, the main rules on adoption are discussed here, they will have to be borne in mind and to some extent reconsidered later under the Law of Succession.[1]

There are very early traces of adoption as an institution in Greece. Thus in *Il.* 9. 494 ff. Phoinix adopts Achilles, though this does not of course mean that he is making him his heir. We are concerned, however, with the law as it was at Athens in the classical period. Basically this law went back to what must have been an innovation of Solon, though there was evidently some change in the way the law was actually applied between his time and that of the orators. Solon seems to have made two closely related rules; he allowed a man who had neither son nor daughter to choose an heir, whom he adopted; and he allowed a man who had only a daughter to choose for her a husband, whom he adopted. There seems now little doubt that this was the essence of what was later regarded as a law conferring complete freedom of testament on a man who had no legitimate issue.[2]

[1] Beauch. ii. 1–72, Bruck, *Schenkung* 94–105, Lips., *AR* 508–20, F. Brindesi, *La famiglia attica* (Firenze, 1961), 31–85. The last is muddled on some vital points; see A. R. W. Harrison, *CR* 13 (1963), 200.

[2] For justification of this view see below (pp. 149 ff.). It is most fully developed in Gernet, *RÉG* 33 (1920), 123 ff., 249 ff. (*DSGA* 121 ff.). That Solon's law was regarded as essentially a law conferring on a man who had no issue the right to adopt someone *inter vivos* comes out plainly in, for example, Isai. 2 *Menekl.* 13 *ὡς οὖν κατὰ τοὺς νόμους ἐγένετο ἡ ποίησις, τοῦτο ὑμᾶς βούλομαι διδάξαι. καί μοι τὸν νόμον αὐτὸν ἀνάγνωθι, ὃς κελεύει τὰ ἑαυτοῦ ἐξεῖναι διαθέσθαι ὅπως ἂν ἐθέλῃ, ἐὰν μὴ παῖδες ἄρρενες ὦσι γνήσιοι. ὁ γὰρ νομοθέτης διὰ τοῦτο τὸν νόμον ἔθηκεν οὕτως, ὁρῶν μόνην ταύτην καταφυγὴν οὖσαν τῆς ἐρημίας καὶ παραψυχὴν τοῦ βίου τοῖς ἄπαισι τῶν*

There has been much controversy as to what was the precise social aim which Solon had in mind here. What is clear is the meaning attached to these rules by the orators of the classical period. For them their purpose was partly the private one of *γηροτροφία*, partly the more public social–religious one of preserving the *οἶκος*, with all that that implied in the perpetuating of family names and family cults. This was felt to be not merely a private interest, but one in which the state had an important stake, witnessed by the duty imposed on the archon *ἐπιμελεῖσθαι τῶν οἴκων τῶν ἐξερημουμένων*.[1] In the classical period there were three different methods by which an adoption could be effected. Probably the normal method, and almost certainly the only method originally contemplated by Solon, was adoption *inter vivos*.[2] A second method, which must have developed out of the first and thus accounted for the fact that Solon's law was thought of as primarily one conveying freedom of testament, was adoption by will.[3] Lastly there was the curious procedure, of which the origins are obscure, by which, when a man died intestate and leaving no son, one of his heirs, usually his heir by the rules of intestate succession, could be made his adoptive son posthumously, having to marry the *ἐπίκληρος* if there was one.[4] The terminology was the same for all three procedures, save that

ἀνθρώπων, τὸ ἐξεῖναι ποιήσασθαι ὅν τινα ἂν βούλωνται. Later in the same speech (24) the law is called *ὁ περὶ τῆς ποιήσεως νόμος*.

[1] Dem. 43 *Makart.* 75. Whether the law referred to in Isai. 7 *Apollod.* 30 (*νόμῳ γὰρ τῷ ἄρχοντι τῶν οἴκων, ὅπως ἂν μὴ ἐξερημῶνται, προστάττει τὴν ἐπιμέλειαν*) is a different law and, if so, what degree of initiative it assigned to the archon in preserving houses in danger of extinction are problems discussed below (pp. 91 f.) in connexion with posthumous adoption.

[2] Isai. 2 *Menekl.* 10 ff.; cf. especially for the motive *ἐσκόπει ὁ Μενεκλῆς ὅπως μὴ ἔσοιτο ἄπαις, ἀλλ' ἔσοιτο αὐτῷ ὅς τις ζῶντά τε γηροτροφήσοι καὶ τελευτήσαντα θάψοι αὐτὸν καὶ εἰς τὸν ἔπειτα χρόνον τὰ νομιζόμενα αὐτῷ ποιήσοι*. Isai. 7 *Apollod.* 13 ff. Dem. 41 *Spoud.* 3 ff. (the adoptee marries one of the adopter's two daughters; the marriage is dissolved during the adopter's lifetime and the adoption presumably annulled, though this is not explicitly stated; see p. 30, above, p. 94, n. 3, below).

[3] Isai. 6 *Philokt.* 6 *Χαιρέστρατον ἐποιήσατο ὑόν· καὶ ἔγραψεν οὕτως ἐν διαθήκῃ, εἰ μὴ γένοιτο αὐτῷ παιδίον ἐκ τῆς γυναικός, τοῦτον κληρονομεῖν τῶν ἑαυτοῦ*.

[4] Dem. 44 *Leoch.* 43 *οὐδέτερος δ' αὐτῶν ζῶντι, ἀλλὰ τετελευτηκότι εἰσποιεῖ αὐτόν. ἡμεῖς δὲ οἰόμεθα δεῖν . . . ἐκ τῶν κατὰ γένος ἐγγυτάτω ἡμῶν εἰσποιεῖν υἱὸν τῷ τετελευτηκότι, ὅπως ἂν ὁ οἶκος μὴ ἐξερημωθῇ*. Dem. 43 *Makart.* 11 *εἰσήγαγον εἰς τοὺς φράτερας τοὺς τοῦ Ἁγνίου Εὐβουλίδῃ τὸν παῖδα τουτονί . . . ἵνα μὴ ἐξερημωθῇ ὁ οἶκος*. Isai. 11 *Hagn.* 49, 7 *Apollod.* 31. Difficult though the case of Leochares is to follow in detail, Gernet, *Dem.* ii. 127 is right to point out that the speaker presupposes it as conceivable that, after the death of the *de cuius*, a relative could get himself adopted as his son and be acknowledged as such without recourse to the courts.

εἰσποιεῖν τινὶ υἱόν is used only of the third. The act is ποίησις or εἰσποίησις.[1] The adoptive father is said εἰσποιεῖσθαι or ποιεῖσθαι, either with or without the word υἱόν.[2] The adoptive son is said εἰσποιηθῆναι or ποιηθῆναι in relation to his adoptive father, ἐκποιηθῆναι in relation to his natural father;[3] he is also ποιητός, εἰσποίητος, or ἐκποίητος, and is sometimes contrasted with the γόνῳ or φύσει γεγονώς.[4] The adoptive father may be called ποιητὸς πατήρ.[5] One other terminological question is of importance, the use of the words διατίθεσθαι and διαθήκη for making a will and the will itself. In anticipation of the full discussion under the law governing wills (below, pp. 149 ff.) it may be noted here that in all probability the use of these terms implies that the will originated in a contract between two parties, an adopter and an adoptee or his representative; in other words, it confirms the view taken above about the nature of Solon's law.

§ 2. *Qualifications for adopter and adoptee*

The qualifications for one who wished to adopt were the same as those for one who wished to make a will. He had to be a male citizen of age who had no legitimate sons alive; whether a son's son disqualified we do not know.[6] If, however, he had a son or

[1] Dem. 44 *Leoch.* 48, Isai. 7 *Apollod.* 20, 10 *Aristarch.* 14.

[2] Isai. 2 *Menekl.* 1, Dem. 44 *Leoch.* 51. Two possible ambiguities must be noted. Throughout Dem. 39 *Boiot.* i Mantitheos uses ποιεῖσθαι and ποίησις of the action of Mantias in introducing Boiotos and his brother into the phratry (see especially 4 and 20 and cf. p. 69, above). As we have seen, it is not likely that this was legitimation by way of adoption; it was simple acknowledgement that they were indeed his legitimate sons; nevertheless the word may have been deliberately chosen by Mantitheos to suggest that this action was more like an adoption than a straightforward enrolment. In 40 *Boiot.* ii. 10 the mother promises, for a consideration, τούτους τοῖς αὑτῆς ἀδελφοῖς εἰσποιήσειν (active, not middle) υἱεῖς; Gernet, *Dem.* ii. 8, n. 2, 36, n. 1. The other ambiguity, in this case perhaps played upon by a speaker (but see p. 86, n. 2), is that ποιεῖσθαι (passive) can be used of being made a citizen, Dem. 46 *Steph.* ii. 15; and so with ποιητός, 45 *Steph.* i. 78. θέσθαι υἱόν, θέτης of the adoptive father, θετός of the adopted son are not found in the orators, with the possible exception of θέτης in Isai. 10 *Aristarch.* 24 (quoted on p. 216, n. 1, cf. p. 266, n. 2).

[3] Dem. 44 *Leoch.* 27 τῷ Ἀρχιάδῃ, πρὸς ὃν εἰσεποιήθης (of a posthumous adoption). Isai. 7 *Apollod.* 25 μητρὸς δ' οὐδείς ἐστιν ἐκποίητος, ἀλλ' ὁμοίως ὑπάρχει τὴν αὐτὴν εἶναι μητέρα, κἂν ἐν τῷ πατρῴῳ μένῃ τις οἴκῳ κἂν ἐκποιηθῇ.

[4] Isai. 2 *Menekl.* 11, 7 *Apollod.* 16.

[5] Lys. 13 *Agorat.* 91, Lykourg. *Leokr.* 48.

[6] Dem. 44 *Leoch.* 49 τὸ δὲ "κυρίως" κατὰ τῶν ποιήσεων ὁ νομοθέτης ἔλαβεν, ὑπολαμβάνων δεῖν, ὅταν τις ὢν ἄπαις καὶ κύριος τῶν ἑαυτοῦ ποιήσηται υἱόν, ταῦτα κύρια

sons who were minors, he could adopt some other person in a will, and this adoption would take effect if, and only if, the natural son or sons died before coming of age.[1] If there were daughters but no sons he could adopt a son on condition that he married her to one of the daughters.[2] If, after adopting a son, he had sons born to him, the adopted son was entitled to share the estate with the others.[3] A man who had himself been adopted might in certain cases be thereby disqualified from adopting a son though qualified in all other respects. There is some dispute as to what these cases were. On one view *no* adopted son could, even in the absence of heirs of his body, himself adopt; though if he availed himself of his right to renounce his adoption, which he could do if he could leave in his adopted house an heir born of his body, he would recover the right to adopt provided he had no other son.[4] On another view an adopted son could acquire the

εἶναι. Ibid. 67 *ὁ τοῦ Σόλωνος νόμος οὐδὲ διαθέσθαι τὸν ποιητὸν ἐᾷ τὰ ἐν οἴκῳ, οἷ ἂν* (Blass: *ὅταν* codd.: *ὅτῳ ἂν* Reiske) *ποιηθῇ.* Dem. 46 *Steph.* ii. 14 *ΝΟΜΟΣ. ὅσοι μὴ ἐπεποίηντο, ὥστε μήτε ἀπειπεῖν μήτ' ἐπιδικάσασθαι, ὅτε Σόλων εἰσῄει τὴν ἀρχήν, τὰ ἑαυτοῦ διαθέσθαι εἶναι ὅπως ἂν ἐθέλῃ, ἂν μὴ παῖδες ὦσι γνήσιοι ἄρρενες, ἂν μὴ μανιῶν ἢ γήρως ἢ φαρμάκων ἢ νόσου ἕνεκα, ἢ γυναικὶ πειθόμενος, ὑπὸ τούτων του παρανοῶν* (Wesseling; *τοῦ παρανόμων* codd.), *ἢ ὑπ' ἀνάγκης ἢ ὑπὸ δεσμοῦ καταληφθείς.* Dem. 20 *Lept.* 102 (p. 88, n. 4).

[1] Dem. 46 *Steph.* ii. 24 (p. 75, n. 3). There is a similar rule in Plato, *Laws* 923 e. In the face of this evidence the argument to the contrary put forward in Isai. 10 *Aristarch.* 9 must be disregarded; cf. Wyse ad loc., Lips., *AR* 511, n. 42. But E. Ruschenbusch, *Z* 79 (1962), 307 f. thinks that a conditional adoption *inter vivos* of this kind would have been unworkable and concludes that *διαθήκη* here must be 'testament' and not 'adoption *inter vivos*'.

[2] Lips., *AR* 511 f., F. Brindesi, *La famiglia attica* (Firenze, 1961), 59, Isai. 3 *Pyrrh.* 68 *ὁ γὰρ νόμος διαρρήδην λέγει ἐξεῖναι διαθέσθαι ὅπως ἂν ἐθέλῃ τις τὰ αὑτοῦ, ἐὰν μὴ παῖδας γνησίους καταλίπῃ ἄρρενας· ἂν δὲ θηλείας καταλίπῃ, σὺν ταύταις. οὐκοῦν μετὰ τῶν θυγατέρων ἔστι δοῦναι καὶ διαθέσθαι τὰ αὑτοῦ· ἄνευ δὲ τῶν γνησίων θυγατέρων οὐχ οἷόν τε οὔτε ποιήσασθαι οὔτε δοῦναι οὐδενὶ οὐδὲν τῶν ἑαυτοῦ.* Isai. 10 *Aristarch.* 13 *καὶ τῷ μὲν πατρὶ αὐτῆς, εἰ παῖδες ἄρρενες μὴ ἐγένοντο, οὐκ ἂν ἐξῆν ἄνευ ταύτης διαθέσθαι· κελεύει γὰρ ὁ νόμος σὺν ταύταις κύριον εἶναι δοῦναι, ἐάν τῳ βούληται τὰ ἑαυτοῦ.* Brindesi, loc. cit., follows Beauch. ii. 71 in distinguishing between a case where a man devolved both his property and his daughter on an adopted son and one where he devolved only his daughter; in the latter case a son born of the marriage would have been the heir of his grandfather, in the former he would have been his father's heir. No specific text is cited to bear out this distinction, and it is difficult to understand how in the latter case the daughter's husband could have been regarded as her father's adopted son.

[3] Isai. 6 *Philokt.* 63 *ἐν τῷ νόμῳ γέγραπται, ἐὰν ποιησαμένῳ παῖδες ἐπιγένωνται, τὸ μέρος ἑκάτερον ἔχειν τῆς οὐσίας καὶ κληρονομεῖν ὁμοίως ἀμφοτέρους.*

[4] Dem. 44 *Leoch.* 63, 67 (quoted in n. 6, above). Ibid. 68 " *ὅσοι μὴ ἐπεποίηντο* " *φησίν (ὁ νόμος)* " *ὅτε Σόλων εἰσῄει εἰς τὴν ἀρχήν, ἐξεῖναι αὐτοῖς διαθέσθαι ὅπως ἂν ἐθέλωσιν* ", *ὡς τοῖς γε* (Q γρ., *τοῖς δὲ* S F Q, *τοῖς δέ γε* A) *ποιηθεῖσιν οὐκ ἐξὸν διαθέσθαι,*

right to adopt in his turn if his own adoption was arrived at by way of ἐπιδικασία. Those who advance this view seem to hold that this procedure was only open to an adoptee who happened also to have the best claim *ab intestato*, whether to the estate or to the hand of the ἐπίκληρος if there was one. They do not seem to have asked themselves what is none the less a relevant question, namely whether one adopted *inter vivos* who had not the best claim *ab intestato* or who, in default of the adoption, would have had to share with other ἀγχιστεῖς related to the *de cuius* in the same degree as himself, could by waiving his right to enter on the inheritance (ἐμβατεύειν) and submitting his claim to a court retain the right to adopt if he begat no sons.[1] On a third view freedom of testament, and with it freedom to adopt, was only denied to those who had been adopted *inter vivos*.[2] This rule might seem strange to us, but possibly it was felt that such an adoptee's right to enter without ἐπιδικασία was based on the assumption that he would produce for the οἶκος heirs of his body and that if he did not do so the ἀγχιστεῖς should recover their rights. With other

ἀλλὰ ζῶντας ἐγκαταλιπόντας υἱὸν γνήσιον ἐπανιέναι, ἢ τελευτήσαντας ἀποδιδόναι τὴν κληρονομίαν τοῖς ἐξ ἀρχῆς οἰκείοις οὖσι τοῦ ποιησαμένου.

[1] This second is the view of F. Schulin, *Gr. Test.* 13, Beauch. ii. 36, Dareste, *Dem.* ii. 307, Bruck, *Schenkung* 53, Lips., *AR* 511, n. 41. See p. 95, n. 1, below.

[2] So Thalheim, *RA* 80, *BPW* 29 (1909), 878, 30 (1910), 371. Crucial is the interpretation of the first eight words of the law in Dem. 46 *Steph.* ii. 14 quoted in p. 84, n. 6, above. To Dareste and those who think with him the words are to be paraphrased as meaning 'all those who had not been adopted or, having been adopted, had either renounced the adoption or had not taken advantage of it by 'entering' on the death of the *de cuius*, but had proceeded by ἐπιδικασία'. Thalheim argued that it would have been otiose to except from the number of adoptees those who had renounced the adoption and that the suppressed object of ἀπειπεῖν should be the same as that of ἐπιδικάσασθαι, viz., not the adoption but the inheritance. To him the phrase means 'those who had not been adopted in such a way that they could neither decline the inheritance nor needed to establish their claim by ἐπιδικασία'. In other words Thalheim assumes (for we have no independent evidence for this) that male children by birth were like Roman *heredes necessarii* and that those adopted *inter vivos* became in this respect on all fours with children by birth. This consorts well with the contractual element in adoption *inter vivos*. Brindesi, op. cit. 41, misunderstands Thalheim here, cf. A. R. W. Harrison *CR* 13 (1963), 200. Modern commentators have perhaps been too ready to dismiss as pure sophistry the argument of Apollodoros in Dem. 46 *Steph.* ii. 15 that Pasion was disqualified from making a will not only because he had sons but also because ἐπεποίητο ὑπὸ τοῦ δήμου πολίτης. From the point of view of the phratry, an important point of view in Solon's day at least, a naturalized foreigner was as much ποιητός as an adopted son, and it is by no means unthinkable that his right to dispose of his property by will in the absence of sons of his body might have been equally restricted.

types of adoption, on the other hand, the ἀγχιστεῖς would necessarily get a chance to put their claims to a court when the adoption took place, and if they then failed it was legitimate to regard the adoptee as having established his right to start afresh, as it were, as head of the οἶκος with all his rights unimpaired. This would be even more plausible if the adoptee *inter vivos* was allowed to waive his right to enter. He would have had to make a delicate choice on the death of his adopted father between entering and thus forfeiting the right to adopt in his turn in case he should have no heirs of his body, and proceeding by ἐπιδικασία, with the risk that the court would not confirm the adoption. If he chose to enter, the ἀγχιστεῖς on their side would have had to decide whether to dispute his claim with the chance that the court might confirm it and thus close the inheritance to them even if he should have no heirs of his body, or let him bide, in the hope that he would produce no heir, in which case on his death the inheritance would come through to them.[1]

Other disqualifications for adopting were mental incapacity caused by madness, senility, drugs, sickness, the undue influence of women, or having acted under duress or loss of personal liberty.[2] Finally, we learn from a passage in Aischines that a magistrate who had not yet rendered his accounts (who was ὑπεύθυνος) could not make dispositions of his property (διαθέσθαι τὰ ἑαυτοῦ).[3] The object of this provision must have been fiscal, to prevent a man who was in default from defrauding the treasury by disposing of his property. Formally the words used must have covered an act of adoption, but in practice it is difficult to see how an adoption could have helped a defaulter, since his estate would have been liable in any case for any debt due from him to the state: this in itself would make it unlikely that anyone would consent to be adopted by a man so circumstanced.[4]

In order to qualify to be adopted a person had to be of Athenian parentage on both sides. It is usually held, though

[1] To Gernet, *RÉG* 33 (1920), 138 (*DSGA* 128) the exclusion of adopted sons from freedom of testament was a concession to tradition.

[2] Dem. 46 *Steph.* ii. 14 cited in p. 84, n. 6, above. Cf. also Hyper. 5 *Athenog.* 17, Lys. F 74 Th., Isai. 6 *Philokt.* 9, 2 *Menekl.* 1, 4 *Nikostr.* 16.

[3] Aischin. 3 *Ktes.* 21 πάλιν ὑπεύθυνον οὐκ ἐᾷ (ὁ νομοθέτης) . . . οὐδὲ ἐκποίητον γενέσθαι οὐδὲ διαθέσθαι τὰ ἑαυτοῦ.

[4] Beauch. ii. 47, Lips., *AR* 512, Brindesi, op. cit., 63. Of course a man could give a dowry to an adopted son, but it would be the dowry-giving rather than the adoption which might defraud the treasury.

perhaps on insufficient grounds, that he or she had to be the child of a union by *ἐγγύη*.[1] Since adoption *inter vivos* was in the nature of a contract it would seem probable that, at least where the child to be adopted was a girl or a boy who was still a minor, its father or guardian would have had to give his consent.[2] Even with a boy who was of age one might have expected that the principle of preserving *οἶκοι* might have dictated a rule allowing the father of an only son to veto that son's adoption, but there is no evidence for such a rule. Daughters could be adopted and thus become *ἐπίκληροι*, though naturally this happened much less frequently than the adoption of sons.[3] Although it was usual to choose a relative to adopt there was no legal bar to adopting a complete stranger.[4] A magistrate who had not rendered his accounts could not be adopted,[5] nor could anyone who had been

[1] See pp. 68, 70, above. The principal passage relied on is Isai. 7 *Apollod.* 16 *ἔστι δ' αὐτοῖς νόμος ὁ αὐτός, ἐάν τέ τινα φύσει γεγονότα εἰσάγῃ τις ἐάν τε ποιητόν, ἐπιτιθέναι πίστιν κατὰ τῶν ἱερῶν ἦ μὴν ἐξ ἀστῆς εἰσάγειν καὶ γεγονότα ὀρθῶς καὶ τὸν ὑπάρχοντα φύσει καὶ τὸν ποιητόν*. The question is whether the words *γεγονότα ὀρθῶς* necessarily mean 'born of a marriage by *ἐγγύη*'. If this were the intention of the clause we might ask why the phrase used is not *ἐξ ἀστῆς καὶ ἐγγυητῆς*. It should be noted that the phrase does not strictly fit an adopted child, since the oath in such cases ought to have guaranteed the citizenship of the father as well as the mother. In relation to the more normal case of a child by blood might not the words *γεγονότα ὀρθῶς* simply indicate that the father was guaranteeing his own paternity of the child? Where the child was adopted they would have been understood, by a natural extension, to mean that he guaranteed that the father was a citizen. This rule can only have been in force at those periods when Perikles' citizenship law was operating (see p. 61, above).

[2] Lips., *AR* 512, arguing against van den Es, *De iure fam.* 92 ff. Isai. 2 *Menekl.* 21 clearly implies the power of a father to prevent the adoption of his son, but there is nothing to show whether the son was a minor at the time.

[3] Isai. 11 *Hagn.* 8, 41, 7 *Apollod.* 9, and Wyse's note ad loc.

[4] Dem. 20 *Lept.* 102 *ὁ Σόλων ἔθηκεν νόμον ἐξεῖναι δοῦναι τὰ ἑαυτοῦ ᾧ ἄν τις βούληται, ἐὰν μὴ παῖδες ὦσι γνήσιοι.* Gernet, *RÉG* 33 (1920), 139 (*DSGA* 129) lists twenty-seven cases of recorded adoptions, of which the greater number are of relatives.

[5] See p. 87, n. 3, above. Here the fiscal object was more obvious; a rich father whose son was a magistrate about to be found in default might have been tempted to persuade some penniless friend to adopt the son so as to avoid the possibility of the family property's becoming liable for the debt to the treasury. It is probably to this manœuvre, and not, as MSL 546, n. 179 suggest, to one by which a defaulting magistrate gets his son adopted, that reference is made in *An. Bekk.* (*Λέξ. Ῥητ.*) 247 *ἐκποίητον γενέσθαι: ἀποκηρυχθῆναι ἐκ τοῦ γένους, ὥσπερ εἰσποίητος ὁ θετός. πολλοὶ δὲ τοῦτο ποιοῦσι τῶν πατέρων τοὺς παῖδας αὐτῶν, ὅταν ἐν ταῖς ἀρχαῖς κλέψαντες ἐλπίσωσιν ἁλώσεσθαι ἐν ταῖς εὐθύναις. ἤτοι οὖν ἐπὶ τοῦ ἄρχοντός ἐστι τὸ ἐκποίητον, ἢ ὑπὲρ τῆς οὐσίας τῆς ὑπερτιθεμένης εἰς ἄλλους διὰ τὴν προσδοκίαν τῶν εὐθυνῶν*. It is true that this involves taking as the subject of *ἐλπίσωσι* the sons and not the fathers, but it is difficult to see how, if it were the fathers who were

condemned to total ἀτιμία, but it is probable that the sons of those thus condemned were eligible; for in the decree pronouncing ἀτιμία against Archeptolemos and Antiphon in 411 B.C. the adoption of any of their children is banned, which implies that this did not follow automatically.[1]

§ 3. *Procedure*

The procedure followed in adoptions naturally differed according to whether the adoption was *inter vivos*, testamentary, or posthumous (see above, p. 83, for these three kinds of adoption). Adoption *inter vivos* had two facets, private and public. Privately it was in principle a contract between the adopter and the adoptee or his father or guardian. This, like other Athenian contracts, needed for its completion no formality beyond a declaration of intent by the two parties. But, although this agreement between the parties was sufficient to validate the adoption, the adopter would normally proceed to enrol an adopted son on his own phratry and deme registers at the appropriate times. His doing or failing to do this would have had much the same effect on the status of the adopted son as if he had been a son by birth; that is to say that it would have tended as a matter of evidence to confirm or to throw suspicion upon the fact of the adoption. The presentation to the phratry was probably as a rule on the third day of the feast of the Apaturia, the normal day for the presentation of natural sons; but in a case of urgency it could take place at some other meeting of the phratry.[2] The father swore to the

defaulting magistrates, they could gain much by getting their sons adopted. On either interpretation the meaning of the last sentence is obscure.

[1] One who was punished with total ἀτιμία in effect ceased to be a citizen and must for that reason have been incapable of being adopted. For the decree against Archeptolemos and Antiphon Plut., *Mor.* 834 b καὶ ἐάν τις ποιήσηταί τινα τῶν ἐξ Ἀρχεπτολέμου καὶ Ἀντιφῶντος, ἄτιμος ἔστω ὁ ποιησάμενος, probably from Krateros' collection of decrees (Jacoby, *F.Gr.H.* 342 F 5); cf. Thalheim, *RA* 82, Lips., *AR* 513, n. 49.

[2] Beauch. ii. 12, Lips., *AR* 514, Bu. Sw. 960 f. In the best-documented case, Isai. 7 *Apollod.* 15 ff., presentation of an adopted son takes place at the Thargelia, but the speaker stresses that Apollodoros, the adopter, was sick, and he in fact died before he could carry out the presentation to the deme (ibid. 27). For presentation of sons by birth to the phratry and its significance see above, pp. 64 ff., especially p. 64, n. 1, p. 79. Cf. *IG* ii². 1237, lines 26 ff. (the 'Demotionid Decree', *SIG* 921), with H. T. Wade-Gery's commentary in *EGH* 118 ff., Pollux 8. 107 *An. Bekk.* (Συν. Λέξ. Χρησ.) 417, lines 12 ff., *Et. Mag.* s.v. ἀπατούρια. Note that the

proper birth qualifications of the child; the phratry members voted on oath whether to admit or reject his name. If they rejected it he could appeal to a dicastery.[1] Presentation to the deme of the adopted father took place at the election of officers (ἀρχαιρεσίαι), whenever that was; again the demesmen voted on the admission and an appeal to a dicastery against an adverse decision was allowed.[2]

Adoption by will differed principally from adoption *inter vivos* in not being a contract, though it was still called διαθήκη. The adoptee need have no knowledge of his adoption till the adopter had died; and either he, or if he was a minor his guardian, would have had to arrange for enrolment on the phratry and deme lists. This could only be done when the archon, and if the will was challenged, a dikastery, had confirmed the will.[3]

Posthumous adoption was a peculiar institution which needs rather more attention. When a man died without male issue and without having made any testamentary disposition either of his property or, if he left daughters, of their hands together with his property there is no doubt that it was possible, and

Isaios passage (quoted on p. 88, n. 1, above) refers to the law of the phratry; this means that we cannot assume absolute uniformity throughout the state on this important piece of procedure, and the procedure in the Demotionid decree clearly has its own idiosyncrasies; so too demes were not always equally strict; cf. Harpokr. s.v. *ποταμός· ἐκωμῳδοῦντο ὡς ῥαδίως δεχόμενοι τοὺς παρεγγράπτους* referred to by Wyse, *Isai*. 560.

[1] Dem. 59 *Neair*. 59; Phrastor presents a son to his phratry, the name is refused, and Phrastor brings suit against the phratry members of the genos Brytidai who had blocked the entry; this suit gets no further than the public arbitrator, though it clearly might have reached a dikastery: *λαχόντος τοῦ Φράστορος αὐτοῖς δίκην, ὅτι οὐκ ἐνέγραφον αὐτοῦ υἱόν, προκαλοῦνται αὐτὸν οἱ γεννῆται πρὸς τῷ διαιτητῇ ὀμόσαι καθ' ἱερῶν τελείων ἦ μὴν νομίζειν εἶναι αὑτοῦ υἱὸν ἐξ ἀστῆς γυναικὸς καὶ ἐγγυητῆς κατὰ τὸν νόμον. προκαλουμένων δὲ ταῦτα τῶν γεννητῶν τὸν Φράστωρα πρὸς τῷ διαιτητῇ, ἔλιπεν ὁ Φράστωρ τὸν ὅρκον καὶ οὐκ ὤμοσεν.* Gernet, however, maintains in *Mél. Desrousseaux* (Paris, 1937), 176, that this is not an appeal but a suit for damages. The Demotionid decree makes no reference to an appeal beyond the phratry.

[2] Isai. 7 *Apollod*. 28 *κἀκεῖνοι (οἱ δημόται) ταῦτα ἀκούσαντες, τούτων ἐν ἀρχαιρεσίαις κατηγορούντων καὶ λεγόντων ὡς οὐκ ἐποιήσατό με ὑόν, καὶ ἐξ ὧν ἤκουσαν καὶ ἐξ ὧν ᾔδεσαν, ὀμόσαντες καθ' ἱερῶν ἐνέγραψάν με, καθάπερ ἐκεῖνος ἐκέλευε.* Dem. 44 *Leoch*. 39 f., Ar., *Ath. Pol*. 42. 1, Lips., *NJ* 117 (1878), 299 ff., *AR* 515, Bu. Sw. 943.

[3] Isai. 3 *Pyrrh*. 1, 56, 4 *Nikostr*. 10 ff., 5 *Dikaiog*. 6 (*ἀποθανόντος αὐτοῦ ἄπαιδος διαθήκην ἀπέφηνε Πρόξενος ὁ Δικαιογένους πατήρ, ᾗ πιστεύσαντες οἱ ἡμέτεροι πατέρες ἐνείμαντο τὸν κλῆρον. καὶ ἐπὶ μὲν τῷ τρίτῳ μέρει τοῦ κλήρου Δικαιογένης ὅδε τῷ Μενεξένου Δικαιογένει, ἡμετέρῳ θείῳ, ὑὸς ἐγίγνετο ποιητός*), perhaps rather a posthumous adoption, 6 *Philokt*. 4 ff. See later under Wills, p. 150 with n. 4, for the significance of the contrast between a joint action such as that involved in adoption *inter vivos* and two unilateral actions such as those involved in adoption by will and acceptance by the adoptee on the death of the adopter.

indeed not unusual, for a man to be made his son by a procedure which is, like normal adoption, called εἰσποίησις. Perhaps the most instructive instance is that of Euboulides III in the famous case of the estate of Hagnias. He was the son of Sositheos and Phylomache II and his father, the speaker in Dem. 43 *Makart.* procured his adoption as son of his wife's father Euboulides II and the due recognition of this adoption by Euboulides II's phratry after the latter's death.[1] Euboulides II was the son of Phylomache I, alleged by Sositheos to be full sister of Polemon, the father of the Hagnias whose estate was in dispute. When that estate was awarded by a court to Theopompos, Euboulides III was not even alive, and the adoption which was supposed to strengthen his claim did not take place till after Theopompos died, having held the estate for some eighteen years. Even though we may doubt whether the adoption did in fact strengthen his claim, we can hardly doubt that it took place.[2] Other instructive examples occur in Dem. 44 *Leoch.* The speaker's phraseology in 19 is equivocal. He seems to be trying to suggest that Leokrates got himself posthumously adopted as the son of Archiades, whose estate is in question, but in 46 he says that Archiades adopted him. It may be that Archiades in fact adopted Leokrates by will and that the latter improperly entered on the estate as if he had been adopted *inter vivos*; but in any case the speaker makes no suggestion that the adoption would have been invalid simply *qua* posthumous. On the contrary in 43 he expressly says that a son ought to be provided posthumously for Archiades, though this should happen after the decision of the present case.[3] The most

[1] Dem. 43 *Makart.* 13 καὶ ἐγὼ ταῦτα ὑπηρέτησα αὐτῷ (Εὐβουλίδῃ II), ὁ τὴν Εὐβουλίδου (II) θυγατέρα ἔχων ἐπιδικασάμενος ὡς γένει ὢν ἐγγυτάτω, καὶ εἰσήγαγον τὸν παῖδα τουτονὶ (Εὐβουλίδην III) εἰς τοὺς Ἁγνίου καὶ Εὐβουλίδου φράτερας . . . καὶ οἱ φράτερες . . . ἐψηφίσαντο τὰ δίκαια, ὀρθῶς καὶ προσηκόντως τὸν παῖδα τουτονὶ εἰσάγεσθαι Εὐβουλίδῃ υἱὸν εἰς τὸν οἶκον τὸν Ἁγνίου.

[2] It might be thought that the significant point was the preservation of an οἶκος, viz., the οἶκος of Hagnias II, or rather its resuscitation after being really swallowed up in that of Theopompos; but this point would have been made more plausible if Euboulides had been adopted as son of Hagnias II. It is true that Sositheos uses rather ambiguous language, speaking of the son sometimes as being adopted into the house of Hagnias (13 in n. 1, above), at other times into the house of Euboulides II (41); but it seems fairly clear that he is to be thought of as the adopted son of his mother's father, Euboulides II.

[3] Dem. 44 *Leoch.* 19 Λεωκράτης . . . εἰσποιεῖ αὑτὸν υἱὸν τῷ Ἀρχιάδῃ, καὶ ἐνεβάτευσεν οὕτως εἰς τὴν οὐσίαν ὡς ὑπ' ἐκείνου ζῶντος ἔτι εἰσποιηθείς. 46 ὁ Ἀρχιάδης ἐκεῖνος, οὗ ἐστιν ὁ κλῆρος, ἐποιήσατο υἱὸν τὸν τοῦ διαμεμαρτυρηκότος νυνὶ πάππον. 43 ἡμεῖς οἰόμεθα δεῖν, ἐπειδὰν περὶ τούτου τοῦ ἀγῶνος ὑμεῖς τὴν ψῆφον ἐνέγκητε,

striking of these adoptions was the last, that of Leochares; he was a grandson of the original adoptee and was the fourth person to be thus posthumously adopted. In these and the other cases which can be cited[1] action seems to be initiated by one of the kindred of the *de cuius*, and though that action had to be confirmed, as in the case of adoption *inter vivos* or by will, by the phratry and presumably the demesmen, there is no suggestion that any public official was involved, though presumably the archon's court would have been brought in in a disputed case. Some scholars, however, have built upon the phrase in Isai. 7 *Apollod.* 30, νόμῳ τῷ ἄρχοντι τῶν οἴκων, ὅπως ἂν μὴ ἐξερημῶνται, προστάττει τὴν ἐπιμέλειαν, a theory that the archon had an initiative in this matter, some restricting this initiative to what must have been the very rare cases of *bona vacantia*, but one at least going much further and suggesting that in the last resort the choice of a son for posthumous adoption rested with the archon.[2] On the other side it is argued that Isaios is slightly twisting for his own purpose the law in Dem. 43 *Makart.* 75 (quoted on p. 39, n. 2) which gives the archon care of 'deserted houses' rather than laying on him the duty of seeing that houses should not be deserted.[3] Few commentators have faced squarely the fact that while κλῆρος in this context had a fairly clearly defined legal sense, the material property of the *de cuius*, οἶκος had a much less clearly defined sense, embracing as it did that cluster of intangibles which constituted the family cult.[4] Strictly speaking there should have been one κλῆρος, one οἶκος. And as no

τηνικαῦτα ἐκ τῶν κατὰ γένος ἐγγυτάτω ἡμῶν εἰσποιεῖν υἱὸν τῷ τετελευτηκότι, ὅπως ἂν ὁ οἶκος μὴ ἐξερημωθῇ.

[1] Dem. 43 *Makart.* 77, Isai. 3 *Pyrrh.* 73 (alludes to the possibility of a man's leaving solemn injunctions that a future son of his heiress daughter should be adopted into his house: as Wyse, ad loc., points out, this passage and that quoted in p. 91, n. 1, above from Dem. 43 *Makart.* 13 f. prove that while there might be a moral, there was no legal obligation on one who married an heiress to transfer a son by the marriage by adoption into the house of his father-in-law), Isai. 7 *Apollod.* 31, 44 (alluding to a posthumous adoption which the speaker asserts should have, but had not taken place), Isai. 11 *Hagn.* 49 (the same adoption as that referred to in Dem. 43 *Makart.* 77), Isai. 10 *Aristarch.* 6.

[2] So Caillemer, *Succession* 133, Beauch. iii. 571, Guiraud, *Prop. fonc.* 224, Brindesi, *La famiglia attica* 49 ff., who assigns a major role in this matter to the archon. See also Jones, *LLTG* 194 and p. 83, above.

[3] So Lips., *AR* 560, n. 51.

[4] Gernet is one of the few. See especially his introduction to Dem. 44 *Leoch.* in *Dem.* ii. 127 ff., ibid. 91, and *RÉG* 33 (1920), 269 ff. (*DSGA* 148 f.). Cf. below, pp. 123 ff.

οἶκος should ever die out both the amalgamation and the unbridled splitting up of *κλῆροι* was to be, so far as possible, avoided. Pressure of economic circumstances in the fourth century was making it more and more difficult to meet these requirements and at the same time keep the rules clear. Posthumous adoption was a rather clumsy device for perpetuating *οἶκοι*, and the Hagnias and Archiades cases show how uncertain the rules were. In such a situation the archon and his court very likely figured more largely than they would have done in other predominantly private matters. But if we take a test case and ask whether, if A dies intestate and childless and his estate is awarded to his next of kin B who has two sons, B could be forced by the archon to adopt one of the sons into A's house, the answer is probably no, though if he did not he might find some other of the kin doing so and then claiming the estate on that basis.[1]

§ 4. *Effects*

The fundamental effect of an adoption was not merely positive, to make the adoptee child of the adopter with precisely the same relation to him as a natural child except that he could not himself adopt if he himself produced no children. It also had the important negative effect of severing all legal ties between the adopted child and his or her natural father. He or she could neither inherit from him nor through him. We should probably include with the legal ties those ties of religion essentially linked with being a member of an *οἶκος*, which meant that an adopted son was not qualified to carry on the cults of the house out of which he had been adopted.[2] On the other hand, a somewhat

[1] See especially the passages cited from Isaios in p. 92, n. 1, above, with Wyse's comments. They make it abundantly clear that the archon neither took nor was expected to take active measures to prevent the desertion of a house if the relatives did not do so.

[2] Isai. 9 *Astyph.* 2 *εἰσποίητος δ' ἦν ὁ πατὴρ ὁ Κλέωνος εἰς ἄλλον οἶκον, καὶ οὗτοι ἔτι εἰσὶν ἐν ἐκείνῳ τῷ οἴκῳ, ὥστε γένει μὲν διὰ τὸν νόμον οὐδὲν προσήκουσιν Ἀστυφίλῳ*, ibid. 33 *οὐδεὶς γὰρ πώποτε ἐκποίητος γενόμενος ἐκληρονόμησε τοῦ οἴκου ὅθεν ἐξεποιήθη, ἐὰν μὴ ἐπανέλθῃ κατὰ τὸν νόμον*, 10 *Aristarch.* 4 *Κυρωνίδης . . . ἐξεποιήθη εἰς ἕτερον οἶκον, ὥστε αὐτῷ τῶν χρημάτων οὐδὲν ἔτι προσῆκεν*. In Isai. 9 *Astyph.* 7 an adoptive son is expected to keep up the ancestral cults of his adoptive father. In Plut., *Mor.* 838 b Isokrates' adopted son, Aphareus, is buried in Isokrates' family tomb. In Dem. 44 *Leoch.* 32 an adoptive son is *συγγενής* of his adoptive father's relatives (*οἰκεῖοι*). He is also *κύριος* of his adoptive sisters and as such is required to dower them, Isai. 3 *Pyrrh.* 51. It appears from Dem. 42 *Phain.* 21 that Phainippos had

surprising rule laid down that adoption did not affect the adopted child's relation to his or her mother,[1] nor, conversely, did it established any relationship to the wife of the adopter.[2] This was important in view of the fact that inheritances could pass to and through women (see below, pp. 132 ff.).

Adoption *inter vivos* differed in its effects from the other forms in two ways. In the first place it was a contract and it could not therefore be revoked by either party without the consent of the other,[3] though we must suppose that this rule was subject to the proviso that a father had the same right of ἀποκήρυξις against an adopted as he had against a natural son; this would have been an important proviso in view of the arbitrary nature of this power (for which see pp. 75 ff., above). But there was probably a rule to prevent one who had appointed an adoptive son by will from cancelling the will and with it the adoption.[4] An adoptee had the right to return to the house of his natural father if he left a son of his body in the house of his adoptive father.[5] There is no reason to suppose that this right could not be

managed to maintain the position of heir both of his natural father, Kallippos, and of his adoptive father, Philostratos; but Philostratos was also his maternal grandfather (27); it is conceivable that he had been posthumously adopted and that, by an exception, the law allowed the son of an ἐπίκληρος who was thus adopted into her father's house to remain also his own father's heir. Lips., *AR* 516, n. 63, A. Ledl, *Jb. des Öst. Staats-Gym. im Graz* (Graz, 1908), 12 ff., Gernet, *Dem.* ii. 84, n. 2.

[1] Isai. 7 *Apollod.* 25 μητρὸς οὐδείς ἐστιν ἐκποίητος. It is probably by virtue of this rule that in Dem. 43 *Makart.* 15 Euboulides III has as his κύριος not his father, though he is still alive, but his elder brother; he had been transferred by adoption from his father's house to that of his maternal grandfather, but his brother remained akin to him through the mother. So Gernet, *Dem.* ii. 92, n. 1.

[2] This rule, though asserted to hold by Schulin, *Gr. Test.* 20 (whom Beauch. ii. 57, Brindesi, op. cit. 74 follow), is to be deduced *a priori*. It seems probable enough on analogy.

[3] In Dem. 41 *Spoud.* 3 f. an adoption seems to be cancelled by mutual consent. See p. 83, n. 2, above.

[4] The events recounted in Isai. 6 *Philokt.* 31 have been taken to prove that alteration of a will, and by implication of an adoption by will, needed the consent of the beneficiaries. Reasons for and against this view are given below under Wills, p. 155.

[5] Isai. 6 *Philokt.* 44 ὁ γὰρ νόμος οὐκ ἐᾷ ἐπανιέναι, ἐὰν μὴ ὑὸν καταλίπῃ γνήσιον, 10 *Aristarch.* 11 αὐτῷ ἐπανελθεῖν εἰς τὸν πατρῷον οἶκον ἐξῆν, ὑὸν ἐγκαταλιπόντα ἐν τῷ Ξεναινέτου οἴκῳ, 9 *Astyph.* 33 (p. 39, n. 2, above), Dem. 44 *Leoch.* 21, 44, 46, Harpokr. s.v. ὅτι οἱ ποιητοί. The speaker in Dem. 58 *Theokr.* 31 is certainly misstating the law when he asserts that no adopted child who returned to his original family was thereby compelled to relinquish property inherited from his adoptive father, though the case of Phainippos (p. 93, n. 2, above) shows that it was sometimes in practice possible to hold property from both houses. Lips., *AR* 518, n. 73, Gernet, *Dem.* iv. 52, n. 1.

exercised by one adopted *inter vivos* even during the life of his adoptive father, though there does not seem to be a recorded instance of this. The second difference between one adopted *inter vivos* and other types of adoptee was that the former was entitled on the death of his adoptive father to enter (ἐμβατεύειν) on his estate and could, like a natural son, meet any other pretendants with a formal declaration (διαμαρτυρία) that the estate was ἀνεπίδικος.[1] Those adopted by will, on the other hand, could not enter, but had to state their claim before the archon, just as did all claimants *ab intestato* other than sons by birth or by adoption *inter vivos. A fortiori* those adopted posthumously could not enter without reference to the archon.[2] Another aspect of this distinction was that one who was adopted *inter vivos* was probably obliged to take up the inheritance, while an adoptee by will could decline. A man who was of age and was posthumously adopted into another's house was presumably bound, as an assenting party, to accept all the consequences of becoming an adopted son; but whether a minor to whom the same thing happened could renounce on coming of age we do not know.[3]

While the normal effect of any adoption was to make the

[1] Dem. 44 *Leoch.* 19 ἐνεβάτευσεν οὕτως εἰς τὴν οὐσίαν ὡς ὑπ' ἐκείνου ζῶντος ἔτι εἰσποιηθείς, Isai. 7 *Apollod.* 3 ἐγὼ δ' εἰ μὲν ἑώρων ὑμᾶς μᾶλλον ἀποδεχομένους τὰς διαμαρτυρίας ἢ τὰς εὐθυδικίας, κἂν μάρτυρα προὐβαλόμην μὴ ἐπίδικον εἶναι τὸν κλῆρον ὡς ποιησαμένου με ὑὸν Ἀπολλοδώρου κατὰ τοὺς νόμους, 3 *Pyrrh.* 60 ὅσοι μὲν ⟨ἂν⟩ καταλίπωσι γνησίους παῖδας ἐξ αὑτῶν, οὐ προσήκει τοῖς παισὶν ἐπιδικάσασθαι τῶν πατρῴων· ὅσοι δὲ διαθήκαις αὑτοῖς (Dobree: αὐτοὶ codd.) εἰσποιοῦνται, τούτοις ἐπιδικάζεσθαι προσήκει τῶν δοθέντων (when the speaker in the next sentence says that *all* adopted sons proceeded by ἐπιδικασία he is probably only exaggerating a tendency of those who were adopted *inter vivos* to proceed thus, which may have been due to the possible fact that thereby they acquired the right to adopt in their turn if they had no sons, cf. pp. 85 ff., above). Isai. 2 *Menekl.* concerns a case where a man had been adopted *inter vivos*; on the death of his adoptive father the next of kin claimed the inheritance, but the adopted son produced a witness to declare (διαμαρτυρεῖν) that the inheritance was not open to adjudgement (2 οὐκ ἔστιν ἐπίδικος ὁ κλῆρος ὁ Μενεκλέους ὄντος ἐμοῦ ὑοῦ ἐκείνου, ἀλλ' ὁ μάρτυς διεμαρτύρησε τἀληθῆ). The entries s.v. ἀμφισβητεῖν in Harpokr., Suda, and *An. Bekk.* (*Λέξ. Ῥητ.*) 197 clearly refer to this rule, though in each case the text is corrupt. Lips., *AR* 541, n. 7, 580, n. 118.

[2] Isai. 3 *Pyrrh.* 60 (n. 1), D.H. *Isai.* 15 οὐ δεῖ τὸν ἐπίδικον κρατεῖσθαι κλῆρον πρὸ δίκης. It is always necessary to keep in mind the distinction between the adoption and the claim to succeed to property which might either precede or come after the adoption; Gernet, *Dem.* ii. 127. For the procedures in detail see pp. 156 ff.

[3] The difficult issue of 'necessary' heirs is discussed in full under Intestate Succession, below, pp. 125 ff. Here it need only be said that it is highly likely that sons adopted *inter vivos* were in this respect on the same footing as natural sons. For the bearing of Dem. 46 *Steph.* ii on the question see above p. 86, n. 2.

adopted son or daughter heir to the whole of the estate of the adopter it was certainly possible in the classical period, though probably even then not common, to adopt a child and leave it only a proportion of one's estate. From Isai. 5 *Dikaiog.* we learn that Dikaiogenes II was alleged to have made a will in which he adopted his cousin, Dikaiogenes III, and left him one-third of his estate and the remainder in equal parts to his four sisters. It makes no difference that, after enjoying one-third of the estate under this will for twelve years, Dikaiogenes III produced another will adopting him and making him heir to the whole property and persuaded a court to reverse the previous settlement. He could scarcely have argued that the first will was invalid because it did not grant him the whole estate, though he may have argued against it on the ground that such a division was not usual.[1]

[1] Isai. 5 *Dikaiog.* 6 *ἀποθανόντος αὐτοῦ (Δικαιογένους* II) *ἄπαιδος διαθήκην ἀπέφηνε Πρόξενος . . . καὶ ἐπὶ μὲν τῷ τρίτῳ μέρει τοῦ κλήρου Δικαιογένης ὅδε* (III) . . . *ὑὸς ἐγίγνετο ποιητός· τῶν δὲ λοιπῶν ἑκάστη τοῦ μέρους ἐπεδικάσατο τῶν Μενεξένου θυγατέρων* . . . 7 (twelve years later) *ἠμφεσβήτει (Δικαιογένης* III) *ἡμῖν ἅπαντος τοῦ κλήρου, φάσκων ἐφ' ὅλῃ ποιηθῆναι ὑὸς ὑπὸ τοῦ θείου τοῦ ἡμετέρου.* Cf. Lips., *AR* 518.

IV · GUARDIANSHIP

§ 1. *Introduction*

EVIDENCE for the Athenian rules on guardianship is comparatively good. Several surviving speeches are concerned wholly or in their greater part with the subject; in many others it forms an important topic; even more are known only by their titles, yet they too (and possibly two plays of the New Comedy) will have been laid under contribution by lexicographers, who furnish some valuable articles on various aspects of guardianship.[1]

[1] Lys. 32 *Diogeit.*, Isai. 11 *Hagn.*, Dem. 27, 28 *Aphob.* i, ii were delivered in suits directly concerned with guardianship. Dem. 29 *Aphob.* iii (of doubtful authenticity and therefore to be used with caution, cf. p. 105, n. 5, below), 30, 31 *Onet.* i, ii, 36 *For Phorm.*, 38 *Nausim.* are concerned with questions closely related to guardianship. D.H., *Lys.* 20, records that *λόγοι ἐπιτροπικοί* formed a group among the speeches of Lysias; besides his 32 *Diogeit.* which is defective at the end we have some bare titles, *κατὰ Φιλίππου ἐπιτροπῆς* (Harpokr. s.v. *Ἀρκτοῦρος, ζειρά, ὁδός, Πεδιακά*), *πρὸς Θεοπείθη ἐπιτροπῆς ἐπίλογος* (id. s.v. *ἐπιδιατίθεσθαι*, a speech for the defence), *πρὸς τοὺς ἐπιτρόπους τῶν Βόωνος παίδων* (probably in a case brought by guardians in the interest of their ward against a third party, Lips., *AR* 521, n. 4), two speeches for the prosecution in the procedure known as *phasis* (on which see below, pp. 115 ff.), viz., *πρὸς Διογένην* (or as it should probably read *κατὰ Διογένους ὑπὲρ μισθώσεως οἴκου*) and *πρὸς τὴν φάσιν τοῦ ὀρφανικοῦ οἴκου*, and two fragments, one from a speech for the prosecution *κατὰ Δημοσθένους ἐπιτροπῆς* (fr. 27 Th., Harpokr. s.v. *καρποῦ δίκη* quoted p. 223), the other from the beginning of a speech for the defence by a guardian being sued by his wards *πρὸς τοὺς Ἱπποκράτους παῖδας* (fr. 43 Th., D.H., *Isai.* 9). There were also speeches by Antiphon *ἐπιτροπικὸς Καλλιστράτου* (codd., *κατὰ Κ.* Sauppe: Harpokr. s.v. *ὅτι οἱ ποιητοί*) and *ἐπιτροπικὸς τιμοκράτης sive τιμοκράτω* (codd., *κατὰ Τιμοκράτους* Maidment: Harpokr. *Σπάρτωλος*); by Hyperides *κατ' Ἀντίου ὀρφανικός* (Harpokr. s.v. *σεσημασμένων κτλ.*) and *πρὸς Χάρητα ἐπιτροπικός* (id. s.v. *ἐπὶ διετὲς ἡβῆσαι*), for the prosecution and the defence respectively in *δίκαι ἐπιτροπικαί*; by Dinarchos *κατὰ Πεδιέως κακώσεως ὀρφανοῦ παιδός* (genuine according to D.H., *Dein.* 12) and *Σατύρῳ πρὸς Χαρίδημον ἀπολογία* (not genuine, ibid. 13); by Aristogeiton *κατὰ Θρασύλλου ὀρφανικός* (Suda s.v. *Ἀριστογείτων*, probably a single speech, not two, as printed, e.g., by Adler: Lips., *AR* 521, n. 8). Two, possibly three, speeches of Isaios on guardianship are known to us by title or very brief fragments only, viz.: (1) *πρὸς Ἁγνόθεον* (frs. 22, 23 Th.) a speech for the defence against Hagnotheos, the guardian's nephew (Harpokr. s.v. *ἐπισημαίνεσθαι*, D.H., *Isai.* 8 and 12, reading in the former passage of D.H. *τοῦ ἰδίου ἀδελφιδοῦ* for *τῶν ἰδίων ἀδελφῶν* and *Ἁγνόθεον* for *ἀγνοηθέντα*). Harpokr., loc. cit., uses of this speech the words *ἐν τῇ ἐξούλης Καλυδῶνι πρὸς Ἁγνόθεον ἀπολογίᾳ*: there seems no need with E. S. Forster, *Isaeus* (Loeb, p. 446),

The subject falls into two well-defined parts, though there is inevitably some overlapping between them, namely the guardianship of male minors, which terminated when they came of age, and the guardianship of women, which lasted all their lives. Whether there were any changes in the nature of guardianship over women when they came of age and if so what these were are matters of debate.[1]

The normal word for the guardian of a male minor was *ἐπίτροπος*, to be a guardian was *ἐπιτροπεύειν*, and the function was *ἐπιτροπή*, or less frequently *ἐπιτροπεία*.[2] A more general word was *κύριος*, which was the only word for the guardian of a woman, at least after she had reached puberty. Both *ἐπίτροπος* and *κύριος* were used more or less indifferently of control of the person and of control of the property of the ward.[3]

and P. Roussel, *Isée* (Budé, p. 218), to suppose a confusion here; the action might well have been on *res iudicata* in a previous guardianship action; see Lips., *AR* 522, n. 9. (2) *πρὸς Διοφάνην ἐπιτροπῆς ἀπολογία* (frs. 7, 8 Th., Harpokr. s.v. *παρηγγύησεν κτλ.*) another speech for the defence. (3) *πρὸς Καλυδῶνα ἐπιτροπῆς*, Harpokr. s.v. *Κεφαλῆθεν*; in other articles of Harpokr. called simply *πρὸς Καλυδῶνα*, viz., s.vv. *ἀφ' ἑστίας μυεῖσθαι, Ἱππία Ἀθηνᾶ, χρῆσται, Ἀνθεμόκριτος*. Unfortunately in the first article there is a variant, *ἐπιστολῆς* for *ἐπιτροπῆς*. On these fragments see Schulthess, *VAR* 247 ff. There is a fairly long fragment from a speech, perhaps by Hyperides, which appears to be for a ward who was suing his guardian, Demeas, and was being barred by a *παραγραφή* (Ox. Pap. 27 (1962), no. 2464). Finally there was a play called *ἐπίτροπος* by Alexis (Athen. x. 61) and one called *ἐπιτροπή* by Diphilos (*An. Bekk.* (*Ἀντιαττικ.*) 96 s.v. *ἐξιδιάσασθαι*).

[1] Schulthess gave a full account of the legal aspects of the guardianship of male minors in *VAR* and was closely followed by Beauch. ii. 147–380 and Lips., *AR* 520–37, who treat guardianship of women as well. Schulthess brought his views up to date in his article in *RE* s.v. *μίσθωσις*. Cf. also Thalheim, *RE* s.v. *ἐπίτροπος*, Finley, *Land* 38–44, below, pp. 293 ff.

[2] *ἐπίτροπος* and *ἐπιτροπεύειν* first appear in this sense in Hdt. 9. 10 and 1. 65 respectively. For *ἐπιτροπή* of guardianship (it can also mean 'arbitration') see, for example, Dem. 27 *Aphob.* i. 39 *ἐν τοῖς λόγοις τῆς ἐπιτροπῆς*, 30 *Onet.* i. 8 *ὀφλόντος δέ μοι τὴν δίκην Ἀφόβου τῆς ἐπιτροπῆς*. For *ἐπιτροπεία* Lys., fr. 43 Th.

[3] In Aischin. 1 *Timarch.* 18 *κύριος* is used to describe all those, the *ἐπίτροπος* included, who may have personal control of a minor: *ἐνταῦθ' ὁ νομοθέτης οὔπω διαλέγεται αὐτῷ τῷ σώματι τοῦ παιδός, ἀλλὰ τοῖς περὶ τὸν παῖδα, πατρί, ἀδελφῷ, ἐπιτρόπῳ, διδασκάλοις καὶ ὅλως τοῖς κυρίοις*. Ibid. 13. Isai. 1 *Kleonym.* 10 *τὸν ἔχθιστον τῶν οἰκείων ἐπίτροπον καὶ κύριον τῶν αὑτοῦ καταλιπεῖν* seems to intend *ἐπίτροπος* for the person and *κύριος* for the property, since probably *οἰκείων* is masculine and *τῶν αὑτοῦ* neuter (but see Wyse ad loc.): so too Dem. 36 *For Phorm.* 22 *τὸν μὲν παῖδ' ὑπὸ πατρὸς καταλειφθέντα, καὶ οὗ τῶν ὄντων κύριος ἦν, ἐπίτροπος καταλελειμμένος*. Similarly 38 *Nausim.* 6. In Isai. 5 *Dikaiog.* 10 *τούτων [τε] ἅμα καὶ ἐπίτροπος καὶ κύριος καὶ ἀντίδικος ἦν* the word *κύριος* is perhaps added as carrying the special sense of legal representative in court proceedings and thus giving point to the contrast with *ἀντίδικος*. On the other hand, *ἐπίτροπος* is used of control of the property in, for example, Lys., fr. 43 Th. *καταλειφθεὶς ἐπίτροπος τῶν Ἱπποκράτους*

§ 2. *Males*

(i) *Appointment*

We may presume, though the principle never seems to be stated in so many words, that all free males, whether citizen or foreign, were held to be under tutelage until they came of age at the beginning of the official year immediately after they had reached the age of seventeen (or possibly eighteen).[1] So long as the father, whether natural or adoptive, was alive, he naturally exercised this tutelage.[2] When he died, either physically or by total ἀτιμία civilly, his place had to be filled. The simplest method of replacing him, and, where at least there was any considerable property, the most common, was through appointment by the father himself. This power was part of the father's general parental authority (see above, p. 73). The appointment could take place *inter vivos*, but it was no doubt usual to confirm such an appointment by provisions in a will. Thus, according to Demosthenes' graphic story, his father had on his death-bed solemnly entrusted his two children and his property to two nephews and a friend, but he had also made his intentions clear in a will. It is no matter that his opponents seem to have contested the existence of the will; the story clearly presupposes the normality of procedure of this kind.[3] The father was apparently allowed unfettered discretion in his choice of guardians (though possibly at least one of the guardians of a citizen boy had to be himself a citizen);[4] one of the guardians of Demosthenes was not related to him, and a passage in Lysias indicates that appointments

χρημάτων, 32 *Diogeit.* 18 ἀνάξιον τῆς οὐσίας τὸν ἐπίτροπον κατέλιπεν, Dem. 27 *Aphob.* i. 55, D.L. 5. 12 (Aristotle's will).

[1] See above, p. 74, n. 3.

[2] For the possibility that a father's tutelage of sons by an ἐπίκληρος had a special character see p. 74, n. 1, above.

[3] Dem. 28 *Aphob.* ii. 5, 14. For another testamentary guardianship see Dem. 36 *For Phorm.* 8. Diogeiton's guardianship in Lys. 32 *Diogeit.* 5 was conferred *inter vivos*, but confirmed by a will: Bruck, *Schenkung* 123.

[4] This proviso, the existence of which is deduced *a priori*, is denied by Beauch. ii. 191 f. and Hruza, *Beitr.* ii. 129, on the ground that Pasion made his freedman, Phormion, guardian of his son and Phormion acted as such although he only became an Athenian citizen ten years after Pasion's death, Dem. 36 *For Phorm.* 8, 45 *Steph.* i. 3, 46 *Steph.* ii. 13. But the first of these three passages, though it says of Phormion τὸν παῖδ' ἐπετρόπευεν, later refers to οἱ ἐπίτροποι, and in 45 *Steph.* i. 37, ἐμαρτύρησε Νικοκλῆς ἐπιτροπεῦσαι κατὰ τὴν διαθήκην, Nikokles appears to be an active guardian and he may well have been a citizen. Given more than one guardian there would seem no *a priori* reason against and certain reasons in favour of being able to include among them a man of Phormion's standing.

outside the family were not uncommon.[1] When the verb *καταλείπειν* is found either in the active or the passive in conjunction with *ἐπίτροπος* we may infer appointment by the father.[2] The less common but more interesting case was where there had been no such appointment by the father. We may assume, though there is no direct evidence on the point, that the law laid down who was to enjoy the privilege or bear the burden of guardianship in such a case. This is implied in Isai. 10 *Aristarch.* Hyp. 10, *Ἀριστομένης ἀδελφὸς ὢν αὐτοῦ καὶ κατὰ νόμον ἐπίτροπος τῶν τοῦ ἀδελφοῦ γινόμενος παίδων*, and by the titles of two actions which fell to the competence of the archon, *εἰς ἐπιτροπῆς κατάστασιν* and *εἰς ἐπιτροπῆς διαδικασίαν*. The exact nature of these actions will be discussed later, but their existence makes it almost certain that, in the absence of appointment by the father, guardianship devolved on the relatives in an established order. We should expect this order to correspond to the order in which the property would have devolved had there been no surviving children, with the necessary proviso that if this process led to a woman, who in the absence of the ward in question would have been the heiress, she would have to be passed over as being incapable of acting as guardian. This order will be discussed in connexion with the law of succession (pp. 143 ff., below). There was apparently no restriction on the number of guardians; Demosthenes had three and Plato's will provides for seven.[3] If then the rule of

[1] Lys. 32 *Diogeit.* 3 *ἀποδείξω οὕτως αἰσχρῶς αὐτοὺς ἐπιτετροπευμένους ὑπὸ τοῦ πάππου ὡς οὐδεὶς πώποτε ὑπὸ τῶν οὐδὲν προσηκόντων.*

[2] Lys. 32 *Diogeit.* 18 (p. 98, n. 3), ibid. 22, Lys., frs. 43, 75, Th., Dem. 36 *For Phorm.* 22, Plat., *Alk.* i. 104 b *Περικλέα τὸν Ξανθίππου, ὃν ὁ πατὴρ ἐπίτροπον κατέλιπε σοί τε καὶ τῷ ἀδελφῷ*, Plut., *Alk.* 1 *τοῦ Ἀλκιβιάδου Περικλῆς καὶ Ἀρίφρων οἱ Ξανθίππου, προσήκοντες κατὰ γένος, ἐπετρόπευον.*

[3] See p. 99, above; D.L. 3. 43 for Plato's will. Aristotle's will provided *ἐπίτροπον εἶναι πάντων καὶ διὰ παντὸς Ἀντίπατρον* and then for five *ἐπιμεληταί*, D.L. 5. 11–16. In the *Laws* Plato has fairly precise rules on the appointment of guardians (924 a, b): *ᾧ δ' ἂν ἐπιτρόπων οἱ παῖδες δέωνται, ἐὰν μὲν διαθέμενος τελευτᾷ καὶ γράψας ἐπιτρόπους τοῖς παισὶν ἑκόντας τε καὶ ὁμολογοῦντας ἐπιτροπεύσειν οὕστινασοῦν καὶ ὁπόσους ἂν ἐθέλῃ, κατὰ ταῦτα τὰ γραφέντα ἡ τῶν ἐπιτρόπων αἵρεσις γιγνέσθω κυρία· ἐὰν δὲ ἢ τὸ παράπαν μὴ διαθέμενος τελευτήσῃ τις ἢ τῆς τῶν ἐπιτρόπων αἱρέσεως ἐλλιπής, ἐπιτρόπους εἶναι τοὺς ἐγγύτατα γένει πρὸς πατρὸς καὶ μητρὸς κυρίους, δύο μὲν πρὸς πατρός, δύο δὲ πρὸς μητρός, ἕνα δ' ἐκ τῶν τοῦ τελευτήσαντος φίλων, τούτους δ' οἱ νομοφύλακες καθιστάντων τῷ δεομένῳ τῶν ὀρφανῶν*, 766 c *ἐὰν ὀρφανῶν ἐπίτροπος τελευτήσῃ τις, οἱ προσήκοντες καὶ ἐπιδημοῦντες πρὸς πατρὸς καὶ μητρὸς μέχρι ἀνεψιῶν παίδων ἄλλον καθιστάντων ἐντὸς δέκα ἡμερῶν, ἢ ζημιούσθων ἕκαστος δραχμῇ τῆς ἡμέρας, μέχριπερ ἂν τοῖς παισὶν καταστήσωσι τὸν ἐπίτροπον.* Cf. Wyse, *Isai.* 190 f.

next of kin produced several males related to the orphan in the same degree it would have been quite natural for them all to be guardians, provided of course that they were themselves of age, though we do not know whether this was actually the rule. We have evidence of guardians related in various degrees to their wards, but it is seldom possible in any given case to rule out the possibility that the guardian was appointed by the ward's father. Eupolis was the guardian of his brother's son in Isai. 7 *Apollod.* 5 f., but there is nothing to indicate definitely that this was not by will. Diokles, in Isai. 8 *Kir.* 41 f., is guardian of his half-sister's son; it seems unlikely that he had been made guardian by will, since he had recently been in litigation with the ward's father. In the famous case of the estate of Hagnias, Theopompos is guardian of his brother's son (Isai. 11 *Hagn.* 10 ff.); but the fact that there was another guardian, apparently not so related, would suggest that they had both been appointed by the father. Deinias is guardian of his brother's sons, and the language of Isai. 1 *Kleonym.* 9 rather suggests that he was so by virtue of that relationship, but if there had been appointment by the father it would have been in the speaker's interest to pass over the fact.[1] The relationship of Dikaiogenes to his wards in Isai. 5 *Dikaiog.* 10 is too obscure to warrant any inference, even if we could be sure that he too was not appointed by the father.[2] In Lys. 10 *Theomn.* i. 5 Pantaleon is guardian of his younger brothers, whether by appointment or not we cannot say. On the other hand in Lys. 32 *Diogeit.* 9 a guardianship which has become a burden because, according to the speaker's story, the original guardian appointed by the father has dissipated the property is passed on by that guardian to the elder son as soon as he is of age. Another probable instance of a guardianship compulsorily laid upon a man is in Lys. 19 *Prop. Arist.* 9, where the speaker says that he has been forced to bring up the three small children of his sister.[3]

With regard to all these sources of guardianship, whether through appointment by the father *inter vivos* or by will, or through some relative claiming to act simply by virtue of his relationship, or in the absence of any such appointee or claimant,

[1] *Δεινίας ὁ τοῦ πατρὸς ἀδελφὸς ἐπετρόπευσεν ἡμᾶς θεῖος ὢν ὀρφανοὺς ὄντας.*

[2] See Wyse ad loc.

[3] *παιδάρια τρία ἠναγκασμένοι τρέφειν.* There seems no reason to suggest, as does Lips., *AR* 525, n. 22, that this liability was something other than guardianship.

we have the difficult task of determining the role played by the archon. Upon him was laid by a law, of which the exact terms are preserved for us, the duty of looking after (ἐπιμελείσθω) orphans, heiresses, houses which were becoming extinct, and women who remained in the house of a dead husband claiming to be pregnant by him. One passage of Lysias speaks of the archon, loosely perhaps, as κύριος of orphans and heiresses.[1] It is generally agreed that part, perhaps the major part, of the archon's function in this respect was to introduce and preside at all court cases which might arise in connexion with the appointment of guardians and their treatment of their wards whilst the wardship still subsisted (whether he was also in charge of cases brought by a ward after the end of the wardship is discussed on p. 119). The difficult question is how far the archon's duty was more executive than that, at least in the classical period; for we can easily imagine that what had at first been an important executive function had become atrophied with the decline of the power of the archonship so that all that was left was the presidency of the relevant court.[2] The evidence from

[1] For the law Dem. 43 *Makart.* 75 (p. 39, n. 2), 35 *Lakrit.* 48, Aischin. 1 *Timarch.* 158, schol., Dem. 24 *Timokr.* 20, Isai. 7 *Apollod.* 30, Lys. 26 *Euandr.* 12 of an archon, ἐπικλήρων καὶ ὀρφανῶν κύριον γεγενημένον. For possible initiative of the archon in posthumous adoptions see above, p. 92.

[2] The most important piece of evidence bearing on this is the rather mutilated passage in Ar., *Ath. Pol.* 56. 6 and 7. This passage begins by listing γραφαί and δίκαι which fall to the archon: these include ὀρφανῶν κακώσεως (αὗται δ' εἰσὶ κατὰ τῶν ἐπιτρόπων), ἐπικλήρου κακώσε[ως . . . αὗτ]αι δ' εἰσὶ κατὰ τῶν ἐπιτρόπων καὶ τῶν συνοικούντων), οἴκου ὀρφανικοῦ κακώσεως (εἰσὶ δὲ καὶ [αὗται κατὰ τῶν] ἐπιτρόπων), then a little later εἰς ἐπιτροπῆς κατάστασιν, εἰς ἐπιτροπῆς διαδικασίαν, εἰς [ἐμφανῶν κατάστασ]ιν, ἐπίτρ[οπ]ον αὑτὸν ἐγγράψαι, κλήρων καὶ ἐπικλήρων ἐπι[δικασίαι. It seems clear that up to this point it is judicial functions which are being described, though there are some infelicities of expression which conceal the exact nature of the procedure, as, for example, when Aristotle starts using εἰς with the accusative instead of the simple genitive for the content of the action and, more gravely, when he suddenly introduces the accusative and infinitive ἐπίτροπον αὑτὸν ἐγγράψαι, a phrase which might cover both a case where a reluctant guardian had been compelled (through the action of ὁ βουλόμενος?) to take on the guardianship and one where a man had assumed the post of guardian, but his right to hold it had been challenged. The really significant point in the passage, however, is that it continues ἐπιμελεῖτ]αι δὲ καὶ τῶν [ὀρφ]ανῶν καὶ τῶν ἐπικλήρων καὶ τῶν γυναικῶν ὅσαι ἂν τελευτ[ήσαντος τοῦ ἀνδρ]ὸς σκή[πτω]νται κύειν, and this indicates clearly that the archon's duty to look after the interests of orphans, heiresses, and pregnant widows was not confined to his direction of court proceedings. Pollux 8. 89 adds nothing to the evidence of *Ath. Pol.* Wolff in his otherwise enlightening discussion of the distinction between the archon's judicial and extra-judicial functions in *Traditio* 4 (1946), 67 ff. (*Beitr.* 59 ff.) does not deal with the archon's duties *vis-à-vis* orphans.

Aristotle's *Ath. Pol.* in the passage quoted on p. 102, n. 2 favours the view that the archon had significant executive duties towards orphans. We should expect these duties to vary with the circumstances, and we must now examine the scanty evidence outside Aristotle for the archon's function in the several cases.

First there is the case where a father appoints a guardian either *inter vivos* or by will (and we may include here the case where such appointment is made by an already established guardian). Two passages in Isaios have sometimes been taken as proving that a guardian appointed *inter vivos* or by will had to get himself registered as such by the archon before he could act; but in both places more than the simple issue of guardianship is involved, and neither is therefore conclusive.[1] On the other hand, there is a very strong presumption that this step would have been required, for without it the general protection of orphans' interests could not have been even nominally discharged by the archon. We may also presume that some publicity attached to this registration and that this gave opportunity for other claimants to stake their claims, or possibly for objectors to intervene without themselves making a claim. In the former event an *ἐπιτροπῆς διαδικασία* would result, in the latter conceivably a case subsumed under Aristotle's head *ἐπίτροπον αὐτὸν ἐγγράψαι*.

Next we have the case where no provision has been made by the father or a previous guardian. The evidence that in that case the next of kin, whether one or a number, might then claim the guardianship is given above (p. 100). Again we must assume that he or they would have had to follow the same procedure before the archon as did the guardian appointed by the father, with the same possibility of a *διαδικασία* if there were other claimants.

Finally we have the case where neither has provision been made by the father nor does any claimant appear. Here we must assume that in theory at least the initiative would lie with the archon to nominate a guardian. There is some slight evidence (see above, p. 101) that guardianship could be imposed upon a man, and, though no instance can be quoted, it seems most likely that this was done by the archon. Doubtless in making his

[1] Isai. 6 *Philokt.* 36 *ἀπογράφουσι τὼ παῖδε τούτω πρὸς τὸν ἄρχοντα ὡς εἰσποιήτω τοῖς τοῦ Εὐκτήμονος ὑέσι τοῖς τετελευτηκόσιν ἐπιγράψαντες σφᾶς αὐτοὺς ἐπιτρόπους.* 4 *Nikostr.* 8 *Ἀμεινιάδης ὑὸν αὐτῷ πρὸς τὸν ἄρχοντα ἧκεν ἄγων οὐδὲ τρί' ἔτη γεγονότα.* Lips., *AR* 526.

choice he was guided by certain principles, but what these were and how closely he was bound by them we cannot say.[1]

(ii) *Functions of guardians*

A guardian's functions were twofold; they related either to the person or to the property of the ward.[2] First he had to provide for the ward's maintenance (*τροφή, σῖτος*).[3] If he failed in this duty the archon was responsible for bringing him to heel; whether he did so by an executive act or as presiding over a *δίκη σίτου* is not clear. There is some evidence that a *δίκη σίτου* was available against a guardian, but it is not easy to see how such a suit could have been set on foot during a ward's minority except where one guardian proceeded against a co-guardian (see below).[4] Besides physical maintenance, which in an account presented by a guardian in Lys. 32 *Diogeit.* 20 included clothing, shoes, laundry, and hair-cutting as well as food, the guardian was expected to provide for his ward's education. Thus in Lys., op. cit. 28 the guardian includes in his expenditure account money for a *παιδαγωγός*, and if we are to believe Demosthenes his guardians engaged teachers for him, though they bilked them of their pay.[5] There seems to have been a view as to what was a reasonable sum to spend on these objects: thus the speaker in Lysias (loc. cit.) reckons that 1,000 drachmai a year would be a generous figure for bringing up two boys and a girl. An important element in

[1] If the first sentence from Plato's *Laws* 924 a quoted in p. 100, n. 3, above, reflects Athenian practice, a guardian appointed by will could decline (*ἑκόντας τε καὶ ὁμολογοῦντας ἐπιτροπεύσειν*). Here too the archon would have had to act; maybe he could compel the reluctant guardian, if as might well be he was related to the ward, to take up a joint guardianship with other relatives. Lips., *AR* 526, fails to raise this issue. On the archon's powers in general with regard to guardians see Bo. Sm. ii. 102 ff.

[2] Dem. 27 *Aphob.* i. 6 *οὗτοι . . . τὴν ἄλλην οὐσίαν ἅπασαν διαχειρίσαντες καὶ δέκα ἔτη ἡμᾶς ἐπιτροπεύσαντες.*

[3] Lys. 32 *Diogeit.* 9, Dem. 27 *Aphob.* i. 36.

[4] Ar., *Ath. Pol.* 56. 7 *καὶ τοὺς ἐπιτρόπους, ἐὰν μὴ διδῶσι τοῖς παισὶ τὸν σῖτον, οὗτος* (sc. *ὁ ἄρχων*) *εἰσπράττει. An. Bekk.* (*Λέξ. Ῥητ.*) 238 *δίκην σίτου: ὄνομα δίκης. συνίσταται δὲ ἡ δίκη κατὰ τῶν ἐπιτρόπων τῶν οὐ τελούντων σῖτον καὶ τροφὰς τοῖς ὀρφανοῖς καὶ ταῖς τούτων μητράσιν.* The passage from the *Ath. Pol.* disposes of the doubt expressed by Schultess, *VAR* 91, whether the *δίκη σίτου* was available against guardians. See further p. 119, below. For the *δίκη σίτου* in connexion with dowries see above, p. 59, and Harpokr. s.v. *σῖτος* quoted p. 57, n. 2.

[5] Dem. 27 *Aphob.* i. 46 *τοὺς διδασκάλους τοὺς μισθοὺς ἀπεστέρηκεν.* Perikles, as guardian of Alkibiades, provided Zopyros, an aged slave, as his *παιδαγωγός*: Plato, *Alk.* i. 122 a.

a guardian's relation to the person of his ward was his control over the ward's domicile. Lys. 32 *Diogeit.* affords clear evidence that Diogeiton was free to determine the domicile of his wards and incidentally that he was under no obligation to secure that they still lived with their mother. Perikles, as guardian of Kleinias, made him for a time go to live with Ariphron in order to remove him from the corrupting influence of his brother Alkibiades.[1] Often the ward would have lived with his guardian, an arrangement especially appropriate when the guardian had married the ward's mother and become his stepfather.[2]

We know rather more about a guardian's duties in relation to the property of his ward. The normal word for his control over that property, κύριος, implies a pretty wide discretion; but there were of course limits to the exercise of that discretion.[3] The most general limit was the obligation placed on the guardian to render an account at the end of his guardianship. For this general accountability the suit of Demosthenes against his guardians provides the best evidence, though there are several references to it elsewhere.[4] It is important to note that the account is rendered, not as one might have supposed to the archon, but directly to the ward. It is less easy to define what conditions the guardian had to satisfy in rendering the account. One thing is clear: a testator who appointed a guardian in his will could give him instructions on how to deal with the ward's property. He could, for example, direct that the estate as a whole (οἶκος) should be leased by the procedure known as μίσθωσις οἴκου. In default of such instruction there is evidence to show that the guardian could use his own discretion in the matter.[5] Something is said about this

[1] Lys., op. cit. 8, 14, 16, Plato, *Prot.* 320 a. Schulthess, *VAR* 92 ff.

[2] We can reject out of hand the authenticity of a law attributed to Solon in D.L. 1. 56 which forbade a guardian to marry his ward's mother or a man to become guardian if he stood to inherit from the ward in the event of his death. See p. 24, n. 1, above.

[3] Isai. 1 *Kleonym.* 10 Deinias is spoken of as κύριος τῆς οὐσίας of his ward's property. Dem. 28 *Aphob.* ii. 16 κύριος τῶν ἐμῶν γενόμενος ἐπὶ τούτοις (conditions laid down, Demosthenes contended, in a will), 36 *For Phorm.* 22 οὗ τῶν ὄντων κύριος ἦν, ἐπίτροπος καταλελειμμένος, 38 *Nausim.* 6.

[4] Dem. 27, 28 *Aphob.* i, ii *passim*, 38 *Nausim.* 14, 15, 36 *For Phorm.* 20 ὁ Πασικλῆς ἀνὴρ γεγονὼς ἐκομίζετο τὸν λόγον τῆς ἐπιτροπῆς, 30 *Onet.* i. 15 ἐγὼ δὲ . . . δοκιμασθεὶς ἐνεκάλουν καὶ λόγον ἀπῄτουν. Cf. pp. 119 ff., below.

[5] On this see O. Schulthess, *RE* s.v. μίσθωσις 2111 ff. The procedure is described in Isai. 6 *Philokt.* 36 ff. Note two points in this passage: the final decision whether the estate was to be leased or not rested with a dikastery, and the putative guardians

procedure in connexion with ἀποτίμημα (pp. 293 ff.). The lease of the estate was auctioned by the archon. The lessee undertook to pay a certain rate of interest for the maintenance of the ward and to surrender the estate at his coming of age. The guardian could himself bid for the lease. The bidder in this 'auction', if it is properly so called, had to satisfy the court that the security he offered for the eventual return of the estate was adequate; subject to that presumably he who offered the largest return was awarded the lease. This rules out the suggestion which has been made that there was a rate of interest laid down by law for such leases.[1] It may well be that, even where leasing had not been

were allowed to bid for the lease. Dem. 27 *Aphob.* i. 40 ἐν ἐκείναις (ταῖς διαθήκαις) ἐγέγραπτο . . .· τὸν οἶκον ὅπως μισθώσουσι. Cf. ibid. 58–60; 28 *Aphob.* ii. 15, of the elder Demosthenes on his death-bed, ἐπισκήπτων μισθῶσαί τε τὸν οἶκον καὶ διασῶσαί μοι τὴν οὐσίαν. That where there were no instructions in a will μίσθωσις οἴκου was permissive, not obligatory, is shown by the words used by the speaker in Lys. 32 *Diogeit.* 23 ἐξῆν αὐτῷ κατὰ τοὺς νόμους οἳ κεῖνται περὶ τῶν ὀρφανῶν καὶ τοῖς ἀδυνάτοις τῶν ἐπιτρόπων καὶ τοῖς δυναμένοις, μισθῶσαι τὸν οἶκον ἀπηλλαγμένον πολλῶν πραγμάτων, ἢ γῆν πριάμενον ἐκ τῶν προσιόντων τοὺς παῖδας τρέφειν and by Demosthenes in 27 *Aphob.* i. 58 τούτῳ γὰρ ἐξῆν μηδὲν ἔχειν τούτων τῶν πραγμάτων μισθώσαντι τὸν οἶκον κατὰ τουτουσὶ τοὺς νόμους: the speakers could hardly have used ἐξῆν if there had been a rule which imposed leasing. The only evidence to the contrary is in Dem. 29 *Aphob.* iii. 29 τὸν οἶκον οὐκ ἐμίσθωσεν τῶν νόμων κελευόντων καὶ τοῦ πατρὸς ἐν τῇ διαθήκῃ γράψαντος. This speech is sometimes rejected as a late rhetorical exercise, as for example by Finley, *Land* 235, following Lipsius, *AR* 523, n. 12, 822, n. 68 (though Lipsius inconsistently makes frequent use of the speech as evidence, e.g. on p. 533, n. 62 for the very point on which he denies its validity on p. 822), Schulthess, *VAR* 225, *RE* 2112. G. M. Calhoun, *TAPA* 65 (1934), 80–102, regards the speech as genuine, and Gernet, *Dem.* i. 63 ff., though he does not think the speech was delivered as it stands, suggests that it contains material amassed for use in speeches by Demosthenes himself. Finley uses this passage as conclusive against the genuineness of the speech, pointing out justly that the two genuine speeches against Aphobos assume that leasing was merely permissive. It may be, however, that the writer of these words was not guilty of the blunder attributed to him; it is odd that he should say 'the law bade him *and* my father had given instructions in his will', since any reader must ask why the father had needed to give these instructions; possibly then καί has here the sense of *id est*; the law so ordered *because* the father had given these instructions. See p. 59, above. For the general binding effect of the instructions in a will Dem. 45 *Steph.* i. 37 ἐμαρτύρησε μὲν Νικοκλῆς ἐπιτροπεῦσαι κατὰ τὴν διαθήκην, ἐμαρτύρησε δὲ Πασικλῆς ἐπιτροπευθῆναι κατὰ τὴν διαθήκην. Dem. 36 *For Phorm.* 8 shows the guardians departing from the terms of the will in order to protect the interests of their ward against the depredations upon the estate of his elder brother.

[1] Demosthenes quotes a case where the lessee of an estate worth 3 talents and 3,000 drachmai had paid over more than 6 talents to his ward after a guardianship of six years and argues from it that his own guardians, who had in defiance of the will not leased out his father's estate, ought during their ten years of guardianship to have trebled the original 14 talents: Dem. 27 *Aphob.* i. 58 f. κατὰ τούτους τοὺς νόμους Ἀντιδώρῳ μὲν ἐκ τριῶν ταλάντων καὶ τριχιλίων ἐν ἓξ ἔτεσιν ἓξ τάλαντα καὶ

prescribed in a will, it was the simplest and safest procedure for a guardian, as is suggested in the passage from Lys. 32 *Diogeit.* 23 quoted on p. 105, n. 5, above. We should naturally conjecture that the lessee would have the procedural rights necessary to maintain his control over the property during the lease, and this conjecture gains some support from a rather difficult passage in Isaios.[1]

Supposing the guardian elected to keep the estate in his own hands, his control over it was fairly wide, though subject to certain limitations. The last few words quoted in p. 105, n. 5, above, from Lys. 32 *Diogeit.* 23 (ἢ γῆν πριάμενον ἐκ τῶν προσιόντων τοὺς παῖδας τρέφειν) can certainly not be pressed to imply that a guardian was bound to invest any cash that formed part of the estate in land, nor does Lys. F 91 Th. support such a rule (see n. 3 on this page). In fact a clause in Plato's will banning the sale of land implies that without such a ban land forming part of the estate could be sold.[2] The limitations were upon the purposes for which cash could be lent. Lys. F 91 Th. just mentioned, if it is a correct statement of the law, means that a guardian was forbidden to lend his ward's money on any but landed security, bottomry loans being specifically excluded.[3] The general duty of the guardian to manage the property in the interests of his ward could be enforced, in theory at least, by the quite wide powers entrusted to the archon to protect orphans.[4]

πλέον ἐκ τοῦ μισθωθῆναι παρεδόθη. There is nothing in these or the succeeding sections to justify the view that there was a percentage prescribed by law. Demosthenes is simply giving an example of what might reasonably be expected. Schulthess, *VAR* 150 ff., Lips., *AR* 347, n. 27. We are not told whether Antidoros' guardians had had to provide for his maintenance as well during the six years: Beauch. ii. 250 assumes not.

[1] 11 *Hagn.* 34. Theopompos, referring to a piece of property which he was accused by his fellow guardian of having filched from their ward, says εἰ δὲ . . . φησι . . . ἤδη εἶναι ταῦτα τοῦ παιδός, ἀπογραψάσθω πρὸς τὸν ἄρχοντα εἰς τὴν μίσθωσιν τῶν ἐκείνου χρημάτων, ἣν ὁ μισθωσάμενος εἰσπράξει με ταῦτα ὡς ὄντα τοῦ παιδός. Unlikely as it may be that any lessee would have come forward in such circumstances we need not doubt that, had he done so, his procedural rights would have been as stated.

[2] D.L. 3. 41.

[3] Suda s.v. ἔγγειον (below, p. 228, n. 3). But Finley, *Land* 235, holds with Gernet, *Lys.* 2. 183, n. 3, that the cases of Diogeiton and Aphobos show that maritime loans were permissible and that this quotation is therefore in some way misleading.

[4] Dem. 43 *Makart.* 75 quoted on p. 39, n. 2: if anyone insults, or commits any unlawful act against, one of the protected parties the archon can fine him up to the allowed limit, or if he thinks a larger penalty appropriate can bring him before a court with a proposal for a penalty. The experience of Demosthenes, however, if

The accountability of the guardians is dealt with below (pp. 119 ff.).

Common to the guardian's responsibility for the person and for the property of the ward was his duty to represent him in every kind of legal transaction. His duties in this respect corresponded exactly with those of a father towards his sons during their minority.[1] The ward could not enter into any contract during his minority, nor could he defend himself in court either actively as plaintiff or passively as defendant against attacks on either his person or his property. In all these respects his guardian had to act for him.[2] He had also to act for his ward *vis-à-vis* the public treasury with regard to the property tax known as εἰσφορά, the only direct tax to which minors would be liable.[3] Finally he was required to perform on his ward's behalf such funeral rites as the latter would have had to carry out if he had been of age.[4]

§ 3. *Females*

(i) *Introduction*

There can be no doubt that a woman remained under some sort of tutelage during the whole of her life. She could not enter into any but the most trifling contract, she could not engage her own hand in marriage, and she could not plead her own case in court. In all these relations action was taken on her behalf by her κύριος, and this was so during her whole life.[5] Had the Athenians been more tidy in their juridical terminology we should have expected to find that when the woman reached a certain age laid down by law the man who was in control of her was transformed from her ἐπίτροπος into her κύριος; or alternatively that a man was described as ἐπίτροπος of a woman as long as she was unmarried, but became her κύριος if he married her. Unfortunately

his account of it is to be accepted and if it was at all typical, indicates that unscrupulous guardians could evade the protective activities of the archon.

[1] For a father's duties see pp. 70 and 73, n. 3, above.

[2] Aischin. 1 *Timarch.* 16 (though this quotation of a law may not be genuine: see Lips., *AR* 422) and a speech 'against the guardians of the children of Boön' which was probably delivered in a case brought by guardians in the interest of their wards (p. 97, n. 1, above).

[3] Dem. 27 *Aphob.* i. 7, 28 *Aphob.* ii. 4, 8.

[4] Isai. 1 *Kleonym.* 10.

[5] For the limitation on a woman's right of contract Isai. 10 *Aristarch.* 10 (p. 73, n. 3, above); for disposal of her hand in marriage, p. 19, above; for her representation in court, schol. Aristoph., *Kn.* 965 (p. 32, n. 2, above).

we do not find any such sharp distinction of terms, though some modern writers have assumed that we do.[1] Yet there must have been some distinction between the relation of a guardian to a male and to a female ward, if only owing to the fact that the female ward could never become a full person in her own right and in particular could never be the uninhibited owner of property, though if she were or became an ἐπίκληρος she was the human vehicle, as it were, through which property passed. We must therefore attempt to distinguish where we can, with rather inadequate evidence, rules which applied specifically to the guardianship of women.

(ii) *Appointment*

So long as he was alive a woman's father exercised parental authority over her, including the right to give her in marriage by ἐγγύη and probably also to terminate her marriage; during the marriage the woman's husband was her κύριος (see above, pp. 30 f.).[2] The father's right to transmit this authority to another either

[1] E. Hafter, *Erbtochter* 30 ff. Beauch. ii. 325 ff. spends some rather fruitless pages of speculation on this subject. Lips., *AR* 534, speaks of a transition from minority guardianship (*Altersvormundschaft*) to the power of the κύριος and suggests that there was a fixed age for this viz., the age at which a girl was ripe for marriage. Isai. 6 *Philokt.* 13 f., however, makes this improbable: there Androkles has alleged that Euktemon had had two sons by Kallippe, ἐξ ἐπιτροπευομένης δὲ τούτω γενέσθαι: to this the speaker answers that Kallippe must have been at least thirty when these sons were born and goes on ὥστ' οὔτ' ἐπιτροπεύεσθαι προσῆκε τὴν Καλλίππην ἔτι, τριακοντοῦτίν γε οὖσαν, οὔτε ἀνέκδοτον καὶ ἄπαιδα εἶναι, where the point surely is, not, as Lips., loc. cit., would have it, that a girl could not legally be ἐπιτροπευομένη at the age of 30 (what would then be the point of the words οὔτε ἀνέκδοτον κτλ?), but the somewhat sophistic one that no girl was likely to remain unmarried to the age of 30; all that the passage shows is that a girl, once married, would not be described any more as ἐπιτροπευομένη. Beauch. ii. 328 is on the right lines, though at the end his account is vitiated by his mistaken view that the husband was not κύριος of his wife. Wyse ad loc. makes the mistake of assuming that ἐπιτροπευομένη must have had the normal connotation of being an orphan minor, though we have no clear indication of what minority indicated in the case of women, so that this is really a *petitio principii*. An important point, which will have to be discussed when we come to deal with the ἐπίκληρος, is whether a girl became ἐπίδικος on her father's death, however young she was; or whether she was only as it were a potential ἐπίκληρος until she reached an age when she could in fact marry. If the former was the rule the successful claimant to her hand was her guardian till she attained puberty, though it must be noted that he himself might be a minor, in which case *his* guardian would presumably have been guardian of the ἐπίκληρος also. If the rule was that her hand could only be claimed at puberty, we have no evidence as to how her guardian was appointed. See p. 138, below.

[2] It is possible, but not probable, that the son of an ἐπίκληρος became her κύριος when he came of age. See p. 113, below.

inter vivos or by will is not so plainly attested for daughters as for sons, though it is highly probable. The issue is complicated by the law quoted in Dem. 46 *Steph.* ii. 18 to which we had to refer several times in considering ἐγγύη.[1] This law is primarily concerned to define the conditions required for a woman to be regarded as ἐγγυητή for the purpose of giving birth to legitimate children; to this end it specifies those who are entitled to give her hand in marriage; in the first group come father, brother by the same father, paternal grandfather; if none of these is alive and if she is an ἐπίκληρος the man who claims her as nearest of kin becomes her κύριος but must marry her;[2] if she is not an heiress she falls under the power of the man appointed by her father (who perhaps stands here as representative of the other two kin in the first group, i.e. if the father failed to appoint the brother could, and failing him the grandfather). On this, in itself highly problematical, interpretation of the law it is not easy to determine whether it is dealing with testacy or intestacy. As far as the words τὸν κύριον ἔχειν it seems to be dealing with intestacy, and it does not contemplate a case where a father, though survived by his son or his own father, had made other provision for the guardianship of his daughter. But when it comes to the case of a girl who has no father, brother, or paternal grandfather alive and who, not being an heiress, does not have her κύριος decided for her by the process of ἐπιδικασία, there seems to be an assumption that the father has appointed a κύριος for her; at any rate the law makes no provision for the case where he has not.[3] Whatever be the correct interpretation of this law, we have in Demosthenes' sister a clear case of a girl's hand being disposed of in her father's will and in his mother a case of a husband disposing of the hand of his wife. Probably the two women were to be under the tutelage of the three guardians until the marriages could be completed. Pasion bestowed his wife on Phormion by

[1] Text quoted on p. 5, n. 2, above: cf. also pp. 19, 20, n. 2.

[2] If a girl became ἐπίδικος only on reaching puberty her guardian might change at that point, but it is not easy to see who it would have been before her marriage. See p. 109, above.

[3] Cf. p. 20, n. 1, above. It is significant that, if the law is correctly quoted, the right, or as it was more likely to be regarded, the duty, of giving in marriage the hand of a girl who was not an heiress did not extend to the kin beyond brothers by the same father and paternal grandfather. We must suppose that cases where none of these relatives had acted either directly by giving her in marriage or by directions in wills were sufficiently rare to be passed over by the legislator.

will.[1] Where a marriage was dissolved by the husband's death and he had not disposed of his wife's hand she would, if she were childless, naturally revert to the power of her original κύριος or his heirs. If, however, she claimed to be pregnant by her husband she could, or perhaps she was bound to, remain in her husband's house, being under the tutelage of the man who would become guardian of the child when born; this could, of course, be an older brother of the child in the event of there being one who was not still a minor; such an older brother might be a son or a step-son of the woman. If she already had sons by her husband she could again probably elect to stay in his house and be under their tutelage or that of their guardian. In any of these cases her action would have been to some extent determined by the presence or absence of a dowry. A dowry was in certain circumstances returnable to him who had provided it, and in such a case the woman whose dowry it was would naturally come again under the tutelage of her original κύριος.[2]

(iii) *Functions of guardians*

Here again we may consider the guardian's duties in relation first to the person of his ward and secondly in relation to property connected with her—to speak of *her* property in this connexion would be to beg an important question.

A duty to provide maintenance and education and a right to determine domicile existed in relation to a female, just as to a male, ward (for these see pp. 104 f., above). There were two main points of difference in a guardian's relations to the person of a female ward. In the first place the duty of maintenance did not automatically come to an end at a determined date, the ward's coming of age. We must presume—and it is a presumption —that it only terminated with her marriage.[3] Secondly, a woman's

[1] Cf. above, pp. 6 ff., 19, 30.

[2] On these various possibilities see above, pp. 20, 38, 44; for the dowry pp. 45, 46, n. 1, 55 ff. Note especially Dem. 40 *Boiot.* ii. 6 f. where a woman, having borne three daughters and one son to a certain Kleomedon, on the death of Kleomedon returns with her dowry to her own house and is then married off by two of her brothers to a second husband with the same dowry. Beauch. ii. 335 ff. puts the possibilities clearly, but see p. 109, n. 1, above. He argues strongly for understanding ὁ ἄρχων as subject of ἐπιτρέψῃ in Dem. 46 *Steph* ii. 18. Lipsius's treatment of this difficulty in *AR* 536 is a little cavalier.

[3] Cf. p. 109, n. 1. In the case there quoted from Isai. 6 *Philokt.* 13 there is the legal possibility, though it is dismissed by the speaker as a practical impossibility, that a woman might be still a ward at the age of thirty.

guardian had the supremely important right and duty to dispose of his ward's hand in marriage. This topic has been dealt with fully under Marriage.[1]

Where property was in question we have to ask first of all in what sense, if at all, a woman could own property; or perhaps rather, since the concept of ownership was apt to mislead in Athenian law (see p. 201), in what degree and in what circumstances a woman could exercise control of property.[2] Things might become the quasi-property of women in a number of ways. First by gift: a general instance of gifts to women would be what were known as ἀνακαλυπτήρια, gifts to newly wed brides from their husbands or relatives which were distinct from the dowry and were in some special but ill-defined sense the property of the woman. Lysias appears to have devoted some argument in a lost speech to discussing whether such gifts were to be 'in the firm possession' of the woman. We may have a concrete instance of such a gift from Pasion to his wife Archippe mentioned in the last clause of his will.[3] With regard to such strictly personal effects we may conjecture that morally they were regarded as belonging to the woman; that her right to do with them what she would ought to have been defended on her behalf, if necessary by proceedings in court, by her guardian against third parties; but that if her guardian himself chose to interfere with her possession of them in his own interests or proved unwilling to take action against third parties on her behalf she would have little hope of redress, unless, if she were an ἐπίκληρος, by means of an εἰσαγγελία κακώσεως.[4] A second possible source of quasi-property

[1] See especially pp. 5 ff., 12, 17 f. with the suggestion on p. 19 that when an ἐπίκληρος was assigned a κύριος by ἐπιδικασία the κύριος in this case and this case only was not at liberty to dispose of her hand freely, but had to marry her himself. For a different view Beauch. ii. 341.

[2] On women's capacity to own see p. 236.

[3] Theon, *Progymn.* 2. (Spengel ii. 69. 7) ἐν τῷ περὶ τῶν ἀνακαλυπτηρίων ἐπιγραφομένῳ Λυσίου ζητεῖται εἰ τὰ δοθέντα ἀνακαλυπτήρια γυναικὶ γαμουμένῃ βεβαίως ἔχειν αὐτὴν δεῖ. Dem. 45 *Steph.* i. 28 after provision for the dowry of Archippe and her ἐγγύη to Phormion the will closes with these words καὶ τἄλλα ὅσα ἐστὶν αὐτῇ ἔνδον, ἅπαντα ταῦτα Ἀρχίππῃ δίδωμι. As Gernet, *Dem.* ii. 163, points out, it is not clear whether Pasion is confirming Archippe in possession of these things or giving them to her by this act; but in any case it is assumed that in some sense she will now possess them as her own. Cf. on ἀνακαλυπτήρια in general E. Gerner, *Beiträge zum Recht der Parapherna* (*Münch. Beitr.*, Hft. 38 (1954), 39 ff.).

[4] Ar., *Ath. Pol.* 56. 6, makes it fairly certain that the only woman who could rely on a γραφὴ κακώσεως was an ἐπίκληρος. Lips., *AR* 342 f. Cf. p. 117.

rights accruing to women was by means of intestate succession. This topic must be reserved for fuller consideration under the Law of Succession. Here it must suffice to say, first, that, as in many other respects, the *ἐπίκληρος* stood in a different relation to the property with which she was connected than any other class of woman. While her guardian up to her marriage and her husband on her marriage[1] had control of the income from the property, though being under a duty to provide for her maintenance out of it, the property passed to the son or sons of the *ἐπίκληρος* when they came of age and with it the duty to provide for the maintenance of the *ἐπίκληρος*; whether control of the person of the *ἐπίκληρος* also passed to her sons at this stage is a difficult question which will be discussed fully later. The probability is that it did not.[2] In the second place a woman might have a claim to property on intestacy without being an *ἐπίκληρος*. If she had brothers they shared out the father's estate, and it is doubtful if she even had a right to be dowered out of it.[3] But a woman without brothers might be entitled to inherit from a relative other than her father, and if she did it is fairly certain that she was not technically an *ἐπίκληρος*.[4] Similarly a woman might, without becoming an *ἐπίκληρος*, receive a gift under a will or a gift *inter vivos*. Finally, her dowry was in some sense *hers*. In

[1] For the possibility that these might not be the same person see p. 109.

[2] Dem. 46 *Steph.* ii. 20 *ΝΟΜΟΣ. καὶ ἐὰν ἐξ ἐπικλήρου τις γένηται καὶ ἅμα ἡβήσῃ ἐπὶ δίετες, κρατεῖν τῶν χρημάτων, τὸν δὲ σῖτον μετρεῖν τῇ μητρί.* When the speaker goes on *οὐκοῦν ὁ μὲν νόμος κελεύει τοὺς παῖδας ἡβήσαντας κυρίους τῆς μητρὸς εἶναι* he is probably putting an unjustified gloss on the law. Isai. 8 *Kir.* 31 *εἰ γὰρ ἔζη μὲν ἡ ἐμὴ μήτηρ, θυγάτηρ δὲ Κίρωνος, μηδὲν δὲ ἐκεῖνος διαθέμενος ἐτελεύτησεν, ἦν δὲ ἀδελφὸς οὗτος αὐτῷ, μὴ ἀδελφιδοῦς, συνοικῆσαι μὲν ἂν τῇ γυναικὶ κύριος ἦν, τῶν δὲ χρημάτων οὐκ ἄν, ἀλλ' οἱ γενόμενοι ἐκ τούτου καὶ ἐξ ἐκείνης, ὁπότε ἐπὶ δίετες ἥβησαν· οὕτω γὰρ οἱ νόμοι κελεύουσιν*: this speaker distinguishes between the sons' control of their mother's property and of her person. Cf. Isai. 10 *Arist.* 12, 3 *Pyrrh.* 50, fr. 25 Th. *ἡγούμεθα γὰρ ἐκείνῃ μὲν τὸν ἐγγυτάτω γένους δεῖν συνοικεῖν, τὰ δὲ χρήματα τέως μὲν τῆς ἐπικλήρου εἶναι, ἐπειδὰν δὲ παῖδες ἐπὶ διετὲς ἡβήσωσιν, ἐκείνους αὐτῶν κρατεῖν*, Hyper., fr. 192 J. *ap.* Harpokr. s.v. *ἐπιδιετὲς ἡβῆσαι· ὁ νόμος . . . ὃς κελεύει κυρίους εἶναι τῆς ἐπικλήρου καὶ τῆς οὐσίας ἁπάσης τοὺς παῖδας, ἐπειδὰν ἐπιδιετὲς ἡβῶσιν*: we cannot press this as evidence that the sons always became guardians of their mother when they came of age, since, as Lips., *AR* 537, n. 80, points out, the father may well have been dead. Cf. Gernet, *RÉG* 34 (1921), 365.

[3] See above, p. 48.

[4] Some scholars, for example, Beauch. i. 415 ff., hold that a woman was not an *ἐπίκληρος* if at the time of her father's death she had alive a brother or paternal grandfather, even if the brother subsequently died without issue or the grandfather died without any other issue. More of this below in connexion with the *epiklerate*; pp. 136 ff. See also above, pp. 9 ff.

all these cases of women who were not ἐπίκληροι but had some entitlement to property we are faced with the difficult question of the powers and duties of their guardians in regard to the property. On control of the dowry sufficient has been said above (pp. 52 ff.). As to other kinds of property we are more in the dark. We may perhaps discount a passage in Demosthenes where a woman makes a loan of 1,800 drachmai; the consent of her κύριος is not mentioned, but there is no compelling reason why it should have been. Nor need we attach much importance to passages from comedy in which women appear to be transacting business on their own.[1] On the whole it seems best to suppose that the law quoted above (p. 73, n. 3) held good and that for any important transaction concerning property the woman would have had to proceed through her guardian. Subject to his consent there is no reason to think that there were any legal restrictions on what she could do with the property, though this is to some extent tied up with the question whether women could bequeath property by will.[2] It is difficult to say how far the consent of the κύριος had become a formality in the fourth century; on the whole it would seem likely that it remained, as a rule, considerably more than this, though obviously in individual cases much would have depended on the force of character of the woman on one side and the guardian on the other.[3]

A woman's guardian had the same general duty to represent her in court as did a man's, whether it was a question of defending her person or her property (above, p. 108). But here once again the position of the ἐπίκληρος was anomalous; for in that

[1] In Dem. 41 *Spoud.* 9, 22 the widow of Polyeuktos lends her son-in-law 1,800 drachmai and the loan is recorded in γράμματα; her brothers are present as witnesses, and it may be that they were in fact assenting κύριοι, though this is not stated. Passages such as Aristoph., *Thesm.* 839 ff., *Ekkl.* 446 ff., where women appear to be transacting business quite freely, are not to be pressed. Nikarete, wife of Hippias, who appears as buyer and seller of young girls in Dem. 59 *Neair.* 18 ff., was not an Athenian, and in referring to one of the sales at least the speaker mentions that it was made under the law of Corinth (loc. cit. 29). Aischin. 1 *Timarch.* 107, though it speaks of women managing property, is self-contradictory and rhetorical.

[2] See below, p. 151.

[3] For the κύριος in other Greek states see Beasley, *CR* 20 (1906) 249 ff. *IJ* 1. vii, 64: in the register of Tenos father, brother, son, and even grandson appear as women's κύριοι: for Amorgos, *IJ* 1. viii, nos. 64, 65, pp. 117 ff. (Finley, Horoi nos. 8, 9). Aristoph., *Plout.* 982 ff., Dem. 40 *Boiot.* ii. 10 for acquisitions of property by women.

very important action which concerned her marriage (ἐπιδικασία) she was the object rather than the subject of rights, and we can find no indication of her being represented in her own right in the proceedings, save in so far as the archon himself had a general duty to protect her.[1]

§ 4. *Actions*

Actions for the defence of the rights of wards fall into two broad groups which may be described as public and private. There is also here at times the need to distinguish cases where the ward was a female. The mark of the public case is that it can be set on foot by any citizen competent to appear in court; such a procedure was, of course, particularly apt for the protection of those who were not in a position to plead in court themselves. There were two main forms of public procedure relevant here, known under the general terms of φάσις and εἰσαγγελία.

(i) φάσις

Our evidence for this procedure is scanty. Two lost speeches of Lysias may have been for the prosecution in cases of *phasis* (p. 97, n. 1, above). These perhaps gave something for the grammarians to work on; but their contributions are somewhat muddled. We have also a few scattered references in Demosthenes, which will be noted as occasion arises.[2]

We are concerned with a particular type of *phasis* here, namely φάσις ὀρφανικοῦ οἴκου, but there are some features of the procedure as such which must be mentioned first. In the first place it was an informant's procedure; as a γραφή was initiated by ὁ βουλόμενος a φάσις was initiated by ὁ φαίνων.[3] The implication is that here is a wrong which the wronged party may not be in a position to bring before a court, but which the state feels to be sufficiently serious to allow some other person to act against the

[1] For the ἐπιδικασία see above, pp. 91 ff., and further below on the *epiklerate*, pp. 158 ff.

[2] Schulthess, *VAR* 209 ff., *RE* s.v. μίσθωσις 2113 (withdrawing his views on φάσις as expressed in *VAR*), Beauch. ii. 294 ff., Lips., *AR* 309 ff., E. Berneker, *RE* 19^2 (1938), 1896 s.v. φάσις.

[3] Dem. 38 *Nausim.* 23 οὐκ ἐμίσθωσαν τὸν οἶκον, ἴσως ἐροῦσιν. οὐ γὰρ ἐβούλεθ' ὁ θεῖος ὑμῶν Ξενοπείθης, ἀλλὰ φήναντος Νικίδου τοὺς δικαστὰς ἔπεισεν ἐᾶσαι αὐτὸν διοικεῖν.

wrongdoer. There is an important difference between certain types at least of *φάσις*—whether our type was one of these is open to discussion—and other public suits; in the former the prosecutor received one-half of the goods forfeited by a convicted defendant or one-half of the penalty imposed on him.[1] On the other hand the prosecutor had in certain types of *φάσις* to deposit a court fee equal to the amount he stood to gain if he proved successful, which he forfeited if he was not.[2] He was also subject, probably in every type, to a penalty of 1,000 drachmai and to partial *atimia* if he did not secure one-fifth of the jurors' votes, and to a like penalty if he failed to bring the case before the court after making his denunciation.[3] The charge in a *φάσις ὀρφανικοῦ οἴκου* was probably that a guardian had failed to put up his ward's estate for leasing by the archon when he had been so instructed in a will or that he had acted in some fraudulent way in connexion with the leasing.[4] It is unlikely that any other

[1] Dem. 58 *Theokr.* 13 *ἐξόν . . . τὰ ἡμίσεα τῶν φανθέντων λαβεῖν*. The reference here is to a case of information against breach of the law imposing on merchants the duty of importing corn to Attica; but that this provision also applied to our type of case is rendered probable by the fact that Plato, *Laws* 928 c, ordains of the penalty for wrongs against orphans *γιγνέσθω τὸ μὲν ἥμισυ τοῦ παιδός, τὸ δὲ ἥμισυ τοῦ καταδικασαμένου τὴν δίκην*.

[2] This rule applied in all types, if we assume that the provisions of a law quoted in Dem. 43 *Makart.* 71, which is concerned with the denunciation of one who had dug up an olive-tree, were common to all kinds of *φάσις*. The relevant clause is *πρυτανεῖα δὲ τιθέτω ὁ διώκων τοῦ αὐτοῦ μέρους*.

[3] Dem. 58 *Theokr.* 6 speaking of a law covering both *γραφαί* and *φάσεις*: *ἔστι δὲ ταῦτα, ὥσπερ ἠκούσατε ἐξ αὐτοῦ τοῦ νόμου, ἐὰν ἐπεξιὼν τις μὴ μεταλάβῃ τὸ πέμπτον μέρος τῶν ψήφων, χιλίας ἀποτίνειν, κἂν μὴ ἐπεξίῃ . . . χιλίας ἑτέρας*.

[4] For the details we have to rely on unsatisfactory articles in the grammarians. Harpokr. s.v. *φάσις* (= Suda 2, *Et. Mag.* 788. 50): *λέγεται μὲν καὶ ἐπὶ δημοσίου ἐγκλήματος ὅταν τις ἀποφαίνῃ τῶν δημοσίων ἔχοντά τινα μὴ πριάμενον, λέγεται δὲ καὶ ἐπὶ τῶν ὀρφανῶν οἴκων. ὅτε γὰρ μὴ ἐκμισθώσαιεν οἱ ἐπίτροποι τὸν οἶκον τῶν ἐπιτροπευομένων, ἔφαινεν αὐτὸν ὁ βουλόμενος πρὸς τὸν ἄρχοντα ἵνα μισθωθῇ· ἔφαινε δὲ καὶ εἰ ἐλάττονος ἢ κατὰ τὴν ἀξίαν* (Suda 2, *ἄδειαν* B.C.F.G.) *μεμίσθωτο. τοῦ μὲν οὖν προτέρου τὰ μαρτύρια ἔνεστιν εὑρεῖν παρά τε Δεινάρχῳ καὶ Δημοσθένει, τῆς δὲ περὶ τῶν ὀρφανικῶν οἴκων φάσεως παρὰ Λυσίᾳ πρὸς τὴν φάσιν τοῦ ὀρφανικοῦ οἴκου*. Suda 1 (= Photius) *φάσις ἐστὶν ἣν ποιεῖταί τις πρὸς τὸν δοκοῦντα ὑπορύττειν δημόσιον μέταλλον ἢ χωρίον ἢ οἶκον ἢ ἄλλο τι τῶν δημοσίων· ἔτι δὲ καὶ οἱ τοὺς ἐπιτρόπους τῶν ὀρφανῶν αἰτιώμενοι παρὰ τοῖς ἄρχουσιν ὡς οὐ δεόντως μεμισθωκότας τὸν ὀρφανὸν οἶκον προφαίνειν λέγονται*. *An. Bekk.* (*Λέξ. Ῥητ.*) 313 *φαίνειν: εἶδος ἐγκλήματος δημοσίου καὶ ἰδιωτικοῦ . . . ὅταν δὲ μὴ ἐκμισθώσωσι τὸν τῶν ὀρφανῶν οἶκον οἱ ἐπίτροποι, ἰδιωτικόν ἐστι τὸ ἀδίκημα*. Ibid. 315 *φάσις: μήνυσις πρὸς τοὺς ἄρχοντας . . . κατὰ τῶν ἐπιτρόπων τῶν μὴ μεμισθωκότων τὰς οἰκίας τῶν ὀρφανῶν*. Pollux 8. 47 *φάσις δὲ ἦν τὸ φαίνειν . . . περὶ τοὺς ὀρφανοὺς ἐξαμαρτάνοντας*. The reading *ἀξίαν* in Suda 2 is difficult; if the leasing had been done by the archon by auction how could its 'worth' be challenged? Lex. Cant. s.v. *ἔνδειξις* has *κατὰ τὴν τάξιν* (on which see

misconduct of the guardian towards his ward could be made the subject of a *φάσις*.[1]

(ii) *εἰσαγγελία*

The principal sanction for wrongs of a guardian against his ward other than those connected with the leasing of the estate was by way of *εἰσαγγελία*. We know from Ar. *Ath. Pol.* 56. 6 (quoted p. 102, n. 2) that guardians could be cited before the archon's court for *ὀρφανῶν κακώσεως*, *ἐπικλήρου κακώσεως*, and *οἴκου ὀρφανικοῦ κακώσεως*. Aristotle includes these in a list of *δίκαι* and *γραφαί*, and this might lead one to conclude that they were in fact simple *γραφαί*. It is clear, however, from a number of references that for wrongs against orphans or against *ἐπίκληροι* the *εἰσαγγελία* was available.[2] The only question is whether Aristotle's language can be pressed to imply that a *γραφή* was

P. S. Photiades, Ἀθ. 13 (1901), 8). The reading *ἄδειαν* would suggest that it was possible to get from the archon an immunity to lease provided that a minimum rate per cent. was achieved; a guardian who defied this provision in leasing could be described as in Suda I as *οὐ δεόντως μεμισθωκὼς τὸν οἶκον*. The definition in Pollux is probably too wide. Lips., *AR* 346, n. 24, Wyse, *Isai.* 526.

[1] Schulthess in his article in *RE* s.v. *μίσθωσις* now doubts whether *φάσις* was even used for this restricted purpose. His doubt is based on the silence of Ar., *Ath. Pol.*, in the passage quoted p. 102, n. 2. Against this view must be set the facts that Aristotle does not mention any of the other types of *φάσις* either, that the grammarians, even though muddled, are hardly likely to have invented the connexion of this procedure with *μίσθωσις οἴκου* (note especially the reference to a speech of Lysias at the end of the Harpokration entry), and that the passage from Demosthenes quoted p. 115, n. 3 is difficult to explain on any other hypothesis. Fine, *Horoi* 113, believes that *φάσις* may have been used for a number of offences connected with the leasing of a ward's estate.

[2] For orphans it is clear that the procedure used against Theopompos which is the subject of Isai. 11 *Hagn.* was *εἰσαγγελία*; cf. 6 *οἴεται δεῖν ὑμᾶς . . . ἐμοῦ καταγνῶναι ταύτην τὴν εἰσαγγελίαν*, 15 *οὗτος ὁ νῦν ἐμὲ εἰσαγγέλλων*: for *ἐπίκληροι* Isai. 3 *Pyrrh.* 46 *καὶ οὐκ [ἂν] εἰσήγγειλας πρὸς τὸν ἄρχοντα κακοῦσθαι τὴν ἐπίκληρον ὑπὸ τοῦ εἰσποιήτου οὕτως ὑβριζομένην καὶ ἄκληρον τῶν ἑαυτῆς πατρῴων καθισταμένην, ἄλλως τε καὶ μόνων τούτων τῶν δικῶν ἀκινδύνων τοῖς διώκουσιν οὐσῶν καὶ ἐξὸν τῷ βουλομένῳ βοηθεῖν ταῖς ἐπικλήροις*; Dem. *ap.* Pollux 8. 53 (p. 10, n. 2, above); the nature of the charge there referred to is not certain; either against a non-relative who, being married to a woman who became an *ἐπίκληρος*, failed to notify the archon of her having become one (so Paoli), or against any husband of an *ἐπίκληρος* who was deliberately refraining from sexual intercourse with her (reading *προσηκόντως* for *προσηκόντων* with Meier); Dem. 37 *Pant.* 45 f. *οὗτος γὰρ ᾐτιάσατ' ἐκεῖνον . . . ἐπὶ τὰς ἐπικλήρους εἰσελθεῖν καὶ τὴν μητέρα τὴν αὑτοῦ, καὶ τοὺς νόμους ἧκεν ἔχων τοὺς τῶν ἐπικλήρων πρὸς τὸ δικαστήριον. καὶ πρὸς μὲν τὸν ἄρχοντα, ὃν τῶν τοιούτων οἱ νόμοι κελεύουσιν ἐπιμελεῖσθαι, καὶ παρ' ᾧ τῷ μὲν ἠδικηκότι κίνδυνος περὶ τοῦ τί χρὴ παθεῖν ἢ ἀποτεῖσαι, τῷ δ' ἐπεξιόντι μετ' οὐδεμιᾶς ζημίας ἡ βοήθεια, οὐδέπω καὶ τήμερον ἐξήτασται, οὐδ' εἰσήγγειλεν οὔτ' ἔμ' οὔτε τὸν Εὔεργον ὡς ἀδικοῦντας.*

available for the same purposes; while we must admit that this is a formal possibility, it is not at all probable, for a reason which will appear immediately. One of the principal distinguishing features of the *εἰσαγγελία* was that in it the prosecutor ran no risk; he neither had to pay a court fee (*πρυτανεῖον* or *παράστασις*) which would be forfeit if he lost the case, nor was he subject to any penalty if he failed to secure a certain proportion of the jurors' votes, as was the prosecutor in a *γραφή*.[1] It seems obvious therefore that, even if there had existed a parallel procedure by *γραφή*, no prosecutor in his senses would have used it. Pleaders in these cases were free of the usual time limits (the cases were *ἄνευ ὕδατος*).[2] The penalty in the event of conviction was fixed by the process of assessment and counter-assessment (they were, that is, *ἀγῶνες τιμητοί*).[3] A convicted guardian was deprived of his guardianship.[4] It is clear that this procedure was available not merely against guardians, but against anyone who was guilty of an offence against an orphan or *ἐπίκληρος*. Whether, when the wrong-doer was other than a guardian, the guardian could proceed alternatively by way of a *δίκη* is not quite so clear; but probably he could not. It is perhaps significant here that in Isai. 11 *Hagn.* Theopompos' fellow guardian uses *εἰσαγγελία* to bring Theopompos to book. We should not, however, rule out the possibility of the guardian proceeding by way of *δίκη* to protect some specific interest of his ward, though there seems no direct evidence for this being done.[5] It would perhaps be difficult to

[1] Isai. 3 *Pyrrh.* 47 *οὔτε γὰρ ἐπιτίμιον ταῖς πρὸς τὸν ἄρχοντα εἰσαγγελίαις ἔπεστιν, οὐδὲ ἐὰν μηδεμίαν τῶν ψήφων οἱ εἰσαγγείλαντες μεταλάβωσιν, οὔτε πρυτανεῖα οὔτε παράστασις οὐδεμία τίθεται τῶν εἰσαγγελιῶν· ἀλλὰ τοῖς μὲν διώκουσιν ἀκινδύνως εἰσαγγέλλειν ἔξεστι, τῷ βουλομένῳ, τοῖς δ' ἁλισκομένοις ⟨αἱ⟩ ἔσχαται τιμωρίαι ἐπὶ ταῖς εἰσαγγελίαις ἔπεισιν.* Dem. 37 *Pant.*, loc. cit. Harpokr. s.v. *εἰσαγγελία*. The view of Bo. Sm. ii. 59 that the prosecutor in a *γραφὴ ξενίας* was immune from these penalties is hardly supported by the passages they cite, viz., Dem. 58 *Theokr.* 32, 59 *Neair.* 53, 121. The use of the phrase *γραφὴ κακώσεως* in Dem. 58 *Theokr.* 32 and Menander, fr. 279 K., can be ignored: the indictment in an *εἰσαγγελία* would be called a *γραφή* and Theopompos uses *γραφή* several times of the action against him, Isai. 11 *Hagn.* 28, 31, 35. See also Gernet, *Recherches* 446 f.

[2] Harpokr. s.v. *κακώσεως*.

[3] Dem. 43 *Makart.* 75 (p. 39, n. 2, above). For the possibility of very severe penalties Isai. 11 *Hagn.* 13, 35, 3 *Pyrrh.* 47 (n. 1, above), 62 (n. 5, below), 1 *Kleonym.* 39, Dem. 37 *Pant.* 46 (p. 117, n. 2, above).

[4] Isai. 11 *Hagn.* 31 *ἐλπίζει χρήματα λήψεσθαι καὶ ἐμὲ τῆς ἐπιτροπῆς ἀπαλλάξειν.*

[5] Isai. 3 *Pyrrh.* 62 *μηδεὶς οὖν ὑμῶν ἡγείσθω, εἰ ἐνόμιζε γνησίαν εἶναι τὴν ἑαυτοῦ γυναῖκα Ξενοκλῆς, λαχεῖν ἂν ὑπὲρ αὐτῆς τὴν λῆξιν τοῦ κλήρου τοῦ πατρῴου, ἀλλ' ἐβάδιζεν ἂν ἡ γνησία εἰς τὰ ἑαυτῆς πατρῷα, καὶ εἴ τις αὐτὴν ἀφῃρεῖτο ἢ ἐβιάζετο,*

suppose that in every case where a ward's interests had to be protected in the courts it would have been plausible to argue that his or her opponent was guilty of *κάκωσις*.

(iii) *δίκη ἐπιτροπῆς and δίκη σίτου*

There is one private suit which was concerned exclusively with guardianship, the *δίκη ἐπιτροπῆς*.[1] We have some very useful information about this suit from Demosthenes' action against one of his guardians, Aphobos, in 27 and 28 *Aphob.* i, ii, and from the action against Diogeiton which is the subject of Lys. 32 *Diogeit.*[2] The object of the action was to compel a guardian to submit accounts for his guardianship and to pay damages if the court determined that he had rendered himself liable to them.[3] Though there is no explicit evidence on the point, it seems likely that the action was not available until the guardianship had come to an end, and that it could only be brought by the ward himself, if he was a male; if the ward was a female we are entirely in the dark as to the age at which and the person through whom a *δίκη ἐπιτροπῆς* could be set on foot. So long as the guardianship, whether of a male or a female, subsisted, it seems certain that the

ἐξῆγεν ἂν ἐκ τῶν πατρῴων, καὶ οὐκ ἂν ἰδίας μόνον δίκας ἔφευγεν ὁ βιαζόμενος, ἀλλὰ καὶ δημοσίᾳ εἰσαγγελθεὶς πρὸς τὸν ἄρχοντα ἐκινδύνευεν ἂν περὶ τοῦ σώματος καὶ τῆς οὐσίας ἁπάσης τῆς ἑαυτοῦ. The speaker is here sketching various possible lines of action Xenokles might have taken on the supposition that his wife had become an *ἐπίκληρος* and someone else had entered on the inheritance. He rejects the possibility that he would have simply brought suit for the estate (*λῆξιν λαγχάνειν*), but this is only because, as an *ἐπίκληρος*, the wife would have had the right of entry. He describes this right of entry, using the word *ἐβάδιζεν*, as being exercised by the woman herself; but we can hardly doubt that it would have been exercised on her behalf by Xenokles; if it had been resisted, he argues, the opponent would have laid himself open not only to a private suit (here the *δίκη ἐξούλης*), but to *εἰσαγγελία*. The implication is that, while Xenokles might have used a private suit, he would more probably have used *εἰσαγγελία*. It is irrelevant to the point here at issue who is the subject of *ἐξῆγεν ἄν*: on this see pp. 313 ff. Beauch. ii. 286 ff.

[1] Schulthess, *VAR* 220 ff.

[2] On the other hand, what might have been a very valuable piece of evidence, the opening words of Demosthenes' actual claim (29 *Aphob.* iii. 31 ἔστιν οὖν τοῦ μὲν ἐγκλήματος ἀρχή "τάδ' ἐγκαλεῖ Δημοσθένης Ἀφόβῳ· ἔχει μου χρήματ' Ἄφοβος ἀπ' ἐπιτροπῆς ἐχόμενα, ὀγδοήκοντα μὲν μνᾶς, ἣν ἔλαβεν προῖκα τῆς μητρὸς κατὰ τὴν διαθήκην τοῦ πατρός"), can only be used on the hypothesis that that speech is from the hand of Demosthenes; on this see above, p. 105, n. 5, and the two contradictory judgements in Lips., *AR* 533, n. 62, and 822, n. 68.

[3] Dem. 38 *Nausim.* 15 ὅτε τοίνυν ἐλάγχανον τῷ πατρὶ τῆς ἐπιτροπῆς, τἀναντί' ἐγράψαντο τούτων· ὡς γὰρ οὐκ ἀποδόντι λόγον τότ' ἐγκαλοῦντες φαίνονται. 21 *Meid.* 78 τὰς δίκας ἔλαχον τῶν πατρῴων τοῖς ἐπιτρόποις.

only protection by legal process for a ward's interests was through the public actions described above.[1] The private actions had to be preceded by a hearing before an arbitrator, either private or public.[2] In the action itself the damages were fixed by the jury's deciding between the assessments of plaintiff and defendant.[3] Frivolous claims were discouraged by a penalty of one-sixth of the value of the claim if the plaintiff failed to secure more than one-fifth of the jurors' votes.[4] The action was probably heard before the archon, though some scholars have argued that, since there is evidence of arbitral procedure in these cases, they must have come before the Forty, not the archon.[5] Statutorily a suit had to be brought within five years of the end of the guardianship.[6] Where there was more than one guardian the ward proceeded against each separately for a specified proportion of the amount claimed, and by analogy if the claim had to be made against the heirs of the guardian owing to the latter's death it was made against each severally. Dem. 38 *Nausim.* shows that the two

[1] Isai. 11 *Hagn.* 27 with Wyse's note ad loc.

[2] Dem. 27 *Aphob.* i. 49 ff.

[3] Dem. 27 *Aphob.* i. 67 *καὶ τούτῳ μέν, ἐὰν καταψηφίσησθε, τιμητὸν . . . ἐμοὶ δ' ἀτίμητον τοῦτ' ἔστιν* (i.e. because of the *ἐπωβελία*; see next note).

[4] The penalty was called *ἐπωβελία*. That this penalty was incurred only by a plaintiff who failed to secure one-fifth of the votes is not directly attested for this suit, but is stated as the rule in *διαμαρτυρίαι* in Isok. 18 *Kallim.* 12. Some scholars, however, maintain that the penalty was incurred by every unsuccessful plaintiff, relying on the words used in Dem. 27 *Aphob.* i. 67 *ἂν γὰρ ἀποφύγῃ μ' οὗτος, ὃ μὴ γένοιτο, τὴν ἐπωβελίαν ὀφλήσω μνᾶς ἑκατόν* and on *An. Bekk.* (*Λέξ. Ῥητ.*) 255 s.v. *ἐπωβελία: ἐπιτίμιόν τι τοῦτό ἐστι τοῖς διώκουσι χρηματικήν τινα δίκην, ἂν μὴ ἕλωσιν*, Harpokr. s.v. *ὅπερ ἐδίδοσαν οἱ διώκοντες τοῖς φεύγουσιν εἰ μὴ ἕλοιεν*. This is the view of Lips., *AR* 939 (he takes the opposite view at 533), but not of Gernet, *Dem.* i. 24. If this was the rule it would have acted as a strong deterrent against wards prosecuting their wrongs in this way; perhaps we may suspect Demosthenes of exaggerated language which has been taken too literally by the lexicographers.

[5] For the Forty, Bo. Sm. ii. 102 ff. (cf. R. J. Bonner, *CP* 2 (1907), 413 f.), followed by Gernet, *Dem.* i. 24.

[6] Dem. 38 *Nausim.* 17 *τὸν νόμον . . . ὃς διαρρήδην λέγει, ἐὰν πέντ' ἔτη παρέλθῃ καὶ μὴ δικάσωνται, μηκέτ' εἶναι τοῖς ὀρφανοῖς δίκην περὶ τῶν ἐκ τῆς ἐπιτροπῆς ἐγκλημάτων*. That speech was for the defence in a *δίκη βλάβης* where two ex-wards were making claims against the sons of their former guardian, now dead, arising out of his guardianship, though they had come of age some twenty-two years before. The speaker, one of the four sons of the guardian, countered with a *παραγραφή* based on two pleas (1) that fourteen years before the wards had made a settlement of their claim with his father (2) that the action was barred by prescription. We cannot say whether it would have been an effective answer to the second plea that in form this was not a *δίκη ἐπιτροπῆς* but a *δίκη βλάβης*. It is important to note, however, that, even by the account of the speaker, his father had somehow been brought to a settlement eight years after the guardianship had terminated.

wards, Nausimachos and Xenopeithes, each made separate claims against each of the four sons of their late guardian; perhaps here too the analogy may be appealed to and the same rule applied when several wards were claiming against a single guardian, but we have no direct evidence of this.[1]

Though it seems certain that a *δίκη σίτου* could be brought against a guardian who failed to maintain his ward, it is not clear who could initiate this suit before the ward came of age or what purpose it would serve thereafter.[2]

There is no reason to suppose that a ward had a legal hypothec on the property of his guardian. The passage from Demosthenes 30 *Onet.* i. 7 sometimes cited to support this thesis in fact disproves it.[3]

Finally, we have no evidence that there was any specific suit through which a guardian could indemnify himself for loss suffered in discharging his duties as guardian.

[1] Demosthenes sued Aphobos, one of his three guardians, for a third of the sum he claimed, Dem. 27 *Aphob.* i, Hyp. 2 *διὸ πρὸς τὸν Ἄφοβον εἰσελήλυθεν ἐπιτροπῆς δέκα ταλάντων τὴν δίκην λαχών, ἐπειδὴ τρίτος ὢν ἐπίτροπος τὸ τρίτον ὀφείλει τῶν χρημάτων.* Cf. Schulthess, *VAR* 236 ff. For the procedure in the Nausimachos case see Dem. 38 *Nausim.* 2 *ὄντες γὰρ δύο τέτταρας εἰλήχασι δίκας ἡμῖν, τῶν αὐτῶν χρημάτων πάσας, τρισχιλίων ἑκάστην, βλάβης.*

[2] See p. 104, n. 4, above.

[3] Lips., *AR* 531, n. 51, Gernet, *Dem.* i. 95, n. 2.

V · SUCCESSION

§ 1. *Introduction*

OUR evidence for the rules governing succession is, comparatively speaking, satisfactory, largely owing to the predominance of this topic in the surviving speeches of Isaios.[1] This pre-

[1] All the eleven surviving speeches of Isaios are concerned directly or indirectly with questions of succession. Throughout his commentary Wyse attempts to discredit Isaios' statements as to what was the law. This scepticism has been much overdone; it is unlikely that Athenian juries were so gullible or so ignorant of the law as it implies. One or two lost speeches of Isaios also dealt with succession, in addition to those listed on p. 97, n. 1, concerned with the allied topic of guardianship: the speech *πρὸς Ἀριστογείτονα καὶ Ἄρχιππον*, though it may have been delivered in what was formally a *δίκη εἰς ἐμφανῶν κατάστασιν* (cf. p. 208), was in effect concerned with an inheritance, as we can see from the argument preserved in D.H., *Isai.* 15 *ὡς ἐν τῇ λήξει τῇ πρὸς Ἀ. καὶ Ἀ. εὑρίσκεται πεποιηκὼς ἐν ᾗ κλήρου τις ἀμφισβητῶν ἀδελφὸς ὢν τοῦ τελευτήσαντος προσκαλεῖται τὸν ἔχοντα τἀφανῆ χρήματα εἰς ἐμφανῶν κατάστασιν, ὁ δὲ τοῦ κλήρου κρατῶν παραγράφεται τὴν κλῆσιν δεδόσθαι λέγων ἑαυτῷ τὰ χρήματα κατὰ διαθήκας*: it is almost certainly this speech which is described in Pollux 10. 15 as *περὶ τοῦ Ἀρχεπόλιδος κλήρου*: two fragments of it survive (1 and 2 Th.): there are also two fragments (24 and 25 Th.) from a speech *πρὸς Λυσίβιον* which dealt with an *ἐπίκληρος*: finally there was a speech against Satyros on behalf of an heiress (Harpokr. s.v. *ἐπίδικος*) and one on behalf of the daughter of Mnesaios (id. s.v. *ἀπορώτατος*, *An. Bekk.*, *Συν. Λέξ. Χρησ.* 434). In the Demosthenic corpus we have 43 *Makartatos* (particularly valuable, since it deals with the same estate as is the subject of Isai. 11 *Hagnias*), 44 *Leochares*, and 48 *Olympiodoros*. A fair number of the lost speeches of Lysias dealt either directly or indirectly with succession: we have some glimpse of the contents of three, viz. (1) *πρὸς Γλαύκωνα περὶ τοῦ Δικαιογένους κλήρου*, to which probably frs. 29–31 as well as 23 and 24 Th. belong (see Gernet, *Lys.* ii. 243, n. 4), (2) *ὑπὲρ Φερενίκου περὶ τοῦ Ἀνδροκλείδου κλήρου*, frs. 78, 79 Th.; the title is probably inaccurate; the suit concerned *τὰ ὑπ' Ἀνδροκλείδου δεδομένα*, i.e. probably a gift in anticipation of death; the case is of particular interest as both Pherenikos and Androkleides were Thebans (see Gernet, *Lys.* ii. 244), (3) a speech on the estate of Polyainos known only from the following reference in Rutilius Lupus, *de fig. sent.* 2. 8 'quaeris a me quo iure obtinere possim. quo iure? mihi Polyaenus reliquit, praetor dedit possessionem, leges me defendunt, ad te non pertinent, hi veritatem sequuntur'; perhaps a testamentary adoption; it appears that the *ἐπιδικασία* by the archon afforded a presumption in the claimant's favour (Gernet, ibid. 243, n. 3): of the rest we have only titles or uninformative fragments; they are *περὶ τῆς 'Επιγένους διαθήκης* (Suda s.v. *ἀνάργυρος*, fr. 35 Th.), *περὶ τοῦ 'Ηγησάνδρου κλήρου* (Harpokr. s.v. *κακώσεως* (118, n. 2, above), Priscian XVIII. 238, 179, frs. 40, 41 Th.), *πρὸς Τιμωνίδην* (Suda s.v. *διάθεσις*, fr. 74 Th.), *περὶ τοῦ Θεοπόμπου κλήρου*

dominance in its turn is probably partly due to the fact that the rules were in the fourth century both complicated and fluid, and this gave play to litigation and the skill of the logographer.[1]

Two general points need to be borne in mind during the following discussion. First, while it is true that legal rules in a vigorous society are seldom static, the rules governing succession were more than ordinarily transitional during this period in Athens. The reason for this emerges clearly from a consideration of the historical development of the will, but this is beyond the scope of the present work. Discussion here is confined as far as possible to the rules obtaining in the classical period.

The second point is that we must constantly be on our guard against the anachronism of regarding succession in classical Athens as a purely economic matter, concerned merely with the transmission of material goods or of rights closely linked with material goods (see p. 92, above). It may well be that Athenian ideas were unconsciously moving in that direction, but there is ample evidence to show that a man's heir was still looked upon as owing to him a primary duty to preserve the *sacra* of the house, and that this aspect of succeeding to a dead man was seldom far from the minds of those who had to determine disputes as to succession (see p. 130, below).[2]

(Harpokr. s.v. *ὀργέων*), *περὶ ἡμικληρίου τῶν Μακαρτάτου χρημάτων* (Harpokr. s.vv. *Προσπάλτιοι, σιπύα*); finally, three speeches on the daughters of Antiphon (the son of Lysonides, not the orator), Onomakles, and Phrynichos (Plut., *Mor.* 833, Harpokr. s.v. *πεντακοσιομέδιμνον*, id. s.v. *ἀρκτεῦσαι* respectively) must have been concerned with succession matters. Hyperides wrote a speech on the inheritance of Pyrrhandros (Harpokr. s.v. *κακώσεως*), fr. 160 J., and two on the inheritance of Hippeus (id. s.v. *παρακαταβολή*), frs. 108–10 J. Dinarchus wrote two on the heiress daughter of Iophon (D.H., *Din.* 12), one or two 'synegoric' speeches (on this type of speech see Bo. Sm. ii. 8 ff.) either for or against Hegelochos about an heiress (D.H., ibid., Harpokr. *ληξιαρχικὸν γραμματεῖον*), one on the estate of Mnesikles (D.H., ibid.), one on the daughters of Aristophon (*διαμαρτυρία ὡς οὐδέ εἰσιν ἐπίδικοι* ⟨*αἱ*⟩ *Ἀριστοφῶντος θυγατέρες*, D.H., ibid., Harpokr. s.vv. *διαμαρτυρία, ἐπίκληρος*), and finally a speech in a *diamarturia* against Chares on the estate of Euippos (D.H., ibid.). The loss of many plays of the New Comedy dealing with heiresses is only poorly offset by the survival of Terence's *Phormio*, based on the *Ἐπιδικαζόμενος* of Apollodoros. See also evidence on guardianship cited p. 97, n. 1, above.

[1] Ar. *Ath. Pol.* 9 *διὰ τὸ μὴ γεγράφθαι τοὺς νόμους ἁπλῶς μηδὲ σαφῶς, ἀλλ' ὥσπερ ὁ περὶ τῶν κλήρων καὶ ἐπικλήρων, ἀνάγκη πολλὰς ἀμφισβητήσεις γίγνεσθαι.* Aristotle takes the sensible view that this was not Machiavellianism on Solon's part, but was due to the difficulty of formulating general rules to govern these complex matters.

[2] Besides the general treatment in Beauch. iii. 423–709 (on the transmission of patrimonies), i. 398–487 (on heiresses), and in Lips., *AR* 537–88 (with references

§ 2. *The estate*

The most general term for a man's heritable estate was κλῆρος. Thus speeches in inheritance cases are normally entitled 'concerning X's κλῆρος', and the heir was called κληρονόμος.[1] We are in some difficulty in determining what in principle was included in this heritable estate and how in particular cases the content of it was delimited for the purposes of litigation.[2] In origin, no doubt, as the word κλῆρος suggests, it was the ancestral plot of land with all that went with it, such as farm implements and livestock, and we may conjecture that in early times it was this which was transmitted to the heir or heirs. By the classical period, however, the inheritance seems to have included all the property of the *de cuius*, movable and immovable, together with debts due to him[3] as well as liability for debts owed by him.[4]

to modern literature on 539, n. 5), the following are especially important: C. Bunsen, *De iure hereditario Atheniensium*, Caillemer, *Succession*, id., 'Le Droit de tester à Athènes', *AEG* 4 (1870), 19 ff., Hafter, *Erbtochter*, Schulin, *Gr. Test.*, Bruck, *Schenkung*, Demisch, *Schuldenerb.*, Gernet, 'La Création du testament', *DSGA* 121 ff., id., 'Sur l'épiclérat', *RÉG* 34 (1921), 337 ff., Paoli, 'L'ἀγχιστεία nel diritto successorio attico', *SDHI* 2 (1936), 77 ff., id., 'L'ἐπίκληρος attica nella palliata Romana', *Atene e Roma* 45 (1943), 19 ff., id., 'La legittima aferesi della ἐπίκληρος nel diritto attico', *Studi e Testi* 125 (1946), 524 ff., Jones, *LLTG* 191 ff., D. Asheri, 'L'οἶκος ἔρημος nel dir. succ. att.', *AG* 159 (1960), 12 ff., id., 'Laws of Inheritance in Anc. Gr.', *Historia* 12 (1963), 1 ff., Kränzlein, *Eig. und Bes.* 94 ff.

[1] The word οἶκος was even more comprehensive, including as it did, besides the property, all the persons who belonged to the 'house' such as the widow, minors, slaves, and in a sense the dead ancestors (through the rites due to them). Plut., *Sol.* 21, speaking of the period before Solon, says ἐν τῷ γένει τοῦ τεθνηκότος ἔδει τὰ χρήματα καὶ τὸν οἶκον καταμένειν. See further pp. 1 and 92 above.

[2] In this connexion our comparative ignorance of the procedure followed in the ἀνάκρισις is particularly unfortunate; but we may conjecture that one function of this preliminary hearing in succession cases was to establish exactly how the κλῆρος in dispute was made up. This would also go some way to explain how a particular κλῆρος could remain an identifiable entity and subject of litigation for many years and after going through several hands. The estates of Hagnias and of Archiades are good instances; their histories are discussed above, pp. 91 ff. For the documentation of an inheritance note the illuminating remark in Dem. 36 *For Phorm.* 19 τίς ἂν ἐνείματο τὰ πατρῷα μὴ λαβὼν γράμματα, ἐξ ὧν ἔμελλεν εἴσεσθαι τὴν καταλειφθεῖσαν οὐσίαν; Cf. also p. 233.

[3] For an inheritance composed largely of debts due see Dem. 38 *Nausim.* 7.

[4] Lys. 17 δημ. ἀδ. 3 ff., Dem. 35 *Lakrit.* 4, 44, 47 *Euerg.* 32, 36 *For Phorm.* 36 οὗτος (Apollodoros) ἐκ μὲν τῶν χρεῶν ὁμοῦ τάλαντ' εἴκοσιν εἰσπέπρακται ἐκ τῶν γραμμάτων ὧν ὁ πατὴρ (sc. Pasion) κατέλιπεν, 49 *Timoth.* 1 μηδενὶ ὑμῶν ἄπιστον γενέσθω εἰ Τιμόθεος ὀφείλων ἀργύριον τῷ πατρὶ τῷ ἐμῷ φεύγει νῦν ὑπ' ἐμοῦ ταύτην τὴν δίκην. On the significance of Isai. 10 *Aristarch.* 15 see below, p. 125.

There are two points of controversy raised by this rather sweeping statement. The first is touched upon in considering the kinds of thing recognized by the Athenian law of property (p. 233). The Athenians made a distinction between a man's inherited property (πατρῷα) and what he had himself added to that property (ἐπικτητά). There seems no reason to suppose that in cases of intestacy this distinction had any juristic significance. Both these kinds of property would have been part of the κλῆρος claimed by the heirs. There is, however, a fairly strong probability that a man had, whether by custom or by statute, a freer right to dispose of ἐπικτητά by will than of πατρῷα.[1]

More complicated is the second point of controversy, which concerns the disposal of the debts of the *de cuius* and the related question as to what heirs, if any, were obliged to take the inheritance.[2] It goes without saying that debts were a first charge upon the estate itself.[3] But it seems clear that, once an heir (or heirs) was established, he (or they, in proportion to what they took) was liable for the debts out of his own property, if the inheritance was not adequate to meet them. This rule can be certainly deduced from at least two passages. In Isai. 10 *Aristarch.* 16 f. the speaker argues that the estate in dispute cannot be insolvent; for if it had been, his opponents would not have

[1] See Gernet, *RÉG* 33 (1920) 266 (*DSGA* 144), and under Wills below, p. 151, n. 4. Custom probably played an abnormally important role in the courts' decision of inheritance cases. One of Aristotle's *Problems* (950^{b}) runs διὰ τί ἐν ἐνίοις δικαστηρίοις τοῖς γένεσι μᾶλλον ἢ ταῖς διαθήκαις ψηφιοῦνται (codd., ψηφίζονται Bekker); His answer is that it may be because wills are more easily falsified than birth qualifications; but the question itself suggests that the courts assumed a fairly wide latitude in these matters. For the use of πατρῷα see especially Isai., fr. 6 Th. (quoted p. 233, n. 4); in connexion with distribution among a number of heirs Dem. 36 *For Phorm.* 19 (p. 124, n. 2, above), 39 *Boiot.* i. 6, ibid. 35 (additionally important for the distinction between succession to the property and to the *sacra*: τῶν πατρῴων ἔχεις τὸ μέρος μετὰ τὴν τοῦ πατρὸς τελευτήν· ἱερῶν, ὁσίων μετέχεις), 40 *Boiot.* ii. 2, 14; in Dem. 45 *Steph.* i. 21 a putative testamentary document (διαθήκη) is included among τὰ πατρῷα.

[2] C. Bunsen, *De iure her. Ath.* 86 ff., R. Dareste, *J. des Sav.* (1885), 269 ff., id., *Dem.* i. xxix and 106, n. 3, Caillemer, *Succession* 149 ff., Beauch. iii. 587, 634, iv. 541, Glotz, *Solidarité* 510, 542, Partsch, *GB* 232, 243, Lips., *AR* 540, n. 6, 572 ff., Demisch, *Schuldenerb*, *passim*.

[3] Thus the speaker in Isai. 10 *Aristarch.* 16 alleges that his opponents had discharged a debt on the estate in order to create a presumption that they were entitled to succeed, and Isai. 1 *Kleonym.* 1 implies that it could be plausibly alleged that a man's inherited πατρῷα might be in debt to another estate: οὐ γὰρ τῶν Κλεωνύμου μόνον ἀμφισβητοῦσιν ἀλλὰ καὶ τῶν πατρῴων, ὀφείλειν ἐπὶ τούτοις ⟨ἡμᾶς⟩ ἐκείνῳ φάσκοντες ἀργύριον. Cf. Partsch, *GB* 240.

wasted money by claiming it and adopting a son into the house of Aristarchos, on whom the debts would fall, but would have left this burden to the next of kin of his mother, who, on his contention, was the ἐπίκληρος. However sophistic this argument may be, it would be utterly pointless unless the rule had been that an heir who took was liable for the debts without limit.[1] The same inference is to be drawn from Dem. 35 *Lakrit.* 3 f. We shall have to examine the details of this difficult case in other connexions. Here it is sufficient to say that the plaintiff, Androkles, claimed to be owed money on a bottomry loan by Artemon, Artemon had died without paying the debt, and since it is clear, despite certain vague suggestions by Androkles to the contrary, that Artemon's brother, Lakritos, was neither bound by direct contract to Androkles nor indirectly as surety, the latter has to fall back on suing Lakritos as Artemon's heir; moreover, Androkles reveals that Lakritos had specifically claimed to have renounced the inheritance, and though he, Androkles, denies the efficacy of this plea, the mere fact that it was advanced proves that potentially Lakritos would have been liable for the debts of Artemon even if the estate was not sufficient to meet them.[2] The real difficulty comes when we inquire whether there was a class of heir who had not the option of declining the inheritance if it seemed likely that the estate would prove insolvent. Here there has been a sharp division of opinion. One school of thought, relying principally on Dem. 38 *Nausim.* 7,[3] holds that even direct

[1] εἰ γὰρ ἦν, ὡς οὗτοι λέγουσιν, ὑπόχρεως οὗτος ὁ κλῆρος, οὔτ' ἂν χρήματα οὗτοι ὑπὲρ αὐτῶν ἐξέτινον (οὐ γὰρ προσῆκεν αὐτοῖς, ἀλλ' οἷς ἐγένετο ἡ ἐμὴ μήτηρ ἐπίδικος, τούτοις ἀναγκαῖον ἦν ὑπὲρ αὐτῶν βουλεύσασθαι), οὔτε ἂν εἰσεποίουν εἰς τοῦτον τὸν κλῆρον υἱὸν Ἀριστάρχῳ, μέλλοντες ὠφεληθήσεσθαι μὲν μηδέν, ζημιωθήσεσθαι δὲ μεγάλα. Partsch, *GB* 233 does not really dispose of this argument; see Demisch, *Schuldenerb.* 17.

[2] Thalheim, *Herm.* 23 (1888), 335, Demisch, *Schuldenerb.* 18 ff., Gernet, *Dem.* i. 169. The case is noteworthy because the plaintiff was an Athenian and the defendant a Phaselite. There is nothing to show what law was applied in such a case; but from the rather curious way in which Androkles refers to the law in relation to this particular point one might gather that normal Athenian practice would obtain unless the defendant could point to some particular enactment to the contrary. Lakritos, he says (4), is the heir to all Artemon's property, whether at Athens or in Phaselis, and he cannot point to any law which gives him authority ἔχειν μὲν τὰ τοῦ ἀδελφοῦ καὶ διῳκηκέναι ὅπως ἐδόκει αὐτῷ, μὴ ἀποδιδόναι δὲ τὰ ἀλλότρια χρήματα, ἀλλὰ λέγειν νῦν ὅτι οὐκ ἔστιν κληρονόμος, ἀλλ' ἀφίσταται τῶν ἐκείνου.

[3] φασὶ γὰρ οὐκ ἀποδόσθαι τὰ πατρῷ' ὧν ἐκομίζοντο χρημάτων, οὐδ' ἀποστῆναι τῶν ὄντων, ἀλλ' ὅσ' αὐτοῖς κατελείφθη χρέα καὶ σκεύη καὶ ὅλως χρήματα, ταῦθ' ἑαυτῶν γίγνεσθαι.

descendants could refuse an inheritance.[1] Nausimachos and Xenopeithes had brought suits βλάβης against the sons of Aristaichmos on the ground that Aristaichmos had, as their guardian, collected a debt due to their father and should have paid over the sum to them. This speech is by one of the sons, who has interposed a παραγραφή based on the pleas first that the action was barred by prescription (this does not concern us here, but see p. 120, n. 6, above) and second that the wards had fourteen years before come to a settlement of their claims with Aristaichmos and received the money or real property agreed in that settlement. Those who wish to bring this particular passage to bear on our present problem would translate it 'my opponents say that they did not sell their patrimony for the sum received under the settlement, nor did they renounce their inheritance'. The words ἀποστῆναι τῶν ὄντων are taken as bearing the technical sense which they do undoubtedly bear in, for example, Dem. 35 *Lakrit.* 4, 44 of a potential heir renouncing the inheritance, and as therefore necessarily implying that they were legally entitled to renounce the estate of their father. But the words need not have this technical sense; they can mean simply 'they were not standing out of their own property'; and this is the more natural sense, for the speaker at no point suggests any valid reason why his opponents should have thus renounced, nor is it plausible that they should have done so, even if the law allowed. It is better then to accept the view that this passage has no relevance to our problem. The general run of the remaining evidence on balance supports the view that direct descendants, among whom should be included those adopted *inter vivos*, had no right to refuse.[2]

We must distinguish at the outset between the public and the private obligations of the *de cuius*. It is all the more necessary to proceed thus because certain scholars have admitted what it is indeed hard to deny, that sons were liable for some at least of a dead father's debts to the state, but have argued that this was simply the state looking after its own interests and should not be taken as presumptive evidence that the sons would also be liable

[1] Dareste, locc. citt. (p. 125, n. 2, above), Beauch., Glotz, Partsch, locc. citt. (ibid.), Guiraud, *Prop. Fonc.* 225.

[2] Caillemer, *Succession*, took this view of Dem. 38 *Nausim.* 7; he was followed by Thalheim, *Herm.* 23 (1888), 335 ff., Lips., *AR.* 540, n. 6, Demisch, *Schuldenerb.* 5 ff., Gernet, *Dem.* i. 254, n. 1.

for private debts.[1] Several passages in Demosthenes indicate in a general way that a son was, as his father's heir, liable for undischarged penalties incurred by his father against the state. Thus in 22 *Androt.* 34 Demosthenes says *κληρονόμον γάρ σε καθίστησ' ὁ νόμος τῆς ἀτιμίας τῆς τοῦ πατρός*,[2] and there are specific cases where the son or his guardian is plainly held to be liable: Demosthenes tells the court that his guardians had tried to excuse certain of their dealings with his father's estate by alleging that his grandfather was a state debtor and the debt was still due out of the estate; Demosthenes challenges the facts but not the statement of what would have been the position had the facts been true: in another case a speaker assumes that it would be the normal practice to sue the sons of a trierarch who was dead for money he was alleged to owe for equipment for a trireme.[3] The best view in the light of this evidence seems to be

[1] Dareste, *Dem.* i. 106, n. 3, Beauch. iii. 587 ff., 634 f., Glotz, *Solidarité* 542, Partsch, *GB* 235 f.

[2] Cf. Dem. 24 *Timokr.* 201 *μέλλων κληρονομήσειν τῆς ἀτιμίας, ἂν ἐκεῖνός* (sc. *ὁ πατήρ*) *τι πάθῃ*. This general liability could descend to a grandson; Dem. 58 *Theokr.* 17 *ὀφείλοντος αὐτῷ τοῦ πάππου πάλαι, καὶ τοῦ νόμου κελεύοντος κληρονομεῖν τοῦτον τῶν ἐκείνου*: though it must be admitted that this speaker's arguments are not above suspicion and that the significance of the word *αὐτῷ* in the above clause is obscure. Dem. 43 *Makart.* 58 contains the following clause from a law: *τοὺς δὲ μὴ ἀποδιδόντας τὰς μισθώσεις τῶν τεμενῶν τῶν τῆς θεοῦ καὶ τῶν ἄλλων θεῶν καὶ τῶν ἐπωνύμων ἀτίμους εἶναι καὶ αὐτοὺς καὶ γένος καὶ κληρονόμους τοὺς τούτων, ἕως ἂν ἀποδῶσιν*: as it stands this clause means that, where a man had died in debt to a temple, any heir, whether direct descendant or not, was personally liable till the debt was discharged. This throws this type of liability so very much wider than is suggested anywhere else that commentators have tried to water the passage down, either by arguing that the phrase *γένος καὶ κληρονόμους τοὺς τούτων* means 'their descendants and heirs of *these descendants*' (Beauch. iii. 635), a most implausible view, or by striking from the text the words *καὶ κληρονόμους τοὺς τούτων* (Partsch, *GB* 236, followed by Gernet, *Dem.* ii. 115). Glotz, *Solidarité* 510 f., holds that originally the *ἀτιμία* fell upon the *γένος* as a whole, but that later liability was limited to those of the *γένος* who by *ἀγχιστεία* were heirs; at that date the words *κληρονόμους τοὺς τούτων* were added in apposition to *γένος*; he therefore would delete the *καί* between *γένος* and *κληρονόμους* and substitute *τούς*; this view has the double disadvantage of entailing an emendation and yet leaving the liability very wide. Gernet, *RÉG* 31 (1918), 187 ff., thought the passage could be interpreted as referring to descendants only, the words *καὶ κληρονόμους τοὺς τούτων* being added to make it clear that a descendant was not liable unless he became heir; a grandson, for example, was not liable so long as his father was alive; but later Gernet changed his view (loc. cit. above).

[3] For Demosthenes' case see 28 *Aphob.* ii. 1. Gernet, *RÉG* 31 (1918), 187 was right to stress the fact that it was the debts of Demosthenes' *maternal* grandfather for which he was allegedly liable; the implication is that for public debts at least liability might pass through a daughter to a grandson, provided of course that that

that a direct descendant, when he was also the heir *ab intestato*, was liable for the public debts of the *de cuius*, and that he could not evade this liability by renunciation; the liability could descend to grandchildren, if their fathers were dead, the sons of any particular son of the *de cuius* being presumably held liable *per stirpes* rather than *per capita*; furthermore it could, under certain conditions, descend to a grandchild through a daughter of the *de cuius*. On the other hand, the very fact that this liability is specially laid down in relation to public debts[1] rather suggests that it did not extend to private debts and that therefore it was open to a direct descendant to evade responsibility for these by not entering upon the inheritance; in such a case the creditors would have had no claim beyond that which could be satisfied out of the estate. There is, however, one piece of evidence which has been held to suggest that a direct descendant could not renounce; in Dem. 46 *Steph.* ii. 14 we have a clause from a law defining those who had the right to make a will; the most satisfactory interpretation of this clause is that it excludes those adopted *inter vivos*, which it does in the words 'those not adopted in such a way that they can neither renounce the inheritance nor need claim it by process before the courts' (ὅσοι μὴ ἐπεποίηντο ὥστε μήτε ἀπειπεῖν μήτ' ἐπιδικάσασθαι); this interpretation loses all plausibility unless the rule was that *natural* sons too were barred from renouncing.[2] It must nevertheless be admitted that the obscurity of this phrase renders it but an insecure foundation for the deduction based on it.

It has sometimes been argued that ἀτιμία arising otherwise than out of indebtedness to the state might pass down to descendants where this was specifically laid down in a particular law. But the passage in Andokides which supports this view has

grandson would have been heir under the rules of intestate succession. For the liability of sons of a dead trierarch see Dem. 47 *Euerg.* 32. It is not certain that the case of Sopolis is relevant here: he was condemned in a court in 325/4 B.C. ὅτι οὐκ ἀπεδίδου τὰ ξύλινα σκεύη ἐπὶ δέκα τριήρεις ὑπὲρ Κηφισοδώρου τοῦ ἀδελφοῦ (*IG* ii². 1631, *c.* 350 ff. = *IJ* xxvi); Boeckh, *Staatsh.* iii. 212, Beauch. iii. 636, and the editors of *IJ* assume that this liability fell on Sopolis as the heir of his brother, but Partsch, *GB* 234 f., rightly points out that nothing in the inscription necessarily implies this and that Sopolis might have taken over his brother's debts in the latter's lifetime or been liable as a surety. Cf. Weiss, *GP* 205.

[1] Although the text of the law refers only to temple debts the other passages cited justify the wider term.

[2] See p. 86, n. 2, above, and note especially Demisch, *Schuldenerb.* 11 ff.

recently been emended in such a way that it too refers only to state debtors.[1]

Finally, as has already been suggested (p. 123, above), succession to a man's estate involved certain religious obligations, and this rule was so well established that participation in the *sacra* is advanced as evidence of relationship giving a claim to succeed (ἀγχιστεία), and the relationship is technically described as ἀγχιστεία ἱερῶν καὶ ὁσίων where ἱερά probably refers to the family cult and ὅσια to the material goods.[2] Conversely, failure to carry out these obligations is urged as a reason against a man's being confirmed as heir to the property by the court.[3]

§ 3. *Intestate succession: order of succession*

(i) *Sons*

First in order of succession came the legitimate sons, whether natural or adopted, of the *de cuius*.[4] All sons shared equally, and

[1] The passage, which is relied upon by Lips., *AR* 573 f., is from 1 *Myst.* 74. The actual words are οὗτοι δ' αὖ ἦσαν ὁπόσοι κλοπῆς ἢ δώρων ὄφλοιεν· τούτους ἔδει καὶ αὐτοὺς καὶ τοὺς ἐκ τούτων ἀτίμους εἶναι. As the text stands it means that direct descendants of all those convicted of theft or bribery inherited their liability. But Paoli, *St. Dir.* 305 f., followed by D. MacDowell, *Andok. Myst.* (Oxford, 1962), ad loc., transposes this clause in the text so that it refers only to those who had stolen from the state.

[2] Isai. 2 *Menekl.* 46 οὗτος νυνὶ ἄκληρον μὲν ἐμὲ ποιεῖν τοῦ κλήρου τοῦ πατρῴου . . . ἄπαιδα δὲ τὸν τελευτήσαντα καὶ ἀνώνυμον βούλεται καταστῆσαι, ἵνα μήτε τὰ ἱερὰ τὰ πατρῷα ὑπὲρ ἐκείνου μηδεὶς τιμᾷ μήτ' ἐναγίζῃ αὐτῷ καθ' ἕκαστον ἐνιαυτόν. 9 *Astyph.* 7, 13. 8 *Kir.* 15. Dem. 39 *Boiot.* i. 35. In the text of the law on intestate succession given in Dem. 43 *Makart.* 51 we have the phrase νόθῳ . . . μὴ εἶναι ἀγχιστείαν μήθ' ἱερῶν μήθ' ὁσίων and it recurs in Isai. 6 *Philokt.* 47; see p. 67, above. These customary duties are described as τὰ νομιζόμενα in, for example, Isai. 2 *Menekl.* 4 (with Wyse ad loc.), 1 *Kleonym.* 10, 9 *Astyph.* 7.

[3] Isai. 4 *Nikostr.* 19 πῶς οὐκ ⟨ἂν⟩ ἀνοσιώτατος εἴη, ὃς τῷ τεθνεῶτι μηδὲν τῶν νομιζομένων ποιήσας τῶν χρημάτων αὐτοῦ κληρονομεῖν ἀξιοῖ; Dem. 43 *Makart.* 65, where a distinction is first drawn between being heir of the deceased's body and being heir of his estate, but it is at once urged that to be the former entails being the latter. Isai. 6 *Philokt.* 51.

[4] The most important piece of evidence for the order of succession is Dem. 43 *Makart.* 51, quoted in full below, p. 138, n. 3: but that law takes for granted and therefore does not mention sons. The rule governing descendants is, however, clearly stated in the following passages: Isai. 6 *Philokt.* 28 τοῖς γὰρ φύσει υἱέσιν αὐτοῦ οὐδεὶς οὐδενὶ ἐν διαθήκῃ γράφει δόσιν οὐδεμίαν, διότι ὁ νόμος αὐτὸς ἀποδίδωσι τῷ υἱεῖ τὰ τοῦ πατρὸς καὶ οὐδὲ διαθέσθαι ἐᾷ ὅτῳ ἂν ὦσι παῖδες γνήσιοι, 8 *Kir.* 34 πάντες γὰρ ὑμεῖς τῶν πατρῴων, τῶν παππῴων, τῶν ἔτι περαιτέρω κληρονομεῖτε ἐκ γένους παρειληφότες τὴν ἀγχιστείαν ἀνεπίδικον, Isok. 1 *Demon.* 2 πρέπει γὰρ τοὺς παῖδας, ὥσπερ τῆς οὐσίας, οὕτω καὶ τῆς φιλίας τῆς πατρικῆς κληρονομεῖν. For the right of adoptees see p. 95, n. 1, above; and of illegitimate children pp. 66 ff., above.

if any son had predeceased the *de cuius* his share was in its turn divided equally between any sons he might have.[1] Adopted sons shared equally with any natural sons born after the adoption.[2] Rights of succession of descendants did not, as some scholars have suggested, run out after the third generation, but the line of heirs continued theoretically *ad infinitum*.[3] In principle all the heirs in this category succeeded *ab intestato*, and the existence of any one such heir ruled out the possibility of a will (for further detail see below, p. 151). All the evidence is against the possibility that primogeniture secured any kind of privilege, though it will be seen later in connexion with wills that in practice a father might by will confer some special advantage on a particular son. It was indeed the absence of a system of primogeniture and the limited powers of a father in this respect which made so precarious the balance between, on the one hand, preserving houses from extinction through lack of descendants, and, on the other, so subdividing the ancestral estate that no part of it was sufficient to provide a living for its occupant.[4] Equal

[1] Isai. 6 *Philokt.* 25 τοῦ νόμου κελεύοντος ἅπαντας τοὺς γνησίους ἰσομοίρους εἶναι τῶν πατρῴων. That grandsons whose fathers had predeceased them took shares *per stirpes* and not *per capita* is nowhere directly vouched for, and the main passage which is held to support the rule by analogy, Isai. 7 *Apollod.* 20, does not do so; the point there being made, though in rather obscure language, is itself quite clear, namely that, if the *de cuius* left no descendants or brothers, but only a sister and a nephew by another sister who had predeceased him, the surviving sister and the nephew had claim to equal shares; to prove that claims in similar cases were *per stirpes* and not *per capita* we should need an example where there were two nephews whose combined share was equal to that of their aunt. Thus the deductions made from this passage by Caillemer, *Succession* 32, followed by Beauch. iii. 472, are not justified. Lips., *AR* 542, n. 9, affords no help. On the other hand, all attempts to show that there were cases where division was *per capita* rather than *per stirpes* have failed, and rationality favours the latter system (p. 144, n. 1).

[2] Isai. 6 *Philokt.* 63 (p. 85, n. 3, above).

[3] Bunsen, *De iur. her. Ath.* 17, argued from Isai. 8 *Kir.* 32 γονεῖς δ' εἰσὶ μήτηρ καὶ πατὴρ καὶ πάππος καὶ τήθη καὶ τούτων μήτηρ καὶ πατήρ, ἐὰν ἔτι ζῶσιν· ἐκεῖνοι γὰρ ἀρχὴ τοῦ γένους ἐστί, ibid. 34 (p. 130, n. 4, above), that the line of heirs stopped at great-grandsons; but the former of these passages cannot be pressed in this sense and the latter tends in the other direction. Although it is not likely that it often happened that a great-great-grandson existed when his great-great-grandfather was still alive while his father, his grandfather, and his great-grandfather were all dead, there is no reason to suppose that the Athenian rule was so irrational as to exclude him. Caillemer, *Succession* 11, Beauch. iii. 447 f., Lips., *AR* 541; but in the contrary sense M. E. Seebohm, *Structure of Gr. Tribal Soc.* (London, 1895), 54 ff.

[4] When in a voluntary division of part of Pasion's estate Apollodoros has first choice between a factory and a bank we can hardly press this as a right secured by his being the elder (Dem. 36 *For Phorm.* 11 νέμονται τὴν τράπεζαν καὶ τὸ ἀσπιδοπηγεῖον, καὶ λαβὼν αἵρεσιν Ἀπολλόδωρος αἱρεῖται τὸ ἀσπιδοπηγεῖον ἀντὶ τῆς τραπέζης).

division was the rule even when the sons were of different marriages.[1]

When the *de cuius* was survived not only by sons or issue of sons but also by daughters the daughters had no right of inheritance. It has been suggested that in such a case the sons or their issue were not merely morally, but legally, bound to provide any daughter with a dowry. There can be no doubt that a daughter had a strong claim by custom to a dowry; but, as is argued in full above (p. 48), the evidence is strongly against her having had any legal right.

(ii) *Heiresses*

If a man died leaving behind him no sons but only a daughter or daughters, and if he had not married off the daughters to men whom he adopted, the daughters became *ἐπίκληροι*, and a number of special rules applied both as to the estate and as to the marriage and the status of the heiress.[2] The rules as to her marriage are discussed in full in the section on *ἐπιδικασία* (pp. 9 f., above), and those on her status before marriage in the section on the guardianship of females (pp. 108 ff., above). Here we have to decide the precise effects of this institution on the passing of property on intestacy.

The distinguishing mark of an *ἐπίκληρος* was that she was also *ἐπίδικος*;[3] that is to say, her hand could be claimed in marriage

But later in the same speech (para. 34) we are told that he received a house as *πρεσβεῖα* (*πρεσβεῖα λαβὼν τὴν συνοικίαν κατὰ τὴν διαθήκην*); it is true that he receives this by a will; but none the less the use of this word is significant. Beauch. iii. 452, Lips., *AR* 542, n. 12, Bruck, *Schenkung* 101, Gernet, *Dem.* i. 216, n. 1, W. Kamps, *AHDO* 3 (1947), 272, Jones, *LLTG* 192. Dem. 39 *Boiot.* i. 27, 29 suggests that the right to bear the name of his paternal grandfather was the *πρεσβεῖα* of the eldest son.

[1] Dem. 36 *For Phorm.* 32 *τὰ μητρῷα πρὸς μέρος ἠξίους νέμεσθαι, ὄντων παίδων ἐκ τῆς γυναικὸς Φορμίωνι.* Apollodoros, son of Pasion, is alleged to have claimed a share in the estate of his mother based on an equal division between her sons by Pasion and those by Phormion.

[2] Hafter, *Erbtochter*, Caillemer, *Succession* 36 ff., Beauch. i. 398 ff., iii. 465 ff., Lips., *AR* 543 ff., Ledl, *Stud.*, Thalheim *RE* s.vv. *ἐπίκληρος*, *ἐπίδικος*. Gernet, *RÉG* 34 (1921), 337 ff. It is assumed for the moment (1) that all male ascendants of the *de cuius* had predeceased him, (2) that he had at no time had any male descendants.

[3] Harpokr. s.v. *ἐπίδικος* (p. 48, n. 3, above). Suda s.v. *ἐπίδικος· ἐπίδικος δὲ ἡ ἀμφισβητουμένη ἐπίκληρος, τίνι χρὴ αὐτὴν γαμηθῆναι. Ἰσαῖος δὲ τὴν ἐπίκληρον ἐν τῷ πρὸς Λυσίβιον ἐπικληρῖτιν ἐκάλεσεν.* Id. s.v. *ἐπίκληρος·* (1) . . . *ὁμοίως δὲ καὶ τὴν ἤδη γεγαμημένην, ὅταν ᾖ ἐπὶ τῇ οὐσίᾳ ὅλῃ καταλελειμμένη. καλεῖται δὲ ἐπίκληρος καὶ ἡ μηδέπω γεγαμημένη, ἀλλὰ παρὰ τῷ πατρὶ οὖσα, καθότι καθήκει αὐτῇ πᾶσα ἡ οὐσία.*

by her father's nearest male kin by the procedure known as ἐπιδικασία. The nearest male kin was decided on the same principles as determined who would be entitled to the estate in the absence of any direct descendants either male or female. By this rule the nearest male relative would have been the brother of the *de cuius*, and, were there more than one, the eldest. What happened if the father of the *de cuius* was still alive is considered below. Next in order came the sons of brothers of the *de cuius*:[1] then sons of his sisters:[2] then the uncles, first paternal and second maternal, of the *de cuius*.[3] After these we have no direct evidence for the order of claimants to the hand of an heiress, but we may assume that it followed the same pattern as the order for claiming an estate where there were no children, male or female.[4]

We have hitherto been considering only the case where there

καλοῦνται δὲ ἐπίκληροι, κἂν δύο ὦσι κἂν πλείους. Pollux 3. 33 καὶ ἡ μὲν ἐπὶ παντὶ τῷ κλήρῳ τρεφομένη μόνη θυγάτηρ ἐπίκληρος, περιόντος τοῦ πατρὸς καὶ ἀποθανόντος· ἐκάλεσαν δέ τινες αὐτὴν καὶ πατροῦχον, 'Ισαῖος δὲ καὶ ἐπικληρῖτιν, ὥσπερ καὶ Σόλων. These definitions are not satisfactory juristically: a woman need not be an orphan to qualify, if that implies the death of her mother as well as her father; the qualification that she must be left ἐπὶ παντὶ τῷ κλήρῳ is not consistent with the Suda's statement that there could be two or more ἐπίκληροι, a statement confirmed by Andok. 1 *Myst.* 117 ff.; and though some women may have been called ἐπίκληρος colloquially while their fathers were still alive, no one could technically be such until the death of her father: Hafter, *Erbtochter* 12 ff. with a useful definition of an ἐπίκληρος at 24. Isai. 3 *Pyrrh.* 43, assumes that where a man left only a legitimate daughter the πατρῷος κλῆρος could only be adjudicated with her. So too Isai. 10 *Aristarch.* 13.

[1] Isai. 10 *Aristarch.* 5 Ἀριστομένης γὰρ ἀδελφὸς ὢν ἐκείνου τοῦ Ἀριστάρχου (the *de cuius*, father of the alleged heiress), ὄντος αὐτῷ ὑέος καὶ θυγατρός, ἀμελήσας ἢ αὐτὸς αὐτὴν ἔχειν ἢ τῷ ὑεῖ μετὰ τοῦ κλήρου ἐπιδικάσασθαι: we can ignore for the moment the difficulty that Isaios may here be cheating in calling the woman an ἐπίκληρος (when her father died she had had a brother, but he subsequently died while still a minor and it may be that this disqualified her for the status of ἐπίκληρος, see below, p. 137); on the assumption that she was we need not doubt that Isaios is correctly stating the rule as being that her hand could be claimed first by her paternal uncle and after him by his son. Isai. 3 *Pyrrh.* 72 ἀλλ' οὔτε ἐγένετο οὔτ' ἔστι, μὴ γενομένων [δὲ] παίδων γνησίων ἐκείνῳ, ἐγγυτέρω ἡμῶν οὐδὲ εἷς· ἀδελφὸς μὲν γὰρ οὐκ ἦν αὐτῷ οὐδ' ἀδελφοῦ παῖδες, ἐκ δὲ τῆς ἀδελφῆς ἡμεῖς ἦμεν αὐτῷ.

[2] Isai. 3 *Pyrrh.* 72 (n. 1, above).

[3] Ibid 63, 74 show that maternal uncles of the *de cuius* could claim where there were no brothers or brothers' sons: in that case there were no paternal uncles, but it is legitimate to assume that they would have had a prior claim.

[4] Ibid. 74 ἢ γὰρ ἡμῶν τινα τῶν ἐγγύτατα γένους ἐπιδικασάμενον ἕξειν γυναῖκα, ἢ εἰ μηδεὶς ἡμῶν ἐβούλετο λαμβάνειν, τῶν θείων τινὰ τούτων τῶν νῦν μαρτυρούντων, εἰ δὲ μή, τῶν ἄλλων τινὰ συγγενῶν τὸν αὐτὸν τρόπον ἐπὶ πάσῃ τῇ οὐσίᾳ ἐπιδικασάμενον κατὰ τοὺς νόμους ἕξειν ταύτην γυναῖκα. Hafter, *Erbtochter* 37, Caillemer, *Succession* 39.

was a single surviving daughter and there had never been any other children. There were, however, other possibilities. There might, in the first place, be more than one surviving daughter. The passages from Andok. 1 *Myst.* and the Suda cited in p. 132, n. 3 suggest that in such a case the property was shared between the surviving daughters and that their hands could be claimed by relatives in the prescribed order. Secondly it might happen that, though there was only one surviving daughter, other daughters had predeceased the *de cuius*, leaving issue; if that issue was female we may conjecture that theoretically these girls would have rights to a share in the estate *per stirpes*,[1] though in practice their chances of securing a share (which were also the chances of the male relatives who would have had a claim to their hands) might depend a good deal on their age and the age of their aunt; if the issue was male we have the difficult problem of determining what were the relative claims of such a boy and of his aunt. Probably he had a claim to what would have been his mother's share of the estate. This rule seems to be laid down unequivocally in Isai. 7 *Apollod.* 19, though as will be seen in another connexion (p. 147, n. 2, below), the argument in which this statement of the law occurs is not above suspicion. Other instances cited to prove the rule do not do so.[2] It is worth recalling here that an adoptee was by his adoption severed from his father's house, but not from that of his mother (see p. 93, above); he would have inherited then by virtue of his continued membership of his maternal grandfather's house. A nephew could of course double his share of the estate by marrying his aunt, and there is no reason to suppose that such a marriage would have been ruled out. On the other hand, there no direct evidence that a nephew had a right to secure this extra share by claiming his aunt's hand, though it seems probable that he could.[3]

[1] Cf. H. Buermann, *RM* 32 (1877), 355 ff.

[2] Beauch. i. 430 wrongly cites Andok. 1 *Myst.* 117 and Isai. 3 *Pyrrh.* 72 as cases where a nephew's claim to his aunt's hand is recognized: in both cases the men are nephews of the *de cuius*, but cousins of the heiresses.

[3] Caillemer, *Succession* 38, holds that the normal disparity of age between nephew and aunt made cases where they might reasonably marry so rare that the law did not provide for them; but the normalcy of this disparity may well be exaggerated: it is not all that rare for nephew and aunt to be reasonably close in age. If they were, it would seem more in consonance with other Athenian rules of succession that a woman's nephew should take precedence over her first cousin, who would come in next (in the absence, that is to say, of paternal uncles).

We have also the difficult case of an ἐπίκληρος who had several sons. It has been argued that unless the heiress's husband had been adopted as son of the *de cuius* in one of the three accepted ways, only one of her sons could succeed, and this had to be by way of adoption posthumously into the house of the heiress's father. This is the most likely view *a priori*, since in the case envisaged the sons would normally be heirs of their father. Had they been entitled to succeed to their father's estate and at the same time share out the estate of their maternal grandfather, one of the main objectives of the *epiklerate* would have been frustrated.[1]

The daughter of a man in the thetic class who survived him and would thus have been an ἐπίκληρος if there had been any estate to inherit was known as a θῆσσα and was the subject of special provisions which are set out in full in Demosthenes, *Makartatos*.[2]

Hafter, *Erbtochter* 36, rules out the nephew's claim to his aunt's hand, not on the same grounds as Caillemer but because, he urges, the relationship must be reckoned not from the heiress herself, but from the *de cuius*; this might justify putting a paternal uncle of the heiress ahead of her nephew, but not excluding the latter altogether as Hafter appears to do. It is worth noting that Isai. 7 *Apollod.* 19 (mentioned in the text above) is referring strictly to the estate not of the woman's father, but of her brother; of this estate she may not have been technically an ἐπίκληρος. It is quite conceivable that the rule was not clear even in the fourth century: as Gernet argued in his article in *RÉG* 34 (1921), 337 ff., there were two conflicting purposes embodied in the rules concerning the *epiklerate*, the desire to maintain existing houses, which would have looked favourably on the solidarity to be gained by a marriage between nephew and aunt, and the desire to protect the interests of the ἀγχιστεῖς, which would have wished to keep a share in the estate available for one of them.

[1] But see Beauch. i. 468 ff., Gernet, *RÉG* 33 (1920), 156 (*DSGA* 137), who take the contrary view.

[2] Dem. 43 *Makart.* 54 *ΝΟΜΟΣ.* τῶν ἐπικλήρων ὅσαι θητικὸν τελοῦσιν, ἐὰν μὴ βούληται ἔχειν ὁ ἐγγύτατα γένους, ἐκδιδότω ἐπιδοὺς ὁ μὲν πεντακοσιομέδιμνος πεντακοσίας δραχμάς, ὁ δ' ἱππεὺς τριακοσίας, ὁ δὲ ζευγίτης ἑκατὸν πεντήκοντα, πρὸς οἷς αὐτῆς. ἐὰν δὲ πλείους ὦσιν ἐν τῷ αὐτῷ γένει, τῇ ἐπικλήρῳ πρὸς μέρος ἐπιδιδόναι ἕκαστον. ἐὰν δ' αἱ γυναῖκες πλείους ὦσι, μὴ ἐπάναγκες εἶναι πλέον ἢ μίαν ἐκδοῦναι τῷ γ' ἑνί (K. F. Hermann: τῷ γένει codd.), ἀλλὰ τὸν ἐγγύτατα ἀεὶ (Blass: δεῖ codd.) ἐκδιδόναι ἢ αὐτὸν ἔχειν. ἐὰν δὲ μὴ ἔχῃ ὁ ἐγγύτατα γένους ἢ μὴ ἐκδῷ, ὁ ἄρχων ἐπαναγκαζέτω ἢ αὐτὸν ἔχειν ἢ ἐκδοῦναι. ἐὰν δὲ μὴ ἐπαναγκάσῃ ὁ ἄρχων, ὀφειλέτω χιλίας δραχμὰς ἱερὰς τῇ Ἥρᾳ. ἀπογραφέτω δὲ τὸν μὴ ποιοῦντα ταῦτα ὁ βουλόμενος πρὸς τὸν ἄρχοντα. D.S. 12. 18. 3 τρίτος δὲ νόμος διωρθώθη ὁ περὶ τῶν ἐπικλήρων, ὁ καὶ παρὰ Σόλωνι κείμενος. ἐκέλευε γὰρ τῇ ἐπικλήρῳ ἐπιδικάζεσθαι τὸν ἔγγιστα γένους, ὡσαύτως δὲ καὶ τὴν ἐπίκληρον ἐπιδικάζεσθαι τῷ ἀγχιστεῖ, ᾧ ἦν ἀνάγκη συνοικεῖν ἢ πεντακοσίας ἐκτῖσαι δραχμὰς εἰς προικὸς λόγον τῇ πενιχρᾷ ἐπικλήρῳ. Cf. Aristoph. Byz. *ap.* Eustath. on *Il.* 21. 449, Harpokr. s.vv. ἐπίδικος and θῆτες, Posidippos, fr. 35 K., Ter., *Phorm.* 410, Suda s.v. θῆττα. The grammarians fix the stipulated dowry as 500 drachmai, irrespective of the census class of the man obligated. Either they have mistakenly generalized from the sum fixed for the *pentakosiomedimnos* or at a date when the

Her nearest male kinsman was required either to marry her himself or to dower her; the dowry was fixed by the census class to which the man belonged, 500 drachmai if he was a *pentakosiomedimnos*, 300 if he was a knight, 150 if he was a *zeugite*. If there was more than one kinsman related to her in the same degree they had to pay in proportion. No man could be forced to dower more than one woman under this rule. The archon was responsible for seeing that the law was obeyed and if he failed was liable to a penalty of 1,000 drachmai. It was open to any citizen (ὁ βουλόμενος) to initiate proceedings against a defaulting kinsman.[1] The law makes no provision for the case where the nearest kinsman was himself in the thetic class, and we cannot say whether he was compelled to marry the θῆσσα without the option of a dowry or whether he was simply passed over, so that the obligation fell on the nearest of kin in one of the top three classes.[2]

It has been assumed so far that all the male ascendants had predeceased the *de cuius* and that at no time had he had any male descendants. If either of these assumptions did not apply, were any surviving female descendants still technically ἐπίκληροι?

There has been much discussion as to whether a surviving paternal grandfather—we need not go higher up the scale—excluded a woman from the class. A superficial reading of the law quoted in Dem. 46 *Steph.* ii. 18 suggests that he did.[3] That law specifies those who had the right to dispose of a woman's hand by ἐγγύη. These are her father, her brother by the same father, and her paternal grandfather. If there are none of these, the law proceeds, then she may either be an ἐπίκληρος, in which case so and so, or she may not, in which case so and so. At first sight this seems to imply that, were any of the aforesaid relatives, including a paternal grandfather, alive, the girl would not be an ἐπίκληρος. But Gernet has shown that this inference is invalid.[4] For it is based on two assumptions: first that, if a grandfather was competent to give a girl in marriage, all the other conditions

value of money had declined the law was changed and the highest sum fixed for all men, irrespective of their census.

[1] The word ἀπογραφέτω probably here simply means 'let him bring a γραφή' and does not imply the use of the special procedure known as ἀπογραφή: Lips., *AR* 352, n. 45.

[2] On purely *a priori* grounds the latter alternative seems more probable: it would better serve the purpose of preserving οἶκοι.

[3] So Hafter, *Erbtochter* 16 f., Beauch. i. 415 f.

[4] *RÉG* 34 (1921), 339 ff.

required to make her an ἐπίκληρος (save of course his own survival) were present; but this need not be so, for it is at least highly probable that where the girl had brothers who were minors the grandfather could dispose of her hand, but she was not an ἐπίκληρος: second, that the list of relatives mentioned in the law is exhaustive, for if other relatives were competent to give a girl in marriage they certainly did not preclude her being an ἐπίκληρος; neither therefore did her grandfather; but there are clear cases where a girl's hand is bestowed by a relative who is not included in the list which figures in the law.[1] But though this law does not of itself furnish conclusive evidence that a woman did not become an ἐπίκληρος if her paternal grandfather survived her father, all probability is against this rule; for it is inconsistent with another rule which, as we shall see, is fairly well established, namely the rule that the father did not inherit from the son. If the *de cuius* had died without issue his κλῆρος would not have passed to his father; it seems therefore unlikely that if he were survived by female issue his father should have had the right to dispose of the property by bestowing their hands as he pleased.

Then there is the question whether a woman was ever ἐπίκληρος to her brother. In Isai. 6 *Philokt.* we have a case where a man, Euktemon, has been predeceased by a son, Philoktemon (among other children who do not concern us here), and is survived by a widowed daughter. At one stage of the proceedings over his estate a claimant sues for her hand as an ἐπίκληρος together with a part of the estate (para. 46 says a fifth part, but the text is probably corrupt). On one interpretation of this very confused story she was in this claim being regarded as ἐπίκληρος

[1] It seems clear from Lys. 32 *Diogeit.* 6 that Diogeiton had disposed of the hand of Diodotos' daughter; Diodotos was brother of Diogeiton and had married his daughter, so that Diogeiton was both paternal uncle and maternal grandfather of the girl whose hand he had given in marriage. He may have done so by virtue of Diodotos' will; if not, he did so as the girl's paternal uncle. The only difficulty about this case is that it is doubtful whether it can be confidently cited, as Gernet, loc. cit., cites it, to support a rule on intestacy. It is better with Isai. 6 *Philokt.* 51, which puts quite clearly a hypothetical case of a woman who is not an ἐπίκληρος, but whose hand is disposed of by collaterals. Note that Plato, *Laws* 744 e, gives the power of ἐγγύη first to the father, then to the paternal grandfather, then to brothers by the same father, then to the same relatives on the mother's side, and finally τοὺς ἐγγύτατα γένους ἀεὶ κυρίους εἶναι μετὰ τῶν ἐπιτρόπων. It seems likely that here Plato is not drawing strictly on the law of Athens; so Gernet, *Plat.* clxvi, taking a rather different view from that which he had adopted in *RÉG* (loc. cit., p. 136, n. 4, above).

of her brother, Philoktemon; more probably the claim was that she was ἐπίκληρος to a part or the whole of Euktemon's estate.[1] On the whole is seems likely that if a man died without issue, but was survived by a sister, that sister was regarded as heiress to her father rather than her brother. But this is largely conjecture.

The evidence is insufficient to determine whether a girl who had not reached puberty on the death of her father became ἐπίδικος on his death or only on reaching puberty. The language of Ar., *Ath. Pol.* 56. 6–7 rather suggests that the guardian of an ἐπίκληρος who was a minor might not be identical with her eventual husband; but neither that passage nor any other gives a clue as to how, in that case, her guardian was chosen. It might of course happen that the properly qualified claimant to her hand was himself a minor at the death of her father. Presumably in such a case *his* guardian would have been guardian of the ἐπίκληρος also.[2]

(iii) *Ascendants*

Although the issue is controversial, it seems highly probable that ascendants were excluded from the succession. This probability cannot be made to rest, as Lipsius makes it rest, purely and simply on the fact that the law quoted in Dem. 43 *Makart.* 51 does not mention ascendants among those who inherited *ab intestato*; for that law does not mention sons or their issue either, but begins with the case where there are daughters.[3] The significant point is that this law is dealing with cases of intestacy; it

[1] Gernet, *RÉG* 34 (1921), 347 f., Hafter, *Erbtochter* 23 f. The whole case is bedevilled by the doubt whether we are dealing with the estate of Euktemon or of Philoktemon. See further on it p. 139, below.

[2] Hafter, *Erbtochter* 15, 31, Hruza, *Beitr.* i. 109, n. 33, Beauch. i. 413 ff., Wyse, *Isai.* 322.

[3] Lips., *AR* 549. The text of the law in Dem. 43 *Makart.* 51 is unfortunately corrupt, though something can be done to emend it by reference to Isai. 11 *Hagn.* 2 and 11 ff. It reads *ΝΟΜΟΣ.* ὅστις ἂν μὴ διαθέμενος ἀποθάνῃ, ἐὰν μὲν παῖδας καταλίπῃ θηλείας, σὺν ταύτῃσιν, ἐὰν δὲ μή, τούσδε κυρίους εἶναι τῶν χρημάτων. ἐὰν μέν ἀδελφοὶ ὦσιν ὁμοπάτορες· καὶ ἐὰν παῖδες ἐξ ἀδελφῶν γνήσιοι, τὴν τοῦ πατρὸς μοῖραν λαγχάνειν· ἐὰν δὲ μὴ ἀδελφοὶ ὦσιν ἢ ἀδελφῶν παῖδες, * * * ἐξ αὐτῶν κατὰ ταὐτὰ λαγχάνειν· κρατεῖν δὲ τοὺς ἄρρενας καὶ τοὺς ἐκ τῶν ἀρρένων, ἐὰν ἐκ τῶν αὐτῶν ὦσι, καὶ ἐὰν γένει ἀπωτέρω. ἐὰν δὲ μὴ ὦσι πρὸς πατρὸς μέχρι ἀνεψιῶν (Wesseling: ἀνεψιαδῶν codd.) παίδων, τοὺς πρὸς μητρὸς τοῦ ἀνδρὸς (τοῦ τελευτήσαντος Isai. 11 *Hagn.* 2, 12) κατὰ ταὐτὰ κυρίους εἶναι. ἐὰν δὲ μηδετέρωθεν ᾖ ἐντὸς τούτων, τὸν πρὸς πατρὸς ἐγγυτάτω κύριον εἶναι. νόθῳ δὲ μηδὲ νόθῃ μὴ εἶναι ἀγχιστείαν μήθ' ἱερῶν μήθ' ὁσίων ἀπ' Εὐκλείδου ἄρχοντος. In the lacuna Meier and Buermann read ἀδελφὰς ὁμοπατρίας καὶ παῖδας, Lipsius reads ἀδελφὰς ὁμοπατρίας καὶ παῖδας ἐξ αὐτῶν λαγχάνειν· ἐὰν δὲ μὴ ἀδελφαὶ ὦσιν ἢ παῖδες ἐξ αὐτῶν, ἀδελφοὺς τοῦ πατρὸς καὶ ἀδελφὰς καὶ παῖδας.

does not mention sons because by the strict letter of the law where there were sons there could not be a will; no one, however, has suggested that a man could not dispose of his property by will if his father survived him, and, that being so, if his father had a right to succeed *ab intestato* at any point in the prescribed order he must have found mention in this law.[1] The arguments on the other side are partly *a priori*. It is asserted that natural justice would have dictated this rule: the claims of a father upon his son were recognized by the institution, which had some legal backing, of γηροτροφία; if a father had a claim upon his son for maintenance in his old age, *a fortiori* he had a claim upon the son's property if the son died first. But the logical deduction from this argument would be that a man was precluded from disposing of his property by will not only when he was survived by sons, but when he was survived by his father, and no one has suggested that there was any such rule. A more persuasive point is that, as we shall see, a man's heir might be his paternal or even his maternal uncle; and it would seem irrational that these relatives should succeed to the exclusion of his father. Those who argue against the father's right have simply to accept this irrationality.

Apart from these *a priori* arguments there are certain specific cases which have been held to prove the father's right. Of these only one (the last here named) stands up to examination. The principle case so used is that of Philoktemon in the sixth speech of Isaios. Philoktemon died without issue; he was survived by two sisters, one of whom had a son, Chairestratos; Chairestratos is the claimant in the case, alleging that he had been adopted by Philoktemon in his will; he did not put in his claim, however, immediately on the death of Philoktemon, but only on the death several years later of Philoktemon's father, Euktemon, and then his claim was to inherit not only Philoktemon's, but also Euktemon's estate. His failure to assert his rights under Philoktemon's will immediately must have been very damaging to his case; it is perhaps explicable on the hypothesis that Philoktemon's estate by itself was not large enough to make

[1] Caillemer, *Succession* 61 ff., puts the full case for the father's right to succeed *ab intestato*. He was answered conclusively by Beauch. iii. 474 ff. Lips., *AR* 550, agrees with Beauch. Mitteis, *RV* 324, leaves the question open. Cf. also Paoli, *SDHI* 2 (1936), 106 f., Jones, *LLTG* 193.

it worth Chairestratos' while to leave his father's house, as he would have to do as an adopted son of Philoktemon; the addition of Euktemon's estate might turn the scales. However that may be, it is strongly in the interests of Isaios' client to blur the distinction between the estate of Philoktemon and that of Euktemon. This he succeeds in doing, and it is natural that he gives no clear answer to the question who owned the estate of Philoktemon between his death and that of Euktemon, though the logic of his position is that Euktemon did and that therefore fathers were heirs of their sons. But we cannot press this logic any more than Isaios did, and it is significant that at one point at least the orator's language suggests that there had never been a formal division of property between Euktemon and his son, Philoktemon.[1] It is no better with the phrase from Dem. 43 *Makart.* 51, *ἐὰν παῖδες ἐξ ἀδελφῶν γνήσιοι, τὴν τοῦ πατρὸς μοῖραν λαγχάνειν* (p. 138, n. 3, above), which does not mean, as it has sometimes been taken, 'if there are legitimate children of brothers of the deceased they shall take the share which would have gone to the *deceased's father*', but 'they shall each take the share of *his father* (assuming that he is dead)'. In other words, the phrase states the principle of division *per stirpes* and not *per capita* and has no bearing on our problem. Finally, the evidence drawn from Dem. 44 *Leoch.* is rather more favourable to the view that the father had a claim. In that case the estate of Archiades had passed by a series of three posthumous adoptions to Leokrates II, the great-great-grandson of Archiades' sister. Leokrates II had then died without issue; he was survived by his father, Leostratos II, and by his brother, Leochares. Leostratos had at one time himself been adopted as the posthumous son of Archiades, but had taken advantage of the provision which allowed a man to

[1] Isai. 6 *Philokt.* 38 οὕτω πολλὴν οὐσίαν ἐκέκτητο Εὐκτήμων μετὰ τοῦ υἱέος Φιλοκτήμονος. G. F. Schoemann disposed of the arguments based on this speech in *Opusc. Acad.* i (Berlin, 1856), 272 ff., and Caillemer, op. cit. 65 ff., admitted that they would not stand. Gernet, *RÉG* 34 (1921), 347 f., suggests that Philoktemon's testamentary adoption of Chairestratos was effective only for that part of his estate which he owned independently of his father, while for the rest of the estate which had remained undivided his sisters became ἐπίκληροι on the death of their father, Euktemon. Of course if Euktemon had died before Philoktemon the latter would have become heir (assuming none of the counter-claimants was a legitimate son of Euktemon) and Chairestratos would then have had a strong claim to the whole estate, though since he had not been adopted *inter vivos* he would not have been entitled to enter without the assent of the court. Cf. also E. Rabel, 'Elterliche Teilung' (*Fest. zur 49. Versammlung deutschen Philologen im Basel*, 1907), 530.

return to his own family if he left a legitimate son in the family of his adoption. On the death of Leokrates II Aristodemos, the plaintiff in this case, who was a grandson of a brother of Archiades, tried to enter upon the estate, but was met by an ἐξαγωγή on the part of Leostratos, and the speaker asks (para. 33) *κατὰ ποῖον νόμον φανεῖται ἐρήμου ὄντος τοῦ οἴκου τοὺς ἐγγυτάτω γένους ἡμᾶς ἐξαγαγὼν ἐκ τῆς οὐσίας;* He answers *ὅτι νὴ Δία πατὴρ ἦν τοῦ τετελευτηκότος. ἀπεληλυθώς γ' εἰς τὸν πατρῷον καὶ οὐκέτι τῆς οὐσίας ἐφ' ᾗ ἐγκατέλιπεν τὸν υἱὸν κύριος ὤν.* The first words of the answer certainly suggest that a father could with some show of plausibility bar entry by other relatives to a deceased son's estate, and it is significant that the speaker does not meet this argument by a plain statement that in no case could a father claim by virtue of that relationship to succeed his son; he meets it by saying that in effect Leostratos in returning to his own house had ceased to be Leokrates' father. It would seem that Leostratos then shifted his ground and claimed as an adopted son of Archiades (para. 34, *Λεώστρατος οὑτοσὶ παρακαταβάλλει ὡς υἱὸς Ἀρχιάδου*), but his so doing does not necessarily mean that, if there had not been the complication that Leokrates held the estate as the adopted son of Archiades, he could not have maintained his claim to bar entry as Leokrates' father.[1]

Even if it be admitted that fathers might succeed their sons, we have absolutely no evidence as to what place they took in the order of succession. Some scholars have supposed that they excluded all collaterals,[2] others that they shared with brothers and sisters of the deceased and their issue, others that they only took in default of that class.[3]

The right of a mother to succeed, *qua* mother, is even more dubious than that of a father. Again the evidence adduced in favour of her right is partly *a priori*; as we shall see later, in default of relatives down to a certain degree on the father's side relatives on the mother's side came in; there would seem to be the same irrationality in excluding the mother in favour of those related through the mother as in excluding the father in favour of, say, the father's brother (see p. 139, above). In fact this point

[1] Caillemer, *Succession* 71 ff., regarded the passage from Dem. 44 *Leoch.* as conclusive in favour of the father's right. Neither Beauch. iii. 491 ff. nor Lips., *AR* 551, n. 36, who controvert him, are persuasive on this passage.

[2] Bunsen, *De iure her. Ath.* 39, Caillemer, op. cit. 77.

[3] E. Schneider, *De iure her. Ath.* (Munich, 1851), 21.

struck a *rhetor* of the second century A.D.[1] Apart from this *a priori* consideration two passages from Isai. 11 *Hagn.* have been adduced as proving that the mother might have a claim *qua* mother. But, although that speech presents some notorious difficulties of interpretation which we shall meet with again, these passages seem on the whole to tell against rather than in favour of the mother's right *qua* mother.[2] If the mother had a place in the succession in her own right we are just as much in the dark as to what that place was as we are in respect of the father. We have the additional problem, to which there is no solution, as to whether in any or all cases in which a mother succeeded she became technically an ἐπίκληρος. Whether she did or not, she must surely have had a κύριος, and it is hard to envisage how a man could be in this position and yet not have the right of succession before her. This topic will need further discussion in connexion with the law of testament.

[1] Theon, *Progymn.* 13 (Spengel, ii. 130. 23) περὶ πλεονασμὸν δὲ γίνεται ἀσάφεια, ὅταν δυνατὸν ᾖ πλέον τι τοῦ γεγραμμένου συλλογίζεσθαι ὡς καὶ αὐτὸ δυνάμει δηλούμενον· οἷον εἴ τις νομοθετήσειε κληρονομεῖν καὶ τοὺς πρὸς μητρός· ἀμφισβητήσειε γὰρ ἂν καὶ ἡ μήτηρ ὡς εἰ τοὺς πρὸς μητρὸς νόμος κληρονομεῖν καλεῖ, πολὺ πρότερον ἂν αὐτὴν τὴν μητέρα καλοίη. For the claims of those inheriting through the mother of the *de cuius* see Dem. 43 *Makart.* 51 (p. 138 n. 3,, above) and p. 144, below.

[2] The first passage is in 17 οἱ δ' ὑπὲρ τῆς Ἁγνίου μητρὸς γένει μὲν ταὐτὸ προσηκούσης—ἀδελφὴ γὰρ ἦν τοῦ Στρατίου—νόμῳ δὲ ἀποκλῃομένης, ὃς κελεύει κρατεῖν τοὺς ἄρρενας, τοῦτο μὲν εἴασαν, οἰόμενοι δ' ἐμοῦ πλεονεκτήσειν μητέρα εἶναι τοῦ τελευτήσαντος ἔγραψαν· ὃ συγγενέστατον μὲν ἦν τῇ φύσει πάντων, ἐν δὲ ταῖς ἀγχιστείαις ὁμολογουμένως οὐκ ἔστιν. The mother of the *de cuius*, Hagnias, was also Hagnias' second cousin on his father's side, and was related to him in this respect in the same degree as was Theopompos, who is speaking. At a first reading the last words quoted seem to clinch the argument; for they appear to mean 'which, though it is the closest natural tie of all, is nevertheless by general consent not within the kin'. But it must be granted that the words could conceivably mean 'which, though it is by nature the closest tie, is not closest within the kin', and it has been so taken by, for example, Caillemer, *Succession* 122 f. Lips., *AR* 552, n. 37 rightly rejects this interpretation. Note also that Theopompos' opponents appear to have argued that the mother had a right on her own account, but the court rejected this contention. The other passage is in 29 f., where Theopompos argues that even if he had ceded to his nephew a half share in the estate, since the nephew was outside the kin this half-share would have been claimed by relatives on the mother's side, viz. Glaukon, the uterine brother of Hagnias; and he goes on τοῦτο δ', εἰ μὴ ἐβούλετο οὗτος, ἡ Ἁγνίου κἀκείνου μήτηρ, προσῆκον καὶ αὐτῇ τῆς ἀγχιστείας τοῦ αὑτῆς υἱέος. This is not, *pace* Wyse in his note on the former passage, in contradiction with that passage. Theopompos is simply saying that, even if Glaukon had not pressed a claim, the mother could have done so by virtue of her second cousinship to Hagnias. He is surely not admitting what he had there denied, that the mother had a right *qua* mother.

(iv) *Collaterals*

There were two terms which were used to embrace relatives other than ascendants or descendants. These were ἀγχιστεία and συγγένεια. The former of these was the narrower and the more technical. It denoted all those who were related to the deceased, whether on the father's or the mother's side, down to and including sons of cousins (i.e. first cousins once removed), or possibly down to and including second cousins. This limit, which, save for the doubt as to the precise end-point, is laid down clearly both in Isai. 11 *Hagn.* and in Dem. 43 *Makart.*, had a double significance.[1] For the law of homicide it determined the body of relatives of a slain man on whom, in the absence of direct descendants, was laid the responsibility of avenging the dead man and whose unanimous consent was needed if the slayer was to be freed by an act of composition (αἴδεσις) from banishment. For the law of succession it determined the limit of relatives of the deceased's father who were entitled before relatives of his mother could come in; a father's first cousin once removed (possibly a father's second cousin) would take before any relative on the mother's side. The term συγγένεια on the other hand had no such restrictive use and would apply to relatives beyond this limit.[2] Thus all ἀγχιστεῖς were συγγενεῖς, but not all συγγενεῖς were ἀγχιστεῖς.[3]

[1] See, for example, Isai. 11 *Hagn.* 11 τὸ μὲν γὰρ εἶναι τὴν ἀχχιστείαν ἀνεψιοῖς πρὸς πατρὸς μέχρι ἀνεψιῶν παίδων ὁμολογεῖται παρὰ πάντων, Dem. 43 *Makart.* 51 (p. 138, n. 3, above). Theopompos succeeded in a claim based on this law in a suit for the estate of Hagnias. The father of Theopompos, however, was not the first cousin of Hagnias, but his first cousin once removed. Theopompos was Hagnias' second cousin. The usual view has been that Theopompos simply hoodwinked the court. But he must have hoodwinked the archon as well, since the relationship on which his claim was based must have been set out at the ἀνάκρισις. For the grave improbability of this see A. R. W. Harrison, *CR* 61 (1947), 41 f., who suggests that ἀνεψιός could mean 'first cousin once removed', and it is significant that in Dem. 43 *Makart.* 49 Philagros, who stands in just the same relationship to Hagnias as does Theopompos' father, is described as ἀνεψιὸς τοῦ Ἁγνίου. This interpretation, which admittedly raises difficulties about the whole order of succession (see below), does not find favour with L. Lepri, *Sui rapporti di parentela in dir. att.* (Milan, 1959), 8 ff.

[2] An instructive instance in Dem. 43 *Makart.* 79 where συγγενεῖς is used of all the descendants of Bouselos, the great-grandfather of Hagnias and Theopompos, whereas on the hypothesis of the speaker only certain of them were ἀγχιστεῖς of Hagnias.

[3] Suda s.v. ἀγχιστεύς· ἀγχιστεῖς οἱ ἀπὸ ἀδελφῶν καὶ ἀνεψιῶν καὶ θείων κατὰ πατέρα καὶ μητέρα ἐγγυτάτω τοῦ τελευτήσαντος. οἱ δὲ ἔξω τούτων, συγγενεῖς μόνον.

Within the ἀγχιστεία there was a fixed order of relatives entitled to succeed on the father's side, and then, if there was no representative of any of these classes on his side, succession passed to relatives on the mother's side in the same order. Anyone in a nearer group excluded all those more distantly related, while those in the same group shared equally; if one in a group had predeceased the *de cuius* leaving children, those children took his share in equal portions. The competing claims of males and females will be discussed later. This is the order: (1) brothers of the deceased by the same father and their descendants without limit; sharing was *per stirpes*;[1] (2) sisters of the deceased by the same father and their descendants without limit, also sharing *per stirpes*;[2] (3) paternal uncles, their children, and grandchildren;[3]

An. Bekk. (*Λέξ. Ῥητ.*) 213, (*Λέξ. Χρησ.*) 333. For the homicide rule Dem. 43 *Makart.* 57 *ΝΟΜΟΙ*. προειπεῖν τῷ κτείναντι ἐν ἀγορᾷ ἐντὸς ἀνεψιότητος καὶ ἀνεψιοῦ, συνδιώκειν δὲ καὶ ἀνεψιοὺς καὶ ἀνεψιῶν παῖδας καὶ γαμβροὺς καὶ πενθεροὺς καὶ φράτερας. Cf. *IG* i². 115. 20–23 (Tod *GHI* 87).

[1] Where there were no surviving brothers the law speaks only of sons of brothers, not of remoter descendants (ἐὰν δὲ μὴ ἀδελφοὶ ὦσιν ἢ ἀδελφῶν παῖδες). It is true that these words are followed by a lacuna, but it is very unlikely that the lacuna contained any reference to remoter descendants of the brothers. Nevertheless on *a priori* grounds it seems extremely improbable that a brother's grandson should have been outside the ἀγχιστεία. That sharing was *per stirpes* and not *per capita* is suggested by the phrase in the law τὴν τοῦ πατρὸς μοῖραν λαγχάνειν. Concrete cases alleged to exemplify this rule do not do so. Thus in Isai. 7 *Apollod.* 5, adduced for this purpose by Lips., *AR* 554, n. 40, we have three brothers, Eupolis, Mneson, and Thrasyllos; Mneson dies childless and the speaker alleges that his estate should have been divided in equal shares between Eupolis and the only son of Thrasyllos, Apollodoros. Even granting with Lips. (against Caillemer, *Succession* 83 f.) that Thrasyllos predeceased Mneson, the passage proves representation, but it would only prove division *per stirpes* if Eupolis had also predeceased him and been survived by two or more children, when the principle would have dictated one half-share for Apollodoros and the other half-share to be divided between the sons of Eupolis. For a similarly misapplied case as between a sister and the son of another sister of the deceased see above, p. 131, n. 1.

[2] In the lacuna in the text of the law (p. 138, n. 3, above) the first words missing are almost certainly ἀδελφὰς ὁμοπατρίας καὶ παῖδας: the paraphrase of the law in Isai. 11 *Hagn.* 2 reads ἐὰν δ' οὗτοι μὴ ὦσι (viz. brothers by the same father and their sons), δεύτερον ἀδελφὰς ὁμοπατρίας καλεῖ καὶ παῖδας τοὺς ἐκ τούτων. The view that where there were sisters and children of sisters, all surviving, all these, both mothers and children, shared *per capita* (advanced by Bunsen, *De iur. her. Ath.* 27 ff.) is refuted (1) by Isai. 7 *Apollod.* 19, 31, 44, from which it seems fairly clear that the estate of Apollodoros II was divided into two equal shares and one was allotted to a surviving sister who had children while the other was allotted to the son of his other sister who had predeceased him: (2) by Isai. 3 *Pyrrh.* 3, which shows that Pyrrhos' sister was his heir, although at the time of the suit she had a son who was of age. On another view where the deceased had had only sisters

[*Footnotes 2 and 3 continued on opposite page*

sharing was *per capita* between surviving sisters and the children of any sisters that were dead. This was the view of Schömann, *Isai.* 288, *Allg. Literaturz.* (1840) 513; but he relies on Isai. 5 *Dikai.* 9, 12, 16, and 26, reading in the last passage instead of the manuscript *Πρωταρχίδῃ . . . ἔδωκε Δικαιογένης τὴν ἀδελφὴν τὴν ἑαυτοῦ* either *τὴν ἀδελφὴν τοῦ . . .*, where the lacuna contains the name of a male first cousin of the speaker, a son of one of the three sisters of Dikaiogenes II other than the speaker's mother, or *τὴν ἀδελφὴν τούτου*, where *τούτου* refers to Kephisodotos, one of his first cousins, who was with him in court. Schömann argues from these passages that each of the children (whether male or female) of a deceased sister inherited the same amount as a living sister. This rule seems irrational in itself and differs from the rule appertaining to the children of brothers: moreover, it assumes that Kephisodotos shared equally with his sister, which is plainly incompatible with the principle *κρατεῖν τοὺς ἄρρενας καὶ τοὺς ἐκ τῶν ἀρρένων*. These *a priori* improbabilities render Schömann's arguments suspect, and he has not taken sufficient account of the fact that at different points the speaker has two distinct situations in mind: in one the estate of Dikaiogenes II was distributed under the terms of a will which gave one-third to Dikaiogenes III and divided the other two-thirds equally among the four sisters of Dikaiogenes II, who were all alive at his death; at this stage some of the estate was in the hands of a daughter of Kephisophon who had married a sister of the *de cuius* Dikaiogenes II; she was ousted from this property by Dikaiogenes III twelve years after Dikaiogenes II's death, when he got a court's verdict that he was the adopted son of the *de cuius* (para. 9); but at that time this lady was holding in virtue of a will under which her mother had received one-sixth of the estate, and her position has therefore no bearing on the rules of intestate succession. In the other situation envisaged by the speaker he and his partners in litigation are no longer relying on a will, but are claiming intestate succession for the four sisters of the *de cuius*; at that stage we may suppose that the claim of the daughter of Kephisophon was subsumed under that of her brother Menexenos (M. III in Wyse's stemma, M. II in Forster's stemma). Even if the wife of Protarchides of para. 26 was, as Schömann supposes, a niece and not a sister of Dikaiogenes II, and if, as he also supposes, she had a brother, Schömann's unwelcome conclusions do not stand, for, although the speaker says of this woman that she was entitled to the same share as was his own mother, the shares he is speaking of are not the shares of the four sisters *ab intestato* but their shares to two-thirds of the estate under the compromise agreement reached in court with Dikaiogenes III (para. 18). All one could safely conclude from Schömann's suppositions would be that, *if* this lady was a niece and *if* she had a brother, the brother for some reason unknown to us did not participate in his mother's share of the estate as divided under the compromise; but in any case these are only suppositions based on an emended text. For a detailed refutation of Schömann see Wyse, *Isai.* 443 ff. Cf. also Caillemer, *Succession* 100 ff., Beauch. iii. 515 f., 524 ff., Lips., *AR* 554, n. 42.

[3] Isai. 10 *Aristarch.* 5 states that Aristomenes could claim the hand of his brother's daughter, who was an *ἐπίκληρος*: 3 *Pyrrh.* 63 and 74 imply that the brothers of a paternal grandmother (i.e. maternal uncles of the deceased) could claim the hand of an *ἐπίκληρος*: 1 *Kleonym.* 44 states that the maternal uncle of the speakers would have been entitled to their estate *ab intestato*, had they died. This is all evidence *a fortiori* that a paternal uncle appeared at some point in the list, and he probably appeared at this point; hence Lipsius's proposal to insert in the lacuna in Dem. 43 *Makart.* 51, in addition to sisters of the deceased by the same father and their children, paternal uncles and aunts and their children (p. 138, n. 3, above), Lips., *AR* 556, n. 43. See also Schömann, *Isai.* 437 f., Caillemer, *Succession* 39, 105 f., Hafter, *Erbtochter* 37, Beauch. i. 430 f., iii. 531 ff. See also Plato, *Laws* 924 e.

(4) paternal aunts, their children and grandchildren;[1] on the doubtful interpretation of Isai. 11 *Hagn.* suggested on p. 143, n. 1, above, there would come next (4*a*) paternal great-uncles with their children and grandchildren and (4*b*) paternal great-aunts with their children and grandchildren;[2] (5) brothers of the deceased by the same mother; (6) sisters by the same mother, both with descendants without limit; (7) maternal uncles; (8) maternal aunts, in both cases with their children and grandchildren; again doubtfully (8*a*) maternal great-uncles; (8*b*) maternal great-aunts, with their children and grandchildren. This exhausted the ἀγχιστεία. If there were no relatives within the ἀγχιστεία the law simply uses for the next entitled the vague phrase 'the nearest on the father's side' (Dem. 43 *Makart.* 51, ἐὰν δὲ μηδετέρωθεν ᾖ ἐντὸς τούτων, τὸν πρὸς πατρὸς ἐγγυτάτω κύριον εἶναι).[3] One would imagine that the first people in this class would be the grandchildren of ἀνεψιοί (viz., either second cousins or second cousins once removed) on the father's side and then perhaps descendants of the deceased's paternal grandmother.[4]

[1] Proved by the same evidence as that cited in the preceding note. But Jones, *LLTG* 194, n. 1, suggests that paternal uncles and aunts, though not mentioned in the law (there is no reference to them in Isai. 11 *Hagn.* 1), took by implication from the right given to first cousins.

[2] If Theopompos' claim to Hagnias' estate in Isai. was justified we must assume that it was derived through Stratios I, his own grandfather and Hagnias' great-uncle (see stemma in Wyse ad loc.). On this view Theopompos' father, Charidemos, was entitled to be called the ἀνεψιός of Hagnias. In our terminology he was his first cousin once removed. The French language has an advantage over English and Greek in describing first cousins once removed; they are called 'oncle' and 'neveu à la mode de Bretagne' according to the generation of each member of the pair. Some scholars have argued that the phrase μέχρι ἀνεψιῶν παίδων in the law does not mean strictly 'down to and including *sons* and *daughters* of ἀνεψιοί 'but 'down to *descendants* of ἀνεψιοί'; in other words, that here too, as in the former categories, representation was *in infinitum* (Caillemer, *Succession* 108, MSL 585, n. 274, Thalheim, *RA* 68, n. 1, Beauch. iii. 536): this argument was disposed of by Wyse, *Isai.* 566, followed by Lips., *AR* 556, n. 44; he pointed out that there could have been no point in a limit which was infinitely extensible.

[3] Paoli, *SDHI* 2 (1936), 78. There is an apparent conflict between this clause in the law and Theopompos' statement of his case in Isai. 11 *Hagn.* 1–3, where, having reached the sons of ἀνεψιοί on the father's and then on the mother's side, he says ταύτας ποιεῖ τὰς ἀγχιστείας ὁ νομοθέτης μόνας, and of his own nephew, who was one degree further from the *de cuius* than himself, he says ἔξω τῆς συγγενείας ἐστίν; but this use of συγγενεία here must be inexact (see p. 143).

[4] Caillemer, *Succession* 108, for no very good reason puts descendants of the deceased's paternal grandmother before his relatives by the same mother; in other words, the half-brother by the same mother of the father of the *de cuius* and his descendants *in infinitum* would have come before the brothers of the *de cuius* by the same mother. Lips. *AR* 559, n. 49.

The possibility that there would be no relatives at all on the father's side, as well as none on the mother's side within the ἀγχιστεία, was sufficiently remote for the legislator to ignore it and also to ignore the possibility of *bona vacantia*.[1] The rule giving precedence to males has been the subject of some controversy. It is stated as follows in the law: κρατεῖν τοὺς ἄρρενας καὶ τοὺς ἐκ τῶν ἀρρένων, ἐὰν ἐκ τῶν αὐτῶν ὦσι, καὶ ἐὰν γένει ἀπωτέρω (see p. 138, n. 3, above). This should be translated 'males and the issue of males, if they are of the same stock (viz., as females and the issue of females), are to have precedence, even if they are more remotely related to the deceased'. The straightforward interpretation of this, followed, for example, by Lipsius, seems the best. To borrow his examples, under this rule the deceased's sister would be excluded by a son of his brother, his paternal aunt by the son of a paternal uncle, the daughter of a paternal uncle by a son of a son of the same paternal uncle, the daughter of a paternal aunt by the son of a son of the same paternal aunt. It is probable, though by no means certain, that when the daughter of a paternal uncle was in competition with the son of a son of a different paternal uncle—and equally with the issue of paternal aunts—the principle of representation prevailed, a principle expressed earlier in the law in relation to the deceased's brothers in the words ἐὰν παῖδες ἐξ ἀδελφῶν γνήσιοι, τὴν τοῦ πατρὸς μοῖραν λαγχάνειν; in other words, the daughter of paternal uncle A would get A's share and the son of the son of paternal uncle B would get B's; for the purposes of this rule this woman and this man were not ἐκ τῶν αὐτῶν.[2]

[1] Caillemer, *Succession* 133, followed by Beauch. iii. 571, believed that the power of the archon 'to look after houses so as to see that they become not void' (Isai. 7 *Apollod.* 30) meant that the archon had to appoint an heir to *bona vacantia*; he cited Anaximenes, *Rhet. ad Alex. Rh. Gr.* p. 22. 14 Hammer in support. Wyse, *Isai.* 576 rightly points out that the passage of Anaximenes has nothing to do with *bona vacantia*. The normal Athenian's eagerness not to leave his house desolate, joined to the ease with which he could adopt a child, must have made *bona vacantia* a very remote possibility.

[2] See Wyse, *Isai.* 560 and 565 (the latter page has a very clear statement of the most probable interpretation of the law). Isai. 7 *Apollod.* 18–20 contains an argument which has led to much controversy on this rule. The estate in that case was that of Apollodoros I, and the speaker is claiming as an adopted son. Apollodoros I had had a paternal uncle, Eupolis, who had three children: (1) Apollodoros II, who had died without issue before A. I; (2) a daughter married to Aischines; she too was dead, but was survived by a son, Thrasyboulos; (3) another daughter married to Pronapes who is claiming the estate by challenging the adoption. In the passage under discussion the speaker is arguing *a fortiori* from the failure of

Something was said earlier (p. 66) of the bearing of legitimacy (γνησιότης) on the right to inherit *ab intestato*. The last clause of the law (quoted p. 138, n. 3) excludes bastards, male and female, from the ἀγχιστεῖς; but they could conceivably have come in after the ἀγχιστεῖς.[1]

We may conjecture that succession *ab intestato* of metics in Athens was governed by the same rules as held for citizens. The relevant court cases were under the direction of the polemarch.[2]

The property of a freedman probably devolved on his children, if any survived him. If he died childless and intestate a passage in Isaios, supported by one in Anaximenes, suggests that his property went to his manumittor or his manumittor's heir.[3] It is an open

Thrasyboulos to contest his claim; for, he says, while the law explicitly states that a sister of the *de cuius* and the nephew of another (predeceased) sister should share equally (*νόμος . . . τήν τε ἀδελφὴν ὁμοίως, κἂν ἐξ ἑτέρας ἀδελφιδοῦς ᾖ γεγονώς, ἰσομοίρους τῶν χρημάτων καθίστησι*), and in fact the estate of Apollodoros II had been divided between Thrasyboulos and the wife of Pronapes accordingly, when it came to remoter kin (viz. *ἀνεψιοί*) the rule *κρατεῖν τοὺς ἄρρενας* prevailed, and, had there been an intestacy in relation to the estate of Apollodoros I (as distinct from A. II), Thrasyboulos would have shut out his aunt, the wife of Pronapes. The last part of this argument is probably a misrepresentation of the law—it is in any case only describing a hypothetical situation. The principle *κρατεῖν τοὺς ἄρρενας* ought perhaps at first sight to have operated to exclude the wife of Pronapes from any share in the estate of Apollodoros II; we may suppose that the reason it did not was that for the purposes of this clause the two claimants were not 'from the same source' (*ἐκ τῶν αὐτῶν*). But the same reasoning would have applied if they had both been claimants *ab intestato* to the estate of Apollodoros I; if on the other hand Thrasyboulos had been son of a *brother* of Apollodoros II he would have excluded his aunt from either estate, since his father, through whom his claim arose, and his aunt were *ἐκ τῶν αὐτῶν*. See P. Roussel, *Isée* 126. Put in another way, the principle 'males have precedence' applied to those persons in the family tree through whom any two or more rival claimants traced their claim: a brother's son ousts a sister because the brother would have done, a sister's son does not because the sister would not; the son of a son of a paternal uncle ousts the daughter of the same paternal uncle because his father would have done so (she would have been his sister). On the other hand, the son of the son of paternal uncle B would not oust the daughter of paternal uncle A because A would not be ousted by his brother B.

[1] See Glotz, *Solidarité* 346, Gernet, *RÉG* 33 (1920), 265 (*DSGA* 143); but these authors are wrong in equating exclusion from the ἀγχιστεία with total exclusion from all inheritance rights.

[2] Ar., *Ath. Pol.* 58. 3 *αὐτὸς* (sc. *ὁ πολέμαρχος*) *εἰσάγει δίκας τὰς . . . κλήρων καὶ ἐπικλήρων τοῖς μετοίκοις*, Dem. 46 *Steph.* ii. 22 *νόμος κελεύει ἐπιδικασίαν εἶναι τῶν ἐπικλήρων ἁπασῶν, καὶ ξένων καὶ ἀστῶν, καὶ περὶ μὲν τῶν πολιτῶν τὸν ἄρχοντα εἰσάγειν καὶ ἐπιμελεῖσθαι, περὶ δὲ τῶν μετοίκων τὸν πολέμαρχον*; Ter., *Andr.* 800; Caillemer, *Succession* 140 ff.

[3] Isai. 4 *Nikostr.* 9 with Wyse's note ad loc., Anaximenes *Rhet. ad Alex.* 1 (*Rh. Gr.* p. 16. 4 Hammer). Dem. 47 *Euerg.* 70 shows that a freedwoman was regarded as no longer belonging to the house of the son of her former master for the purposes of determining whether he was required to prosecute in the case of her death by

question whether a childless freedman was permitted to dispose of his property by will. This may have depended on the terms of his manumission. Whether children born before his manumission qualified as his heirs we do not know. They probably did not, but this and other matters were no doubt often provided for by agreement at the time of the manumission.[1]

§ 4. *Wills*

(i) *Introduction*

The evolution of the will is of great importance sociologically, and it happens that we have the evidence to trace this evolution at Athens rather more clearly than that of many other legal institutions. It would not be in keeping with the plan of this book to trace the history of this evolution here, and the following paragraphs are confined to giving the rules as they were at the time of the orators. But it is particularly true of this topic that that period was one of transition and that the rules then prevailing can only be fully understood in the light of the evolution as a whole.[2]

For the understanding of the rules that obtained in the fourth century the most significant facts that emerge from an historical survey are that originally a man could in no circumstances determine the ownership of things belonging to his patrimony after he should die; that Solon took the first legislative step to granting testamentary rights to an owner; but that even by the fourth century these rights were still severely limited.[3]

violence; but we are not entitled to deduce from this that the man would not have had a claim to any property she might have left. Caillemer, *Succession* 136, Lips., *AR*. 560, n. 54.

[1] Mitteis, *RV* 384 ff., Beauch. ii. 491 ff., iii. 573 ff., Thalheim, *RA* 25 ff. We shall have more to say on this topic in connexion with the general status of metics and of slaves (pp. 185, 195, below). If Athenian law here followed the pattern which can be traced elsewhere in Greece from numerous manumission documents, there were many more shades of status between slavery and complete freedom, and these were sketched in by the agreements made on the liberation of the slave.

[2] To the works cited on p. 123, n. 2, add: F. O. Norton, *Lexicog. and Hist. St. of* διαθήκη (Chicago, 1908), Partsch, *GB* 228 ff., Thalheim, *Z* 31 (1910), 398–401, *BPW* 40 (1920), 1103 f., Weiss, *GP* 235 ff., F. Kraus, *Form. de Gr. Test.* (Giessen, 1915), J. V. A. Fine, *Hesperia*, Suppl. 9 (1951), 185 ff., F. S. Boncompte, *St. Paoli* (Firenze, 1955), 629–42, E. Ruschenbusch, *Z* 79 (1962), 307, Ziebarth, *RE* s.vv. διαθήκη, δόσις (1903).

[3] Isai. 9 *Astyph.* 12, 4 *Nikostr.* 12 show the sort of prejudice against devising

The normal words for a will and for making a will were διαθήκη (the plural διαθῆκαι is often used, especially by Isaios, for a single will) and διατίθεσθαι.[1] The words δόσις and διδόναι were also used.[2] We can be fairly confident that the formula τὰ ἑαυτοῦ διαθέσθαι ὅπως ἂν ἐθέλῃ goes back to Solon and that the noun διαθήκη owes its origin to this use of the verb διατίθεσθαι.[3] It is, however, unsafe to build too much on the meaning of this word in constructing a view of the original, or of the eventual, nature of the Athenian will. All we can say is that the use of the word in his law is perfectly compatible with the theory that originally Solon did nothing more than allow a man who had no sons to adopt whom he pleased *inter vivos*; but it is equally compatible with the view that he allowed such a man complete testamentary freedom.[4]

property by will which still existed in the early fourth century. Cf. also Ar., *Probl.* 950^b (p. 125, n. 1, above).

[1] See especially s.vv. in Goligher and Maguiness, *Index to the Speeches of Isaeus* (Cambridge, 1961, reprinted from *Hermathena* 51 (1938), and later vols.).

[2] Isai. 4 *Nikostr.* 22, 24, 25, 9 *Astyph.* 8; Ar., *Pol.* 1309^{a}24, for inheritance κατὰ γένος contrasted with inheritance κατὰ δόσιν.

[3] The actual law is cited in Dem. 46 *Steph.* ii. 14 (see p. 84, n. 6, above). E. F. Bruck, *Zur Gesch. der Verfügungen von Todeswegen im altgr. R.* (Breslau, 1909), 13 f., questions whether the words διαθέσθαι τὰ ἑαυτοῦ (described by Wyse, *Isai.* 326, as 'the consecrated phrase of Solon's law') go back as far as Solon. Whether they do or do not, they are certainly the words which appeared in the law as it stood in the classical period, and the orators thus quote it, as in Isai. 2 *Menekl.* 13, 3 *Pyrrh.* 68, 6 *Philokt.* 9, Dem. 44 *Leoch.* 67 f., Hyper. 5 *Athenog.* 17. In other passages purporting to refer to the law the words used are δοῦναι τὰ ἑαυτοῦ, as in Isai. 4 *Nikostr.* 16, Dem. 20 *Lept.* 102, Ar., *Ath. Pol.* 35. 2, Plut., *Sol.* 21: this indicates that by the fourth century the words διαθέσθαι and δοῦναι were in this context synonymous; but it remains probable that the word in the original law of Solon was διαθέσθαι.

[4] Bruck, loc. cit. (n. 2, above), argues convincingly that the word is quite appropriate to describe a transaction between two parties (which is what adoption *inter vivos* was), as against Thalheim, who had claimed that the word necessarily implied disposal of one's property after death (*BPW* (1909), 877 ff.). On the other hand, the word need not imply two parties, and the inclusion of διάθηκαι among συμβόλαια in Isai. 4 *Nikostr.* 12 (cf. 10 *Aristarch.* 10) lends no support to the view that it does; the latter word has the very wide sense of 'legal transaction': so Wyse, *Isai.* 384, quoting Schulin, *Gr. Test.* 8, n. 6, Schultess, *VAR* 104, Beauch. ii. 364, n. 3 (cf. also Lips., *AR* 562, n. 59, 568, n. 77); Bunsen, *De iur. her. Ath.* 53 had argued from the passage in Isai. 4 *Nikostr.* 12 that an Athenian will was a contract, and this is on the whole the view of Bruck in *Schenkung* 115 ff. Ruschenbusch argues against Bruck in *Z* 79 (1962), 307 ff. Note that Isai. 2 *Menekl.* 13 gives as an equivalent for the phrase in the law τὰ ἑαυτοῦ ἐξεῖναι διαθέσθαι ὅπως ἂν ἐθέλῃ, ἐὰν μὴ παῖδες ἄρρενες ὦσι γνήσιοι the words τοῖς ἄπαισι τῶν ἀνθρώπων τὸ ἐξεῖναι ποιήσασθαι ὅν τινα ἂν βούλωνται. We can conclude from this that the right of adoption *inter vivos*, was part of what Solon's law conferred upon the childless, but not that it was necessarily all that it conferred: but see p. 82, n. 2.

(ii) *Capacity*

Neither minors nor women were qualified to make a will.[1] We have little direct evidence for the testamentary rights, if any, of those of foreign, metic, or other non-citizen status; but there is slight *a priori* probability that the rules here followed the same pattern as the rules for their succession to estates *ab intestato* (set out on pp. 148 ff., above). This would mean that the polemarch's court would have admitted the validity of wills made by foreigners, metics, or freedmen provided that other conditions analogous to those required of citizens were present.[2]

No man could dispose of his property by will if he had legitimate sons. If he had only legitimate daughters he could, but it had to be 'with them', that is, by marrying them to men whom he adopted.[3] There can be no doubt that this was the strict letter of the law. It is, however, clear that in the fourth century at least it was possible for a man who had sons to make some dispositions of his property by will. Thus, if we are to believe Lysias, Konon out of an estate of which the value was some forty talents left no less than twenty-three talents away from his son.[4] Demosthenes' father had made a will including considerable bequests for the dowries of his widow and his daughter; Demosthenes when he came of age did not contest the validity of these bequests.[5]

[1] Isai. 10 *Aristarch.* 10 παιδὸς γὰρ οὐκ ἔξεστι διαθήκην γενέσθαι· ὁ γὰρ νόμος διαρρήδην κωλύει παιδὶ μὴ ἐξεῖναι συμβάλλειν μηδὲ γυναικὶ πέρα μεδίμνου κριθῶν. Bunsen, *De iur. her. Ath.* 56, followed by Bruck, *Schenkung* 111, questioned the incapacity of women to testate on the ground that they seem to do so in Dem. 36 *For Phorm.* 14, 41 *Spoud.* 9; but the first of these was probably a gift *inter vivos* and the second a devise through the lady's κύριος: see Schulin, *Gr. Test.* 11 f., Lips., *AR* 566, n. 68.

[2] The wills of the philosophers Aristotle, Theophrastos, Lykon, and Straton, all metics, described in D.L. 5. 11, 51, 61, 69, must all have had validity at least as to certain of their conditions in Athens: Bruns, *Z* 1 (1880), 1 ff., Dareste, *AEG* 16 (1882), 1 ff., Lips., *AR* 564, n. 63, Wyse, *Isai.* 379 ff., Bu. Sw. 984 f.

[3] Isai. 3 *Pyrrh.* 68 ὁ γὰρ νόμος διαρρήδην λέγει ἐξεῖναι διαθέσθαι ὅπως ἂν ἐθέλῃ τις τὰ αὑτοῦ, ἐὰν μὴ παῖδας καταλίπῃ ἄρρενας· ἂν δὲ θηλείας καταλίπῃ, σὺν ταύταις, ibid. 42 οὔτε γὰρ διαθέσθαι οὔτε δοῦναι οὐδενὶ οὐδὲν ἔξεστι τῶν ἑαυτοῦ ἄνευ τῶν θυγατέρων, ἐάν τις καταλιπὼν γνησίας τελευτᾷ, 6 *Philokt.* 28 (p. 130, n. 4, above), 2 *Menekl.* 13, 10 *Aristarch.* 13 καὶ τῷ μὲν πατρὶ αὐτῆς, εἰ παῖδες ἄρρενες μὴ ἐγένοντο, οὐκ ἂν ἐξῆν ἄνευ ταύτης διαθέσθαι· κελεύει γὰρ ὁ νόμος σὺν ταύταις κύριον εἶναι δοῦναι, ἐάν τῳ βούληται, τὰ ἑαυτοῦ. See Wyse, *Isai.* 248, 325.

[4] Lys. 19 *Prop. Aristoph.* 39 ff. Gernet ad loc. suggests that the bulk of Konon's fortune consisted in additions to his patrimony (acquêts) and that this accounts for the large sum at his free disposal.

[5] Dem. 27 *Aphob.* i. 5, 42 f., 28 *Aphob.* ii. 15.

Pasion, who had two sons, left a will securing some advantage to the elder (πρεσβεῖα) and containing other dispositions.[1] Polyeuktos, who had no sons but was survived by two daughters, disposed of some of his property by will without making either of their husbands his adopted son.[2] These concrete cases show that the simple principle 'no man shall "dispose of his own" (τὰ ἑαυτοῦ διαθέσθαι) if he has legitimate sons' had been considerably eroded by the fourth century, and it must have been a matter for the courts to decide in any particular case whether a man had gone too far in leaving property away from legitimate sons. Testators would have had to make nice calculations on the matter, bearing in mind the known propensity of the courts to override wills.[3]

There was another respect in which the full rigour of the rule that no one with sons could make a will was modified. A law expressly laid down that a man who had legitimate sons could make a will which would become valid if the sons died while still minors.[4]

The law required that a testator's judgement should not have been clouded by madness, senility, drugs, sickness, undue influence of women, force, or restriction of liberty.[5] A public

[1] Dem. 36 *For Phorm.* 34 f., 45 *Steph.* i. 28 which gives the text of the will: on this see H. Schucht, *BPW* 39 (1919), 1120 f., 1143 ff.

[2] Dem. 41 *Spoud.* 6. We should perhaps add the case of Diodotos, who was survived by two sons and a daughter, but had none the less on leaving for an expedition during which he died left with his brother a διαθήκη which among other provisions directed that legacies should be paid out of his estate to his wife and his daughter (Lys. 32 *Diogeit.* 6); Bruck, *Schenkung* 123 f., followed by Gernet, *Lys.* ii. 185, n. 4, regards this transaction as a hybrid form between a will proper and *donatio mortis causa*; but see Lips., *AR* 566, n. 67. On the general validity of the law see also Wyse, *Isai.* 515.

[3] Bruck, *Schenkung* 149, and for a comparable problem in the development of the Roman will H. J. Jolowicz, *Hist. Intr. R. Law* 131 f.

[4] Dem. 46 *Steph.* ii. 24; see p. 75, n. 3, p. 85. To E. Ruschenbusch, *Z* 79 (1962), 307 f., the wording of this law indicates that when it was made the word διατίθεσθαι could not have been used of adoption *inter vivos*, since such an adoption, involving as it did the severance of the adoptee from his natural family, could hardly have been made with the condition that it would become invalid if any of the existing sons reached majority. This really begs the question, since, if a will leaving property to a man adopted *inter vivos* was in fact a kind of contract, an adoptee would *ex hypothesi* have had to accept this risk. It does, however, seem probable that this particular clause dates from a period when disposition of property by will was not restricted to cases of adoption *inter vivos*.

[5] Dem. 46 *Steph.* ii. 14 (p. 84, n. 6, above). The phraseology of the law there cited is fairly closely confirmed by actual phrases of the orators as in Dem., ibid. 16, Lys., fr. 74 Th. (Suda s.v. διάθεσις), Isai. 6 *Philokt.* 9, 4 *Nikostr.* 16, Hyper. 5 *Athenog.* 17. Ar., *Ath. Pol.* 35. 2, speaking of the Thirty's attempt to lessen the power

official who had not yet cleared his accounts could not make a will until he had done so.[1]

It is possible that a freedman without children could not make a will, but was necessarily succeeded by his former master (p. 148, above).

There were cases where the right to take under a will was denied. Thus in wills involving adoption a man could only take if he was qualified to be adopted (see p. 87, above). No foreigner or metic could take a gift of land by will unless he had the right of ἔγκτησις.[2]

(iii) *Form*

In consonance with the general looseness of Athenian legal institutions, there seem to have been no strict rules as to the form a will must take. Normally no doubt it was in writing, though there is one passage in Demosthenes which strongly suggests an oral will.[3] Again, it was normal practice to have witnesses at the making of a will; not to do so would have been very unwise in view of the general prejudice against wills.[4] But there is no conclusive evidence that witnesses were needed to make the will valid, and there is some slight evidence that they were not.[5]

of the dikasteries by removing causes of litigation which might arise out of Solon's laws, gives the following example: *οἷον περὶ τοῦ δοῦναι τὰ ἑαυτοῦ ᾧ ἂν ἐθέλῃ κύριον ποιήσαντες καθάπαξ, τὰς δὲ προσούσας δυσκολίας "ἐὰν μὴ μανιῶν ἢ γηρῶν ἢ γυναικὶ πιθόμενος" ἀφεῖλον, ὅπως μὴ ᾖ τοῖς συκοφάνταις ἔφοδος*. See Bruck, *Schenkung* 55, Weiss, *GP* 235, Wyse, *Isai.* 223, H. Meyer-Laurin, *Gesetz und Billigkeit im attischem Prozess* (Weimar, 1965), 20 f.

[1] See above, p. 87, where it is argued that the same limitations were imposed on the right to adopt *inter vivos*. See ibid. for the object of the last limitation.

[2] See below, p. 237.

[3] Dem. 41 *Spoud.* 16 *οὐ δήπου καὶ τοὺς μάρτυρας ἔπεισα ψευδῆ μοι μαρτυρεῖν . . . τοὺς ταῖς διαθήκαις παραγενομένους*, the implication being that the dispositions of the alleged will could only be discovered by questioning witnesses; cf. Lips., *AR* 568, n. 78, Gernet, *Dem.* ii. 55.

[4] Isai. 4 *Nikostr.* 12, 9 *Astyph.* 7 ff.

[5] Id. 9 *Astyph.* 12 *εἰ μὲν ὁ Ἀστύφιλος μηδένα ἐβούλετο εἰδέναι ὅτι τὸν Κλέωνος ὑὸν ἐποιεῖτο μηδ' ὅτι διαθήκας καταλίποι, εἰκὸς ἦν μηδὲ ἄλλον μηδένα ἐγγεγράφθαι ἐν τῷ γραμματείῳ μάρτυρα· εἰ δ' ἐναντίον μαρτύρων φαίνεται διαθέμενος, τούτων δὲ μὴ τῶν μάλιστα χρωμένων ἀλλὰ τῶν ἐντυχόντων, πῶς εἰκός ἐστιν ἀληθεῖς εἶναι τὰς διαθήκας;* See Wyse ad. loc. The speaker is trying to prove that a will purporting to make Kleon's son the son of Astyphilos was a forgery; either, he argues, Astyphilos wished his testamentary adoption of Kleon's son to remain secret or he did not; if he did not, he would have had his will witnessed by relatives, members of his phratry and deme and the like, not by a random collection of strangers; if he did, he would have had no name inserted in the will *as a witness*, but only the name of Kleon's son

Where there were witnesses they did not necessarily, though they might, know the contents of the will. They were simply witnesses that a will had been made, and, when it was in writing, it is at least doubtful whether they could vouch for the fact that the document produced was the document which they had witnessed.[1] A more practical precaution against forgery was the sealing of the will by the testator.[2] It could also be deposited for safe keeping either with an official or with a friend or relative.[3]

There were certainly circumstances in which it was possible to add to or modify the terms of a will. In Isaios' first speech Kleonymos tries to recover the will which he had deposited with the astynomoi, either in order to revoke it—so the speaker—or in order to alter it—so his opponents.[4] It is doubtful whether a will could be revoked merely by making a subsequent will. The actual document had to be recovered or a solemn declaration made before witnesses that it no longer represented his will.[5] Although

whom he was adopting: thus those who use this passage to prove that a will might be valid without witnesses; but the word *ἄλλον* is difficult, and the phrase could mean that he would have inserted no name as witness *other than Kleon.*

[1] Isai. 4 *Nikostr.* 13 *τῶν διατιθεμένων οἱ πολλοὶ οὐδὲ λέγουσι τοῖς παραγιγνομένοις ὅ τι διατίθενται, ἀλλ' αὐτοῦ μόνου, τοῦ καταλιπεῖν διαθήκας, μάρτυρας παρίστανται, τοῦ δὲ συμβαίνοντός ἐστι καὶ γραμματεῖον ἀλλαγῆναι καὶ τἀναντία ταῖς τοῦ τεθνεῶτος διαθήκαις μεταγραφῆναι· οὐδὲν γὰρ μᾶλλον οἱ μάρτυρες εἴσονται, εἰ ἐφ' αἷς ἐκλήθησαν διαθήκαις, αὗται ἀποφαίνονται.*

[2] Isai. 7 *Apollod.* 1 *εἴ τις τελευτήσειν μέλλων διέθετο, εἴ τι πάθοι, τὴν οὐσίαν ἑτέρῳ καὶ ταῦτ' ἐν* (Reiske: *ταύτην* codd.) *γράμμασι κατέθετο παρά τισι σημηνάμενος.* The will of Theophrastos, given in D.L. 5. 57, concludes thus: *αἱ διαθῆκαι κεῖνται ἀντίγραφα τῷ Θεοφράστου δακτυλίῳ σεσημασμέναι, μία μὲν παρὰ Ἡγησίᾳ Ἱππάρχου· μάρτυρες κτλ. τὴν δ' ἑτέραν ἔχει Ὀλυμπιόδωρος· μάρτυρες δ' οἱ αὐτοί. τὴν δ' ἑτέραν ἔλαβεν Ἀδείμαντος, ἀπήνεγκεν δὲ Ἀνδροσθένης ὁ υἱός· μάρτυρες κτλ.* Aristoph., *Wasps* 583 ff. *κἂν ἀποθνήσκων ὁ πατήρ τῳ δῷ καταλείπων παῖδ' ἐπίκληρον, / κλάειν ἡμεῖς μακρὰ τὴν κεφαλὴν εἰπόντες τῇ διαθήκῃ / καὶ τῇ κόγχῃ τῇ πάνυ σεμνῶς τοῖς σημείοισιν ἐπούσῃ.*

[3] Theophrastos' procedure (n. 2, above) shows that there might be more than one copy of a will and that the witnesses to the different copies might be different. Diodotos had a copy of his will made, Lys. 32 *Diogeit.* 7, and when Apollodoros in Dem. 46 *Steph.* ii. 28 says *διαθήκης οὐδεὶς πώποτε ἀντίγραφα ἐποιήσατο* he is either lying or expressing in a very misleading way the fact that no one was obliged to make public a copy of what was written in his will. Cf. Isai. 4 *Nikostr.* 13 (n. 1, above) and Wyse ad loc. Kleonymos deposited his will with the astynomoi, Isai. 1 *Kleonym.* 15, though those officials had no specific connexion with such matters: for deposit of a will with relatives or friend see Lys. 32 *Diogeit.* 5, Isai. 7 *Apollod.* 1 (n. 2, above), 6 *Philokt.* 7, 9 *Astyph.* 5, Dem. 45 *Steph.* i. 18.

[4] Isai. 1 *Kleonym.* 14 *ἐβουλήθη ταύτας τὰς διαθήκας ἀνελεῖν*, ibid. 18 *ἰσχυρίζονται ταῖς διαθήκαις, λέγοντες ὡς Κλεώνυμος μετεπέμπετο τὴν ἀρχὴν οὐ λῦσαι βουλόμενος αὐτὰς ἀλλ' ἐπανορθῶσαι καὶ βεβαιῶσαι σφίσιν αὐτοῖς τὴν δωρεάν.*

[5] In Isai. 6 *Philokt.*, if we are to believe the speaker, Euktemon had deposited

there was clearly no rule that a beneficiary under a will could veto the revocation of that will—indeed, it must have been common for beneficiaries not to know that they had been named in a will until the death of the testator—where a will gave posthumous effect to an adoption *inter vivos* we must suppose that it could not be revoked without the consent of the adoptee, since he by his adoption had sacrificed all rights of inheritance from his natural father.[1]

a διαθήκη with Pythodoros; two years later he wished to annul (ἀνελεῖν) this deed, and he called upon Pythodoros to hand it over for destruction; the latter urged that this should only be done in the presence of the guardian of a daughter of one of Euktemon's daughters, and the archon upheld this plea; Euktemon then (para. 32) διομολογησάμενος ἐναντίον τοῦ ἄρχοντος καὶ τῶν παρέδρων καὶ ποιησάμενος πολλοὺς μάρτυρας ὡς οὐκέτ' αὐτῷ κέοιτο ἡ διαθήκη, ᾤχετο ἀπιών. This document had been drawn up as the instrument of a rather sordid bargain between Euktemon on the one side and his son, Philoktemon, and his sons-in-law on the other, and no doubt this granddaughter was a beneficiary under it. Wyse in his commentary on the speech holds that the document was not, properly speaking, a will, in this agreeing with Schulin, *Gr. Test.* 9, and Lips., *AR* 571, n. 87. But this is really a *petitio principii*; διαθήκη is certainly in Isaios' usage normally 'a will'; we cannot be sure whether in this particular instance the testator had an absolute right of revocation, and the action of Pythodoros, backed as it was by the archon, suggests that it was a moot point. Kleonymos tried to recover his will from the astynomoi with whom he had deposited it either, as the speaker alleges, because he wanted to cancel it or, as his opponents maintained, because he wanted to alter it in their interests; see locc. citt. in n. 4, above. The meaning of para. 25 of that speech has been obscured by commentators. The speaker is inviting the jury to guess why Kleonymos wanted to get hold of the actual will; it cannot have been, as his opponents suggest, in order to make modifications in it, since that he could have done by drawing up another document; it must have been that he wanted to cancel it: so Wyse ad loc., disagreeing with Lips., *AR* 571, n. 85. The argument, sophistic though it be, would be grotesque unless there had been a rule that one will could not be automatically cancelled by a later one.

[1] Wyse, *Isai.* 518, and Lips., *AR* 571, following Beauch. iii. 670, are too dogmatic in asserting that, to quote Wyse, 'the idea that at Athens a man could not revoke a will without the consent of the heirs therein instituted does not deserve refutation'. The *a priori* reasons for thinking that testamentary dispositions made when adopting a son *inter vivos* were on a par with a contract with that son and could not therefore be unilaterally revoked are confirmed by the case of Polyeuktos and Leokrates in Dem. 41 *Spoud.* 3 ff. On this case see p. 30, above. Polyeuktos had married one of his daughters to Leokrates, and at the same time adopted him, having no sons of his own; Leokrates was specifically made his heir and is described as κληρονόμος in para. 5. The two men fell out, the marriage was dissolved, and Leokrates sued Polyeuktos; the precise grounds are not stated, but they evidently included matters of property, for the difference was finally settled by Leokrates' recovering the property which he had introduced into the house (a dowry presumably) and ceasing to be a member of it (ἐξεκεχωρήκει ibid.). Although it is not stated in so many words, it is clear that there was a will which had to be revoked because it was tied up with Leokrates' position as heir and adoptive son of Polyeuktos.

§ 5. *Entry*

(i) *Immediate*

There were two ways in which a claimant could assert his right to property passing on a man's death. If he was a direct descendant by birth of the deceased he was entitled to enter upon the property (ἐμβατεύειν) without legal formality, and he could meet any attempt to resist his entry by a δίκη ἐξούλης.[1] If some counter-claimant wished to contest his right in the courts he could meet that claim by a solemn statement (διαμαρτυρία) that the estate was not assignable by a court, since there was a legitimate son living.[2] If his opponent took no further step he remained in possession; but it was open to the counter-claimant to make a formal objection (ἐπισκήπτεσθαι), which he then had to follow up by a suit for false declaration (δίκη ψευδομαρτυρίων) in which the defendant was the man who had made the διαμαρτυρία, whether that man was the alleged son of the deceased or someone else who had made the declaration on his behalf.[3] Most modern authorities have held that the trial of such a suit was necessarily

[1] Isai. 3 *Pyrrh.* 59 ὅτῳ γόνῳ γεγόνασι γνήσιοι παῖδες, οὐδενὶ ἐπιδικάζεσθαι τῶν πατρῴων προσήκει . . . ἅπαντες ὑμεῖς καὶ οἱ ἄλλοι πολῖται ἀνεπίδικα ἔχουσι τὰ ἑαυτῶν ἕκαστοι πατρῷα, 8 *Kir.* 34 πάντες ὑμεῖς τῶν πατρῴων, τῶν παππῴων, τῶν ἔτι περαιτέρω κληρονομεῖτε ἐκ γένους παρειληφότες τὴν ἀγχιστείαν ἀνεπίδικον. The passage from the Suda s.v. ἀνεπίδικα (cf. *An. Bekk.* [*Λέξ. Χρησ.*] 398. 2) usually quoted in this context adds nothing and is itself unintelligible unless the word πλήν is conjectured to have dropped out before ὅσα ὡς. The passage reads τῶν μὴ θεμένων διαθήκας ἐπιδικάζεσθαι τοῖς κλήροις (a genitive would have been more natural) ὁ νόμος συγχωρεῖ τοὺς ἐγγυτάτω γένους, ὅσα ὡς υἱός τις ἢ υἱδοῦς τοῦ τετελευτηκότος ἀξιοῖ κατέχειν. ταῦτα ἀνεπίδικα λέγεται. For the controversial problems connected with entry and its legal enforcement see below, pp. 217 ff.; in spite of what is said in Appendix C (p. 313) Isai. 3 *Pyrrh.* 62 does at least indicate that the δίκη ἐξούλης would have been available to a direct descendant whose entry on the inheritance was being resisted. Beauch. iii. 594, Lips., *AR* 577, Kränzlein, *Eig. und Bes.* 94.

[2] Isai. 6 *Philokt.* 4 διεμαρτύρησεν Ἀνδροκλῆς οὑτοσὶ μὴ ἐπίδικον εἶναι τὸν κλῆρον, ibid. 43 εὐθυδικίᾳ μὲν οὐκ ἐτόλμησαν εἰσελθεῖν, ἀλλὰ διεμαρτύρουν ὡς ὑπὲρ γνησίων. Androkles is acting on behalf of two putative sons of Euktemon whose estate is at issue (though the speaker tries to make it appear that it is Philoktemon's estate). Dem. 44 *Leoch.* 46 διαμεμαρτύρηκεν οὑτοσί, ὡς ἀκηκόατε, "μὴ ἐπίδικον εἶναι τὸν κλῆρον τὸν Ἀρχιάδου, ὄντων αὐτῷ παίδων γνησίων κυρίως κατὰ τὸν θεσμόν": ibid. 42, 55 ff. See also Isai. 3 *Pyrrh.* 3, 5 *Dikaiog.* 16 (next note).

[3] Isai. 5 *Dikaiog.* 16 μελλόντων δ' ἡμῶν ἀντόμνυσθαι διεμαρτύρησε Λεωχάρης οὑτοσὶ μὴ ἐπίδικον εἶναι τὸν κλῆρον ἡμῖν. ἐπισκηψαμένων (Ald.: ἐπισκεψαμένων codd.) δ' ἡμῶν ἡ μὲν λῆξις τοῦ κλήρου διεγράφη, ἡ δὲ τῶν ψευδομαρτυρίων δίκη εἰσῄει: for the reading ἐπισκηψαμένων cf. Ar., *Ath. Pol.* 68. 4, *Pol.* 1274^{b}5, Plato, *Laws* 937 b: for ψευδομαρτυρίων genitive of ψευδομαρτύριον rather than ψευδομαρτυριῶν from ψευδομαρτυρία cf. Ar., *Ath. Pol.* 59. 6, Plato, *Theait.* 148 b, and Wyse, *Isai.* 288. See also Isai. 3 *Pyrrh.* 3 f.

antecedent to, and also quite separate from, the trial of the substantive issue whether A or B had the better right: they assert that while, if the defendant in the δίκη ψευδομαρτυρίων was acquitted, *cecidit quaestio*, if he was convicted a διαδικασία would ensue.[1] U. E. Paoli, on the other hand, has argued with considerable persuasiveness that the trial of the δίκη ψευδομαρτυρίων was itself the trial of the substantive issue; a verdict for the defendant would mean that *ipso facto* the putative son was confirmed as heir, at least *vis-à-vis* that plaintiff, for the plaintiff that the putative son had to cede a better right to the plaintiff.[2] It is important to bear in mind that in judgements of this kind at Athens all that is decided is the relative rights of the parties, not an absolute right against the whole world, so that whichever way the verdict went the successful litigant might have to deal with other claimants subsequently. Thus, even if we accept Paoli's view, the successful plaintiff in a δίκη ψευδομαρτυρίων, though he would be able to oust the defendant from the property, might well find himself engaged in a διαδικασία with some third claimant.

This right of immediate entry and of making a διαμαρτυρία in reply to a counter-claim was extended also to sons adopted *inter vivos*,[3] and to daughters if there were no surviving sons or issue of sons. A daughter's claim was made through her κύριος.[4]

Claimants who had this right of immediate entry were not obliged to meet a counter-claim by means of the διαμαρτυρία. They could, if they chose, submit to an immediate trial of the issue by a court (εὐθυδικία). There are occasional suggestions, perhaps mere rhetoric, that procedure by εὐθυδικία showed a greater reliance on the justice of one's claim.[5] A man who was

[1] Beauch. iii. 597, Thalheim, *RE* 5 (1905), 324 s.v. διαμαρτυρία, Lips., *AR* 778 ff., 856, Glotz, DS s.v. *paragraphe*.

[2] Paoli, *St. Proc.* 143 ff. The issue is still open. Paoli fails to mention the first passage from Isaios quoted in p. 156, n. 3, above.

[3] See p. 95, n. 1, above.

[4] Isai. 3 *Pyrrh.* 3 ὁ κύριος τῆς εἰληχυίας τοῦ κλήρου γυναικὸς ἐτόλμησε διαμαρτυρῆσαι μὴ ἐπίδικον τῇ ἡμετέρᾳ μητρὶ τὸν τοῦ ἀδελφοῦ κλῆρον εἶναι, ὡς οὔσης γνησίας θυγατρὸς Πύρρῳ, οὗ ἦν ἐξ ἀρχῆς ὁ κλῆρος: the context makes it clear that the procedure would have been appropriate if the daughter had been in fact legitimate. For the heiress's right of entry see ibid. 62.

[5] Isai. 7 *Apollod.* 3 (p. 95, n. 1, above), 6 *Philokt.* 3 λαχόντος δὲ τοῦ Χαιρεστράτου κατὰ τὸν νόμον τοῦ κλήρου, ἐξὸν ἀμφισβητῆσαι Ἀθηναίων τῷ βουλομένῳ καὶ εὐθυδικίᾳ εἰσελθόντι εἰς ὑμᾶς, εἰ φαίνοιτο δικαιότερα λέγων, ἔχειν τὸν κλῆρον, διεμαρτύρησεν Ἀνδροκλῆς οὑτοσὶ μὴ ἐπίδικον εἶναι τὸν κλῆρον, ἀποστερῶν τοῦτον τῆς ἀμφισβητήσεως καὶ ὑμᾶς τοῦ κυρίους γενέσθαι ὅντινα δεῖ κληρονόμον καταστήσασθαι τῶν Φιλοκτήμονος (cf. Wyse ad loc.); Dem. 44 *Leoch.* 59 προελόμενος γὰρ ἕκαστος αὐτῶν τὸν ἐκ τοῦ

adopted *inter vivos* might certainly have felt it safer to proceed by εὐθυδικία, and it is conceivable that by doing so he would acquire the right, which was denied him if he merely entered on the estate, of disposing of the estate by will (see p. 86, above). Certainly the διαμαρτυρία was simpler, for if other claimants acquiesced no further proceedings were called for. It did, however, involve a risk, a risk referred to in Dem. 44 *Leoch.* 59 (quoted on p. 157, n. 5, above). Anyone who entered a διαμαρτυρία had to make a deposit (παρακαταβολή) equivalent to one-tenth of the value of the estate: if he lost the δίκη ψευδομαρτυρίων he lost this deposit, which almost certainly went to the state. There can be little doubt that this was a rule designed to discourage the use of this procedure except in the most cast-iron cases.[1]

(ii) ἐπιδικασία

Any claimant to an inheritance who neither was a direct descendant of the deceased nor had been adopted *inter vivos* had to make application in writing to the archon, whether he was claiming as a relative or under a will; claimants under a will included specifically those who claimed to have been adopted by will.[2] Such claims could be entered at any time of the year save in

διαμαρτυρῆσαι κίνδυνον, οὐκ ἀναγκασθεὶς εἰσέρχεται. On διαμαρτυρία in general see also Gernet, *Dem.* ii. 128, Bo. Sm. ii. 76 ff., Paoli, loc. cit. (n. 2, above), Gernet, *RHD* 6 (1927), 5 ff. (*DSGA* 83 ff.); for Gernet the διαμαρτυρία was in origin a simple 'protestation' that the estate was not open to adjudication because there existed legitimate offspring. It was a later development when this turned into a piece of sworn testimony including such details as that X was a legitimate son of the *de cuius*, and only at this stage was the deponent liable, if challenged, to a δίκη ψευδομαρτυρίων.

[1] Paoli, op. cit. (p. 157, n. 2) 157 ff. suggests that there were three and only three types of inheritance case in which a παρακαταβολή was demanded: (1) when, in face of a λῆξις, a διαμαρτυρία was presented to the archon asserting μὴ ἐπίδικον εἶναι τὸν κλῆρον; (2) when, in face of a λῆξις, the right to succeed as an adoptive son was asserted; (3) when, in face of a previous assignment of the inheritance, a fresh ἐπιδικασία was set on foot by means of an ἀντιγραφή. He is followed by E. Berneker, *RE* s.v. παρακαταβολή (1949). For differing views see G. Steigertahl, *De vi et usu* παρακαταβολῆς (Celle, 1832), Caillemer, DS s.v. *amphisbetesis*, Boeckh, *Staatsh.* i. 430 f., Beauch. iii. 604 ff., Lips., *AR* 579 f., 933 ff. The lexicographers, Harpokr. s.v. ἀμφισβητεῖν, Suda s.v. ἀμφισβητεῖν 2, *An. Bekk.* (*Λέξ. Ῥητ.*) 197, Pollux 8. 32, though confused do at least confirm, *pace* Wyse, *Isai.* 374, that παρακαταβολή was only demanded in a limited category of cases, not of every litigant in an inheritance suit. For the bearing on this topic of Dem. 43 *Makart.* 5, which none of the moderns deals with satisfactorily, see p. 159, below.

[2] D.H., *Isai.* 15 οὐ δεῖ τὸν ἐπίδικον κρατεῖσθαι πρὸ δίκης, Dem. 46 *Steph.* ii. 22 *ΝΟΜΟΣ.* κληροῦν δὲ τὸν ἄρχοντα κλήρων καὶ ἐπικλήρων, ὅσοι εἰσὶ μῆνες, πλὴν τοῦ

the last month, Skirophorion; the reason for this limitation was probably that the proceedings preliminary to trial in such cases were apt to be protracted, and it was essential that the case should be brought before the court by the archon under whom it had been initiated.[1] Publicity for claims was secured in three ways: first they were posted up on the magistrate's notice-board (*σανίς*);[2] secondly they were read out at the first full assembly (*κυρία ἐκκλησία*) after they had been entered with the archon;[3] finally, at some stage which cannot be certainly identified, a herald made an announcement the terms of which are preserved in Dem. 43 *Makart.* 5 (*εἴ τις ἀμφισβητεῖν ἢ παρακαταβάλλειν βούλεται τοῦ κλήρου τοῦ* [*δεῖνος*] *ἢ κατὰ γένος ἢ κατὰ διαθήκας*).[4]

Suppose there was only one claimant, or a number with identical claims—three brothers, for example, of the deceased—the archon's court formally awarded the inheritance to him or to them.[5] If, on the other hand, opposing claims were entered,

σκιροφοριῶνος. ἀνεπίδικον δὲ κλῆρον μὴ ἔχειν. To enter such a claim was *ἐπιδικάζεσθαι τοῦ κλήρου* or *λαγχάνειν λῆξιν τοῦ κλήρου* or *λαγχάνειν τοῦ κλήρου*; the process was *ἐπιδικασία* or *λῆξις*: Isai. 3 *Pyrrh.* 2, 43, 5 *Dikaiog.* 6. Where suit was brought against one already in possession the term was *δίκην κλήρου λαγχάνειν*, as in Isai. 11 *Hagn.* 13. Chairestratos had been adopted by will by Philoktemon, and the speaker in Isai. 6 *Philokt.* 3 says of him *λαχόντος τοῦ Χαιρεστράτου κατὰ τὸν νόμον τοῦ κλήρου.* For application in writing see Isai. 3 *Pyrrh.* 30, 4 *Nikostr.* 2. For *ἐπιδικασία* of an *ἐπίκληρος* see pp. 9 ff., above.

[1] Dem. 46 *Steph.* ii. 22, p. 158, n. 2, above.

[2] Isok. 15 *Antid.* 237.

[3] Ar., *Ath. Pol.* 43. 4 *κυρίαν ἐν ᾗ δεῖ . . . τὰς λήξεις τῶν κλήρων καὶ τῶν ἐπικλήρων ἀναγιγνώσκειν, ὅπως μηδένα λάθῃ μηδὲν ἔρημον γενόμενον.*

[4] Sositheos, the speaker here, alleges that Theopompos did not dare to make the deposit and thus showed that he had no confidence in his claim to Hagnias' estate. If the deduction is to hold we must conclude that only by making a deposit could Theopompos stake a claim and that in this context *ἀμφισβητεῖν ἢ παρακαταβάλλειν* are not alternative procedures, the one involving, the other dispensing with, a deposit; the phrase will mean 'if anyone wishes to contest, viz. to make a deposit in connexion with, the inheritance'. If this, rather forced, interpretation is correct—and it seems the only feasible one—we can infer that this announcement by the herald was made at the moment when the court had made its adjudication, and that if Theopompos had chosen to make a deposit it would have been through an *ἀντιγραφή*, case (3) envisaged on p. 158, n. 1, above. Sositheos' story is confused, however, and it would seem that eventually Theopompos must in fact have made a deposit, since he did get the case reopened.

[5] That this was formally the act of the court, not merely of the archon himself, was argued by Heffter, *Ath. Gerichtsverf.* (Cöln, 1822), 385, followed by Lips., *AR* 581, Paoli, *St. Proc.* 154, n. 2. Paoli quotes Isai. 11 *Hagn.* 15 f., 26, 6 *Philokt.* 51 to show that *ἐπιδικασία* was regarded as the function of the jury whether a *κλῆρος* or an *ἐπίκληρος* was in question. It is true that these were cases where there had been a *διαδικασία*, but the terminology does suggest that formally *ἐπιδικασία* was the act

there ensued a διαδικασία τοῦ κλήρου, in which there was no defendant or plaintiff or any πρόσκλησις, nor was there, as in most civil suits, any preliminary arbitration procedure; but the parties were summoned to the ἀνάκρισις by the archon.[1] Rights in the inheritance were conferred by the judgement of the court in the διαδικασία; the view that this judgement was merely declaratory of a right originally acquired by the simple act of entering a claim with the archon is due to a misunderstanding of the phrase λῆξιν λαγχάνειν τοῦ κλήρου and of a law cited in Dem. 43 *Makart.* 16.[2]

Success in a διαδικασία did not ensure a claimant undisturbed ownership. Another διαδικασία could be set on foot, not only by litigants who had not been parties to the original suit, but even by parties who had failed in that suit but now either advanced

of the court even where a διαδικασία had not been necessary. For a different view see p. 10, n. 3, above.

[1] Dem. 44 *Leoch.* 7, 13, 40. Dem. 48 *Olymp.* 5 ff., 20 ff. shows us Olympiodoros and Kallistratos as relatives (in what degree we do not know) to the childless Komon performing funeral rites for him and dividing up his φανερὰ οὐσία between them, though in the expectation that there would be other claimants in the field. When these duly appeared and the case was about to open (23 ἐπειδὴ ἀνεκρίθησαν πρὸς τῷ ἄρχοντι ἅπασαι αἱ ἀμφισβητήσεις), Olympiodoros had been called away on an expedition and Kallistratos tried to get the hearing postponed, but the court rejected this plea and the estate was adjudged to the other claimants (26 ἐπεδίκασεν ὁ ἄρχων τοῖς ἀντιδίκοις τοῖς ἡμετέροις τὸν κλῆρον τὸν Κόμωνος: this phrase should not be pressed to mean that the archon acted independently of the jury). When Olympiodoros returned to Athens he succeeded in getting the case reopened, no doubt under the law cited in Dem. 43 *Makart.* 16 (p. 161, n. 1): on this occasion summonses were issued to all who held the estate under the previous judgement (30 προσεκλήθησαν ἅπαντες οἱ ἔχοντες τὰ τοῦ Κόμωνος κατὰ τὸν νόμον), there was another ἀνάκρισις, and the estate was adjudged to Olympiodoros. We must assume that on this occasion both he and Kallistratos would have had to make deposits.

[2] Strictly the phrase means 'to have one's claim to an inheritance entered (with the archon for subsequent adjudication)', the subsequent adjudication being a matter of form if there were no conflicting claims; but, partly perhaps because this subsequent adjudication was sometimes a matter of form, the phrase can be used to mean 'to acquire the inheritance' (in all other cases except entry by a direct descendant). Beauch. iii. 616, following Hruza, *Beitr.* i. 100 f., admits these two meanings, but holds that the second is the basic meaning and that it could never have become so but for the fact that a right in the inheritance was conferred by the mere act of entering a claim. This is a *petitio principii*, as can be clearly seen in Beauchet's treatment of Isai. 11 *Hagn.* 10: there Theopompos is arguing that his nephew, the son of Stratokles, has no claim to a share of Hagnias' estate because Stratokles had died πρὶν γενέσθαι τὰς λήξεις τῶν δικῶν: it is begging the question to deduce from this phrase that the mere entry of a claim would have conferred on Stratokles rights which would then have been transmitted to his son. For the law in *Makart.* 16 see next note. It is concerned with the special case of an estate or heiress already adjudicated but which had become the object of a second suit.

a different ground for their claim or complained that the original suit had been wrongfully decided in their absence.[1] It is not clear whether, apart from the special case of the *διαμαρτυρία*, a *δίκη ψευδομαρτυρίων* if it succeeded upset the original *διαδικασία* or merely entailed damages.[2] It was a rule in this kind of suit, which was also entitled a *διαδικασία*, that the new claimant should issue formal summonses to all those who were occupying the estate in virtue of the first suit. There was thus in this type of *διαδικασία* alone someone who was very much like a plaintiff, and it is highly probable that only the plaintiff—or plaintiffs—in such cases were required to furnish a *παρακαταβολή*.

As we learn from Isai. 3 *Pyrrh.* 58, the time limit within which such actions had to be brought was extremely liberal; they were permissible at any time during the life of the first heir or heirs and within five years of his or their death. (For a fuller discussion of this rule see pp. 220, 247f.)

The rules for claiming an inheritance by way of *ἐπιδικασία*

[1] Dem. 43 *Makart.* 16 *ΝΟΜΟΣ. ἐὰν δ' ἐπιδεδικασμένου ἀμφισβητῇ τοῦ κλήρου ἢ τῆς ἐπικλήρου, προσκαλείσθω τὸν ἐπιδεδικασμένον πρὸς τὸν ἄρχοντα, καθάπερ ἐπὶ τῶν ἄλλων δικῶν· παρακαταβολὰς δ' εἶναι τῷ ἀμφισβητοῦντι. ἐὰν δὲ μὴ προσκαλεσάμενος ἐπιδικάσηται, ἀτελὴς ἔσται ἡ ἐπιδικασία τοῦ κλήρου. ἐὰν δὲ μὴ ζῇ ὁ ἐπιδικασάμενος τοῦ κλήρου, προσκαλείσθω κατὰ ταὐτά, ᾧ ἂν ἡ προθεσμία μήπω ἐξήκῃ. τὴν δ' ἀμφισβήτησιν εἶναι τῷ ἔχοντι, καθότι ἐπεδικάσατο οὗ ἂν ἔχῃ τὰ χρήματα.* Isai. 4 *Nikostr.* 25 states explicitly that, even if the estate is awarded to the speaker's clients, other claimants could subsequently bring suit on the ground that they were nearer of kin to the *de cuius*. In Dem. 48 *Olymp.* 29 ff. (see p. 160, n. 1) one can see that Olympiodoros had some claim in equity to have the case reopened on the ground of his enforced absence during the earlier trial, but Kallistratos, who was also allowed to sue on this occasion, had no such ground. The courts must have been very tolerant in such matters. See Gernet, *Dem.* ii. 229 f. According to Isai. 5 *Dikaiog.* 7 Dikaiogenes III, having for twelve years enjoyed one-third of the estate of Dikaiogenes II under a will, then produced another will and successfully secured the whole of the estate. In Dem. 43 *Makart.* 4 ff. Glaukos and Glaukon, having failed to secure Hagnias' estate under a will, were permitted to enter a plea to the estate as relatives under an intestacy.

[2] One passage in Isai. (11 *Hagn.* 46 *κελεύει δ' ὁ νόμος, ἐὰν ἁλῷ τις τῶν ψευδομαρτυρίων, πάλιν ἐξ ἀρχῆς εἶναι περὶ αὐτῶν τὰς λήξεις*) suggests at first reading that the conviction of a single witness on the opposing side for perjury automatically allowed an unsuccessful claimant to reopen an inheritance case; but the language is not precise enough to justify this *a priori* improbable conclusion: cf. Wyse ad loc., Lips., *AR* 958, n. 11. In Isai. 5 *Dikaiog.* 12 ff. the conviction for perjury of one of the witnesses to a will encourages a litigant to sue, with others of the same degree of kinship, for the estate as under an intestacy: from the narrative it would not seem that the sentence for perjury automatically overturned the previous adjudication, but that it would provide valuable evidence in support of the claims of those who reopened the case under the law in *Makart.* 16. The rule in Plato, *Laws* 937 c, anfl schol. ad loc. are of little help for Athenian law (Lips., *AR* 955 f.).

applied *mutatis mutandis* to claiming the hand of an heiress. It should be noted in particular that the rules in *Makart.* 16 about reopening an adjudged issue applied specifically to heiresses as well as estates. (For further discussion see the section on heiresses, pp. 132 ff., above.)

VI · SLAVERY

§ 1. *Introduction*

THE discussion of the law of slavery which follows has been designedly placed here, under the Law of the Family, rather than under the Law of Property.[1] To some extent this is an arbitrary choice. From many points of view slaves in fourth-century Athens were chattels (see p. 230). Aristotle describes a slave as 'a live possession' or 'a live tool'.[2] On the other hand, as will emerge later, there were many respects in which a slave was treated for legal purposes in a way different from the treatment of, say, a beast of burden, and he owed this different treatment to the fact of his being a human person. It is a mistake to lay too much emphasis on either one of these viewpoints and thus argue that cases where the other viewpoint has dictated a rule must be regarded as departures from a principle.[3] Instead we should recognize that there was a pervasive ambiguity about the legal status of a slave which made him both a chattel and something more than a mere chattel. It is this very ambiguity which

[1] Beauch. ii. 393–545 rightly treats slaves as an extension of the family. The arrangement of Lipsius, *AR* precludes his treating the law of slavery in a distinct section, but in the third book, on procedure, he discusses the slave's status *vis-à-vis* the courts (pp. 793–99). H. A. Wallon, *Histoire de l'esclavage dans l'antiquité* (2nd ed., Paris, 1879), is still useful. See also Bu. Sw. 272–88, 979–84, R. Schlaifer, *HSCP* 47 (1936), 176–84, Morrow, 'Murder of Slaves in Att. L.', *CP* 32 (1937), 210, id., *Slavery*, Gernet, *Plat.* cxix–cxxxii.

[2] Ar., *Pol.* 1253^b32, ὁ δοῦλος κτῆμά τι ἔμψυχον; but it is worth noting that earlier in the same sentence Aristotle instances the look-out man on a ship as a 'live tool' in contrast to the rudder, a 'lifeless tool'; these are tools in the art of piloting a ship; the slave is a 'live tool' in the art of managing a family; the point of the comparison is really economic and sheds little or no light on the legal status of the slave. Ar., *Nic. Eth.* 1161^b4, ὁ γὰρ δοῦλος ἔμψυχον ὄργανον, τὸ δ' ὄργανον ἄψυχος δοῦλος. ᾗ μὲν οὖν δοῦλος, οὐκ ἔστι φιλία πρὸς αὐτόν, ᾗ δ' ἄνθρωπος: this passage is equally inconclusive, since in the second sentence Aristotle indicates that in relation to the topic he is considering, friendship, the position of the slave is ambiguous.

[3] Lips., *AR* 794, for example, calls the admissibility of the γραφὴ ὕβρεως for maltreatment of a slave an 'Abfall vom Prinzip', and is rightly criticized for this by Morrow, *Slavery* 26, n. 5.

justifies the decision not to treat the law of slavery as part of the law of property.

§ 2. *Origin of status*

A man might be a slave by birth or he might lose his freedom from one cause or another. Children whose parents were both slaves were themselves slaves. Where one parent was slave the other free the position is not so clear. We know from Dio Chrysostom that in the first century A.D. at Athens the child of a free woman who was a citizen was free (though not a citizen) even if the father was a slave and regardless of whether the woman was or was not aware of the father's slave status.[1] Where the father was free and the mother a slave there is a slight probability that the offspring was slave, though some scholars have argued that here too Athenian law took the liberal view and allowed the offspring the status of the more privileged parent.[2]

In pre-Solonian Athens it must have been fairly common for free men to fall into slavery. They might be sold into slavery by their parents; they might pledge their persons as security for loans; or they might be hailed into servitude for failing to pay a debt. All these procedures were expressly forbidden by Solon, and from the date of his legislation early in the sixth century a free Athenian could not become a slave in Athens.[3] There were

[1] Dio Chrys. 15. 446 R. ἢ οὐ πολλαὶ ἀσταὶ γυναῖκες δι' ἐρημίαν τε καὶ ἀπορίαν, αἱ μὲν ἐκ ξένων ἐκύησαν, αἱ δὲ ἐκ δούλων, τινὲς μὲν ἀγνοοῦσαι τοῦτο, τινὲς δὲ καὶ ἐπιστάμεναι; καὶ οὐδεὶς δοῦλός ἐστιν, ἀλλὰ μόνον οὐκ Ἀθηναῖος τῶν οὕτω γεννηθέντων.

[2] Beauch. ii. 407 takes this latter view, basing himself on Ar., *Pol.* 1278a32, εὐποροῦντες δὴ ὄχλου κατὰ μικρὸν παραιροῦνται τοὺς ἐκ δούλου πρῶτον ἢ δούλης, εἶτα τοὺς ἀπὸ γυναικῶν, τέλος δὲ μόνον τοὺς ἐξ ἀμφοῖν ἀστῶν πολίτας ποιοῦσιν. This passage may suggest that in some cities at some time in their history children of mixed parentage would be free whether it was the father or the mother who was a slave; but the passage is concerned with citizen versus non-citizen status rather than free versus slave, and it may be that in the more liberal periods acts of enfranchisement preceded grants of citizenship; moreover, there is nothing to indicate that Athens was one of these cities, or if so at what period of its history this rule applied. Morrow, *Slavery* 92, takes the other view, citing the proviso of Drakon's homicide law from Dem. 23 *Aristok.* 55 ἐπὶ παλλακῇ ἣν ἂν ἐπ' ἐλευθέροις παισὶν ἔχῃ. There is certainly the implication here that some children of marriages between a free man and a concubine were not free, and these would presumably be where the concubine was a slave: it is puzzling that the proviso does not run ἐπὶ παλλακῇ ἣ ἂν ἐλευθέρα ᾖ, which would have avoided the ambiguity noted above, pp. 13 ff. Morrow, loc. cit., confuses 'citizen' with 'free' status when he contrasts slave παλλακαί with ξεναί rather than with ἐλευθέραι παλλακαί. On the whole question see also Hitzig, *Z* 18 (1897), 167.

[3] Ar., *Ath. Pol.* 2. 2, 4. 5, 6. 1, 9. 1, Plut., *Sol.* 15.

only two exceptions to this rule. If an Athenian paid the ransom for a fellow citizen who had been captured in war and the latter did not repay him the ransomed man became the slave of his ransomer. In certain circumstances, to be discussed in detail later, a freedman might as a result of losing a *δίκη ἀποστασίου* be reduced to slavery again.[1] In this field Athens was markedly more liberal than many other Greek states where debt slavery was a normal phenomenon.[2]

Another source of slave status was capture, either in war or by piracy. Although there was a certain feeling in fourth-century Greece that Greek should not enslave Greek—Plato, *Rep*. 469 b, for example, deprecates the practice—it is certain that there was no legal bar to the citizen of another Greek state becoming a slave at Athens. In actual fact the majority of captured slaves were probably of barbarian origin.[3]

Finally, for certain offences slavery might be imposed as a penalty on foreigners or metics, but not on citizens. A foreigner who was convicted in a *γραφὴ ξενίας* of masquerading as a citizen was enslaved.[4] A foreign man or a foreign woman who entered into a permanent union (*συνοικεῖν*) with an Athenian woman or man was liable to prosecution by a *γραφή* and, if convicted, became a slave.[5] A metic who failed to pay the *μετοίκιον* could be sold into slavery, as could one who was convicted in a *γραφὴ ἀπροστασίου* of failing to acquire a *προστάτης*.[6]

Athenian citizens were undoubtedly protected against wrongful enslavement by a stringent penal action, though whether this was only by the procedure known as *ἀπαγωγή* or there was also available a *γραφὴ ἀνδραποδισμοῦ* is not clear. Strictly *ἀπαγωγή*

[1] Dem. 53 *Nikostr*. 11 *οἱ νόμοι κελεύουσιν τοῦ λυσαμένου ἐκ τῶν πολεμίων εἶναι τὸν λυθέντα, ἐὰν μὴ ἀποδιδῷ τὰ λύτρα*. Harpokr. s.v. *ἀποστασίου· δίκη τίς ἐστι κατὰ τῶν ἀπελευθερωθέντων δεδομένη ἀπελευθερώσασιν, ἐὰν ἀφιστῶνταί τε ἀπ' αὐτῶν ἢ ἕτερον ἐπιγράφωνται προστάτην καὶ ἃ κελεύουσιν οἱ νόμοι μὴ ποιῶσιν. καὶ τοὺς μὲν ἁλόντας δεῖ δούλους εἶναι, τοὺς δὲ νικήσαντας τελέως ἤδη ἐλευθέρους*. On the *δίκη ἀποστασίου* see below, p. 182.

[2] Lys. 12 *Ag. Eratosth*. 98 and many instances cited by Glotz, *Solidarité* 366.

[3] Xen., *Kyrop*. 7. 5. 73, Polyb. 2. 58. 9 vouch for the general rule throughout Greece that enslavement was the expected result of capture in war, and in fact this general rule is presupposed by the passage from Plato cited above. Cf. Bu. Sw. 276.

[4] Dem., *Ep*. 3. 29, schol. Dem. 24 *Timokr*. 131.

[5] Dem. 59 *Neair*. 16; pp. 25 ff., above.

[6] Dem. 25 *Aristogeit*. i. 57, Harpokr. s.v. *μετοίκιον*, Pollux 8. 99, Bu. Sw. 295, n. 3. Harpokr. s.v. *ἀπροστασίου*, and for the penalty Suda s.v. *πωληταί* 2, Bu. Sw. 294, n. 3.

was only applicable to those caught in the act, and we should expect *a priori* that a *γραφή* would have been available for cases where the wrongful seizure was in the past, but we have no direct evidence for it; perhaps the continued holding of a free man in bondage was regarded as a prolonged act of seizure. We have no evidence whether this procedure was available for the protection of other than Athenian citizens.[1] Another line of defence open to one wrongfully enslaved was the procedure known as *ἀφαίρεσις εἰς ἐλευθερίαν* (on which see p. 178, below).

§ 3. *Legal status*

(i) Vis-à-vis *the state*

In very general terms there were fewer distinguishing marks between slave and free at Athens than was normal in Greek cities. This was somewhat sardonically stressed by the late fifth-century writer known as the Old Oligarch.[2] Though slaves were excluded from certain religious festivals and temples, this was the exception; they could be initiated into the Eleusinian mysteries and could and did establish their own private cults.[3] There were, however, a number of legal disabilities from which slaves in Athens suffered. They were excluded from the citizens' gymnasia and palaistrai. They were forbidden under pain of scourging to have homosexual relations with, or to solicit, free boys.[4] No slave

[1] Isok. 15 *Antid.* 90 *καὶ εἰ μέν τις τοῦτον ἀπαγαγὼν ἀνδραποδιστὴν καὶ κλέπτην καὶ λωποδύτην κτλ.*, Dem. 35 *Lakrit.* 47 *ἀλλὰ τοιχωρύχους καὶ κλέπτας καὶ τοὺς ἄλλους κακούργους τοὺς ἐπὶ θανάτῳ οὗτοι* (sc. *οἱ ἕνδεκα*) *εἰσάγουσιν*, Ar., *Ath. Pol.* 52. 1. Beauch. ii. 413, n. 1, refers to Caillemer, DS s.v. *andrapodismou graphe*, MSL 275, 458, Wallon, *Esclavage* 168 f., and other modern authorities for a *γραφὴ ἀνδραποδισμοῦ*: but none of these provides any ancient evidence for such a suit, and it is not assumed by Lips. in *AR* 639 ff. or in Bu. Sw. 532, 1107 in their treatment of *ἀνδραποδισμός*. Bu. Sw. in the latter passage rightly point out that in Lys. 13 *Agorat.* 86 ff., Dem. 54 *Kon.* 1, 24 *ἐπ' αὐτοφώρῳ* is watered down to mean any public, unconcealed act. Harpokr. s.v. *ἀνδραποδιστής* quotes from Lykourgos a statement that *ἀνδραποδισταί* were punished with death; in this passage *ἀνδραποδισταί* are defined as those who steal others' slaves, but the term also included those who abducted free men.

[2] Ps.-Xen., *Ath. Pol.* 1. 10.

[3] Isai. 6 *Philokt.* 48 ff. cites a law, probably dealing with the Thesmophoria, under which slaves were excluded from ceremonies in honour of Demeter and Persephone. Dem. 59 *Neair.* 21 for a slave's initiation into the mysteries. S. Lauffer, *Bergwerkssklaven* ii. 177, for epigraphic evidence of slave cults of Artemis, Athena, Men, and other gods at Laureion.

[4] Aischin. 1 *Timarch.* 138 "*δοῦλον*", *φησὶν ὁ νόμος*, "*μὴ γυμνάζεσθαι μηδὲ ξηραλοιφεῖν ἐν ταῖς παλαίστραις*". 139 *πάλιν ὁ αὐτὸς εἶπε νομοθέτης· "δοῦλον ἐλευθέρου παιδὸς μήτ' ἐρᾶν μήτ' ἐπακολουθεῖν, ἢ τύπτεσθαι τῇ δημοσίᾳ μάστιγι πεντήκοντα πληγάς."*

could bear the name Harmodios or Aristogeiton.[1] Nor could he attend the ekklesia.[2] In two passages Demosthenes says that the most important difference between a slave and a free man was that the former had to answer for all his wrongdoings in his person (*τὸ σῶμα τῶν ἀδικημάτων ἁπάντων ὑπεύθυνόν ἐστιν*); this only happened to a free man in the very last resort.[3] Apart from this very general distinction, we have to consider the slave's position in the administration of justice first as a possible plaintiff, second as a defendant, and third as a witness.

As a general rule a slave could not appear in court as a plaintiff. Plato explicitly says that a wronged slave could not come to his own assistance (sc. as a plaintiff at law), and Demosthenes gives as a sign of one Kerdon being the slave of Arethousios that, when a delict occurred in which Kerdon was the wronged or the wrongdoer, Arethousios acted as plaintiff or defendant as the case might be.[4] There was one important exception to this rule. A clearly distinguishable category of slaves was made up of those who were not part of their master's household at least in the narrow physical sense. These were called *χωρὶς οἰκοῦντες*.[5] There is some, not altogether satisfactory, evidence that they could acquire property, with which they might in some cases purchase their liberty, and that they could in certain circumstances appear as parties in court.[6] Certain publicly owned slaves also probably enjoyed these privileges (p. 177).

[1] Aul. Gell., *N.A.* 9. 2.

[2] Aristoph., *Thesm.* 294.

[3] Dem. 24 *Timokr.* 167, 22 *Androt.* 55.

[4] Plato, *Gorg.* 483 b ἀνδραπόδου . . . ὅστις ἀδικούμενος καὶ προπηλακιζόμενος μὴ οἷός τέ ἐστιν αὐτὸς αὑτῷ βοηθεῖν μηδὲ ἄλλῳ οὗ ἂν κήδηται, Dem. 53 *Nikostr.* 20 τοὺς μισθοὺς Ἀρεθούσιος ἐκομίζετο ὑπὲρ αὐτοῦ, καὶ δίκας ἐλάμβανε καὶ ἐδίδου, ὁπότε κακόν τι ἐργάσαιτο, ὡς δεσπότης ὤν: it may, however, be slightly straining the phrase δίκας ἐλάμβανε καὶ ἐδίδου to take it as proof that the master must actually always represent the slave in court; the phrase could stand if all that was meant was that the master eventually received or paid any resulting penalties or damages.

[5] There has been some dispute as to whether men so described were in fact slaves or freedmen. Dem. 4 *Phil.* i. 36 uses the phrase, but (*pace* Lips., *AR* 622, n. 6, 798, n. 29) there is nothing in that passage to determine whether he is referring to slaves or freedmen, and Dem. 47 *Euerg.* 72, though it says of a freedwoman χωρὶς ᾤκει, does not clinch the question. The grammarians differ: Suda and Harpokr. s.v. τοὺς χωρὶς οἰκοῦντας restrict the phrase to freedmen, but *An. Bekk.* (*Λέξ. Ῥητ.*) 316 s.v. χωρὶς οἰκοῦντες has οἱ ἀπελεύθεροι, ἐπεὶ χωρὶς οἰκοῦσι τῶν ἀπελευθερωσάντων. ἢ δοῦλοι χωρὶς οἰκοῦντες τῶν δεσποτῶν. Partsch, *GB* 136, equates the χωρὶς οἰκῶν with the δοῦλος μισθοφορῶν and describes him as 'ein halbfreier Sklave': so too M. Clerc, *Les Métèques athéniens* 281. But Lips., locc. citt., and Bu. Sw. 274, n. 3, 985, n. 5, believe the phrase was restricted to freedmen.

[6] For the right to appear in court the principal evidence is the case of Lampis,

But though as a general rule the slave could not protect his person or property (in the limited sense in which he could have any) as a plaintiff, it does not follow that he was wholly outside the protection of the courts. We learn from the Old Oligarch that slaves could not be struck in Athens (with the probable proviso that they could be beaten by their masters, on which see below, pp. 171 f.). Striking a slave would in certain circumstances have rendered a man liable to prosecution by a *γραφὴ ὕβρεως*, which anyone could institute. Probably, though less certainly, he might be sued by the slave's master through a *δίκη αἰκείας*.[1] Slaves were specifically protected from *ὕβρις*, and Demosthenes even alleges that men had been condemned to death on this charge.[2] The concept of *ὕβρις* was rather indeterminate and will be discussed more fully under the Law of Obligations. Here it will suffice to say that not all physical assault was necessarily *ὕβρις*, and, on the

probably a slave of Dion, in Dem. 34 *Ag. Phorm.* 5, 18, 46: the reference here is only to giving evidence, but there is the clear implication that Lampis might have been a party to the proceedings; the case would be conclusive but that some scholars have denied that the words *παῖς* and *οἰκέτης* used of Lampis necessarily imply that he was a slave. Paoli, *St. Dir.* 106, Partsch, *GB* 136, hold that Lampis was a slave; against that view Lips., *AR* 797, n. 28 (but it is arguing in a circle to state that para. 37 proves him to be a freedman); Westermann, *The Slave Systems of Greek and Roman Antiquity* 17, n. 106; doubtful, Jones, *LLTG* 141, n. 3. In Menand., *Arbitr.*, Syriskos, who is shown by 203 f. K. to be a *δοῦλος μισθοφορῶν*, is clearly thought by the poet to be competent to bring suit to protect his right to retain possession of some trinkets belonging to a foundling who had come into his care (226 *δικάσομαι ἅπασι καθ' ἕνα*, 242 *δεῖ δίκας μελετᾶν*); but Gernet, *AHDO* 5 (1950), 175, n. 3 (*DSGA* 163, n. 4) thinks the word *δικάζεσθαι* here may be simply a joke. Theophr., *Char.* 30. 9, 15 assumes slaves with a right to (1) their findings, (2) their earnings; Kränzlein, *Eig. und Bes.* 41, 43. *IG* i². 374 lists slaves receiving the same wages as free men on public works; it is probable that though part of this pay went as *ἀποφορά* to their owners a part was retained by the slaves. The whole tone of Ps.-Xen., *Ath. Pol.* 1. 11 implies that slaves at Athens could sue in the courts. Aischin. 1 *Timarch.* 54 for a public slave *εὐπορῶν ἀργυρίου*. For slaves at Athens purchasing their liberty see the evidence of the so-called 'freedmens' bowls' in *IG* ii². 1553–78 discussed in Westermann, op. cit. 25 f., id., *JNES* 5 (1946), 94–96, Finley, *Land* 104, and below, p. 182.

[1] Ps.-Xen., *Ath. Pol.* 1. 10. For the *γραφὴ ὕβρεως* see next note. Lips., *AR* 428, n. 34, asserts against Beauch. ii. 431, n. 2, that the *δίκη αἰκείας* was available against one who struck a slave: he states no grounds, but it seems *a priori* likely that a master should have had a right—or duty—towards his slave parallel to the right of *ὁ βουλόμενος*.

[2] Dem. 21 *Meid.* 47–49, Aischin. 1 *Timarch.* 15. The law, quoted in full in the former passage, casts its net very wide: *ἐάν τις ὑβρίσῃ εἴς τινα, ἢ παῖδα ἢ γυναῖκα ἢ ἄνδρα, τῶν ἐλευθέρων ἢ τῶν δούλων, ἢ παράνομόν τι ποιήσῃ εἰς τούτων τινά, γραφέσθω πρὸς τοὺς θεσμοθέτας ὁ βουλόμενος Ἀθηναίων οἷς ἔξεστιν.* Note that in the last clause of the law there is slight discrimination against a slave victim of *ὕβρις*: *ἐὰν δὲ ἀργυρίου τιμηθῇ τῆς ὕβρεως, δεδέσθω, ἐὰν ἐλεύθερον ὑβρίσῃ, μέχρι ἂν ἐκτείσῃ.*

other hand, it might include actions which did not amount to physical assault, though in relation to slaves it is not easy to imagine what such actions might be.

But of course the literally vital interest of a slave was the preservation of his life, and we have to consider what attitude the law took to the killer of a slave.[1] The first point that emerges is that, though the death of a slave might have been regarded as nothing more than damage to the property of his master and thus as giving rise simply to a *δίκη βλάβης* instituted by the master against the killer, the law went further. It certainly prescribed that the killer must go through the form of purification, and we may suppose that failure to do this would render him liable to a *γραφὴ ἀσεβείας*.[2] This, however, would have been a somewhat weak protection for the slave. That the master could presumably —and it is only a presumption—bring a *δίκη βλάβης* against the killer of his slave was of course some protection, and there are two reported cases where a normal *δίκη φόνου* was brought against killers of slaves, probably though not certainly by their masters.[3] The relatives of a slave could bring moral pressure to bear on his master to prosecute his killer, but probably could do no more.[4] The most conclusive evidence that the killing of a slave was on an entirely different level from the killing of a beast of burden is the fact that the Palladion, one of the traditional homicide courts, was laid down as the court for trying those who killed slaves, whether the killing was premeditated or unpremeditated; the same court tried cases of unpremeditated homicide

[1] See MacDowell, *Homicide*, Index s.v. Slave, Morrow, *CP* 32 (1937), 210 ff.

[2] Ant. 6 *Chor.* 4 shows that even a master who had killed his slave was bound by sacred custom—just as imperative a tie as written law—to purify himself. A 'flagrant' killer (*ἐπ' αὐτοφώρῳ*) could certainly be arraigned if he were found in the market-place or any sacred place, Dem. 23 *Aristokr.* 80, Lys. 13 *Agorat.* 85–87.

[3] The two cases are Isok. 18 *Kallim.* 52 ff., Dem. 59 *Neair.* 9 f. According to Dem. 47 *Euerg.* 70 the law imposed the duty of prosecuting on a man if a woman (and we may assume a man also) was killed who was either related to him (*ἐν γένει*) or his servant (*θεράπαινα*): although the context is about a freedwoman the word *θεράπαινα* would surely embrace a slave.

[4] Dem. 47 *Euerg. and Mnes.* 72 *κελεύει ὁ νόμος τοὺς προσήκοντας ἐπεξιέναι μέχρι ἀνεψιαδῶν (καὶ ἐν τῷ ὅρκῳ διορίζεται ὅ τι προσήκων ἐστίν), κἂν οἰκέτης ᾖ, τούτων τὰς ἐπισκήψεις εἶναι.* MacDowell, *Homicide* 20, rightly urges that the last four words do not mean, as they have usually been taken, 'prosecutions shall belong to the masters' (for which the natural Greek would have been *τοὺς δεσπότας ἐπεξιέναι*), but 'his relatives shall urge vengeance'; he quotes Ant. 1 *Stepmother* 29, Lys. 13 *Agorat.* 41 for a dying man who *ἐπισκήπτει* his family to take vengeance. See, however, J. H. Kells, *CR* 15 (1965), 207.

of citizens and of all homicide of metics and foreigners. There is a slight presumption—no more—from this venue that the penalty was less severe than for the premeditated killing of a free citizen.[1] Other evidence suggests that there was no one penalty laid down by law for killing a slave, whereas for premeditated and unjustifiable killing of a free citizen the penalty was death, which could only be avoided by voluntary exile for life.[2]

All this, however, still left the slave in a very weak position if his master was not prepared to avenge his death, and of course still more so if his master were himself the killer. Here too the slave was not left entirely defenceless, but the rules can be more conveniently examined in discussing the slave's status *vis-à-vis* his master in the next section. That too will be the best place to discuss the rules where a slave was a wrongdoer and therefore a potential defendant in a suit. We turn therefore now to the slave as a possible witness in court. Normally a slave's evidence could only be produced in court if it had been given under torture; this was due to the irrational but strongly held view that a slave would only speak the truth under torture. We have to decide whether there were cases in which a slave might appear as a witness on just the same footing as a free man. It has usually been held on the basis of two passages in Antiphon that in homicide cases a slave's evidence was permissible, but MacDowell has shown that neither passage bears out this contention, and he comes to the cautious but correct conclusion that the evidence available does not permit of a decision either way.[3] There was,

[1] Ar., *Ath. Pol.* 57. 3, Isok. 18 *Kallim.* 52, Dem. 47 *Euerg. and Mnes.* 70, Aischin. 2 *False Emb.* 87 with schol. See below, pp. 196f.

[2] Lykourg., *Leokr.* 65, says that in early days the penalty for killing a slave was not merely a fine, which seems to imply that in his day it might be. In Dem. 59 *Neair.* 10 the penalty may be either banishment or disfranchisement. In *An. Bekk.* (*Δικ. 'Ονομ.*) 194 the penalty for killing a citizen is given as death, for killing a metic it is exile; there is no mention of the killing of a slave.

[3] MacDowell, *Homicide* 102–9: in Ant. 2 *1st Tetr.* 3. 4 (*οὐ γὰρ ἐπὶ ταῖς τοιαύταις μαρτυρίαις βασανίζονται, ἀλλ' ἐλεύθεροι ἀφίενται*) a slave with his dying breath revealed the name of his killer; the phrase quoted implies that had the slave lived he would have been freed and then he could have given evidence in the ordinary way; it is therefore on the whole adverse to the view that he could have given this evidence in court while yet a slave. Ant. 5 *Her.* 48 *εἴπερ καὶ μαρτυρεῖν ἔξεστι δούλῳ κατὰ τοῦ ἐλευθέρου τὸν φόνον*: these words have usually been translated 'if it is allowed that a slave shall give evidence against a free man in a murder case', which would be conclusive; but MacDowell rightly points out that this does not fit the context, and he translates 'if it is permissible to give evidence for a slave against a free man of his being killed'. If we accept this translation we can ignore

however, one type of case in which a slave might play a role analogous to that of a witness, namely in cases of treason, sacrilege, or theft of public money: there was a special procedure known as μήνυσις (denunciation) which was available against the perpetrators of such wrongs. The denouncer, who must be distinguished from the prosecutor in an εἰσαγγελία, might be a slave, and he earned his freedom if the proceedings ended in a conviction; if they did not he might be liable to the death penalty.[1]

(ii) Vis-à-vis *masters*

We have first to determine in what respects the master's absolute dominion over his slave was restricted. We have seen in the last section that the law provided for the trial of anyone who killed a slave and that the slave's relatives could bring at least moral pressure to bear on the master to avenge his slave's death (p. 169, above). It would in any case have usually been in the master's own interest to avenge the killing of his own slave by a third party. If he were himself tempted to kill him there is no doubt that the act was illegal. The speaker in Ant. 5 *Her.* 47 is most explicit that the owners of a slave were not entitled to put him to death, though he gives no indication what sanctions could be applied against them.[2] If this had not been the law the offer of freedom to slave informers (see this page above) would have

the somewhat desperate attempts of those who try to reconcile the traditional translation with the view that a slave's evidence was no more permissible in homicide than in other cases except under torture. J. H. Kells, reviewing MacDowell in *CR* 15 (1965), 207, rejects his translation of Ant. 5 *Her.* 48, but does not really dispose of his argument against the accepted translation. For various other theories see M. Guggenheim, *Bedeutung der Folterung in a. Proc.* (Zurich, 1882), 10 ff., Leisi, *Zeuge* 12 ff., 21 ff., R. J. Bonner, *CP* 1 (1906), 131, 7 (1912), 450 ff., id., *Evidence in Ath. Courts* 34, 36, J. Deutzsch, *De δίκη ψευδομαρτυρίων* 15, Lips., *AR* 873, Bo. Sm. ii. 126 ff., 221 ff., Gernet, *AHDO* 5 (1950), 159 ff. (*DSGA* 151 ff.).

[1] Thuc. 6. 27. 2, Ant. 5 *Her.* 34, 2 *1st Tetr.* 3. 4 (p. 170, n. 3), Lys. 7 *Sacr. Ol.* 16, 5 *Kall.* 5, Lips., *AR* 208. The phrasing of Andok. 1 *Myst.* 20 suggests that the penalty for false denunciation had been, but no longer was, death (ὁ νόμος οὕτως εἶχεν).

[2] The slave in question had been suspected of collaborating with the speaker in killing Herodes; he had been bought by Herodes' relatives, was alleged by them to have confessed to the murder and to have incriminated the speaker, and had then been put to death by them in Mytilene as a murderer; the speaker uses very strong words of this act: ὃ οὐδὲ πόλει ἔξεστιν, ἄνευ Ἀθηναίων οὐδένα θανάτῳ ζημιῶσαι. But G. de Ste Croix, *CQ* 11 (1961), 271, believes the orator is here falsely assuming that a law forbidding the imposition of the death penalty by the courts of Athens' subject allies covered the killing of slaves as well as free men.

tended to be nugatory, since a master who suspected that a slave had a hold over him would have been strongly tempted to do away with him. Thus slaves were not entirely without a legal guard against death at their masters' hand. But the guard was at best flimsy; indeed, the passage from Ant. 6 *Chor.* 4 which states that a master who killed his own slave must undergo purification suggests by its wording that this might be all that he did,[1] though if he failed even to do that he would be in peril (p. 169, above with n. 2).

When we turn to bodily mischief short of killing it seems probable—decisive evidence is lacking—that as against his master the slave could not rely even on the somewhat slender chance of getting a sympathetic citizen to bring a *γραφὴ ὕβρεως* if he suffered bodily violence at his master's hands. Certainly the rationale given by the Old Oligarch for the legal protection given to slaves in Athens—that slaves there were indistinguishable in appearance from free men and there was therefore a risk of outraging a free man under the misapprehension that he was a slave—might have tended of itself to exempt owners from liability, since they could not be victims of this possible mistake.[2] Moreover, it might well have been held that the necessary ingredient for *ὕβρις* of intention to insult could by a sort of fiction be supposed between a third party and slave, but could not between a master and a slave. This is, however, mere speculation. One remedy against cruel usage by a master lay in a slave's right to take asylum either at the Theseion or at the altar of the Eumenides on the Areopagos; he could from there beg a third party to buy him from his master, and there was probably some official intervention which justified a grammarian's use of the word *δίκαι* in connexion with the procedure, though this has been denied.[3]

[1] *καὶ ἄν τις κτείνῃ τινὰ ὧν αὐτὸς κρατεῖ καὶ μὴ ἔστιν ὁ τιμωρήσων, . . . ἀγνεύει τε ἑαυτὸν καὶ ἀφέξεται ὧν εἴρηται ἐν τῷ νόμῳ.* Lips., *AR* 605, 794, takes this passage as conclusive that a master who killed his own slave was liable to nothing more than purification. Kränzlein, *Eig. und Bes.* 51, disagrees, but is criticized for this by Wolff, *Z* 81 (1964), 335.

[2] Ps.-Xen., *Ath. Pol.* 1. 10. Aischin. 1 *Timarch.* 17 gives a slightly different reason for the surprising fact that the protection of the *γραφὴ ὕβρεως* covered slaves; it was not for the sake of the slaves, but to accustom men to abstain from outraging free men.

[3] Aristoph., fr. 567 K. *ἐμοὶ κράτιστόν ἐστιν εἰς τὸ Θησεῖον δραμεῖν, ἐκεῖ δ' ἕως ἂν πρᾶσιν εὕρωμεν μένειν*, Eupolis, fr. 225 K. *κακὰ τοιάδε πάσχουσα μηδὲ πρᾶσιν αἰτῶ*, *Et. Mag.* 451, 40 *Θησεῖον· τέμενός ἐστι τῷ Θησεῖ, ὃ τοῖς οἰκέταις ἄσυλον ἦν (ἐλέγοντο δὲ δίκαι ἐνταῦθα), ἢ ναὸς τοῦ Θησέως, ἐφ' ὃν οἱ ἀποδιδράσκοντες δοῦλοι*

We now turn to the master's relation to his slave in cases where the slave had become liable either to punishment or to payment of damages as a result of delictual or contractual obligations.[1]

We are ill informed as to the procedure when a slave was suspected of homicide, of whatever category. Ant. 5 *Her.* 47 certainly implies that procedure against him in legal form was prescribed. It would presumably have been set on foot by the relatives of the deceased man; but we cannot say what, if any, part was played in the trial by the slave's master. Again we must assume, in default of any evidence of the fact, that penalties were more severe for the slave: it is difficult, for example, to imagine that the same pleas in justification were available to him as to a free man.

As regards other delicts, in very general terms a law attributed to Solon in Hyper. 5 *Athenog.* 22 lays down that loss or damage due to a slave's delict had to be compensated by the man who owned the slave at the time of the delict.[2] The same general rule—the master's liability at law—emerges from the case of Kerdon referred to on p. 167, above. There was, however, if we may rely on passages from two speeches of Demosthenes, a refinement on this general rule. Where the slave had acted on his master's instructions the master was sued direct. So we find Pantainetos in his statement of claim in a *δίκη βλάβης* suing Nikoboulos for a wrongful act done at Nikoboulos' behest by a slave of Nikoboulos to a slave of Pantainetos.[3] Nikoboulos

προσέφευγον: Philoch., *F.Gr.H.* 328. 177, with Jacoby's notes ad loc. Jacoby believes there was some judicial procedure and refers also to schol. Aischin. 3 *Ktes.* 13; for the contrary view Lips., *AR* 643. For the altar of the Eumenides Aristoph., *Kn.* 1312, *Thesm.* 224.

[1] See especially Gernet, *AHDO* 5 (1950), 184 ff. (*DSGA* 155 ff.), Lips., *AR* 660, 794, Pringsheim, *GLS* 453 ff., Wyse, *Isai.* 506, Partsch, *GB* 135.

[2] *Σόλων . . . ἔθηκε νόμον δίκαιον . . . τὰς ζη[μίας ἃς ἂν] ἐργάσωνται οἱ οἰκέται καὶ τὰ ἀ[ναλώμ]ατα* (Revillout: *ἀ[δικήμ]ατα* Jensen) *διαλύειν τὸν δεσπότην παρ' ᾧ [ἂν ἐργάσ]ωνται οἱ οἰκέται.* Gernet, loc. cit. n. 1 prefers the reading *ἀναλώματα* on the somewhat dubious ground that many *ἀδικήματα* might be wrongs against the state and not against private individuals and in these cases the master would not be liable. The speaker is trying to disclaim liability for debts incurred by Midas, a slave whom he had bought from Athenogenes as part of a perfumery business; he had accepted liability for them in a contract, but in terms too vague to show whether they were delictual or contractual (para. 10 *καὶ εἴ τῳ ἄλλῳ ὀφείλει τι Μίδας*). We are not here concerned with problems which arose if ownership of the slave passed to a third party after the delict.

[3] Dem. 37 *Pant.* 21 *ΕΓΚΛΗΜΑ. ἔβλαψέ με Νικόβουλος ἐπιβουλεύσας ἐμοὶ καὶ*

countered with the plea that as he was absent from Athens at the time of the alleged wrong he could not have given any such orders to his slave, and later in the speech says that the proper procedure for Pantainetos would have been to sue the slave and by this means get a judgement against himself as the slave's master.[1] There is a concrete instance of a slave's being sued in his own person in Dem. 55 *Kallikl.* 31 ff.: in that case the speaker argues that suing the slave was inappropriate because no slave would have been likely to do the act without his master's orders.[2] We may then state the rule as being that where the master's complicity was alleged the master was to be sued direct, where the slave had acted on his own the slave was to be sued, but judgement would go against both him and his master. Whether the master could discharge his liability by surrendering his slave either temporarily or permanently to the wronged party and if so what the exact rules were are matters of serious doubt. Some scholars confidently assert that 'noxal surrender', as it is called, obtained in Athenian law. On comparative grounds this is *a priori* likely, but there is almost no direct evidence.[3] (For certain special penal regulations dealing with slaves' delicts see p. 166, above).

Where an obligation had arisen out of contractual dealings by a slave the rules are far from clear, and they had certainly not been worked out at Athens with anything like the detail and subtlety that obtained in Roman law. We may assume that originally a slave was totally incapable of contracting and that his acts were regarded simply as being the acts of his master.

τῇ οὐσίᾳ τῇ ἐμῇ, ἀφελέσθαι κελεύσας Ἀντιγένην τὸν ἑαυτοῦ οἰκέτην τὸ ἀργύριον τοῦ ἐμοῦ οἰκέτου.

[1] Dem. 37 *Pant.* 51 *ἔδει . . . λαχόντ' ἐκείνῳ τὴν δίκην τὸν κύριον διώκειν ἐμέ. νῦν δ' εἴληχεν μὲν ἐμοί, κατηγορεῖ δ' ἐκείνου. ταῦτα δ' οὐκ ἐῶσιν οἱ νόμοι.*

[2] Op. cit. 31 *ἐρήμην μου καταδεδιῄτηται τοιαύτην ἑτέραν δίκην, Κάλλαρον ἐπιγραψάμενος τῶν ἐμῶν δούλων.* 32 *καίτοι τίς ἂν οἰκέτης τὸ τοῦ δεσπότου χωρίον περιοικοδομήσειεν μὴ προστάξαντος τοῦ δεσπότου;* Cf. Gernet, *Dem.* i. 228, *Dem.* iii. 119.

[3] Beauch. ii. 456 arguing from Plato, *Laws* 936 c, the law governing the mysteries at Andania, *SIG* 736. 78, and the analogy of the law of Solon governing the noxal surrender of animals, Plut., *Sol.* 24 (*ἔγραψε δὲ καὶ βλάβης τετραπόδων νόμον, ἐν ᾧ καὶ κύνα δάκνοντα παραδοῦναι κελεύει κλοιῷ τριπήχει δεδεμένον*). For the rule in Greece generally see Glotz, *Solidarité* 177 ff., J. Partsch, *AP* 6 (1912), 65 ff. The one piece of direct evidence for Athens is *An. Bekk.* (*Δικ. 'Ον.*) 187 *ἐγγυῆσαι· ὅταν τις κρινόμενος παράσχῃ δοῦλον ἀνθ' ἑαυτοῦ τιμωρηθῆναι.* There is a strong presumption that such an entry is derived from an Athenian source.

This crude point of view is envisaged in Dem. 53 *Nikostr.* 21, where the slaves are described as buying up a crop (ὀπώραν πρίαιντο) or hiring themselves out for a harvest (θέρος μισθοῖντο ἐκθερίσαι), but the master is the actual buyer or hirer on their behalf (ὁ ὠνούμενος καὶ μισθούμενος ὑπὲρ αὐτῶν). Even here, however, the slaves are described as 'buying' and as 'hiring themselves out', and the use of the middle, μισθούμενος, for the master's part in the hiring indicates that his act differed from the hiring out of a chattel, for which the active form would have been appropriate.[1] These were agricultural workers, but the situation became more complex with the development of industry, particularly when managerial responsibilities were undertaken by slaves. In this sphere it seems that the statute law lagged behind the needs of the commercial community. This emerges from one aspect of the case at issue in Hyper. 5 *Athenog.* (above, p. 173 and n. 2). Midas, one of the slaves in the case, had incurred certain obligations, some no doubt, though not necessarily all, contractual, as manager of the perfumery business.[2] Athenogenes, by a stratagem to evade liability for these debts, had sold the business with Midas included to Epikrates. Obviously noxal surrender was not open to either master here, for the total of the debts far exceeded the value of the slaves and they would have been surrendered. One or other of the masters therefore was clearly liable for the debts. The significant point is that the only law Epikrates can quote in relation to the matter is a rather archaic law of Solon which seems to have been framed primarily to deal with a slave's delicts; it is only by a sort of analogy that the law can be applied to contractual debts. It is further significant that Epikrates has to sue Athenogenes for damages (βλάβη); he has been unable to meet the creditors with a reference to Athenogenes as the originator through Midas of the contracts.[3]

It may be that here as elsewhere the rules governing overseas commerce were more advanced than the rest and that in this sphere the agency of the slave was more clearly recognized. The case of Lampis (referred to on p. 167, n. 6, above) almost certainly proves that in commercial cases at least a slave could

[1] Gernet, *AHDO* 5 (1950), 171 (*DSGA* 160) 'l'esclave est un intermédiaire, il n'est pas un simple instrument: de la part du maître, il ne s'agit plus d'un louage de choses'.

[2] In 6, 10, 20 the slave is spoken of as the debtor.

[3] Pringsheim, *GLS* 454 f.

appear as a party: naturally the proceeds of his commercial operations would fall as to the greater part to his master.[1] Further, in Dem. 34 *Ag. Phorm.* 31 the speaker suggests that in a commercial transaction abroad his opponent would have been wise to have called in witnesses both slave and free; the implication is certainly that such a slave witness would have been able to give evidence on just the same footing as a free man. This somewhat liberal attitude to slaves in the world of commerce is to be seen as part of the special legal machinery devised by Athens to deal with commercial suits, the δίκαι ἐμπορικαί. In the allied sphere of banking the heirs of Pasion leased his bank to four slaves who were only subsequently enfranchised.[2]

Subject to the above provisions a master could treat his slave as a chattel in all legal relationships with third parties. He could transfer his ownership of him by sale, gift, or testament. There were rules governing the sale of slaves analogous to rules about the sale of beasts, and it is possible, though unlikely, that some rule about prior publicity was in force similar to the rule about publicity in the sale of land (for which see p. 308).[3] A master could also hire out his slaves,[4] or loan them,[5] or pledge them either separately or as an integral part of a business.[6] (For the limits of a master's rights over property acquired by his slave see p. 167, n. 6, above.)[7]

(iii) Vis-à-vis *third parties*

Where the third party was a free man the legal relationships between him and a slave have been dealt with by implication in

[1] Paoli, *St. Dir.* 105 ff.

[2] Dem. 36 *For Phorm.* 13 f.; the phrase ἐλευθέρους ἀφεῖσαν should certainly be translated 'enfranchised them' and not 'released them from their obligations'; Gernet, *Dem.* i. 209, n. 2, *AHDO* 5 (1950), 175 (*DSGA* 163).

[3] Hyper. 5 *Athenog.* 15 μετὰ δὲ] ταῦτα ἕ[τερο]ς νόμος [ἐστὶ περὶ ὧν ὁμολογοῦν]τες ἀλλήλοις συμβάλλουσιν, ὅταν τις πωλῇ ἀνδράποδον προλέγειν ἐάν τι ἔχῃ ἀρρώστημα, εἰ δ[ὲ μ]ή, ἀναγωγὴ τούτου ἀστίν, Suda s.v. ἐναγωγὴ οἰκέτου, *An. Bekk.* (Λέξ. Ῥητ.) 207. 23, 214. 16.

[4] Xen., *Por.* 4. 14 f. for Nikias and others hiring out slaves to work in the mines; for other instances Dem. 27 *Aphob.* i. 20, 53 *Nikostr.* 20 f., Lys. 12 *Ag. Eratosth.* 19, Isai. 8 *Kir.* 35, Aischin. 1 *Timarch.* 97.

[5] Ant. 6 *Chor.* 23.

[6] Dem. 27 *Aphob.* i. 9 for the former, *IG* ii². 2747, 2748, 2749, 2751 (Finley, nos. 88, 89, 90, 178) for the latter; see Finley, *Land* 73.

[7] The δίκαι φορᾶς ἀφανοῦς and μεθημερινῆς of Pollux 8. 31 are certainly not suits of master against slave; perhaps we should read φωρᾶς in the sense of κλοπῆς: so Lips., *AR* 758, n. 306, MSL 728.

the previous two sections. Where the third party was also a slave the only remaining point which needs mention is the possibility of some form of marriage between slaves. Although relatively permanent unions were in fact formed between slaves it is very doubtful whether these had any juristic validity. Two passages in Plautus which might be taken to suggest that they had are probably satiric exaggerations.[1] Nor can we press too hard the statement that Lampis, probably a slave (p. 167, n. 6, above), had a wife and children (Dem. 34 *Ag. Phorm.* 37 οὔσης αὐτῷ γυναικὸς ἐνθάδε καὶ παίδων).

§ 4. *Public slaves*

The state was an owner of slaves on a considerable scale (p. 224), and these, who were known as δημόσιοι, formed a privileged class.[2] Their legal status approximated closely to that of metics. We find a public slave, Pittalakos, in Aischin. 1 *Timarch.* 54 described as rich (εὐπορῶν ἀργυρίου), he has a house (59),[3] and when he has been beaten up by Hegesandros and Timarchos he brings suit against them (62 δίκην ἑκατέρῳ αὐτῶν λαγχάνει): we cannot be absolutely sure that this last phrase means that Pittalakos sued without the intervention of a patron, since the phrase is in other places used of minors or women who could not sue in their own persons; but there is at least no hint of such intervention here.[4]

It has been plausibly suggested, though there is no direct proof, that not all slaves who came into the state's hands were *ipso facto* privileged in this way, but that those who were not needed for the public service would have at once been sold off to private persons.[5]

[1] It is not safe to conclude from Plut., *Mor.* 751. 12 (Σόλων) δούλοις μὲν ἐρᾶν ἀρρένων παίδων ἀπεῖπε καὶ ξηραλοιφεῖν. χρῆσθαι δὲ συνουσίαις γυναικῶν οὐκ ἐκώλυσε that there was any specific enactment on the Athenian statute book sanctioning unions between slaves; Plutarch could well have been arguing from silence. For unions between slave and free see p. 15, above. The Plautus passages are *Casin.* 68 ff., *Mil. Glor.* 1006. Cf. Beauch. ii. 451.

[2] *An. Bekk.* (Λέξ. Ῥητ.) 234 s.v. δημόσιος. Beauch. ii. 461 ff., S. Waszýnski, *Herm.* 34 (1899), 553 ff., id., *De servis Atheniensium publicis* (Berlin, 1898), B. Büchsenschütz, *Bes. u. erw.* 164 ff.

[3] Probably not as owner but as tenant: Kränzlein, *Eig. und Bes.* 41.

[4] Dem. 43 *Makart.* 15 of a minor, Isai. 3 *Pyrrh.* 2 of a woman; cf. 11 *Hagn.* 9.

[5] Lips., *AR* 799, n. 34 referring to MSL 664. Caillemer, *Succession* 147, says of public slaves 'ils pouvaient sans doute contracter mariage, et les enfants nés de leur union recueillaient leur fortune', but he offers no evidence for these statements: cf. Waszýnski, *Herm.* 34 (1899), 556.

Special provision for the punishment of public slaves for misdemeanours in discharge of their duties is made in a decree of Lykourgos.[1]

§ 5. *Actions*

The slave's ambiguous position as a chattel and as a possible subject of rights stands out when we come to discuss the actions relating to his status. This ambiguity was a natural outcome of the fact that a *de facto* slave's right to be free entailed, on the one hand, a denial of his alleged master's property rights in him and, on the other, the assertion of his own right to stand in court as a free man. We are here concerned with the legal procedures by which a *de facto* slave could establish an alleged right to be free.[2]

We saw above (p. 165) that there was a strict penal action known as *ἀπαγωγή* available against one who wrongfully enslaved a free Athenian (this at least—possibly against one who enslaved any free man). There may also have been a *γραφὴ ἀνδραποδισμοῦ*. We must assume that for either of these procedures the intervention of *ὁ βουλόμενος* was necessary, and that a conviction would mean, besides a serious penalty for the defendant, the release of the slave.

Another procedure was available, the *ἀφαίρεσις εἰς ἐλευθερίαν*.[3] This was likely to be more practicable, since it did not impose on the slave's friend the invidious task of bringing a penal charge against the master. In fact all that was required of him was the symbolic act of taking the alleged slave away into liberty (*ἀφαιρεῖσθαι εἰς ἐλευθερίαν*). Technically this was the counter-move to the master's haling the man into slavery (*ἄγειν*). The actual legal process began when the master then brought suit against the

[1] See *IG* ii². 333 and from the second century B.C. ibid. 1013.

[2] In dealing with the procedure known as *ἀφαίρεσις εἰς ἐλευθερίαν* under the Law of Property (p. 221) we look at the matter from the point of view of the master asserting his rights of property in a slave.

[3] Harpokr. s.v. *ἀφαίρεσις· ἰδίως λέγεται ἡ εἰς ἐλευθερίαν· Ὑπερείδης ἐν τῷ κατ' Ἀρισταγόρας.* Id. s.v. *ἐξαιρέσεως δίκη: ὁπότε τις ἄγοι τινὰ ὡς δοῦλον, ἔπειτά τις αὐτὸν ὡς ἐλεύθερον ἐξαιροῖτο, ἐξῆν τῷ ἀντιποιουμένῳ τοῦ ἀνθρώπου ὡς δούλου λαγχάνειν ἐξαιρέσεως δίκην τῷ εἰς τὴν ἐλευθερίαν αὐτὸν ἐξαιρουμένῳ· Ἰσαῖος ἐν τῇ ὑπὲρ Εὐμάθους εἰς ἐλευθερίαν ἀφαιρέσει.* It is unfortunate that neither of these speeches survives, but there are some fragments both from the former (13–26 J.) and from the latter (Isai., frs. 15–17 Th.), among them what is probably an extract from the statement of claim of the master (fr. 16) *ἔβλαψέ με Ξενόκλης ἀφελόμενος Εὐμάθην εἰς ἐλευθερίαν, ἄγοντος ἐμοῦ εἰς δουλείαν κατὰ τὸ ἐμὸν μέρος.*

'assertor', the slave's friend: the latter furnished sureties before the polemarch for the appearance of the alleged slave in court. The resulting suit was a delictual one in which a convicted defendant had to pay a fine of the value of the slave to the state.[1] This is the generally accepted account of the procedure, but there are variant views both as to the exact stages in it and as to its significance. In the first place there is a question whether once the 'assertor' has made his *ἀφαίρεσις* he remains a party to the ensuing suit or relinquishes this role to the alleged slave, and as a corollary to this whether he or the slave normally furnishes the sureties: the language of Lys. 23 *Pankl.* 12 suggests the latter answer in both cases; there Pankleon had been haled into slavery by Nikomedes, but because, so the speaker alleges, he knew he had no case he resisted forcibly and was afraid to furnish sureties and then engage in a struggle for his freedom.[2] A more important question is whether there were two separate issues giving rise to two alternative suits, namely the status of the alleged slave, decided by a *δίκη ἀφαιρέσεως*, and the damages due to his master from the 'assertor' supposing the court concluded in the master's favour, decided by a *δίκη βλάβης*. The most probable answer is that there was but one suit and that the system did not make, as perhaps logically it should have done, any distinction between an 'assertor' who acted in good faith and therefore did not merit a penalty and one who acted 'unjustly'; it assumed that if the court decided that the man was a slave the 'assertor' must have acted 'unjustly'. The harshness of this rule was, however, mitigated by the fact that the court could by its assessment (*τίμημα*) fix the scale of the penalty.[3]

[1] For the evidence see passages cited below, p. 221.

[2] *εὖ εἰδὼς ἑαυτὸν ὄντα δοῦλον ἔδεισεν ἐγγυητὰς καταστήσας περὶ τοῦ σώματος ἀγωνίσασθαι.* It must be admitted that the words do not absolutely exclude the possibility that the action desiderated by the speaker was the appearance of an 'assertor' and the provision by him of sureties: this failure could by brachylogy by spoken of as a failure of Pankleon himself. On this speech see Wilamowitz, *A. und A.* ii. 368 ff.

[3] Partsch, *GB* 296 ff., argued that besides a *δίκη ἀφαιρέσεως* against the 'assertor' a master could sue his alleged slave direct by a *δίκη δουλείας*. He relied chiefly on Aischin. 1 *Timarch.* 66 *ἔφη βούλεσθαι . . . ἄρασθαι τὰς δίκας, ἥν τε αὐτὸς ἐνεκαλέσατο Ἡγησάνδρῳ καὶ Τιμάρχῳ* (Franke: *Ἡγήσανδρον καὶ Τίμαρχον* codd.), *καὶ ἥν Ἡγήσανδρος τῆς δουλείας αὐτῷ*, Ar., *Probl.* 29. 13, 951[b] *οἷον εἴ τις φεύγει δουλείας ἢ ἀνδροφονίας*. But Lips., *AR* 642, n. 21, rightly objected that the Aischines passage is interpolated and that the other passage is clearly not using terms of art: there was certainly no suit named *ἀνδροφονίας*. Gernet has a lengthier refutation based

There was one other possible, though rather problematic, recourse to the courts, namely when a slave took asylum at the Theseion or the altar of the Eumenides. (On this see p. 172, above.)

to some extent on *a priori* considerations, *AHDO* 5 (1950), 176 ff. (*DSGA* 164 ff.). When the law stipulates that he who has 'unjustly' acted as 'assertor' shall pay a penalty (Dem. 58 *Theokr.* 21 κελεύει τὸ ἥμισυ τοῦ τιμήματος ὀφείλειν τῷ δημοσίῳ ὃς ἂν δόξῃ μὴ δικαίως εἰς τὴν ἐλευθερίαν ἀφελέσθαι) the assumption is that the 'assertor' must prove that the man is rightly free; if he cannot do this he was himself guilty of a wrong in taking him into freedom. In other words, there was no test of a just ἀφαίρεσις other than the decision whether the man was entitled to be free. So Lips., *AR* 641. Morrow, *Slavery* 113, on the other hand, holds that the penalty was only incurred by one who had acted in bad faith. Cf below, p. 221, n. 1.

VII · FREEDMEN

§ 1. *Introduction*

FREEDMEN and freedwomen enjoyed a definable status under Athenian law, although the somewhat scanty evidence makes it difficult for us to recover the details of this definition.[1] The status was partly a matter of custom formed by individual acts of manumission which involved agreements between the slave and his master when he was manumitted. But that there was some statutory regulation of the status is proved by the fact that, according to Pollux, Demosthenes referred to laws dealing with freedmen. These laws fell into two categories, those dealing with ἀπελεύθεροι and those dealing with ἐξελεύθεροι.[2] Though Athenian writers did not maintain the distinction in terminology strictly, there is no reason to doubt that it existed; the lexicographers may well be right in stating that the ἐξελεύθεροι were those freedmen who had originally been free, had fallen into slavery, and then been manumitted, and also the sons of manumitted slaves.[3] Men who had originally been free reverted to their former status (ξένος, metic, or citizen), though as we saw above (p. 165) a citizen who had been ransomed by a fellow citizen might become the latter's slave if he did not pay him the amount of the ransom.[4] How far conditions imposed upon a slave at his manumission were inherited by his sons will be discussed later.

[1] On freedmen in general see Beauch. ii. 467 ff., G. Foucart, *De libertorum conditione apud Athenienses* (Paris, 1896), Caillemer, DS s.v. *apéleuthéroi*, A. Calderini, *La manomissione e la condizione dei liberti in Grecia* (Milan, 1908), Thalheim, *RE* s.v. *Freigelassene*, Bu. Sw. 288 ff., 984 ff., H. Francotte, *Mél. de dr. pub. gr.* (Liège, 1910), 207 ff.

[2] Pollux 3. 83 Δημοσθένης φησὶν ἐξελευθερικοὺς νόμους καὶ ἀπελευθερικοὺς νόμους.

[3] Harpokr. s.v. ἀπελεύθερος: ὁ δοῦλος ὤν, εἶτα ἀπολυθεὶς τῆς δουλείας, ὡς καὶ παρ' Αἰσχίνῃ, ἐξελεύθερος ὁ διά τινα αἰτίαν δοῦλος γεγονώς, εἶτα ἀπολυθείς· ἔστι δ' ὅτε καὶ οὐ διαφέρουσι. Hesych. s.v. ἐξελεύθεροι: οἱ τῶν ἐλευθερουμένων υἱοί. Lips., *AR* 621, n. 3, discounts this evidence, Thalheim (loc. cit. in n. 1), Bu. Sw. 288 accept it. Athen. 3. 82 adds nothing.

[4] Dem. 53 *Nikostr.* 6 ff., 57 *Eubul.* 18 for reversion to citizen status.

§ 2. *Origin of status*

There were occasions in the history of Athens when the state for reasons of public policy freed a group of slaves. There were also cases where a slave might earn manumission either as a witness in a homicide case or as informer against certain wrongdoers (p. 171, above). We may suppose, though we are not told, that in that event some compensation was offered to their owners if they were not state-owned.[1]

We are here concerned rather with the regular avenues to manumission. The gate to these would in normal circumstances be under the control of the slave's master. He could confer freedom either during his life or by testament. In doing so he could lay certain conditions upon the ex-slave, and these conditions could be enforced by the *δίκη ἀποστασίου*. It was a probably fairly common practice for a slave to purchase his freedom out of accumulated earnings.

Two noteworthy freedmen who were manumitted by their masters in their lifetime were Pasion and Phormion. They both later became Athenian citizens.[2] Each of them before his manumission had been working in his master's bank, and it is a conjecture—no more—that each had paid something to his master out of his earnings when he was manumitted. The case of Neaira must be used with caution, as she was manumitted in Corinth, and we cannot be certain that the same rules applied there as in Athens. It is, however, clear that her enfranchisement was recognized as valid in Athens. We learn from Dem. 59 *Neair.* 29 ff. that Neaira's owners expressed willingness to free her if she could raise twenty minai. She raises the money partly from her earnings as a prostitute and partly from contributions from an *ἔρανος*. The money is paid to her owners by a free man, Phrynion, probably as head of the *ἔρανος*, and she is freed, but with the condition that she is not to practise as a prostitute in Corinth.[3] The

[1] For enfranchisements in connexion with the battle of Arginusai (407/6 B.C.) see Aristoph., *Fro.* 694 with schol. (Hellanikos, *F.Gr.H.* 323a F 25 with Jacoby ad loc.). Freedom earned by informing against certain wrongdoers: Lys. 5 *Kall.* 3, 5 (sacrilege), 7 *Sacr. Ol.* 16 (destroying a sacred olive), *IG* ii². 1128 (Tod, *GHI* 162: export of ruddle from Koresos in Keos elsewhere than to Athens; the rule is Kean, but seems to have been enforceable at Athens; the inscription is mid fourth-century; on it see A. Pridik, *De Ceae Insulae rebus* (Berlin, 1892), 108 ff.).

[2] Dem. 36 *For Phorm.* 47, 46 *Steph.* ii. 13, 15, 59 *Neair.* 2.

[3] Cf. Gernet, *Dem.* iv. 80, n. 1, Finley, *Land* 105.

freedmen's bowls (φιάλαι ἐξελευθερικαί) have been plausibly interpreted as indicating a similar pattern of procedure in Athens in the latter half of the fourth century. The φιάλη was probably equivalent to a registration fee whose aim it was to secure a public record of the result of a δίκη ἀποστασίου. If the defendant had won it served as public evidence of his right to be free, including freedom from any restrictions laid upon him at his original manumission and possibly freedom to choose a new patron (see below, p. 185). If the plaintiff had won it publicized the renewed slave status of the defendant.[1] In seventeen cases an ἔρανος, usually with a named leader, is mentioned; these were probably creditors who put up money on loan for the manumission. Other recorded purchases of freedom are that of Phila by Hyperides (mentioned by Idomeneus, *F.Gr.H.* 338 F 14) and the proposed sale of Midas and his two sons by Athenogenes with a view to manumission (Hyper. 5 *Athenog.* 5).

Although there is nothing to suggest that at Athens any strict form was required in manumitting a slave, a master would often take steps to see that his act received some publicity. Thus Eumathes was liberated by Epigenes in a court, and the practice of announcing enfranchisements in the theatre became so common that it had to be prohibited by law some years before 330 B.C.[2]

The wills of the philosophers as reported by Diogenes Laertios provide examples of manumissions by testament. Plato thus frees Artemis; Aristotle frees Ambrakis, Tuchon, Philon, Olympios and his son, and leaves instructions that no child who is serving him is to be sold and they are all on coming of age to be freed 'at their worth' (ὅταν ἐν ἡλικίᾳ γένωνται, ἐλευθέρους ἀφεῖναι κατ' ἀξίαν: the last words presumably mean that the slaves are to be allowed to buy their freedom); Theophrastos and Straton make similar provisions; Lykon, besides freeing several slaves, remits the ransom money (λύτρα: or perhaps simply the balance of the price at which they had bought freedom) due from two men who

[1] The inscriptions are *IG* ii². 1553–78. On them see M. N. Tod, *BSA* 8 (1901/2), 197 ff., W. L. Westermann, *JNES* 5 (1946), 92 ff., id., *Slave Systems* 25, who, following Kahrstedt, *Staatsg.* 307, regards the trials as legal fictions to validate manumissions.

[2] Isai., fr. 15 Th., Aischin. 3 *Ktes.* 41, 44. According to Ar., *Rhet.* 1408^{b}25 a frequent herald's cry was τίνα αἱρεῖται ἐπίτροπον ὁ ἀπελευθερούμενος; This, however, may have been part of the procedure of a δίκη ἀποστασίου.

had been freed earlier.[1] Theophrastos 'and Lykon's wills grant freedom to certain slaves provided that they do satisfactory service for a number of years after the testator's death. Plato was the only one of these who was an Athenian citizen, but the wills were no doubt drawn up in conformity with Athenian practice.[2]

There is no satisfactory evidence that a slave who wished to purchase his freedom could force his master's hand.[3] But as we have seen (p. 172, above) it is possible that a slave who was cruelly used by his master might be able to extract his manumission through the intervention of a third party.

§ 3. *Characteristics of status*

Certain disabilities under which a freedman laboured were imposed by the law of the state, but they could be either abated or enhanced by the particular act of manumission in any given case. The principal disabilities imposed by law were those which all freedmen shared with metics. Thus a freedman could not own land in Attica and as a consequence could not lend money on the security of land. He could not (at least from the middle of the fifth century onwards) contract a marriage whose offspring would be Athenian citizens, nor could a freedwoman do so, and from an unknown date earlier than about 340 B.C. freedmen and freedwomen were liable to severe penalties if they married Athenians (p. 26, above). Like metics they could not attend or vote in the ekklesia or at elections or hold office. On the other hand, they were liable to certain liturgies and to the payment of a special tax (μετοίκιον). Most important of all, they were subject to certain rules in relation to the courts. In the first place certain suits relating to them were taken to the court of the polemarch, and secondly in all judicial business they had to be represented by a patron (προστάτης). The evidence for all this is discussed later in the section on metics (pp. 189 ff.). There were two respects in which the rules laid down by law for freedmen differed from those governing other metics. The first was rather trivial,

[1] D.L. 3. 42, 5. 14–15, 55, 63, 72–73, 10. 21, K. G. Bruns, *Z* 1 (1880), 1 ff., R. Dareste, *AEG* 16 (1882), 1 ff.

[2] D.L. 5. 55, 73 f., cf. p. 151, n. 2, above.

[3] Beauch. ii. 470 f., Lips., *AR* 643, n. 23. The two passages advanced as evidence, Plaut. *Cas.* 315 ff., Dio Chr. 15. 22, do not prove the point.

though it might have had some psychological significance. Harpokration, basing himself on Menander, says that freedmen paid in addition to the twelve-drachmai *μετοίκιον* a sum of three obols, 'perhaps to the tax-farmer (*τελώνης*)'. There is no evidence whether this trifling sum was payable once for all or annually.[1] More important was the rule that the freedman had to have his former master as *προστάτης*, unlike other metics, who were free to choose.[2] The master's rights in this respect were protected by the *δίκη ἀποστασίου*, a suit which according to Harpokration was open to manumittors against those they had manumitted if the latter deserted them or registered some other person as patron and failed to do what the laws prescribed; if the defendant was convicted he relapsed into slavery, if he was acquitted he became wholly free. We do not know whether the laws prescribed any particular duties besides that of registering the master as *προστάτης*; it may be that this phrase implies no more than that the laws imposed on the freedman the duty of doing all those things which he had agreed to do at his manumission.[3] No doubt an acquitted defendant had the right to choose his *προστάτης*, and it may be that some publicity was given to his choice.[4] In one other important respect freedmen differed from other

[1] Harpokr. s.v. *μετοίκιον* (= Suda): *οἱ δοῦλοι ἀφεθέντες ὑπὸ τῶν δεσποτῶν ἐτέλουν τὸ μετοίκιον. Μένανδρος δέ φησι πρὸς ταῖς ιβʹ δραχμαῖς καὶ τριώβολον τούτους τελεῖν, ἴσως τῷ τελώνῃ.* Cf. Hesych. s.v., Pollux 3. 55. Clerc, *Les Métèques athéniens* 284 ff., regards the three obols as a once-for-all payment to the clerk for enrolment on the metic list. Bu. Sw. 984, Kahrstedt, *Staatsg.* 294, take it to be an annual payment.

[2] The manumittor might be himself of metic status, as, for example, in *IG* ii². 1553. 11 f., 26 ff. But according to Harpokr. s.v. *ἀπροστασίου* and other grammarians cited below (p. 189, n. 4) the patron had to be a citizen. It is a plausible guess, though no more, that in such cases the *προστάτης* of the manumittor became *προστάτης* of the freedman as well; Kahrstedt, *Staatsg.* 306, n. 3.

[3] Harpokr. s.v. *ἀποστασίου· δίκη τίς ἐστι κατὰ τῶν ἀπελευθερωθέντων δεδομένη τοῖς ἀπελευθερώσασιν, ἐὰν ἀφιστῶνταί τε ἀπ' αὐτῶν ἢ ἕτερον ἐπιγράφωνται ἐπιστάτην* (Suda *προστάτην*) *καὶ ἃ κελεύουσιν οἱ νόμοι μὴ ποιῶσιν. καὶ τοὺς μὲν ἁλόντας δεῖ δούλους εἶναι, τοὺς δὲ νικήσαντας τελέως ἤδη ἐλευθέρους.* Cf. Suda s.v. (20–23 Adler), *An. Bekk.* (*Λέξ. Ῥητ.*) 201, (*Συν. Λέξ. Χρησ.*) 434, Poll. 8. 35. The grammarians had a good many speeches to go on which are now lost: Lysias, *For Dexios* and *Against Pythodemos* (Gernet, *Lys.* ii. 242), Isaios, *Against Apollodoros, For* or *Against Python, Against Andokides* (possibly to be attributed to Lysias), Deinarchos, *Against Archestratos, For Aischylos, Against Hedyle*, Hyperides, *Against Demetria.* Cf. Foucart, *De libertorum conditione* 61 ff., Calderini, *Manomissione* 330 ff. Dem. 25 *Aristogeit.* i. 65 implies that a freedman convicted in such a suit was publicly sold, the money presumably going to the prosecutor: but evidence from this speech is of doubtful authority (Lips., *AR* 625).

[4] See p. 183, n. 2, above.

metics: if they died childless and intestate they were succeeded not by their nearest relatives but by their former masters, and it is possible that they could not evade this by making wills (p. 148, above).

There is much epigraphic evidence for conditions of various kinds laid upon freedmen at the time of their manumission, but unfortunately it comes for the most part from places other than Athens. We can, however, be fairly confident that the pattern in Athens showed much the same variations as elsewhere.[1]

[1] Bu. Sw. 290 f.

VIII · METICS

§ 1. *Terminology*

As we might expect, the term *μέτοικος* has in Greek literature both a generalized sense, denoting a man who has settled more or less permanently in the territory of a city not his own, and a specialized sense, denoting a man—or woman—who has a defined legal status in the city of his present domicile. We are here concerned with the latter sense as it applied in Athens in the classical period.[1]

It is probable, though not demonstrable, that articles in the grammarians dealing with metics are referring to Athens, though it is more doubtful whether they give the situation as it was in the classical period and not rather that of Hellenistic times. The principal lexicographical entries on the subject are Harpokr. s.v. *μετοίκιον*: *μέτοικος μέν ἐστιν ὁ ἐξ ἑτέρας πόλεως μετοικῶν ἐν ἑτέρᾳ καὶ μὴ πρὸς ὀλίγον ὡς ξένος ἐπιδημῶν, ἀλλὰ τὴν οἴκησιν αὐτόθι κατακτησάμενος*; and Aristoph. Byz., *Λέξεις*, Fr. 38 N. *μέτοικος δέ ἐστιν ὁπόταν τις ἀπὸ ξένης ἐλθὼν ἐνοικῇ τῇ πόλει τέλος τελῶν εἰς ἀποτεταγμένας τινὰς χρείας τῆς πόλεως· ἕως μὲν οὖν ποσῶν ἡμερῶν παρεπίδημος καλεῖται καὶ ἀτελής ἐστιν, ἐὰν δὲ ὑπερβῇ τὸν ὡρισμένον χρόνον, μέτοικος ἤδη γίνεται καὶ ὑποτελής.*[2] We shall have to return to the detail of these definitions later. The immediate point to be made is that the main body of metics was from foreigners who had specifically changed their domicile to Attica and that they formed a separate class for taxation purposes: neither definition includes freedmen as such among the metics, but the articles in Harpokration and the Suda go on to say that they paid the metic tax (see p. 185, n. 1, above). Strictly interpreted, this might be taken to imply that they were not in

[1] Wilamowitz, *Herm.* 22 (1887), 107 ff., 211 ff., Clerc, *Les Métèques athéniens*, id., DS s.v. *Metoikoi* (1904), H. F. Hitzig, *Z* 28 (1907), 211 ff., Francotte, *Mél. de dr. pub. gr.* 202 ff., Bu. Sw. 292 ff., 984 ff., Kahrstedt, *Staatsg.* 276 ff., H. Hommel, *RE* s.v. *μέτοικος* (1932), Weiss, *GP* 176, C. Mossé, *Fin de la dém. ath.* (Paris, 1962) 167 ff.

[2] Cf. Suda, Phot. s.v. *μετοίκιον*, Hesych. s.v. *μέτοικοι*. The earliest surviving use of the word in a technical sense is in the law of the deme Skambonidai from mid fifth century in *IG* i². 188. 52.

other respects metics, but modern scholars have tended to draw the contrary conclusion, namely that they were metics with certain added disabilities (p. 184, above).[1] These scholars are probably right, and this means that when a statute either conferred privileges or imposed duties on metics freedmen would have been included unless an exception was expressly made. As M. Clerc (*Mét. Ath.* 288) formulated the position a freedman was a metic *vis-à-vis* the city, a freed slave *vis-à-vis* his patron. Since the difference was mostly one of his private relations with his former master it is unlikely that the freedman's name was entered separately on any public register.

Over against the metic there was on the one side the fully qualified citizen, the πολίτης or ἄστος.[2] Sometimes the word ἐλεύθερος is used in an extended sense for a free man with full citizen rights, so that δουλεία could be used of all those falling short of that status.[3] On the other side was the ξένος. In a very strict sense ξένοι included μέτοικοι, so that there is nothing strange in the locution ξένος μέτοικος as in Aristoph., *Kn.* 347, Soph., *O.T.* 452.[4] The term could, however, be used of foreigners as distinct from either citizens or metics.[5] Ps.-Ammonios seems to have arrived at the most happy general definition of the status, περὶ ὁμοίων καὶ διαφόρων λέξεων (p. 75 Valckenaer): μέτοικος ὁ μετοικήσας εἰς ἑτέραν πόλιν ἐκ τῆς ἑαυτοῦ καὶ τοῦ μὲν ξένου πλέον τι ἔχων, τοῦ δὲ πολίτου ἔλαττον. It would perhaps be safe to say that in a legal context the word ξένος will be held to include metics unless they are specifically excluded.

[1] Clerc, op. cit. 286 ff., Kahrstedt, *Staatsg.* 327 (though the passages he cites are by no means persuasive: in particular Dem. 22 *Androt.* 61 is just as ambiguous as the grammarians' entries). Bu. Sw. 985, n. 5 conclude from Dem. 4 *Phil.* i. 36 ἐμβαίνειν τοὺς μετοίκους ἔδοξε καὶ τοὺς χωρὶς οἰκοῦντας that official terminology made a distinction between metics and freedmen: but χωρὶς οἰκοῦντες may not mean 'freedmen' (see p. 167, above).

[2] For the distinction between these terms see Paoli, *St. Dir.* 258 ff.

[3] Dem. 57 *Eubul.* 45, Ar., *Ath. Pol.* 42. 1, Ps.-Dikaiarch., fr. 59 (*FHG* 2, p. 254), Hommel, *RE* s.v. μέτοικος 1415.

[4] In Dem. 23 *Aristokr.* 47, 48 ξένος ἢ πολίτης is clearly meant to cover the whole range of possible defendants in a homicide case, and therefore ξένος includes metics. Dem. 57 *Eubul.* shows up well the ambiguity of the terms: thus in 19 ξένος is used as the simple contrary of πολίτης; but in 48 we find ξένον καὶ μέτοικον in the sense of 'foreigner, viz. metic' and in 55 the phrase εἶτ' ἐγὼ ξένος; ποῦ μετοίκιον καταθείς; Cf. also Dem. 46 *Steph.* ii. 22, 23 and p. 193, n. 1, below.

[5] In Dem. 23 *Aristokr.* 23 where the speaker is spelling out the proper legal way of describing all possible defendants he says εἰ σκέψαισθ' ἐν τίνι τάξει ποτ' ἔσθ' ὑπὲρ οὗ τὸ ψήφισμ' εἴρηται, πότερα ξένος ἢ μέτοικος ἢ πολίτης ἐστίν.

A privileged class within the metics was formed by the *ἰσοτελεῖς*. Their status was on all fours with that of other metics save that they paid exactly the same taxes as citizens: as a sub-class, therefore, they have little juristic significance.[1] Some metics, a growing number during the fourth century to judge by inscriptions, were granted the title of *πρόξενος*. It is doubtful whether this title in itself conferred anything but an honorary rank, though it was often linked with tangible privileges such as *ἰσοτέλεια* and *ἔγκτησις γῆς* and *ἔγκτησις οἰκίας* which of course were important juristically.[2]

§ 2. *Characteristics of status*

We have now to discuss the juristic aspects of the metic's status. One general point should be grasped at the outset: in relation to other *ξένοι* the metic enjoyed a privileged position;[3] the contrary view, which seems to be implied in the latter half of the entry in Aristophanes of Byzantium (p. 187, above), is not confirmed by the literary and epigraphic evidence; possibly Aristophanes' statement is a misunderstanding of some rule laying down the period of residence required to qualify for the status.

An important, though highly controversial, issue is the relation between the metic and his patron or *προστάτης*. At one stage in the history of the institution this relation was central, and from this stage dates the requirement that every metic must have a patron or be liable to prosecution by a *γραφὴ ἀπροστασίου*.[4]

[1] Xen., *Hell.* 2. 4. 25, Harpokr. s.v. *ἰσοτελὴς καὶ ἰσοτέλεια*, *An. Bekk.* (*Λέξ. Ῥητ.*) 267, 298. 27, *IG* ii². 83, 287, 505. 51 ff., 554, and *IG* ii/iii². 4, fasc. 1, p. 52, Index. That the sub-class had *some* juristic significance is shown by the following verbal quotation from a law in Dem. 20 *Lept.* 29 *μηδένα μήτε τῶν πολιτῶν μήτε τῶν ἰσοτελῶν μήτε τῶν ξένων εἶναι ἀτελῆ* and by the fact that in Ar., *Ath. Pol.* 58. 2, they form one of the classes who appeared in the polemarch's court if they were defendants in private suits (p. 193, n. 1, below). It may be significant that in Dem. 34 *Ag. Phorm.* 18, 44 Theodotos, who has been appointed private arbitrator, is twice designated *ἰσοτελής*, but it would not be safe to conclude that it was his membership of the sub-class which made him eligible as a private arbitrator: cf. Clerc, op. cit. 180, Hommel, *RE* s.v. *metoikos* 1421, Thalheim, *RE* s.v. *ἰσοτελεῖς*.

[2] Clerc, op. cit. 218 ff., Hommel, *RE* s.v. *metoikos* 1421, Kahrstedt, *Staatsg.* 288 ff., *IG* ii/iii². 4, fasc. 1, p. 57, Index.

[3] Kahrstedt, *Staatsg.* 276.

[4] Harpokr. s.v. *ἀπροστασίου· εἶδος δίκης κατὰ τῶν προστάτην μὴ νεμόντων μετοίκων· ᾐρεῖτο γὰρ ἕκαστος ἑαυτῷ τῶν πολιτῶν τινὰ προστησόμενον περὶ πάντων τῶν ἰδίων καὶ τῶν κοινῶν. Ὑπερείδης ἐν τῷ κατ' Ἀρισταγόρας ἀπροστασίου β'*. *An. Bekk.* (*Λέξ. Ῥητ.*) 201 s.v. *ἀπροστασίου· . . . προστάτην τὸν ἐπιμελησόμενον καὶ τῶν ἰδίων καὶ τῶν δημοσίων ὑπὲρ αὐτοῦ, ὥσπερ ἐγγυητὴν ὄντα.* Suda s.v. *νέμειν προστάτην· ἀντὶ τοῦ ἔχειν προστάτην· τῶν γὰρ μετοίκων ἕκαστος μετὰ προστάτου τῶν ἀστῶν τινος τὰ πράγματα αὐτοῦ συνῴκει* (codd., *διῴκει* Kuster: cf. *An. Bekk.* [*Λέξ. Ῥητ.*] 298. 3)

It is possible that the penalty on conviction was confiscation of property and enslavement.[1]

The main problem is to decide what precisely 'having a patron' involved. The technical term for it was clearly *νέμειν προστάτην*. Some scholars hold that this phrase was indistinguishable from *ἔχειν προστάτην*, in this agreeing with, for example, the Suda and Pollux.[2] This would imply a lasting relation between the metic and his patron such that it was an offence for a metic at any time not to be able to name his *προστάτης*, though it would reveal nothing positive about the nature of this relation. On the other side are scholars who allege that the phrase is only suitable for one determinate act, namely the choice of a patron at the moment when the resident alien opted for the status of metic; with the freedman it was the moment when he was freed and his ex-master became his patron automatically, or when he was acquitted in a *δίκη ἀποστασίου* and could choose his own patron.[3] This view is thought to be borne out by an alternative phrase, *ἐπιγράφεσθαι προστάτην*, found, for example, in Soph., *O.T.* 411, Aristoph., *Peace* 684, both clearly allusions to the relation of a metic to his patron; this phrase certainly is appropriate only to the initial act of enrolment as a metic. On this view the offence is procuring enrolment without the intervention of a citizen who acted as sponsor; once the enrolment was secured, no further or lasting tie was assumed between the metic and his patron unless the former had been manumitted by the latter, in which case there were the legal ties which might give rise to a *δίκη ἀποστασίου*.

καὶ τὸ μετοίκιον κατετίθει. καὶ τὸ ἔχειν προστάτην καλεῖται νέμειν προστάτην. Ὑπερίδης· ὥστε κελευστέον τοὺς μαρτυροῦντας τὰ τοιαῦτα καὶ τοὺς παρεχομένους μάτην ἀπατᾶν ὑμᾶς, μὴ τυγχάνωσι δικαιότερα λέγοντες· καὶ νόμον ἡμῖν ἀναγκάζετε παρέχεσθαι, τὸν κελεύοντα μὴ νέμειν προστάτην (Hyper., fr. 21 J.: probably a lacuna should be marked after *παρεχομένους*, *μή* be inserted before *μάτην*, and *ἐάν* before *μὴ τυγχάνωσι*). See also *An. Bekk.* (*Συν. Λέξ. Χρησ.*) 440. 24, Hesych. s.v. *ἀπροστασίου* and *προστάτου*, Harpokr. s.v. *προστάτης*, Pollux 8. 35. Isok. 8 *Peace* 53 *καὶ τοὺς μὲν μετοίκους τοιούτους εἶναι νομίζομεν, οἵους περ ἂν τοὺς προστάτας νέμωσιν*, Ar. *Pol.* 1275a11 *πολλαχοῦ μὲν οὖν οὐδὲ τούτων τελέως οἱ μέτοικοι μετέχουσιν, ἀλλὰ νέμειν ἀνάγκη προστάτην*. For modern discussions see references p. 187, n. 1, above.

[1] Suda s.v. *πωληταί*.

[2] Pollux says the suit was available *κατὰ τῶν οὐ νεμόντων προστάτην μετοίκων*: the present participle could hardly have been used of a once-for-all act. In favour of this meaning of the phrase Lips., *AR* 370, n. 5, Bu. Sw. 294, and apparently Kahrstedt, *Staatsg.* 302.

[3] In favour of this meaning Wilamowitz, *Herm.* 22 (1887), 232, W. L. Newman, *Pol. of Ar.* iii (Oxford, 1902), 133, M. L. W. Laistner, *Isoc. De Pace* (New York, 1927), 95, Hommel, *RE* s.v. *metoikos* 1443.

The statement in Λέξ. Ῥητ. 201 (p. 189, n. 4) that the *prostates* was a kind of surety (ὥσπερ ἐγγυήτην ὄντα) has been held, but without justification, to confirm this second view: the phrase would be equally applicable on the other view. Those who hold the former of these two views believe that not only was it always an offence for a metic not to be able to declare his *prostates*, but also that, at least in the fifth and early fourth centuries, a metic could not appear in court either as plaintiff or defendant without the intervention of his *prostates*, though they admit that in the course of the fourth century this requirement came to be waived. As the passages quoted in p. 189, n. 4 show, the grammarians represented the *prostates* as playing a continuing role in the metic's life; he chose him 'to be his guardian in all matters both private and public'. The view of Wilamowitz, supported by Hommel (locc. citt., p. 190, n. 3), that the grammarians were misled, perhaps by Roman analogies with the relation of *patronus* and *cliens*, into a distortion of the relation between *prostates* and metic, which was never more than the act of the *prostates* in introducing the metic into the body politic as a 'quasi-citizen'—to use a phrase of Wilamowitz—is probably refuted by the fragments of Lysias' speech against Hippotherses (Ox. Pap. 13. 1606). The precise dating of that speech and the issues involved are matters of dispute; but it is certainly not long after the restoration of the democracy in 403 B.C., and it was certainly not delivered by Lysias himself; it is conceivable, though hardly probable with an expert orator like Lysias, that it was simply a συνήγορος, or advocate, who was speaking for him, but more likely that at that time there was a rule that a metic could only appear through his *prostates*.[1] Thereafter we find no contemporary evidence for the intervention of a *prostates* in a suit either for or against a metic, but on the contrary instances where metics act without such intervention, as indeed do ξένοι.[2] The question must be regarded as still open; but two points have tended to be overlooked in its

[1] On this speech see Lips., *BSGW* 71 (1919), 93 ff., Weiss, *GP* 181, Kahrstedt, *Staatsg.* 302, A. Körte, *AP* 7 (1923), 156. Gernet, *Lys.* ii. 226, takes a different view: 'c'est un de ses amis qui présente sa défense.'

[2] The somewhat earlier speech of Lysias, 12 *Ag. Eratosth.*, was delivered in such special circumstances that we can deduce no permanent rule from the fact that it was from Lysias' own mouth. On the other hand such speeches as Dem. 32 *Zenoth.*, 33 *Apatour.*, 34 *Ag. Phorm.*, 56 *Dionysod.* provide evidence of foreigners and metics appearing as litigants without hint of the intervention of a *prostates*.

discussion. The first is that metic status should rather be looked on as a privilege than a burden; the metic is a privileged foreigner rather than an underprivileged citizen. It was natural when this privileged status was first recognized that the formal backing of a citizen should have been required both for entry into it and for the exercise of any privilege *vis-à-vis* the courts which it entailed; but with the liberalizing of judicial procedure at Athens which resulted from her pre-eminence as a commercial city the access of all foreigners to the courts was eased, and it might have been a side-issue of that development that the requirement upon a metic to plead through a *prostates* fell into abeyance. The second point which has not been allowed for is one that may have affected the evidence for the institution. That evidence is, as always in our field of study, predominantly the speeches in court, whether at first hand or through the medium of the grammarians. We have very little evidence on what must none the less have been a very important element in the judicial process, the stages preliminary to the trial and in particular the ἀνάκρισις. It is conceivable, though this is mere conjecture, that although the *prostates* ceases to take any part when the case reaches the dikastery his appearance was still mandatory at the preliminary stage; that is to say that if a metic was plaintiff he could not set his suit in motion unless he brought his *prostates* with him, and if he was defendant he ran the risk of having judgement given against him by default if his *prostates* did not appear at the ἀνάκρισις. This would only be a plausible conjecture on the assumption, not easy to substantiate, that something more exacting was required of the ξένος.[1]

There is one further argument against the view that the offence charged in a γραφὴ ἀπροστασίου was simply that of not procuring a *prostates* to sponsor enrolment on the official list of metics. It is difficult to envisage circumstances in which a man could have laid himself open to such a charge. There must surely have been

[1] As we shall see, for certain cases μέτοικοι, ἰσοτελεῖς, and πρόξενοι had resort to the court of the polemarch. This was a privilege; but we have no direct evidence what tangible advantage it conferred. G. E. M. de Ste Croix, *CQ* 11 (1961), 101, suggests that it may have been that the polemarch's court was likely to have less business and therefore provide a speedier trial. H. T. Wade-Gery makes another, but less plausible, suggestion in *EGH* 188, n. 2, that in this court an alien needed no *prostates*; the trouble with this is that we have no evidence that an alien who was not a metic ever needed one.

some recognized procedure for enrolment in the deme which included the effective sponsorship of a *prostates*: a man could only bypass this procedure with the guilty complicity of the official in charge of the list. It was different, however, on all subsequent occasions when the metic was taking advantage of his privileged position. If his status was challenged the evidence of the list was not enough; he had to produce an actual, living *prostates*. It was much as if a citizen had been required on the death of his father, who was the most effective witness to the enrolment on the phratry and deme lists which was the condition of his exercising his full citizen rights, to find some surviving person to act as his κύριος.

It seems probable then that in the fifth and early fourth centuries the metic had to have a *prostates*, not only to effect his enrolment as a metic, whenever that took place, but also during the whole of his life, and that he could not himself plead in court, but only through the mouth of his *prostates*; early in the fourth century this last requirement fell into abeyance, though there is the possibility that a *prostates* was still needed in the preliminaries to a trial. We are unfortunately almost wholly in the dark on the duties of a *prostates* beyond that of appearing in court. One might have deduced from the fact that it was an offence not to have one that the *prostates* could in some way be made liable, in part at least, for the wrongs, public or private, of a metic, but there is not the slightest evidence for this except the grammarian's phrase that the *prostates* was a kind of surety (p. 189, n. 4).

We can now deal with the peculiarities of metic status in relation to the administration of justice. Metics, together with ἰσοτελεῖς and πρόξενοι, had the privilege of resorting in certain cases to the court of the polemarch.[1] It is highly probable that this jurisdiction arose out of, but must none the less be distinguished from, an executive function which at one time devolved upon the polemarch, the function of protecting the interests of this privileged group of foreigners, much as the archon had in early days the

[1] See p. 192, n. 1. Ar., *Ath. Pol.* 58. 2 δίκαι δὲ λαγχάνονται πρὸς αὐτὸν (sc. τὸν πολέμαρχον) ἴδιαι μέν, αἵ τε τοῖς μετοίκοις καὶ τοῖς ἰσοτελέσι καὶ τοῖς προξένοις γιγνόμεναι. καὶ δεῖ τοῦτον λαβόντα καὶ διανείμαντα δέκα μέρη, τὸ λαχὸν ἑκάστῃ τῇ φυλῇ μέρος προσθεῖναι, τοὺς δὲ τὴν φυλὴν δικάζοντας τοῖς διαιτηταῖς ἀποδοῦναι. αὐτὸς δ' εἰσάγει δίκας τάς τε τοῦ ἀποστασίου καὶ ἀπροστασίου καὶ κλήρων καὶ ἐπικλήρων τοῖς μετοίκοις, καὶ τἄλλ' ὅσα τοῖς πολίταις ὁ ἄρχων, ταῦτα τοῖς μετοίκοις ὁ πολέμαρχος. In Dem. 46 *Steph.* ii. 22, 23 ξένων and ξένης are, as the context shows, loosely used for those of metic status. See further p. 10, n. 1.

executive duty of protecting the rights of property owners and of orphans and heiresses from which his jurisdiction in these spheres derived.[1] Thus in a large category of private suits involving metics[2] (all those suits which were the domain of the Forty) informations had to be laid before the polemarch, and he had the task of dividing them up into ten sections and distributing these among the ten tribes by lot; the appropriate four of the Forty then submitted the cases allotted to their tribe to the public arbitrators. We cannot be sure to what extent preliminary reference to the polemarch in these cases was the equivalent of the *ἀνάκρισις* in trials of the same category concerning citizens, but it

[1] For the archon see Ar., *Ath. Pol.* 56. 2 *καὶ ὁ μὲν ἄρχων εὐθὺς εἰσελθὼν πρῶτον μὲν κηρύττει, ὅσα τις εἶχεν πρὶν αὐτὸν εἰσελθεῖν εἰς τὴν ἀρχήν, ταῦτ' ἔχειν καὶ κρατεῖν μέχρι ἀρχῆς τέλους* and pp. 92, 102, above.

[2] A designedly vague phrase, since it is matter of dispute whether the rule applied only where the metic was defendant or also to cases where he was plaintiff. For the former Lips., *AR* 65, n. 49, H. F. Hitzig, *Z* 28 (1907), 219, Bu. Sw. 1095, n. 4, Hommel, *RE* s.v. *metoikoi* 1444; for the latter Clerc, op. cit. 91, G. de Ste Croix, *CQ* 11 (1961), 100. The evidence from Ar., *Ath. Pol.* 58. 2, considered in the light of 53. 2, has been taken by the supporters of the former view as conclusive in their favour, without justification. It is true that from 53. 2 we learn that in citizens' cases coming under the Forty, if after they had been submitted to a public arbitrator either party appealed from his decision, the case was remitted to the four members of the Forty who belonged to the tribe of the defendant and they introduced the case to a dikastery; but a close examination of the two passages in Aristotle shows that nothing can be deduced from comparing them, for in 53 we are told that the cases there under discussion—citizens' cases—were divided tribe-wise only after a decision by an arbitrator had been given and rejected by one or other party, whereas in 58 the division of metics' cases takes place before the cases are remitted to the arbitrators. We should therefore reject the *a priori* argument of Hitzig, loc. cit., that a rule which allowed a metic plaintiff to initiate proceedings against a citizen in the polemarch's court is unthinkable, since it would have deprived the citizen defendant of the privilege of having his case dealt with by judges of his own tribe: it is very dubious whether the rule applying to citizens was dictated by a desire to protect the interests of defendants and was not simply a rule of thumb for distributing the cases among the Forty: it would have been odd if in this instance alone a litigant could have been thought to derive some advantage by belonging to the same tribe as the magistrate presiding at the trial by dikastery. Direct evidence from the orators is inconclusive; Lys. 23 *Pankl.* 2, 13, proves that a metic had to be sued before the polemarch, but Kahrstedt, *Staatsg.* 299, n. 5, should not cite Dem. 32 *Zenoth.* 29 f. to prove that a metic plaintiff had resort to the polemarch, since the imagined defendant in that passage may well have been a metic. On the other hand, there is direct evidence in inscriptions that *πρόξενοι* sometimes received the right to appear as plaintiffs in the polemarch's court (and if *πρόξενοι* why not metics?); cf. *SEG* 10. 108 (*ATL* 2 D 23), 20–24, a decree in honour of Proxenides, a *proxenos*, probably dated 416/15 B.C.: *ἐὰ[ν δὲ ἀδικεῖ τις ἒ Ἀθεναίον] | ἒ τô[ν σ]ụ[μμάχον τôν Ἀθεναίον κατὰ] | [τ]ούτον λ[αγχανέτο Ἀθένεσιν πρὸς] [τ]ὸμ πολέ[μαρχον τὰς δίκας ἄνευ πρ]|υτανείο[ν*, *SEG* 10. 23. 2–7, in honour of Acheloion, dated in the 440s, and others cited by de Ste Croix, loc. cit. 273.

would seem a reasonable conjecture that the polemarch's principal role here was to give an official *imprimatur* to the litigant's claim that he belonged to the privileged class. Probably in the early days of the dikasteries this official *imprimatur* sufficed, but later it could no doubt have been challenged by way of a παραγραφή. This conjecture, if accepted, tends to support the view that in this type of case first resort was to the polemarch both for the plaintiff metic and for the defendant metic; for it is not easy to see how in the great majority of cases of this type, cases arising out of contractual or delictual obligations, a metic defendant would have been any better off *qua* metic than a ξένος; it would therefore have been of no particular advantage to him that his opponent should be required to lay the information before a special magistrate. With a plaintiff, on the other hand, the right to sue would always be in issue. We can assume that this right was inherent in the metic status, but that with ξένοι it would depend on treaty relationships between Athens and the city of the particular ξένος. In this situation the *imprimatur* of a magistrate on a man's claim to the privileged status would have been important.

Besides the cases we have hitherto been discussing, in which the polemarch's role seems to have been to take the initial depositions and then hand the cases over to the Forty, there were some metics' cases in which the polemarch not only received the depositions but also acted as president of the court which, if things so turned out, finally tried them. These cases were, first, δίκαι ἀποστασίου: the wording of Aristotle (p. 193, n. 1) and of Dem. 35 *Lacr.* 48 taken together suggests that these went to the polemarch irrespective of the status of the plaintiff—the defendant as a freedman would always have been of metic status; second, γραφαὶ ἀπροστασίου: the defendant here was by definition a metic, the plaintiff was ὁ βουλόμενος, and metics could probably not appear in this role;[1] finally, the polemarch took all cases of

[1] The regular formula for prosecuting by way of a γραφή was γραψάσθω ὁ βουλόμενος Ἀθηναίων οἷς ἔξεστιν, as, for example, in Dem. 21 *Meid.* 47 (ὕβρις), 24 *Timokr.* 63 (εἰσαγγελία), Aischin. 1 *Timarch.* 32 (ἐπαγγελία δοκιμασίας). This formula would seem to exclude metics (and *a fortiori* ξένοι): but in Dem. 59 *Neair.* 52 in the law directed against those who gave foreign women in marriage to Athenian citizens the formula reads γραφέσθων πρὸς τοὺς θεσμοθέτας οἷς ἔξεστιν, καθάπερ τῆς ξενίας. The omission of Ἀθηναίων here may be significant and indicate that in these cases exceptionally, where the information in a foreigner's hands might often be decisive, one who was not a citizen might sue (if successful he

inheritance and heiresses and stood in relation to metics just where the archon stood in relation to citizens. We may perhaps deduce from this very general remark in Aristotle (loc. cit.) that the substantive rules in the law of succession and marriage as between metics were the same as for citizens, and further that the polemarch had some administrative responsibility towards widows and orphans of metics and for seeing that, where possible, a metic's house was perpetuated. On this last point there must be considerable doubt; it would, for example, logically entail that such suits as the *γραφὴ κακώσεως ὀρφανῶν* would lie for wrongdoing to a metic's orphan, but we have no direct evidence for this and there is an *a priori* presumption against it: metic children were probably not protected from procuration or violation by the *γραφὴ ἑταιρήσεως* (p. 37, n. 5, above), and it is therefore improbable that they had the protection of the *γραφὴ κακώσεως ὀρφανῶν*.

In certain of the private cases where a metic was defendant, if not in all, the prosecutor could cite him before the polemarch and demand sureties up to a sum related to the value of the matter in dispute.[1]

Homicide cases as usual need separate treatment. We have to consider cases where the victim, the possible plaintiff, or the possible defendant was a metic. For a metic as victim we have only one direct piece of evidence.[2] In Dem. 47 *Euerg.* 68–73 we have the story of the death of an aged freedwoman whose status was probably, though not certainly, metic. She had

received a third of the convicted defendant's property). In Dem. 59 *Neair.* 66 a foreigner sues in a *γραφὴ ἀδίκως εἰρχθῆναι ὡς μοιχόν*: he was the victim of the illegal restraint, and Lips., *AR* 244, deduces from the case a general rule that where a *γραφή* was concerned with a wrong to an individual the victim of the wrong could sue even if he were a foreigner (and *a fortiori* a metic, Clerc, op. cit. 113); but if the rule had been as general as this it would be hard to explain the word *Ἀθηναίων* in the formula relating to the *γραφὴ ὕβρεως*. It is better to assume that in this type of case too there were reasons which we cannot uncover for an exception to be made allowing foreigners to prosecute, though it should be noted that, judging from Ar., *Ath. Pol.* 43. 5, metics were quite commonly suspected of sycophancy, and by and large they could only practise this by prosecuting in public suits.

[1] Isok. 17 *Trapez.* 12 *εἷλκέ με πρὸς τὸν πολέμαρχον ἐγγυητὰς αἰτῶν καὶ οὐ πρότερον ἀφῆκέ με, ἕως αὐτῷ κατέστησα ἓξ ταλάντων ἐγγυητάς*: ibid. 41 shows that the speaker was probably a metic. Dem. 32 *Zenoth.* 29 should not be cited in this connexion, as it is not certain that Protos was a metic. Lips., *AR* 811, Partsch, *GB* 292, Hommel, *RE* s.v. *metoikos* 1445.

[2] For a full discussion of this piece of evidence see MacDowell, *Homicide* 12 ff. Lys. 12 *Ag. Eratosth.* deals with the killing of a metic, but the circumstances are so exceptional that the speech yields no evidence on general rules.

died as the result of mishandling in a forcible execution upon property. Her manumittor was dead, and his son in whose house she was living, acting presumably as her προστάτης, though he does not say so, asks the ἐξηγηταί, the expounders of sacred law, what his duties are arising out of her death, since she was not related to him by blood. Their answer is that it is his duty to bring a spear to the funeral—a symbol that she had died a violent death—and to make proclamation at her tomb for any relative and keep watch there for three days (the implication being that if a relative turned up that relative would be obliged to prosecute); this, they say, is the sacred law (*τὰ νόμιμα*); at his request they add some advice on his subsequent actions; since he had not been present at the incident himself and the only witnesses were his wife and children he should make proclamation against 'the perpetrators of the deed, the killers', but without naming them (ὀνομαστὶ μὲν μηδενὶ προαγορεύειν, τοῖς δεδρακόσι καὶ κτείνασιν)—this proclamation is to be distinguished from the first one and would normally be made as a preliminary to prosecution by the victim's relatives, who would name the accused and warn him to keep away from τὰ νόμιμα; finally the expounders advise that since the woman was neither related to the inquirer nor his slave he has no obligation to bring a case before the basileus. Although the proper procedure in this case was obscure—only the first part of the expounders' answer is stated as undoubted law—the uncertainty was due to the old woman's having no known relative: but we can safely deduce from the story that the relatives of a freedman or woman (and therefore probably of a metic) who was killed were required to do the things which were not done on this occasion, that is, make a proclamation warning the killer by name to keep away from the places laid down by law and then prosecute him at the Palladion before the basileus. In other words, the only difference in procedure up to the beginning of the trial proper when the victim was a metic and not a citizen was that the venue was the Palladion, whatever the type of homicide, whereas with the killing of a citizen only the trial of unpremeditated homicide was heard there.[1] It has been argued that one consequence of this difference of venue was that the penalty for the premeditated killing of a metic (and by the same token of a slave or a foreigner) was less than that for killing

[1] Ar., *Ath. Pol.* 57. 3.

a citizen; the latter penalty was death, which, however, could be converted into banishment for life if the defendant fled the country before the end of the trial. This is a probable though not absolutely certain deduction. We cannot be entirely dogmatic on the precise procedure in prosecutions for homicide, nor therefore on the rationale which lay behind it. We know that the main function of the Palladion was to try cases of unpremeditated (or involuntary) homicide, the Delphinion of justifiable homicide, and the Areopagos of what we should call murder; cases were taken to the Delphinion when the accused pleaded justification; we do not know how it was decided which cases should go to the Palladion, but it seems most likely that in those cases too the defendant's plea decided; the penalty for unpremeditated killing of a citizen was exile, with the possibility of return if composition (αἴδεσις) could be arranged with the dead man's relatives; but we must surely suppose that if the court decided that the killing had in fact been premeditated the sentence must either have been death or at least banishment for life. If this reasoning is on the right lines it suggests that when a slave, metic, or foreigner was killed there was no distinction of penalty between premeditated and unpremeditated killing, but the milder penalty was laid down; here too, however, we must suppose that, if the defendant had elected to go before the Palladion on the ground that the dead man was a slave, metic, or foreigner, the court could decide against him on that plea and therefore impose the harsher penalty. By the same reasoning it would seem natural that if a defendant was going to plead justification he should have been heard in the Delphinion, whatever the status of his victim; certainly the circumstances held to justify homicide cannot have been more rigorous—and were likely if anything to have been less rigorous—for the death of a slave, metic, or foreigner than for the death of a citizen, and therefore a different venue can have had little significance. We may conclude then tentatively that the premeditated killing of a metic was less severely punished than that of a citizen; we simply cannot say whether the punishment for killing one unpremeditatedly was also scaled down, nor whether there were circumstances which justified killing a metic which would not have justified killing a citizen.[1]

[1] See above, pp. 169 f., for the killing of a slave. The statement of MacDowell, *Homicide* 69, that the Palladion court was reserved for less important cases of

The evidence considered in the preceding paragraph is sufficient to show that a metic was not merely allowed, but was expected to bring a *δίκη φόνου* when a relative had died a violent death; the court in which he proceeded would be determined by the plea of the defendant; it would normally be the Palladion, since the dead man would normally, but not inevitably, be himself a metic. We are as ignorant of the rules which applied when a metic was defendant in a homicide case as of those which applied to a slave defendant (p. 173); in particular we cannot say whether the rules for justifiable homicide were the same for a metic as for a citizen.

We can now turn to the peculiarities of metic status other than those directly related to judicial procedure. We shall restrict discussion to matters of private law, if it is permissible to use the term in this context; we shall ignore, that is, their disabilities in regard to holding office or voting or speaking in the assembly and their special liabilities in the field of taxation and of military service.[1] Metics, like other non-citizens, were prohibited from owning land or houses in Attica unless they had this special privilege conferred on them (*ἔγκτησις γῆς καὶ οἰκίας*).[2] While, as we saw above (p. 196), the law of marriage as between metics was probably the same as for that between citizens, the rules governing marriages between a metic woman and a citizen man and a metic man and citizen woman differed at various periods. (They have been discussed above at pp. 24 ff., 61 ff.[3]) The right to contract fully valid marriages with citizens was sometimes conferred on groups of metics, but not, it seems, on individuals (p. 29, above).

homicide is slightly misleading; it seems to be based on the assumption that the venue was determined by the charge put forward in the prosecution; it is doubtful if this could have been practicable and more likely that it was determined as suggested above. The statement in *An. Bekk.* (*Δικ. 'Ον.*) 194 *Φονικόν: ἐὰν μέτοικόν τις ἀποκτείνῃ, φυγῆς μόνον κατεδικάζετο· ἐὰν μέντοι ἀστόν, θάνατος ἡ ζημία* refers clearly to premeditated homicide and is correct so far as it goes.

[1] On these see Kahrstedt, *Staatsg.* 296, Hommel, *RE* s.v. *metoikoi* 1446 ff.

[2] For the evidence see below, p. 237.

[3] Add to the literature there cited Wilamowitz, *Herm.* 22 (1887), 227, A. Ledl, *WS* 30 (1908), 211, 227, P. S. Photiades, *Ἀθ.* 32 (1920), 139 ff.

PART II

LAW OF PROPERTY

I · OWNERSHIP AND POSSESSION

§ 1. *Introduction*

THE law of property is one of the most difficult branches of Athenian law. In the first place the chances of survival have dealt harshly with the subject. Though we have the titles of several speeches which suggest that they were concerned directly with property issues, no surviving speech deals with such an issue pure and simple.[1] There are one or two invaluable articles in the lexicographers, but these are a poor substitute for contemporary speeches. And, secondly, even in the dim light shed by this evidence it seems fairly clear that the Athenians of the fourth century were still at a relatively simple stage in their legal thinking about property; so much so that they had no general term which could describe this branch of the law. It might therefore seem an anachronism to deal with it as a separate topic. Nevertheless we are bound to isolate the legal problems arising out of the having or transmitting of a thing in Athens, since the

[1] The list of speeches given by Lips., *AR* 681 f. shows how much we have lost. There were speeches (1) περὶ χωρίου by Lysias *For Diophantos* (39a Th.), *Against Diogenes* (36 Th.), by Isaios *Against Diokles* (9 Th.), *Against Medon* (29 Th.), *Against Nikokles* or *Neokles* (34 Th.), *Against Timonides* (43 Th.), *Against the Demesmen* (7 Th.; the hypothesis and opening paragraph survive); (2) περὶ οἰκίας by Hyperides *Against Epikles* (22 Jensen, 27 Kenyon), by Lysias *Against Asopodoros* (23 Th.); (3) ὑπὲρ ἀνδραπόδων by Deinarchos *Against Daous* or *Daon* (κατὰ Δάους or πρὸς Δάωνα 66 Sauppe); (4) περὶ νεώς by Deinarchos *Against Dioskourides* (61 S.); (5) περὶ ἵππου by Deinarchos *Against Antiphanes* (64 S.). Two speeches περὶ οἰκίας *Against Alkibiades* attributed to Lysias are probably apocryphal (see Gernet, *Lys.* ii. 246). The speech of Isaios *Against Eukleides* (14 Th.) is called περὶ τῆς τοῦ χωρίου λύσεως and was no doubt concerned with the release of a piece of land from a mortgage.

Athenians themselves in their day-to-day life must have been constantly confronted with such problems.

§ 2. *Ownership*

The first question we have to answer is what modes of 'having a thing' were recognized for legal purposes by the Athenians, and, as a subsidiary question to this, what kinds of 'thing' were so recognized. Now not only had the Athenians no general term to describe the law of property; they had no abstract word for ownership. In legal terminology οὐσία never meant 'ownership', but was always used in a concrete sense of a thing or collection of things owned by someone. The words ἔχειν and κρατεῖν have always a factual, concrete, non-juristic connotation; they are not used, for example, to describe the owner who is not the occupier or the occupier who is not the owner, nor in combination to describe one who is both. The same is true of the word κεκτῆσθαι.[1] There is a strong contrast here with Roman legal thought, with its firm and clear-cut concept of '*dominium*'. Both that word itself (though it is never defined in Roman sources) and the actual law relating to ownership serve to underline the strongly individualistic character of Roman ownership, which comes out forcibly in the plaintiff's words in a *vindicatio*, 'hunc fundum meum esse aio ex iure Quiritium'. The Roman citizen asserts a claim against all the world, based on an act of his own will. There is nothing at all corresponding to this in Athens. The Athenian in claiming a right to a thing seems to have been merely asserting a better right than A or B or C.[2]

[1] For the meaning of οὐσία see Leist, *Att. Eig.* 43, E. Rabel, *Z* 36 (1915), 342, n. 2, Lips., *AR* 674, n. 1, Suda s.v., J. Korver, *De Terminologie van het Creditwesen in het Griekschk* (Amsterdam, 1934), 12 f. On property terminology in general Finley, *Land* 53 ff., Kränzlein, *Eig. und Bes.* 13 ff. On Dem. 41 *Spoud.* 10 Finley, ibid. 245, n. 61, writes 'τοὺς ἔχοντας cannot mean those in physical possession of the property but those who "have" the *apotimema* in the sense of "having the contingent right to the property" '. Again, ibid. 12 and 204, n. 11, discussing the phrase ὥστε (or ἐφ' ᾧτε) ἔχειν καὶ κρατεῖν in *horoi* nos. 1, 2, and 10 in his collection, 'that κρατεῖν does not necessarily mean "to own" is clear from such passages as Hdt. 2. 136, Isai. 8 *Kir.* 2, Dem. 35 *Lakr.* 25, 49 *Timoth.* 11, Xen. *Mem.* 2. 7. 2, Polyb. 12. 16. 4'. For a different view of the meaning of this phrase H. J. Wolff, *Z* 70 (1953), 423, *Fest. Rabel* (1954), ii. 331, n. 166, Gernet, *Iura* 4 (1953), 365. For the concept of κυριεία see Wolff, *Traditio* 2 (1944), 63 (*Beitr.* 187), *RE* s.v. προίξ 148. For κρατεῖν, Kränzlein, op. cit. 17, and for κεκτῆσθαι, ibid. 19.

[2] This difference serves to explain differences in the remedies provided for the protection of ownership in Rome and in Athens; but the importance of the distinction

This is all negative. Positively, one of the few passages which shed any light on the general concept of ownership in ancient Greece is Aristotle's remark in *Rhet.* $1361^{a}21$, ὅρος τοῦ οἰκεῖα εἶναι ὅταν ἐφ' αὑτῷ ᾖ ἀπαλλοτριῶσαι ἢ μή. λέγω δὲ ἀπαλλοτρίωσιν δόσιν καὶ πρᾶσιν. It is noteworthy that Aristotle should single out the power to alienate as the true sign of a thing being one's own (οἰκεῖον). In Athens at any rate the power to alienate heritable estates had at one time been very restricted, though it is a matter of continued debate when the principal restrictions were removed. Even in the fourth century the power to alienate by will—and the term δόσις covers this as well as gifts *inter vivos*—was restricted to cases where there was no surviving legitimate son.[1]

This power to alienate may be said to include all lesser rights of disposal, but we are singularly ill informed as to what this amounted to in detail at Athens. We can only assume that ownership of land, for example, carried with it ownership of buildings on the land, for there is no text which bears on the subject. On ownership of minerals below privately owned land there is more evidence, but its interpretation is highly controversial. It was for long rendered unnecessarily so by a failure to distinguish in the sources between μέταλλον, the comprehensive term for a mine including approach works and galleries, and

so far as it concerns the basic conception of ownership has perhaps been exaggerated; cf. G. Simonetos, *Fest. Koschacker* iii (1939), 172. For the Roman conception F. Schulz, *Principles of Roman Law* (Oxford, 1936), 151 ff.; 'a Roman principle must have existed to the effect that the right of ownership was to be as unrestricted as possible and the greatest possible latitude given to individual action and initiative'. Vinogradoff, *HJ* 198, criticizes the theory of Beauch. iii. 52 that the absence of Greek terms corresponding to *dominium* was due to insufficient development in Greece of the rules as to occupation and usucapion, which meant, on this theory, that a Greek wishing to assert absolute ownership against the whole world would have had to refer to an endless series of *auctores*. But, as Vinogradoff points out, in the Greek world property was frequently to be traced to definite acts of state—for example, the distribution of lots in a colony—and in such cases nothing could have been easier than to assert absolute *dominium*, if the concept had been there.

[1] Plato, *Euthyd.* 301 e describes what is 'your own' in rather different terms (ἆρ' οὖν ταῦτα ἡγῇ τὰ σὰ εἶναι, ὧν ἂν ἄρξῃς καὶ ἐξῇ σοι αὐτοῖς χρῆσθαι ὅτι ἂν βούλῃ; οἷον βοῦς καὶ πρόβατον, ἆρ' ἂν ἡγοῖο ταῦτα σὰ εἶναι, ἃ σοι ἐξείη καὶ ἀποδόσθαι καὶ δοῦναι καὶ θῦσαι ὅτῳ βούλοιο θεῶν;). Kränzlein, *Eig. und Bes.* 33, sees the essence of the Greek idea of ownership as the power to use. For further more general discussions of ownership see Guiraud, *Prop. fonc.* 53 ff., 170 ff., 178 ff., Glotz, *Solidarité* 325 ff., Pringsheim, *GLS* 9 ff., Jones, *LLTG* 198 ff., V. Arangio-Ruiz, *AG* 23 (1932), 248, E. Rabel, *Seminar* 1 (1943), 41. For restriction on the right of testament see above, p. 151.

ἐργαστήριον, a workshop where an industry is carried on, in the case of a mine an ore-crushing mill or smelting furnace. This confusion has now been cleared up, and the best view seems to be that, as far at any rate as the mines at Laureion go, the mines under private land were not in the full sense owned by the landlords of the surface, but the state exercised a measure of control over them, whether or not we choose to call this the equivalent of a Bergregal.[1]

Full rights of ownership might be restricted in a number of other ways. Thus a thing might belong to more than one person. We consider the effects of this in connexion with both succession (pp. 124 ff.) and associations (pp. 240 ff.). Again, easements (see below, pp. 249 ff.) restricted the rights of the owner. Finally, the state might regulate the exploitation of privately owned land.[2]

[1] On the law relating to mines see R. J. Hopper, *BSA* 48 (1953), 200–9, drawing on the poletai lists published by M. Crosby in *Hesp.* 19 (1950), 189–312. Much of the evidence advanced for the private ownership of the mines is based on the mistaken identification of ἐργαστήριον with μέταλλον in, for example, Dem. 37 *Pantain.*, *passim*, Aeschin. 1 *Timarch.* 101, Isai. 3 *Pyrrh.* 22. Hence too the view of Boeckh, *Staatsh.* 377 ff., followed by Miles, *Hermathena* 78 (1951), 50–56, that the state was the original owner of the mines, but that it granted to individuals perpetual leases, or freeholds subject to a perpetual debt-charge. Other evidence for private ownership is also weak. (1) the ἴδιον of Hyper. 3 *Euxen.* 36 could only be used to support it by a *petitio principii*, since on any view Epikrates was being accused of having extended his workings beyond the proper boundary; by acquitting him, the speaker argues, the jury decided that the μέταλλον was ἴδιον; he had not encroached, it was 'his', and the word would have been equally appropriate whether the mine was private property or he was entitled to work it under a concession of 'mineral rights' by the state. Hopper is not clear when he says (op. cit. 206) 'ἴδιον does not mean "own property", but "their concern" as opposed to someone else's, since the *metallon* was alleged to have been extended ἐντὸς τῶν μέτρων': but it is sufficient for his purpose that it *need* not mean 'own property'. See also Schönbauer, *Z* 55 (1935), 193 ff., Lauffer, *Bergwerkssklaven* i. 117, n. 2, J. Labarbe, *Loi navale de Thémistocle* (Paris, 1957), 56, Kränzlein, *Eig. und Bes.* 26. (2) It is a similar *petitio principii* to take the word δημευθέν applied to a μέταλλον in Dem. 42 *Phain.* 3 as implying private ownership. The poletai 'sold' or 'leased' mines—the words used are ambiguous, Ar., *Ath. Pol.* in c. 47, for instance, using derivatives of ὠνεῖσθαι and μισθοῦσθαι indifferently for the process. When the 'purchaser' or 'lessee' was unable to meet his obligations the state rescinded the 'sale' or 'lease'. The word δημευθέν was appropriate whatever the nature of the tenure which was being cancelled. So Gernet, *Dem.* ii. 79, against Lips. who writes in *AR* 311, n. 8 'die Entziehung eines auf 3, bzw. 10 Jahre verpachteten Bergwerks kann keinesfalls als Konsfiskation bezeichnet werden'. (3) Dem. 40 *Boiot.* ii. 52 is equally inconclusive. Money is borrowed εἰς ὠνήν τινα μετάλλων, but the term ὠνή is ambiguous, see (2), above. On the question of the state ownership of mines see further below, pp. 234 f. and Appendix D, p. 315.

[2] Peisistratos, for example, imposed the planting of olives, Dio Chrys. 25. 3. Cf. Dem. 43 *Makart.* 71.

§ 3. *Possession*

Just as the Athenian concept of ownership was blurred in comparison with the Roman, so it was with the concept of possession. In Roman law of the classical period *possessio* meant physical control of a corporeal thing, in contrast to ownership and other kinds of relationships to things. It was 'a matter of fact and not of right, but it was a fact which was, within certain limits, endowed with legal consequences'.[1] The reasons which led the Romans to develop their rules about possession are in dispute, but the general effect of the rules in protecting factual possession and thus preserving the peace is clear. If, for example, A buys a thing in good faith from a thief and B, the owner, finds the thing in A's possession and takes it from him, A can recover possession by an interdict and B's remedy is then to sue A with a *rei vindicatio*, in which A has the advantage of being defendant. This distinction gave rise to two quite separate forms of procedure, the *iudicium possessorium* and the *iudicium petitorium*, the former being a shorter and more summary process, since in it the *right* to possess was not at issue.

Of course any but the most rudimentary system of law must recognize the factual difference between possessing a thing and owning it; and two texts at least are cited to show that the Athenians were fully aware of the juridical importance of the distinction. Hegesippos in Dem. 7 *Hal.* 26 says: ἔστι γὰρ ἔχειν καὶ τἀλλότρια, καὶ οὐχ ἅπαντες οἱ ἔχοντες τὰ αὑτῶν ἔχουσιν, ἀλλὰ πολλοὶ καὶ τἀλλότρια κέκτηνται. This passage refers to relations between states and therefore has only the force of analogy. The more interesting passage is from a fragment of Theophrastos dealing with sale (Stob., *Florileg.* 44. 22; the best text now in Arangio-Ruiz and Olivieri, *Inscr. Gr. Sic. et inf. It. ad ius pert.* (Milan, 1925), pp. 240 ff.). Theophrastos is discussing the legal conditions of sale and, in particular, the effects of the payment of the price. He says, κυρία ἡ ὠνὴ καὶ ἡ πρᾶσις εἰς μὲν κτῆσιν, ὅταν ἡ τιμὴ δοθῇ καὶ τὰ ἐκ τῶν νόμων ποιήσωσιν . . . πότερον δὲ ἕως ἂν κομίσηται κύριον εἶναι τοῦ κτήματος; οὕτω γὰρ οἱ πολλοὶ νομοθετοῦσιν. The last two sentences mean 'shall the vendor be owner of the property until he gets the price? This is the rule of most legislators.' This clearly recognizes a distinctive legal situation

[1] Schulz, *CRL* 428, and the whole chapter on possession.

where a man has sold something, but has not yet received the price, and though he may have lost possession, the law still regards him as owner.[1]

It is, however, one thing to recognize a difference between possession and ownership and quite another to elaborate the distinction into a whole body of separate rules for protecting the two different relations to a thing. This the Romans did and the Athenians failed to do.[2]

[1] G. Simonetos, loc. cit. (p. 201, n. 2), Pringsheim, *GLS* 136.

[2] Vinogradoff, *HJ* 228, J. C. Naber, *Mnem.* 57 (1929), 181 ff., Schulz, op. cit. 432, for the view that the Roman elaboration was not necessarily pure gain. A. Kränzlein, *Eig. und Bes.* 11 ff., 33 ff., 38 ff., 157 ff., tries to show that, in spite of inadequate technical terminology, the Athenian system did recognize quite clearly possession without title as in certain circumstances something to be protected by procedural forms. H. J. Wolff disagrees in *Z* 81 (1964), 337 f.

II · PROCEDURAL PROTECTION

§ 1. *Introduction*

THE law of actions will be treated in a later volume; but in regard to property discussion of the remedies plays such an important part in discovering the rules of the substantive law that it seems best to begin our examination of those rules with a study of the actions concerned with property.

It will not be necessary to anticipate what will be said about the general course of a suit and, in particular, about the preliminary stages of arbitration and *anakrisis* which were common to most of the suits we are here concerned with. Consideration is at the moment limited to those procedures specially connected with property.[1]

At once we come up against a recurrent difficulty, that what are now fairly well-defined categories of procedure, for example civil as distinct from criminal actions, either did not exist in the Athenian system or corresponded very imperfectly with similar categories in Roman or English law. Thus it is misleading to equate, as is often done, the distinction between a *δίκη* and a *γραφή* with the distinction between a civil and a criminal suit. In considering remedies in the field of property we must guard against entertaining any preconceived categories.

§ 2. *Movables: ἀπαγωγή, ἐφήγησις*

There is a good practical reason for considering the protection of movables and land separately, since under any system of law the practical problem of identifying and recovering a movable and a piece of land must differ materially. We may begin therefore with the procedure available to an owner who wished to recover a movable of which he had lost possession.

If we can trust at all to analogies with the history of other legal systems, we should expect to see this procedure arising out

[1] See Kaser 134 ff., Vinogradoff, *HJ* 218 ff.

of and going along with the procedure for recovering a stolen object. A man who finds someone else in possession of a thing which belongs to him starts with the assumption that the thing has been stolen, and, conversely, the man who prosecutes for theft not only expects the thief to be punished, but also looks to get back from him the thing stolen.

The simplest case is where the owner catches the thief in the act, ἐπ' αὐτοφώρῳ. He can then bring him before the Eleven and secure his punishment by the procedure known as ἀπαγωγή. Or, if he feels himself unequal to the task of haling the thief before the magistrate, he can by ἐφήγησις bring the magistrate to the thief. In either case the stolen object would be before the magistrate and its restoration to the owner a simple matter.[1]

A similar summary form of procedure is the formal house search, φωρᾶν, described by the lexicographers as τὸ τὰ κλοπιμαῖα ζητεῖν. Presumably, if found, the thing was restored to the owner forthwith, though we are not specifically told this. The possessor was punished, the assumption being perhaps that, had he had a clear conscience, he would have delivered up the thing and then asserted his own claim to it by a suit at law.[2]

§ 3. δίκη εἰς ἐμφανῶν κατάστασιν

These direct and somewhat primitive remedies are supplemented in the developed law of the fourth century by a δίκη εἰς ἐμφανῶν κατάστασιν. The description of this suit as εἰς ἐμφανῶν κατάστασιν

[1] Kaser 144. For ἀπαγωγή Dem. 45 *Steph.* i. 81, Isai. 4 *Nikostr.* 28, Aischin. 3 *Ktes.* 10. Dem. 24 *Timokr.* 113 states that by a law of Solon this procedure was restricted to thefts by night or from a gymnasium by day or of sums over ten drachmai in a harbour or over fifty drachmai elsewhere. For ἐφήγησις Dem. 22 *Androt.* 26, Poll. 8. 50. The two last cited passages from Demosthenes show that a δίκη and a γραφὴ κλοπῆς were available side by side with these remedies.

[2] On the earlier history of the house search see Glotz, *Solidarité* 201 ff., F. de Visscher, *TR* 6 (1925), 264. The procedure described in Plato, *Laws* 954 a may well be Athenian (Gernet, *Plat.* clxxii); cf. Isai. 6 *Philokt.* 42, schol. Aristoph., *Cl.* 498, *An. Bekk.* (Λέξ. Ῥητ.) 314 s.v. φωρᾶν. It is doubtful whether the fragment of an archaic law quoted in Lys. 10 *Theomn.* i. 17 (ὅστις δὲ ἀπίλλει τῇ θύρᾳ, ἔνδον τοῦ κλέπτου ὄντος) refers to house search for the reasons given by Kaser 145, n. 32, against Lips., *AR* 440, n. 78. A law quoted in Dem. 24 *Timokr.* 105 reads Ὅ τι ἄν τις ἀπολέσῃ, ἐὰν μὲν αὐτὸ λάβῃ, τὴν διπλασίαν καταδικάζειν, ἐὰν δὲ μή, τὴν διπλασίαν (Heraldus: δεκαπλασίαν codd.) πρὸς τοῖς ἐπαιτίοις, i.e. a penalty of double the thing's value if the plaintiff recovered the thing; if he did not, double the value (with Heraldus's emendation) in addition to the value of the thing (accepting with Lips., *AR* 441, n. 79 Reiske's rendering of πρὸς τοῖς ἐπαιτίοις 'praeter illam rem de qua contenditur').

is rather puzzling, and still more so is the variant in *An. Bekk.* (*Λέξ. Ῥητ.*) 246 ἐξ ἐμφανῶν καταστάσεως, though this may be simply a misunderstanding of Dem. 53 *Nikostr.* 14, where ἐξ ἐμφανῶν καταστάσεως ἐπιβολή may perhaps be a short way of saying 'a fine due to condemnation in a δίκη εἰς ἐμφανῶν κατάστασιν.'[1] But the general sense of the abstract phrase is no doubt expressed in such concrete phrases as ἐμφανῆ καταστῆσαι τὰ χρήματα (Dem. 52 *Kallip.* 10), and it means a suit for the production of a thing. The fullest account we have of the purpose of this suit is in *An. Bekk.* (*Λέξ. Ῥητ.*), loc. cit. A man has lost something; he knows who has it; by this suit he can compel the possessor both to produce the 'stolen' thing (αὐτὰ τὰ σῦλα) and to state from whom he acquired it (παρὰ τίνος ὠνήσατο). If the possessor indicates a 'seller' (or perhaps better, 'warrantor'; the word is πρατήρ)[2] then the claimant sues *him*, as having sold what was not his. If he does not indicate a 'seller', then he is sued himself. *Lex. Cant.* 669. 10 makes the suit cover inherited property (κλῆρος ἀμφισβητήσιμος) as well as stolen goods, and Pollux 8. 33 extends it to the person or thing the production of whom, or of which, has been guaranteed by a surety (ὁπότε τις ἐγγυήσαιτο ἢ αὐτόν τινα ἢ τὰ χρήματα, οἷον τὰ κλοπαῖα). In the orators we find the suit mentioned or implied for the production of the 'undisclosed' part of an inheritance; in Isaios' lost speech *Against Aristogeiton and Archippos* (D.H. *Isai.* 15), the brother of the deceased προσκαλεῖται (codd., προκαλεῖται Sylburgius) τὸν ἔχοντα τἀφανῆ χρήματα εἰς ἐμφανῶν κατάστασιν. Kallippos threatens to use the suit against the banker, Pasion, to compel him to produce a sum of money deposited with Pasion by Lykon, now dead, with instructions, Kallippos alleges, to give the sum to Kallippos in case of his death; if the money has already been paid, Pasion is to declare the name of the recipient (ἐμφανῆ καταστῆσαι τὰ χρήματα ἢ τὸν κεκομισμένον Dem. 52 *Kallip.* 10). In Isai. 6 *Philokt.* 31 a testator used it in an attempt to recover and destroy a will he had made. We can infer the possibility of its use in bottomry loans, where the pledged ship, on its return to the home port, is to be held by the creditor until the secured debt is paid; Dem. 35 *Lakrit.* 11 παρέξουσι τοῖς δανείσασι τὴν ὑποθήκην ἀνέπαφον κρατεῖν, 56 *Dionysod.* 38 ἐὰν δὲ μὴ παράσχωσι τὰ ὑποκείμενα ἐμφανῆ καὶ ἀνέπαφα . . .

[1] Lips., *AR* 588, n. 142.

[2] For the meaning of πρατήρ see below, p. 275, n. 1.

ἀποδιδότωσαν διπλάσια τὰ χρήματα (both quotations from documents).[1]

Disregarding refinements, it seems, then, that the purpose of this suit was to secure the production of an object to enable the claimant to lay hands on it.[2] If the possessor was prepared to acquiesce in the surrender of the thing the whole procedure could presumably be completed out of court. If, however, he wished to dispute the claimant's right to have the thing, he had not merely to produce it on the spot out of court, but also be ready to produce it in court before the magistrate, when the issue of right was to be settled. So Lex. Cant., loc. cit., says *εἰς τὸ ἐμφανὲς καθίστασθαι τοῖς δικασταῖς*, and *An. Bekk.* (*Δίκ. 'Ονομ.*) 187 *ὅταν τὰ ἐπιδικαζόμενα τεθῶσιν ἐπὶ τοῦ ὑπάρχου.*[3] The suit produced its effect by a penal element. On the most probable interpretation of a difficult passage in Dem. 53 *Nikostr.* 14 f. a condemned defendant, besides being required to surrender the thing, had to pay the plaintiff a sum in damages and a fine of equal amount to the state. The suit was in fact delictual, the delict being on one view not the original concealing or taking of the thing, but declining to make it available on demand, on another view the presumption

[1] *An. Bekk.* (*Λέξ. 'Ρητ.*) 246 *Εἰς ἐμφανῶν κατάστασιν καὶ ἐξ ἐμφανῶν καταστάσεως: ὄνομα δίκης ἐστίν, ἣν ἐποιοῦντό τινες ἀπολέσαντές τι τῶν ἰδίων σκευῶν ἢ ἀνδραπόδων ἢ κτηνῶν ἤ τι τῶν οἰκείων, γνωρίσαντες ὅπερ ἀπώλεσαν παρά τινι. διὰ ταύτης οὖν τῆς δίκης ἐπηνάγκαζον τὸν ἔχοντα ἐμφανῆ καταστῆσαι αὐτά τε τὰ σῦλα, καὶ παρὰ τίνος ὠνήσατο ταῦτα. καὶ δῆλον ὅτι, εἰ μὲν πρατῆρα ἐπεδείκνυεν ὁ ἄλλου τι ἔχων, πρὸς ἐκεῖνον ἐγίνετο τῷ ἀπολέσαντι ὁ λόγος, ὡς τὸ ἀλλότριον πωλήσαντα· εἰ δὲ μὴ ἀπεδείκνυε, πρὸς αὐτὸν τὸν ἔχοντα.* Harpokr. s.v. *ὄνομα δίκης ἐστὶν ὑπὲρ τοῦ τὰ ἀμφισβητήσιμα εἶναι ἐν φανερῷ.* On these passages see Kaser 148, E. Rabel, *Z* 36 (1915), 382 ff. Even supposing that we restore Ar., *Ath. Pol.* 56. 6, to read *εἰς ἐμφανῶν κατάστασιν* after *διαδικασίαν*, this is no good reason for putting this suit among those dealing with the family, as does Lips., *AR* 585; certainly it belonged to the archon (Isai. 6 *Philokt.* 31), but rather in his capacity as protector of the rights of property, for which see Ar., *Ath. Pol.* 56. 2. On the passage from Isai. 6 see Wyse ad loc.; the *διαθήκη* which the testator sought to recover was not a straightforward will, but one which had been made part of a wider agreement. On Pollux 8. 33 see Partsch, *GB* 206, 308.

[2] It is doubtful if this suit could be used to compel the production of documents needed for some other litigation, though this might perhaps be implied in Dem. 33 *Apatour.* 38. Gernet, *Dem.* iii. 84 f. takes a different view of this suit; it is not an action to secure that a thing is produced ('la procédure athénienne ne parait pas faite pour assurer l'exécution d'obligations de faire'), but rather aims at a pecuniary penalty for opposition to the exercise of a private right. For further literature see Weiss, *GP* 334, n. 290.

[3] This is roughly the procedure laid down in Plato, *Laws* 914 c, which very probably derived from Athenian practice. Gernet, *Plat.* clxxi, points out that physical seizure is part of the formal procedure for asserting a claim to a thing.

of theft, which could have been avoided by the production of the thing. The only point which the plaintiff had to establish was previous possession of the thing. He need not prove his right to possess; conversely, the actual possessor could not make the direct counter-plea that he had the right; he had to enter a special plea or παραγραφή with the disadvantages which that procedure entailed. This is clear from the words which follow those quoted on p. 208 from D.H., *Isai.* 15, ὁ δὲ τοῦ κλήρου κρατῶν παραγράφεται τὴν κλῆσιν, δεδόσθαι λέγων ἑαυτῷ τὰ χρήματα κατὰ διαθήκας.

The possessor had fulfilled his obligations so far as the suit was concerned by the production of the thing. The references in *An. Bekk.* (Λέξ. Ῥητ.) 246 to a seller (παρὰ τίνος ὠνήσατο) and in Dem. 52 *Kallip.* 10 to a subsequent possessor (τὸν κεκομισμένον) merely indicate means whereby a man could divert liability from himself.

It is doubtful whether the distinction made in the passage from Dionysius between things ἐμφανῆ and ἀφανῆ has anything to do with the common division of property into φανερά and ἀφανὴς οὐσία. As will be argued later (pp. 230 ff., below), this division had no specific juristic significance.

When in the two bottomry loans referred to above it is laid down that the pledge must be handed over to the creditor free from any legitimate claim by a third party (ἀνέπαφον), this is probably a condition laid down in the contract, not a legal requirement automatically falling upon anyone summoned to produce a thing by the procedure of δίκη εἰς ἐμφανῶν κατάστασιν.

§ 4. *Formal seizure, warranty, summons*

A plaintiff, having secured the presence before a magistrate of a defendant and of the thing being claimed, proceeds to the formal act of seizing the thing, ἐφάπτεσθαι. Although there is no direct evidence for this step in the procedure for Athens, we may perhaps assume its existence there from a passage in Plato's *Laws*, backed up by closely similar provisions in two inscriptions, one from Miletos, the other from Delphi. Plato, *Laws* 915 c, reads ἐὰν δὲ ὡς αὑτοῦ ἐφάπτηται ζῴου καὶ ὁτουοῦν ἤ τινος ἑτέρου τῶν αὑτοῦ χρημάτων, ἀναγέτω μὲν ὁ ἔχων εἰς πρατῆρα ἢ τὸν δόντα ἀξιόχρεών τε καὶ ἔνδικον ἤ τινι τρόπῳ παραδόντα ἄλλῳ κυρίως. In reply to this formal seizure the possessor could either acquiesce and deliver up the thing, in which case, so at least the Delphi inscription suggests, he was liable to the penalty for theft. Or he could contest the claim in one of two ways; either by referring the claimant to his predecessor in title, *ἀνάγειν*, or by undertaking himself to show that he had a better title than the claimant, *αὐτομαχεῖν*.

For *ἀνάγειν ἐπὶ τὸν πρατῆρα* we have, in addition to the passage from Plato's *Laws* quoted above, two citations from the lexicographers. Harpokr. s.v. *ἀνάγειν· τὸ μηνύειν τὸν πεπρακότα καὶ ἐπ' ἐκεῖνον ἰέναι· Λυσίας ἐν τῷ πρὸς Βοίωνα, εἰ γνήσιος, καὶ Δείναρχος. An. Bekk.* (*Λέξ. Ῥητ.*) 214 *ἀνάγειν εἰς πράτην καὶ ἀνάγειν ὠνήν: δίκης ὄνομα, ὅταν ἀμφισβητῇ τις περὶ οἰκέτου ὡς οὐ δεόντως πραθέντος, ὁ τὸν οἰκέτην διακατέχων παραγίνεται ἐπὶ τὸν πεπρακότα, καὶ ἀναγκάζει αὐτὸν συνίστασθαι τὴν δίκην πρὸς τοὺς ἀμφισβητοῦντας. καὶ τοῦτο καλεῖται ἀνάγειν εἰς πράτην.*[1] These passages refer to two distinct uses of the procedure, its use to provide a purchaser with warranty against eviction and its use to provide him with a remedy against secret defects. There is little doubt that originally in both these uses the object was physically retransferred to the seller (*ἀνάγειν*), and it is probable that the first use is the older of the two. The purchaser, whose right to possess a thing is challenged, delivers the thing back to the seller, and the latter has to take over the defence. On his side the claimant could presumably decline to accept this substitution of one defendant for another; this is implied in the condition mentioned in Plato (*Laws* 915 c) that the warrantor must be both solvent (*ἀξιόχρεως*) and subject to the jurisdiction of a court accessible to the claimant (*ἔνδικος*). We must also presume, though there is no evidence from Athens on the point, that if the claimant took this course there was a preliminary procedure to decide whether he was justified in so doing; if he was, then the original defendant had to answer. For further protection of the claimant Plato lays down a limit of time within which the possessor must refer the claimant to a warrantor. We cannot say whether the warrantor who was named by the possessor could in his turn refer to a warrantor or whether he was compelled to take on the defence (*αὐτομαχεῖν*).[2]

[1] Cf. *An. Bekk.*, ibid., s.v. *ἀναγωγὴ οἰκέτου*, 207 s.v. *ἀναγωγή*, Hesych. s.v. *ἀναγωγή*.

[2] The two inscriptions are (1) *Inscr. Cret.* iv (Guarducci), no. 161 *Ἐάν τις Μιλησίων ἐν Γόρτυνι ἢ Γορτυνίων ἐμ Μιλήτωι / ἐφάπτηται σώματος ἢ δούλου ἢ ἐλευθέρου, ἆμ μὲν ἀνά/γηι ὁ ἔχων πράτορι ἀξιόχρεωι ἢ εἰς πόλιν ἔνδικον, ἀποδοὺς / τὴν τιμὴν τὴν ἀρχα[ί]αν ἀποδότω τὸ σῶμα ὁ ἐφαψάμε/νος· ἂν δὲ μὴ ἀνάγηι, ἀποδότω*

The possessor whose right to possess had been challenged could compel his warrantor to take over the defence by a *δίκη βεβαιώσεως*, most fully described in Pollux 8. 34 f. *ἡ δὲ βεβαιώσεως δίκη, ὁπότ' ἄν τις πριάμενος οἰκίαν ἢ χωρίον, ἀμφισβητοῦντός τινος, ἀνάγῃ ἐπὶ τὸν πρατῆρα, τὸν δὲ προσήκει βεβαιοῦν ἢ μὴ βεβαιοῦντα ὑπεύθυνον εἶναι τῆς βεβαιώσεως. καὶ εἰ ὁ ἀνάγων ἐπὶ τὸν πρατῆρα ἡττηθείη, τὸ μὲν ἀμφισβητηθὲν τοῦ κρατήσαντος ἐγίγνετο· ὁ δὲ ἡττηθεὶς τὴν τιμὴν τοῦ συκοφαντήσαντος ἐκομίζετο.*[1] Here again we have a penal suit in which the warrantor, if unsuccessful, is fined, in Athens perhaps the simple value of the thing. Necessary conditions for success in this suit were that there had been a valid sale, that the price had been paid, and that the possessor had tried the procedure of *ἀναγωγή* without success. The delict consisted either in failure to take on the defence, in which case the suit might presumably be brought even if the possessor had decided to take on the defence (*αὐτομαχεῖν*) and had won; he would recover the costs of the action which the warrantor would have borne had he done his duty. Or, more probably, the delict was receiving the price for a thing belonging to someone else which the possessor now had to hand over to that person. In that case the *δίκη βεβαιώσεως* would have had to wait upon the

τὸ σῶμα ὁ ἔχων τῶι ἐφαψα/μένωι αὐθημερόν. On this see Pringsheim, *GLS* 432 f. (2) Treaty between Delphi and Pellana, published by Haussoulier in *Bibl. Éc. Hautes Ét.* 222 (1917), ii A 14 ff. *[αἰ δ]έ κα ἔξοθεν [ἅψηται* (*φωρᾶι* Partsch) *Δελφὸς παρὰ Πελλα/νεῖ ἢ Πελλανεὺς παρὰ Δ]ελφῶι, ὁ ἔχων ἀναγέτω, τῶι ἐφαπτομέν[ωι] ἔγγυον καταστάσ[ας ποὶ τὰν ἀρχὰν τὰν εἰσάγουσαν τὰν δίκαν ἔ]νδικον καὶ ἄνδρα ἀξιόχρεον, ἃ μὲν ἐν [Δ]ελφοῖς ἢ Πελλανε[ῦσιν ἔχει ἐμφανέα καταστᾶσαι* (*δικαίως πεπάσθαι* Haussoullier) *κατὰ / τοὺς νόμους τᾶς πόλιος· ἐξέσ]τω δὲ τῶι μὲν μὴ δέξασθαι τὰν ⟨ἀν⟩αγωγὰν εἰπόντι καθ' [ὅτι δικαίως ἐφάπτοιτο / τῶι δὲ ἀποδείξασθαι ὅτ]ι ἀνάγοι καθότι πέπαται*. On this see Pringsheim, ibid., Partsch, *Z* 43 (1922), 578 ff. In this inscription the possessor must (*a*) provide a surety (that he or a warrantor will appear in court to defend his possession), (*b*) refer, if he wishes, to a warrantor who will take on the defence (and is to be distinguished from the surety). On the possessor's duty to provide sureties Partsch, *GB* 344 ff. Kaser 164 says that he has not found the abstract *ἀναγωγή* used for reference to a warrantor except in the second inscription above, but Pringsheim rightly sees it in Plato, *Laws* 916 a. Pringsheim, op. cit. 474, argues, against Lips., *AR* 744, that *ἀνάγειν εἰς τὸν πράτηρα* was intended originally to protect against eviction and was later applied to protection against secret defects. For the claimant's right to decline substitution of defendants see Kaser 167; he extends it to cases where the claimant contested the validity of an alleged sale and therefore of the transfer of the defence to the warrantor. Similarly Naber, *Mnem.* 41 (1913), 125, who vainly tries to extract from Dem. 30 *Onet.* i. 2 f. the conclusion that reference to a warrantor was only on the motion of the claimant.

[1] Cf. also Harpokr., *An. Bekk.* (*Λέξ. Ῥητ.*) 219 s.v. *βεβαιώσεως*.

decision of the main action. We cannot say whether this action was available by law to any purchaser or whether specific terms to that effect had had to be agreed by the parties to the sale.[1]

If the warrantor, having taken over the defence, lost the case against the claimant, he was probably not only liable as if for theft, but had to deliver the thing to the claimant. There is a theory that one who had purchased from a solvent and suable vendor was protected from eviction, however bad the vendor's title to the thing sold was, provided that the relevant rules as to publicity had been complied with at the time of the sale. A third party who had a claim to the thing and failed to intervene at the sale could not attack the purchaser's right; his only redress was against the vendor. This theory has been rightly criticized on the ground that such an indefeasible right of a purchaser is incompatible with the *ἀναγωγή* procedure outlined above, since it was of the essence of that procedure that if the possessor refused to refer to his warrantor, or if the reference broke down in some way, a claimant should be entitled to proceed against the possessor. Moreover, it would seem illogical that the claimant's failure to state his claim at the time of the sale should bar his proceeding against the purchaser while allowing him to proceed against the vendor.[2]

Although direct evidence is scanty, there are some indications that in Athenian law usucapion could in certain circumstances confer ownership. (On this see below on modes of acquisition, pp. 245 ff.)

[1] On the *δίκη βεβαιώσεως* in general see Beauch. iv. 134 ff., Lips., *AR* 746 ff., J. Partsch, *Nachgel. u. kl. Schr.* (Berlin, 1931) 264 ff. (= *GGA* 1911, 713 ff.), G. Husserl, *Rechtskraft u. Rechtsgeltung* (1925) 191 ff., Pringsheim, *GLS* 356 ff., Kaser, *Z* 64 (1944), 168, M. Talamanca, *L'arra della compravendita in dir. gr. e dir. r.* (Milan, 1953), 17 ff. For the fine of the simple value see Husserl, loc. cit. 195. Apart from the passage from Pollux quoted in the text Beauch. iv. 136, n. 2, and Lips., *AR* 747, n. 260, base their view that '*simplum*' applied in Athens on Isai. 5 *Dikaiog.* 21 *οἱ παρὰ τούτου πριάμενοι καὶ θέμενοι οἷς ἔδει αὐτὸν ἀποδόντα τὴν τιμὴν ἡμῖν τὰ μέρη ἀποδοῦναι*, but Kaser 169 is probably right in thinking, with Wyse, *Isai.* 429 ff., that the reference here is not to the *δίκη βεβαιώσεως*, but to the releasing of a property mortgaged by *πρᾶσις ἐπὶ λύσει* by repayment of the loan. For the possessor who *αὐτομαχεῖ* successfully and recovers the cost of the action from the defaulting warrantor see Beauch. iv. 135, Lips., *AR* 747, Partsch, *GB* 345. See also p. 264, below.

[2] Kaser 176, n. 137, follows Lips., *AR* 676, n. 5, E. Caillemer, *La Prescription à Athènes* 6 f., in the view that Plato, *Laws* 954 c (*τῶν ἀμφισβητησίμων χρόνου ὅρος ὃν ἐάν τις ᾖ κεκτημένος, μηκέτ' ἀμφισβητεῖν ἐξεῖναι*) gives a rule on prescription derived from Athenian law: on the other side Leist, *Att. Eig.* 60. See also Beauch. iii. 142, J. Partsch, *Longi temp. praescr.* 120 ff., Gernet, *Plat.* clxxiii.

If for any reason no reference is made to a warrantor or the reference breaks down, then the possessor has to defend, αὐτομαχεῖν. He could in this case no doubt still make use of a vendor in the capacity of a witness.[1]

The procedures we have been considering related to movables; land cannot be carried off or hidden, and these procedures would therefore have been inappropriate for asserting a claim to it. How could a man who found another in occupation of land which he claimed to be his reach a position parallel to that of an owner of a movable who has lost possession of it, but has managed to get himself, the present possessor, and the thing assembled together before the magistrate? He could not make a forcible entry, but he could by πρόσκλησις cite the occupier to appear in court. It is doubtful whether such a summons could ever give rise to an action *in rem*, though we find a law quoted in Dem. 43 *Makart.* 16 laying down πρόσκλησις for a case where an inheritance has been adjudicated and another wishes to oust the man to whom it has been adjudged. It is conceivable that a plaintiff in a case of landed property could, in the appropriate circumstances, bring a δίκη βιαίων against a wrongful occupier, though we have no direct evidence for the use of this action in property cases.[2] The δίκαι καρποῦ, οὐσίας, and ἐνοικίου, and, on top of these, the δίκη ἐξούλης, were also available in certain contingencies. These suits were all *in personam* and therefore provided for summoning a defendant. Their relations one to another and their place in the protection of property in land will be discussed below (pp. 217 ff.).

Once the preliminaries appropriate to movables or land had been completed, issue was joined between the claimant and the possessor or his warrantor. The judicial process which decided this issue was a διαδικασία.

§ 5. διαδικασία

The διαδικασία is the form of procedure central to the law of actions concerning property. It has at the same time a number of

[1] For αὐτομαχεῖν see Harpokr. and Suda s.v. and *An. Bekk.* (Δικ. 'Ον.) 184 s.v. ἀντιμαχῆσαι. Isai. 10 *Aristarch.* 24 implies the calling on a vendor as a witness.

[2] Kaser 158 ff. argues that as forcible seizure of a movable could be remedied by a δίκη βιαίων this remedy would *a fortiori* have been available against forcible ejection from a piece of land. With him is Pappoulias, *Z* 26 (1905), 552; against, Caillemer, DS s.v. βιαίων δίκη, Lips., *AR* 637, n. 4, Photiades, *Ἀθ.* 17 (1905), 35.

peculiarities which have given rise to differences of opinion about its true significance in that context. As a form of procedure it was not limited to property cases, and in fact we know less about its use in them than about any of its other uses. These other uses will be discussed in their several places; here it will suffice to say that all cases have these characteristics in common: a right or a duty is in dispute between two or more parties, each party claiming either to have a better right to a thing than any of the other parties or to have a less obligation to perform a duty; as a consequence there is strictly speaking in such cases neither plaintiff nor defendant, but all parties start on the same footing.[1]

There is general agreement that a διαδικασία concerning property shared these characteristics with the other types. Differences appear when the attempt is made to assess the significance of these peculiarities. Leist, starting from a distinction between δίκη in its specialized sense and ἀμφισβήτησις, holds that there were no δίκαι for the protection of ownership, inheritance rights, or status. These are the subject of ἀμβισβητήσεις. The distinction between the two forms of procedure corresponds to a distinction expressed by Justinian, *Inst.* 4. 6. 1, when he says 'agit unusquisque aut cum eo, qui ei obligatus sit, vel ex contractu vel ex maleficio' (δίκη) . . . 'aut cum eo agit, qui nullo iure ei obligatus est' (ἀμφισβήτησις). In a δίκη there is an alleged legal bond requiring the defendant to perform some duty towards the plaintiff; the main business of the action is to establish the existence or non-existence of this bond. In a διαδικασία, though it may be that a possessor is being required to deliver up a thing to his opponent, this is secondary. The primary function of the court is to decide which of the two has a better right to own the thing (or, if it is that kind of διαδικασία, to enter on an inheritance or to use a particular name or not to perform a liturgy). This gave to the procedure its characteristic features: there was no plaintiff and no defendant; the two parties stood side by side, trying each to show that his relation to the thing or duty gave him a better right to own the thing or to escape the duty than his opponent; the procedure was essentially pre-judicial and in kind similar to the Roman *praeiudicium*. Certainly a non-possessor might secure

[1] Leist, *Att. Eig.*, remains indispensable as a starting-point for discussion. See also Beauch. iii. 375 ff., Lips., *AR* 463 ff., 678 ff., Kaser, Pringsheim, *GLS* 10, n. 3, with further citations, Gernet, *AHDO* 1 (1937), 111 ff. (*DSGA* 70 ff.).

the appearance of a possessor in court by *πρόσκλησις*; but it is wrong to conclude from this that the possessor could play a purely passive role, leaving it to his opponent to show title and then merely rebutting this attack. He had no such advantage; for the function of the court was always to decide which of the two had the better right, and each party therefore had to expound and justify *his own* claim to ownership.[1]

There has on the whole been substantial agreement with the general outlines of Leist's treatment up to this point.[2] The final turn he gave to his theory has received less attention and is much more questionable. He has a section which aims at proving that in a *διαδικασία* the issue is not that of a right or of the violation of a right; when the judges decided that one or the other party had the better claim, they were not guided by any objective rules, whether laid down by law or custom; they were themselves by their decision creating the 'better' right for that particular concrete occasion. It is difficult to go all the way with him here. Suppose, for example, that A wishes to oust B from

[1] Leist, *Att. Eig.* 31 ff. Cf. *An. Bekk.* (*Λέξ. 'Ρητ.*) 236 *διαδικασία: οὐχ ἅπλως πᾶσα δίκη διαδικασία καλεῖται, ἀλλ' ἐν αἷς περί τινος ἀμφισβήτησίς ἐστιν, ὅτῳ προσήκει μᾶλλον. σημειωτέον δὲ ὅτι διαδικασία λέγεται καὶ ὅταν δημευθείσης οὐσίας δικάζεταί τις πρὸς τὸ δημόσιον ὡς ὀφειλομένων αὐτῷ χρημάτων ἐν τῇ δημευθείσῃ οὐσίᾳ.* Cf. also *Et. Mag.* 267, 7, schol. Dem. 24 *Timokr.* 13, schol. Aischin. 3 *Ktes.* 146, schol. Dem. 8 *Chers.* 57. A key passage is Isai. 10 *Aristarch.* 24 *τῶν ἀμφισβητησίμων χωρίων δεῖ τὸν ἔχοντα ἢ θέτην ἢ πρατῆρα* (edd., *πρακτῆρα* codd.) *παρέχεσθαι ἢ καταδεδικασμένον φαίνεσθαι*, which is probably best translated 'when lands are in dispute the possessor must either produce the one who has mortgaged the land to him or sold it or show that it has been adjudicated to him'. So Wyse ad loc., P. Roussel (Budé, 1922) ad loc., E. S. Foster (Loeb, 1927) ad loc. (save that he translates *θέτην* 'mortgagee', surely by a slip). Leist, *Att. Eig.* 37, followed by Mitteis, *RV* 501, translates the last three words 'otherwise he must lose his case', taking *καταδεδικασμένον* as passive, not middle. K. Münscher, *Z. vergl. Rechtsw.* 37 (1919), 283, followed by Finley, *Land* 233, takes *θέτην* to mean 'one who has bequeathed it to him as an adopted son', referring to Harpokr., Phot., *An. Bekk.* (*Λέξ. 'Ρητ.*) 264 s.v. *θέτης*. Whatever the translation, two things are clear about the passage: (1) the speaker is not giving an exhaustive list of possible titles; he does not refer, for example, to gift or direct inheritance; (2) it strongly suggests that an *ἀμφισβήτησις* was to decide a relative right to possess and that for that purpose the possessor had to state and defend his claim. See Kaser 183 ff., who compares the Roman procedure of *legis actio sacramento in rem*. Lips. on the other hand seeks to disprove the relative character of the Athenian conception of ownership, *AR* 463, n. 3 (with addition on p. 983), 465, n. 8, 676. Kaser doubts whether *πρόσκλησις* was available in a property *διαδικασία* (loc. cit. 185 f.).

[2] But Kränzlein, *Eig. und Bes.* 140 ff., notes the lack of any direct evidence for a *διαδικασία* on an issue between individuals on property and doubts whether it was in fact available either for movables or for immovables.

a piece of land on the ground that he has bought it from C, and that B, in accordance with the procedure sketched in Isai. 10 *Aristarch.* 24, alleges that C had mortgaged the land to him, B; we can surely believe that the judges had to examine both these assertions side by side and determine which of them constituted the stronger claim without also having to believe that there were no objective rules to guide their determination.[1]

§ 6. δίκη ἐξούλης, δίκη ἐξαιρέσεως

Assuming that the decision in a διαδικασία was declaratory, we have next to ask how the party whose right to a thing had been declared the better secured the possession of it if he did not already possess it. This would in many cases have been covered by the provision of sureties.[2] But in any case the successful litigant would have been required to proceed in the first instance by legalized self-help. If he was resisted in this he could have recourse to the penal δίκη ἐξούλης.[3]

[1] Leist, *Att. Eig.* 38 ff. He is followed on this point by Kaser 185: 'die von beiden Parteien vorgebrachten Titel für ihren Besitz, werden vom Gericht *nach freiem Ermessen* [my italics] gegeneinander abgewogen, der dem konkreten Gegner gegenüber 'besser' Berechtigte wird im Urteil als Eigentümer befunden.' Kaser, ibid., basing himself on his own account of the Roman interdicts *uti possidetis* and *utrubi* (*Eigentum und Besitz* (Weimar, 1943), 277 ff.), discounts the idea that Roman analogy would lead one to expect in Greek systems any possessory procedure to determine in advance of a property case which party was to have the advantage of being defendant; he rightly denies the relevance to this question of Polyb. 12. 16, as also the contention of Naber, *Mnem.* 43 (1915), 196 ff., that the archon's oath, Ar., *Ath. Pol.* 56. 2, is evidence for an official procedure to protect interim possession. Gernet, *AHDO* 1 (1937), 129, n. 2 (*DSGA* 72, n. 2), asks whether the decision in a διαδικασία is 'constitutif' or 'déclaratif de droit' and decides tentatively for the latter; cf. id., *AHDO* 2 (1938), 287. U. E. Paoli, in *St. Albertoni* ii (Padua, 1937), argues confidently that in Athenian law there was no protection of possession as such. Cf. Kränzlein, *Eig. und Bes.* 165 f.

[2] Partsch, *GB* 294 ff., Kaser 190. There is no Athenian evidence for the use of sureties in this connexion, but cf. Polyb. 12. 16, *Lex Gort.* 1. 1. 23, Plato, *Laws* 914 d. The ἐγγύηται were in such circumstances similar to the Roman *praedes litis et vindiciarum.*

[3] On the δίκη ἐξούλης in general see E. Rabel, *Z* 36 (1915), 340 ff., with earlier literature there cited, 340, n. 1. This article was severely criticized by Lipsius in *Z* 37 (1916), 1 ff. Rabel retorted in *Z* 38 (1917), 296 ff., and Lipsius again in *Z* 39 (1918), 36 ff. For more detail on this controversy see Appendix B, below. On the whole, Rabel's thesis has stood its ground. See also Jörs, *Z* 40 (1919), 5, 13, 77 ff., Weiss, *GP* 455 ff., 484 f., Juncker, *Ged.-schr. Seckel* (1927), 230 ff., U. E. Paoli, *St. Albertoni* ii. 313 ff., Kaser 191 ff., Gernet, *AHDO* 1 (1937), 132 (*DSGA* 74), Pringsheim, *GLS* 286 ff., Gernet, *Lys.* ii. 229, on the speech against Hippotherses, Jones, *LLTG* 203 ff., K. J. Wolff, *Traditio* 4 (1946), 52 (*Beitr.* 38), id., *Z* 74 (1957), 40 ff., E. Schönbauer, *Πραγ. Ἀκαδ. Ἀθ.* 18 (1954), 5 ff.

The precise scope of this action has long been a matter of controversy, but learned opinion has hardened round the theory first fully worked out by Rabel on the foundations laid by Leist, that it was nothing more and nothing less than a delictual action for the protection of justified self-help, principally, if not exclusively, in regard to the occupation of land. Self-help was held to be justified for people in at least four groups, namely (1) one who had been adjudged to have a better right than the present possessor by a judgement of a court or was entitled by some general rule to distrain upon a piece of land in satisfaction of a claim; (2) a mortgagee; (3) the *suus heres* (γνήσιος); (4) one who had rented or bought land from the state. The delict consisted in excluding from a piece of land one who was entitled to enter upon it for the purposes of execution, whether it were to occupy the land itself or to recover possession of a movable that was upon the land. Whether it was available also to an occupier who was forcibly ejected from his land, was in fact a protection of possession as such, is debated. Perhaps the best view is that it was so only when the expelled possessor fell under one of the four privileged groups.[1] On this view the δίκη ἐξούλης presupposes in the successful claimant a 'right to possess' either (1) as having been adjudged a thing by a court or as creditor having attempted to levy distress upon a particular thing which he was entitled by some special provision to seize; or (2) as mortgagee entitled by default of the mortgagor to seize the object mortgaged; or (3) as heir by right of succession; or (4) as tenant or purchaser of state

[1] So Kränzlein, *Eig. und Bes.* 166 f. The key passage is Harpokr. s.v. ἐξούλης: ὄνομα δίκης ἣν ἐπάγουσιν οἱ φάσκοντες ἐξείργεσθαι τῶν ἰδίων κατὰ τῶν ἐξειργόντων. εἴρηται μὲν οὖν τοὔνομα ἀπὸ τοῦ ἐξίλλειν ὅ ἐστιν ἐξωθεῖν καὶ ἐκβάλλειν· δικάζονται δὲ ἐξούλης κἀπὶ τοῖς ἐπιτιμίοις οἱ μὴ ἀπολαμβάνοντες ἐν τῇ προσηκούσῃ προθεσμίᾳ, ὑπερημέρων γιγνομένων τῶν καταδικασθέντων. οἱ δὲ ἁλόντες ἐξούλης καὶ τῷ ἑλόντι ἐδίδοσαν ἃ ἀφῃροῦντο αὐτόν, καὶ τῷ δημοσίῳ κατετίθεσαν τὰ τιμηθέντα. ἐδικάζετο δὲ ἐξούλης καὶ ὁ χρήστης κατέχειν ἐπιχειρῶν χρῆμα τοῦ χρεωστοῦντος καὶ κωλυόμενος ὑπό τινος. καὶ ἐπεργασίας δέ τις εἰ εἴργοιτο, δίδωσιν ὁ νόμος δικάζεσθαι πρὸς τὸν εἴργοντα ἐξούλης. καὶ περὶ ἀνδραπόδου δὲ καὶ παντὸς οὗ φησί τις αὑτῷ μετεῖναι. ταῦτα δὲ σαφῶς Ἰσαῖος διδάσκει καὶ Λυσίας ἐν τῷ κατὰ Στρατοκλέους ἐξούλης. Δείναρχος μέντοι ἐν τῇ Κροκωνιδῶν διαδικασίᾳ ἰδίως κέχρηται τῷ τῆς ἐξούλης ὀνόματι ἐπὶ τῆς ἱερείας τῆς μὴ βουλομένης τὰ ἴδια δρᾶν. ὅτι δὲ ἐπὶ παντὸς τοῦ ἐκ τῶν ἰδίων ἐκβαλλομένου τάττεται τοὔνομα καὶ οὐχ ὡς οἴεται Καικίλιος μόνων τῶν ἐκ καταδίκης ὀφειλόντων καὶ Φρύνιχος ἐν Ποαστρίαις δῆλον ποιεῖ. On this passage see further Appendix B. Cf. also Suda s.v. ἐξούλης δίκη, Pollux 8. 59, and other grammarians' notices collected in Rabel, *Z* 36 (1915), 356. For procedure (1) by a successful litigant Dem. 30, 31 *Onet.* i, ii (2) by mortgagee Isai. 5 *Dikaiog.* 22 (3) by *heres suus* id., 3 *Pyrrh.* 62 (4) by purchaser from the state Dem. 24 *Timokr.* 54, 37 *Pant.* 19.

land. A claimant who wished to assert his right to possess on any other ground than these would have to proceed first by one of the other forms, *διαδικασία* or *δίκη καρποῦ, οὐσίας*, or *ἐνοικίου*. Only if he were successful in one or other of these actions and his opponent still failed to give up possession could he have recourse to the *δίκη ἐξούλης*.[1]

Fundamental to the understanding of the procedure by *δίκη ἐξούλης* is the question of the process known as *ἐξαγωγή*. In origin this was no doubt a forcible preventing of a man who was trying to exercise his right of self-help. By the fourth century it has become a formal act by which the possessor indicates to a claimant that he intends to dispute his claim and thus compels him to desist from self-help and have recourse to the *δίκη ἐξούλης* on the pain of himself becoming liable to a *δίκη βιαίων*. The trial of the ensuing *δίκη ἐξούλης* is then the determination of the issue as to which of the two parties has the better right to the thing.[2]

It has been maintained that the *ἐξαγωγή* could be assigned to one of the parties by agreement in order to give opportunity to decide an issue of property by the *δίκη ἐξούλης*, on the analogy of the Roman *deductio quae moribus fit*. This view ignores the fact that in a *δίκη ἐξούλης* a penalty, equivalent to the assessed value of the thing in question, went to the state and was thus lost to both parties. This would make it unlikely that the parties would use the procedure simply to agree in advance as to which of them should be cast for the role of defendant in the ensuing action.[3]

[1] Kaser 192 ff. The authorities speak mostly only of land in this connexion probably because it was customary for arrangements to be made for movables in dispute to be held by a third party and for sureties to be provided.

[2] For the very detailed treatment of *ἐξαγωγή* by U. E. Paoli in *St. Albertoni* ii. 313 ff. see Appendix C.

[3] The case for a mutually agreed *ἐξαγωγή* was strongly put by L. Mitteis, *Z* 23 (1902), 288 ff. For Athens he relied on Dem. 32 *Zenoth.* (outside Athens P. Grenf. I. 11, Polyb. 12. 16). The position of the parties in that speech is complex, but Mitteis's main point was simple, that on a straightforward reading of the *ἐξαγωγή* in 17 ff. Zenothemis, by declining *ἐξάγεσθαι* by Protos, is in fact, as he desires, subjected to *ἐξαγωγή* by Demon, *ἐξῆγεν αὐτὸν Πρῶτος . . . οὑτοσὶ δ' οὐκ ἐξήγετο, οὐδ' ἂν ἔφη διαρρήδην ὑπ' οὐδενὸς ἐξαχθῆναι, εἰ μὴ αὐτὸν ἐγὼ ἐξάξω*, and this implies virtually an agreement between the parties. But, as Rabel, loc. cit. 367 shows, the position was reached by Zenothemis' tactics, playing on Protos' lack of confidence in his case. When Zenothemis said to Protos 'I refuse *ἐξάγεσθαι* by you', he was simply indicating that he proposed to ignore his formal *ἐξαγωγή* and proceed with his seizure of the corn. In reply Protos could either himself ignore the action of

If this account of the δίκη ἐξούλης is approximately correct, that suit was not merely a method of giving sanction to a decision reached in a διαδικασία. It also served to bypass a preliminary διαδικασία altogether in the privileged cases. A man who was basing his claim on one of these titles could, by seizure, either gain possession at once, if the possessor did not meet him with ἐξαγωγή, or, if he did, he could ensure the trial of the case by a δίκη ἐξούλης. We cannot say whether he was himself liable to a penalty if he failed to make good his case by this procedure.[1] If, on the other hand, his title was not one of the privileged, then he had first to establish that it was better than that of the possessor by a διαδικασία.[2]

The essentially relative character of these procedures for establishing a right to a thing is startlingly illustrated by the rules governing prescription in inheritance cases. Isai. 3 *Pyrrh.* 58 tells us that a claimant could sue for an estate at any time during the lifetime of one who held it as heir and for five years after his death (ὁ νόμος πέντε ἐτῶν κελεύει δικάσασθαι τοῦ κλήρου ἐπειδὰν τελευτήσῃ ὁ κληρονόμος). We have in Isai. 5 *Dikaiog.* 7 and 35 the case of a man whose title to an inheritance is attacked in court twenty-two years after he had originally entered on it. Moreover, not only is a judgement in court not binding, at least so it seems, on third parties, but even a litigant whose claim on one ground has been rejected by a court is not debarred from suing for the same thing on some other ground.[3]

Zenothemis or he could bring against him the δίκη βιαίων. He does neither, and Demon's only recourse then is himself ἐξάγειν. See further Kaser 195, n. 197, and on Dem. 32 *Zenoth.* A. C. Costman, *Dem. Rede tegen Zen.* (Leiden, 1939), P. Vinogradoff *TR* 3 (1921), 163 ff. H. Meyer-Laurin, *Gesetz und Billigkeit im attischem Prozess* 5 ff. agrees with Lips., *AR* 656 f. (especially n. 77), against the general view, that the Zenothemis suit was not a δίκη ἐξούλης but a δίκη βλάβης, since Zenothemis was the possessor whom Demon was trying to oust and not vice versa.

[1] Yes, Leist, *Att. Eig.* 51; no, Hitzig, *Pfand.* 139, n. 3, MSL 967 ff. The affirmative is more likely *a priori*. Unless he staked something a plaintiff would have been tempted always to use the penal procedure.

[2] Kaser 196 ff., emphasizing the close resemblance between the διαδικασία and the Roman *vindicatio*, claims for the former a considerable antiquity. As a procedure it has from the first an independent existence of its own with a purpose quite distinct from the δίκη ἐξούλης. The διαδικασία is in essence free from all touch of delict and there is nothing to justify the view that the δίκη ἐξούλης was ever the only means by which a claimant could secure the validation of his ownership and the right to assert it by self-help, or that the declaratory procedure of the διαδικασία was a younger offshoot of the delictual procedure.

[3] Gernet, *AHDO* 1 (1937), 128 (*DSGA* 71). If we can trust the speaker in Isai. 6

The procedure known as ἀφαιρεῖσθαι or ἐξαιρεῖσθαι εἰς ἐλευθερίαν of slaves shows analogies with, but also differences from, the procedure of ἐξάγειν of land. A man who wished to claim as his own slave another man who was either going free or was a state slave haled him off (ἄγειν) with the declaration αὐτοῦ δεσπότης εἶναι (Lys. 23 *Pankl.* 9) or ἑαυτοῦ εἶναι δοῦλον (Aischin. 1 *Timarch.* 62). An *adsertor* might now come forward ἀφαιρεῖσθαι or ἐξαιρεῖσθαι εἰς ἐλευθερίαν, providing at the same time three sureties for the appearance of the alleged slave in court (Dem. 59 *Neair.* 40, 45, Lys. 23 *Pankl.* 9, 12, Isok. 17 *Trapez.* 14). In this case the vindicator must hold his hand (if we may here follow Plato, *Laws* 914 e, μεθιέτω ὁ ἄγων) or be liable to a δίκη βιαίων. To pursue his claim he must now bring a suit which Harpokration calls ἐξαιρέσεως δίκη against the *adsertor* for having wrongfully championed the man's liberty (μὴ δικαίως εἰς τὴν ἐλευθερίαν ἀφελέσθαι: cf. Dem. 58 *Theokr.* 21). This was a delictual action in which the defendant, if condemned, had to pay a fine of the value of the slave to the state. The successful plaintiff perhaps had the choice of recovering ownership of the slave or receiving his value in money. Conceivably there was cumulation of the two.[1]

Philokt. 52, his adversary intended, and would by law have been entitled, to have two attempts at securing the whole or part of the inheritance in question. He had put in a διαμαρτυρία that the inheritance was not ἐπίδικος on the ground that there were legitimate sons of the *de cuius* alive. If he lost the διαμαρτυρία, he was going to claim the hand of a daughter of the *de cuius* as an ἐπίκληρος (ἵνα . . . ἀντιγραψάμενοι δὶς περὶ τῶν αὐτῶν ἀγωνίζωνται).

[1] Rabel, loc. cit. 379 ff., Kaser 202 ff., Kränzlein, *Eig. und Bes.* 159 ff. When Dem. 58 *Theokr.* 21 says that the law bids the condemned defendant in a δίκη ἐξαιρέσεως to owe half the τίμημα to the state, the τίμημα will be the assessed value of the slave, as settled by the jury, doubled (this assumes that the issue is simply the depriving the owner of ownership of the slave). The words of the law (ὃς ἂν δόξῃ μὴ δικαίως εἰς τὴν ἐλευθερίαν ἀφελέσθαι) could be taken as limiting the penalty to those who had acted in bad faith (M. Nicolau, *Causa liberalis* (Paris, 1933), 301), but they need not. The words περὶ τοῦ σώματος ἀγωνίσασθαι in Lys. 23 *Pankl.* 12 suggest that the result of the action might be the re-enslavement of the man: Lips., *AR* 641, n. 18. Kaser, loc. cit., notes the following difference between ἐξαιρεῖσθαι and ἐξείλλειν or ἐξάγειν. ἐξαιρεῖσθαι is itself a form of aggressive seizure, not, like ἐξείλλειν or ἐξάγειν, a mere hindering of an act of seizure. It need not therefore follow immediately upon the ἄγειν, but could be set in motion at any time. The possessor could put up a defence, and the status of the man was then settled by a court. What he could not do was to wait for the *adsertor* to free the man and then proceed again. Plato at least, in *Laws* 914 e (μεθιέτω μὲν ὁ ἄγων), provides against this threat to public order. Against the possibility that there was a δίκη δουλείας see Gernet, *AHDO* 5 (1950), 176 ff. (*DSGA* 164 ff.). See also Partsch, *GB* 295 ff. and above, p. 178.

§ 7. δίκαι οὐσίας, καρποῦ, ἐνοικίου

This is a group of actions for which the evidence is very largely drawn from various articles in the lexicographers under the respective titles of the actions. The principal of these articles are the following.

A. Under *οὐσίας δίκη* or *οὐσία*: (1) *An. Bekk.* (*Λέξ. 'Ρητ.*) 285 (= Harpokr. = Phot., Art. 2 = Suda, Art. 2), *οἱ δικαζόμενοι περὶ χωρίων ἢ οἰκιῶν πρὸς τοὺς ἔχοντας ⟨ἀλλότρια καὶ καρπουμένους⟩ οὐσίας ἐδικάζοντο τὴν δευτέραν δίκην. ἡ δὲ προτέρα ἦν τῶν μὲν οἰκιῶν ἐνοικίων, τῶν δὲ χωρίων καρποῦ. τρίτη δὲ ἐπὶ τούτοις ἐγίνετο ἐξούλης. καὶ ἐξῆν τοῖς ἑλοῦσι* (codd., *ἔχουσι* edd.) *κρατεῖν τῶν κτημάτων τούτων, εἰ ἡττηθεῖεν τὴν πρώτην δίκην τοῦ καρποῦ ἢ τὴν τοῦ ἐνοικίου. εἰ δὲ καὶ τὴν δευτέραν ἡττηθεῖεν, τὴν τῆς οὐσίας, ἐξούλης λαχεῖν. εἰ δὲ καὶ τὴν ἐξούλης ἁλοῖεν, οὐκ ἔτι ἐξῆν ἐπικρατεῖν, ἀλλ' ἐξίστασθαι ἤδη τῶν κτημάτων τοῖς δικασαμένοις.* 'Those who were bringing actions for estates or houses against the possessors (and usufructuaries of property not their own: *these words in Λέξ. 'Ρητ. only*) would bring a suit *οὐσίας* in the second instance. In the first instance they would bring a suit *ἐνοικίου* for houses, *καρποῦ* for estates. On top of these there was a third suit available, *ἐξούλης*. And it was open to possessors (reading with most editors *ἔχουσι* for *ἑλοῦσι*) to retain possession of the thing in question if they lost the first suit, whether *καρποῦ* or *ἐνοικίου*. And if they lost the second suit, *οὐσίας*, (they could not be evicted but) they could resist eviction by means of a *δίκη ἐξούλης*. If, however, they lost the *δίκη ἐξούλης*, they could no longer retain possession, but had to give it up to those in whose favour judgement had been given.' (2) Phot., Art. 1 (= Suda, Art. 1), *οὐσίας εἰσάγουσι δίκην πρὸς τοὺς ἑαλωκότας ἐν προτέρᾳ δίκῃ χρέους ἢ καρποῦ ὡς δέον ἀπολαμβάνειν ἐξ ὅλης τῆς οὐσίας ἃ κατεδικάσαν⟨το⟩.* 'They introduce a suit *οὐσίας* against those who have been condemned in a former suit *χρέους* or *καρποῦ* on the ground that it was fitting that men should be able to get what had been adjudged to them from the whole property of the defendant.' (3) *An. Bekk.* (*Δικ. 'Ον.*) 192, *οὐσία*: *ὅταν μὴ σώζωσί τινες τοὺς καρποὺς ἀποδοῦναι, ἐκ πάσης αὐτοὺς τῆς οὐσίας ἀπαιτοῦνται.* 'When people fail to give up the fruits, claims are made on the whole of their property.'

B. Under *καρποῦ δίκη*: (1) Phot. (= Harpokr., s.v. = Suda,

Art. 2), οἱ γῆς ἀμφισβητοῦντες ὡς προσηκούσης αὐτοῖς λαγχάνουσι τοῖς διακρατοῦσιν· εἶτα ἑλόντες λαγχάνουσι καὶ περὶ ἐπικαρπίας. τοῦτο καρποῦ δίκη ἐπικαλεῖται. καὶ Λυσίας ἐν τῷ κατὰ Δημοσθένους ἐπιτροπῆς· "Εἰ γάρ τι ἐγκαλεῖς τῷδε τῷ μειρακίῳ καὶ τῶν σῶν τι ἔχει δίκασαι αὐτῷ κατὰ τοὺς νόμους, εἰ μὲν χωρίου ἀμφισβητεῖς καρποῦ, εἰ δὲ οἰκίας, ἐνοικίου, ὥσπερ οὗτος σοὶ νῦν ἐπιτροπῆς δικάζεται." 'Those who claim that a piece of land is theirs bring suit against the possessors; then if they win they sue for the fruits too. This is called a καρποῦ δίκη. And Lysias in his speech against Demosthenes on the Guardianship says: "If you are bringing a charge against this young man and he has something of yours, bring an action against him in accordance with the laws, an action καρποῦ if you are claiming land, an action ἐνοικίου if you are claiming a house, just as he is now bringing an action ἐπιτροπῆς against you."' (2) Suda, Art. 1, καρποῦ δίκη: τῷ βλάψαντι καρποὺς δίκας ἐπετίθουν. 'They made a man who did damage to crops liable to δίκαι: Hesych., τῷ βλάψαντι καρπὸν οὕτως ἐδίκαζον. (3) *An. Bekk.* (Δικ. 'Ον.) 190, καρποῦ: ὅταν τινὲς ξένην γῆν ἐργάζωνται, εἶτα διωχθέντες ἀπαιτῶνται τὰς ἐπικαρπίας. 'It is a suit καρποῦ when men have been working land that is not their own, are evicted from it, and then sue for the fruits.'

C. For the δίκη ἐνοικίου we have an important sentence in Dem. 48 *Olymp.* 45, where the speaker, Kallistratos, is trying to show that the house which he was occupying did not belong to Olympiodoros, his opponent, as the latter alleged, for if it had done Olympiodoros would have sued him for the rent. διὰ τί σὺ οὐδεπώποτέ μοι ἔλαχες ἐνοικίου δίκην τῆς οἰκίας ἧς ἔφασκες μισθῶσαί μοι ὡς σεαυτοῦ οὖσαν; 'Why did you never bring a suit ἐνοικίου against me for the house which, so you said, belonged to you and was leased by you to me?'[1]

The legitimate deductions from the evidence about these suits have long been, and still are, a matter of lively controversy. Many scholars, among them Lipsius and Vinogradoff, basing themselves on the Harpokration passage (A (1), above), argue that we have here a genuine procedure *in rem*, though arranged in a curious three-tiered structure. A man who wished to claim as his own a house or a piece of land would begin by suing for the

[1] Beauch. iii. 363 ff., Lips., *AR* 678 ff., Rabel, *Z* 36 (1915), 342, n. 2, Vinogradoff, *HJ* 223 ff., Weiss, *GP* 494, Gernet, *AHDO* 1 (1937), 129, n. 1 (*DSGA* 72, n. 1), Kaser 136 ff.

fruits by a δίκη ἐνοικίου or καρποῦ as the case might be. If the possessor lost the case but remained in possession the claimant then sued for the substance (οὐσία) of the property. If he was again successful in the action, but the possessor remained recalcitrant, he could finally have recourse to the δίκη ἐξούλης. If successful here he could oust the possessor, and the latter had to pay the fine as well.

Even if we could be sure that this is the necessary interpretation of the Harpokration passage, there are grave *a priori* objections to the resulting scheme of actions. What, for example, happened if a condemned defendant in a δίκη ἐνοικίου paid up the rent but declined to vacate the house? What was the need for the threefold procedure? What was the relation between this procedure and procedure by διαδικασία?[1] Kaser has a deeper *a priori* objection, based on comparison with early Roman law. Assuming, he argues, that in their earliest stages both Greek and Roman law regarded ownership as nothing more than the right to possess, we ought not to go on to the conclusion, at first sight obvious, that the owner had a claim against the unjustified or less justified possessor to the surrender of the thing, that the possessor was under an *obligation* to surrender. Such a conception, which introduces an element of obligation into the scheme of property relations, is comparatively late. It appears first in Rome in the *formula petitoria* at the turn of the second and first centuries B.C., being based on the fusion of two originally independent

[1] Lips., *AR* 680, expresses a doubt (shared by H. J. Wolff, *Z* 74 (1957), 40 ff., Kränzlein, *Eig. und Bes.* 141) whether it was necessary to proceed through the δίκη οὐσίας to the δίκη ἐξούλης or whether it was not possible to go straight from the δίκη καρποῦ or ἐνοικίου to the δίκη ἐξούλης. But on the latter hypothesis how could the δίκη ἐξούλης have given the plaintiff anything but the rent, plus the appropriate fine? Or to put the objection in another way, how on this view of the three-tiered procedure did a man go to work who was simply suing another for rent and nothing more? Conversely, how did he proceed if he wanted to evict a tenant who was quite willing to go on paying the rent (cf. below, p. 227)? Reinach, DS s.v. *enoikiou diké* sees in the triple procedure a desire to provide the strongest possible bastion to actual possession; he suggests that a possessor who lost a δίκη καρποῦ or ἐνοικίου had the choice of vacating the property or paying the rent demanded, but this would surely have been hard on a rightful owner who wished to secure possession. Weiss, *GP* 494, n. 146, takes the Photios passage (A 2) quite literally; the creditor has the right to recover the thing due *from* the property of the debtor (*aus* dem Vermögen), which is not the same thing as satisfaction *by means of* the whole property (*mit* dem Vermögen). For a different view see Schönbauer, *AAW* 89 (1952), 1 ff. For the use of the δίκη ἐνοικίου in succession cases see Gernet, *Dem.* ii. 31, 59. For earlier literature on all these actions Beauch. iii. 365 ff.

institutions, the declaratory process establishing ownership on the one hand and on the other the obligation, voluntarily assumed by an interim possessor through *cautio pro praede*, to surrender the thing to one who has been declared owner. Before this stage was reached procedure to secure ownership was limited to the declaratory process, and the actual taking over of the thing was left to the self-help of the owner. The basic conception is that the owner has a right only *vis-à-vis* the thing, not *vis-à-vis* the possessor, and that the latter is not under an obligation to perform a definite act of restitution, but only to refrain from resistance to the justified act of self-help. Kaser concludes that it is practically impossible that ancient Greek law recognized a 'vindication' in the form of a real action for the surrender of the thing.[1]

The alternative, and more probable, view starts from the fact, admitted even by Lipsius,[2] that the *δίκαι ἐνοικίου* and *καρποῦ* are personal actions. Both the title of the first and the reference to it in Dem. 48 *Olymp.* 45 show that it was an action for rent of a house available to the lessor. That the *δίκη καρποῦ* was similarly a personal action for rent, available to the lessor of a piece of land, is not specifically stated in the three passages from the lexicographers which refer to it (B 1, 2, and 3, above), but is alleged to be a safe deduction from the close association of the two actions in the Harpokration passage (A 1) and from the use of *ἐγκαλεῖν* in connexion with both suits in the Lysias fragment (B 1). There is a possibility, it can be nothing more, that by a natural extension, even when there was no lease, an owner who was being wrongfully excluded from his property by an unjustified possessor could use one or other of these actions against the latter *as if* he had leased the property to him and were owed rent for it. But if these suits are essentially personal rather than real the probability is that the same is true of the *δίκη οὐσίας*. It will have been a personal action for the property as a whole as opposed to one for the fruits only, and, on the view here being considered, its purpose is expressed in the clause *ὡς δέον ἀπολαμβάνειν ἐξ ὅλης τῆς οὐσίας ἃ κατεδικάσαν⟨το⟩* (A 2 above; cf. also A 3). We are to imagine that the lessor of a piece of land has sued the lessee for the rent. Success in the suit allows him to distrain upon the fruits, and in this instance the name of

[1] So too Kränzlein, *Eig. und Bes.* 139.

[2] Lips., *AR* 757 f., *Z* 37 (1916), 10.

the suit describes the object that can be seized by a successful plaintiff (καρπός). But supposing the fruits were not sufficient to satisfy the plaintiff's claim, he could then bring a δίκη οὐσίας, which would allow him to distrain upon the property of the lessee as a whole, the suit here too getting its name from the object to be distrained upon. If now the possessor did not yield possession the plaintiff could have recourse to the δίκη ἐξούλης with its penal element.

Slightly different, on this view, was procedure in the case of house property. Here the name of the action, ἐνοικίου, indicated not the object to be distrained upon but the ground of the plaint. This arose from the fact that here the 'fruits' were represented, not by objects which could be seized, but normally by the use of the thing, namely the house. Distress could therefore be levied directly upon the house itself without the need for the interposition of a δίκη οὐσίας before the δίκη ἐξούλης became available. It was an error, though an easily intelligible one, when some of the lexicographers assumed that the δίκη ἐνοικίου was on all fours with the δίκη καρποῦ in leading on to a δίκη οὐσίας.

On this view then the primary purpose of these three actions was to provide the lessor of a house or of land with the means of recovering his rent. The procedure was then extended to cover cases where an owner had been wrongfully dispossessed of his property. Such an owner could, if he liked, start by suing the possessor for rent or fruits, of which he was being unjustly deprived by the wrongful detention. If the possessor resisted to the point of the δίκη ἐξούλης the court would have already determined in the previous hearings the issue of ownership, so that there would have been no need of a declaratory process such as the διαδικασία to justify the δίκη ἐξούλης. The reasons which might have induced litigants to adopt this indirect method of approach rather than proceed by way of διαδικασία were perhaps two. In the first place the claimant could get the issue of ownership tried in the first instance at much less monetary risk, since the court fee which had to be deposited in such cases by a claimant and which he forfeited if he lost the case was related in value to the estimated value of the thing claimed. In the second place, the suits being personal, the claimant had the advantage both of πρόσκλησις (he may not always have had this in a διαδικασία, see above, p. 214) and of immediate right of entry, if he won the case, on to the property in question.[1] Kaser stresses the point that the use of this indirect procedure was manifestly an advocate's trick and must have emerged at a comparatively late stage in legal development.

Although this view has points of advantage over the other it has certain difficulties of its own. In particular, it is not easy to see how the suits *ἐνοικίου* and *καρποῦ* could, without considerable confusion, have been made to serve two not wholly consistent aims. For after all an owner whose main object is to regain actual possession of a house or piece of land cannot be simply equated with one who has let a house or piece of land and merely wants to get the rent due to him. This incompatibility is brought out when one considers the effect of the *δίκη οὐσίας*. If it was a genuine action for rent how did the right to distrain really help the claimant, who was *ex hypothesi* owner, if the *οὐσία* was the actual piece of property the rent of which was at issue? In this case surely the *οὐσία* ought at least to include property *owned* by the defendant and therefore other than the piece of property at issue. Kaser (pp. 141 ff.) rather slurs two different distinctions, the distinction between the fruits and the property itself (viz., the property in dispute) and the distinction between the property in dispute and other property owned by the defendant.[2]

On the other hand, when the *δίκη οὐσίας* was an action for the recovery of possession how could a *δίκη ἐξούλης* lie from the mere refusal of the defendant to vacate the property, if after losing the case he paid up the sum claimed as fruits? Kaser himself (p. 142) emphasizes that the action is for the fruits only ('wegen der entzogenen Nutzungen — und nur wegen dieser').

In view of the difficulties which confront both of the theories considered above it must be recognized that so far no wholly satisfactory explanation of these three suits and their relationship to one another and to the *διαδικασία* has been put forward.

[1] Naber, *Aeg.* 11 (1930/1), 40 ff., *Mnem.* 43 (1915), 193 ff., for a wrongfully dispossessed owner suing *as if* a lessor for rent. Rabel, *Z* 36 (1915), 342, n. 2. for rights to distrain laid down in various leases, citing *IG* ii². 1241. 33 ff. (cf. Partsch, *GB* 221), *IG* ii². 2492. 7 ff., *Inscr. Délos* (Durrbach–Roussel), n. 503 (cf. Partsch, *GB* 267).

[2] Another weakness in Kaser's argument is the somewhat cavalier treatment he gives to the articles on the *δίκη καρποῦ* from the Suda (Art. 1) and Hesychios in B 2. These make that action available against a man who has damaged crops, conceptually something quite distinct from an action to allow distraint upon the crops. One might of course have developed out of the other, but it is not easy to imagine by what steps.

III · KINDS OF THING

§ 1. *Land and chattels*

THERE was a marked lack of juristic definition in Athenian terminology during the classical period for the various types of things that could be owned. Practical considerations, of course, led both orators and philosophers to distinguish between these various types, but on the whole the distinctions remained purely factual and did not build up into legal categories resulting in different legal treatment for the different types.[1]

The distinction between landed and all other types of property was one of fact and was bound to have some influence on the rules of law concerning land as distinct from other types (see above, pp. 206 ff., 214 ff.). There is, however, no very clear-cut terminology to express this distinction in the classical period. The suggestion in the lexicographers that *οὐσία ἔγγειος* and *ἔπιπλα* are a neat pair of opposites in this sense is not borne out by classical usage.[2] On the one hand, *ἔπιπλα* is often used to cover certain movables, to the exclusion of others such as slaves, animals, or money. Only in two passages, Lys. 19 *Prop. Arist.* 29, 31, does the word seem to be used comprehensively of all property that was not land or houses. On the other hand, the word *ἔγγειος* is rendered somewhat equivocal by the fact that its contrary is often not 'movable' but 'maritime', in such phrases as *ἔγγειοι τόκοι*, interest on money lent in other than bottomry transactions.[3]

[1] Beauch. iii. 5 ff., Caillemer, DS s.v. *bona*, Lips., *AR* 674 ff., Vinogradoff, *HJ* 199 ff., Finley, *Land* 54.

[2] For lexicographers' definitions see *Et. Mag.*, Harpokr., Sud., Hesych. s.v. *ἔπιπλα*, Pollux 10. 10, Eustath., *Od.* 3. 302, 1469. 28 (*ἔπιπλα κατὰ Παυσανίαν τὰ μὴ ἔγγαια κτήματα*). For the use of *ἔπιπλα* in the orators see especially Isok. 21 *Euth.* 2, which divides a man's property up into *οἰκία, οἰκεται, ἔπιπλα*, and *ἀργύριον*, Lys. 12 *Ag. Eratosth.* 19, 32 *Diogeit.* 15, 19 *Prop. Arist.* 29, 31 (on these two passages see text above), Isai. 8 *Kir.* 35, 11 *Hagn.* 41, 43, Dem. 27 *Aphob.* i. 10, Aischin. 1 *Timarch.* 97.

[3] Dem. 34 *Ag. Phorm.* 23, 24 *ἔγγειοι τόκοι*, 33 *Apatour.* 3 *συμβολαίου . . . οὔτε ναυτικοῦ οὔτ' ἐγγείου*, 35 *Lakrit.* 12 (text of a contract) *ἔστω ἡ πρᾶξις . . . ἐκ τῶν τούτων ἁπάντων, καὶ ἐγγείων καὶ ναυτικῶν*; Lys. *ap.* Sud. s.v. *ἔγγειον*: *τοῦ νόμου κελεύοντος*

This evidence adds up to a fairly strong argument from silence that there was in the classical law of Athens nothing so clear-cut juristically as the distinction, for example, between real and personal property in English law or between *res mancipi* and *res nec mancipi* in Roman.

Nevertheless there were at least three directions in which the distinction between landed and other property did in fact have legal consequences. First there were the differences already discussed (pp. 206 ff., 214 ff.) between the procedures for the protection of landed and of other property, differences due to the nature of these two kinds of thing. Secondly there is the treatment of things which, though movable, are bound up with the exploitation of the land, implements, slaves, cattle, things which the French civil code describes as *immeubles par destination.* A passage in Plato (*Laws* 856 d) laying down that a banished family should be allowed to take its property into exile with it, but excepting the accessories of the estate (πλὴν ὅσον κατεσκευασμένου τοῦ κλήρου παντέλως), indicates that Plato was aware of the importance of treating these accessories as integral parts of the property. There are passages in the orators which tend in the same direction, referring, for example, to the appurtenances of a farm (σκεύη) or the slaves of a factory as making up an economic unit with the farm or factory.[1] Even so, the evidence falls short of showing that Athenian lawyers had evolved anything as subtle as the concept of *immeubles par destination*,[2] and it was probably

τοὺς ἐπιτρόπους τοῖς ὀρφάνοις ἔγγειον τὴν οὐσίαν καθιστάναι, οὗτος [δὲ] ναυτικοὺς ἡμᾶς ἀποφαίνει, cf. p. 107. In Dem. 30 *Onet.* i. 30 it is used of objects attached to the soil. In Dem. 36 *For Phorm.* 5 ἔγγειος οὐσία is set beside ἀργύριον δεδανεισμένον as constituting Pasion's property. Cf. Korver, *De Terminologie van het Creditwesen in het Griekschk* 125 ff.

[1] Dem. 30 *Onet.* i. 28, 29 clearly implies that, if a farm was hypothecated, τὰ σκεύη τὰ γεωργικά would be regarded as an integral part of the pledge; Onetor by not resisting the removal of these had tacitly admitted that the farm was not standing as security for a dowry. Dem. 37 *Pant.* 4 and *passim* deals with a loan secured on a mill with slaves, cf. Finley, *Land* 32 ff. Three *horoi*, all recording πράσεις ἐπὶ λύσει, couple ἐργαστήρια and ἀνδράποδα, *IG* ii². 2747 to 2749 (Finley, nos. 88 to 90). Lauffer, *Bergwerkssklaven* i. 97 ff., discussing these *horoi* and Dem. 37 *Pant.*, shows how slaves and mill were often regarded as one unit for purposes of sale, hypothecation, and the like.

[2] Guiraud, *Prop. fonc.* 171 ff., argued that they had. Beauch. iii. 9 cited against him Ar., *Pol.* 1267ᵇ περὶ τὴν τῆς γῆς κτῆσιν ἰσάζει μόνον, ἔστι δὲ καὶ δούλων καὶ βοσκημάτων πλοῦτος καὶ νομίσματος, καὶ κατασκευὴ πολλὴ τῶν καλουμένων ἐπίπλων. But though here Aristotle puts land in one category and slaves and cattle in another, he is merely making the simple point that, of two men with farms of equal size, the

a matter for *ad hoc* decision whether in any given case these accessories were or were not regarded as one with the property to which they were attached.

Thirdly the incapacity of a foreigner to own land or houses in Attica, except by special concession, shows how important in practice the distinction between this and all other types of property might be. See further below (pp. 236 ff.) on the capacity to own.

Although slaves were from many points of view chattels there were important respects in which they were not *mere* chattels. For this reason the law of slavery is dealt with not under the law of property but under the law of the family (pp. 163 ff.).

§ 2. *Visible and invisible*

Another pair of opposites which recurs frequently is *οὐσία φανερά* or *ἐμφανής* and *οὐσία ἀφανής*. But here again the categories are scarcely juristic in character, despite the suggestion of the lexicographers to the contrary.[1] To these latter the distinction was again a simple one, between land and all other types, and again they are not borne out by the usage of the orators. There, though landed property is always *φανερὰ οὐσία*, this category may also include slaves, cattle, and furniture; its contrary, *ἀφανὴς οὐσία*, may either be simply claims (*δανείσματα* or *χρέα*) or it may include ready money (*ἀργύριον*). In all cases we have to look at the context to determine what practical issue is involved in regarding these particular things as readily attributable to an owner (*φανερά*) or readily concealed (*ἀφανή*). The most usual practical issue is whether the things in question can be easily attributed to a man's property for the purpose of estimating his liability to a tax or to a liturgy. Or the distinction may be within an inherited estate

man with a better-stocked farm will be better off. This would be just as true if the Greeks had in fact conceived the idea of *immeubles par destination*. That they had not conceived it rests on *a priori* considerations. An Athenian lease of 305/6 B.C., *IG* ii². 2499, 11–14, 30–37, authorizes the tenant at the expiry of the lease to take with him the woodwork, the roof-tiles, and the doors with their frames, but this is a unique provision and suggests that normally these things would have been regarded as integral with the house; so Finley, *Land* 72. *Horoi* occasionally mention the roof as specifically included in the property hypothecated, more usually not.

[1] Guiraud, *Prop. fonc.* 173, Beauch. iii. 13 ff., Caillemer, DS s.v. *aphanes ousia*, Lips., *AR* 677, Finley, *Land* 54 and n. 10, Wyse, *Isai.* 516, Kaser, 154 ff., Weiss, *GP* 173, 491, J. C. A. M. Bongenaar, *Isok. Trapez.* (Utrecht, 1933), 234 ff., Pringsheim, *GLS* 69.

between what can be easily divided up (ἀφανή) and what it is more convenient for a number of heirs to hold in common (φανερά); or between cash handed over in the presence of witnesses (ἀργύριον φανερόν) and mere promises to pay or repay.[1]

Clearly, then, there was no cut-and-dried classification of property into 'visible' and 'invisible'. All that the use of these terms allows us to say is that for the Athenians among the things that a man could say were his some were more obviously and absolutely attributable to him than others, and that the most important practical result of this distinction was in relation to a man's liability to tax or the performance of liturgies or to the confiscation of property. That they left the concept in this rather

[1] Harpokr. s.v. ἀφανὴς οὐσία καὶ φανερά: ἀφανὴς μὲν ἡ ἐν χρήμασι καὶ σώμασι καὶ σκεύεσι, φανερὰ δὲ ἡ ἔγγειος· Λυσίας ἐν τῷ πρὸς Ἱπποθέρσην. Cf. Suda, *An. Bekk.* (Συν. Λέξ. Χρησ.) 468, s.v. The surviving fragments of Lysias' speech against Hippotherses do not help much, but see Gernet in *Lys.* ii. 230. The lexica are confuted by, for example, Isai. 8 *Kir.* 35, where φανερά comprised land and houses, slaves and furniture, all set over against δανείσματα. Dem. 38 *Nausim.* 7 opposes χρέα to the φανερὰ οὐσία, including in this latter σκεύη and ἀνδράποδα. Citations may be segregated roughly as follows: (1) Passages where the predominant issue is some sort of public liability: Lys. 12 *Ag. Eratosth.* 83 (confiscation), 20 *Polystr.* 23, 33 (*eisphorai* and liturgies); Isok. 7 *Areop.* 35 (public liabilities); Isai. 7 *Apollod.* 35–39 (liturgies), 11 *Hagn.* 47 (public liabilities); Dem. 28 *Aphob.* ii. 2–4, 7–9 (public liabilities), 45 *Steph.* i. 66 (liturgies), 50 *Polykl.* 8 (*eisphora*), 5 *Peace* 8 (public liabilities), *Ep.* 3. 41 (public liabilities); Din. 1 *Dem.* 70 (public liabilities). (2) Passages where the make-up of an inherited estate is in question: Isai. 6 *Philokt.* 30–34 (the φανερὰ οὐσία in an estate will be more certainly assured to the necessary heirs than will the money realized by selling this φανερὰ οὐσία; in it was included a farm, a bath-house, a mortgage on a house, some goats and a goat-herd, mules, and slaves), 8 *Kir.* 35 (see above), 11 *Hagn.* 43 (τὰ φανερά is here simply that part of the estate which was acknowledged to belong to it by the speaker's opponents); Dem. 27 *Aphob.* i. 57 (ἡ φανερὰ οὐσία is that part of the estate which belonged to it by common knowledge, as opposed to that ὧν οὐκ ἐμέλλεθ' ὑμεῖς ἔσεσθαι μάρτυρες), 38 *Nausim.* 7, 45 *Steph.* i. 66 (see also under (1)), 48 *Olymp. Hyp.* 2, 9, 33, 35 (ἡ φανερὰ οὐσία is the part of the estate which was there, available for division between the two claimants, as opposed to those parts with regard to which claims had to be made good); Andok. 1 *Myst.* 118 (φανερὰ οὐσία is opposed to the debts); Lys. 32 *Diogeit.* 4, 23 (two brothers divide up the ἀφανὴς οὐσία and hold the φανερά in common), fr. 79 Th. (a difficult snatch of argument to the effect that the actual holder of ἀφανὴς οὐσία such as ἀργύριον or χρύσιον will find it easier to establish his right to these than the occupier of a farm or other φανερὰ οὐσία). (3) Passages where the emphasis is on cash in hand as opposed to credits: Dem. 48 *Olymp.* 12 (ἀργύριον φανερὸν ἐπὶ τῇ τραπέζῃ τῇ Ἡρακλείδου); Isai. fr. 15 Th. (a depositee, hearing of the death of the depositor, ἐνεφάνισε τὰ χρήματα and handed it over to the relatives); Isok. 17 *Trapez.* 7 (τὰ φανερὰ τῶν χρημάτων is opposed to a deposit in a bank); Dem. 56 *Dionysod.* 1 (the ἀργύριον φανερὸν καὶ ὁμολογούμενον which a borrower receives is contrasted with the piece of paper on which the creditor has to depend); Hyper. 5 *Athenog.* 9 (within three months after a shop has been purchased ἅπαντα τὰ χρέα φανερὰ ἐγεγόνει).

loose and untidy state is one more indication of their tendency not to define or elaborate concepts, but to leave a great deal to be settled by decisions in court or by administrative action.[1]

§ 3. *Productive and unproductive*

Demosthenes, in his first speech against Aphobos, divides the property left by his father into ἐνεργά and ἀργά.[2] The general sense of this distinction does not correspond to the modern distinction between productive and dead capital. The term ἐνεργά is confined to capital which is actually at work in industry, while under ἀργά are included not only the raw materials in stock at the factories, but also at least one item bringing in interest.[3] It is not possible to discern either in this speech or in the few other scattered references to property as ἐνεργόν or ἀργόν any specifically juristic significance in the distinction. In particular, there is no ground for the view that the duty of investing the property of orphans in land, imposed on guardians in a law quoted in a fragment of Lysias, could have been expressed as a duty to make their capital ἐνεργόν rather than ἀργόν. On the contrary, that law is simply prescribing investment in land as against investment in bottomry loans, and Demosthenes, in a later passage of the same speech, while he implies that his guardians were remiss and foolish in not converting that part of his inheritance which was ἀργά into being ἐνεργά, does not claim that their action was illegal, as he surely would have done if such had been the case.[4]

[1] Gernet, *Rev. philosoph.* 146 (1956), 81 ff.: 'c'est l'histoire d'une catégorie manquée'.

[2] Dem. 27 *Aphob.* i. 7–11. Beauch. iii. 22.

[3] Gernet, *Dem.* i. 29 ff., notes that the term ἐνεργά is restricted to the capital which 'works' in industry (cf. the use of the word in Dem. 56 *Dionysod.* 29, 36 *For Phorm.* 5), but in the *Aphob.* i passage it unexpectedly includes a sum lent out at interest at 12 per cent. per annum. This loan, or these loans, Gernet suggests (op. cit. 261), were for objects sold; since the law did not recognize credit sales it was evaded by the fiction of a loan at interest to the purchaser; cf. Pringsheim, *GLS* 245. J. Korver, *Mnem.* 10 (1942), 8 ff., inquires why the ἀργά listed in Dem. 27 *Aphob.* i. 10–11 include a bottomry loan, a talent lent (διακεχρημένον) in sums of 200 to 300 drachmai, and three deposits, one with a banker. He suggests that bottomry loans were so classed because there was special risk of loss of capital and the interest was normally paid when the capital was returned; if the deposits were for safe-keeping, they would not probably have borne interest, and the same may be true of the 200 to 300 drachmai loans.

[4] Sud. s.v. ἔγγειον, quoted p. 228, n. 3, above, Dem. 27 *Aphob.* i. 61, Beauch. ii. 229.

§ 4. *Ancestral and acquired*

More important, at least in the view of some scholars, is the distinction between πατρῷα and ἐπικτητά. The distinction, though without the use of these terms, is perhaps most clearly made in Lys. 19 *Prop. Arist.* 37, a reference to a hypothetical division of property by a father among his sons. Lysias distinguishes between the sort of division you would expect according to whether the property had been acquired or inherited by the father in question (εἴ τις μὴ κτησάμενος ἀλλὰ παρὰ τοῦ πατρὸς παραλαβών).[1] Elsewhere the term πατρῷα is fairly common for 'inheritance'. The question is how far the distinction in fact was a distinction in law. It has been argued that, even in the classical period, a man had a much freer right of disposal over acquired than over ancestral property, that, for example, it was only for the πατρῷα that the law imposed equal division among the sons and that the penalties for dissipating a fortune would not apply to the dissipation of acquired property.[2] The further implication of this is that by strict law the πατρῷα remained inalienable right down into the fourth century. We had to deal more fully with this topic in connexion with the law of succession (p. 125). Here it must suffice to say that, though it is not possible to demonstrate this principle *totidem verbis* in the texts, its existence is made probable by the law imposing a maximum on gifts in favour of bastards[3] and by the rule for prescription in inheritance cases. This rule gave a claimant the right to sue for an estate at any time during the lifetime of the heir and for five years after his death, and it implies the maintenance of the estate as a unit for at least that period.[4]

[1] Guiraud, *Prop. fonc.* 59 ff., 95 ff.; Beauch. iii. 23 ff.; Gernet, *RÉG* 33 (1920), 267 (*DSGA* 144). A similar distinction appears in other Greek systems. At Sparta it was considered improper to sell land and definitely forbidden to sell any part of 'the ancient portion'; Herakl. Pont. 2. 7 πωλεῖν δὲ γῆν Λακεδαιμονίοις αἰσχρὸν νενόμισται· τῆς δὲ ἀρχαίας μοίρας οὐδὲν ἔξεστιν. The latter rule was fairly general according to Ar., *Pol.* 1319ª, ἦν δὲ τό γε ἀρχαῖον ἐν πολλαῖς πόλεσι νενομοθετημένον μηδὲ πωλεῖν ἐξεῖναι τοὺς πρώτους κλήρους: cf. *Pol.* 1266ᵇ. Epikteta of Thera towards the end of the third century refers in her will to αὐτόκτητα χωρία, *IJ* xxiv A 1 32.

[2] Isai. 6 *Philokt.* 25 τοῦ νόμου κελεύοντος ἅπαντας τοὺς γνησίους ἰσομοίρους εἶναι τῶν πατρῴων; Aischin. 1 *Timarch.* 30 τὰ πατρῷα κατεδηδοκώς. Cf. Pollux 8. 45.

[3] On this see p. 67.

[4] Gernet, loc. cit., takes this view, summing up 'même sous le régime de la famille étroite, les biens patrimoniaux formaient la réserve des descendants'. While warning against the danger of equating the distinction with that between

§ 5. *Public, sacred*

The Athenian state was a considerable property owner. Besides the money held in the public treasuries, it owned slaves and extensive public buildings. Private property also could be transferred to it by gift, legacy, or confiscation, though such acquisitions were normally converted at once into cash by sale at public auction, since the state had no convenient organ for managing property.[1] In what sense the state owned minerals under Attic soil and how precisely it exploited this ownership are highly controversial issues. There is a fair amount of evidence in connexion with the silver mines at Laureion, but it has not yet produced clear and generally accepted conclusions. The main question is whether the Athenians achieved the abstraction of separating out from rights of ownership in the soil the right to exploit the minerals below the surface and vesting this latter right as such in the state. If they did this, it is held that they were alone in anticipating the medieval system of Bergregal. The evidence has been used to support three different views. Either the whole mining area, both surface and mines, belonged to the state; or there were some state and some private mines; or the surface was normally in the hands of private owners, but all mineral products were owned by the state and the state leased the right to exploit them for varying periods on varying terms. On the whole the evidence seems to favour the third view, but it is not so simple as some of its supporters seem to think. In particular, such a system must have raised very serious legal problems as between the owners of the surface and those who had acquired mining concessions from the state, but we are entirely in the dark as to the exact nature of these problems and how they were dealt with.[2]

immovables and movables, he points out that πατρῷα are usually in fact immovables, and draws attention to the machinations of Euktemon's sons-in-law in Isai. 6 *Philokt.* 30 ff. as indicating that Euktemon could expect to have greater freedom of disposal of his property by converting it from immovables to movables. Cf. E. F. Bruck, *Totenteil u. Seelgerat im Gr. R.* (*Münch. Beitr.* 9, 1926), 41–74. For πατρῷα as a separate category of property cf. Isai., fr. 6 Th. τὸ χωρίον . . . ἦν πατρῷον Λυσιμένει τῷ πατρὶ Μενεκράτους· ὁ δὲ Λυσιμένης ἔσχε τὰ πατρῷα πάντα. On prescription see pp. 220 and 246.

[1] Beauch. iii. 28 ff., Kahrstedt, *Staatsg.* 42 ff. For a potential legacy to the state Andok. 4 *Alk.* 15. For confiscation as a source of public ownership Aristoph., *Wasps* 659, Lys. 30 *Nikom.* 22, *Caillemer*, DS s.v. *demioprata*. Finley, *Land* 91 ff., for the state and its subdivisions as property owners.

[2] There was a special law on mining which, according to Dem. 37 *Pant.* 35, ἐάν τις ἐξίλλῃ τινὰ τῆς ἐργασίας, ὑπόδικον ποιεῖ. That it needed this special provision to

There were two particularly important legal effects of state ownership of property. Lessees or purchasers of state-owned property could assert their right to possess or own by self-help and in case of resistance were protected by the *δίκη ἐξούλης*.[1] Secondly, theft of state property was punished with special severity; a person convicted of such theft was fined ten times the value of the stolen property.[2]

Property could also be owned by constituent parts of the state such as tribes or demes. But since the rules governing such ownership were the same as those which applied to individual ownership, this topic can be reserved for consideration in connexion with the problem of legal personality.[3]

Although some things were sacred, there is no need to posit 'sacral property' as a separate legal category. Some sacred things belonged to the state, the rest to groups subordinate to the state. The law applying to ownership of these things would be determined, not by whether they were or were not sacred, but by whether they were or were not owned by the state.[4]

make the *δίκη ἐξούλης* available to one who was ousted from a mine working indicates that the occupation of such workings was in a sense anomalous; the occupier was put on the same footing as one who had bought a thing outright from the state. A speech falsely ascribed to Dinarchos, D.H., *Din.* 13, was probably delivered in such a case: *Πρὸς Μήκυθον μεταλλικός· Πριάμενοι μέταλλον, ὦ ἄνδρες. Ἐπὶ Νικομάχου ἄρχοντος εἴρηται ὁ λόγος οὗτος. φησὶ γὰρ ὁ λέγων ἐπ' Εὐβούλου μὲν μισθώσασθαι τὸ μέταλλον, τρία δὲ ἔτη ἐργασάμενος, ἐκβαλλόμενος ὑπὸ τοῦ πλησίον ἔχοντος μέταλλα, λαχεῖν αὐτῷ τὴν δίκην κατὰ Νικόμαχον ἄρχοντα.* Note *πρίασθαι* and *μισθώσασθαι* used with apparent indifference of acquiring the right to work the mine. See p. 202, above and Hopper's article cited on p. 203, n. 1 with Appendix D, below.

[1] See above, p. 218, and passages cited at the end of n. 1. ibid.

[2] For the *γραφὴ κλοπῆς δημοσίων χρημάτων* see Ar., *Ath. Pol.* 54, Dem. 24 *Timokr.* 112, 127, Lips., *AR* 399.

[3] On the subdivisions of state as owners of property see Finley, loc. cit. (p. 234, n. 1, above).

[4] Finley, *Land* 285, n. 45, with a warning against Guiraud, *Prop. fonc.* 362, and von Bolla, *RE* s.v. *Pacht*, who fail to make the distinction, and K. Latte, *Heil. R.* 51–54, who does not maintain it. Beauch. iii. 35 also misses this point.

IV · CAPACITY TO OWN

Restriction on the capacity to own might be total or partial. Privately owned slaves were incapable of owning any property at all. The degree to which the extremity of this rule was modified by a system similar to the Roman *peculium* is discussed in the section on slavery. Public slaves, on the other hand, could own property other than land.[1]

A citizen who had been condemned to total ἀτιμία was excluded from the agora and from access to the courts. This would naturally impair very seriously his capacity to own; for if his ἀτιμία had not been accompanied, as it usually was, by confiscation of all his possessions, he would not have been able to protect his rights of ownership by legal process. Beauchet is wrong, however, to state that total ἀτιμία specifically involved incapacity to own. State debtors were totally ἄτιμοι until they had discharged their debt, but it would be wrong to suppose that they in fact owned nothing in the interim.[2]

It is largely a matter of definition whether we say that in Athens a woman's or a minor's capacity to own was restricted. Women, like minors, could not make legally valid agreements for the disposal of goods above the value of one *medimnos*, except through the agency of their κύριοι. This limitation apart—and its significance in detail has been discussed in connexion with guardianship—a woman's or a minor's capacity to own either chattels or land was on all fours with that of a man who was of age, provided she or he was a properly qualified citizen.[3]

[1] Beauch. iii. 84 and for slaves' incapacity id. ii. 444 ff., Guiraud, *Prop. fonc.* 146; for public slaves Beauch. ii. 463. See also Kränzlein, *Eig. und Bes.* 40 f.

[2] Lys. 6 *Andok.* 24 αὐτὸν εἴργεσθαι τῆς ἀγορᾶς καὶ τῶν ἱερῶν ὥστε μηδ' ἀδικούμενον ὑπὸ τῶν ἐχθρῶν δύνασθαι δίκην λαβεῖν. Isai. 10 *Aristarch.* 20; Dem. 21 *Meid.* 87; Beauch. iii. 85 'il se trouve déjà, en fait, incapable de rien posséder'. So too Guiraud, *Prop. fonc.* 149.

[3] Beauch. iii. 85 and for guardianship id. ii. 351 ff., Kränzlein, *Eig. und Bes.* 45 f., Kahrstedt, *Staatsg.* 271, Isai. 10 *Aristarch.* 10. See above, pp. 73, n. 3, 108, 112 ff. Finley, *Land* 78 f., for the evidence of the *horoi*: from Amorgos three *horoi* name women in other contexts than that of a dotal *apotimema*, in Athens not a single

Of partial limitations on capacity to own a possible one is on the total amount of land a man could hold. Aristotle alleges that Solon was among a number of ancient legislators who imposed such a limit. There is no indication what the limit was, nor is there any evidence for the application of the rule; it is highly probable that, if it ever existed, it fell into disuse early.[1]

Much more important was the rule which prohibited any but full citizens from owning land or houses. The existence of this rule at Athens is proved by the numerous decrees from the last quarter of the fifth century onwards conferring on foreigners, often *proxenoi*, the right to own land and houses in Attica—ἔγκτησις γῆς καὶ οἰκίας. Sometimes, at a rather later period, a limit was set on the amount of land a grantee could hold. Xenophon suggests that a more liberal policy in granting ἔγκτησις to metics would benefit the state by encouraging them to develop house property in Athens. This incapacity, extending as it did to metics, had far-reaching effects on the economic structure of Athenian society, since it meant that the very men who were the backbone of the trading and banking community were precluded from owning, and therefore borrowing or lending on the security of, land.[2] It is probable that ἔγκτησις was not automatically included in grants of ἰσοτελεία and προξενία, but that it had to be specifically conferred on the recipients of these two privileges.[3] It is perhaps

horos names a woman in any context other than a dowry. This contrast, however, should not be overstressed. In some other inscriptions women are named as property owners: *SEG* xii. 100. 67–69, *IG* ii². 2765, 2766 (Finley, nos. 176, 174): minors are named as property owners in *IG* ii². 2658 (Finley, no. 57), *SEG* xii. 100. 78–80: Menand., *Arbitr.* 142 K., suggests that the trinkets were the property of the child.

[1] Ar., *Pol.* 1266ᵇ νόμος ὃς κωλύει κτᾶσθαι γῆν ὅσην ἂν βούληταί τις. Cf. *Pol.* 1319ᵃ and, significantly perhaps for Athens, a similar law at Thurioi, *Pol.* 1307ᵃ. Dem. 23 *Aristokr.* 208, 13 *Synt.* 30 for apparent absence of restrictions on ownership of land in the fourth century.

[2] For decrees see, for example, *IG* i². 83, 110, ii². 8, 86 and for further instances the indexes s.v. ἔγκτησις. Xen., *Por.* 2. 6. Dem. 36 *For Phorm.* 6; Phormion, so long as he is not a citizen, will not accept real property as security, since his incapacity to own it renders it useless for the purpose. Cf. Guiraud, *Prop. fonc.* 146, Finley, *Land* 74 and index s.v. 'Land, Monopoly of by Citizens'; id., *Pol. Sc. Q.* 68 (1953), 263 f., Kränzlein, *Eig. und Bes.* 38 ff. It is significant that in the Second Athenian Confederacy no Athenian was to own real property in any allied state whether by purchase, by hypothecation, or by any means whatsoever, *IG* ii². 43 (Tod, *GHI* 123), 35 ff. *An. Bekk.* (Λέξ. Ῥητ.) 251 s.v. ἐγκτήματα for the distinction between κτήματα and ἐγκτήματα. Cf. also Dem. 7 *Hal.* 42.

[3] So Beauch. iii. 90, Caillemer, DS s.v. *egtêsis*. Boeckh, *Staatsh.* i. 177, takes the contrary view. Lys. 12 *Ag. Erat.* certainly shows Lysias and his brother,

significant of the agricultural economics of Attica that no decree has survived which adds the right of pasturage—ἐπινομία—to that of owning land and houses.[1]

A foreigner's capacity to own was not hereditary, since there are decrees which specifically confer it on a man *and* his descendants; but we must suppose that property acquired by a foreigner in virtue of a decree could be retained by his heirs. Capacity to own could also be conferred for a period shorter than the life of the grantee, and, from the middle of the third century at least, a monetary limit on the value of property allowed to be held could be imposed.[2]

Citizens who held land in other demes than their own were called ἐγκεκτημένοι, and, unless they had been granted exemption by those demes, they had to pay a tax, τὸ ἐγκτητικόν. This seems to have been simply a fiscal matter, and there is no evidence that tenure of land thus held differed in any other way from tenure of land by a man in his own deme.[3]

Polemarchos, to have been owners of three houses in Athens, and they were ἰσοτελεῖς. But there are decrees conferring *both* ἰσοτελεία *and* ἔγκτησις which would have been superfluous if one included the other; and we may conjecture that Lysias and Polemarchos had been given ἔγκτησις specifically. Similarly προξενία decrees sometimes confer ἔγκτησις specifically, e.g. *IG* ii². 287.

[1] Finley, *Land* 246, n. 6, and works there cited.

[2] Beauch. iii. 93, *IG* ii². 706. Clerc, *Les Métèques athéniens* 207. Guiraud, *Prop. fonc.* 154. Certain refugees granted ἔγκτησις till their return home *IG* ii². 237. 24. For the monetary limit (separate maxima for land and house) see Finley, op. cit. 252, n. 47.

[3] Caillemer, DS s.v. *egtêsis* 495; Dem. 50 *Polykl.* 8.

V · JOINT OWNERSHIP

ATHENIAN law made some provision for a thing, whether movable or immovable, to be owned jointly. Indeed in the embryonic period of the legal system common ownership both of land and of chattels by families must have been the rule so that the succession of sons on the death of their fathers was in principle not succession at all, but simply the continuation of joint ownership. Such heirs were precisely similar to Roman 'sui heredes' though the Athenians had no corresponding term.[1] Expressions found in the orators indicate that even in the fourth century it was common enough for sons to remain joint owners of the family property on their father's death: the property (*οὐσία*) is then called *ἀνέμητος* and the implication is that the dividing up of an estate was anything but automatic. A good example of indivision is Dem. 44 *Leoch.* 10, 18. In that case Euthymachos left three sons and one daughter. On his death the sons marry off their sister; then one of them dies; a second, Meidylides, marries; the third, Archiades, remains a bachelor. Meidylides then begets a daughter whom in due course he offers in marriage to Archiades; the latter replies that he does not want to marry and for that reason agrees that the property should continue undivided (10 *οὐκ ἔφη προαιρεῖσθαι γαμεῖν, ἀλλὰ καὶ τὴν οὐσίαν ἀνέμητον διὰ ταῦτα συχωρήσας εἶναι ᾤκει καθ' αὑτὸν ἐν τῇ Σαλαμῖνι*) and so it did (18 *οὐδέπω τὴν οὐσίαν ἐνέμοντο*). We may infer from Archiades' reply that if he had been willing to marry the girl no division would have been necessary, since the estate would remain as a whole within the family (consisting of him, the girl and Meidylides); if on the other hand he was contemplating marriage to some other girl he would have had to insist on a division of the estate (this would have been a likely condition of his getting a dowry with his intended wife); but as he had no intention of marrying *anyone* he could

[1] Beauch. iii. 638 ff., Lips., *AR* 575 (on coheirs), Finley, *Land* 71, A. Biscardi, *Labeo* 1 (1955), 156 ff., id., *St. Paoli* (Firenze), 105 ff., id., *RHD* 36 (1958), 321 ff., Jones, *LLTG* 210 ff., Kränzlein, *Eig. und Bes.* 130 ff.

allow the estate to remain undivided between himself and Meidylides.[1]

It seems probable, though it cannot be proved, that other kinds of joint ownership were derived from this model. One feature of it deserves special attention. It is of its essence that the thing owned—usually, but not exclusively, a landed estate—is owned as a whole by the joint owners and not in proportions varying as between one and another of them. It would also seem that each and every of the joint owners had such control over the use and disposal of the thing as to enable him to interdict, for example, its hypothecation or sale.[2] Dem. 36 *For Phorm.* 8 provides an instance for Athens. Apollodoros was dissipating the capital of the hitherto undivided estate of his father, Pasion: the guardians of his younger brother, Pasikles, who was still a minor, came to the conclusion that the only way to put a stop to this was to insist upon a distribution between the two brothers. It seems likely that in this case it was predominantly cash that was being dissipated and that this made it difficult for Pasikles' guardians to intervene by way of *ἀπόρρησις* (on which see next paragraph); they obviously believed that they could stop Apollodoros from similarly disposing of a bank and a shield factory and that they need not therefore include them in the division (see n. 2 on this page). A passage from Seneca, *Contr.* vii. 4, undoubtedly represents

[1] See for another instance Aischin. 1 *Timarch.* 102. Cf. also Dem. 47 *Euerg.* 34, Harpokr. s.v. *κοινωνικῶν*: *Δημοσθένης ἐν τῷ περὶ τῶν συμμοριῶν, κοινωνικοὺς ἂν λέγοι τάχα μὲν τοὺς ἀνέμητον οὐσίαν ἔχοντας ἀδελφούς, ὧν ὁ μὲν πατὴρ ἐδύνατο λειτουργεῖν, οἱ δὲ κληρονόμοι τῶν ἐκείνου καθ' ἕνα τριηραρχεῖν οὐκ ἐξήρκουν· τάχα δὲ καὶ περὶ τῶν ἑκούσιον κοινωνίαν συνθεμένων ἐμπορίας ἤ τινος ἄλλου, ὧν ἕκαστος οὐκ εἶχε τὸ ὅλον τίμημα τῆς κοινῆς οὐσίας.*

[2] It is a modification of this pattern when part of an estate is divided up and another part continues to be held in joint ownership. In Lys. 32 *Diogeit.* 4 the *ἀφανὴς οὐσία* is divided up while the *φανερὰ οὐσία* is held under joint ownership (*τὴν ἀφανῆ οὐσίαν ἐνείμαντο, τῆς δὲ φανερᾶς ἐκοινώνουν*). Again, in Dem. 36 *For Phorm.* 9 the whole estate is divided except a bank and a shield factory which remain leased to Pasion and the revenue from which continues to be divided between the two brothers. It might be held that the pattern was also modified where an inheritance was not divided and the *de cuius* was survived by grandsons as well as sons; for as we have seen (pp. 144 ff.), in such a case, if a division took place, it was *per stirpes*, not *per capita*. Thus if A dies leaving a childless son, B, and two grandsons, C and D, by another son who had predeceased A, if the estate is divided B will get a half and C and D a quarter each; if the estate remains undivided we may assume that the fruits will be divided in those proportions, but we cannot further assume that B or C or D can of his own motion sell or hypothecate one half or one quarter of the estate as the case might be. See especially A. Biscardi, *Labeo*, loc. cit. p. 239, n. 1.

Greek rather than Roman law, though we cannot say it was necessarily Athenian. It states that where a thing is the property of two owners the control of it shall rest entirely with that one of the two who is present ('potestas eius tota fieret qui praesens esset'), giving as examples a slave ('puta servum te esse communem huic domino servies qui praesens est') and an estate ('puta fundum esse communem is fructus percipiet qui praesens'). Two Attic boundary stones bearing an identical inscription show a small cult group, the Eikadeis, drawing public notice to the fact that no one—and this must mean no member of the group—is entitled to borrow on the security of the land on which the stones stood: this implies that without such specific ban money could have been raised by any individual member on this security.[1]

It is probable that the procedure known as ἀπόρρησις was available to a joint owner who wished to interdict the sale or hypothecation of the joint property. It is true that this rule should not, as it sometimes is, be deduced from Isai. 2 *Menekl.* 28 where Menekles' brother intervenes to prevent the sale of some property by his brother, since we cannot be sure that he does so by virtue of being joint owner with him.[2] But it can be indirectly deduced from Plaut. *Merc.* 451 ff. which undoubtedly gives Athenian law. In that scene the young Charinus is trying to avoid having to sell a slave girl at his father's behest: he pretends that there is a joint owner who is not present and who might not agree to the sale; 'communest illa mihi cum alio. qui scio / quid sit ei animi, uenirene eam uelit an non uelit?' and a little later 'communis mihi illa est cum illo: is hic nunc non adest... nescio, inquam, uelit ille illam necne abalienarier.' This shows that transfer of property (here a chattel) by one joint owner was liable to be held invalid unless other joint owners had been given the opportunity to intervene against the sale.

Though in origin joint ownership may have been principally, if not exclusively, ownership by members of a family, by the fourth century it had a much wider use. Besides ownership by such groups as the Eikadeis (above) or by tribes, demes, *orgeones*,

[1] *IG* ii². 2631, 2632 ὅρος χωρίου κοινοῦ Εἰκαδείων· μὴ συμβάλλειν εἰς τοῦτο τὸ χωρίον μηθένα μηθέν. This is the most probable, though not absolutely certain, interpretation of the inscription: Finley, *Land* 98, Kränzlein, *Eig. und Bes.* 132.

[2] Ibid. 132 f. and below, pp. 291, 307. See also p. 267, n. 1.

thiasoi, and the like, groups formed for commercial purposes could and frequently did own things jointly, though it is important to note that the Athenians never achieved the convenient fiction of regarding such a group of joint owners as a single person juristically. They remained joint several owners.[1] It is more difficult to determine whether Athens did or did not achieve another distinction of some subtlety, that between joint ownership of a thing as an undivided whole and joint ownership of a thing divided up whether actually or ideally into parts in the ratio of the joint owners' original contributions. It has been argued from Aristotle's use of the analogy of *κοινωνίαι χρημάτων* to illustrate one aspect of friendship (*Nik. Eth.* 1163^{a} *καθάπερ ἐν χρημάτων κοινωνίᾳ πλεῖον λαμβάνουσιν οἱ συμβαλλόμενοι πλεῖον*) that this concept was familiar in fourth-century Greece, if not specifically in Athens. But the passage says nothing directly about the ownership or control of the thing; it only refers to the distribution of the fruits and it is quite possible to conceive of a system which, while it allowed for the distribution of the fruits by quotas among a number of participants, did not recognize the right of any participant to hypothecate or sell any part of the single common thing.[2] Nor can the passage from Harpokration quoted on p. 240,

[1] This is the commonly held view, but it seems based on the rather slender argument that documents speak indifferently of the members of a body (e.g. tribe) and of the body itself in the singular. Thus in *IG* ii^{2}. 2670 (Finley, *horos* no. 146) land is hypothecated to the Kekropidai (members of a tribe), the Lykomidai (members of a genos), and the Phlyans (members of a deme); in *IG* ii^{2}. 2699 (Finley, no. 30) land is sold *ἐπὶ λύσει* to *ἐρανισταῖς τοῖς μετὰ Ἀριστοφῶντος Εἰρεσίδου*; in *IG* ii^{2}. 2631 (p. 241, n. 1), on the other hand, the land is described as belonging to the *κοινόν* of the Eikadeis, and in *Hesp.* 5 (1936), 397, lines 175 f. a tribe itself is described as creditor (*ἐνοφείλεσθαι τῆι Αἰαντίδι φυλῆι*). Finley, *Land* 260, n. 114, Kränzlein, *Eig. und Bes.* 136. It may be significant that Merton College is described in conveyances as 'The Warden and Scholars of the House or College of Merton in the University of Oxford'; it is none the less a juristic person.

[2] Kränzlein, *Eig. und Bes.* 134, P. J. T. Endenburg, *Koinoonia. En gemeenschap van zaken bij de Grieken in den klassieken tidj* (Amsterdam, 1937), 146. For leases granted by various kinds of body see, e.g., *IG* ii^{2}. 1241 (*c.* 300 B.C.: a phratry: the lessors are described as *οἱ φρατρίαρχοι καὶ τὸ κοινὸν Δυαλέων*), 2492 (345 B.C.: a deme: note the provision *ἐάν τις εἰσφόρα ὑπὲρ τοῦ χωρίου γίγνηται εἰς τὴν πόλιν Αἰξωνέας εἰσφέρειν*), 2493, 2497, 2498 (demes: last half of the fourth century), 2499 (*SIG* 1097, 306 B.C.: *orgeones*: the rent is paid *τῷ ἀεὶ ταμιεύοντι τῶν ὀργεώνων*), 2501 (end of the fourth century: *orgeones*: the rent is paid *τοῖς [ὀργεῶσι]*). In *IG* ii^{2}. 2496 (*SIG* 1216) a perpetual lease is granted by eight men who are called *Κυθηρίων οἱ μερῖται*: here any *εἰσφορά* or other charge (*ἀπ[ότ]εισμα*) is to be paid by the lessee. In 2499 any *εἰσφορά* is to be paid *ἀπὸ τοῦ τιμήματος τοῖς ὀργεῶσιν*: this may mean either that the chest of the *orgeones* had to pay the tax as assessed for the

n. 1, above be taken as unequivocal recognition of joint ownership by quotas, though on one interpretation it might be so taken.[1] On the other hand, in the Tenos land register of the third century B.C. we find that it was possible to own part of a building (expressed as a fraction) or even a part of a water-supply.[2] Perhaps it is not too bold to surmise that fourth-century Athens had a similar concept, though the argument from silence against this surmise is not entirely without weight.

One or more joint owners could enforce distribution of the joint property by bringing a *δίκη εἰς δατητῶν αἵρεσιν*. This suit was probably in origin confined to joint family property, since it came under the archon. But it may well have been extended later to property of any kind.[3]

property in question as a whole or that the share of each *orgeon* in the property was assessed in with his property and he had to pay the relative amount of tax.

[1] A. Biscardi, *RHD* 36 (1958), 346, interprets Harpokr. thus: co-owners might, on the one hand, be brothers holding an estate undivided, whose father had been able to bear a liturgy whereas the heirs were not of sufficient wealth to discharge the trierarchy severally; on the other hand, they might be those who had entered into title to the common property (taking *ἔχειν τὸ ὅλον τίμημα τῆς κοινῆς οὐσίας* to mean 'avoir la titularité du patrimoine commun pour le tout'). But it is better with Boeckh, *Staatsh.* 633, and Kränzlein, op. cit. 134, to take the last words to mean 'none of whom severally had the whole value of the property assessed to him (viz. for a liturgy)' and none of whom therefore, just as in the other kind of *κοινωνία*, was liable for the trierarchy by virtue of joint ownership of that property alone. The only point Harpokration is making is that with either kind of *κοινωνία* the estate would not be valued as a whole for liturgy purposes. We may assume that in either case the estimated value of each joint owner's share would have been reckoned in his individual *τίμησις*. The meaning of *κοινωνικῶν* in Dem. 14 *Sym.* 16, on which Harpokr. is commenting, is too obscure to be of much help: on it see Endenburg, op. cit. (preceding note) 54.

[2] *IG* xii. 5. 872 (*IJ* vii), 22, 24, E. Weiss, *AP* 4 (1908), 331, Finley, *Land* 260, n. 114.

[3] Ar., *Ath. Pol.* 56. 6 *δίκαι λαγχάνονται πρὸς τὸν ἄρχοντα . . . εἰς δατητῶν αἵρεσιν ἐάν τις μὴ θέλῃ κοινὰ τὰ ὄντα νέμεσθαι*, Harpokr. s.v. *δατεῖσθαι*: *ὁπότε γὰρ κοινωνοῖέν τινες ἀλλήλοις καὶ οἱ μὲν βούλοιντο διανέμεσθαι τὰ κοινά, οἱ δὲ μή, ἐδικάζοντο οἱ μὲν βουλόμενοι τοῖς μὴ βουλομένοις προκαλούμενοι εἰς δατητῶν αἵρεσιν*. Beauch. iii. 643 ff., Pappulias *Ζ* 26 (1905) 550 f., Jones *LLTG* 210. Lips. *AR* 576 f. insists that the suit was always restricted to family property.

VI · MODES OF ACQUISITION

Two general distinctions may be made at the outset. For the convenience of treatment of the topics we can distinguish between those cases where ownership of the thing has passed on the death of the previous owner and all other cases. It is convenient to discuss the former cases under the law of succession, which of course embraces other topics besides that of ownership.

Secondly, we may distinguish between what may be called original acquisition, where the thing has never belonged to an owner before, and acquisition by the transmission of ownership from one owner to another.

Originally ownership might spring from an act of assignment by the state. This would not be an important source of ownership in Attica itself during the classical period; but the original colonists and cleruchs of the sixth, fifth, and fourth centuries would all have acquired the ownership of their land in this way.[1] We have no direct evidence of the use of such a title in a concrete case in Athens. Ownership acquired by purchase from the state was pretty nearly on all fours with ownership by original allotment. Thus a purchaser from the state could assert his right to own by self-help, with the protection of the δίκη ἐξούλης if he were resisted (p. 218, above), and he could call upon the poletai to warrant his ownership.[2]

Apart from these acts of state we should expect occupation or appropriation by a private individual to be the main source of original acquisition. Here again we have no direct evidence from Athens. Aristotle (*Pol.* 1256[a,b]) recognizes fishing, hunting, and war as distinct sources of property, but he is not, in that passage, concerned specifically with Athens, nor with the juristic

[1] Vinogradoff, *HJ* 202 f., Guiraud, *Prop. fonc.* 33 ff. A good example is the Athenian colony at Brea of about 447/6 B.C. with its ten *geonomoi* who distribute the land, *IG* i². 45 (Tod, *GHI* 44), 6 ff.

[2] Dem. 24 *Timokr.* 54, 37 *Pant.* 19, Ar., *Ath. Pol.* 47. 2, Gernet, *RHD* 29 (1951), 574 (*DSGA* 214), Kränzlein, *Eig. und Bes.* 117.

aspect of the matter.[1] For objects found we have a law attributed to Solon reserving the ownership absolutely to the depositor, if there were such a one. We do not know what the rule was when the depositor could not be identified, but Plato rules that such findings should be devoted to the goddess of the roads.[2] Menander (*Arbitr.* 64 ff. K.) and Theophrastos (*Char.* 30. 9) assume that ownership could pass to the finder of a thing not deposited.[3]

Though there is no direct evidence for Athens we cannot rule out the possibility that piracy or robbery might be the origin of the legitimate ownership of a thing, but not of course if the thing had previously belonged to an Athenian citizen.[4]

The two main derivative modes of acquisition were gift and sale. It is not easy to decide what is the most appropriate place to discuss these transactions. Sale is a transfer of property; but it is also, in any but the most primitive stage of society, a contract, and the contractual element in the Athenian law of sale is a thorny topic. Gift too, though primarily a transfer of property, has important connexions with sale. It must suffice here merely to mention these two modes of acquisition, reserving detailed discussion of them for treatment under the law of contract.[5]

There is one other mode of acquisition which falls between original and derivative modes, that is, acquisition by undisputed occupation for a prescribed term. The Romans had well-defined

[1] Vinogradoff, *HJ* 213, from an alleged law of Solon, Plut., *Sol.* 23, that a new hive of bees must be not less than 300 feet from an existing hive on a neighbour's land, infers that the domestication of bees gave a right of property in them; but on this see Kränzlein, *Eig. und Bes.* 103. Plaut., *Rud.* 971–5, if it represents Athenian law, establishes the fisherman's legal ownership of his catch; Kränzlein, op. cit. 72 regards the hypothesis as shaky, but it is accepted by H. J. Wolff, *Z* 81 (1964), 335, n. 5.

[2] D.L. 1. 57 gives as a law of Solon ἃ μὴ ἔθου, μὴ ἀνέλῃ· εἰ δὲ μή, θάνατος ἡ ζημία. Plato, *Laws* 913 c–914 b, Beauch. iii. 50, Kränzlein, *Eig. und Bes.* 105 ff.

[3] Kränzlein, op. cit. 106: but for a different view Taubenschlag, *Z* 46 (1926), 76, R. Düll, *Z* 61 (1941), 41 ff.

[4] Most revealing is the mid-fifth-century treaty between Oianthea and Chaleion, Tod, *GHI* 34, which specifically allows citizens of the one city to seize (συλᾶν) goods belonging to citizens of the other except on the territories or in the harbours of the two cities. We can assume that this right of seizure as between citizens of different states was a general one in the Greece of the time: Kränzlein, op. cit. 110.

[5] Beauchet treats of gift in his chapter on the acquisition of property (iii. 122–42); he devotes ten pages (112–22) to sale in the same chapter, but his main discussion of sale is in iv. 104–56. See Gernet, *RHD* 29 (1951), 571 (*DSGA* 211), for the view that the real ancestor of sale is not barter but the exchange of gift for gift. Pringsheim, *GLS* 13, 86, discusses the contractual and the conveyancing element in Greek sale.

rules for acquiring ownership by *usucapio* and *longi temporis praescriptio*. Before examining the position at Athens we should distinguish between a rule which bars action at law after a certain lapse of time and a rule which confers absolute ownership after such a lapse.[1] These two kinds of rule serve different purposes and will tend to arise in differing social circumstances. The object of the first is, to quote Vinogradoff, 'to put an end to vexatious demands and to fraudulent devices of pettifoggers'. It is particularly prominent in connexion with debt claims, where the defendant cannot fall back on an assertion of title. The latter, on the other hand, aims at establishing firm rights of ownership for those who have occupied and brought under cultivation hitherto unoccupied tracts of land. Roman rules on *usucapio* and *longi temporis praescriptio* had the second object mainly in view. The Athenian rules, however, seem to be of the first kind;[2] the Athenians perhaps did not feel the same need as the Romans for the second kind of rule, since they tended to think of a man's ownership of his land as due to an original act of allotment by the state.[3]

Some modern scholars have maintained that in effect there was in Athens nothing to correspond to the Roman *usucapio*. An examination of the very scanty direct evidence on the matter suggests that this is largely a question of definition.

Rules on the limitation of actions clearly varied with the types of action. Here we are only concerned with the law as it applied to property actions. Not very much can be made of the statement in Isok. 6 *Archidam.* 26 τὰς κτήσεις καὶ τὰς ἰδίας καὶ τὰς κοινὰς ἂν

[1] See above, p. 201, n. 2, and Vinogradoff, *HJ* 213 ff. For the importance of the distinction here Kränzlein, op. cit. 121, H. J. Wolff, *Eranion Maridakis* i (Athens, 1963), 87 ff.

[2] But note the view of Kränzlein (loc. cit.) that the objective of the Athenian rule cannot have been merely to avoid litigation, since a defence based on προθεσμία would have come before a court by way of παραγραφή: rather the aim was relatively speedy trial of cases in order to facilitate the production of reliable evidence. This explanation does not fit the rule in inheritance cases, which left the period open during the whole lifetime of the first heir and for five years after his death. H. J. Wolff (loc. cit. in previous note) argues that, *pace* Dem. 36 *For Phorm.* 25, there was no general νόμος τῆς προθεσμίας or any general principle of equity by which the Athenians recognized that a claimant should bring a claim within a certain time or forfeit his right to sue. Each type of case had its rule, or had no rule, for specific reasons, though he suggests as a common factor the protection of defendants from excessive difficulty in producing evidence to rebut a claim or a charge.

[3] The whole of Dem. 44 *Leoch.* is striking testimony to the Athenian reluctance to admit the idea of prescription: Gernet, *Dem.* ii. 128, n. 1.

ἐπιγένηται πολὺς χρόνος κυρίας καὶ πατρῴας εἶναι νομίζουσιν, except that in a very general way Greek states at the time considered a long period of possession of private property as conferring ownership. We get no help here in discovering how this general idea was clothed in specific rules. Nor do we get much further with Plato, *Laws* 954 c, e, where Plato gives for movables certain limits of time within which suits have to be brought—periods varying from one to ten years according to the degree of publicity which has attended the possession of the thing. There is nothing to indicate whether his rules were based on actual rules—they do not sound highly practical—and, even if they were, whether the actual rules were Athenian.

One or two passages in the orators shed a little rather fitful light on the Athenian rules. Dem. 36 *For Phorm.* 25 speaks of 'the law of prescription'—τὸν τῆς προθεσμίας νόμον: he says that Solon's object in making the law was to prevent sycophancy and that a period of five years was sufficient to allow for injured parties to secure redress. In that context Demosthenes is speaking of contracts in general (τοὺς συμβάλλοντας). In 33 *Apatour.* 27 we find that an action based on a guarantee must be brought within one year, and in 38 *Nausim.* 17 that an orphan must bring an action against his guardian within five years, presumably from the date of his coming of age. The passage most relevant to our present purpose is Isai. 3 *Pyrrh.* 58, which tells us that a claimant could sue for an estate at any time during the lifetime of one who held it as heir and for five years after his death (p. 220, above). This somewhat peculiar rule has been called in evidence both by those who assert and by those who deny that the Athenians had an equivalent to the Roman *usucapio*. The effect of the rule would seem to be that, if B has inherited property from A, as soon as five years have elapsed from B's taking the property no claim can be advanced which is based on the faulty title of A. To that extent the five years' unchallenged possession by B strengthens his title. On the other hand, he is never protected during the whole of his life from a claim based on the allegation, for example, that he did not rightfully inherit from A. This is pretty remote from the Roman rules, under which possession of a movable for one year and an immovable for two conferred ownership, provided the thing had not been acquired by theft or force. No very convincing rationale for the peculiarities of the Athenian rule has been offered. The idea that it was intended to protect the interests of minors who might have had a good claim to succeed to an estate hardly satisfies. This protection would surely have been better given by a period of eighteen years from the date when the *κληρονόμος took* rather than five years from the date when he *died*. For suppose that A dies and B secures the inheritance; then B dies immediately and the property passes to C. After five years it will be impossible to attack C's title on the ground that B's title was faulty; but D, who was, say, two years old at B's death, may have had a better claim than B.

What the position was when a man was not a *κληρονόμος*, but a purchaser, for example, we simply cannot say; but the often quoted passage in Isai. 10 *Aristarch*. 24,[1] according to which a possessor, if challenged, must produce a mortgagor, or a warrantor, or the judgement of a court, though it is patently not exhaustive, would in its context lose much of its point if a common method of acquiring ownership had been by a fairly short period of undisputed possession.[2]

On the whole, the best view seems to be that Athenian law did not recognize usucapion as a method of acquiring ownership in any sense closely analogous to the Roman *usucapio*.

On the acquisition of ownership of fruits we have literally no evidence for Athens.[3]

[1] See p. 216, n. 1, above.

[2] J. F. Charles, *Statutes of Limitation at Athens* (Chicago, 1938), especially 53–59. He argues that Isai. 3 *Pyrrh*. 58 is conclusive that Athenian law knew usucapion. But he fails to notice that under the rule as there stated the κληρονόμος never acquires an indisputable title *for himself* by long possession. For earlier discussions see K. F. Hermann, *De vestigiis institutorum veterum* (Marburg, 1836), 66, Leist, *Att. Eig.* 60, Beauch. iii. 142, Caillemer, *La Prescription à Athènes*, Lips., *AR* 676, and later Kaser 137, 176, Kränzlein, Wolff (locc. citt., p. 246, n. 1).

[3] Kränzlein, *Eig. und Bes.* 75.

VII · EASEMENTS

We have some very scanty evidence for the existence at Athens of rules corresponding in general purpose with the servitudes of Roman, or the easements of English law. The Roman praedial servitude was a right over a piece of land which was vested not in the owner of that land, but in the owner of a piece of land adjacent to it, and vested in him solely as owner of that piece of land, so that if he alienated the land he alienated the right with it.[1] Such rights might exist universally as of law or they might be created specifically by private legal acts. A number of rules of the first kind are attributed to Solon by Plutarch, confirmed and expanded by Gaius. A man whose property was more than 4 stades from the nearest public well and who, having dug 10 fathoms, had failed to find water on his own land, could draw up to 6 *choai* (about 4½ gallons) twice a day from his neighbour's well. Fig and olive trees had to be planted not less than 9 feet from a neighbour's boundary, all other trees not less than 5 feet. A ditch had to be as far from the boundary as it was deep. A hive of bees had to be at least 300 feet from a neighbour's hive. Gaius adds that a rubble wall (*αἱμασία*) must not cross the boundary, an ashlar (?) wall (*τειχίον*) must be 1 foot from it, a building (*οἴκημα*) 2 feet, and a well 1 fathom.[2] Demosthenes' speech 55, *Against Kallikles*, though in detail not easy to interpret, shows clearly that where one property lay lower down a slope than another it had to accommodate any natural flow of water from the higher property. This rule is taken over by Plato (*Laws* 844 c), with the proviso that the owner of the higher property must do

[1] Schulz, *CRL* 381 ff. for Roman servitudes created by private legal acts. A. Berger, *Encyclopedic Dictionary of Roman Law* (Philadelphia, 1953) 702 ff. lists about twenty such servitudes.

[2] Plut., *Sol.* 23, *Dig.* 10. 1. 13, Pap. Hal. 80 ff., *Dikaiomata* (Berlin, 1913) 65 ff., J. Partsch, *AP* 6 (1914), 46. It is not very clear what was the distinction between *αἱμασία* and *τειχίον*. The former was certainly not a 'hedge', though it might perhaps have been a rubble wall with scrub occasionally growing out of it. Cf. Lips., *AR* 682, 985, U. E. Paoli, *RHD* 27 (1949), 505 ff., Kränzlein, *Eig. und Bes.* 58 ff.

his best to minimize damage by flood water flowing down from it. A passage in the same speech (§ 14) suggests that there might be a right of way over another's land to a family tomb.

Much more difficult is the question, raised but not solved in Demosthenes 55 *Kallikl.*, of the method of redress for breaches of these rules. In that case Kallikles is suing the son of Tisias on the allegation that a wall built round his property by Tisias some fifteen years earlier had caused flood water in a recent storm to flow over and damage Kallikles' land. The son of Tisias, who is speaking as defendant, describes the action as βλάβης and as χιλίων δραχμῶν ἀτίμητος (18, 25, 28). He also discloses that he has had two judgements given against him in arbitrations, in one of which the plaintiff was Kallikles and the sum awarded was 1,000 drachmai (2 δύο δίκας ἐρήμους μου κατεδιῃτήσατο, τὴν μὲν αὐτὸς χιλίων δραχμῶν). It is probable, though by no means certain, that the case in which the speech was delivered was an appeal from the award by the arbitrator of 1,000 drachmai. Some scholars have argued from this case that the law fixed a payment of 1,000 drachmai as a penalty for such action as Kallikles attributes to Tisias, irrespective of the damage.[1] A variant of this view holds that the penalty was forfeiture of the delinquent property, which could be avoided by the defendant's paying 1,000 drachmai.[2] Neither of these views is plausible, the second even less than the first. It is hard to believe that a community of practical farmers, such as the Athenians must have been when this law was forming, could have put up with a system which imposed a penalty totally unrelated to the damage done; and on the variant view there would have been the added illogicality that the 1,000 drachmai would have borne no relation to the value of the property which it was designed to release from forfeiture; nor is it easy to imagine how the extent of the forfeited property was to be determined, or what was to be done if there were more than one plaintiff. On another view the 1,000

[1] So MSL 224 f., Beauch. iv. 402, Dareste, *Dem.* i. 166, Gernet, *Dem.* iii. 118.

[2] So H. J. Wolff, *AJP* 64 (1943), 316 ff. (*Beitr.* 91 ff.); cf. also id., *Traditio* 4 (1946), 51 ff. (*Beitr.* 36), Kränzlein, *Z* 79 (1962), 353. Wolff's most telling point is that, in one or two places (1–2, 34, for example) the speaker alleges that Kallikles' object is to get hold of his land. But if the speaker was a poor man and if he was condemned in the sum of 1,000 drachmai there might have been a serious danger that Kallikles would be able to secure possession of his land by way of distraint for a judgement debt. At least this possibility would be sufficient basis for an Athenian orator to make the suggestion which this speaker does make.

drachmai was a penalty for not appearing before the arbitrator.[1] But this will hardly do either. We must surely suppose that the absence of the defendant in an arbitration simply involved judgement for the plaintiff; this would itself be the penalty for non-appearance. It is perhaps more likely that the arbitrator had fixed 1,000 drachmai as the amount due, and that on the appeal the court was limited to annulling or confirming this award and could not vary the amount.[2] If this is right, the procedure would have been for the wronged owner to bring the defaulting owner before a public arbitrator, who would make the award that seemed fitting to him. Whether this award, besides in appropriate cases being of money, could also include a direction, for example to remove a wall, we cannot say. The son of Tisias speaks only of the penalty of 1,000 drachmai as the result if he lost this particular case.[3]

So far we have dealt only with rights conferred by law. We have now to consider those conferred by private legal acts, the most significant difference being that an owner who wished to plead one of these would have to show title. Our evidence for these at Athens is even more scanty. In Dem. 55 *Kallikl.* 19 the speaker refers to the existence on some estates of acknowledged water-courses (ὁμολογούμεναι χαράδραι) by means of which water was passed on from the land of one owner to that of another, just as the water from the gutter of a house might be passed on.

[1] So Thalheim, *RA* 6.

[2] So A. W. Heffter, *Ath. Gerichtsverf.* (Cöln, 1822), 117, Lips., *AR* 662, n. 97, J. Partsch, *AP* 6 (1914), 51. Cf. also J. E. Sandys and F. A. Paley, *Demosthenes, Sel. Priv. Or. Pt.* ii[4] (Cambridge, 1910), lxx ff. No satisfactory explanation has so far been offered why the son of Tisias makes so much play with the fact that the suit was for a fixed amount of 1,000 drachmai, whereas the damage was, according to him, a minute fraction of that amount. We may not be right in thinking that this case was an appeal from an arbitrator's award given in default—and there is the difficulty that the speaker makes no attempt to explain his earlier failure to appear. But supposing that we are right, might it not possibly have been the rule that when a defendant appealed from an arbitrator's award the plaintiff had the choice between making the case on appeal τίμητος or ἀτίμητος, the amount in the latter case being that fixed by the arbitrator? If he adopted the latter alternative he would be gambling on all or nothing. If he adopted the other, the defendant might be able to cut his losses by putting in a substantially lower estimate and, if condemned, getting the jury to accept it. Thus here Kallikles would have been within his rights in insisting on the suit being χιλίων δραχμῶν ἀτίμητος, but the defendant on his side could make play with the alleged fact that the damage was far less than this.

[3] See on easements in general Beauch. iii. 155 ff., Lips., *AR* 655, 682, 985, Caillemer, DS s.v. *aqua*, Guiraud, *Prop. fonc.* 189 ff., Kränzlein, *Eig. und Bes.* 59 ff.

This seems to be a servitude in the full Roman sense. There is also epigraphical evidence from mortgage-stones and leases which suggests a right to the use of water as something distinct from the property which is serving as security or being leased.[1]

Whether there is anything in Athenian law corresponding to the so-called personal servitude of usufruct in Roman law is a matter of doubt. Usufruct is defined as 'the right of using and taking the fruits of property belonging to another, *salva rerum substantia*'. It was usually, though not necessarily, for the lifetime of the person entitled, and he enjoyed it personally, not by being owner of a particular piece of property. It probably occurred first as the result of legacies. The only trace of such an institution in Athenian law is the provision in the will of Demosthenes' father by which he granted to his friend, Therippides, seventy minai from the estate to be used for Therippides' profit till Demosthenes came of age. This seems closely analogous to the Roman usufruct, though in the developed Roman system, since this was the ususfruct of money, Therippides would have had to furnish security for the return of the seventy minai at the expiry of the term.[2]

[1] Finley, *Land* 72, quoting *horoi IG* ii². 2759 (Finley, no. 2), *IG* ii². 2657 (Finley, no. 116 ὅρο/[ς] χωρίων καὶ οἰ/[κ]ίας καὶ τοῦ ὕδα/[τ]ος τοῦ προσόν/[τ]ος τοῖς χωρίοι/[ς]), *IG* ii². 2655 (Finley, no 159), and leases *IG* i². 94. 34–37, ii². 2494. 8–11 (the last of somewhat doubtful value owing to difficulties of restoration: see A. Wilhelm, *AP* 11 (1933), 205, G. Klaffenbach, *SbB* (1936), 382, n. 2).

[2] For the Roman rules see H. F. Jolowicz, *Hist. Intr. R. Law*² (Cambridge, 1952), 282. For Demosthenes' estate Dem. 27 *Aphob*. i. 5 *κἀκείνῳ ἔδωκεν ἐκ τῶν ἐμῶν ἑβδομήκοντα μνᾶς καρπώσασθαι τοσοῦτον χρόνον ἕως ἐγὼ ἀνὴρ δοκιμασθείην.*

VIII · REAL SECURITIES

§ 1. *Introduction*

REAL security is another topic which does not fall neatly under the law of property. A real security has been defined as 'a right over a thing (movable or immovable) granted to a creditor in order to secure his claim against a debtor'. Since the creation of such a right necessarily affects the control of the thing which may be exercised by the debtor and the creditor respectively, it falls to be considered under the law of property. On the other hand, it may be created in a number of ways, by a process of execution, for example, or by a will or by the contract of loan, and comes up for treatment therefore under the law of procedure and the law of obligations also.[1]

In comparison with some other parts of the law of property the evidence for real security is relatively plentiful. The various kinds of real security are referred to fairly frequently in the orators, sometimes in considerable detail; and these references are invaluably confirmed and supplemented by the *horoi*, or mortgage stones, more than two hundred of which have been found, the majority in Attica, the rest in places in the Aegean which were at one time or another closely connected with Athens.[2]

[1] Definition from Schulz, *CRL* 400. Beauchet deals with real securities mainly under the law of property, iii. 176–317; real securities arising out of contracts are dealt with ibid. 195–223 and glanced at under the law of obligations in connexion with the contract of loan, iv. 237 and 279 ff. (bottomry); the executory function of real securities he deals with both under the law of property at iii. 223–34 (*la prise de gage*) and under the law of obligations at iv. 415. Vinogradoff, *HJ* 250 ff. subsumes the subject under contract. Lipsius treats *Pfandrecht* with the private suits of the Forty, *AR* 690–705. The most important special studies are Hitz., Papp., E. Rabel, *Die Verfügungsbeschränkungen des Verpfänders* (Leipzig, 1909), Weiss, *Pfand.*, L. Raape, *Der Verfall des gr. Pfandes* (Halle, 1912), A. Manigk, *RE* s.v. *hyperocha* (1914) 292–321, Weiss, *RE* s.v. *katenechyrasia* (1919), 2495–512, id., *GP*, Bk. 4 on execution, Paoli, *St. Dir.*, reviews of Paoli by V. Arangio-Ruiz, *AG* 23 (1932), 245–53 and G. La Pira, *BIDR* 41 (1933), 305–20, Paoli, *AG* 24 (1932), 161–78, id., *SIFC* 10 (1933), 181–212, Fine, *Horoi*, Finley, *Land*, H. J. Wolff, *Fest. Rabel* ii (Tübingen, 1954), 293 ff.

[2] Dem. 33 *Apatour.* and 37 *Pant.*, for example, contain a good deal on real security. The texts of the *horoi* are most conveniently consulted in Finley's book. He prints

Once more we are hampered by the absence of a developed technical terminology. This makes it difficult to mark in as sharp outline as we should like the distinctions between the various kinds of real security. Nevertheless, we must start with a brief discussion of the principal terms.

The word for a pledge is ἐνέχυρον. Its predominant use, when it is not being applied to an object seized by way of distraint, is to denote a thing offered and accepted as security for a loan. Usually the thing is a movable held in the possession of the creditor during the term of the debt. But we cannot press the term as describing a particular type of real security (such as the Roman *pignus*) of which the essence is the transfer of the possession of the thing pledged to the creditor; for in at least one instance it is used of the thing pledged in a πρᾶσις ἐπὶ λύσει (see below), where the thing had clearly been for some time during the term of the debt in the possession of the debtor.[1]

No more clear-cut are the uses of various derivatives of τίθημι in the context of real security. The simple verb and its compound ὑποτίθημι are used in the active voice for the debtor in various kinds of real security, in the middle voice for the creditor.[2]

all the texts then available, gives a statistical analysis of 144 of them in four main categories, and discusses in the body of the book the legal and economic deductions which can be drawn from them. He was only able to take note of Fine's publication (see n. 1) in an appendix.

[1] Dem. 49 *Timoth.* 52, a banker has slaves οἳ τὰ ἐνέχυρα τῶν δανεισμάτων παρελάμβανον. Here the ἐνέχυρον is a quantity of copper. The creditor is ὁ ὑποτιθέμενος and the debtor ὁ ὑποτιθεὶς τὸν χαλκόν. Dem. 41 *Spoud.* 11 φιάλην λαβόντες παρὰ τῆς Πολυεύκτου γυναικὸς καὶ θέντες ἐνέχυρα μετὰ χρυσίων: a pawning operation; the creditor is ὁ θέμενος. In Dem. 49 *Timoth.* 2 and 53 ἐπ' ἐνεχύρῳ is used in the general sense of lend or borrow 'on security'. Dem. 56 *Dionysod.* 3 a ship in a bottomry loan is ἐνέχυρον. Dem. 33 *Apatour.* 10 ἐνέχυρον used of a ship that has been the object of what is obviously from 8 a πρᾶσις ἐπὶ λύσει even though not so described; in 12 the transaction is called θέσις. *IG* xii. 7, 58 (Finley, no. 8) ὅρος χωρίων . . . καὶ οἰκίας καὶ κ[ήπων] . . . καὶ τῶν ἐπικυρβίων ἐνεχύρων ὑποκειμένων from a third-century stone found in Amorgos; for the difficult phrase ἐπικύρβια ἐνέχυρα—perhaps 'recorded pledges'—see Finley, *Land* 219, n. 81, and literature there cited. In Harpokr. s.v. ἀποτιμηταί (quoted on p. 257, n. 1) property offered as security by the lessee of an orphan's estate is called τὰ ἐνέχυρα. Hdt. 2. 136, describing how at a certain period in Egypt, when money was tight, men were allowed to borrow on the security of their father's corpses, uses the phrase ὑποτίθεντι τοῦτο τὸ ἐνέχυρον. Quite distinct is the use of ἐνέχυρον and its cognates for seizure in distraint, as, for example, in Dem. 47 *Euerg.* 37, 38, 41, 42. For further references see Papp. 13 ff., Fine, *Horoi* 61, n. 4, Finley, *Land* 221 ff., nn. 4, 6, 7, 17.

[2] See the first two citations from Demosthenes in n. 1. Add Dem. 35 *Lakrit.* 11 (cf. also 21) ὑποτιθέασι δὲ ταῦτα οὐκ ὀφείλοντες ἐπὶ τούτοις ἄλλῳ οὐδενὶ οὐδὲν ἀργύριον, οὐδ' ἐπιδανείσονται. Dem. 50 *Polykl.* 55 ὑποθέμενον τὰ σκεύη τῆς νεώς of a creditor.

ὑποκεῖσθαι is used of the thing pledged or hypothecated.[1] θέτης is an ambiguous word, but was probably used of a mortgagor.[2] The act of pledging or hypothecating is θέσις or ὑπόθεσις.[3] The word ὑποθήκη appears to be restricted in the classical period to the thing offered and accepted as security. It is not used to describe the act, still less to differentiate one kind of security transaction from other kinds. It is in fact significant that the Athenians seem to have had no word for 'hypothec' as a distinct type of real security.[4]

Dem. 53 *Nikostr.* 10 τὸ χωρίον οὐδεὶς ἐθέλοι οὔτε πρίασθαι οὔτε θέσθαι (edd., τίθεσθαι codd.), ibid. 13 τίθημι τὴν συνοικίαν ἑκκαίδεκα μνῶν Ἀρκέσαντι, ibid. τὸ ἀργύριον οὗ ἡ συνοικία ἐτέθη. In *IG* ii². 2758 (Finley, no. 1) the creditor is τὸν θέμενον, ibid. 2759 (Finley, no. 2) the creditor is τὸν ὑποθέμενον. The exact meaning of θέμενοι in Isai. 5 *Dikaiog.* 21 is disputed; see Wyse ad loc., Finley, *Land* 232, n. 51, Paoli, *St. Dir.* 155. In *IG* ii². 43 (Tod, *GHI* 123) ὑποθέσθαι and τίθεσθαι are both used to indicate acceptance of real property as security by Athenians in the territory of the allies during the Second Athenian Confederacy. Harpokr. s.v. θέσθαι· ἀντὶ μὲν τοῦ ὑποθήκην λαβεῖν Ὑπερείδης ἐν τῷ πρὸς Ὑγιαίνοντα.

[1] Dem. 56 *Dionysod.* 4 τὴν ναῦν τὴν ὑποκειμένην. Dem. 27 *Aphob.* i. 9 κλινοποιοὺς εἴκοσι . . . τετταράκοντα μνῶν ὑποκειμένους (cf. ibid. 24). Dem. 56 *Dionysod.* 38 ἐὰν μὴ . . . παράσχῃς τὰ ὑποκείμενα ἐμφανῆ καὶ ἀνέπαφα. The timber alleged in Dem. 49 *Timoth.* 35 to be ὑποκείμενα to Pasion was a cargo on which, so the argument seems to imply, Pasion could distrain to recover the freight which he had paid; see Dareste, *Dem.* ii. 230, n. 20, Lips., *AR* 699, Gernet, *Dem.* iii. 23, n. 1, Pringsheim, *KFG* 27. The following *horoi* use various cases of the participle ὑποκείμενος to qualify the property charged: *IG* ii². 2758, 2759, 2761 A and B, Δελτ. 14 (1931/2), παρ. 31, no. 4, *IG* ii². 2760, *IG* xii. 7, 58, *Annuario* 15/16 (1932/3, pub. 1942), 298, no. 6 (Finley, nos. 1, 2, 4, 5, 6, 7, 8, 10 respectively; the last from Lemnos, the last but one from Amorgos, all the rest from Attica).

[2] Isai. 10 *Aristarch.* 24, quoted and discussed above, p. 216, n. 1.

[3] Lys. 8 *Ag. Coass.* 10 περὶ τῆς θέσεως τοῦ ἵππου: it is uncertain whether the reference is to pledge or πρᾶσις ἐπὶ λύσει; see Finley, *Land* 232, n. 50, who refers to Guenter, *Sicherungsübereignung* (Königsberg, 1914), 44–47. Dem. 33 *Apatour.* 12 πραθείσης τῆς νεὼς τετταράκοντα μνῶν, ὅσουπερ ἡ θέσις ἦν: the money had been raised by πρᾶσις ἐπὶ λύσει (but see Finley, *Land* 225, n. 17). ὑπόθεσις is less certainly vouched for. *An. Bekk.* (Ἀντιαττ.) 115 s.v. has ἀντὶ τοῦ ὑποθήκην· Μένανδρος, where ὑποθήκη presumably could mean the act of pledging or hypothecating, though that is not its classical meaning (see below). Menand., *Arbitr.* 329 K. has ὑπόθημα of a ring pledged to cover a gambling debt.

[4] ὑποθήκη is used to describe or qualify either goods alone or goods and ship in bottomry loans in Dem. 35 *Lakrit.* 11 (contract document) παρέξουσι τοῖς δανείσασι τὴν ὑποθήκην ἀνέπαφον κρατεῖν. Ibid. 18 ὑπαρχούσης αὐτοῖς ὑποθήκης ἑτέρων τριάκοντα μνῶν. Ibid. 52 οὐ φάσκοντος . . . δανείσειν ἐὰν μὴ ὑποθήκην λάβῃ ἅπαντα ὅσα κτλ. . . . ἐπέτρεψαν ταῦτα ὑποθήκην γενέσθαι. Dem. 34 *Ag. Phorm.* 7, 8, 22 (οὐκ ἐνθέμενος εἰς τὴν ναῦν τὰ χρήματα καὶ ὑποθήκην οὐκ ἔχων), 50 (τοῖς δανεισταῖς οὐ παρασχόντα τὰς ὑποθήκας). The phrase ibid. 6 ἐπὶ ἑτέρᾳ ὑποθήκῃ is too obscure to furnish any conclusion; cf. Dareste, *Dem.* i. 310, Paley–Sandys, *Dem. Select Priv. Or.* i ad loc., Fine, *Horoi* 62, Finley, *Land* 223, n. 7, Jones, *LLTG* 236 (where the last sentence of n. 1 should read 'the noun is not found *in this sense* in the time of the orators').

It may be no coincidence that they also failed to use any abstract word to describe that common form of real security, sale subject to redemption. The phrase πρᾶσις ἐπὶ λύσει does not occur in the orators, though the institution turns up recognizably in a number of speeches. Various parts of the verbs πιπράσκω and ἀποδίδομαι are used by Demosthenes to describe selling with the right of redemption; only the context can indicate whether they have this sense rather than that of selling outright. In one instance the adverb κάθαπαξ is added to πιπράσκω to mark its use in the latter sense. On a very large number of *horoi* the participial phrase πεπραμένας or πεπραμένων ἐπὶ λύσει attests the presence of sale with right of redemption. It is perhaps natural that the procedure is normally described in terms referring to the borrower, though occasionally ὤνη and ὠνοῦμαι are used.[1]

ἀποτιμᾶν and kindred words have a specialized sense in the context of real security. The basic conception here seems to be that a piece of property is marked off to serve as security, being given at the time the business is negotiated an exact value, either in terms of money or as being adjudged equivalent to the whole estate of a ward. This group of words is used predominantly in two particular types of transaction, security given by the lessee of an orphan's estate to cover the payment of interest and the eventual return of the capital and security for the return of a dowry. To provide the security is ἀποτιμᾶν, to accept it is ἀποτιμᾶσθαι, the property charged is ἀποτίμημα or τὰ ἀποτιμηθέντα. The official valuers sent by the archon to confirm that property offered as security for the lease of an orphan's estate was

[1] Dem. 37 *Pant.* 17, 30 (ἐφ' οἶσπερ ἐωνήμεθ' αὐτοὶ πάλιν ἀπεδόμεθα), where there was a contract providing for λύσις ἔν τινι ῥητῷ χρόνῳ (5). Ibid. 50, of outright sale of the property, πέπρακας καθάπαξ. On the other hand in 31 ἀπεδόμεθα (some MSS. read ἐωνήμεθα) and ἀπέδου without qualification are used in the same sentence to describe sale with right of redemption and sale outright respectively. Dem. 33 *Apatour.* 8 ὠνὴν ποιοῦμαι τῆς νεὼς καὶ τῶν παίδων ἕως ἀποδοίη τάς τε δέκα μνᾶς κτλ., ibid. 25 ἐπεπράκει perhaps of the same operation; on the other hand, ibid. 12 πραθείσης τῆς νεώς is outright sale. Dem. 37 *Pant.* Hyp. 2 has γραμματεῖον οὐχ ὑποθήκης, ἀλλὰ πράσεως γράφεται, post-classical language of course. For the *horoi* see Finley, nos. 11–115 (the last four possibly sale outright as they do not contain the words ἐπὶ λύσει) and in Appendix III twenty additional stones with ἐπὶ λύσει and two without. In *Hesperia* 10 (1941), 14, no. 1 (poletai record for 367/6), we get in line 23 ἀπεδομένο and in lines 33–34 πριαμένων ἐπὶ λύσει to describe the same transaction; in line 6 ἀπέδοντο is used for sale outright. Pollux 8. 142 (Hyper., fr. 193 J.) Ὑπερείδης δὲ ἐν τῷ πρὸς Χάρητα ἔφη ἀποδόμενος ἀντὶ τοῦ ὑποθείς. On terminology for sale in general see Pringsheim, *GLS* 92–102, 111–26, P. Chantraine, *RP*, N.S. 14 (1940), 11–24, Finley, *Land* 31 with nn., 296, n. 16.

adequate were ἀποτίμηται, and their activity was also ἀποτιμᾶσθαι. Exceptionally we find the simple words τιμᾶν and τίμημα and the compound ἐναποτιμᾶν used analogously.[1]

Finally we have the words ὅρος and ὁρίζω. The word ὅρος for a stone marking an encumbrance on a building or piece of land (to be distinguished sharply from its meaning 'boundary stone') goes right back to Solon: his so-called *Seisachtheia* ('throwing off of burdens') was symbolized by the uprooting of these mortgage stones.[2] The word then disappears from surviving literature, to reappear at the beginning of the fourth century on a large number of such stones[3] and in speeches of Isaios and Demosthenes. The verb ὁρίζω is used in the passive of the property mortgaged, in the middle of the debtor, with the property mortgaged in the accusative and the amount of the loan in the genitive.[4]

[1] Dem. 30 *Onet.* i has a good selection of uses of the word ἀποτιμᾶν as applied to a dowry; see 4, 7, 8, 18, 26, 28, 29, and 31 *Onet.* ii. 3, 4, 11. *Horoi* recording security for dowries are collected in Finley, *Land*, nos. 132–65, Appendix III, 152A (some dubious, about twenty-seven usable as evidence, of which twenty-four are from Athens). For these words in connexion with the estates of wards Isai. 6 *Philokt.* 36 μισθοῦν ἐκέλευον τὸν ἄρχοντα τοὺς οἴκους ὡς ὀρφανῶν ὄντων, ὅπως ἐπὶ τοῖς τούτων ὀνόμασι τὰ μὲν μισθωθείη τῆς οὐσίας, τὰ δὲ ἀποτιμήματα κατασταθείη καὶ ὅροι τεθεῖεν, Dem. 49 *Timoth.* 11 ὁ ἐν πεδίῳ ἀγρὸς ἀποτίμημα τῷ παιδὶ τῷ Εὐμηλίδου καθειστήκει, Ar., *Ath. Pol.* 56. 7, of the archon, μισθοῖ δὲ καὶ τοὺς οἴκους τῶν ὀρφανῶν καὶ τῶν ἐπικλήρων . . . καὶ τὰ ἀποτιμήματα λαμβάνει. *Horoi* Finley, *Land*, nos. 116–31 and in Appendix III, 120A–29A (twenty-one in all, of which nineteen are from Athens). Both these kinds of security are dealt with in Harpokr. s.v.: ἀποτιμηταὶ καὶ ἀποτίμημα καὶ ἀποτιμᾶν καὶ τὰ ἀπ' αὐτῶν· οἱ μισθούμενοι τοὺς τῶν ὀρφανῶν οἴκους παρὰ τοῦ ἄρχοντος ἐνέχυρα τῆς μισθώσεως παρείχοντο· ἔδει δὲ τὸν ἄρχοντα ἐπιπέμπειν τινὰς ἀποτιμησομένους τὰ ἐνέχυρα. τὰ μὲν οὖν ἐνέχυρα τὰ ἀποτιμώμενα ἐλέγοντο ἀποτιμήματα, οἱ δὲ πεμπόμενοι ἐπὶ τῷ ἀποτιμήσασθαι ἀποτιμηταί, τὸ δὲ πρᾶγμα ἀποτιμᾶν. εἰώθεσαν δὲ καὶ οἱ τότε, εἰ γυναικὶ γαμουμένῃ προῖκα διδοῖεν οἱ προσήκοντες, αἰτεῖν παρὰ τοῦ ἀνδρὸς ὥσπερ ἐνέχυρόν τι τῆς προικὸς ἄξιον, οἷον οἰκίαν ἢ χωρίον. . . . ὁ δ' αὐτὸς λόγος καὶ ἐπὶ τῶν ἄλλων ὀφλημάτων. For the words τιμᾶν and τίμημα Lys., fr. 52 Th. οὗτοι δὲ φάσκοντες πλείονος μισθώσασθαι καὶ τίμημα καταστήσασθαι, Dem. 31 *Onet.* ii. 6, possibly *horoi* Finley, nos. 131 and 147 and *IG* ii². 1172. 20–22 (on which see Finley *Land* 242, n. 51). Dem. 53 *Nikostr.* 20 has ἐναπετίμησε (on which see Paley and Sandys, *Dem. Select Priv. Or.* ii ad loc., Finley, *Land* 241, n. 44, Fine *Horoi* 132, n. 58; probably not a security transaction). Distinguish ἐντιμᾶν in Dem. 41 *Spoud.* 27, 28, Pollux 8. 142, Harpokr., Suda s.v. ἐνετιμᾶτο, passages discussed in Fine, *Horoi* 118, Finley, *Land* 240, n. 41, 245, n. 63, Wolff, *Traditio* 2 (1944), 54, n. 60, id., *Fest. Rabel* ii. 314, n. 86. Dem. 41 *Spoud.* 10 νόμος ὃς οὐκ ἐᾷ τῶν ἀποτιμηθέντων ἔτι δίκην εἶναι πρὸς τοὺς ἔχοντας: on the difficult question what τὰ ἀποτιμηθέντα ἔχειν could mean see Fine, *Horoi* 129 ff., Finley 245, n. 61 ('to "have" the *apotimema* in the sense of "have the contingent right to the property" '), Wolff, *Fest. Rabel* ii. 331, n. 166, Gernet, *Iura* 4 (1953), 365.

[2] Solon 24. 5 Diehl Γῆ μέλαινα, τῆς ἐγώ ποτε / ὅρους ἀνεῖλον πολλαχῇ πεπηγότας, / πρόσθεν δὲ δουλεύουσα, νῦν ἐλευθέρα.

[3] See Fine, *Horoi*, Finley, *Land passim*.

[4] For ὅρος Isai. 6 *Philokt.* 36, Dem. 25 *Aristogeit.* i. 69, 42 *Phain.* 5, 28 (absence of

§ 2. *Types*

Nowhere perhaps is the danger of thinking too closely in terms of Roman law more apparent than in the realm of real securities. This is primarily due to the fact that here more than anywhere else the distinction between possessing and owning was of paramount importance and that, whereas the Romans worked out wholly distinct procedures for the protection of possession and of ownership, we can find no evidence of a corresponding distinction in Athenian procedure (see above, pp. 204 ff.).

It has been usual to distinguish four main types of real security in Athenian law. The simplest is pledge. This is the handing over of a thing, usually a movable, by the debtor into the possession of the creditor, the latter being required to restore the thing on the discharge of the debt. Ownership remained with the debtor. The second type is hypothec. Here the thing, usually a piece of real property, remains in both possession and ownership of the debtor, but a right is conferred on the creditor in case of default by the debtor to enter on the property and, if resisted, to have recourse to the courts by a *δίκη ἐξούλης*. Thirdly there was *πρᾶσις ἐπὶ λύσει*—sale subject to redemption—again normally of an immovable, in which, to use what may turn out to be question-begging terminology, ownership was transferred from the debtor to the creditor subject to the debtor's right to reacquire the property by repayment of the loan either by a fixed date or at any time in the future. Possession here might be with either party, though we shall see that probably it was normally with the debtor. The fourth type is bottomry.[1] *ἀντίχρησις* as a separate

ὅροι proves that the land is unencumbered), 49 *Timoth.* 11, 12 *δάνεισμα ποιεῖται ἰδίᾳ παρ' ἑκάστου αὐτῶν τὰς ἑπτὰ μνᾶς καὶ ὑποτίθησιν αὐτοῖς τὴν οὐσίαν, ἃς νῦν αὐτοὺς ἀποστερεῖ καὶ τοὺς ὅρους ἀνέσπακεν*, 31 *Onet.* ii. 1 *τίθησιν ὅρους ἐπὶ μὲν τὴν οἰκίαν δισχιλίων (δραχμῶν), ἐπὶ δὲ τὸ χωρίον ταλάντου*, ibid. 3, 4, 12, 41 *Spoud.* 6, 16. For *ὁρίζω* 31 *Onet.* ii. 5 *δισχιλίων ὡρισμένος τὴν οἰκίαν, ταλάντου δὲ τὸ χωρίον*, 49 *Timoth.* 61 *ἴστε μὲν καὶ αὐτοὶ ὅσοις αὐτοῦ ἡ οὐσία ὡρισμένη ἦν, οὓς νῦν ἀποστερεῖ.*

[1] Guiraud, *Prop. fonc.* 103 ff. Beauch. iii. 176 ff. in a rather confusing chapter entitled 'De l'hypothèque', after beginning with a fairly clear differentiation between pledge, hypothec, and *πρᾶσις ἐπὶ λύσει*, tends to let his treatment of them run together until he comes to the effects, which he deals with in three separate sections (ibid. 236 ff.). Cf. Lips., *AR* 690 ff., Fine, *Horoi* 61 ff., Finley, *Land* 8 f., 28 ff. On p. 56 Finley argues that bottomry loans and loans on the security of slaves had so many peculiarities that they should be considered in isolation from loans on the security of land; cf. p. 304, n. 1, below. Finley himself has little to say on pledge, naturally since his book is concerned with land. Jones, *LLTG* 235–47 has a chapter

type has been omitted designedly.[1] The provision of security for the return of a dowry and for the administration of a ward's estate by what was known as ἀποτίμημα can perhaps be regarded as special cases of hypothec.

Much discussion has centred round the chronological development of these institutions. On the whole it seems likely that simple pledge was the earliest form of real security; but whether πρᾶσις ἐπὶ λύσει developed out of hypothec or vice versa, or whether their development was parallel and independent, are still quite open questions, only to be answered on highly dubious *a priori* grounds.[2]

In the discussion which follows it will become plain that the following are among the more important *differentiae* which can

on mortgages and leases in which he gives clear definitions of ἀποτίμημα, hypothec, and πρᾶσις ἐπὶ λύσει; he touches only lightly on pledge and bottomry. For Paoli's schema see Appendix E below, p. 316. Kränzlein, *Eig. und Bes.* 82 ff., makes one of the *differentiae* of hypothec the fact that ownership of the thing mortgaged remains with the debtor: the creditor has only an expectancy.

[1] ἀντίχρησις is a special type of security, in which the creditor has the usufruct of the thing in lieu of interest. The word does not occur in classical Greek, and Occam's razor may be allowed to dispose of the thing. Beauch. iii. 212 ff. expresses firm belief in it, but cites no instance. Dareste finds it in Dem. 27 *Aphob.* i. 9 (Moiriades' 20 bed-makers), 30 *Onet.* i. 26 ff. (alleged security for dowry), Dem. 41 *Spoud.* 3 ff. (security for payment of dowry) in *Dem.* i ad loc. None of these instances is convincing, but Manigk, *Glaubigerbefriedigung durch Nutzung* (Berlin, 1910), 27, 39, 43, takes the first to be ἀντίχρησις, as had Hitz. 95 f. Paoli, *St. Dir.* 158, n. 2, sees it in two *horoi*, *IG* ii². 2758, 2759 (*IJ* 1. viii. 62, 63, Finley, nos. 1, 2), as did the editors of *IG* ii² and *IJ*. These stones (and Finley, no. 10) contain the puzzling formula ὥστε or ἐφ' ᾧτε ἔχειν καὶ κρατεῖν, on which see p. 270, n. 2. Fine justly criticizes Paoli on this point; for in saying 'quando il pegno era una cosa fruttifera, si intende che il frutto tenesse luogo degl' interessi' Paoli is turning all hypothecs which offer what he defines as a 'real right', or at least all those which consisted in real property, into cases of ἀντίχρησις. Fine himself, 70 ff., is doubtful; the only marked difference between ἀντίχρησις and πρᾶσις ἐπὶ λύσει would have been that the former conferred provisional possession, the latter provisional ownership. But we shall see reason to believe that normally in πρᾶσις ἐπὶ λύσει possession remains with the debtor; he may have paid the creditor rent on the property which would have been in lieu of interest, but that is fundamentally different from the creditor's occupying the property and retaining the fruits as interest. Fine regards Moiriades' bed-makers as an instance of either ἀντίχρησις or πρᾶσις ἐπὶ λύσει. Finley, *Land* 205, n. 12, is sceptical of ἀντίχρησις as a category.

[2] Szanto, *WS* 9 (1887), 279 ff., Hitz. 4 ff., Weiss, *Pfand.* 9 ff., Papp. 46, Beauch. iii. 180 ff., Lips., *AR* 693. For a full discussion see Fine, *Horoi* 90–94, 156; pledge first, then πρᾶσις ἐπὶ λύσει, probably in origin a legal fiction to circumvent the inalienability of land (which persisted according to Fine down to the last quarter of the fifth century, as he argues in his ch. 8: controverted by Wolff, *Z* 70 (1953), 422, n. 25), finally hypothec. Much the same view is taken by Gernet, *St. Paoli* (1955), 347. Jones, *LLTG* 237, says πρᾶσις ἐπὶ λύσει was 'the earliest method of securing the payment of money', but he does not argue the point. Vinogradoff, *HJ* 252, puts hypothec before πρᾶσις ἐπὶ λύσει.

serve to distinguish one type of security from another. Was the thing offered as security a movable or an immovable? Did ownership or possession or both or neither pass from the debtor to the creditor when the security operation took place? Was there any fixed term for repayment of the debt? If there was a fixed term, what effect had failure to pay on ownership and possession?

§ 3. *Pledge*

The practice of offering movables as security for repayment of a debt in all probability originated in the practice of seizing debtor's property in satisfaction of a debt, which had in Athens since the days of Solon replaced the still older practice of seizing the debtor's person. Although the property thus seized by a process of execution may in some respects be on all fours with property which falls to a creditor through a security operation, so that there is to this extent a close link between execution and security, the fact that in the latter case the piece of property which is to pass to the creditor has been agreed in advance by the parties, while in the former it has not, entails so many consequential differences that it will pay to treat the two institutions in isolation. Here, therefore, execution is ignored.[1]

Unequivocal instances of pledge are few and far between in the orators. In Lys. 19 *Prop. Arist.* 25 Demos offers to hand over to Aristophanes a gold cup, which he himself held as a σύμβολον from the Great King, in return for a loan of 16 minai to be used for his trierarchic expenses. He undertook to redeem the pledge for twenty minai on his arrival in Cyprus (ἐπειδὴ εἰς Κύπρον ἀφίκοιτο λύσεσθαι ἀποδοὺς εἴκοσι μνᾶς). In 26 the four minai are described as interest. The offer was refused, and the incident tells us little about the law on the subject.[2] Lys. 8 *Ag. Coass.* 10 is not much more helpful. The speaker, X, has lent Polykles twelve minai on the security of a horse (provided, it would seem, by

[1] Fine, *Horoi* 90, n. 108, Finley, *Land* 28, 221, nn. 1, 2 and the works there cited, especially (for execution), Weiss, *GP*, Bk. 4, id., *RE* 10 (1919) s.v. κατενεχυρασία 2495 ff., Mitteis, *RV* 413 ff., Partsch, *GB* 193 ff.

[2] Beauch. iii. 284 strains the passage too far in deducing from it a general rule about the use of a pledge while it was held by the creditor. The most we can say is that (1) Demos claimed that he himself would be able to put the cup to profitable use as a sort of letter of credit when he redeemed it, (2) that he was not suggesting that the creditor should make a similar use of it as a means of providing interest on the loan.

a third party). The operation is described as *θέσις τοῦ ἵππου*. When the horse became sick, X wished to recover the loan by returning the horse (*τὸν ἵππον ἀνάγειν*). He was dissuaded by one of his co-associates, but when the horse died the same man told him that he had no claim to repayment of the loan. We should be cautious in using this passage. This is not a forensic speech, and we are less than usually justified in expecting juristic precision in the terms used. Moreover, it is not absolutely clear that it is a case of pledge; it has been argued that the use of the word *ἀνάγειν* suggests the *ἀναγωγὴ εἰς πρατῆρα* of sale and that we have here *πρᾶσις ἐπὶ λύσει*. Assuming, however, as we probably should, that this is pledge, and assuming that the co-associate was right in telling X that he had no claim, there is the further question whether this was because there was a limit of time within which such a claim had to be made and this time had elapsed or whether, as is more probable, it was because there was a general rule that in pledge the risk lay with the creditor who held the pledge. This passage, with one doubtful exception, is our only evidence for such a rule at Athens.[1] More useful is Dem. 27 *Aphob*. i. 9, 24 ff. Demosthenes' father had lent Moiriades forty minai on the security of twenty bed-makers—they are described as *τετταράκοντα μνῶν ὑποκείμενοι*. Demosthenes complains that his guardians had charged the estate with 1,000 drachmai for the keep of these slaves, had set nothing on the credit side, though his father was known to have netted twelve minai a year from their products, and had lost possession of the slaves into the bargain; in 27–28 he adds that Aphobos had lent Moiriades a further 500 drachmai on the security of these same slaves and had received interest on the loan. It is fairly widely held that this is pledge; the creditor holds the pledge for years on end and retains the products in lieu of interest; at some stage after the first loan the creditor (now the young Demosthenes' guardian) makes a further loan on the same security, this time exacting interest.[2]

[1] Hitz. 96, Beauch. iii. 284, Lips., *AR* 705, n. 105, Pringsheim, *GLS* 478, n. 1, Finley, *Land* 232, n. 50 (tentatively), all take this as a case of pledge against Papp. 120, Guenter, *Sicherungsübereignung* 44–47 (Königsberg, 1914 with full bibliography), who argue for *πρᾶσις ἐπὶ λύσει*. Even if we take the former view we might still hold that a pledgee, in case of some defect in the pledge, had a redress analogous to *ἀναγωγὴ εἰς πρατῆρα* in sale (for which see p. 221, above); so Lips. and Finley against Pringsheim, locc. citt.

[2] So Beauch. iii. 283, Lips., *AR* 705, n. 104, Finley, *Land* 205, n. 12, 262, n. 124 (an almost unique case of pledging of slaves), 274, n. 69 (where he seems to hint

In Dem. 53 *Nikostr.* 9 Apollodoros deposits cups and a gold crown with a banker as security for 1,000 drachmai which are to be paid over to Nikostratos as a gift. We hear nothing of the conditions of this loan by the bank to Apollodoros.

These seem to be the only reasonably certain instances of simple pledge in the classical period which need be considered.[1]

§ 4. *Hypothec*

We must be cautious in reconstructing an institution for which, as we saw above (p. 255), the Athenians had no name. We may begin by considering the sort of *differentiae* we should need in order to distinguish hypothec from pledge, on the one hand, and from sale with right of redemption on the other. As against pledge, the security in hypothec would normally not be a specific movable thing, and it would normally not be transferred to the possession of the creditor. As against sale with right of redemption, there would be in hypothec no element, genuine or fictitious, of sale; this may, with some risk of question-begging, be developed by saying that in hypothec ownership remains with the debtor, whichever party possesses, and in sale with right of redemption ownership passes to the creditor, whichever possesses. To this last distinction we might like to add *differentiae* based on the possibility or impossibility of raising a second loan on property already charged, on the presence or absence of a maturity date for the debt, on the different results which might ensue if the debt was paid off, on where the loss fell if the security was damaged, and so on. Unfortunately we shall find that it is just here that our evidence breaks down. Even such a simple conjecture as that repayment of the loan in sale with right of redemption would

at the possibility that there had been default and forfeit with the right still reserved to the debtor to redeem the pledge by payment of the debt). Paoli, *St. Dir.* 155 f., regards this as a case of hypothec and as confirming his view that hypothec, like pledge, in the classical period had a continuative character. Fine, *Horoi* 75 ff., points out the weakness of Paoli's argument here and suggests that the transaction might be ἀντίχρησις or πρᾶσις ἐπὶ λύσει. Lauffer, *Bergwerkssklaven* i. 82 ff. argues that, since the security here was slaves, not real property, the transaction was not hypothec, in effect a circular argument. On the second loan see Gernet, *Dem.* i. 41, n. 1: 'une opération dont on peut contester l'opportunité et la délicatesse, mais dont la correction juridique peut être admise', but cf. p. 292, n. 2.

[1] Dem. 41 *Spoud.* 11 and 49 *Timoth.* 48 really add nothing to our knowledge. Beauch. iii. 286, n. 1, seems to infer, wrongly, that Dem. 50 *Polykl.* 28 and Isai. 6 *Philokt.* 33 are instances of pledge.

entail reconveyance of the security, while in hypothec it would not, must remain a pure conjecture, and in our general ignorance of the modes of conveyance a pretty barren conjecture at that.[1]

When we try to isolate specific instances of hypothec, whether in literature or inscriptions, it is seldom obvious what the nature of the transaction was, and often a case has been assigned to one category or another by what turns out on examination to be a circular argument. There is in the literary sources only one unequivocal case. Aischines (3 *Ktes.* 104) tells us that the city of Oreos hypothecated (ὑπέθεσαν) the public revenues of the city to Demosthenes to cover the loan of one talent. Interest was at the rate of 12 per cent., and principal and interest were duly paid. Here the security is not a presently existing determinate thing, but an indeterminate future claim; and by its very nature it could neither be handed over into the possession of the creditor nor be the subject of a real or fictitious sale to him. Strictly, this is evidence for the law of Oreos rather than that of Athens. Moreover, we should not too readily draw conclusions for private law from what was in essence little more than a budget device for earmarking a part of the revenue for a special purpose.[2]

The orators provide a fair number of cases which have been assumed by one scholar or another to be hypothec, but which might none the less be πρᾶσις ἐπὶ λύσει. In Isok. 21 *Euth.* 2 a certain Nikias, in order to avoid the predatory attentions of the Thirty, τὴν οἰκίαν ὑπέθηκε: he also conveyed his slaves out of the country, emptied the house of furniture, and went himself to live in the country. This is possibly hypothec, but the use of the word

[1] Much of Kränzlein's discussion in *Eig. und Bes.* 82 ff., is vitiated by circular argument.

[2] Hitz. 19, Papp. 70 f. For references to similar budgeting devices elsewhere Finley, *Land* 279, n. 18. Paoli, *St. Dir.* 144 f., gives this as an instance of hypothec without transfer of possession and therefore not conferring a 'real' right. Fine, *Horoi* 64, misses Paoli's point when he argues that there is no evidence here for the contention that this contract 'afforded inadequate protection against the claims of other possible creditors'. It is not the adequacy but the nature of the protection which is in question, and Paoli is surely so far right that there is a fundamental difference between a guarantee which takes the form of a thing handed over into the possession of the creditor on the formation of the contract and one where the creditor is simply given first claim on a future revenue. Precisely the same arguments apply to the securing of loans to the city of Arkesine on Amorgos of about 300 B.C. recorded in *IG* xii. 7, 66–70, on which see Paoli and Fine, locc. citt., Finley, *Land* 198, n. 17, 278, nn. 15, 16, with further references.

ὑπέθηκε does not rule out *πρᾶσις ἐπὶ λύσει*, and we are no more entitled with Paoli to take this as tending to prove that in hypothec which provided a 'real right' possession passed immediately to the creditor than we are to assume with the French translators of Isokrates (Budé ed. ad loc.) that this is *πρᾶσις ἐπὶ λύσει*.[1] Isaios provides several cases of the same kind. In 5 *Dikaiog.* 21, a highly controversial passage, the speaker is alleging that, in compromising a previous suit, Dikaiogenes had undertaken to hand over, free of charges (*ἀναμφισβήτητα*), two-thirds of the inheritance in dispute; a good part of this two-thirds had either been sold outright, sold with the right of redemption, or hypothecated—it is a matter of conjecture whether he implies all or any one or two of these processes—to third parties; Dikaiogenes was now claiming that he had carried out this undertaking by simply refraining from laying any claim himself to the properties in question which had been sold or hypothecated; to this the speaker replies that an undertaking of that kind would have been meaningless, since it would have cost Dikaiogenes nothing, and he goes on as follows: *οὐδὲ γὰρ πρὶν ἡττηθῆναι τὴν δίκην εἶχεν ὧν ἡμεῖς δικαζόμεθα, ἀλλ' οἱ παρὰ τούτου πριάμενοι καὶ θέμενοι, οἷς ἔδει αὐτὸν ἀποδόντα τὴν τιμὴν ἡμῖν τὰ μέρη ἀποδοῦναι*, and a little later *πλὴν γὰρ δυοῖν οἰκιδίοιν . . . οὐδὲν κεκομίσμεθα, ἀλλ' οἱ παρὰ τούτου θέμενοι καὶ πριάμενοι*. Various interpretations have been put upon the words *οἱ παρὰ τούτου πριάμενοι καὶ θέμενοι*. On one view these are (1) purchasers, and (2) mortgagees who had foreclosed as a result of the failure of Dikaiogenes to repay the loans by the stipulated dates. We should then have to suppose either that the speaker is asking Dikaiogenes to do the impossible or that a purchaser could be required to sell back a piece of property for the price he had paid for it and a mortgagee to release a piece of property on which he had foreclosed if repayment of the original loan was offered. Moreover, *τιμή* will have to do double duty as the original price and the amount of the loan. All this is so improbable that this view can be ruled out.

On another view we have here (1) purchasers *ἐπὶ λύσει* and (2) creditors who had been given possession of the property to secure a loan and held it under a continuative hypothec. On

[1] Paoli, *St. Dir.* 154, rebutted by Fine, *Horoi* 73. Finley, *Land* 12, deprecates the use of this passage as evidence in view of the wholly exceptional circumstances; cf. id. 205, n. 13.

this view it would clearly have been in Dikaiogenes' power to recover possession and ownership of the properties by repayment of the loans. The word *τιμή* still has to do double duty, but the hendiadys is less forced, since the 'price' in a sale with the right of redemption is virtually equivalent to the sum lent in an hypothec. In fact, if we had other evidence for a continuative hypothec of this sort, this interpretation would be perfectly feasible. We are not justified, however, in arguing that we have here independent evidence for such an institution.

On a third view we have (1) purchasers ἐπὶ λύσει and (2) creditors in possession under a hypothec which was not continuative in character, but on which either there had not been foreclosure or, if there had, a period of grace was still left allowing the debtor to recover the property by payment of the sum due. Much the same considerations apply to this as to the second view. We should certainly not rule it out, as some have done, by the circular argument that here the creditor appears to be in possession while it is of the essence of hypothec that until foreclosure possession remains with the debtor.

On the fourth, and on the whole most probable, view the words οἱ πριάμενοι καὶ θέμενοι are a composite phrase for purchasers ἐπὶ λύσει.[1] If this view is correct we can deduce nothing from the passage as to the nature of hypothec at Athens.[2]

In Isai. 6 *Philokt.* 33 it is alleged that Euktemon, with the object of turning as much as possible of his property from οὐσία φανερά into οὐσία ἀφανής, made a number of sales and further οἰκίαν ἐν ἄστει τεττάρων καὶ τετταράκοντα μνῶν ὑποκειμένην ἀπέλυσε τῷ ἱεροφάντῃ. The general sense here is clear enough. The hierophant had borrowed forty-four minai from Euktemon on the security of a house. Euktemon recovers the money and

[1] There is no parallel for the phrase in this sense; but in the comparative paucity of references to any of these institutions this means little. The addition of θέμενοι may have been one way of indicating that πρίασθαι was not being used for sale outright where that was not plain from the context. But should we then find θέμενοι καὶ πριάμενοι in that order?

[2] So Wyse ad loc., with whom Kränzlein, *Eig. und Bes.* 80, n. 73, seems to agree. Paoli, *St. Dir.* 155, uses the passage to support his theory of continuative hypothec, rebutted by Fine, *Horoi* 74 f. Both the legal and the factual positions are very obscure. Even the one point on which all the above views agree, namely that the creditors were in possession, is not absolutely certain. It depends on pressing εἶχεν in 21 to mean 'was in possession of'; but perhaps it need not mean that: cf. the suggestion on p. 314, below. See also p. 213, n. 1, for this case.

releases the house. But there is nothing to indicate the exact nature of the contract, and we should neither conclude from the use of the word ὑποκειμένην that it must have been hypothec nor from ἀπέλυσε that it must have been πρᾶσις ἐπὶ λύσει.[1]

The last relevant passage from Isaios is 10 *Aristarch.* 24, where, on one interpretation at least, a regular way of proving title, or the right to possess, was to produce a mortgagor (θέτης). Quite apart from the doubt as to the meaning of the word θέτης here, the passage cannot be tortured into telling us anything significant about the institution of hypothec.[2]

The Demosthenic corpus yields a few more of these embarrassingly ambiguous cases. In Dem. 50 *Polykl.* 61 we find an encumbered property in possession of the debtor; the creditors are pressing for payment of interest if what is due to them under a contract is not paid up. This could equally refer to hypothec or πρᾶσις ἐπὶ λύσει. If it was the latter, since the debtor was in possession, payments by way of interest to the creditors would more strictly be called rent. But we certainly cannot classify this case confidently as hypothec simply on the basis of the words ἐπὶ τοὺς τόκους.[3]

[1] Hitz. 9, n. 1, 106, n. 1 πρᾶσις ἐπὶ λύσει, followed by Fine, *Horoi* 74 and Kränzlein, *Eig. und Bes.* 29: Wyse ad loc. hypothec. Finley, *Land* 36 and 232, nn. 48, 49, takes the view adopted in the text, but adds that if this is πρᾶσις ἐπὶ λύσει it is probably the only case where the creditor-buyer in such a case acquires possession. But we cannot be certain that Euktemon was in possession. The word ἀπέλυσε would be equally appropriate in either case, and there is nothing in Fine's argument (loc. cit.) that, because there is no mention of interest and the house is apparently redeemed for the exact amount of the loan, Euktemon must have possessed it and had the usufruct in lieu of interest. If, as seems to have been common practice, the hierophant had retained possession and had been paying rent-interest, the release would have involved simple repayment of the original loan.

[2] Passage quoted above (p. 216, n. 1). We cannot say whether τὸν ἔχοντα means 'owner' or 'possessor'. Paoli, *AG* 24 (1932), 171 f., takes the passage as confirming continuative hypothec. He is rebutted by Fine, *Horoi* 78 f., who puts two possibilities: (1) a (former) mortgagee establishes his title to property on which he has foreclosed by referring to the mortgagor (θέτης); in this case the word πράτηρ will cover both the seller outright and the seller ἐπὶ λύσει; or (2) the word πράτηρ means only the seller outright, and the θέτης is the debtor in any kind of contract with real property as security, i.e. in effect hypothec or πρᾶσις ἐπὶ λύσει. For Finley, *Land* 228, n. 33, 232, n. 51, the passage is irrelevant here, since for him πράτηρ means 'warrantor' and θέτης 'adopter'. See p. 275, n. 1.

[3] The relevant sentence reads οἱ δὲ δεδανεικότες ἧκον ἐπὶ τοὺς τόκους, ἐπειδὴ ὁ ἐνιαυτὸς ἐξῆλθεν [ἐξήει D], εἰ μή τις ἀποδοίη [ἀποδιδοίη SD] αὐτοῖς κατὰ τὰς συγγραφάς. The sense of the dependent clauses is far from clear, and we do not know the terms of the contract. Fine, *Horoi* 81, though treating the case in his chapter on hypothec, leaves the question open. Finley, *Land* 25 suggests that the terms of this

In Dem. 53 *Nikostr.* 10 Nikostratos is represented as saying that, pressed though he was for money, no one would either buy or lend money on a certain property (οὔτε πρίασθαι οὔτε θέσθαι) because his brother, Arethousios, would not allow anyone to buy or lend on it, alleging that money was owed to him on the same security (οὐδένα ἐῴη οὔτε ὠνεῖσθαι οὔτε τίθεσθαι, ὡς ἐνοφειλομένου αὐτῷ ἀργυρίου). It seems clear from 28 that the brothers held their properties severally, that this estate was owned by—though not necessarily in the possession of—Nikostratos, and that there was some charge on it in favour of Arethousios. Although we cannot exclude the bare possibility that θέσθαι and τίθεσθαι here mean purchase ἐπὶ λύσει, this seems highly improbable seeing that they are coupled with the words πρίασθαι and ὠνεῖσθαι. Only on the unlikely supposition that at the time of the speech πρᾶσις ἐπὶ λύσει was virtually the only method of borrowing on the security of land and that therefore in such contexts τίθημι and kindred words denoted πρᾶσις ἐπὶ λύσει and nothing else could the combination πρίασθαι and θέσθαι mean 'purchase outright' and 'purchase ἐπὶ λύσει'. We have here then one of the least ambiguous literary references to hypothec. This is important, since the passage further gives us, on the most likely interpretation, the rule that the first creditor in whichever type of security this is could ban both the sale of the property charged and the raising of a further loan on it.[1] A few lines later in the same speech (12–13) Apollodoros, being short of cash, offers to

contract were probably unusual. In the difficult passage Dem. 53 *Nikostr.* 12 (above) Apollodoros undertakes to make what would in effect have been a loan of money and to charge no interest for a year. The loan to Apollodoros in the Polykles speech may have been similar, and this might explain the enigmatic reference to 'the year'.

[1] So Hitz. 121 f., followed by Lips., *AR* 700, nn. 87, 89, who regards this right of the first creditor as one of the hall-marks of hypothec. Fine, *Horoi* 81, 94, is inclined to see this as hypothec, but is wrong to deduce from Nikostratos' desire to sell or mortgage that he 'was in possession' of the property and that this is therefore a fairly strong instance of the debtor in hypothec retaining possession. Others are doubtful whether Arethousios held a mortgage on the land and suggest that his right was either in virtue of co-ownership or because a loan had given him a kind of general hypothec on the property of his brother. Cf. Rabel, *Die Verfügungsbeschränkungen* 16. Pringsheim, *GLS* 164, sees no indication that Arethousios held a mortgage on the land; the word ἐνοφείλω here means 'a simple debt, which is, however, so to speak secured by the land which can be recovered if the debt is not paid'; but on p. 498 he seems to suggest that Arethousios barred alienation as a co-owner. Finley, *Land* 271, n. 51 regards the case as indecisive. Cf. Weiss, *GP* 335 f., and further references there.

lend Nikostratos some property on which Nikostratos could raise a loan, but without the obligation to pay interest on it (τῶν κτημάτων σοι τῶν ἐμῶν κίχρημι ὅ τι βούλει, θέντα τοῦ ἐπιλοίπου ἀργυρίου ὅσου ἐνδεῖ σοι, ἐνιαυτὸν ἀτόκῳ χρῆσθαι τῷ ἀργυρίῳ). When it comes to the point Apollodoros himself borrows on the security of a multiple dwelling; he hands the money over to Nikostratos while undertaking to pay the interest himself at the rate of 16 per cent. The words used are *τίθημι τὴν συνοικίαν* and *τὸ ἀργύριον οὗ ἡ συνοικία ἐτέθη*. There is nothing which rules out *πρᾶσις ἐπὶ λύσει* absolutely.[1]

Dem. 42 *Phain.* raises one issue which is relevant to the topic of real security. The speech is our principal source for the somewhat obscure procedure of *antidosis*, the details of which do not concern us here. The speaker is trying to shift the liturgy known as *proeisphora* from himself to Phainippos. As a preliminary step in the procedure each party had to give the other access to his property, so that when the two parties put in inventories of their estates on the basis of which their relative liabilities were determined each had some check on the figures of the other. According to the speaker, he had made a thorough search on what was apparently the principal estate of Phainippos to discover if there were any *horoi* upon it. He discovered none, and he solemnly adjured Phainippos to confirm that there were none, in case it might later turn out that there was a debt secured on the property—5 *ὅπως μὴ ὕστερον ἐνταῦθα χρέως γενόμενον* [*ἐπὶ τῷ χωρίῳ*] *ἀναφανήσεται*. Later, at 28, the speaker complains that despite this disclaimer of Phainippos he subsequently maintained that he had debts to the tune of three talents. Two deductions, one secure the other less so, can be drawn from the incident as a whole. The certain deduction is that it was impossible to infer from the fact that the owner was in occupation of the land that the land was unencumbered; otherwise the search for *horoi* would have been meaningless. The other deduction, which the speaker wished the jury to make, perhaps in defiance of the facts, is that for the purpose of valuation for liturgies secured debts only would be reckoned as diminishing the value of the debtor's

[1] Paoli, *St. Dir.* 73 ff., whose account is confused by glossing over the fact that Apollodoros does something rather different from what he undertakes to do. Cf. Finley, *Land* 272, n. 59, Weiss, *GP* 334 f. Fine, *Horoi* 81, sees here another fairly clear case of hypothec with the debtor in possession.

estate. However that may be, there is absolutely nothing in the references to real security in this speech to tie them down to one type rather than another.[1]

In 28 *Aphob.* ii. 17–18 Demosthenes relates how, in order to discharge a liturgy, he had been forced to hypothecate all his possessions (*ἀπέτεισα τὴν λητουργίαν ὑποθεὶς τὴν οἰκίαν καὶ τἀμαυτοῦ πάντα*: the last three words are clearly rhetorical exaggeration). He goes on to ask to what resources he can look if the present suit goes against him. *εἰς τὰ ὑποκείμενα τοῖς δανείσασιν; ἀλλὰ τῶν ὑποθεμένων ἐστίν. ἀλλ' εἰς τὰ περιόντ' αὐτῶν; ἀλλὰ τούτου γίγνεται, τὴν ἐπωβελίαν ἐὰν ὄφλωμεν.* Again there is nothing in the words used to exclude *πρᾶσις ἐπὶ λύσει*.[2]

Finally, Dem. 36 *For Phorm.* 6 draws attention to the incapacity of Phormion, as a non-citizen, *εἰσπράττειν ὅσα Πασίων ἐπὶ γῇ καὶ συνοικίαις δεδανεικὼς ἦν*. Here too the words could fit either kind of security.

When we turn to the evidence of the *horoi* for hypothec three striking facts emerge. First only eleven *horoi*, eight from Athens, two from Amorgos, and one from Lemnos, have been claimed as marking hypothec obligations. The reason for so classifying them is that almost all of them have a formula of the type *ὅρος χωρίου καὶ οἰκίας ὑποκειμένων* 𐅅HH𐅄.[3] The small number of *horoi* in this class compared with the number—about 122—of those marking *πρᾶσις ἐπὶ λύσει* must indicate either that the latter was a far more common method of furnishing real security than the former or that, for some reason that we cannot divine, there was less need of a *horos* where the type of security was hypothec. In the

[1] Finley, *Land* 3, 17; Gernet, *Dem.* ii. 80, n. 3. Fine, *Horoi* 80 discusses the case in his chapter on hypothec, though admitting that it might be *πρᾶσις ἐπὶ λύσει*. He wrongly deduces that a mortgagor normally remained in possession. His argument on p. 85 that in 28–29 we have evidence for foreclosure in hypothec is purely circular. In this case, perhaps exceptionally, it would clearly have been in the interest of Phainippos, the *debtor*, to have been able to point to *horoi* if in fact the land was encumbered. In general *horoi* seem to have been designed to protect the interests of the creditor.

[2] Hitz. 21, Papp. 81, 144, Lips., *AR* 702, n. 95, Paoli, *St. Dir.* 160, agree in seeing this as hypothec, though not in the deductions to be drawn from it. Fine, *Horoi* 87 f., takes it tentatively as hypothec and, on that supposition, draws conclusions about foreclosure from it. Finley, *Land* 203, n. 7, follows Paoli. Kränzlein, *Eig. und Bes.* 20, thinks it may have been *πρᾶσις ἐπὶ λύσει*.

[3] Finley, nos. 1–10 and in App. III, no. 3A. In no. 3 the formula is *ὅρος χωρίου τιμῆς ἐνοφειλομένης Φανοστράτῳ . . . XX*. In no. 9 *ὅρος οἰκιῶν καὶ κήπου ὧν κατέθηκεν Ἀντήνωρ κτλ.*

present state of our knowledge the former alternative should be accepted. The second fact, also statistical, is that as many as six of the hypothec *horoi* contain references to written contracts—the type of formula is κατὰ τὰς συνθήκας τὰς κειμένας παρὰ Θεοδώρῳ—whereas only eight of the πρᾶσις ἐπὶ λύσει *horoi* contain such a reference. This disparity can hardly be accidental, but it is not easy to see what it implies. If we adopt the view that during the classical period πρᾶσις ἐπὶ λύσει was the normal method of furnishing real security and hypothec was only just beginning to be developed as an alternative, then we might suppose that the former type had acquired by custom or legislation a fairly well-established body of rules which would be assumed to apply in all cases, whereas the latter was a more flexible instrument and allowed scope for variations, which then had to be incorporated in written contracts.[1] Thirdly, in three of the hypothec *horoi* we find the baffling phrase ὥστε or ἐφ' ᾧτε ἔχειν καὶ κρατεῖν, but we find it nowhere else. Here again, though with slightly less assurance, the statistics allow us to infer that this formula would have been quite common in hypothec, rare if not wholly absent in πρᾶσις ἐπὶ λύσει. This inference would be more important if we could be more clear what the precise significance of the formula was.[2]

One further piece of epigraphical evidence is relevant. In the poletai records for 367/6 B.C. (*Hesperia* 10 (1941), 14) the sale of a confiscated house is recorded, and the record refers to certain charges which have been recognized as encumbering the house before it was confiscated. In the original denunciation the denouncer had declared a debt of 150 drachmai to be due to a creditor on the security of the house, so that the value of the house was to be reckoned as less by that amount: οἰκίαν . . . δημοσίαν εἶναι . . . ὅσῳ πλείονος ἀξία ἢ ὑποκεῖται Σμικύθῳ Τειθρασίῳ ΗΠ δραχμῶν (lines 10 ff.). Three other creditors also put

[1] So Finley, *Land* 24. His book first suggested and made possible this statistical approach.

[2] For ἔχειν καὶ κρατεῖν see p. 201, n. 1, above; Hitz. 9 ff.; Finley, *Land* 12 and 204, n. 11. The three *horoi* are Finley, nos. 1, 2, and 10. For a different view of them see Wolff, *Z* 70 (1953), 423; in his view πρᾶσις ἐπὶ λύσει gave the creditor immediate possession; hypothec did not: the clause ἐφ' ᾧτε κτλ. gave a right of seizure after a period specified in the contract; the practical effect of hypothec was to protect the interests of the debtor; hence it is later to develop than πρᾶσις ἐπὶ λύσει. Cf. also V. Arangio-Ruiz, *AG* 11 (1952), 170, Kränzlein, *Eig. und Bes.* 19 (the formula means 'eine zukünftige physische Sachherrschaft' and κρατεῖν is 'ein Zugriffsrecht').

in claims, two of them (for 100 and 34 drachmai respectively) based on πρᾶσις ἐπὶ λύσει (ἀποδομένου ἐμοὶ καὶ τοῖς φράτερσιν τὴν οἰκίαν ταύτην Θεοφίλου (line 23) and πριαμένων ἡμῶν τὴν οἰκίαν ταύτην παρὰ Θεοφίλου . . . ἐπὶ λύσει (line 33)), the other for funeral expenses of the previous owner of the house (lines 25 ff.). The house was sold for 575 drachmai. Out of this sum were to be met certain public charges and also, quite specifically, the repayment of the 150 drachmai to Smikythos. Although the record admits the validity of the other claims (ἔδοξεν ἐνοφείλεσθαι), only Smikythos' claim apparently is immediately satisfied, and it seems reasonable to deduce that he was a preferred creditor. We cannot, however, further conclude that this had anything to do with the distinction between hypothec and πρᾶσις ἐπὶ λύσει. For, though it is true that ὑποκεῖται is used of Smikythos' claim, this cannot be pressed to imply that his was hypothec as against the other two, which were expressly πρᾶσις ἐπὶ λύσει.[1]

Looking at the evidence for hypothec as a whole, we can, for the classical period at least, rarely identify cases which indubitably belong to the category, and the cases identified yield little which is demonstrably peculiar to the category.

§ 5. *Sale with right of redemption*

If what is argued in the preceding section is right, sale with right of redemption is, for the classical period, the predominant and typical form of real security. But before attempting to discern the main outlines of the institution we must briefly enumerate

[1] Cf. p. 256, n. 1. Fine 94, n. 116, 150 ff., confidently classifies the Smikythos transaction as hypothec, though he has himself on p. 62 stressed that the use of the word ὑποκεῖται may well have been compatible with any type of real security. The classification is important to him, since he holds that in πρᾶσις ἐπὶ λύσει the debtor lost ownership and with it the power to raise any further loan on the same property, whereas this did not apply to hypothec (143). His attempt to explain two separate debts on the same house by πρᾶσις ἐπὶ λύσει as recorded in this inscription is unconvincing. Finley, *Land* 111, 295, n. 13, is more cautious, but he too assumes that the word ὑποκεῖται here indicates hypothec. Cf. his fuller treatment of the inscription in *St. V. Arangio-Ruiz* (Naples, 1953), iii. 473 ff. Kränzlein, *Eig. und Bes.* 84 f., is not clear, though he specifically denies that Smikythos owed his position as preferred creditor to the nature of his security; rather it may have been that his debt alone had reached its fixed term. Cf. ibid. 125. The fact that this is a case of a confiscated property should make us wary of generalizing too freely from it.

the instances of indubitable *πρᾶσις ἐπὶ λύσει*, which are to be added to the ambiguous instances dealt with above (pp. 263–9).

Two speeches in the Demosthenic corpus contain unmistakable references to the institution, though in both the phraseology is more than usually exasperating in its vagueness. The first is Dem. 33 *Apatour.* 5–12. In that case Apatourios, a Byzantine, had borrowed forty minai on the security of his ship. The period of the loan had run out. His creditors were pressing and had got to the point of attaching the ship (*ἐνεβάτευον εἰς τὴν ναῦν*).[1] He satisfied these creditors by raising a fresh loan, and it is this loan which concerns us here. He got a promise of ten minai from a fellow Byzantine, Parmenon, three minai of which was paid down. He also approached the speaker in this suit (X), who, having no ready money, induced his banker to advance thirty minai with himself as surety. Parmenon then got involved in a quarrel with Apatourios. He still wished, however (possibly he was contractually bound),[2] to complete the loan he had promised, while escaping any contractual relation with Apatourios. He therefore paid the balance of seven minai to X, and the latter entered into a contract with Apatourios by which he purchased with right of redemption the ship and its slave crew: the terms in which the conditions for redemption were expressed are significant: *ὠνὴν ποιοῦμαι τῆς νεὼς καὶ τῶν παίδων, ἕως τάς τε δέκα μνὰς ἃς δι' ἐμοῦ ἔλαβεν καὶ τὰς τριάκοντα ὧν κατέστησεν ἐμὲ ἐγγυητὴν τῷ τραπεζίτῃ*. The bank now went bankrupt and Apatourios tried to make off with the ship. X, informed of this by Parmenon, set guards on the ship and handed it over to the guarantors (*ἐγγυηταί*) of the bank as security for the thirty minai owing to it, warning them that it also served as cover for ten minai due to Parmenon (10 *παρέδωκα τὸ ἐνέχυρον, εἰπὼν αὐτοῖς ὅτι δέκα μναῖ ἐνείησαν τῷ ξένῳ ἐν τῇ νηί*). There follows the cryptic sentence *ταῦτα δὲ πράξας κατηγγύησα τοὺς παῖδας, ἵν' εἴ τις ἔνδεια γίγνοιτο, τὰ ἐλλείποντα ἐκ τῶν παίδων εἴη*. Apatourios protests against this procedure in the following terms, as reported by X: 11 *ἠρώτα εἰ οὐχ ἱκανόν μοι εἴη αὐτῷ ἀπολυθῆναι τῆς ἐγγύης τῆς πρὸς τὴν τράπεζαν, ἀλλὰ καὶ ὑπὲρ τοῦ ἀργυρίου τοῦ Παρμένοντος τὴν ναῦν κατεγγυῶ καὶ τοὺς παῖδας*. Eventually X recovers the whole

[1] There is no means of determining the nature of this original loan. It could have been hypothec, bottomry, or *πρᾶσις ἐπὶ λύσει*. Bottomry is most probable.

[2] This aspect of the case is relevant to the law of contract.

of the forty minai by the sale of the ship (there is no further mention of the crew), which realizes exactly that sum: μόλις εἰσέπραξα τὸ ἀργύριον, πραθείσης τῆς νεὼς τετταράκοντα μνῶν, ὅσουπερ ἡ θέσις ἦν. This whole incident bristles with unanswered, perhaps unanswerable, questions. The security seems to be the ship and crew; it secures two debts of ten and thirty minai respectively; X is surety for the thirty minai advanced by the bank and debtor to Parmenon for the ten advanced by him. X 'makes a purchase' (ὠνὴν ποιοῦμαι) of the security until the two sums are repaid. This clearly implies that, if the whole sum was repaid, Apatourios would regain unfettered control of the ship and crew. It does not tell us what term, if any, was fixed within which Apatourios had to pay up on pain of losing all rights in the security. Nor can we tell precisely what power over the security X gained by having 'purchased' it. He certainly prevents it putting to sea, and by doing so and by transferring physical control of it to the representatives of the bank he appears to have been quit of his suretyship for the thirty minai. This attachment of the security is described by the word κατεγγυᾶν.[1] Apatourios, if X is to be believed, did not contest the legality of this attachment, but suggested that X was being quixotic in insisting that the security should cover not only his surety obligation to the bank but also the debt due to a mere foreigner like Parmenon. Now, even though it must be admitted that πρᾶσις ἐπὶ λύσει of a movable, such as a ship, would probably be governed by stricter rules to protect the creditor than would be needed for land, it is difficult to believe that the normal rule would have allowed the creditor not merely to hold the security but to recover the loan by a forced sale almost as soon as it had been contracted. It is significant that in the end X's action

[1] Partsch, *GB* 90, notes that in Dem. 32 *Zenoth.* 29, 59 *Neair.* 40, Isok. 17 *Trapez.* 12 κατεγγυᾶν is specially used of compelling a foreign defendant to provide before the polemarch a surety for his conforming to the decision of the case if it went against him (κατεγγυᾶν πρὸς τὸν πολέμαρχον). Here we have an analogous case; sureties are demanded to undertake that the object serving as security continues to be available for seizure in the event of a judgement against the debtor. But Partsch does not explain why in the former cases the object of the verb is the person who has to furnish the sureties, whereas in our case the object is the things serving as security. Lips., *AR* 701, n. 93, differs from Partsch on other, not very clear, grounds. See further Partsch, op. cit. 286, Rabel, *Z* 28 (1907), 328, n. 1, Gernet, *Dem.* i. 129, T. W. Beasley, *Bib. Ec. Hautes Ét.* 143 (1902), 31, 54, n. 3, Kränzlein, *Eig. und Bes.* 81.

frustrated the very purpose of the loan, which was to save Apatourios from losing the ship by forced sale. This suggests the possibility that X's right to attach the ship and crew was derived not from the simple fact that he had bought them with the right of redemption, but from Apatourios' attempt at a clandestine departure. There is a further difficulty. X mentions the attachment of the crew as subsequent to and separate from that of the ship and as having the specific purpose of covering any deficit if the value of the ship did not provide for the repayment of both loans. This is strange, since ship and crew seemed at the outset to be joint security for both loans. Here again it may be that this attachment is something exceptional not envisaged in the original contract. When it takes place X warns the representatives of the bank, who are releasing him from his suretyship in return for possession of the ship as a pledge, that the ship is also encumbered with the debt of ten minai due to Parmenon. Since normally in loans of this kind the value of the security would considerably exceed the amount of the debt, this might have been a plausible proposition, and it would protect X's interests in case the ship should prove to be worth more than the thirty minai owed to the bank. On the other hand X had to provide for the possibility that the ship would be worth less than the whole forty minai, and it is to meet this contingency that he also attaches the slaves. In the end the ship did in fact fetch forty minai, and the slaves were perhaps reconveyed to Apatourios. The facts that we are dealing here with πρᾶσις ἐπὶ λύσει of a movable, that the security is composite (ship and crew), that it secures two debts, that the creditor is surety to a bankrupt banker for one of the debts and is acting as a go-between in the other, and, finally, that there seems to be no provision for any interest on the loans, all contribute to making this case much less informative on the nature of the institution than at first sight it promised to be.[1]

The other relevant Demosthenic speech (37 *Pant.*) is more

[1] Besides locc. citt. in p. 273, n. 1 see Fine, *Horoi* 144 ff., whose discussion is impaired by being largely directed against the implausible surmises of I. A. Meletopoulos in *Πολέμων* 4 (1949), 41–72. Fine wrongly explains X's action in seizing the ship and crew as simply the exercise of his rights as owner; he himself has argued strongly for the view that πρᾶσις ἐπὶ λύσει is in essence a security transaction rather than a genuine sale. Finley, *Land* 35 and 231, n. 42, deprecates any attempt to generalize from the sale of Apatourios' ship. See also Hitz. 147, Pringsheim, *GLS* 117, n. 5, 192, n. 5.

rewarding, though it too presents a number of unsolved problems. The facts seem to be as follows. Pantainetos had obtained from a certain Telemachos rights in an *ergasterion*, a crushing mill with thirty slaves for working ore from a mining concession which he rented from the state at Maroneia. So far as we can tell, Telemachos owned the *ergasterion* unencumbered. We do not know what sum he was paid, but we may be certain that it was 105 minai plus *x*; for we find that Pantainetos had raised a loan of 105 minai from Mnesikles and two other creditors on the security of the property, and *x* would be the additional sum needed to make up the purchase price. When we last hear of the property it is sold unencumbered for 206 minai. The precise legal position before Pantainetos borrowed from Mnesikles cannot be stated. We are simply told that Mnesikles 'bought the property for Pantainetos from Telemachos who had it before' (5 ἐώνητ' ἐκεῖνος αὐτὰ τούτῳ παρὰ Τηλεμάχου τοῦ πρότερον κεκτημένου). Pantainetos now wishes to discharge his debt to Mnesikles and his two co-creditors and to do so borrows 105 minai from Nikoboulos, who delivers this speech, and Euergos. We have more details of this transaction. Mnesikles becomes warrantor, at the express wish of Pantainetos, to Nikoboulos and Euergos for the mill and slaves (5 πρατὴρ τοῦ ἐργαστηρίου καὶ τῶν ἀνδραπόδων ἡμῖν γίγνεται: cf. 29). These two then make a contract with Pantainetos under which he has a lease of the mill and slaves at a rent equivalent to interest at the rate of 12 per cent. per annum on the loan. He also has the right to release the property within a stated time (ibid., μισθοῦται οὗτος παρ' ἡμῶν τοῦ γιγνομένου τόκου τῷ ἀργυρίῳ: the contract refers to λύσις τούτῳ παρ' ἡμῶν ἔν τινι ῥητῷ χρόνῳ).[1] Nikoboulos then left Athens, and during his

[1] Probably the difference between the full purchase price of the security and the loan of 105 minai raised first from Mnesikles and co-creditors and then from Nikoboulos and Euergos (*x* above) was paid by Pantainetos himself, and it was this consideration which gave him a right to the property if he paid off the loan by the due date. See Hitz. 74 f., 117 ff., for the legal relationship of the parties at this point. Fine, *Horoi* 147, suggests that Telemachos was the first of the πρᾶσις ἐπὶ λύσει creditors and therefore stood at one point in the same relation to Mnesikles as later Mnesikles stood to Nikoboulos and Euergos. If we could be sure that Telemachos received only 105 minai this would be the best explanation for the difference between this sum and the final sale price of 206 minai; but we cannot be sure, and there seems just as much to be said for the view taken above, which makes Telemachos the original owner. So Hypoth. 1, Partsch, *GB* 355, n. 1, Pringsheim, *GLS* 206 ff., though the last named ignores the fact that 105 minai can hardly have been the full purchase price; this vitiates his view of Mnesikles'

absence Euergos, alleging that Pantainetos had defaulted on his rent-interest and on other obligations under the contract, took over possession of the *ergasterion* (6–7). In doing so he committed certain acts which led to his being condemned in a δίκη βλάβης. He continued, however, in possession of the mill, and Pantainetos still had the right to redeem within the appointed time.[1] Nikoboulos on his return is faced with an unwelcome alternative. If he wishes to receive interest on his loan, he must either join with Euergos in running the mill or he must make with Euergos a contract similar to the former contract he and Euergos had made with Pantainetos. To add to his discomfiture, some other alleged creditors of Pantainetos turned up claiming that they too had lent him money on the security of the mill; the precise nature of this alleged contract is not revealed. Nikoboulos calls on his warrantor, Mnesikles, to 'confirm' (βεβαιοῦν), presumably to confirm that the property was not charged with these other debts. This Mnesikles does. The other creditors none the less maintain their claim and make Nikoboulos a formal offer. Let him either take payment of his loan and be quit of the affair or let him pay to them what they alleged was due to them on the property. The latter proposal they justified by pointing out that the property was worth much more than the sum due to Nikoboulos and Euergos.[2] Nikoboulos and Euergos accept the former

legal position ('certainly not a mortgagee', yet surely Nikoboulos and Euergos are mortgagees, and they are creditors of Pantainetos for precisely the same sum). Finley, *Land* 32 ff., has a full analysis of the case: see especially 228, n. 33, for the view that the proper translation of πρατήρ is warrantor; note Dem. 37 *Pant.* 31, where ἀποδίδοσθαι (ἐωνήμεθα in some MSS.) and πρατὴρ εἶναι are contrasted.

[1] In other words this seizure by Euergos did not arise from default on the principal of the loan. It is clear from the context that Pantainetos' right of redemption remains throughout. Euergos' exploitation of the mill is the nearest approach to *antichresis* which we find in the sources.

[2] Hitz. 126 f., Rabel, *Die Verfügungsbeschränkungen* 22 ff. Strictly speaking the argument attributed to the other creditors by Nikoboulos in 12 is a *non sequitur*; they should have urged that the value of the property exceeded by a safe margin the amount of *all* the loans taken together, if they wished the proposal that Nikoboulos should discharge their debt to appear at all plausible. This *non sequitur* would be removed if we could take the subject of ἐδεδώκεμεν to be *all* the creditors, but this is scarcely possible. It becomes even more glaring if we assume, with Gernet, *Dem.* i. 263, n. to p. 235, that the rule implied here is that in such cases the creditor could only reimburse himself to the amount of his debt; for what possible inducement could there then have been for Nikoboulos to take upon himself the added risk, and what relevance in saying that the value of the property far exceeded the amount of his loan? If on the contrary the rule was that on default the creditors enjoyed the advantage of any excess, Nikoboulos, in paying off the other

proposal, but when the other creditors appear with the money a hitch occurs. They insist, very wisely according to Nikoboulos, that they will only hand over the money if Nikoboulos will become warrantor. He reluctantly consents in deference to an earnest plea from Pantainetos that he should. His debt is discharged, he becomes warrantor to the other creditors, but insists at the same time on getting from Pantainetos a formal release from any liability towards him. This attempt to guard his position availed him little, for we find later (29) that Pantainetos includes in his statement of claim a charge that Nikoboulos, in 'selling' the security, had violated his contract. The behaviour of the parties in this particular transaction needs careful analysing. The other creditors insist on Nikoboulos as warrantor (just as we may suppose he insisted on Mnesikles), not, as has been suggested, because Nikoboulos 'owned' the security and this ownership was a legal bar which prevented a sale ἐπὶ λύσει by Pantainetos to the other creditors, but because, as Nikoboulos says, no one had sufficient faith in Pantainetos to accept him as warrantor. Nikoboulos would no doubt have preferred, on receipt of his 105 minai, simply to release the property to Pantainetos, who would then have entered into a contract with the other creditors similar to his contract with Nikoboulos. This would have meant, however, that the other creditors would have had to rely upon the warranty of Pantainetos for the πρᾶσις ἐπὶ λύσει to them, and this risk they declined to take.[1] Finally the property is sold

creditors, would be speculating on the possibility of default with a large ὑπεροχή which he would not have to share with the other creditors. If such was the case the excess value of the property over the amount of Nikoboulos' debt was relevant, though it would still have been more logical to state the excess over all the debts taken together.

[1] Fine, *Horoi* 148, tries to prove from this case that in πρᾶσις ἐπὶ λύσει ownership passes to the creditor. 'Unless words have no meaning, Pantainetos would not have been described as lessee of property of which he still retained the ownership'; and later the reason that no one will accept Pantainetos as vendor (πρατήρ) must be that, since he had already sold the property ἐπὶ λύσει for 105 minai, 'the ownership of the *ergasterion* and slaves had been transferred to his creditors'. This is a circular argument and leaves out of account the fact that Pantainetos was not an ordinary lessee but had a redemption right to the property. The truth is that we really have to do here with the sale and resale of two different things, the property wholly unencumbered and the property with the condition attached that it must be released to Pantainetos if he could repay 105 minai within a stated time. (We can imagine a third saleable thing in this context, the right of Pantainetos to redeem the property, but we cannot say whether the Athenians would have entertained this concept.) Nikoboulos is exploiting the possible confusion of thought between

outright for 206 minai (31). In this sale Pantainetos is either not warrantor or not sole warrantor.[1] Three important and inter-related points must be kept constantly in mind for a proper understanding of this case. The first is that the 'price' or 'loan' for which the property stands security has been paid over not to the debtor, but, at the debtor's request, to a previous creditor. It is therefore a fiction within a fiction to regard the debtor here as 'seller'. The right of release (*λῦσις*) is provided for in the subsequent (or contemporaneous) lease of the property by the new creditor to the debtor. Secondly, the right of release had to be exercised within a certain period. We are not told what was to happen if the debt was not repaid within the period. On one view the creditor could then sell the property outright, but was obliged to pay the debtor any excess (*ὑπεροχή*) of the sale price over the amount of the debt; if there was any deficiency he could still take what other means were open to him to recover the deficiency from the debtor. The better view seems to be (see p. 276, n. 2) that the property then became the creditor's absolutely, and that, if he then chose to sell it, he would keep the excess but would not be able to recover a deficiency. The third point is the enormous margin between the 'price' of the property when 'sold' *ἐπὶ λύσει* and its price when sold outright.

these essentially different things when he says in 31 *ἃ γὰρ ἡμεῖς πέντε καὶ ἑκατὸν μνῶν ἀπεδόμεθα* (SA, *ἐωνήμεθα* vulg.), *ταῦθ' ὕστερον τριῶν ταλάντων καὶ δισχιλίων καὶ ἑξακοσίων ἀπέδου σύ*. This sentence illustrates admirably the dual nature of *πρᾶσις ἐπὶ λύσει*, half sale, half mortgage.

[1] *καίτοι τίς ἂν καθάπαξ πρατῆρά σ' ἔχων σοὶ δραχμὴν ἔδωκε μίαν;* (31, the sentence immediately following that quoted above). Nikoboulos is rebutting the charge that by 'selling' the property he had broken his contract (and thus presumably damaged Pantainetos' interests). He does so partly by producing witnesses to show that this 'sale' was at Pantainetos' request, partly by a twofold inference from the final sale; first that, since eventually 206 minai was realized by the sale outright, there was no reason to question the probability of Pantainetos' urging him to 'sell' *ἐπὶ λύσει* for about half that sum; second that, since Pantainetos could not sell the property outright on the strength of his own warranty, he would naturally have needed the warranty of Nikoboulos for the 'sale' *ἐπὶ λύσει*. The precise meaning of the sentence quoted above is doubtful. The French translators take *καθάπαξ* with *πρατῆρα* to mean 'you only, without other warrantors' (Dareste 'sans offrir d'autre garantie', Gernet 'sans autre garantie'). Others compare the use of *καθάπαξ* in 50 meaning 'sale outright' and suppose the sense here is 'warrantor of a sale outright' (Sandys, *Dem. Select Priv. Or.* i ad loc., Finley, *Land* 229, n. 38). This fits less well. *καθάπαξ* is emphatic by position; but Nikoboulos is not saying 'who, having you as warrantor *for a sale outright* . . .?'; rather, 'who, having *you* as a warrantor . . .?'. It would ruin his argument to imply that Pantainetos might have been satisfactory as warrantor in a sale *ἐπὶ λύσει*.

This gives a rough measure of what would have been the ὑπεροχή if the debt had not been paid within the agreed period. The behaviour of Pantainetos, Nikoboulos, and the other creditors in this incident suggests—it cannot be said to do more—that in that event the ὑπεροχή would have gone to Nikoboulos, with a dubious claim of the other creditors to recover their alleged debt out of it.[1]

Horoi marking πρᾶσις ἐπὶ λύσει transactions number 122 (112 from Athens, 1 from Amorgos, 8 from Lemnos, 1 from Skyros). Of these 10 yield nothing beyond their bare classification under this category. In the remaining 112 only 8 refer to a written agreement (p. 270, above). The usual formula is the word ὅρος, followed by the property in the genitive with πεπραμένου (-ης) ἐπὶ λύσει agreeing with it, the creditor or creditors in the dative, and a numeral for the amount of the debt. In fourteen cases (eleven from Athens) the inscription begins with the archon's name. Only once is there the bare possibility that the debtor's name has been included. Three (possibly four) state specifically that the πρᾶσις ἐπὶ λύσει is to guarantee a dowry.[2] Apart from the statistical information which this large body of inscriptions furnishes, individual *horoi* in this class shed occasional light on the kinds of property involved, the types of creditor, whether single or in groups, the question of multiple creditors, and other like topics.

Finally, the sale of a confiscated house in the poletai records for 367/6 B.C., discussed above in connexion with hypothec (p. 270), is equally relevant here.

[1] Fine, *Horoi* 149, 160, following Hitz. 77 f., Beauch. iii. 249 ff., Lips., *AR* 704, argues that, because πρᾶσις ἐπὶ λύσει was in form a sale, the ὑπεροχή naturally went to the creditor. Though the conclusion is probably right the argument again seems to be circular. He makes the important point (149) that Nikoboulos never counters the claim of the other creditors that they too had a debt charged on the property with the assertion that this was legally impossible. This proves that it was permissible for a property which had been 'sold' ἐπὶ λύσει to stand security for another debt. We cannot tell whether this other debt was alleged to have been contracted before or after that of Nikoboulos, nor what its precise form was. Fine argues strongly that it was hypothec, but πρᾶσις ἐπὶ λύσει cannot be absolutely ruled out.

[2] Finley, *Land*, nos. 11–111, 18A–101C in App. III and Table B on p. 173. For the significance of the archon dating Finley 177 ff. For the possible instance of a debtor's name ibid., no. 39 (rejected by Finley 202, n. 2). Nos. 49, 82, 82A, and possibly 93 concern dowries. In no. 57 the 'sale' is παιδὶ Καλλιστράτου. If this is an instance of πρᾶσις ἐπὶ λύσει in place of ἀποτίμημα for securing the leasing of an orphan's estate it is unique; on it see Finley 244, n. 59, Fine, *Horoi* 161 f.

§ 6. *Rules in pledge, hypothec, and sale with right of redemption*

For pledge the evidence affords only the scantiest details. A gold cup is offered as pledge for a loan of 16 minai. It is to be redeemed on payment of 20 minai, the 4 minai being described as interest. The date for repayment is only vaguely fixed, but we may assume that if the contract had been negotiated it would have stipulated a more exact time limit, after which, on default, the cup would have become the absolute property of the pledgee.[1] In another case a body of industrial slaves is pledged to Demosthenes' father for a loan of 40 minai. The pledgee uses these slaves for a number of years, making from their products as much as 12 minai a year (or perhaps 11 minai allowing for the maintenance of the slaves) to serve as interest on the loan. At the pledgee's death his heir's guardian (Aphobos) has possession of the slaves and lends a further 5 minai on them to the original pledger, charging him interest. Principal and interest of this second loan seem to have been repaid before the guardian came to account. When the heir came of age the slaves had disappeared, and the heir includes in his claim against his guardian the value of the original loan (40 minai) plus 2 talents for the income brought in by the slaves' products during the preceding ten years. It is safe to assume that the pledge was worth considerably more than the amount of the loan, at least when the loan was first made. For in the first place the pledge earned for the pledgee so much that, reckoning 12 per cent. as a normal rate of interest, he would have enjoyed that rate of interest and recovered his capital within seven years. And in the second place the pledgee's willingness to lend a further 5 minai on the security of the same pledge is strong evidence that in his judgement the pledge was worth more than the original loan. This disparity must have had important consequences, but we cannot tell what they were, since we do not know what were the conditions for redemption; in particular we do not know whether there was any limit of time, either before which the pledger should not be permitted to redeem or after which, if he had not redeemed, the pledge became the pledgee's property. This in turn makes it difficult to understand why Demosthenes claimed from his guardian the

[1] For the details see p. 260.

amount of the original loan rather than the value of the missing slaves. All that we can safely say about this is that if the pledger still had the right to redeem from Demosthenes by payment of 40 minai slaves of the same value as those he had originally pledged, Demosthenes is unaccountably modest in limiting his claim on the guardian under this head to 40 minai. It is better on the whole to suppose that either the pledger or some other of his creditors had recovered possession of the pledge before Demosthenes began his suit. This case can only with violence be used to prove that in Athenian law the loss of the pledge fell on the pledgee.[1] Rather better, though by no means conclusive, evidence for the existence of this rule is the case of the horse (perhaps pledged, but possibly sold ἐπὶ λύσει) which died in the creditor's possession.[2] The second loan in the Aphobos case is, in effect, a loan by the original pledgee to the original pledger. It sheds no light on the rules which governed the pledging of the same object to a second creditor.[3]

[1] For the details see p. 261 and ibid., n. 2, above. None of the authors there cited has wholly resolved the difficulty. Fine, *Horoi* 77, suggests that possibly the 40 minai had been repaid and pocketed by Aphobos. This is not precisely what Demosthenes says, but it could be reconciled with what he does say. § 25 of the speech shows that Aphobos had succeeded in shedding darkness round the circumstances in which he had lost possession of the slaves; Hitz. 26 suggests that he may have alleged that the slaves had never belonged to the pledger and that the real owner had claimed them. Demosthenes may therefore have felt it safer to limit his claim to the forty minai, which Aphobos clearly owed, since he could not produce the pledge which originally guaranteed the loan. Lips., *AR* 705, n. 105, deduces from this passage, together with the passage from Lys. 8 *Ag. Coass.* 10, that in pledge loss of the thing had to be borne by the creditor. He is followed by Lauffer, *Bergwerkssklaven* i. 83. They do not take sufficient account of the fact that the Aphobos suit is not between pledgee and pledger, but between pledgee and his ward; for no matter what the position was between Aphobos and the pledger, Demosthenes claimed that his father's estate at his death included a pledge securing a debt to him of 40 minae, and for this sum Aphobos had to account. A similar criticism applies to Finley, *Land* 116, when he relies heavily on this passage as evidence that the Athenian idea of hypothecation, like the reality, was purely substitutive; for he assumes that in actual fact Demosthenes' loss was much greater than the 40 minae, but that, blinded by the substitutive concept, he did not recalculate the value of the slaves on the market; but we cannot be sure that Demosthenes' loss was in fact greater. See also W. Felgentrager, *Antikes Lösungsrecht* (Berlin and Leipzig, 1933) 71 f., J. Korver, *Mnem.* 10 (1942), 15 f., Kränzlein, *Eig. und Bes.* 88, 115, Hitz. 95, Rabel, *Die Verfügungsbeschränkungen* 16.

[2] See pp. 260 and 261, n. 1.

[3] See p. 261, n. 2 and n. 1, above. Where, as in this case, the pledge is something whose value depends on its productiveness and that value is greatly in excess of the loan the pledger will stand a reasonable chance of raising a further loan on the same pledge, since it will be in the interest of the pledgee to hold on to it.

Turning to the other two types of real security here in question we shall first examine the rules normally followed in connexion with repayment of the debt. Often a term for repayment would have been agreed in the contract. Some writers assume that this was always the case. It need not have been, and the failure of any *horos* to refer to a terminal date may suggest that in πρᾶσις ἐπὶ λύσει at least it was not even usual, since it would have been in the interest of the creditor to publicize a terminal date if there was one. When there was no terminal date the debtor, whether in hypothec or in πρᾶσις ἐπὶ λύσει, would have retained indefinitely the right to release the property from the charge on it by repaying the debt, so long of course as he was punctual in the payment of interest. Default in the payment of interest, as distinct from capital, might lead to the creditor's taking over possession of the security, while the debtor still retained his right of redemption. This seems to have occurred in the Pantainetos case. Where a term of payment was fixed and the debtor was in default, he was described as ὑπερήμερος and his default as ὑπερημερία, though these words occur more frequently in surviving speeches to describe failure to pay a judgement debt.[1] We have at least two examples in the literature where a term is implied, though in neither can we say what precisely it was. In the Apatourios case the speaker says he 'made a purchase' of the security 'until the debtor should repay' the money lent. This vague phrase must cover some, probably rather short, term for repayment, since clearly neither creditor nor debtor was contemplating a loan for an indefinite period; the security, a ship and its crew, would have been quite unsuited for such a loan. In the Pantainetos case the contract provided for redemption within a stated period, but we are not told how long the period was.[2] These are both

[1] Lips. *AR* 701, Fine, *Horoi* 85 ff., for the ὑπερήμερος. In England 'chief rents', in Scotland the mortgage known as 'absolute disposition with back-bond' are parallels for real security in which the debtor has a continuing right to redeem but no fixed term within which he must repay. The creditor can only recover his capital by transferring his rights for a lump sum to a third party; see W. H. Buckler and D. M. Robinson, *AJA* 16 (1912), 62. For the possibility of a permanent right of redemption see Fine, *Horoi* 159 quoting Hitz. 80 against Lips., *AR* 703, n. 99. For the life-term of loans Finley, *Land* 86 f. For Pantainetos' default on interest payments see above, p. 276, n. 1. Fine, op. cit. 85, holds that in Dem. 45 *Steph.* i. 70 ὑπερήμερος is used of default on capital as opposed to default on interest.

[2] See pp. 272 ff., 274 ff.

πράσεις ἐπὶ λύσει. We have no specific instance of hypothec with a terminal date, and therefore no direct evidence for the procedure followed when the debtor in hypothec was in default. With evidence as scanty as this it is largely on *a priori* grounds that we conclude that where there was a terminal date either in hypothec or in πρᾶσις ἐπὶ λύσει the creditor in cases of default acquired unrestricted ownership of the property, though there is a certain amount of indirect evidence to confirm the conclusion. On the other hand, we cannot draw any valid distinctions between procedures proper to hypothec and to πρᾶσις ἐπὶ λύσει. We cannot, for example, say that in hypothec the creditor must 'enter' (ἐμβατεύειν) whereas in πρᾶσις ἐπὶ λύσει his ownership, hitherto restricted by the debtor's right to redeem, automatically became absolute, and that therefore the latter type of security was safer and more convenient for the creditor.[1] Probably the debtor in πρᾶσις ἐπὶ λύσει was normally in possession, and, if the creditor wished to evict him, he would have had to adopt some procedure very similar to 'entering', while, on the other hand, we cannot rule out the possibility that in some cases the creditor in hypothec was already in possession and therefore would not need to 'enter'. Whichever the type of security, the creditor could no doubt use the δίκη ἐξούλης against a debtor who either refused to yield possession or attempted to reassert it.[2]

We must next consider whether, when there was a terminal date and the debtor defaulted, the creditor was bound to sell the security and pay the debtor any excess over the debt, while retaining a claim against him if the security realized less than the amount of the debt, or whether the security was purely substitutive, so that its seizure by the creditor obliterated the debt, whatever their respective values. This is a most important issue. Basically it is the issue whether the classical law of Athens had

[1] Paoli, *St. Dir.* 157 f., argued that in pledge and hypothec under the civil (as opposed to the commercial) law there was never a maturity date and that is why we never hear of foreclosure in connexion with them. This view was refuted by Fine 84 ff. on the basis of Dem. 36 *For Phorm.* 4–6, 42 *Phain.* 9, 28 f., 45 *Steph.* i. 70, 28 *Aphob.* ii. 17 f., *IG* ii². 43 (Tod, *GHI* 123), 36–42, passages which all imply foreclosure; the refutation depends on assuming that some at least of the cases are in fact hypothec. It applies equally to La Pira's modified version of Paoli's theory in *BIDR* 41 (1933), 314–16, which held that in hypothec, if the debtor defaulted at maturity, the creditor took possession but the debtor retained a permanent right of redemption.

[2] See p. 218, above, and on 'entry' Jörs, *Z* 40 (1919), 77 ff.

achieved the relatively advanced economic contrivance of second or third hypothecs, which enables one piece of property to guarantee more than one loan, or whether it remained under the ban of the much cruder substitutive principle. Both views have been, and still are, strongly held. In considering the evidence it is well to keep in mind the distinction between established rules of law, whether customary or statutory, which would be held to bind the parties in the absence of specific agreements between them to the contrary, and rules made by parties for themselves in particular contracts. These latter rules might, by following a certain pattern over a period of time, modify the former.[1]

Turning to the evidence, a good deal of weight has been placed by those who believe that return of the ὑπεροχή was normal practice on Dem. 31 *Onet.* ii. 5 f. This much-disputed text will have to be considered in connexion with dotal ἀποτίμημα, but something must be said of it here. Demosthenes was owed ten talents by his guardian, Aphobos, as a result of his successful suit against him. In attempting to execute the judgement he tried to occupy some land and a house belonging, he alleged, to

[1] Hitz. 82 ff., 87 ff., 121 ff., 131 f.; in the classical period the concept is basically substitutive, but contractual practice (provision, for example, for second hypothecs or for the creditor to sell the security and claim any deficit from the debtor) is beginning to sap its foundations. So Beauch. iii. 272 ff. Papp. 141 ff. contends that already in the fourth century the substitutive principle is outmoded and that, save in cases of ἀποτίμημα, the creditor in cases of default was bound to sell the security and pay the debtor the excess, if any. Lips., *AR* 702, agrees, save that he would not except ἀποτίμημα cases; so too Mitteis, *Z* 30 (1909), 447. L. Raape, *Der Verfall des gr. Pfandes* (Halle, 1912), 10 ff., returned to the view of Hitzig (cf. review by Koschaker, *KVGR* 14 (1912), 508), as did Manigk, *RE* s.v. *hyperocha* (1914), 306 ff., though he considerably widens the extent of the exceptions to the substitutive principle, holding that wherever a *horos* mentions the amount of the loan—and that is in the majority of cases—the contract would have provided for the excess to be paid to the debtor and the deficit to be claimable; this last is a plausible point, since on any other assumption the debt secured was of little interest to third parties. Paoli, *St. Dir.* 160, believing in a continuative hypothec, cannot agree wholly with either view, but is nearer to Hitzig than to Pappoulias. Fine, *Horoi* 62 f., 94 f., 160 f., argues that since in hypothec the debtor retained possession and ownership of the security he could borrow further on the ὅσῳ πλείονος ἄξιον: this implies that in the event of foreclosure he could claim the ὑπεροχή; πρᾶσις ἐπὶ λύσει by its very nature ruled out such a claim (quoting Lips., *AR* 704, 'das folgt aus der Verkaufsnatur des Geschäfts'). Finley, *Land* index s.v. 'Security, value, substitution, surplus and foreclosure', especially 116 f. 'the idea of hypothecation, like the reality, was purely substitutive'; 294, n. 7, failure of the word ὑπεροχή to displace the clumsy ὅσῳ πλείονος ἄξιον 'is a clear sign that pure substitution remained the overwhelmingly prevalent form of security'. Kränzlein, *Eig. und Bes.* 86 'das griechische Pfand jener Zeit war Ersatz- und Verfall- nicht Sicherungspfand'.

Aphobos. His entry to the land was barred by *ἐξαγωγή* on the part of Onetor, who asserted that he had had this land hypothecated to him (*ἀποτιμήσασθαι*) as security for the dowry of his sister on her marriage to Aphobos and that the land was now forfeit to him because his sister had been divorced (30 *Onet.* i. 2, 8). Demosthenes then brought a *δίκη ἐξούλης* against him. His case was that the hypothecation of the property to Onetor and his occupancy of it were a collusive fraud; the dowry had never been paid and there had not been a divorce. Onetor had made inconsistent claims. At first he had claimed that the dowry was 80 minai, secured as to 1 talent on the land and as to 20 minai on the house. Thinking that this demand might seem exorbitant to a jury, he changed his tune and claimed that the dowry amounted to 1 talent secured on the land; but he also at this stage claimed that the land was worth at least 3 talents and the house (which apparently he had ceded to Demosthenes) 1 talent, and he implies that, could he but recover the 1 talent due to him for the dowry and cede the land as well as the house, he would be allowing Demosthenes to acquire by his distraint property worth about 3 talents net. Dem. 31 *Onet.* ii. 6 *ἐν ὑμῖν ἐτόλμησεν εἰπεῖν ὡς οὐκ ἀποστερεῖ μ' ὅσῳ πλείονος ἄξιόν ἐστι ταλάντου, καὶ ταῦτ' αὐτὸς τιμήσας οὐκ ἄξιον εἶναι πλείονος. . . .* 7 *ὅταν δέ σοι μὴ συμφέρῃ, τἀναντία πάλιν ἡ μὲν οἰκία ταλάντου, διότι νῦν ἐγὼ ταύτην ἔχω, τοῦ δὲ χωρίου τὸ περιὸν οὐκ ἐλάττονος ἢ δυοῖν ἄξιον.* The crux is what we are meant to understand Onetor as implying by the statement attributed to him that 'he will not be depriving me of what the land is worth above the sum of one talent', when he himself, Demosthenes adds, had valued it as not worth more than that sum. Two views have been held. According to one Onetor is being made to say that in fact the land is not worth more than the one talent owed to him and that he is therefore not depriving Demosthenes of the excess, since it did not exist. According to the other view, Onetor is insisting that the land is worth considerably more than the one talent for which he alleges it stood security for the dowry; this excess, he implies, will be available for Demosthenes. It is the latter who counters with the point that, on Onetor's own showing, the land is not worth more than one talent and that the excess is therefore illusory. The passage is difficult to evaluate, since Demosthenes' main concern is to throw suspicion on the whole proceeding by stressing the inconsistencies in Onetor's pleadings, and he may well have been guilty himself of some sophistry in doing this. Allowing for that, it still seems that the second view is right, especially in the light of the sentence quoted from 7; and, if it is, the clear implication is that in this kind of security (ἀποτίμημα for return of a dowry on divorce) the husband (here represented by his creditor) had a claim on the ὑπεροχή. Had it not been so, Demosthenes' answer to this point would not have been 'at one time you valued the security at quite another figure', but rather 'the value of the security is quite irrelevant, since, if you win the case, it will be wholly yours'.[1] Since securing the return of a dowry in this way was probably a common occurrence in the fourth century, it may have exerted considerable influence on methods of securing loans.

The contract document cited in Dem. 35 *Lakrit.* 10 ff. furnishes another piece of indirect evidence, indirect because it is a bottomry contract. The document is now generally agreed to be genuine. The loan is to be repaid within twenty days of the safe arrival of the ship at Athens. The creditors are to have unrestricted control of the security (τὴν ὑποθήκην ἀνέπαφον κρατεῖν) from the time of arrival till the debt is paid. If the loan is not paid by the due date the creditors may hypothecate the security or sell it at the prevailing price (τὰ ὑποκείμενα ἐξέστω ὑποθεῖναι καὶ ἀποδόσθαι τῆς ὑπαρχούσης τιμῆς). If by the sale they recover less than their loan they may distrain for the deficit on all the property of the debtors. Thus we have here not pure substitution, since that takes no account of the relative values of pledge and debt, nor collateral security in the modern sense, since that involves compulsory sale of the pledge and payment to the debtor of any excess of the price realized above the amount of the debt. Here the creditors are allowed, not compelled, to sell, and there is no mention of a possible excess. If they choose to sell they retain by the contract the right to recover any deficit, if they can, from the debtor, but only on condition that they have sold at the market price. What is meant by the right of the creditors in case of default to hypothecate (ὑποθεῖναι) the pledge

[1] Hitz. went astray on this case; cf. Lips., *AR* 702, n. 95, Paoli, *St. Dir.* 182 f., Fine, *Horoi* 125, 139 f. Finley, *Land* 294, n. 7, is not clear: 'On the surplus Demosthenes had full freedom of action', yet he does not seem to take this as an exception to the rule of pure substitution. Cf. Wolff, *Fest. Rabel* ii. 299 ff., who also seems to reject the view that this is an exception to that rule.

is less easy to say. We must suppose that they would only have been tempted to do this if the value of the pledge at the time of default was less than the debt, and we may conjecture that in effect it would have involved inducing a third party to advance a sum of money to them for the transference to him of their rights *vis-à-vis* the debtors, or, in other words, hypothecating to him their right to distrain for the ἔλλειπον. This might through bargaining be more attractive to them than themselves selling the pledge and distraining.[1] We have here then a modification of the system of pure substitution, made by means of a special clause in a bottomry contract and serving principally the interests of the creditor, though the debtor is protected against a collusive sale at a low price aimed at increasing the ἔλλειπον. If such clauses were at all common, they too would have tended to widen the breach in the system of pure substitution in other types of security.[2]

The cases which have been assigned above (pp. 262–79) to hypothec or sale with right of redemption (only very few with any certainty to one rather than the other) yield little on the question of ὑπεροχή and ἔλλειπον. The details of the Dikaiogenes case (Isai. 5 *Dikaiog.* 21 ff., pp. 264 ff. above) are too confused to be used with confidence.[3] In Isai. 6 *Philokt.* 33 a creditor

[1] Hitz. 86, Beauch. iii. 271 ff., J. C. Naber, *Mnem.* 32 (1904), 87, who points out that τῆς ὑπαρχούσης τιμῆς must go with ἀποδόσθαι alone, Manigk, *RE* s.v. *hyperocha* 309, Finley, *Land* 298, n. 28. Manigk appears to doubt the explanation suggested in the text of the creditor's right to hypothecate the pledge.

[2] But there is special need for caution in generalizing from bottomry to loans secured on landed property. The latter were perforce loans made by citizens to citizens, since only citizens could own land. This restriction did not apply to bottomry loans; in the Lakritos case, for example, one creditor is an Athenian, the other an Euboean, the two borrowers are Phaselites. Where the creditor in such a case was an Athenian he had, in addition to the risks of a maritime enterprise, to reckon the risks attendant on recovering from a foreign debtor. No wonder then that the substitution should be modified in his favour in such a way as to give him some chance of passing on at a price his somewhat speculative right of distraint on the debtor's property in the event of an ἔλλειπον.

[3] We have supposed (loc. cit.) that the property there referred to had been sold with right of redemption by Dikaiogenes and that he had had value (τιμή) for it. Menexenos, the plaintiff, claims two-thirds of the property free of all encumbrance. He is demanding that Dikaiogenes should repay the value to the creditors and then divide out the property thus released in the proportion of two to one between himself and his opponents. This might be taken to imply the absence of any concept of ὑπεροχή; otherwise why does not the plaintiff content himself with a straightforward claim against Dikaiogenes for the value of two-thirds of the property? It is even possible that there was no terminal date for the loan. But all

recovers a loan secured on a house by releasing the house, but we cannot say whether this was by bargaining with the borrower or by virtue of some clause in the contract, nor what was the ratio of the debt to the value of the house when released.[1] On the better view of Dem. 28 *Aphob.* ii. 17–18 the 'remainder' of his property to which Demosthenes refers (τὰ περιόντ' αὐτῶν) is not the excess value of the property if sold up over the debt incurred for his liturgy, but such of his property as he had not hypothecated, the words τἀμαυτοῦ πάντα being rhetorical exaggeration (p. 269, above). Dem. 33 *Apatour.* 5–12 describes the sale of a ship by, or with the consent of, the purchaser ἐπὶ λύσει which brings in the exact amount of two separate debts secured jointly on the ship and its slave crew. We do not know what happened to the slaves; but if they were returned to the borrower, and if this could be regarded as a normal instance of default by a debtor who was ὑπερήμερος, then we should have here the equivalent of the return of the excess value to the defaulting debtor. But there is no evidence to support the first hypothesis and the balance of evidence is against the second.[2] The Pantainetos case is, on the whole, easier to understand on the assumption that if the debtor failed to exercise his right of redemption within the stated time

this is bedevilled by the subsequent suggestion that Menexenos would have been satisfied by Dikaiogenes' declining to confirm the title of the holders of the property if he, Menexenos, tried to evict them. How could Menexenos have expected Dikaiogenes to do this when he himself says that the latter had had value for the property? And what would have been the position about the ὑπεροχή if Menexenos had been able to evict the creditors through Dikaiogenes' refusal to confirm their title? A conceivable explanation is that Dikaiogenes was conceding to his opponents the right to redeem, but insisting that they would in that case have to provide the redemption money (τιμή), while Menexenos maintains that the alleged compromise put upon Dikaiogenes the onus of redeeming and redividing. In other words perhaps the key to the puzzle lies in the risk and cost of redeeming the property. This explanation would only make sense if this case was governed by the principle of pure substitution.

[1] The wording suggests, though it does not absolutely necessitate, the principle of substitution.

[2] For the details of the case see pp. 272 ff., above. It could be argued that Apatourios' protest (*Apatour.* 11) against the speaker's insistence that the pledge should cover the 10 minai owing to the foreigner as well as the 30 owing to the bank (ἠρώτα κτλ. quoted on p. 272) is incompatible with the substitution principle, since on that principle the amount of the debt was irrelevant. If the reply to this is that this is not a normal case of a debtor who is in default, but that the creditors are recovering their loan by a forced sale because the borrower had attempted illegally to make off with the pledge, we then get the somewhat anomalous conclusion that the borrower in these circumstances was better off than one who was merely in default.

the creditor would enjoy the benefit of the considerable excess of the value of the pledge over the amount of the debt (see above, pp. 274 ff., especially 278, 276, n. 2). The epigraphic evidence on this problem is best considered in connexion with the closely related problem of multiple creditors (p. 290, n. 3), to which we now turn.

Besides the simple case where a piece of property serves as security for a debt to a single creditor, it may secure debts to more than one creditor either jointly or severally and, if severally, for loans contracted simultaneously or successively. The orators provide several instances of property securing more than one loan in this way, but none of the instances reveals very much as to the relationships between the several creditors. In the Pantainetos case (Dem. 37) Nikoboulos and Euergos advanced to Pantainetos forty-five and sixty minai respectively on the security of the mill by *πρᾶσις ἐπὶ λύσει*. In the absence of Nikoboulos from Athens Euergos felt bound to take over possession of the mill from Pantainetos owing to the latter's default in the payment of interest and other breaches of his contract. On his return Nikoboulos is vexed to find this change in the situation, but makes no suggestion that Euergos was not entitled to take possession of the mill on their joint behalf. We may assume therefore that he was so entitled. Nikoboulos alleges that he then had two alternatives open to him; he could either join with Euergos in exploiting the mine, sharing the profits presumably in proportion to his share of the loan; or he could enter into a new contract in which Euergos stood towards him in the same relation as Pantainetos had previously stood. We cannot say whether these rights accrued to the two creditors by virtue of general rules or of particular terms embodied in the original contract.[1]

In Dem. 35 *Lakrit.* 12 the two joint creditors in a bottomry loan are allowed by the contract to seize and dispose of the pledge jointly or severally in case of default (*ἔστω ἡ πρᾶξις . . . καὶ ἑνὶ ἑκατέρῳ τῶν δανεισάντων καὶ ἀμφοτέροις*). Joint loans on real security are also referred to in Dem. 42 *Phain.* 28, where the words used are *Παμφίλῳ φησὶν καὶ Φειδώλεῳ Ῥαμνουσίοις κοινῇ ἐνοφείλειν* (Bekker: *ἒν ὀφείλειν* or *ὀφείλειν codd.*), in Dem. 50 *Polykl.* 13 and 28, and in Dem. 56 *Dionysod.* 6, another bottomry

[1] Hitz. 118, Dareste, *Dem.* i. 272, Beauch. iii. 293 f. Note that Euergos' seizure is not for default on repayment of the capital; cf. p. 276, n. 1, above.

loan, in which, though there are two joint creditors, only one of them is entered in the contract. These passages give little more than the bare fact of joint creditorship.[1]

There are also references in the orators to the practice of borrowing from a separate, independent creditor on the security of property already standing security for a debt. To lend thus was ἐπιδανείζειν, to borrow ἐπιδανείζεσθαι. Demosthenes uses the word in two bottomry cases, 34 *Ag. Phorm.* 6, 22, 50 and 35 *Lakrit.* 21, 22; in both cases it is claimed that the second loan was illicit because ruled out by the contract with the first creditor, which may, though it does not necessarily, imply that but for the term in the contract the second hypothec would have been valid.[2] In this context, however, it is particularly dangerous to argue from bottomry to landed security, since the risks of the first creditor would differ so widely in the two types of loan.[3]

Our sources do not permit us to say with any certainty how far an owner's right to alienate property which he had pledged in any of the above ways was limited. On one view he could do so, and the property passed to the buyer with the encumbrance attached. On another and on the whole better-supported view a sale without the consent of the mortgagee was invalid. A passage in the Paroemiographers (*Corp. Paroem. Gr.* i. 405, Hesych. s.v. ἐν λευκώμασι: quoted below on p. 306) refers to the practice

[1] Beauch. iii. 295 f., Finley, *Land* 108 f. That the loan in the Phainippos passage was on the security of land can only be taken for certain if we accept Bekker's reading and translate ἐνοφείλειν 'owe upon the land'. Demosthenes 32, 33, and 34 against Zenothemis, Apatourios, and Phormion respectively all raise issues of joint loans, but are reserved for consideration under bottomry. Gernet, *Dem.* i. 147, sharply distinguishes the rules of commercial from those of civil law in this matter: 'le droit commercial, à la différence du droit civil, admet qu'en vertu du lien d'association, l'action ne se divise ni activement ni passivement.'

[2] *An. Bekk.* (*Λέξ. Ῥητ.*) 259 ἐπιδανεῖσαι τί ἐστιν· ὅταν δεδανεικότος τινὸς καὶ ἐνεχυριάσαντος οἰκίαν ἢ χωρίον, ἐπιδανείσῃ τις ἕτερος ἐπὶ τοῖς αὐτοῖς ἐνεχύροις, ἐπιδανεῖσαι λέγεται. But ἐπιδανείζειν sometimes means nothing more than δανείζειν ἐπί 'to lend on'; see T. Reinach, *RÉG* 22 (1909), 242, n. 1 on *IG* xii. 7. 515, Korver, *De Terminologie van het Creditwesen in het Griekschk* 131 ff., Finley, *Land* 297, n. 21. Dem. 35 *Lakrit.* 36 and 52 suggest that in cases of emergency in bottomry a second hypothec was allowed without the concurrence of the first creditor; see Gernet, *Dem.* i. 177, 192, 197.

[3] For the evidence of the *horoi* on multiple creditors see Finley, *Land*, Ch. viii and Tables A and B on pp. 172 f. They give the impression that it was not uncommon for one piece of property to secure loans by several creditors; but owing to their extreme brevity they can shed very little light on the relationships between the several creditors. For the evidence of the poletai records of 367/6 see above, p. 270. We seem there to have evidence for a preferred creditor.

of publishing on whitened boards details of proposed sales of property or slaves ἵνα εἴ τις αἰτιάσασθαι βουληθείη ἐπ' ἀδείας ἔχοι ἐντυχὼν τῷ λευκώματι. There is no specific reference in the passage to Athens. Theophrastos, in a passage from his *Laws* (quoted in Stobaeus, *Floril.* xliv. 22 Meineke, 20 Hense), in describing rules obtaining in various cities for publicity before the sale of property, has the following sentence: παρὰ δὲ τισὶ προκηρύττειν κελεύουσι πρὸ τοῦ κατακυρωθῆναι πένθ' ἡμέρας συνεχῶς, εἴ τις ἐνίσταται ἢ ἀντιποιεῖται τοῦ κτήματος ἢ τῆς οἰκίας· ὡσαύτως δὲ καὶ ἐπὶ τῶν ὑποθέσεων, ὥσπερ καὶ ἐν τοῖς Κυζικηνῶν. Later he implies that the purpose of such rules was to make plain εἰ ἐλεύθερα καὶ ἀνέπαφα καὶ τὰ αὑτοῦ πωλεῖ δικαίως. Reading these passages together we can perhaps say that there were cities in Greece (certainly Kyzikos among them) where notice of an intended sale had to be given in order that not only a putative rival owner of the property, but also one who had a mortgage on it, might intervene. The resulting dispute between the intervener and the seller would then have to be settled judicially before the sale could proceed.[1]

It is more difficult to decide with what probability we can assign a rule of this kind to Athens. None of the cases cited from the orators is conclusive. In Isai. 2 *Menekl.* 28 ff. Menekles proposed to sell some land in order to satisfy the claim of an orphan of whom he had been the guardian. His brother, wishing to embarrass him, successfully banned the sale. διεκώλυε τὸ χωρίον πραθῆναι, ἵνα κατοκώχιμον γένηται καὶ ἀναγκασθῇ τῷ ὀρφανῷ ἀποστῆναι . . . ἀπηγόρευε τοῖς ὠνουμένοις μὴ ὠνεῖσθαι. Because of this intervention Menekles later brought a δίκη ἀπορρήσεως against his brother.[2] There is, however, absolutely nothing to suggest that the brother's claim to intervene rested on any kind of mortgage interest in the land. He may well, for example, have been claiming that he was joint heir to the land, or sole owner of that particular part of the inherited estate.[3] A rather more promising case comes in Dem. 53 *Nikostr.* 10. Nikostratos wished to raise money either by selling or by mortgaging a farm. His brother, Arethousios, successfully prevented him from doing so

[1] Papp. 122 ff., Rabel, *Verfügungsbeschränkungen* 12 ff. For Partsch's interpretation of the somewhat obscure final clause quoted from the Paroemiographers see p. 306, n. 1, below.

[2] On ἀπόρρησις in general see Paoli, *St. Dir.* 187 ff.

[3] For a further discussion of this passage see below, p. 307 and compare A. Biscardi, *RHD* 36 (1958), 336, Kränzlein, *Eig. und Bes.* 132.

on the ground that money was owing to him (perhaps on the security of the farm, though this is in dispute). *ὁ Ἀρεθούσιος . . . οὐδένα εἴα οὔτε ὠνεῖσθαι οὔτε τίθεσθαι, ὡς ἐνοφειλομένου αὐτῷ ἀργυρίου.* The words used certainly could mean that there was an absolute legal bar on Nikostratos' alienating or hypothecating the farm without the consent of Arethousios because the latter had a mortgage on it. This in fact seems the most natural view. On the other hand, it has been maintained that the words need mean nothing more than that Arethousios succeeded in fact in putting off prospective buyers or creditors, or that there was a special clause in his loan agreement with his brother which reserved to him the right to ban sale or further hypothecation, or finally that the money owed to Arethousios need not have been *secured by a mortgage.*[1] The last, and perhaps the most persuasive, item of evidence from the orators comes in Dem. 27 *Aphob.* i. 27. In the estate left by Demosthenes' father there were twenty industrial slaves which were held by him as security for a loan of forty minai. Demosthenes alleges that his guardian had lent a further 500 drachmai on the security of these same slaves, whereas his duty as guardian required him actually to prevent any further loan being raised on the security of these slaves (*δέον αὐτόν, εἰ καί τις ἄλλος ἐβούλετ' εἰς ταῦτα συμβαλεῖν, τοῦτον διακωλύειν ἐπίτροπόν γ' ὄντα*). There seems a fairly clear implication that the guardian, as first creditor, had power to stop a second hypothec on the slaves.[2]

We cannot say whether failure to intervene when a sale or second hypothec had taken place after due notice barred a mortgagee from action subsequently. (On this see below, p. 306.)

There is little direct evidence whether a person not legally entitled could confer on one of his creditors any rights in law over a thing, whether movable or immovable, but the probability is that he could not.[3] The only exception would have been that

[1] Lips., *AR* 700, and Weiss, *GP* 335 ff., take this case as conclusive for a legal ban as against Papp., Rabel (locc. citt. 291, n. 1), and Gernet, *Dem.* iii. 86. Gernet's contention that the second interpretation is 'plus compatible avec les données du droit de l'époque classique' seems a circular argument. Pringsheim, *GLS* 164: 'no indication of a mortgage'.

[2] Gernet, *Dem.* i. 41, is hardly justified in the comment that the guardian consented to an operation 'dont on peut contester l'opportunité et la délicatesse, mais dont la correction juridique peut être admise'.

[3] So Kränzlein, *Eig. und Bes.* 115; but it is rather a strain on Dem. 27 *Aphob.* i. 24 to make it prove this.

the ownership of things purchased at auction from the state could not be challenged on the grounds of the state's deficient title or of faulty sales procedure.[1]

§ 7. ἀποτίμημα

There was a distinctive type of real security referred to by the word ἀποτίμημα and its derivatives. (Its terminology has been described above on pp. 256 ff. and 257, n. 1.) As its name implies, its main characteristic was that at the initial stage of the transaction in question a value was set upon the piece of property which was going to serve as security. Difficulties arise when we try to determine what was the purpose and effect of this valuation. ἀποτίμημα is found principally, though not exclusively, in connexion with two institutions, the leasing of the estates of orphans during their minority, μίσθωσις οἴκου (pupillary), and the giving of dowries (dotal). The rules governing these two institutions in general are discussed in their respective sections of the law of the family. Here we are only concerned with the security aspect of them. It will be best to consider the evidence for pupillary, dotal, and other kinds of ἀποτίμημα separately, and then see what conclusions, if any, emerge for this type of security as a whole.[2]

(i) *Pupillary*

In certain circumstances, more closely examined in connexion with the law of guardianship pp. 105 ff., it was the duty of the archon to let out the estate of an orphan. This he did at a public auction in the presence of dikasts. Unless any objection was raised the lease went to the highest bidder, who then might be—perhaps necessarily was—required to furnish security, probably in the form of land, to cover both the capital value of the orphan's estate and the rate of interest represented by his bid, or, in some circumstances, to cover a lesser amount. The archon sent valuers to value the property so offered, and, if it appeared adequate, the

[1] Dem. 24 *Timokr.* 54, 37 *Pant.* 19.

[2] On the institution in general *IJ* viii, Hitz. 38 ff., Beauch. iii. 183 f., 207, 281 f., Weiss, *Pfand.* 67 ff., 129 ff., Paoli, *St. Dir.* 164 ff., id., *AG* 24 (1932), 161 ff., *SIFC* 10 (1933), 181 ff., Lips., *AR* 695 ff., Fine, *Horoi*, chs. 5 and 6, Finley, *Land*, ch. 4, Wolff, *Fest. Rabel* ii. 311 ff.

lease was confirmed and *horoi* were set up upon it. More than one lessee could participate. The orphan's guardian or guardians could bid for and be granted the lease. If the guardian retained management of the property without applying for the lease of it it seems unlikely that he was still required to provide security in the form of ἀποτίμημα, though it may well be that to protect himself against future litigation by his ward he often did so.[1]

Unfortunately we are told nothing about the principles which governed the ἀποτίμησις. There are, however, one or two more or less certain facts that we should bear in mind in determining what its precise significance was. In the first place the orphan's οἶκος (the word must be sharply distinguished from the word οἰκία in this context) was a single whole, comprising, it might be, land, chattels, cash in hand, and money owing to the estate. It was this whole which was leased and for which, if there was no lease, the guardian had to account when his ward came of age. For either of these purposes a valuation of the estate at the time it was leased or came under control of the guardian was necessary, and this meant in effect a valuation of that part of the estate which did not consist in cash or claims expressed in cash. In μίσθωσις οἴκου the valuers would have had to value first the estate and then the property offered as security by the would-be lessee. In the simplest case the value of the security would have been roughly equal to the value of the estate, and where the estate

[1] Add to works cited in 293 n. 2 Schulthess, *VAR* 191 ff., id., *RE* 15 (1932) s.v. μίσθωσις, Beauch. ii. 238 ff., Lips., *AR* 346 ff., Wolff, *Fest. H. Lewald* 201 ff. For procedure before the archon Ar., *Ath. Pol.* 56. 7, Isai. 6 *Philokt.* 36, 37 (with Wyse ad loc. and W. Kamps in *Ann. de l'inst. de phil. et d'hist. or. et slav.* 6 (1938), 15 ff.), Pollux 8. 89, Harpokr. s.v. ἀποτίμηται (quoted above p. 257, n. 1). Fine, *Horoi* 108 f., Finley, *Land* 42, for the view that ἀποτίμημα was required by law (but cf. Wolff, *Fest. Rabel* ii. 297). Finley, *Land* 43, holds it probable that the security was always in land and that it covered both capital and interest. On the last point see the Naxian *horos*, Finley, no. 131, and Fine, *Horoi* 103, thereon (surely all that this stone proves is that in Naxos an ἀποτίμημα *might* cover both principal and interest). For guardian as lessee Isai. 6 *Philokt.* 36, Schulthess, *VAR* 146, n. 2, followed by Finley, *Land* 236, n. 16 against Wyse ad loc. Wolff, *Fest. H. Lewald* 201 ff., points out that Wyse's doubts ignore the fact that μίσθωσις οἴκου is quite different from a contract between two parties. In favourable circumstances a guardian might gain by becoming lessee, if, for example, the returns on the property considerably exceeded the interest he had offered in his bid; unless he had become lessee he would theoretically be accountable to his ward for the whole fruits. Fine, *Horoi* 111, n. 71, may be right in holding that a guardian who was not lessee did not have to furnish ἀποτίμημα, but Dem. 30 *Onet.* i. 7 does not prove this; for a different view Wolff, *Fest. Rabel* ii. 297.

consisted wholly of cash it would have been entirely reasonable to insist on this degree of cover. We need not, however, assume that this always happened. Where an estate consisted largely of real property it would have been oddly unimaginative to have insisted that a lessee must tie up real property of his own of equal value, provided steps were taken to prevent his alienating or hypothecating the orphan's real property which he was leasing. We should therefore keep open the possibility that in such a case the value of the security offered was equated with the value of the liquid part of the orphan's estate only. Such a system would have enabled a guardian who had not much real property of his own to become lessee. Indeed, without it it might have proved difficult to get a lessee where an orphan had large landed estates.[1] However that may be, it seems reasonably certain that the most important distinguishing mark of this kind of security was the attaching of a monetary value to it by a state official at the time of the original transaction. It is less certain, though still highly probable, that there was a law which prohibited any legal dispute about the value placed on the ἀποτίμημα.[2]

When the ward came of age he might have a claim either against a guardian or against a lessee or conceivably against both. We are not concerned here with these distinctions. What we have to note is that normally the claim would be for the handing over to him of the οἶκος. In so far as any part of this was land one would expect that his claim would be for the actual land. The immense importance attached to maintaining ancestral shrines makes it improbable that another similar piece of land could ever have been regarded as an acceptable substitute. The usual case involving *apotimema* therefore was probably where security had been given for the liquid assets of the οἶκος. We must surely suppose that, if the lessee was able and willing to pay down the cash value of these assets as assessed when he took over the lease, that closed the matter. If, on the other hand, he

[1] Wolff has put forward the view that where a ward's estate included substantial real property and this property was leased by μίσθωσις οἴκου it could itself be made into an *apotimema* in the technical sense. This would presumably have meant attaching *horoi* to it. Whether in Wolff's view it would also have involved making a valuation of it he does not say. If it would not we can only conclude that it had the name *apotimema* by analogy. See further on p. 297 under dotal *apotimema*.

[2] So Finley, *Land* 52 and 245, nn. 61, 62, basing himself on Dem. 41 *Spoud.* 7, 10. See the literature there cited and add Gernet, *Dem.* ii. 56 ff. That is a case of dotal *apotimema* and will be discussed later.

was not able or willing, then surrender of the *apotimema* was a complete discharge of his liability, whether or not its value at that stage was equal to the value of the liquid assets as originally assessed. If this is how the system worked—and in the absence of any actual case in which the surrender of a pupillary *apotimema* is described it is largely speculation—it must have protected the interests of the lessee rather more than those of the ward, since the lessee would obviously not have surrendered the *apotimema* if its value was in excess of the amount due, whereas the ward would have to accept a deficiency.[1]

There remains one puzzling feature of the evidence for pupillary *apotimema* as it is preserved on the *horoi*. Of the 21 *horoi* which certainly record this type only 2 (1 from Athens and 1 from Naxos) specify the sum of money secured, whereas of the 27 which record the dotal type 17 specify the sum of money, and 6 more may have done so. A possible explanation of this difference, which can hardly be accidental, is that the pupillary *apotimema*, having been valued for this specific purpose by an official, was presumably precluded from being used for a second hypothec, and therefore the amount secured by it was of no interest to third parties, whom it was the main function of the *horoi* to warn.[2] The point will be further discussed in connexion with dotal *apotimema*.

(ii) *Dotal*

The second main sphere in which we meet this precise valuation of the security at the time of the original transaction is in

[1] Paoli, *St. Dir.* 166 ff., for cases where assets of the estate were primarily not in land. Finley, *Land* 43 f., errs in my view in insisting that the pupillary *apotimema* would cover land as well as cash when land was part of the ward's estate. I cannot therefore accept his view that often the archon's assessors had no need to attach a money value to the *apotimema*, but might, for example, have determined that the lessee's farm A was equal in value to the ward's farm B plus his liquid assets of *x* minai, without determining money values for A and B.

[2] Finley, horoi nos. 116–29, 120A, 126A, B, C, 129A (Athens), 130 (Amorgos), 131 (Naxos), for pupillary type: 127 and 131 record the amount of money covered. Finley, *Land* 43, argues that, whenever the ward's estate consisted of realty, *whether in whole or in part*, since the *apotimema* had to cover both liquid assets and realty, it would have been a useless fiction to attach a monetary value to the *apotimema*. Note 'or in part' (my italics). Would not the whole procedure of valuation have been nugatory if, in the quite possible eventuality that the lessee returned the ward's real estate but had made away with the liquid assets, there was nothing to show how much of the *apotimema* covered these latter? Cf. also n. 1, above.

connexion with dowries.[1] Here valuation could conceivably have been made for three distinct purposes, and we have to determine first to which of these purposes the technical valuation known as *apotimesis* was relevant. A piece of real property might have been valued as forming part or the whole of the dowry itself; or as forming part or the whole of security offered by the *κύριος* of the bride to guarantee the eventual payment of a promised dowry or part of a dowry; or thirdly as forming part or whole of the security offered by the husband to guarantee the return of the dowry in case the marriage should be dissolved or there should be other cause requiring its return. There is general agreement that *apotimema* in the technical sense was applicable where the return of the dowry was in question. On the most probable view it was common practice, though not obligatory, for the husband who had received a dowry in contemplation of marriage to furnish real property as security for its return. The piece of property was assigned a monetary value agreed between the parties and normally closely approximating to the value of the dowry itself.[2] The lexicographers suggest that this was the only use of *apotimema* in connexion with dowries; but the prevailing modern view is that it was often used in the reverse direction, to

[1] Harpokr. s.v. *ἀποτιμηταί κτλ.* (quoted p. 257, n. 1, above), *An. Bekk.* (*Συν. Λέξ. Χρησ.*) 423. 13 *εἰώθασιν οἱ τῇ γυναικὶ γαμουμένῃ προῖκα διδόντες αἰτεῖν παρὰ τοῦ ἀνδρὸς ὥσπερ ἐνέχυρόν τι τῆς προικὸς ἀντάξιον, ὃ νῦν ὑπάλλαγμα λέγεται. ἐκλήθη δὲ τὸ ὑπάλλαγμα ἀποτίμημα, διότι ἐτιμᾶτο πρὸς τὴν προῖκα, ἵνα μὴ ἔλαττον ᾖ ἀλλὰ πλέον αὐτῆς*, Pollux 8. 142 *ἀποτίμημα δ' ἐστὶν οἷον ὑποθήκη, κυρίως μὲν πρὸς τὴν προῖκα*. Cf. also *An. Bekk.* (*Λέξ. ῾Ρητ.*) 200. 30 ff., 201. 30, Suda s.v. *ἀποτιμηταί*, Hesych. s.v. *ἀποτιμήματα*, Finley, horoi nos. 132 to 156, 152A, Dem. 30 and 31 *Onet.* i and ii *passim*, 41 *Spoud.* 5–7, 10 (on which R. Burgkhardt, *De Causa Or. Ad. Spud. Dem.* (Leipzig, 1908)). Add to opp. citt. p. 293, n. 2 Arangio-Ruiz, *A G*23 (1932), 245 ff., La Pira, *BIDR* 41 (1933), 305 (both critical of Paoli), Wolff, *R.E.* s.v. *προίξ*, especially cc. 159 ff.

[2] The main dissentient is Paoli in locc. citt. (p. 293, n. 2). His view is that *apotimema* was strictly not a security, but a piece of property handed over, in this case to the woman's *κύριος*, to discharge an obligation (*datio in solutum*). Thus theoretically it would not come into existence till the moment came for the restitution of the dowry. But by a legal fiction an *apotimema* could be used to secure the return of the dowry; when the dowry was given, the husband made a fictitious transfer of possession of the *apotimema* to the woman's *κύριος* and it was the function of the *horos* to mark this transfer; if and when the dowry was due to be restored, the *κύριος* was already in possession—howbeit fictitiously—of the property, which therefore fulfilled Paoli's condition for being genuine real security (see below, Appendix E). For criticisms see Arangio-Ruiz and La Pira as cited in n. 1, Fine, *Horoi* 120 ff., Finley, *Land* 200, n. 28, 202, n. 1, 237, n. 23. Wolff, *R.E.* s.v. *προίξ* 161, while agreeing with the critics that the concept of a fictitious possession is too Roman to be Greek, sees a kernel of truth in Paoli's view; on this see below.

guarantee the payment of a promised dowry or of part of it by the bride's κύριος. *Apotimema* may on occasion have served this purpose, but there is no evidence to support the conclusion that it was common practice.[1] Valuation of the dowry itself derived importance from a procedural peculiarity of the δίκη προικός. We learn from Isai. 3 *Pyrrh.* 35 that, if a marriage was dissolved, the bestower of the dowry could not legally enforce the return of anything which had not been originally assessed as part of the dowry: ἐάν τίς τι ἀτίμητον δῷ . . . οὐκ ἔξεστι πράξασθαι τῷ δόντι ὃ μὴ ἐν προικὶ τιμήσας ἔδωκεν. The implication of this would seem to be that the δίκη προικός was always a suit for the sum of money specified in the dowry contract; when the dowry included objects as well as cash, the cash value of the objects had to be stated if the bestower wished to retain the right to recover their value, should the occasion arise, by means of this suit. It is a debatable

[1] The horoi do not help much as their normal form was ὅρος χωρίου | καὶ οἰκίας ἀπ|οτίμημα προ|ικὸς Ἀρχίππηι | TXX (*IG* ii². 2659, Finley, no. 133), where the wording does not tell us whether the debtor was the husband or the κύριος. The sole literary instance adduced for *apotimema* as security for payment of dowry is from Demosthenes' 41st speech, against Spoudias. The speaker, who is plaintiff, had married the elder daughter of Polyeuktos with a dowry agreed at the sum of 4,000 drachmai, of which 3,000 were paid down in cash and the balance was to be paid on the death of Polyeuktos. At the time when the marriage contract was made the payment of this balance was secured by the personal guarantee of Leokrates, adopted son of Polyeuktos and husband of his younger daughter. Then Leokrates quarrelled with Polyeuktos, his adoption was revoked, the younger daughter's marriage was dissolved, and she married Spoudias. Leokrates' personal guarantee of the balance of the elder daughter's dowry naturally lapsed, and her husband, in view of the imminent death of Polyeuktos, induced him to secure payment by a provision in his will which made a house *apotimema* for this sum with *horoi* to mark the fact: τὴν οἰκίαν ταύτην ἀποτιμῶμαι πρὸς τὰς δέκα μνᾶς (op. cit., para. 5); Πολύευκτος . . . τελευτῶν διέθεθ' ὅρους ἐπιστῆσαι χιλίων δραχμῶν ἐμοὶ τῆς προικὸς ἐπὶ τὴν οἰκίαν (ibid. 6). Spoudias, the plaintiff complains, is preventing him from collecting the rents due on the house: (οἰκίαν) ἐξ ἧς διακωλύει με τὰς μισθώσεις κομίζεσθαι Σπουδίας (ibid. 5). The precise legal position of the plaintiff and of Spoudias *vis-à-vis* this house is not relevant here. For our present purpose it seems fair to say that, if we accept the substance of the plaintiff's story, the house was *apotimema* in the technical sense for payment of the balance of the dowry, that it was so made by testament by the bride's *kyrios*—incidentally the only known instance of an hypothec created by testament—and that the husband was now claiming the right to the rents as 'holder' of the security (cf. para. 10 τὸν νόμον ὃς οὐκ ἐᾷ τῶν ἀποτιμηθέντων ἔτι δίκην εἶναι πρὸς τοὺς ἔχοντας). Nevertheless Finley (48 ff. with literature there cited) is right to point out that this was a very special case, that for long there had been no real security for the payment of the balance, and that therefore the passage is quite inadequate as the main evidence for this particular use of *apotimema* as a regular practice. See also Bruck, *Schenkung* 93 and the very important *Notice* to the speech by Gernet, *Dem.* ii. 56 ff. Wolff, *Fest. Rabel* ii. 312.

question whether a piece of real property thus valued as part of a dowry was normally, or even was ever, an *apotimema*. There is certainly a distinction between ἐντιμᾶν (occasionally the simple τιμᾶν) and ἀποτιμᾶν when they are found in a context dealing with a dowry. The first means simply 'to value as part of (the dowry)', the second 'to value and set apart as security for (the return of or, possibly, the payment of) a dowry'.[1]

The more widely held view is that, though both words are found in this kind of context, they always describe entirely distinct functions, the valuation of a non-monetary dowry and the valuation of a security.

On another view it was common practice, especially where real property formed a substantial part of the dowry, for the two operations to merge. The real property was valued as part of the dowry. It passed into the control (κυριεία) of the husband, but to restrict his unfettered rights over it it was simultaneously converted into an *apotimema* and so marked with an *horos*. The effect of this was that, so long as there was a possible liability on the husband to return the dowry, this particular piece of property was to remain available for immediate seizure by the bride's κύριος should the liability arise. If the second step was omitted the husband would still be liable for return of the value of the dowry, including the value of the real property; but this specific piece of property would have been merged with his, and, unless he had offered part of his own property as *apotimema*, the bride's κύριος would have had to depend entirely on a favourable verdict in a δίκη προικός to recover the monetary value of the dowry. Thus on this view ἀποτιμᾶν was always also ἐντιμᾶν, but it would be quite normal ἐντιμᾶν some things (chattels in particular) and not also ἀποτιμᾶν them.[2] In the words of the author of this view

[1] For the distinction Suda ἐνετιμᾶτο διαφέρει τοῦ ἀπετιμᾶτο· ὅταν μὲν γάρ τις ὥς τι ποσὸν ἀργύριον λαμβάνῃ, ἀποτιμᾶσθαι λέγεται· ὅταν δὲ ἐν εἴδεσί τισι λογίσηταί τις μέρος τι τοῦ ἀργυρίου, τοῦτο λέγεται ὡς ἐνετιμήσατο. Pollux 8. 142 ἐντιμήσασθαί ἐστιν ὅταν τις προῖκα διδοὺς τιμήσηται ὁπόσου δεῖ.

[2] Wolff put forward the view that property given as dowry could serve at the same time to secure the claim for restitution of the dowry first in *Traditio* 2 (1944), 54 ff. (*Beitr.* 174 ff.). He was criticized for confusing ἐντιμᾶν and ἀποτιμᾶν by Finley, *Land* 239, n. 32 (cf. id. 240, n. 41, 245, n. 63). Wolff replied in *Z* 70 (1953), 411 ff. (a review of Finley), *Fest. Rabel* ii. 298, n. 17, 307, n. 58, 314, n. 86, *RE* s.v. προίξ (1957) 137 (where he seems to give his whole case away when he says 'die Schätzung entfallen konnte, wenn der zu Mitgift gegebene Gegenstand zum ἀποτίμημα gemacht worden war'), 156, 159 ff. He finds instances of the dowry itself forming an *apotimema* in Finley, horoi nos. 150 (Athens), 156 (Naxos), 155

(H. J. Wolff, *R.E.* s.v. προίξ, c. 161), an *apotimema* was a thing the surrender of which, irrespective of any fall in its value, to one who was entitled to reclaim the dowry could release the husband or his heir from any liability from a δίκη προικός: at the same time the *horos* marked the thing as a real security, available for direct seizure by the claimant for the return of the dowry and freeing him on his side from what might be troublesome procedure by such a δίκη. Thus an *apotimema* might on occasion (viz. when it formed part of the dowry itself) be, in effect, a *datio in solutum*, though in rather a different sense from that suggested by Paoli, for whom *datio in solutum* means a final and definitive payment and who is therefore hard put to it to explain the necessity for *horoi*. Wolff even goes so far as to deduce from the wording of the law in Dem. 41 *Spoud.* 10 that the normal case of *apotimema* envisaged by the legislator was that of the bride's κύριος handing over real property as part of the dowry. This is on the assumption that the δίκη there referred to is the δίκη προικός and that the holder of the *apotimema* is the husband. The law forbids the party which has furnished the *apotimema* (ὁ ἀποτιμήσας) to bring suit against the holder of it (τοὺς ἔχοντας), and in the Spoudias case (see p. 298, n. 1) ὁ ἀποτιμήσας was the bride's father, Polyeuktos, now represented by his heirs, and the speaker, the bride's husband, must be thinking of himself as 'holding' the *apotimema*, though he is being prevented by Spoudias from collecting the rents on it.[1] This is probably to lean too

(Amorgos), the Greek phrases being [ὅρ]ος οἰκίας ἐν προικὶ ἀποτιμημένης, [ὅ]ρος οἰκίας . . . καὶ σκευ[ῶν . .] . . . [τῶν] ἀποτετιμημ[ένων . . .] ἐν προικί, [ὅρος οἰκιῶν καὶ κήπων τῶν . .] . . . τῶν ἀποτετιμημένων Νικησαρέτηι εἰς τὴν προῖκα. The words ἐν προικί and εἰς τὴν προῖκα accord better with Wolff's than with Finley's view (cf. the latter's translation of his no. 155 on p. 26, 'put up as security to Nikesarete for her dowry'; he begs the question when in 239, n. 32, he says that Wolff mistranslates 'valued for N. into' her dowry). For Paoli's theory see references in p. 239, n. 2 and p. 297, n. 2, above.

[1] Note that strictly speaking Spoudias is not bringing suit against the speaker, but vice versa. The speaker omits a stage in the argument, which should run 'Spoudias, as heir to one who had provided an *apotimema*, is barred by statute from suing me, the holder of the *apotimema*, for recovery of the 1,000 drachmai of dowry which this *apotimema* represents. *This implies that he cannot either raise legal objection to my collecting the rents*'; a compressed, but not impossible argument *a fortiori*. 'He could not sue me for the capital value of the house; still less can he contest my claim to draw the rent.' Note, with Fine, who discusses the case at length (*Horoi* 127–32), that the speaker is only paraphrasing the law, which he does in different words in para. 7, τὸν νόμον ὃς οὐκ ἐᾷ διαρρήδην, ὅσα τις ἀπετίμησεν, εἶναι δίκας, οὔτ' αὐτοῖς οὔτε τοῖς κληρονόμοις. The question arises whether the main purpose of this provision

heavily on a law the precise purpose of which is in doubt. Nevertheless, we should do well to keep open the possibility that a dotal *apotimema* might on occasion be a piece of property handed over by the bride's *κύριος* to the husband as part or the whole of her dowry. If, in such a case, the dowry became returnable, we must suppose that the *κύριος* had to accept that piece of property as the equivalent of the amount at which it had been valued even if it had declined in value. We simply cannot say whether it was open to the husband to retain the property and return its monetary value. Similarly, where the husband had furnished *apotimema* for the return of the dowry we may assume that the surrender of the *apotimema* discharged his obligation. In this case it is likely that he had the option of recovering full ownership of the *apotimema* by paying up its equivalent value.

Two of the *horoi* connected with dowries raise a special problem. The first marks a house as *apotimema* for the dowry of Eirene, daughter of Antidoros of Leukonoe, to the value of 1,000 drachmai; by whatever it is worth more than this valuation, the house is hypothecated to (or for) Aglaotime for 200 drachmai and to the Gephyraeans for a sum which is not fully preserved on the stone. The other marks land as (*apotimema* for) the dowry of Hippokleia, daughter of Demochares of Leukonoe, to the value of one talent; by whatever it is worth more than this, it is hypothecated to the Kekropidai, the Lykomidai, and the demesmen of Phlya.[1] Here we have real property set apart, in the first

was to protect the interests of the 'holder' of the *apotimema* during the continuance of the marriage. This must be so if it is to have any relevance to the Spoudias case; but, if it is so, we may ask why the 'holder' of an *apotimema* needed any more protection against a process started by the provider of the *apotimema* than one who 'held' any other form of security. Alternatively the legislator had in mind the position when the dowry had to be returned—or for that matter when a minor came of age, since there is nothing in the words quoted to suggest that they refer only to dotal *apotimema*. At that point *ὁ ἀποτιμήσας* was barred from suing the 'holder' of the security. That means that if he was the bride's *kyrios* he could not sue the husband for any deficiency if the husband surrendered the *apotimema*, while if it was the husband who had furnished the *apotimema* and the bride's *kyrios* who 'held' it, the husband could not sue the *kyrios* for any excess. This seems to be roughly Finley's view of the passage; but it is difficult to get it out of the words quoted and it makes the use of the law by the speaker of Dem. 41 *Spoud.* pure sophistry.

[1] Finley, no. 147 (*Hesp.*, Suppl. 7 (1943), 1, no. 1) *ὅ[ρ]ος οἰκίας ἀποτε[τιμ]/ημένης προικὸς Ε[ἰρη?]/νεὶ Ἀντιδώρου Λευ[κονοι]/έως θυγατρὶ Χ δρα[χμῶν·] / ὅσωι πλέονος ἀξία ἐ[τιμήθ]/η Ἀγλαοτίμει ὑπόκε[ιται] / Η Η καὶ Γεφυραίοις Η Η [. . .] / ⊢⊢⊢⊢ | καὶ ἐπὶ τοῖς α[. . .]/[. .]ụ[. . . . .]τευμ[. . . . . .]*. Finley, no. 146 (*IG* ii². 2670) *ὅρος χωρίο*

case certainly, in the second probably, as *apotimema* for a dowry of a stated value. The property is then further hypothecated to other parties for its value above the stated value of the dowry. We cannot tell in either case whether the original owner of the property was the husband or the bride's father, but for our present purpose this is immaterial. What matters is that apparently in each of these two cases the exact value of the *apotimema* is left indeterminate, and that is contrary to the very nature of an *apotimema* as we have conceived it. We can only suppose—and there is no great difficulty in the supposition—that Athenian practice and terminology were sufficiently fluid in this matter to make it possible for a husband and his bride's father to agree on a security for the dowry of greater value than the dowry itself, to agree that there should be a second hypothec upon it, and to call it by the name used for the more usual type of dowry security, *apotimema*.

There are two important respects in which the conditions which would normally obtain in dotal *apotimema* would differ from those likely to obtain in pupillary *apotimema*. First, a pupillary *apotimema* would inevitably have a fixed terminus, the coming of age (or the death, if he died a minor) of the ward; the dotal *apotimema*, at least if it were for the return of the dowry, had no such fixed ending point. Second, the acceptance of a pupillary *apotimema* on behalf of the ward is in a sense an act of state; there is no contractual element in it, and we may assume that its basically substitutive character would have been pretty

προικὸς / Ἱπποκλεία Δημοχά/[ρ]ος Λευκονοιῶς Τ· / [ὅσ]ωι πλείονος ἄξι/[ον] Κεκροπίδαις / [ὑπό]κειται καὶ Λυκ/[ομί]δαις καὶ Φλυεῦ/[σι]. On these *horoi* see Fine, *Horoi* 141, Finley, *Land* 98 f., 108, 113, 293, n. 1, 294, n. 7, id., *St. Arangio-Ruiz* iii. 482, Wolff, *Fest. Rabel* ii. 295, n. 5, 298, 312, n. 77, 328, Paoli, *St. Dir.* 191. Finley draws attention to the closely parallel language of the poletai record for the year 367/6 (*Hesp.* 10 (1941), 14, no. 1), discussed above, pp. 270 and 271, n. 1; there, as here, cult groups are creditors on the remainder of the property and Finley, *Land* 99, suggests that these may be fictitious loans to secure divine protection for the owner's enjoyment of his property. If that were so, these two *horoi* would be merely nominal exceptions to the rule that an *apotimema* was given and always retained an exact monetary value. Finley's formulation (294, n. 7) is not satisfactory: 'the procedure in the *apotimema* was a redefinition of the property. The part excluded from the evaluated portion remains clear and unencumbered property, as if no obligation existed at all.' If I have a farm of three fields, I can hypothecate two for their full value and leave the third unencumbered or I can hypothecate all three in the first instance for the value of two; but these are quite distinct operations. Only the latter raises serious problems about the surplus and only it is compatible with second or third hypothecs.

strictly adhered to; the dotal *apotimema*, on the other hand, was essentially a contract—note the word *συμβόλαιον* used of the dotal transaction in Dem. 41 *Spoud.* 5—and, although no doubt a general pattern of behaviour developed, there would have been room for variations both at the formation of the contract and during its existence. This may help to explain the puzzling fact referred to on p. 296, above, that it was much more usual to record the sum of money secured in the dotal than in the pupillary type of *apotimema*; in the latter a second hypothec was practically ruled out, in the former, though it was perhaps unusual, it was always a possibility.

(iii) *Miscellaneous*

Harpokration's article on *ἀποτιμηταί*, after dealing with pupillary and dotal *apotimema*, goes on *ὁ δ' αὐτὸς λόγος καὶ ἐπὶ τῶν ἄλλων ὀφλημάτων*. Epigraphy confirms the fact that, although the predominant use of this type of security was for the family transactions of guardianship and dowry, it was not confined to such family matters. We find it used, for example, to guarantee payment of the rent of sacred enclosures, to guarantee loans by the officials of a deme, and for other purposes unstated, but almost certainly not connected either with guardianship or with dowry.[1]

§ 8. *Security in maritime loans*

We have quite a fair knowledge of the rules and general practice which obtained in regard to loans secured on a ship, or on its cargo, or on both, principally because several speeches in the Demosthenic corpus are devoted wholly to such cases. It is,

[1] In about 321 B.C. the deme Peiraeus stipulates that lessees of any sacred enclosure with rent of more than 10 drachmai a year must provide an adequate *apotimema*: *IG* ii². 2498. 3–5 *τοὺς μισθω/[σ]αμένους ὑπὲρ Δ δραχμὰς καθιστάναι ἀποτίμημα τῆς μ/[ι]σθώσεως ἀξιόχρεων*. Similar perhaps *IG* ii². 2494. 7–8 as read by Wilhelm in *AP* 11 (1935), 189 ff. In about 400 B.C. the deme Plotheia lends money on the security of an *apotimema*: *IG* ii². 1172. 20–22 *ὃς ἂ[ν πείθ]ηι τὸς δανείζοντας ἄρχοντα[ς τιμή]ματι ἢ ἐγγυητῆι*. In two Athenian *horoi* the word *apotimema* is found where there can be no question of wardship or dowry: *IG* ii². 2767 (Finley, no. 163) *ὅρος χωρίου ἀποτίμημα ἐπὶ συνθήκαις / Διονύσωσι* 𐅅 H H 𐅄.; ibid. 2701 (Finley, no. 32) *ὅρος χωρίου καὶ οἰκ/ίας πεπραμένου ἐπ/ὶ λύσει Ἱερομν/ήμονι Ἁλαεῖ /* 𐅅 *κατὰ τὰς συνθ/ήκας τὰς παρὰ Λυσι/στράτωι κειμένα[ς] / καὶ δεκαδισταῖς Η / ΔΔΔ καὶ ἀποτίμημ/α ἐρανισταῖς τοῖ[ς] / μετὰ Θεοπείθους / Ἰκαριῶς*. See Finley, *Land* 45 f., Wolff, *Fest. Rabel* ii. 323 f.

however, a debatable point whether the security aspect of these loans merits discussion in close connexion with real security or whether the peculiar characteristics of such loans, with their exceptionally high degree of risk and the element of insurance in them, does not make it more appropriate to deal with them exclusively in a separate section under the law of contract. Here the second alternative has been adopted.[1]

[1] Finley, *Land* 202, n. 1 ('bottomry . . . should not be introduced into an analysis of the nature of real security'). Wolff, on the other hand, suggests that the rules worked out on maritime loans may well have served as models for rules in hypothec, *Z* 70 (1953), 424. Historically this does not seem very probable. For Paoli's view see Appendix E, p. 316.

IX · PUBLIC NOTICE

MANY legal systems have rules, more or less elaborate, for giving public notice when transfers of property are going to be made, whether by sale, by gift, or by succession. By a further refinement the state may maintain a register of all property in land, which may include or be supplemented by a record of all encumbrances on landed property. Athenian rules on the matter were comparatively simple.[1]

Our chief evidence for the practice of Greek cities in general and for Athens in particular comes from a passage from Theophrastos' work on laws (quoted in Stobaeus, *Floril.* xliv. 22 Meineke, 20 Hense). The relevant sentences run as follows. *οἱ μὲν οὖν ὑπὸ κήρυκος κελεύουσι πωλεῖν καὶ προκηρύττειν ἐκ πλειόνων ἡμερῶν, οἱ δὲ παρ' ἀρχῇ τινι, καθάπερ καὶ Πιττακὸς παρὰ βασιλεῦσι καὶ πρυτάνει. ἔνιοι δὲ προγράφειν παρὰ τῇ ἀρχῇ πρὸ ἡμερῶν μὴ ἔλαττον ἢ ἑξήκοντα, καθάπερ Ἀθήνησι, καὶ τὸν πριάμενον ἑκατοστὴν τιθέναι τῆς τιμῆς, ὅπως διαμφισβητῆσαί τε ἐξῇ καὶ διαμαρτύρασθαι τῷ βουλομένῳ, καὶ ὁ δικαίως ἐωνημένος φανερὸς ᾖ τῷ τέλει . . . οὐ χρὴ δ' ἀγνοεῖν, ὅτι αἱ προγραφαὶ καὶ αἱ προκηρύξεις καὶ ὅλως ὅσα πρὸς τὰς ἀμφισβητήσεις ἐστὶ πάντ' ἢ τὰ πλεῖστα δι' ἔλλειψιν ἑτέρου νόμου τίθεται· παρ' οἷς γὰρ ἀναγραφὴ τῶν κτημάτων ἐστὶ καὶ τῶν συμβολαίων, ἐξ ἐκείνων ἔστι μαθεῖν, εἰ ἐλεύθερα καὶ ἀνέπαφα καὶ τὰ αὑτοῦ πωλεῖ δικαίως· εὐθὺς γὰρ καὶ μετεγγράφει ἡ ἀρχὴ τὸν ἐωνημένον.*[2] Another important passage, though not specifically

[1] An important recent discussion of this topic is in Finley, *Land* (index s.v. 'notice, public', and especially 13–21). Earlier discussions in Boeckh, *Staatsh.* 594 ff., Beauch. iii. 319–60, Rabel, *Die Verfügungsbeschränkungen* 12 ff., Lips., *AR* 739 f., Papp. 197 ff., Partsch, *Fest. Lenel* 79 ff., especially 98 ff., F. von Woess (*Münch. Beitr.* 6, 1924), 127 ff., Pringsheim, *GLS* 134 ff. Continental writers, especially German, have tended to speak rather pityingly of the simplicity of the Athenian attitude towards publicity and registration, but the merits of elaborate state registration can be exaggerated and the classical law of Rome got on well enough without. See the sensible remarks of Schulz, *CRL* 353.

[2] Text and commentary in V. Arangio-Ruiz and A. Olivieri, *Inscr. Gr. Sicil. et inf. It. ad ius pert.* (Milan, 1925), 240–9. Cf. Finley, *Land* 208, n. 23, for other references.

related to Athens, comes from the Paroemiographers (i. 405, repeated in Hesych s.v. ἐν λευκώμασι). ἔθος ἦν τὰ πιπρασκόμενα χωρία σώματα δημοσίᾳ ἐγγράφεσθαι ἐν σανίσι λευκαῖς ἢ πυξίοις κεχρισμένοις λευκῇ γῇ καὶ τὰ ὀνόματα καὶ τῶν κτημάτων καὶ τῶν ἀνδραπόδων καὶ τῶν πριαμένων αὐτά, ἵνα εἴ τις αἰτιάσασθαι βουληθείη ἐπ' ἀδείας ἔχοι ἐντυχὼν τῷ λευκώματι.

The general sense of the Theophrastos passage is clear, though certain points in it are controversial. In some cities a sale (he is probably referring to land only) had to be announced by herald several days in advance; in others it had to take place in the presence of an official; in others—among them Athens—notice in writing had to be given at a magistrate's office at least sixty days in advance and the buyer had to pay a tax of 1 per cent. of the purchase price. The purpose of this procedure, according to Theophrastos, was that anyone who pleased might dispute the sale and put in a plea in bar and that the rightful buyer might be clearly identified by payment of the tax; or, on another interpretation, that the rightful buyer might become identifiable by the authority responsible for collecting the tax. Later he adds that notice in advance in writing or by herald was an attempt to fill the gap caused by the absence of a register of properties and contracts, for such a register made it possible to find out whether a seller was entitled to sell and whether the property was unencumbered.[1]

From this passage of Theophrastos we make the following deductions with fair confidence. Though there were in the fourth century cities which had land registers, Athens was not one of them.[2] There an owner or a mortgagee had to rely on the sixty

[1] We need not worry overmuch which is the right interpretation of the words ὁ δικαίως ἐωνημένος φανερὸς ᾖ τῷ τέλει. They express, after all, not a rule, but the reason supposed to lie behind the rule. On the whole the former interpretation seems more natural; the other requires us to connect this reason with the sixty days' notice only, since payment of a tax can hardly be regarded as a way of making the tax collector aware of who is liable to pay it. F. von Woess, loc. cit. p. 305, n. 1, supported by Rabel in *Z* 45 (1925), 521, takes the view that τῷ τέλει must be *dativus commodi*. He also takes the Theophrastos passage in close connexion with that from the Paroemiographers, assuming that the latter has reference to Athens. Partsch, *Fest. Lenel* 99 ff., argues that τῷ τέλει is an instrumental dative, but he too applies the Hesychios passage to Athens and freely renders the last sentence of it 'der Aushang erfolgte, damit derjenige, der Einspruch einlegen wolle, sein recht sichere (ἐπ' ἀδείας ἔχοι), nachdem er auf den Aushang aufmerksam geworden sei'.

[2] The clear testimony of Theophrastos has been questioned on two equally

days' notice ending with the payment of the 1 per cent. tax to ensure that his land or land on which he had a mortgage was not sold wrongfully. Incidentally the sixty days' notice would have also protected the interests of the buyer. Whether either the failure to give the notice or the failure to pay the tax invalidated the sale we cannot say. *A priori* considerations suggest the former, but not the latter. For it would be a reasonable sanction against both parties to cancel the transaction if the notice had not been given, but it would have been rather harsh on the seller to punish him for the failure of the buyer to pay the tax.[1]

It is not clear what exact form an aggrieved owner's or mortgagee's interdiction of a sale took. It is technically described as *ἀπόρρησις*, or by Theophrastos as *διαμαρτύρασθαι*. Isai. 2 *Menekl.* 29 suggests that wrongful use of the procedure could lay the user of it open to a *δίκη ἀπορρήσεως*, though some scholars have thought that such a wrong was remedied by a *δίκη βλάβης*. It is equally uncertain what was the effect of failure to interdict a sale during the period of notice, though it would seem likely that an

inadequate grounds. Harpokr. s.v. *δήμαρχος* says *τὰς ἀπογραφὰς ἐποιοῦντο τῶν ἐν ἑκάστῳ δήμῳ χωρίων*. But Lips., *AR* 302, n. 12, rightly argued that these *ἀπογραφαί* are much more likely to be records of confiscated properties than of all properties in the deme. The formulation in Suda s.v. *δήμαρχος* confirms this: *τὰς ἀπογραφὰς ἐποιοῦντο τῶν προσόντων ἑκάστῳ δήμῳ χωρίων*. Hyperides' speech 5 against Athenogenes makes it quite clear that there was no period of sixty days' notice when Athenogenes' perfumery business was sold. But in that case no landed property was involved—Athenogenes was a foreigner—the sale was confined to three slaves and some supplies. This instance cannot weaken the evidence of Theophrastos, so long as we assume that the rules he gives were for the sale of land, though it admittedly weakens the force of the Hesychius passage. P. Vogt's arguments in *WS* 16 (1894), 212 f., were disposed of by Lipsius, *Philologus* 55 (1896), 45. Cf. Finley, *Land* 209, n. 24.

[1] Some scholars have rather uncritically assumed that notice plus payment of tax could be looked on as a single piece of procedure, required (or not required) to make a sale valid. This is unrealistic and is hardly demanded by the text of Theophrastos, unless we take him to mean that the tax had to be *deposited* by the buyer at the beginning of the sixty-day period. Partsch, *Fest. Lenel* 100, supported by Pringsheim, *GLS* 233, argued that ownership did not pass unless the whole procedure had been carried out, against Lips. 739 f., who gives no adequate reason for the contrary view. Records at Athens from the latter half of the fourth century of the payment of the 1 per cent. tax (not to be equated with the *ἐπώνια*, as Lips. 740, n. 236, pointed out) in *IG* ii². 1594–602. How far these very summary records were from providing any substitute for a land register can be seen by comparing them, for example, with the much more detailed records of changes in real property recorded in the third century by the astynomoi at Tenos (*IG* xii. 5, n. 872, *IJ*, no. vii). These contain, among other details, exact descriptions of the location of the property and sometimes of the encumbrances upon it.

aggrieved owner or mortgagee would have jeopardized, if not wholly forfeited, his rights by such failure.[1]

The rules so far discussed referred to the sale of land. We may conjecture, though there is no evidence, that some similar requirement of notice held with regard to gifts of land.

On the other hand, it is improbable (though there is no direct evidence either way) that public notice had to be given of encumbrances on land, at least if these were by way of hypothec: for this purpose πρᾶσις ἐπὶ λύσει may have been looked upon as sale, which juristically at least it was.[2]

We cannot suppose that any such requirement obtained for the sale of chattels. But, as usual, slaves come in the rather uneasy limbo between land and chattels, and there is some doubt what the rule was in connexion with their sale—we must keep quite separate the procedure in manumission. The passage cited above from the Paroemiographers, if it applied to Athens, would imply the requirement of notice for the sale of slaves similar to that for the sale of land. But there is no direct evidence for any such requirement, and we should have expected to find direct reference to its application to the sale of slaves both in Theophrastos and in Dem. 53 *Nikostr.*[3]

When property passed by succession notice by herald played a part. Thus in Dem. 43 *Makart.* 5 a herald calls on anyone who wishes to make a claim or put down a deposit (ἀμφισβητεῖν ἢ παρακαταβάλλειν) for the estate of Hagnias based either on kinship or on testament. The failure of the speaker's opponents to take advantage of this invitation is held by him to be a strong argument against the validity of their claim, but it clearly did not legally bar them from making one.[4]

[1] For discussion of ἀπόρρησις so far as it concerned mortgage see above, pp. 290 ff., and literature there cited.

[2] Kränzlein, *Eig. und Bes.* 83: Theophrastos, loc. cit., says there was such a rule at Kyzikos, and this probably implies that there was not at Athens.

[3] See Finley, *Land* 209, n. 24.

[4] Publicity is dealt with also under the law of succession, the law of slavery, and the law of marriage, in so far as it affects those several institutions.

APPENDIX A

Judicial dissolution of marriage of ἐπίκληρος

WYSE in his note on Isai. 3 *Pyrrh.* 64 (p. 351) argues the possibility that, where there was a legitimate son, the next of kin could not enforce the dissolution of the marriage. He relies almost wholly on a comparison with the law of Gortyn under which a married woman who became an heiress was not forced to dissolve her marriage, though she might do so subject to provisos differing according to whether there were or were not children; *Gortyn* viii. 20–23, with comments of Bücheler–Zitelmann 154, Köhler–Ziebarth 69, 112. There is nothing in his point that of the two daughters of Euktemon, one married and with two sons, the other a widow and with a daughter, the widow is claimed by a relative as ἐπίδικος, while we hear of no such claim on the other daughter (Isai. 6 *Philokt.* 46, 51, 57, 58); a hundred reasons other than a legal bar could be found for this failure to claim. Here, as too often elsewhere, Wyse overestimates the degree to which an orator could deliberately misrepresent facts, facts here which must have been perfectly familiar to the jurors. That the speeches were published makes such misrepresentation even less probable. Lips., *AR* 545, n. 20, is also sceptical of the rule. He bases himself principally on two articles by A. Ledl (*Stud.*). In these Ledl argues as follows from the law on ἐγγύη referred to in n. 2 on p. 5, above: the law implies (in the words which follow those there quoted, ἐὰν δὲ μηδεὶς ᾖ τούτων, ἐὰν μὲν ἐπίκληρός τις ᾖ) that so long as father, brother by the same father, or paternal grandfather was alive a woman was not ἐπίκληρος. Suppose the case of a girl who has never had a brother and whose father dies before her grandfather. The grandfather is now empowered to give her in marriage by ἐγγύη. But on the death of the grandfather she will *become* an ἐπίκληρος. Who, other than her next of kin, would be likely to take her hand in such circumstances, knowing that on the death of the grandfather she might be taken from him by ἐπιδικασία brought by the next of kin? *A priori*, then, a marriage sanctioned by ἐγγύη by the grandfather was not likely to have been dissoluble, and much less therefore one sanctioned by the father. This is a weak argument from probability, particularly as Athenian fathers could, and often did, avoid these disagreeable consequences by adopting and marrying their daughters to their next of kin: cf. Isai. 3 *Pyrrh.* 72–73 and other instances cited by Gernet, *RÉG* 33 (1920), 139 ff. (*DSGA* 129 f.). Ledl (*Stud.* i. 13) asks ironically whether a man so married would have been required on the death of the father or grandfather to remarry his wife by the procedure of *ἐπιδικασία*. The answer is, of course not. In such a case the significance of the *ἐγγύη* would have been that if there were some other of her kin who thought he was nearer in blood than the actual *ἐγγυώμενος* he would have had to wait for the death of the father or grandfather before he could make a claim to her hand. If no such claimant appeared the original marriage subsisted, as it did on the view taken in the text if it had produced a male child. For this view U. E. Paoli, *Scritti Ferrini* (Milan, 1946), 584 (cf. id., *Studi e Testi* 125 (Vatican, 1946), 530), adds a piece of specific evidence from Terence on the probably justified assumption that in this passage the rules of Athenian law are referred to. In Ter., *Ad.* 657 ff., a girl's mother is represented as urging that the girl could not be claimed by the next of kin because she already had a son by a former husband: 'commenta mater est esse ex alio viro / nescio quo puerum natum, neque eum nominat; / priorem esse illum, non oportere huic dari.' Micio pretends to discredit the mother's argument, but only because he doubts the legitimacy of the original marriage; cf. ibid. 670, 'quis despondit? quis dedit? quoi quando nupsit?' In Ter., *Phorm.* 125–6, there is almost certainly a reference to the Athenian law on heiresses, though there, since the context did not require it, no reference is made to the exemption of women already married and with male children: 'lex est ut orbae, qui sint genere proxumi, / eis nubant, et illos ducere eadem haec lex iubet.' Paoli would extend the protection to the wife who was pregnant, until the birth disclosed whether the child was male or female. He argues on the analogy of the widow, who was allowed to remain in the *οἶκος* of her husband if she claimed to be pregnant (Dem. 43 *Makart.* 75).

Ledl (*Stud.* i) admits that juries may often have interpreted the law as giving the next of kin the right to dissolve the marriage, though it did not really do so. If this was a regular practice it would raise the interesting question, what was in fact the law, the strict terms of the *νόμος* or the interpretation put on it by the courts.

Isai. 10 *Aristarch.* 19 has been used to prove that the next of kin had an absolute right to dissolve the marriage of an *ἐπίκληρος*. The speaker says *ὁ πατὴρ οὑμὸς ἐπὶ προικὶ ἐγγυησάμενος τὴν ἐμὴν μητέρα συνῴκει, τὸν δὲ κλῆρον τούτων καρπουμένων οὐκ εἶχεν ὅπως εἰσπράξαιτο· ὅτε γὰρ περὶ αὐτοῦ λόγους ἐποιήσατο τῆς μητρὸς κελευούσης, οὗτοι ταῦτα αὐτῷ ἠπείλησαν, αὐτοὶ ἐπιδικασάμενοι αὐτὴν ἕξειν, εἰ μὴ βούλοιτο αὐτὸς ἐπὶ προικὶ ἔχειν. ὁ δὲ πατήρ, ὥστε τῆς μητρὸς μὴ στερηθῆναι, καὶ δὶς τοσαῦτα* χρήματα εἴασεν ἂν αὐτοὺς καρποῦσθαι. But the details of this case are not clear enough to allow it to stand in evidence. For (1) it is not certain whether the woman was to be regarded as succeeding to her father or to her brother. The latter had died in childhood after the death of the father. But if she was to be regarded as succeeding her brother, some scholars would hold that, whatever the speaker here says, she was not in fact an ἐπίκληρος, her hand could not be claimed, and the supposed threat was nugatory. (2) On the speaker's own admission it was his mother's paternal uncle who, as her guardian, had given her in marriage by ἐγγύη to the speaker's father, although he could either have claimed her hand himself or married her to his own son. Can we believe that the law would have allowed him later on to go back on all this? In fact it is possible that the marriage took place after the father's but before the brother's death, and that on the latter event a composition was reached between the speaker's father and his mother's family of which para. 19 is a distorted account. In any case the speaker is trying to have it both ways when he implies in para. 5 that either his mother's uncle or her cousin should have married her; for in that case his own father could not have done so. (3) Finally there is nothing to suggest that, at the time when the alleged threats took place, the mother had yet borne any children, so that the passage can certainly not be used to prove the extreme rigour of the rule. U. E. Paoli, *Studi e Testi* 125 (Vatican, 1946), 535 ff., has a detailed analysis of this passage.

Wolff, *TR* 20 (1952), 19, n. 54, argues for the next of kin's unrestricted right to have the marriage dissolved from Isai. 10 *Aristarch.* 5, 12, where the speaker merely says that the ἀγχιστεύς *did* not, not that he *could* not claim; and from ibid. 19, which seems to presuppose that he *could* have claimed even after the speaker's birth.

Gernet, *RÉG* 34 (1921), 349 ff., argues that by the strict letter of the law the next of kin had a right whether the heiress had children or not.

APPENDIX B

δίκη ἐξούλης

Rabel, *Z* 36 (1915), 349, made the following points about the Harpokration passage quoted on p. 218, n. 1, above. (1) In so far as it suggests that the δίκη ἐξούλης was for the protection of possession as such its authority is to be rejected. The clause καὶ περὶ ἀνδραπόδου . . . μετεῖναι, which has possibly become misplaced, does not mean, as Lipsius would have it, that a δίκη ἐξούλης would lie in any case where a man was claiming a slave or any other chattel, but simply that slaves or other chattels which a man might be claiming might, in the appropriate circumstances, be the subject of a δίκη ἐξούλης. Little weight should be attached to the last sentence, in which the refutation of Caecilius's statement that the action was restricted to judgement debts and the assertion that it applied ἐπὶ παντὸς τοῦ ἐκ τῶν ἰδίων ἐκβαλλομένου rest on nothing better than a reference to a comic poet. (2) The two sentences δικάζονται . . . τιμηθέντα refer to a judgement for a sum of money and entirely pass over the execution of a judgement assigning a thing to a plaintiff. The words ἃ ἀφηροῦντο αὐτόν are meaningless as they stand, but hint at the case where a successful plaintiff levies distress on a thing in execution of a judgement for a sum of money. The sentence ἐδικάζετο . . . ὑπό τινος, on the other hand, has in mind the mortgagee who is seizing the object mortgaged and is being resisted. Rabel denies that an ordinary creditor, whose claim rested neither on a judgement nor on an executive clause in a contract, had the right of seizure. He refers to the law of Solon's fifth *axon* as quoted in Ox. Pap. 221, c. 14, l. 12, ἐάν τις ἐξείλλῃ ὧν ἂν δίκην νικήσῃ ὅτου ἂν ἄξιον ᾖ, καὶ εἰς δημόσιον ὀφλεῖν καὶ τῷ ἰδιώτῃ ἑκατέρῳ ἴσον, where, on the one hand, no distinction is made between an original duty to give up a thing and liability to pay a sum of money, while, on the other hand, the result of an adverse judgement in the δίκη ἐξούλης is explicitly a money fine. Now clearly the word ἐξείλλειν in this and similar contexts implies exclusion from a thing; it cannot mean mere failure to pay a sum of money. Either this law, then, is thinking only of things *adjudged* to a litigant, or it is also thinking of things which the winner of a judgement for a money payment has seized by way of distress. Rabel holds that the orators prove the latter to be true for their time, though at this point he only quotes a number of lexicographers, some of whom speak only of a money fine, others of the thing adjudged, schol. Dem. 21 *Meid.* 44 of both. For Rabel the successful plaintiff in a δίκη ἐξούλης must have had the choice between accepting a money payment as assessed by the court, and the exercise of his continuing right, now backed by the state, to seize upon the thing by self-help (Gernet, *AHDO* 1 (1937), 133, n. 3 (*DSGA* 75, n. 1), believes in the cumulation of the two). Rabel's conclusive point against Lipsius is that we have clear evidence that claimants to possess under the four special groups enjoyed a privileged position in regard to self-help. But on Lipsius's view of the availability of the δίκη ἐξούλης it is impossible to see in what their privilege could have consisted. G. von Beseler, however, in *St. Bonfante* 2 (1930), 55 returned to the view that Harpokration and Isai. 5 *Dikaiog.* 22 prove that the δίκη ἐξούλης was available against any unlawful ejection from property in legal and established possession.

APPENDIX C

ἐξαγωγή

U. E. Paoli, *St. Albertoni* ii (Padua, 1937), 313 ff., saw in the rules governing formal ἐξαγωγή the resolution of an apparent contradiction between authorized self-help and the elimination of violence in the settlement of disputes. He insists that ἐξαγωγή can be used as a formal act both by a possessor and by a non-possessor. When it is put in motion ὁ ἐξαγόμενος must abstain, if he is possessor, from forcible resistance to the transfer of the thing, if he is non-possessor, from trying to secure the transfer by force; otherwise he lays himself open to a δίκη βιαίων. His reply to ὁ ἐξάγων is therefore limited to bringing against him a δίκη ἐξούλης. Paoli proposes the following scheme in which A is possessor and B claims to be entitled to ἐμβατεία or ἐνεχυρασία. (*a*) A ἐξάγει. B takes the thing by force. B is liable to a δίκη βιαίων. (*b*) A ἐξάγει. B abstains from force, but he can bring a δίκη ἐξούλης against A; Isai. 3 *Pyrrh.* 62, taking the subject of ἐξῆγεν ἂν to be the possessor who is excluding the heiress. Cf. also the action of Demosthenes in 30, 31 *Onet.* i, ii. (*c*) B ἐξάγει. A holds on to the thing. A is liable to a δίκη βιαίων. This is the case presupposed in Isai. 5 *Dikaiog.* 22. (*d*) B ἐξάγει. A yields the thing, but can bring a δίκη ἐξούλης against B. Dem. 47 *Euerg.* 38. (*e*) Neither A nor B ἐξάγει. Then A must abstain from violence in resisting the self-help of B, and B must abstain from acts of violence not rendered necessary by the behaviour of A. Transgression in either case would make the delinquent liable, not to a δίκη ἐξούλης, but to a δίκη βιαίων. Both these suits are penal and in both the penalty is *in duplum*. But whereas the effect of the δίκη βιαίων is exhausted by the penalty, and the question of right which was defended by the ἐξαγωγή is left unsettled, the δίκη ἐξούλης settles this question. Thus if ὁ ἐξαγόμενος does not bring a δίκη ἐξούλης he provisionally acknowledges the right of ὁ ἐξάγων, and conversely if the possessor or the claimant by self-help renounces the ἐξαγωγή he admits the other party's right.

Kaser 193, n. 194, rightly criticizes this as too schematic: it would imply that a non-possessor could put an ἐξαγωγή in motion, get possession of the thing without opposition from the possessor, and be immune from prosecution by δίκη ἐξούλης unless the possessor happened to be in one of the four privileged classes. Paoli has been misled by ignoring the fact that in the fourth century it was still possible to use ἐξάγειν to describe literally forcible seizure of a thing as well as to describe the formal, legalistic act. Thus in the two passages put forward as evidence for the use of ἐξαγωγή as a formal act by a non-possessor, Isai. 5 *Dikaiog.* 22 and 3 *Pyrrh.* 62, what we really have are simply forcible, illegal ejections.

Although Kaser's criticism is in the main justified, we should be cautious of the use of either Isaios passage in this controversy. In 5 *Dikaiog.* can we really suppose that the ἐξαγωγή is, as Kaser describes it, 'eine gewaltsame Verdrängung aus dem Besitz' and nothing more? The speaker there seems to think it almost essential to explain why he has not used ἐξαγωγή to get possession of a property which he claimed he had a right to; he had in fact used it in an attempt to get hold of part of the property, with the result that he had not only not got hold of it but had had to pay a penalty of forty minai into the bargain. The *only* conclusion which it seems safe to draw from this passage is that, in the situation in which the speaker was, ἐξαγωγή was the method by which he would have been expected to assert his right. We cannot even say for certain that Mikion was in actual *possession* of the bath in question. If, as seems probable, Mikion's rights were those of a creditor-purchaser by πρᾶσις ἐπὶ λύσει, it would be quite possible, normal in fact, for the debtor, Dikaiogenes, still to be in occupation, in which case the ἐξαγωγή might perhaps have consisted in a formal removal from the bath of a ὅρος stone. Menexenos removes it, relying on the assurance of Dikaiogenes that he will not βεβαιοῦν, that is that he will not confirm in evidence that he had in fact 'sold' the bath to Mikion. But when the matter came to trial (Mikion would, as mortgagee, have had available the δίκη ἐξούλης) Dikaiogenes, perhaps in fear of a δίκη βεβαιώσεως, does βεβαιοῦν, Menexenos loses his case, and is fined forty minai. Isai. 3 *Pyrrh.* 62 is no more helpful: for in the first place it is impossible from the Greek to be certain whether it is the heiress or her opponent who is the subject of ἐξῆγεν ἄν in this hypothetical case, and in the second place, whichever it is, it is impossible to tell which of the two the speaker imagines to be in possession when the ἐξαγωγή takes place. See also Kränzlein, *Eig. und Bes.* 166, on these two cases.

Kaser (194, n. 194) is probably right against Paoli (loc. cit. 321, n. 3) in thinking that Dem. 47 *Euerg.* 38 is not a case of ἐξαγωγή at all.

On the connexion between ἐξαγωγή and διαμαρτυρία in inheritance cases see Gernet, *RHD* 6 (1927), 19 ff. (*DSGA* 90 ff.), and cf. p. 156.

APPENDIX D

Mineral Rights

E. Schönbauer has consistently advocated the view that in all cases the state owned both surface and mine. He first stated his position in *Münch. Beitr. Pap. Forsch.* 12 (1929) and elaborated it in *Z* 55 (1935), 13–32, encouraged by A. Wilhelm's interpretation of *IG* ii². 411 as a mining lease of a mine under state land in *AP* 11 (1935), 206 ff. Schönbauer assumes that on the whole the land concerned had practically no agricultural value. He asks pertinently how, if the Athenians recognized the state's rights to the minerals as something distinct from ownership of the land, they described the former rights. And what were the rules for compensation as between private surface owners and holders of mining leases? G. M. Calhoun criticized Schönbauer's earlier formulation in *J. Ec. Bus. Hist.* 3 (1930), 333 ff., arguing for the concept of the eminent right of the state to mineral wealth beneath private holdings and surmising that the concept was invented by Peisistratos, such a concept being more likely to originate with a personal ruler than with the impersonal polis. The same view was supported by A. Momigliano, *Ath.* 10 (1932), 247 ff. Kahrstedt, *Straatsg.* 19–31, took up a rather unsatisfactory middle position. In his view the system started with the acquisition by the state of the mining domain of Peisistratos at Laureion. Laureion is not incorporated in the deme system, hence no deme Laureion. The location described on the poletai records as *ἐπὶ Θρασύμῳ* was in a similar position ('ein exemtes Gebiet'), save that there the state owned the mines without owning the surface. In other areas both surface and mines were private property, but the owner had to pay to the state one twenty-fourth of the gross product of the mines. Thus for Kahrstedt there were in the end (1) state-owned mines leased out to individuals, the state sometimes owning the surface and sometimes not, (2) privately owned mines subject to a tax of one twenty-fourth of the mineral product. Hopper (loc. cit. pp. 203, n. 1, 209) rightly points out that in effect these two categories together come to much the same thing as Bergregal. Cf. also J. Labarbe, *La Loi navale de Thémistocle* (Paris, 1957), 33 ff. For Kränzlein, *Eig. und Bes.* 26, 167, Athenian law regarded lessees of mines as 'temporary owners' ('Eigentümer auf Zeit').

APPENDIX E

U. E. Paoli on types of real security

Paoli's elaborate schema is set out most simply in *St. Dir.* 118–20, 141 ff.; cf. also articles cited p. 253, n. 1 above. He starts with two important presuppositions; first that there was a clear distinction between the commercial and the civil law of Athens, the rules in the former being considerably more elastic and adaptable than those in the latter; second that it was basic to Athenian law of the classical period that a 'real right', a right to a thing valid against all the world as opposed to a right valid only against the debtor, could only accrue to one who possessed the thing. In bottomry the guarantee afforded by the goods passes through two phases. While the ship is still at sea the goods cover an obligation on the debtor to repay the loan, predetermining what the creditor can eventually seize to secure payment, but giving no preferential right as against other parties. But when the ship arrives, if the creditor then seizes the goods the possession thus acquired brings with it a 'real right'. In commercial law the creditor could sell the goods, but when he had satisfied his claim out of the proceeds he had to return the excess, if any, to the debtor. In civil law the security is continuative; there is no maturity date for the debt; the creditor never acquires more than possession; he cannot sell, and therefore no question of the difference between the value of the security and the amount of the debt could arise. Thus for Paoli bottomry is a distinct type of borrowing with its own rules, and he devotes a separate study to it (*St. Dir.* 9–137).

In the civil law the first distinction made by Paoli is between a security which does and one which does not provide a 'real' guarantee. A 'real' guarantee could arise in three ways. (1) By pledge (ἐνέχυρον) or, whenever transfer of possession took place, by ὑποθήκη. (2) By ἀποτίμημα, when this reached its natural consummation in possession. (3) By πρᾶσις ἐπὶ λύσει, in which ownership and *ius possidendi* pass to the creditor and the debtor retains only physical possession of the thing and the right to reacquire ownership by repayment within a certain term. Pledge is always of a specific, movable thing handed over to the creditor and giving him a 'real' right. Hypothec, which for Paoli is any operation where ὑποτίθημι or its derivatives are used, may be of movables or immovables, of one thing or a number of things, determinate or indeterminate, and it may or may not involve the handing over of the thing to the creditor and therefore may or may not confer a 'real' right. The evidence hardly supports this elaborate structure. In particular it necessitates assuming in πρᾶσις ἐπὶ λύσει a distinction between *ius possidendi* and physical possession, which is most improbable for Athenian law. Nor is there any foundation for the view that this type of security was always for a fixed term (ἔν τινι ῥητῷ χρόνῳ). See reviews by Arangio-Ruiz and La Pira cited p. 253, n. 1, above.

ADDENDA

p. 5 n. 3: see now W. K. Lacey, *JHS* 86 (1966) 55 ff.

p. 6: for a different view of the *ἐγγύη* of Demosthenes' mother, see Lacey, art. cit. 60 n. 28.

p. 47 n. 1: Lacey, art. cit. 57.

p. 57 n. 2: see now E. Ruschenbusch, *ΣΟΛΩΝΟΣ ΝΟΜΟΙ*, *Historia Einzelschrift* 9 (Wiesbaden, 1966) 65.

p. 73 n. 1: see also L. Edelstein, 'The Hippocratic Oath', *Bull. Hist. Med. Supp.* 1 (Baltimore, 1943) 13.

p. 126 n. 2: see H. J. Wolff, *Die attische Paragraphe* (Weimar, 1966) 76.

p. 127 n. 2: see H. J. Wolff, op. cit. 58.

p. 129: add between the first and second paragraphs: 'According to Dem. 52 *Kallip.* 17 an heir could be challenged to take an oath on matters which had arisen in an uncompleted suit against the *de cuius*.'

p. 156 n. 2: see now H. J. Wolff, *Die attische Paragraphe* 121 ff.

p. 209 n. 2: see also Thalheim, *RE* v (1903) s.v. *εἰς ἐμφανῶν κατάστασιν δίκη*.

p. 219 n. 3: see now H. J. Wolff, *Die attische Paragraphe* 35 f.

p. 246 n. 2: see H. J. Wolff, op. cit. 84.

INDEX OF SOURCES

Where a note extends over more than one page, the reference is given to the first page only.

INSCRIPTIONS

Annuario 15/16 (1932/3), 298, no. 6: 255 n. 1
Athenian Tribute Lists, ii 4 D 23, 20–24: 194 n. 2

Δελτίον 14 (1931/2), *παρ.* 31, no. 4: 255 n. 1

Finley, *Land*, nos. 1–10: 269 n. 3
1: 201 n. 1, 254 n. 2, 255 n. 1, 259 n. 1, 270 n. 2
2: 201 n. 1, 252 n. 1, 254 n. 2, 255 n. 1, 259 n. 1, 270 n. 2
3: 269 n. 3
3A: 269 n. 3
4: 255 n. 1
5: 255 n. 1
6: 255 n. 1
7: 255 n. 1
8: 52 n. 4, 114 n. 3, 254 n. 1, 255 n. 1
9: 114 n. 3, 269 n. 3
10: 201 n. 1, 255 n. 1, 259 n. 1, 270 n. 2
11–111: 279 n. 2
11–115: 256 n. 1
18A–101C: 279 n. 2
30: 242 n. 1
32: 303 n. 1
39: 279 n. 2
49: 279 n. 2
57: 236 n. 3, 279 n. 2
82: 279 n. 2
82A: 279 n. 2
88: 176 n. 6, 229 n. 1
89: 176 n. 6, 229 n. 1
90: 176 n. 6, 229 n. 1
93: 279 n. 2
102: 52 n. 4
116–29: 296 n. 2
116–31: 257 n. 1
116: 252 n. 1
120A–9A: 257 n. 1
120A: 296 n. 2
126A: 296 n. 2
126B: 296 n. 2
126C: 296 n. 2
127: 296 n. 2
129A: 296 n. 2
130: 296 n. 2
131: 257 n. 1, 294 n. 1, 296 n. 2
132–56: 297 n. 1
132–65: 257 n. 1
133: 298 n. 1
146: 242 n. 1, 301 n. 1
147: 257 n. 1, 301 n. 1
150: 299 n. 2
152A: 257 n. 1, 297 n. 1
155: 52 n. 4, 299 n. 2
156: 299 n. 2
159: 252 n. 1
163: 303 n. 1
174: 236 n. 3
176: 236 n. 3
178: 176 n. 6

Gortyn, law of, i. 1. 23: 217 n. 2
ii. 46 ff.: 43 n. 2
vi. 9 ff.: 53 n. 2
viii. 20–23: 309

Hesperia 5 (1936), 397: 242 n. 1
Suppl. 7 (1943), 1, no. 1: 301 n. 1
10 (1941), 14, no. 1: 256 n. 1, 270 f., 290 n. 3, 301 n. 1
19 (1950), 189–312: 203 n. 1

IG i². 45. 6 ff.: 244 n. 1
83: 237 n. 2
94. 34–37: 252 n. 1

IG i² (*cont.*)
110: 237 n. 2
115. 18: 64 n. 1
115. 20–23: 143 n. 3
188. 52: 187 n. 2
374: 167 n. 6
ii². 8: 237 n. 2
10: 2 n. 1, 29 n. 2
43: 254 n. 2
43. 35 ff.: 237 n. 2
43. 36–42: 283 n. 1
83: 189 n. 1
86: 237 n. 2
237. 24: 238 n. 2
287: 189 n. 1, 237 n. 3
333: 178 n. 1
411: 315
505. 51 ff.: 189 n. 1
554: 189 n. 1
1013: 178 n. 1
1128: 182 n. 1
1172. 20–22: 257 n. 1, 303 n. 1
1237: 12 n. 2
1237. 26 ff.: 89 n. 2
1241: 242 n. 2
1241. 33 ff.: 227 n. 1
1553. 11 ff.: 185 n. 2
1553. 26 ff.: 185 n. 2
1553–78: 167 n. 6, 183 n. 1
1594–602: 307 n. 1
1631, *c.* 350 ff.: 128 n. 3
2492: 242 n. 2
2492. 7 ff.: 227 n. 1
2493: 242 n. 2
2494. 7–8: 303 n. 1
2494. 8–11: 252 n. 1
2496: 242 n. 2
2497: 242 n. 2
2498: 242 n. 2
2498. 3–5: 303 n. 1
2499: 242 n. 2
2499. 11–14, 30–37: 229 n. 2
2501: 242 n. 2
2631: 241 n. 1, 242 n. 1
2632: 241 n. 1
2655: 252 n. 1
2657: 252 n. 1
2658: 236 n. 3
2659: 298 n. 1
2670: 242 n. 1, 301 n. 1
2699: 242 n. 1
2701: 303 n. 1
2747: 176 n. 6, 229 n. 1
2748: 176 n. 6, 229 n. 1
2749: 176 n. 6, 229 n. 1
2751: 176 n. 6
2758: 254 n. 2, 255 n. 1, 259 n. 1
2759: 252 n. 1, 254 n. 2, 255 n. 1, 259 n. 1
2760: 255 n. 1
2761A: 255 n. 1
2761B: 255 n. 1
2765: 236 n. 3
2766: 236 n. 3
2767: 303 n. 1
xii. 5. 872: 243 n. 2, 307 n. 1
7. 55: 52 n. 4
7. 57: 52 n. 4
7. 58: 52 n. 4, 254 n. 1, 255 n. 1
7. 66–70: 263 n. 2
7. 515: 290 n. 2
IJ i. 52: 8 n. 3
vi: 46 n. 3
vii: 50 n. 3, 307 n. 1
22, 24: 243 n. 2
viii. 62: 259 n. 1
63: 259 n. 1
64: 114 n. 3
65: 114 n. 3
xxiv A 1 32: 233 n. 1
xxvi: 128 n. 3
Inscr. Cret. iv (Guarducci), no. 161: 211 n. 2
Inscr. Délos (Durrbach–Roussel), n. 503: 227 n. 1
Bibl. Éc. Hautes Ét. 222 (1917), ii A 14 ff.: 211 n. 2

SEG iii. 70: 29 n. 2
x. 23. 2–7: 194 n. 2
108: 194 n. 2
xii. 100. 67–69: 236 n. 3
100. 78–80: 236 n. 3
SIG 364. 59: 55 n. 2
496. 19: 48 n. 1
736. 78: 174 n. 3
921: 12 n. 2, 89 n. 2
1097: 242 n. 2
1216: 242 n. 2

Tod, *GHI* 34: 245 n. 4
44: 244 n. 1
87: 64 n. 1, 143 n. 3
100: 2 n. 1, 29 n. 2
123: 237 n. 2, 254 n. 2, 283 n. 1
162: 182 n. 1

LEXICA

Anecdota Bekker 96: 97 n. 1
115: 255 n. 3
184: 214 n. 1
187: 174 n. 3, 209
190: 223, 225
192: 222, 225
194: 170 n. 2, 198 n. 1
197: 95 n. 1, 158 n. 1
200. 30 ff.: 297 n. 1
201: 40 n. 2, 185 n. 3, 189 n. 4, 191, 193
201. 30: 297 n. 1
207: 211 n. 1
207. 23: 176 n. 3
213: 143 n. 3
214: 211, 211 n. 1
214. 16: 176 n. 3
215: 77 n. 1
219: 212 n. 1
234: 177 n. 2
236: 216 n. 1
238: 104 n. 4
246: 208, 209 n. 1, 210
247: 77 n. 1, 88 n. 5
250: 54 n. 3
251: 237 n. 2
255: 120 n. 4
256: 48 n. 3
259: 290 n. 2
264: 216 n. 1
267: 189 n. 1
274: 65 n. 2
285: 222
298. 3: 189 n. 4
298. 27: 189 n. 1
310: 80 nn. 1, 2
313: 116 n. 4
314: 207 n. 2
315: 116 n. 4
316: 167 n. 5
333: 143 n. 3
398. 2: 156 n. 1
417, lines 12 ff.: 89 n. 2
421: 40 n. 2
423. 13: 297 n. 1
434: 122 n. 1, 185 n. 3
440. 24: 189 n. 4
468: 231 n. 1
Aristophanes of Byzantium, *Λέξεις*, fr. 38 N.: 187, 189
fr. 39 N.: 46 n. 2, 135 n. 2

Etymologicum Magnum, ἀμφιδρόμια: 71 n. 1
ἀπατούρια: 89 n. 2
διαδικασία: 216 n. 1
ἐκποίητον γενέσθαι: 77 n. 1
ἔπιπλα: 228 n. 2
Θησεῖον: 172 n. 3
φάσις: 116 n. 4

Harpokration, ἀμφιδρόμια: 71 n. 1
ἀμφισβητεῖν: 95 n. 1, 158 n. 1
ἀνάγειν: 211
ἀνδραποδιστής: 166 n. 1
Ἀνθεμόκριτος: 97 n. 1
ἀπελεύθερος: 181 n. 3
ἀποπεφασμένως: 37 n. 2
ἀπορώτατος: 122 n. 1
ἀποστασίου: 165 n. 1, 185 n. 3
ἀποτιμηταί: 254 n. 1, 257 n. 1, 294 n. 1, 297 n. 1, 303
ἀπροστασίου: 165 n. 6, 185 n. 2, 189 n. 4
ἀρκτεῦσαι: 122 n. 1
Ἀρκτοῦρος: 97 n. 1
αὐτομαχεῖν: 214 n. 1
ἀφαίρεσις: 178 n. 3
ἀφανὴς οὐσία καὶ φανερά: 231 n. 1
ἀφ' ἑστίας μυεῖσθαι: 97 n. 1
γαμηλία: 7 n. 2
δήμαρχος: 306 n. 2
διαμαρτυρία: 122 n. 1
ἑβδομευομένου: 71 n. 1
εἰσαγγελία: 118 n. 1
εἰς ἐμφανῶν κατάστασιν: 209 n. 1
ἐνετιμᾶτο: 257 n. 1
ἐξαιρέσεως δίκη: 178 n. 3, 221
ἐξούλης: 218 n. 1, 311 f.
ἐπιδιατίθεσθαι: 97 n. 1
ἐπιδιετὲς ἡβῆσαι: 97 n. 1, 113 n. 2
ἐπίδικος: 48 n. 3, 122 n. 1, 132 n. 3, 135 n. 2
ἐπίκληρος: 122 n. 1
ἔπιπλα: 228 n. 2
ἐπισημαίνεσθαι: 97 n. 1
ἐπωβελία: 120 n. 4
ζειρά: 97 n. 1
θέσθαι: 254 n. 2
θέτης: 216 n. 1
θῆτες: 135 n. 2
Ἱππία Ἀθηνᾶ: 97 n. 1
ἰσοτελὴς καὶ ἰσοτέλεια: 189 n. 1

Harpokration (*cont.*)
- *κακώσεως*: 44 n. 1, 78 n. 1, 118 n. 2, 122 n. 1
- *καρποῦ δίκη*: 97 n. 1, 222 f., 225
- *Κεφαλῆθεν*: 97 n. 1
- *κοινωνικῶν*: 240 n. 1, 242, 243 n. 1
- *ληξιαρχικὸν γραμματεῖον*: 122 n. 1
- *μετοίκιον*: 165 n. 6, 185 n. 1, 187
- *νεμέσεια*: 52 n. 1
- *νοθεῖα*: 67 n. 3
- *ὁδός*: 97 n. 1
- *ὀργέων*: 122 n. 1
- *ὅτι οἱ ποιητοί*: 94 n. 5, 97 n. 1
- *ὅτι παιδί*: 73 n. 3
- *οὐσίας δίκη*: 222, 223 f., 225
- *παρακαταβολή*: 122 n. 1
- *παρηγγύησεν*: 97 n. 1
- *Πεδιακά*: 97 n. 1
- *πεντακοσιομέδιμνον*: 122 n. 1
- *ποταμός*: 89 n. 2
- *Προσπάλτιοι*: 122 n. 1
- *προστάτης*: 189 n. 4
- *πωλῶσι*: 37 n. 2
- *σεσημασμένων*: 97 n. 1
- *σιπύα*: 122 n. 1
- *σῖτος*: 57 n. 2, 104 n. 4
- *Σπάρτωλος*: 97 n. 1
- *τοὺς χωρὶς οἰκοῦντας*: 167 n. 5
- *φάσις*: 116 n. 4, 117 n. 1

Hesychius s.v. *ἀναγωγή*: 211 n. 1
- *ἀποκήρυκτος*: 77 n. 1
- *ἀποτιμήματα*: 297 n. 1
- *ἀπροστασίου*: 189 n. 4
- *δεκάτην θύομεν*: 71 n. 1
- *ἐγχυτρίζειν*: 71 n. 2
- *ἐν λευκώμασι*: 290 f., 306, 306 n. 2
- *ἐξελεύθεροι*: 181 n. 3
- *ἔπιπλα*: 228 n. 2
- *καρποῦ δίκη*: 223, 225, 227 n. 2
- *μέτοικοι*: 187 n. 2
- *μετοίκιον*: 185 n. 1
- *προστάτου*: 189 n. 4

Lex. Cant. s.v. *ἀργίας δίκη*: 79 n. 2
- *εἰς ἐμφανῶν κατάστασιν*: 208, 209
- *ἔνδειξις*: 116 n. 4

Photius s.v. *θέτης*: 216 n. 1
- *καρποῦ δίκη*: 222 f., 225
- *μετοίκιον*: 187 n. 2
- *οὐσίας δίκη* Art. 1: 222, 224 n. 1, 225
- *οὐσίας δίκη* Art. 2: 222
- *φάσις*: 116 n. 4

Pollux 3. 21: 61
- 3. 33: 132 n. 3
- 3. 47: 60 n. 1
- 3. 48: 19 n. 1
- 3. 55: 185 n. 1
- 3. 83: 181 n. 2
- 4. 93: 77 n. 1
- 8. 31: 43 n. 2, 44 n. 1, 176 n. 7
- 8. 32: 158 n. 1
- 8. 33: 208, 209 n. 1
- 8. 34 f.: 212, 213 n. 1
- 8. 35: 185 n. 3, 189 n. 4, 190 n. 2
- 8. 42: 80 n. 1
- 8. 45: 233 n. 2
- 8. 47: 116 n. 4
- 8. 50: 207 n. 1
- 8. 53: 19 n. 2, 32 n. 3, 117 n. 2
- 8. 59: 218 n. 1
- 8. 61: 54 n. 3
- 8. 89: 44 n. 1, 102 n. 2, 294 n. 1
- 8. 99: 165 n. 6
- 8. 107: 89 n. 2
- 8. 142: 256 n. 1, 257 n. 1, 297 n. 1, 299 n. 1
- 10. 10: 228 n. 2
- 10. 15: 122 n. 1

Suda s.v. *ἀγκιστεύς*: 143 n. 3
- *ἀμφιδρόμια*: 71 n. 1
- *ἀμφισβητεῖν*: 95 n. 1
- *ἀμφισβητεῖν* Art. 2: 158 n. 1
- *ἀναγωγὴ οἰκέτου*: 176 n. 3
- *ἀνάργυρος*: 122 n. 1
- *ἀνεπίδικα*: 156 n. 1
- *ἀποστασίου*: 185 n. 3
- *ἀποτιμηταί*: 297 n. 1
- *Ἀριστογείτων*: 97 n. 1
- *αὐτομαχεῖν*: 214 n. 1
- *ἀφανὴς οὐσία καὶ φανερά*: 231 n. 1
- *δεκάτην ἑστιᾶσαι*: n. 71 n. 1
- *δήμαρχος*: 306 n. 2
- *διάθεσις*: 122 n. 1, 152 n. 5
- *ἔγγειον*: 107 n. 3, 228 n. 3, 232 n. 4
- *ἐγχυτρίστριαι*: 71 n. 2
- *ἐκποίητον γενέσθαι*: 77 n. 1
- *ἐνετιμᾶτο*: 257 n. 1, 299 n. 1
- *ἐξούλης δίκη*: 218 n. 1
- *ἐπίδικος*: 132 n. 3, 134
- *ἐπίκληρος*: 67 n. 3, 132 n. 3, 134
- *ἔπιπλα*: 228 n. 2
- *θῆττα*: 135 n. 2
- *κακώσεως*: 44 n. 1
- *καρποῦ δίκη* Art. 1: 223, 225, 227 n. 2

καρποῦ δίκη Art. 2: 222 f., 225
Κυνόσαργες: 65 n. 2
μετοίκιον: 185 n. 1, 187, 187 n. 2
νέμειν προστάτην: 189 n. 4
οὐσία: 201 n. 1
οὐσίας δίκη: 222
πωληταί Art. 2: 165 n. 6, 190 n. 1
σίτου: 40 n. 2
τοὺς χωρὶς οἰκοῦντας 167 n. 5
φάσις: 116 n. 4

Thomas Magister s.v. ἀποκήρυκτος: 77 n. 1
ἀπολείπει: 40 n. 2

LITERARY TEXTS

Achilles Tatius 8. 8. 13: 55 n. 2
Aelianus, *Varia Historia*, 2. 12: 76 n. 1
Aischines, 1 *Against Timarchos* 12: 37
13: 38 n. 1, 98 n. 3
14: 14 n. 3, 37 n. 4
15: 168 n. 2
16: 108 n. 2
17: 172 n. 2
18: 73 n. 3, 98 n. 3
19: 37 n. 5
21: 37 n. 5
28: 78 n. 1, 78 n. 2
30: 80 n. 1, 233 n. 2
32: 195 n. 1
54: 167 n. 6, 177
59: 177
62: 177, 221
66: 179 n. 3
87: 37 n. 5
97: 176 n. 4, 228 n. 2
101: 203 n. 1
102: 240 n. 1
138: 166 n. 4
139: 166 n. 4
158: 102 n. 1
170: 114 n. 1
182: 74 n. 2
183: 36 n. 1
184: 14 n. 3, 37 n. 4
195: 38 n. 1
2 *False Embassy* 87: 170 n. 1
3 *Against Ktesiphon* 10: 207 n. 1
21: 87 n. 3
41: 183 n. 2
44: 183 n. 2
104: 263
251: 80 n. 3
Aischines: scholia to 2 *False Embassy* 87: 170 n. 1
3 *Against Ktesiphon* 13: 172 n. 3
146: 216 n. 1
Aischylos, *Eumenides* 657 ff.: 23
Ps.-Ammonios (p. 75 Valckenaer): 188
Anaximenes, *Rhet. ad Alex.* 1: 147 n. 1, 148 n. 3
Andokides, 1 *De Mysteriis* 20: 171 n. 1
74: 130 n. 1
100: 37 n. 5
117: 132 n. 3, 134 n. 2
118: 231 n. 1
119: 20 n. 1
124: 16 n. 2
125 ff.: 44, 45 n. 1
127: 69
4 *Against Alkibiades*: 41
13: 50 n. 1
14: 40 n. 3
15: 234 n. 1
Antiphanes, fragment 212 K.: 14 n. 3
Antiphon, 1 *Against a Stepmother* 29: 169 n. 4
2 *1st Tetralogy* 3. 4: 170 n. 3, 171 n. 1
5 *Murder of Herodes* 34: 171 n. 1
47: 171, 173
48: 170 n. 3
6 *On the Choreutes* 4: 169 n. 2, 172, 172 n. 1
23: 176 n. 5
Apollodoros, Ἐπιδικαζόμενος: 122 n. 1
Ariston *ap.* Stobaeus, *Flor.* 67. 16: 19 n. 1
Aristophanes, *Birds* 494: 71 n. 1
922: 71 n. 1
1354: 78 n. 1
1649 ff.: 25
1660 f.: 62, 66, 67
Clouds 844 ff.: 80 n. 2
Ekklesiazusae 446 ff.: 114 n. 1
Frogs 694: 182 n. 1
Knights 347: 188
1312: 172 n. 3
Peace 684: 190
Plutus 982 ff.: 114 n. 3
Thesmophoriazusae 224: 172 n. 3
294: 167 n. 2
839 ff.: 114 n. 1
Wasps 583 ff.: 154 n. 2
659: 234 n. 1
fragment 567 K.: 172 n. 3

Aristophanes: scholia to *Birds* 1655: 67 n. 3
Clouds 498: 207 n. 2
1083: 33 n. 2
1371: 22 n. 3
Frogs 694: 182 n. 1
Knights 965: 32 n. 2, 108 n. 5
Aristotle, *Athenaion Politeia* 2. 2: 164 n. 3
4. 2: 12 n. 2
4. 5: 164 n. 3
6. 1: 164 n. 3
9: 123 n. 1
9. 1: 164 n. 3
26. 4: 25
35. 2: 150 n. 3, 152 n. 5
42. 1: 64 n. 1, 74, 74 n. 3, 90 n. 2, 188 n. 3
42. 5: 18 n. 5
43. 4: 10, 159 n. 3
43. 5: 195 n. 1
47: 203 n. 1
47. 2: 244. 2
52. 1: 166 n. 1
52. 2: 50, 51 n. 1
53. 2: 194 n. 2
54: 235 n. 2
56. 2: 194 n. 1, 209 n. 1, 217 n. 1
56. 6: 44 n. 1, 77, 80, 112 n. 4, 117, 209 n. 1
56. 6 and 7: 102 n. 2, 103, 117 n. 1, 138
56. 7: 21 n. 1, 104 n. 4, 257 n. 1, 294 n. 1
57. 3: 170 n. 1, 197 n. 1
58. 2: 189 n. 1, 193 n. 1, 194 n. 2, 195, 196
58. 3: 148 n. 2
59. 3: 34 n. 1
59. 6: 156 n. 3
68. 4: 156 n. 3
Nikomachean Ethics 1161^{b}4: 163 n. 2
1163^a: 242
Politics 1253^{b}32: 163 n. 2
1256$^{a, b}$: 244
1266^b: 233 n. 1, 237 n. 1
1267^b: 229 n. 2
1268^b: 5 n. 3
1274^{b}5: 156 n. 3
1275^{a}11: 189 n. 4
1278^{a}32: 164 n. 2
1280^b: 29 n. 1
1307^a: 237 n. 1
1309^{a}24: 150 n. 2
1319^a: 233 n. 1, 237 n. 1
1335^b: 73 n. 1
Problems 950^b: 125 n. 1, 149 n. 3
951^b: 179 n. 3
Rhetoric 1361^{a}21: 202
1401^b: 31 n. 1
1408^{b}25: 183 n. 2
Athenaeus 3. 82: 181 n. 3
6. 26: 65 n. 2
10. 61: 97 n. 1
13. 2: 15 n. 2, 16 n. 3, 19 n. 1
13. 38: 26 n. 1
13. 58: 76 n. 1
Aulus Gellius, *Noctes Atticae* 9. 2: 167 n. 1
15. 20: 16 n. 3

Cicero, *De Senectute* 7. 22: 81 n. 2

Demosthenes, 4 *Philippic* i. 36: 167 n. 5, 188 n. 1
5 *Peace* 8: 231 n. 1
7 *Halonnesos* 26: 204
42: 237 n. 2
13 *Syntaxis* 30: 237 n. 1
14 *Symmories* 16: 243 n. 1
18 *Crown* 91: 29 n. 1
187: 29 n. 1
20 *Leptines* 29: 189 n. 1
102: 84 n. 6, 88 n. 4, 150 n. 3
21 *Meidias* 47: 195 n. 1
47–49: 168 n. 2
78: 119 n. 3
87: 236 n. 2
22 *Androtion* 26: 207 n. 1
34: 128
55: 167 n. 3
61: 188 n. 1
23 *Aristokrates* 23: 188 n. 5
47: 188 n. 4
48: 188 n. 4
53: 13, 33 n. 1
55: 33 n. 1, 164 n. 2
80: 169 n. 2
208: 237 n. 1
213: 65 n. 2
24 *Timokrates* 54: 218 n. 1, 244 n. 2, 293 n. 1
60: 78 n. 2
63: 195 n. 1
103: 78 n. 1, 78 n. 2
105: 78 n. 2, 207 n. 2
107: 78 n. 1

112: 235 n. 2
113: 207 n. 1
118: 34 n. 2
127: 235 n. 2
167: 167 n. 3
201: 128 n. 2
203: 27 n. 1
25 *Aristogeiton* i. 55: 27 n. 1
57: 165 n. 6
65: 185 n. 3
69: 257 n. 4
27 *Aphobos* i: 74 n. 3, 97 n. 1, 105 n. 4, 119
Hyp. 2: 121 n. 1
4–9: 54
4: 8 n. 1, 21 n. 1
5: 8 n. 1, 24 n. 1, 48 n. 2, 151 n. 5, 252 n. 2
6: 104 n. 2
7–11: 232 n. 2, 232 n. 3
7: 108 n. 3
9: 176 n. 6, 255 n. 1, 259 n. 1, 261, 280, 281
10: 228 n. 2
10–11: 232 n. 3
15: 8 n. 2
17: 8 n. 2, 47 n. 2, 55 n. 1, 57 n. 2, 58
20: 176 n. 4
24 ff.: 261
24: 255 n. 1, 280, 281, 292 n. 3
25: 281 n. 1
27–28: 261
27: 292
36: 104 n. 3
39: 98 n. 2
40: 105 n. 5
42 f.: 151 n. 5
46: 104 n. 5
49 ff.: 120 n. 2
55: 98 n. 3
57: 231 n. 1
58 f.: 106 n. 1
58–60: 105 n. 5
58: 105 n. 5
61: 232 n. 4
67: 120 n. 3, 120 n. 4
28 *Aphobos* ii: 97 n. 1, 105 n. 4, 119
1: 128 n. 3
2–4: 231 n. 1
4: 108 n. 3
5: 99 n. 3
7–9: 231 n. 1
8: 108 n. 3
14: 99 n. 3
15 f.: 6 n. 1
15: 105 n. 5, 151 n. 5
16: 105 n. 3
17 f.: 283 n. 1
17–18: 269, 288
29 *Aphobos* iii: 97 n. 1
29: 105 n. 5
31: 119 n. 2
33: 59
43: 6 n. 1, 48 n. 2
30 *Onetor* i: 41 f., 97 n. 1, 218 n. 1, 297 n. 1, 313
2 f.: 211 n. 2
2: 285
4: 257 n. 1
7: 121, 257 n. 1, 294 n. 1
8: 98 n. 2, 257 n. 1, 285
11: 46 n. 3
12: 52 n. 2
15: 105 n. 4
17: 41 n. 1
18: 257 n. 1
19 f.: 50 n. 2, 50 n. 4
21: 18 n. 2
26 ff.: 259 n. 1
26: 41 n. 1, 257 n. 1
28: 229 n. 1, 257 n. 1
29: 229 n. 1, 257 n. 1
30: 228 n. 3
31: 41 n. 1, 228 n. 3
33: 38 n. 2
31 *Onetor* ii: 97 n. 1, 218 n. 1, 297 n. 1, 313
1: 257 n. 4
3: 257 n. 1, 257 n. 4
4: 257 n. 1, 257 n. 4
5 ff.: 284
5: 257 n. 4
6: 257 n. 1, 285
7: 285 f.
11: 257 n. 1
12: 257 n. 4
32 *Zenothemis*: 191 n. 2, 219 n. 3, 290 n. 1
17 ff.: 219 n. 3
29: 196 n. 1, 273 n. 1
29 f.: 194 n. 2
33 *Apatourios*: 191 n. 2, 253 n. 2, 290 n. 1
3: 228 n. 3
5–12: 272–4, 288

Demosthenes, 33 *Apatourios* (*cont.*)
8: 254 n. 1, 256 n. 1
10: 254 n. 1
11: 288 n. 2
12: 254 n. 1, 255 n. 3, 256 n. 1
25: 256 n. 1
27: 247
38: 209 n. 2
34 *Against Phormion*: 191 n. 2, 290 n. 1
5: 167 n. 6
6: 255 n. 4, 290
7: 255 n. 4
8: 255 n. 4
18: 167 n. 6, 189 n. 1
22: 255 n. 4, 290
23: 228 n. 3
24: 228 n. 3
31: 176
37: 28 n. 1, 57 n. 2, 167 n. 6, 177
44: 189 n. 1
46: 167 n. 6
50: 255 n. 4, 290
35 *Lakritos* 3 f.: 126
4: 124 n. 4, 126 n. 2, 127
10 ff.: 286
11: 208, 254 n. 2, 255 n. 4
12: 228 n. 3, 289
18: 255 n. 4
21: 254 n. 2, 290
22: 290
25: 201 n. 1
36: 290 n. 2
44: 124 n. 4, 127
47: 166 n. 1
48: 102 n. 1, 195
52: 255 n. 4, 290 n. 2
36 *For Phormion*: 97 n. 1
4–6: 283 n. 1
5: 228 n. 3, 232 n. 3
6: 237 n. 2, 269
8: 21, 24 n. 1, 99 n. 3, 99 n. 4, 105 n. 5, 240
9: 240 n. 2
11: 131 n. 4
13 f.: 176 n. 2
14: 151 n. 1
19: 124 n. 2, 125 n. 1
20: 105 n. 4
22: 98 n. 3, 100 n. 2, 105 n. 3
25: 246 n. 2, 247
28: 21
29: 21
32: 132 n. 1
34 f.: 152 n. 1
34: 131 n. 4
36: 124 n. 4
47: 182 n. 2
37 *Pantainetos*: 203 n. 1, 229 n. 1, 253 n. 2, 274, 282, 289
4: 229 n. 1
5: 256 n. 1, 275
6–7: 276
12: 276 n. 2
17: 256 n. 1
19: 218 n. 1, 244 n. 2, 293 n. 1
21: 173 n. 3
29: 275, 277
30: 256 n. 1
31: 256 n. 1, 275 n. 1, 277 n. 1, 278 n. 1
35: 234 n. 2
45 f.: 117 n. 2, 118 n. 1
46: 118 n. 3
50: 256 n. 1, 278 n. 1
51: 174 n. 1
Hyp. 1: 275 n. 1
Hyp. 2: 256 n. 1
38 *Nausimachos*: 97 n. 1, 120
2: 121 n. 1
6: 98 n. 3, 105 n. 3
7: 124 n. 3, 126, 126 n. 3, 127 n. 2, 231 n. 1
14: 105 n. 4
15: 105 n. 4, 119 n. 3
17: 120 n. 6, 247
23: 115 n. 3, 117 n. 1
39 *Boiotos* i: 15, 63, 79, 84 n. 2
2: 63, 79 n. 1
4: 84 n. 2
6: 125 n. 1
20: 84 n. 2
22: 71 n. 1
26: 17 n. 1
27: 131 n. 4
29: 131 n. 4
31: 63
34: 63
35: 125 n. 1, 130 n. 2
39: 75 n. 2, 76, 77
40 *Boiotos* ii: 15, 55, 57, 63, 79
2: 63 n. 3, 125 n. 1
4: 18 n. 5
6 f.: 111 n. 2
6: 39 n. 2, 44
7: 20 n. 1
9 ff.: 79 n. 1

10: 63, 84 n. 2, 114 n. 3
11: 69
14 f.: 57
14: 125 n. 1
16–17: 51 n. 1
19: 48 n. 3
20: 55
25: 49 n. 1, 52 n. 2
28: 71 n. 1
35: 79 n. 1
50: 57
52: 203 n. 1
59: 55 n. 1
61: 2 n. 3
41 *Spoudias*: 51, 52 n. 1, 298 n. 1, 300, 300 n. 1
3 ff.: 83 n. 2, 94 n. 3, 155 n. 1, 259 n. 1
4: 30
5–7: 297 n. 1
5: 50 n. 4, 51 n. 2, 155 n. 1, 298 n. 1, 303
6: 2 n. 1, 49, 152 n. 2, 257 n. 4, 298 n. 1
7: 295 n. 2, 300 n. 1
9: 114 n. 1, 151 n. 1
10: 201 n. 1, 257 n. 1, 295 n. 2, 297 n. 1, 298 n. 1, 300
11: 254 n. 1, 254 n. 2, 262 n. 1
12: 79 n. 1
16: 257 n. 4
22: 114 n. 1
26: 48 n. 3, 49 n. 2
27: 257 n. 1
28: 257 n. 1
42 *Phainippos*: 268
3: 203 n. 1
5: 257 n. 4, 268
9: 283 n. 1
21: 93 n. 2
27: 54, 55 n. 1, 57, 93 n. 2
28 f.: 269 n. 1, 283 n. 1
28: 257 n. 4, 268, 289
43 *Makartatos*: 122 n. 1
4 ff.: 161 n. 1
5: 11 n. 1, 158 n. 1, 159, 308
11: 83 n. 4
13: 91 n. 1, 91 n. 2, 92 n. 1
15: 94 n. 1, 177 n. 4
16: 11 n. 1, 160, 160 n. 1, 160 n. 2, 161 n. 1, 161 n. 2, 162, 214
41: 91 n. 2
49: 143 n. 1
51: 62, 67, 130 n. 2, 130 n. 4, 138, 138 n. 3, 140, 142 n. 1, 143 n. 1, 145 n. 3, 146, 147, 148
54: 20 n. 1, 46 n. 2, 135 n. 2
58: 128 n. 2
57: 64 n. 1, 143 n. 3
65: 130 n. 3
71: 116 n. 2, 203 n. 2
75: 39 n. 2, 83 n. 1, 92, 102 n. 1, 107 n. 4, 118 n. 3, 310
77: 92 n. 1
79: 143 n. 2
44 *Leochares*: 19 n. 1, 122 n. 1, 140, 246 n. 3
7: 160 n. 1
9: 20 n. 1
10: 23 n. 2, 239
13: 160 n. 1
17: 20 n. 1
18: 239
19: 91, 91 n. 3, 95 n. 1
21: 94 n. 5
27: 84 n. 3
32: 93 n. 2
33: 141
34: 141
39 f.: 90 n. 2
40: 160 n. 1
42: 156 n. 2
43: 83 n. 4, 91, 91 n. 3
44: 94 n. 5
46: 91, 94 n. 5, 156 n. 2
48: 84 n. 1
49: 5 n. 2, 9 n. 1, 84 n. 6
51: 84 n. 2
55 ff.: 156 n. 2
59: 157 n. 5, 158
63: 85 n. 4
67 f.: 150 n. 3
67: 84 n. 6, 85 n. 4
68: 85 n. 4
45 *Stephanos* i. 3: 99 n. 4
18: 154 n. 3
21: 125 n. 1
28: 46 n. 3, 47 n. 1, 48 n. 2, 49 n. 2, 112 n. 3, 152 n. 1
37: 99 n. 4, 105 n. 5
66: 231 n. 1
70: 282 n. 1, 283 n. 1
78: 84 n. 2
81: 207 n. 1
46 *Stephanos* ii. 13: 99 n. 4, 182 n.
14: 84 n. 6, 86 n. 2, 87 n. 2, 129,

Demosthenes, 46 *Stephanos* ii (*cont.*)
150 n. 3, 152 n. 5
15: 84 n. 2, 86 n. 2, 182 n. 2, 95 n. 3
16: 152 n. 5, 153 n. 3
18: 5, 5 n. 2, 9, 19, 20 n. 1, 30 n. 1, 61, 110, 111 n. 2, 136, 154 n. 3
20: 60 n. 1, 113 n. 2
22: 10 n. 1, 148 n. 2, 158 n. 2, 159 n. 1, 188 n. 4, 193 n. 1
23: 10 n. 2, 188 n. 4, 193 n. 1
24: 75 n. 3, 85 n. 1, 152 n. 4
28: 154 n. 3
47 *Euergos and Mnesibulos* 32: 124 n. 4, 128 n. 3
34: 240 n. 1
37: 254 n. 1
38: 254 n. 1, 313, 314
41: 254 n. 1
42: 254 n. 1
57: 46 n. 3, 53
68–73: 196
70: 148 n. 3, 169 n. 3, 170 n. 1
72: 167 n. 5, 169 n. 4
48 *Olympiodoros*: 122 n. 1
5 ff.: 160 n. 1
12: 231 n. 1
20 ff.: 160 n. 1
23: 160 n. 1
26: 11 n. 1, 160 n. 1
29 ff.: 161 n. 1
30: 160 n. 1
45: 223, 225
Hyp. 2: 231 n. 1
Hyp. 9: 231 n. 1
Hyp. 33: 231 n. 1
Hyp. 35: 231 n. 1
49 *Timotheos* 1: 124 n. 4
2: 254 n. 1
11: 201 n. 1, 257 n. 1, 257 n. 4
12: 257 n. 4
35: 255 n. 1
48: 262 n. 1
52: 254 n. 1, 254 n. 2
53: 254 n. 1
61: 257 n. 4
50 *Polykles* 8: 231 n. 1, 238 n. 3
13: 289
28: 262 n. 1, 289
55: 254 n. 2
61: 266, 266 n. 3
52 *Kallippos* 10: 208, 210
17: 318
53 *Nikostratos*: 308
6 ff.: 181 n. 4
9: 262
10: 254 n. 2, 267, 291 f.
11: 39 n. 3, 165 n. 1
12–13: 267 f.
12: 266 n. 3
13: 254 n. 2
14 f.: 209
14: 208
20 f.: 176 n. 4
20: 167 n. 4, 257 n. 1
21: 175
28: 54 n. 3, 267
54 *Konon* 1: 166 n. 1
24: 166 n. 1
55 *Kallikles*: 249 f.
1–2: 250 n. 2
14: 250
18: 250
19: 251
25: 250
28: 250
31 ff.: 174
31: 174 n. 2
34: 250 n. 2
56 *Dionysodoros*: 191 n. 2
1: 231 n. 1
3: 254 n. 1
4: 255 n. 1
6: 289
29: 232 n. 3
38: 208 f., 210, 255 n. 1
57 *Eubulides*: 63 f., 188 n. 4
18: 181 n. 4
19: 188 n. 4
20: 22 n. 3
30: 26 n. 1
32: 79
40 ff.: 44
40–43: 64
41: 6 n. 2, 18 n. 2
43: 7 n. 2, 64
45: 188 n. 3
46: 64
48: 188 n. 4
53: 65 n. 2
54: 9 n. 1
55: 188 n. 4
58 *Theokrines* 6: 116 n. 3
13: 116 n. 1
17: 128 n. 2
19: 71 n. 3

21: 179 n. 3, 221 n. 1
31: 94 n. 5
32: 118 n. 1
59 *Neaira*: 26
2: 23 n. 2, 182 n. 2
8: 2 n. 3
9 f.: 169 n. 3
10: 170 n. 2
16: 26 n. 2, 165 n. 5
18 ff.: 114 n. 1
21: 166 n. 3
22: 23 n. 2
29 ff.: 182
29: 114 n. 1, 182
40: 71 n. 3, 221, 273 n. 1
45: 221
50: 49
51: 40 n. 2
52: 6 n. 2, 26 n. 2, 47 n. 2, 55, 57 n. 2, 195 n. 2
53: 6 n. 2, 118 n. 1
59: 90 n. 1
60: 9 n. 1
64: 33 n. 2
66: 33 n. 3, 195 n. 1
67: 37 n. 2
70: 48 n. 1
75: 38 n. 2
85: 22 n. 3
87: 36 n. 1
92: 9 n. 1
93: 2 n. 2
106: 9 n. 1
121: 118 n. 1
122: 2 n. 4, 28 n. 1
Epistulae 3. 29: 165 n. 4
3. 41: 231 n. 1
Demosthenes: Scholia to 8 *Chersonese* 57: 216 n. 1
21 *Meidias* 44: 312
24 *Timokrates* 13: 216 n. 1
20: 102 n. 1
131: 165 n. 4
Digest 10. 1. 13: 249 n. 2
48. 5. 24 pr.: 33 n. 1
Ps.-Dikaiarchos, fr. 59: 188 n. 3
Dinarchos, *Demosthenes* 60: 34 n. 2
70: 231 n. 1
71: 19 n. 1
Dio Chrysostom 15. 3: 164 n. 1
15. 22: 184 n. 3
25. 3: 203 n. 2
74. 9: 73 n. 3

Diodorus Siculus 12. 18: 46 n. 2, 135 n. 2
Diogenes Laertius 1. 55: 78 n. 1, 79 n. 2
1. 56: 24 n. 1, 105 n. 2
1. 57: 245 n. 2
2. 26: 16 n. 3
3. 41: 107 n. 2
3. 42: 184 n. 1
3. 43: 100 n. 3
5. 11: 151 n. 2
5. 11–16: 100 n. 3
5. 12: 98 n. 3
5. 14–15: 184 n. 1
5. 51: 151 n. 2
5. 55: 184 n. 1, 184 n. 2
5. 57: 154 n. 2
5. 61: 151 n. 2
5. 63: 184 n. 1
5. 69: 151 n. 2
5. 72–73: 184 n. 1
5. 73 f.: 184 n. 2
10. 21: 184 n. 1
Dionysios of Halikarnassos, *Antiquitates Romanae* 2. 26: 70 n. 3, 74 n. 2, 75 n. 1, 76
On Deinarchos 12: 97 n. 1, 122 n. 1
13: 97 n. 1, 234 n. 2
On Isaios 8: 97 n. 1
9: 97 n. 1
12: 97 n. 1
15: 95 n. 2, 122 n. 1, 158 n. 2, 208, 210
On Lysias 20: 97 n. 1

Eumelos F 2: 26 n. 1, 62 n. 1
Eupolis, fragment 225 K.: 172 n. 3
Euripides, *Andromache* 173 ff.: 22 n. 2
Orestes 552: 23 n. 1
Eustathius, *On Iliad* 21. 449: 135 n. 2
On Odyssey 3. 302: 228 n. 2

Festus, p. 95: 22 n. 3

Gaius 1. 55: 70 n. 3
Galen 19. 177: 73 n. 1

Hellanikos, F 25: 182 n. 1
Heraklides Ponticus 2. 7: 233 n. 1
Hermogenes, *De inventione* 1. 1: 74 n. 2
Περὶ τῶν στάσεων 10: 19 n. 2
Herodotos 1. 65: 98 n. 2
2. 92: 15 n. 2
2. 136: 201 n. 1, 254 n. 1

Herodotos (*cont.*)
2. 177: 80 n. 1
6. 39: 25 n. 1
6. 126: 25 n. 1
6. 130: 5, 18
9. 10: 98 n. 2
Hippocratic oath: 73 n. 1
Homer, *Iliad* 8. 281: 13 n. 3
9. 494 ff.: 82
11. 243 ff.: 5 n. 3
16. 190: 5 n. 3
22. 472: 5 n. 3
Odyssey 8. 347: 3
8. 351: 3–5
11. 117: 5 n. 3
11. 282: 5 n. 3
14. 202: 13 n. 3
Hyperides, 2 *Lykophron* 20: 34 n. 2
3 *For Euxenippos* 36: 203 n. 1
5 *Against Athenogenes*: 175, 306 n. 2
5: 183
6: 175 n. 2
9: 231 n. 1
10: 173 n. 2, 175 n. 2
15: 176 n. 3
16: 5 n. 2, 9 n. 1
17: 87 n. 2, 150 n. 3, 152 n. 5
20: 175 n. 2
22: 173, 173 n. 2, 175
Hyperides Fragments (Jensen) 13–26: 178 n. 3
21: 189 n. 4
108–10: 122 n. 1
160: 122 n. 1
192: 113 n. 2
193: 256 n. 1

Idomeneus, F 14: 183
Isaios, 1 *Kleonymos* 1: 125 n. 3
9: 101
10: 98 n. 3, 105 n. 3, 108 n. 4, 130 n. 2
14: 154 n. 4
15: 154 n. 3
18: 154 n. 4
39: 118 n. 3
44: 145 n. 3
2 *Menekles* 1: 84 n. 2, 87 n. 2
2: 95 n. 1
3 ff.: 20 n. 1
4: 130 n. 2
5: 49, 49 n. 1, 49 n. 2
7 ff.: 40 n. 1
9: 47, 47 n. 1
10 ff.: 83 n. 2
11: 84 n. 4
13: 82 n. 2, 150 n. 3, 150 n. 4, 151 n. 3
21: 88 n. 2
24: 82 n. 2
28 ff.: 291
28: 241
29: 307
46: 130 n. 2
3 *Pyrrhos*: 41 f.
1: 90 n. 3
2–3: 30
2: 158 n. 2, 177 n. 4
3 f.: 156 n. 3
3: 144 n. 2, 156 n. 2, 157 n. 4
8–9: 49 n. 1
8: 2 n. 3, 40 n. 2, 42
9: 39 n. 1, 56
18 ff.: 18 n. 2
22: 203 n. 1
28–29: 49 n. 1
28: 56
29: 18 n. 2, 49, 49 n. 1
30: 10 n. 2, 71 n. 1, 158 n. 2
35: 47 n. 2, 55, 298
35–39: 49 n. 1
36: 52 n. 3, 56
39: 13–14, 46 n. 3
42: 151 n. 3
43: 132 n. 3, 158 n. 2
45 ff.: 66
45: 20 n. 1
46: 44 n. 1, 117 n. 2
47: 118 n. 1, 118 n. 3
50: 113 n. 2
51: 93 n. 2
53: 2 n. 1
56: 90 n. 3
58: 161, 220, 247, 248 n. 2
59: 156 n. 1
60: 95 n. 1, 95 n. 2
62: 118 n. 3, 118 n. 5, 156 n. 1, 157 n. 4, 218 n. 1, 313 f.
63: 133 n. 3, 145 n. 3
64: 11 n. 2, 12, 309
68: 85 n. 2, 150 n. 3, 151 n. 3
70: 2 n. 1, 6 n. 2, 18 n. 1, 71 n. 1
72–73: 310
72: 133 n. 1, 133 n. 2, 134 n. 2
73–76: 65 n. 1
73: 92 n. 1

74: 133 n. 3, 133 n. 4, 145 n. 3
76: 7 n. 2
78: 39 n. 1, 40 n. 2, 42, 49 n. 1, 56, 57 n. 2
4 *Nikostratos* 2: 10 n. 2, 158 n. 2
8: 103 n. 1
9: 148 n. 3
10 ff.: 90 n. 3
12: 149 n. 3, 150 n. 4, 153 n. 4
13: 154 n. 1, 154 n. 3
16: 87 n. 2, 150 n. 3, 152 n. 5
19: 130 n. 3
22: 150 n. 2
24: 150 n. 2
25: 150 n. 2, 161 n. 1
28: 207 n. 1
5 *Dikaiogenes*: 96
6: 90 n. 3, 96 n. 1, 158 n. 2
7: 96 n. 1, 161 n. 1, 220
9: 144 n. 2
10: 98 n. 3, 101
12 ff.: 161 n. 2
12: 144 n. 2
16: 144 n. 2, 156 n. 2, 156 n. 3, 157 n. 2
18: 144 n. 2
21 ff.: 287
21: 213 n. 1, 254 n. 2, 264 f.
22: 218 n. 1, 312, 313 f.
26: 144 n. 2
27: 53
35: 220
6 *Philoktemon*: 16, 139, 154 n. 5
3: 157 n. 5, 158 n. 2
4 ff.: 90 n. 3
4: 156 n. 2
6: 83 n. 3
7: 154 n. 3
9: 87 n. 2, 150 n. 3, 152 n. 5
10–16: 16 n. 1
13 f. 109 n. 1
13: 24 n. 1, 111 n. 3
14: 2 n. 4, 11 n. 1, 12 n. 2, 28 n. 1
19 ff.: 69
22: 16 n. 1
25: 131 n. 1, 154 n. 5, 233 n. 2
28: 130 n. 4, 151 n. 3
30 ff.: 233 n. 4
30–34: 231 n. 1
31: 94 n. 4, 208, 209 n. 1
32: 154 n. 5
33: 262 n. 1, 265, 287
36 ff.: 105 n. 5
36: 103 n. 1, 257 n. 1, 257 n. 4, 294 n. 1
37: 294 n. 1
38: 140 n. 1
39–40: 16 n. 1
42: 207 n. 2
43: 156 n. 2
44: 94 n. 5
46: 137, 309
47: 26 n. 1, 62, 130 n. 2
48 ff.: 166 n. 3
51: 130 n. 3, 137 n. 1, 159 n. 5, 309
52: 220 n. 3
57: 309
58: 309
63: 85 n. 3, 131 n. 2
7 *Apollodoros* 1: 154 n. 2, 154 n. 3
3: 95 n. 1, 157 n. 5
5 f.: 101
5: 144 n. 1
9: 20 n. 1, 88 n. 3
13 ff.: 83 n. 2
15 ff.: 89 n. 2
16: 84 n. 4, 88 n. 1, 89 n. 2
18–20: 147 n. 2
19: 134, 134 n. 3, 144 n. 2
20: 84 n. 1, 131 n. 1
25: 84 n. 3, 94 n. 1
27: 89 n. 2
28: 90 n. 2
30: 83 n. 1, 92, 102 n. 1, 147 n. 1
31: 83 n. 4, 92 n. 1, 144 n. 2
35–39: 231 n. 1
44: 92 n. 1, 144 n. 2
8 *Kiron* 2: 201 n. 1
8: 2 n. 3, 2 n. 4, 28 n. 1, 39 n. 2
14: 6 n. 2, 18 n. 2
15: 130 n. 2
18: 7 n. 2
19: 2 n. 1, 9 n. 1, 69
29: 2 n. 1, 6 n. 2
31: 113 n. 2
32: 60 n. 1, 78 n. 1, 131 n. 3
34: 130 n. 4, 131 n. 3, 156 n. 1
35: 176 n. 4, 228 n. 2, 231 n. 1
41 f.: 101
43: 26 n. 1
9 *Astyphilos* 2: 93 n. 2
5: 154 n. 3
7 ff.: 153 n. 4
7: 93 n. 2, 130 n. 2
8: 150 n. 2

Isaios, 9 *Astyphilos* (*cont.*)
12: 149 n. 3, 153 n. 5
13: 130 n. 2
27: 24 n. 1
29: 20 n. 1
33: 93 n. 2, 94 n. 5
10 *Aristarchos* 4: 93 n. 2
5: 23 n. 2, 133 n. 1, 145 n. 3, 311
6: 92 n. 1, 93 n. 1
9: 85 n. 1
10: 73 n. 3, 108 n. 5, 150 n. 4, 151 n. 1, 236 n. 3
11: 94 n. 5
12: 113 n. 2, 311
13: 85 n. 2, 132 n. 3, 151 n. 3
14: 84 n. 1
15: 124 n. 4
16 f.: 125, 126 n. 1
16: 125 n. 3
19: 310 f.
20: 236 n. 2
24: 84 n. 2, 214 n. 1, 216 n. 1, 217, 248, 255 n. 2, 266, 266 n. 2
Hyp. 10: 100
11 *Hagnias*: 97 n. 1, 118, 122 n. 1
1–3: 146 n. 3
1: 146 n. 1
2: 138 n. 3, 144 n. 2
6: 117 n. 2
8: 88 n. 3
9: 177 n. 4
10 ff.: 101
10: 160 n. 2
11 ff.: 138 n. 3
11: 143 n. 1, 146
12: 138 n. 3
13: 118 n. 3, 158 n. 2
15 f.: 117 n. 2, 159 n. 5
17: 142 n. 2
26: 11 n. 1, 159 n. 5
27: 120 n. 1
28: 118 n. 1
29 f.: 142 n. 2
31: 118 n. 1, 118 n. 4
34: 107 n. 1
35: 118 n. 1, 118 n. 3
41: 88 n. 3, 228 n. 2
43: 228 n. 2, 231 n. 1
46: 161 n. 2
47: 231 n. 1
49: 83 n. 4, 92 n. 1, 93 n. 1
12 *Euphiletos* 9: 12 n. 2
Against the Demesmen: 200 n. 1
Fragments (Thalheim) 1: 122 n. 1
2: 122 n. 1
6: 125 n. 1, 233 n. 4
7: 97 n. 1
8: 97 n. 1
15: 183 n. 2, 231 n. 1
15–17: 178 n. 3
16: 178 n. 3
22: 97 n. 1
23: 97 n. 1
24: 122 n. 1
25: 113 n. 2, 122 n. 1
Isokrates 1 *Demonikos* 2: 130 n. 4
6 *Archidamos* 26: 246 f.
7 *Areopagitikos* 35: 231 n. 1
8 *Peace* 53: 189 n. 4
14 *Plataikos* 51: 29 n. 1
15 *Antidosis* 90: 166 n. 1
237: 159 n. 2
17 *Trapezitikos* 7: 231 n. 1
12: 196 n. 1, 273 n. 1
14: 71 n. 3, 221
41: 196 n. 1
18 *Kallimachos* 12: 120 n. 4
52 ff.: 169 n. 3
52: 170 n. 1
21 *Euthynos* 2: 228 n. 2, 263 f.

Justinian, *Institutes* 4. 6. 1: 215

Karystios, f. 11: 26 n. 1
Krateros, F 4: 26 n. 1, 64 n. 1
5: 89 n. 1
Kyros 8: 43 n. 2

Lucian, *Abd.* 8: 77 n. 1
Eunuchos 10: 33 n. 1
Lykourgos, *Leokrates* 48: 84 n. 5
65: 170 n. 2
fr. 91: 2 n. 2
Lysias, 1 *Killing of Eratosthenes*: 33
25: 33 n. 2
30 f.: 13 n. 1, 14
31: 2 n. 2
32 ff.: 35 n. 1
32: 34, 34 n. 2
33: 32 n. 6
37: 33 n. 4
49: 33 n. 2
5 *Kallias* 3: 182 n. 1
5: 171 n. 1, 182 n. 1
6 *Andokides* 24: 236 n. 2
7 *Sacred Olive* 16: 171 n. 1, 182 n. 1

8 *Coass.* 10: 255 n. 3, 260 f., 281 n. 1
10 *Theomnestos* i. 5: 101
17: 207 n. 2
19: 37 n. 2
12 *Against Eratosthenes*: 191 n. 2, 196 n. 2, 237 n. 3
19: 176 n. 4, 228 n. 2
83: 231 n. 1
98: 165 n. 2
13 *Agoratos* 41: 169 n. 4
66: 34 n. 2
85–87: 169 n. 2
86 ff.: 166 n. 1
91: 78 n. 1, 84 n. 5
14 *Alkibiades* i. 28: 40, 40 n. 2
16 *Mantitheos* 10: 49 n. 2
17 δημ. ἀδ. 3 ff.: 124 n. 4
19 *Property of Aristophanes* 9: 101
14: 49 n. 1
15: 49 n. 1
17: 49 n. 2
25: 260, 280
26: 260
29: 228, 228 n. 2
31: 228
37: 233
39 ff.: 151 n. 4
59: 48 n. 1
20 *Polystratos* 22: 231 n. 1
33: 231 n. 1
23 *Pankleon* 2: 194 n. 2
9: 221
12: 71 n. 3, 179, 179 n. 2, 221, 221 n. 1
13: 194 n. 2
26 *Euandros* 12: 102 n. 1
30 *Nikomachos* 22: 234 n. 1
32 *Diogeiton*: 97 n. 1, 105, 119
1–9: 20 n. 1
3: 100 n. 1
4: 23 n. 2, 231 n. 1, 240 n. 2
5–14: 44
5: 99 n. 3, 154 n. 3
6: 47 n. 1, 137 n. 1, 152 n. 2
7: 154 n. 3
8: 105 n. 1
9: 101, 104 n. 3
14: 105 n. 1
15: 228 n. 2
16: 105 n. 1
18: 98 n. 3, 100 n. 2
20: 104
22: 100 n. 2
23: 105 n. 5, 107, 231 n. 1
28: 104
34 *Patrios Politeia* 3: 29 n. 1
Against Demosthenes: 223, 225
Against Hippotherses: 191, 217 n. 3, 231 n. 1
Theozotides: 65 n. 2
Fragments (Thalheim) 8: 72, 73 n. 1
8a: 73 n. 1
18–21: 34 n. 1
23: 122 n. 1
24: 18 n. 5, 122 n. 1
27: 97 n. 1
29–31: 122 n. 1
35: 122 n. 1
40: 122 n. 1
41: 122 n. 1
43: 97 n. 1, 98 n. 2, 98 n. 3, 100 n. 2
52: 257 n. 1
74: 87 n. 2, 122 n. 1, 152 n. 5
75: 100 n. 2
78: 122 n. 1
79: 122 n. 1, 231 n. 1
91: 107.

Menander, *Arbitrants*: 19 n. 2, 71 n. 3
64 ff. K.: 245
142 K.: 236 n. 3
165 ff. K.: 22 n. 3
201 f. K.: 167 n. 6
226 f. K.: 167 n. 6
242 f. K.: 167 n. 6
329 K.: 255 n. 3
381 ff. K.: 70 n. 2
480 K.: 31
510 K.: 31
Ἐπιδικαζόμενος: 16
Fabula Incerta 30: 19 n. 2
Περικειρομένη 435 K.: 18, 18 n. 1, 50
Fragments, 220 K.: 18 n. 1
279 K.: 118 n. 1
Minucius Felix, *Octavius* 31. 3: 22 n. 3

Nepos, *Cim.* 1. 2: 22 n. 3
Them. 1: 25 n. 1, 76 n. 1

Corpus Paroemiographorum Graecorum 1. 405: 290 f., 306, 306 n. 1, 308
Pausanias 2. 21. 7: 38 n. 2
Phanodemos F 17: 7 n. 2
Philo, *De specialibus legibus* iii. 4, p. 303 M.: 22 n. 3, 23

Philochoros F 35a: 64 n. 1
F 177: 172 n. 3
Plato, *Alkibiades* 1. 104b: 100 n. 2
122a: 104 n. 5
Euthydemos 301e: 202 n. 1
Gorgias 483b: 167 n. 4
Krito 50d: 78 n. 3
Laws 744e: 137 n. 1
766c: 100 n. 3
774e: 20 n. 1
838b: 22 n. 2
844c: 249
856d: 229
913c–914b: 245 n. 2
914c: 209 n. 3
914d: 217 n. 2
914e: 221, 221 n. 1
915c: 210 f.
916a: 211 n. 2
923e: 85 n. 1
924a: 104 n. 1
924a, b: 100 n. 3
924e: 145 n. 3
928c: 116 n. 1
928d: 77 n. 1
929d–e: 80 n. 3
936c: 174 n. 3
937b: 156 n. 3
937c: 161 n. 2
954a: 207 n. 2
954c: 213 n. 2, 247
954e: 247
Protagoras 320a: 105 n. 1
Republic 461b: 22 n. 2
469b: 165, 165 n. 3
Theaitetos 148b: 156 n. 3
160e: 71 n. 2
Scholium to Plato, *Laws* 936c: 161 n. 2
Plautus, *Aulularia* 793 ff.: 19 n. 2
Casina 41: 71 n. 2
68: 177 n. 1
315 ff.: 184 n. 3
Cistellaria 124: 71 n. 2
Mercator 451 ff.: 241
Miles Gloriosus 1006: 177 n. 1
Rudens 971–5: 245 n. 1
Plutarch, *Alkibiades* 1: 100 n. 2
3: 76 n. 1
8: 40 n. 3, 50 n. 1
Aristeides 27: 16 n. 3
Kimon 4: 22 n. 3, 25 n. 1
Lykourgos 15: 19 n. 1
Lysander 30: 19 n. 1
Perikles 24: 21, 40 n. 1
37: 25, 64 n. 1
Solon 13: 73 n. 2
15: 164 n. 3
20: 32 n. 5
21: 124 n. 1, 150 n. 3
22: 17, 78 n. 3, 80 n. 1
23: 19 n. 2, 33 n. 1, 34, 34 n. 2, 37 n. 2, 73 n. 2, 245 n. 1, 249 n. 2
24: 174 n. 3
Themistokles 1: 25 n. 1, 65 n. 2
2: 76 n. 1
32: 22 n. 3
Theseus 13: 29
Moralia 751. 12: 177 n. 1
785a: 81 n. 2
833: 122 n. 1
834b: 89 n. 1
838b: 93 n. 2
849d: 76 n. 1
Polybius 2. 58. 9: 165 n. 3
12. 16: 201 n. 1, 217 n. 1, 217 n. 2, 219 n. 3
Poseidippos, F 11 K.: 71 n. 2
35: 135 n. 2
Priscian XVIII. 179: 122 n. 1
238: 122 n. 1

Quintilian, *Declamationes* 349: 19 n. 2
Institutio oratoria 9. 2. 90: 19 n. 2

Rutilius Lupus, *De figuris sententiarum* 2. 8: 122 n. 1

Seneca, *Contr.* ii. 3: 19 n. 2
vii. 4: 240 f.
Sextus Empiricus, *Hypot. Pyrrh.* 3. 211: 71 n. 2, 74 n. 2
Solon 24. 5 Diehl: 257 n. 2
Sophokles, *Oedipus Coloneus* 367 ff.: 22 n. 3
830–3: 22 n. 3
Oedipus Tyrannus 411: 190
452: 188
1214: 22 n. 3
1256: 22 n. 3
Stobaeus, *Florilegium* xliv. 22 Meineke, 20 Hense: 204, 291, 305–8, 306 n. 2, 307 n. 1, 308 n. 2
Syrianus on Hermog. 2. 72 Rabe: 24 n. 1

Terence, *Adelphi* 657 ff.: 310
Andria 780 f.: 19 n. 2
800: 148 n. 2
Heautontimorumenos 625: 71 n. 2
Phormio: 16, 122 n. 1
114: 16 n. 2
125–6: 310
410: 135 n. 2
958: 16 n. 2
972: 16 n. 2
1009: 16 n. 2
Theon, *Progymnasmata* 2: 72, 112 n. 3
13: 142 n. 1
Theophrastos, *Characters* 30. 9: 167 n. 6, 245
30. 15: 167 n. 6
Laws: see under Stobaeus *Floril.* xliv
Thucydides 6. 27. 2: 171 n. 1

Valerius Maximus 6. 9, *ext.* 2: 76 n. 1
Vita Sophocl. 13: 81 n. 2

Xenophon, *Hellenika* 2. 4. 25: 189 n. 1
Kyropaedia 7. 5. 73: 165 n. 3
Memorabilia 1. 2. 49: 80 n. 2
2. 2. 13: 78 n. 1
2. 7. 2: 201 n. 1
4. 4. 20: 22 n. 2
Por. 2. 6: 237 n. 2
4. 14 f.: 176 n. 4
Ps.-Xen. *Ath. Pol.* 1. 10: 166 n. 2, 168 n. 1, 172 n. 2
1. 11: 167 n. 6

PAPYRI

Didot 34 ff.: 31 n. 1
Grenfell 1. 11: 219 n. 3
Halensis 80 ff.: 249 n. 2
Ox. Pap. 221: 312
Ox. Pap. 2464: 97 n. 1

GENERAL INDEX

Page references to single words such as *marriage*, which occur in the list of contents on pp. x ff., are not repeated in this Index.

Where an entry refers to a note the page given is that on which the note begins.

ἄγειν εἰς δουλείαν, 71, 178.
ἀγχιστεία, concubine's child, 15.
  νόθοι, 62, 63, 67.
  adoptee, 86.
  succession, 123 n. 2, 128 n. 2, 134 n. 3, 138 n. 3, 311.
  sacra, 130.
  mother, 142 n. 2.
  συγγένεια, 143.
  composition, 146, 148.
ἀγών, ἀτίμητος, τιμητός, 34 n. 2, 118, 250.
αἴδεσις, 143, 198.
ἄμβλωσις, 72.
ἀμφιδρόμια, 70, 76, 78.
ἀμφισβήτησις, 215.
ἀνάγειν, 210, 261.
ἀνακαλυπτήρια, 112.
ἀνάκρισις, 124 n. 2, 143 n. 1, 160, 192, 194.
ἀνδραποδισμός, 165.
ἀνέπαφος, 208, 210, 255 n. 1, n. 4, 286, 291, 305.
ἀνεπίδικος, estate, 95, 156 n. 1.
ἄνευ ὕδατος, 118.
ἀνεψιός, meaning, 143, 146 n. 2.
ἀνήρ, 1, 40 n. 2, 47 n. 2.
ἀντίδοσις, 54, 268.
ἀντίχρησις, 258, 261 n. 2, 276 n. 1.
ἀπαγωγή, 35 n. 1, 78, 165, 178.
ἀπελεύθεροι, 181; *see also* freedman.
ἀπογραφή, 136 n. 1, 306 n. 2.
ἀποδίδοσθαι, 256, 275 n. 1; *see also* πρᾶσις, ὠνή.
ἀποκηρύττειν, 75, 79 n. 1, 94.
ἀπολείπειν, 40.
ἀποπέμπειν, 40.
ἀπόρρησις, 240, 291, 307.
ἀποτίμημα, dotal, 47, 51, 52, 53, 54, 57, 106, 284.
  general, 201 n. 1, 256, 284 n. 1, 316.
  pupillary, 279 n. 2.
ἀργία, 79.
ἄστος, 188.
ἀτιμία, false representation, 26.
  adultery, 35.
  prostitution, 37.
  effect on marriage, 39.
  partial, 39, 116.
  γονέων κακώσεως, 78.
  ἀργία, 79.
  Antiphon, 89.
  succession, 128, 129.
  ownership, 236.
αὐτομαχεῖν, 211.
ἀφαιρεῖσθαι εἰς ἐλευθερίαν, 71, 166, 178, 221.
ἀφαίρεσις, 30, 43, 123 n. 2.

βεβαιοῦν, 212, 276, 314.

γαμετή, 2, 6, 13 n. 1, 17, 40 n. 2, 61, 69 n. 1.
γαμηλία, 7.
γάμος, 1, 2 n. 2, 6, 7, 18, 58.
γηροτροφία, 17, 38, 83, 139.
γνησιότης, 9, 61, 67, 68, 70, 85, 148.
γραφὴ ἀγαμίου, 19.
  ἐξαγωγῆς, 27.
  κακώσεως ἐπικλήρων, 112, 117.
  ἀδίκως εἱρχθῆναι ὡς μοιχόν, 33, 195 n. 1.
  μοιχείας, 34, 36.
  ὕβρεως, 34, 36 n. 2, 163 n. 3, 168, 172, 195 n. 1.
  ἑταιρήσεως, 37, 196.
  προαγωγείας, 37.
  κακώσεως ὀρφανῶν, 39, 117, 196.
  κακώσεως γονέων, 60 n. 1, 77.
  ἀμβλώσεως, 73 n. 1.
  ἀργίας, 79.
  παρανοίας, 80.
  ἐπίτροπον αὐτὸν ἐγγράψαι, 103.
  ξενίας, 118, n. 1, 165.
  ἀνδραποδισμοῦ, 165, 178.

γραφή (*cont.*)
ἀπροστασίου, 165, 189, 192, 195.
ἀσεβείας, 169.
κλοπῆς, 207 n. 1.
κλοπῆς δημοσίων χρημάτων, 235 n. 2.
γυνή, 1, 40 n. 2, 47 n. 2.

δάμαρ, 1 n. 2, 5, 33 n. 1.
δημόσιοι, 177.
διαδικασία, heiress, 11, 32, 43 n. 1.
guardian, 100, 103.
estates, 157, 160.
general, 220.
διαθήκη (testament), 7, 84, 85 n. 1, 90, 125 n. 1, 150, 152, 154 n. 5, 209 n. 1, 210.
διαμαρτυρία, succession cases, 95, 156, 220 n. 3, 314.
διατίθεσθαι, *see* διαθήκη.
δίκαι ἔμμηνοι, προικός, 50.
ἐμπορικαί, 176.
φορᾶς (?φωρᾶς) ἀφανοῦς, μεθημερινῆς, 176 n. 7.
δίκη προικός, 8, 50, 53, 298.
ἐξαγωγῆς, 27.
βιαίων, 34, 36, 214, 219, 221, 313.
ἀπολείψεως, 43.
ἀποπέμψεως, 43.
παραβάσεως συμβολαίων, 51.
ἐνοικίου, 52 n. 1, 214.
βλάβης, 52 n. 1, 79 n. 1, 120 n. 6, 127, 169, 173, 175, 179, 219 n. 3, 250, 276, 307.
ἀργυρίου, 52 n. 1.
ἐξούλης, 97 n. 1, 156, 214, 234 n. 2, 235, 244, 258, 283, 285, 313.
εἰς ἐπιτροπῆς κατάστασιν, 100.
σίτου, 104.
εἰς ἐμφανῶν κατάστασιν, 122 n. 1.
ψευδομαρτυρίων, 156, 161.
ἀποστασίου, 165, 182, 183, 190, 195.
αἰκείας, 168.
φόνου, 169, 199.
ἀφαιρέσεως, 179.
δουλείας, 179 n. 3, 221 n. 1.
κλοπῆς, 207 n. 1.
βεβαιώσεως, 212, 314.
οὐσίας, 214.
καρποῦ, 214.
εἰς δατητῶν αἵρεσιν, 243.
ἀπορρήσεως, 291, 307.
δοκιμασία ῥητόρων, 80 n. 1
δόσις, testament, 150; *see also* διαθήκη.
gift, 202; *see also* gift.

ἔγγειος, 228.
ἐγγύη, betrothal, 1, 2 n. 1, 10, 12, 14, 18, 21, 24, 28, 30, 32 n. 1, 42, 45, 46, 49, 58, 62, 68, 88, 136, 309.
surety 3, 33 n. 3, 179 n. 2,
ἐγγύησις, 2 n. 1, 29 n. 1.
ἐγγυητή, 11, 40 n. 2, 69, 110.
ἔγκλημα, Demosthenes' *v.* guardians, 119 n. 2.
δίκη βλάβης, 173.
ἔγκτησις, 153, 189, 199, 237, 238.
ἔδνα, 45.
εἰσαγγελία, κακώσεως, 32 n. 5, 44, 48 n. 3, 112.
general, 34 n. 2, 171, 195 n. 1.
εἰσποίησις, 84, 88 n. 5, 91.
εἰσφόρα, minors' liability, 108.
ἐκβάλλειν, 40, 45.
ἐκδιδόναι, 2, 6, 18, 21, 32 n. 1, 48, 49.
ἐκκλησία, κυρία, 159.
slaves, 167.
freedmen, 184.
ἐκπέμπειν, 40.
ἐκποίητος, 77 n. 1, 84, 88 n. 5, 93 n. 2, 94 n. 1.
ἐλεύθερος, 188.
ἔλλειπον, 272, 278, 287.
ἐμβατεύειν, 86, 91 n. 3, 95, 156, 272, 283, 313.
ἐνεπισκήψασθαι, 54.
ἐνέχυρον, 254, 272, 313, 316.
ἐντιμᾶν, 299.
ἐξαγωγή, 118 n. 5, 141, 219, 285.
ἐξελεύθεροι, 181; *see also* freedman.
ἐξηγηταί, 197.
ἐπιδανείζειν, 290.
ἐπιδιδόναι, dowry, 49.
ἐπιδικασία, form 18, 115, 122 n. 1, 132, 310.
decides κύριος, 19, 30, 110.
status of parties, 24, 62.
adoptee, 86, 95 n. 1, 129.
ἐπίδικος, κλῆρος, 95, 156 n. 2, 157 n. 5, 220 n. 3.
ἐπίκληρος, 10, 48 n. 3, 109 n. 1, 132, 138, 309.
ἐπίκληρος, marriage, 10, 23 n. 1, 39, 43 n. 1, 44, 66, 145 n. 3, 162, 220 n. 3, 309.
κύριος, 19, 32 n. 1, 110, 117.

endogamy, 22.
 dowry, 48, 56.
 sons, 59, 74 n. 1, 92 n. 1, 93 n. 2, 99 n. 2, 109 n. 2, 113.
 adoptee, 83, 86, 88.
 ownership, 109, 112, 113.
 metic, 196.
ἐπικτητά, 125, 151 n. 4, 233.
ἐπινομία, 238.
ἔπιπλα, 228.
ἐπίπροικος, 48 n. 3.
ἐπισκήπτεσθαι, 156.
ἐπίτροπος, 98, 108; *see also* guardian.
ἐπωβελία, δίκη ἐπιτροπῆς, 120, 269.
ἔρανος, manumission, 182.
εὐθυδικία, 95 n. 1, 157.
ἐφάπτεσθαι, 210.

θέτης (mortgagor), 216 n. 1, 255, 266.
θετός, 84 n. 2, 88 n. 5.
θῆσσα, marriage, 46, 48, 135.

ἰσοτελής, 189, 192 n. 1, 193, 237.

κακοῦργος, 35 n. 1.
κληρονόμος, 124, 128, 155 n. 1 220, 247.
κλῆρος (estate), 92, 95 n. 2, 96 n. 1, 124, 156 n. 3, 157 n. 5, 208, 210, 220, 233, 247, 308.
κοινωνία, 240, 242.
κρατεῖν, 201.
κυριεία (ownership), 201 n. 1, 204.
κύριος, women, 12, 27, 28, 42.
 brother, 22 n. 3, 93 n. 2.
 in court, 36, 108, 157.
 minors, 38, 73, 74, 88, 90, 94 n. 1, 105, 138, 240, 294.
 divorce, 39.
 dowry, 46, 48, 52 n. 4, 53, 56, 58, 59, 299.
 husband, 54.
 See also guardian.

λῆξις, 10, 118 n. 5, 158 n. 2, 160 n. 2.
λύσις, χωρίου, 200 n. 1.
 ἔν τινι ῥητῷ χρόνῳ, 256, 275, 278, 282, 317.
λύτρα, *see* ransom.

μείλια, 45.
μέταλλον, 202, 234, 315.
μετοίκιον, 165, 184, 185, 187.
μήνυσις, 171, 182.
μητρόξενος, 61, 64 n. 1.
μίσθωσις, οἴκου, 105, 117 n. 1, 257 n. 1, 293.
 of mines, 203 n. 1.
μοιχεύειν, 2.
μοῖχος, 19, 32, 33, 36.

νοθεῖα, 61, 67, 233.
νόθοι, 13, 25, 70, 138 n. 3, 148, 233.

ξένος, marriage, 24, 26, 28, 29, 38 n. 1, 39, 61, 65 n. 2, 195 n. 1.
 wills, 151, 153.
 fraud, 165.
 homicide, 170, 198.
 manumitted, 181.
 and metic, 188, 189.
 litigation, 191, 192, 195.
 land, 237.
 loans, 287 n. 2.

ὁ βουλόμενος, adultery, 33, 35.
 abortion, 72.
 γονέων κακώσεως, 77.
 ἀργία, παρανοία, 80.
 ἐπιτροπή, 102 n. 2.
 φάσις, 115.
 dowry for θῆσσα, 136.
 ὕβρις, 168 n. 1.
 ἀπαγωγή, 178.
 metic, 195.
οἶκος (household), preservation, 1, 36 n. 2, 38, 46 n. 1, 48, 83, 86, 88, 91 n. 2, n. 3, 93, 131, 134 n. 3, 136 n. 2, 147 n. 1.
 husband's, 15, 39 n. 2, 42, 45, 57, 310.
 unit of city, 63, 66, 68.
 ἀποκήρυξις, 77 n. 1.
 and κλῆρος, 92, 124 n. 1.
 metic, 196.
οἶκος (estate), 105, 116, 294.
ὁμολογία, 51, 59.
οὐσία, meaning, 201.
 ἀνέμητος, 239.
 φανερά, ἀφανής, 160 n. 1, 240 n. 2, 265.

παιδοποιεῖν, 2 n. 4, 17.
παλλακή, 2, 13, 33 n. 1, 46 n. 3, 61, 164 n. 2.
παραγραφή, 97 n. 1, 120 n. 6, 127, 195, 210.

παρακαταβολή, 158, 159, 161.
παρανοία, 80.
παράστασις, 118.
παράφερνα, 45, 112 n. 3.
πάρεδροι, of archon, 154 n. 5.
πατρῷα, 125, 126 n. 3, 151 n. 4, 233.
ποίησις, adoption, 84.
πρᾶξις, *see* execution.
πρᾶσις, sale, 202, 204.
 ἐπὶ λύσει, 213 n. 1, 229 n. 1, 254, 256, 308, 314, 316.
πρατήρ, 208, 210, 216 n. 1, 266 n. 2, 275, 277.
πρεσβεῖα, 131 n. 4, 152.
προαγωγεία, 14 n. 3, 37.
προθεσμία, *see* prescription.
προίξ, *see* dowry.
πρόξενος, 189, 192 n. 1, 193, 194 n. 2, 237.
πρόσκλησις, 160, 214, 216, 226.
προστάτης, 165, 184, 185, 189.
πρυτανεῖον, court fee, 116, 118.

σῖτος (maintenance), 8, 104, 113 n. 2.
συγγενής, 93 n. 2, 143, 146 n. 3.
συκοφάντης, 152 n. 5.
συλᾶν, 245 n. 4.
συμβόλαιον, 51 n. 2, 150 n. 4, 303.
συνοικεῖν, 2, 26 n. 2, 28, 36 n. 1, 40 n. 2, 41, 135 n. 2, 165.

τίθημι, mortgage, *see* ὑποθήκη.
τίμημα, manumission, 179.

ὕβρις, to slaves, 168, 172.
 See also γραφὴ ὕβρεως.
ὑπερήμερος, 282, 288.
ὑπεροχή, 276 n. 2, 278, 284.
ὑπεύθυνος, disabilities, 87, 88, 153.
ὑποθήκη, bottomry, 208.
 mortgage, 254, 255 n. 4, 316.
ὑποκεῖσθαι, mortgage, 255.
ὑποτίθημι, mortgage; *see* ὑποθήκη.

φθορὰ ἐλευθέρου, 37.
φιάλαι ἐξελευθερικαί, 183.
φωρᾶν, 207.

χωρὶς οἰκοῦντες, 167, 188 n. 1.

ὠνή, 203 n. 1, 204, 210, 256, 272, 275.

abortion, 72.
adoption, and marriage, 23.
 legitimation by, 69.
 foundlings, 71.
 succession, 129, 130, 134, 157, 158.
 wills, 153, 155.
adultery, homicide law, 14, 32.
 γραφὴ μοιχείας, 34.
 woman's penalty, 36, 39.
Agariste, marriage, 5.
Aigina, marriage law, 21.
Alkibiades, divorce, 40, 43.
 dowry, 50 n. 1.
 ἀποκήρυξις, 76.
 ward, 104, 105.
Amorgos, women's guardians, 114 n. 3.
 security law, 263 n. 2.
Antiphon, ἀτιμία, 89.
Apaturia, 89.
Aphobos, litigation, 7, 58, 261, 280, 284.
 marriage, 41.
Apollodoros, son of Pasion, inheritance, 124 n. 4, 131 n. 4, 154 n. 3, 240.
arbitrator, δίκη ἐπιτροπῆς, 120.
 ἰσοτελής as, 189 n. 1.
 general, 194 n. 2, 250.
Archeptolemos, ἀτιμία, 89.
archon, ἐπιδικασία, 10, 18, 115, 122 n. 1.
 ἐγγύη, 12.
 ἐπίκληρος, 20, 136.
 widows and orphans, 38, 39 n. 2, 102, 106, 107, 111 n. 2, 116 n. 4, 117, 154 n. 5, 193, 293.
 divorce, 40–44.
 preservation of οἶκοι, 48, 83, 92, 257 n. 1.
 γρ. γονέων κακώσεως, 77.
 γρ. παρανοίας, 80.
 adoption, 95.
 δίκη ἐπιτροπῆς, 120.
 bona vacantia, 147.
 κλῆρος, 159.
 property, 193, 209 n. 1.
Areopagos, 198.
Aristophon, citizen law, 26.
Aristotle, will, 151 n. 2, 183.

basileus, wife of, 38 n. 2.
 court of, 197.
bastards, *see* νόθοι.
bona vacantia, 92, 147.
boule, enrolment of citizens, 74.

capture, 165.
Chaleion, seizure in, 245 n. 4.
Chalkis, ἐπιγαμία with, 29.
chattels, slaves as, 163, 176, 178.
 in dowry, 46 n. 3.
 hire, 175.
 sale, 308.
citizenship, qualification, 75, 89 n. 1.
 guardianship, 99.
 manumission, 164 n. 2, 181.
 metic status, 188.
 See also Perikles.
contract, minors' incapacity, 73, 81.
 women's incapacity, 73.
 adoption as, 89, 94.
 of slave, 174.
 sale, 245.
 prescription, 247.
Corinth, law of sale, 114 n. 1.
 manumission, 182.
corn, import, 116 n. 1.
creditors, multiple, 289, 301.

debt, succession to, 124.
 of slaves, 173 n. 2.
 as ἀφανὴς οὐσία, 231 n. 1.
delict, slaves, 167, 173.
 public slaves, 178.
 metics, 195.
 procedural, 209, 212, 218.
Delphi, law of sale, 211 n. 2.
Delphinion, 198.
demes, intermarriage, 29.
 enrolment, 74, 79, 90.
 owners, 235, 242 n. 2.
 ἔγκτησις, 238.
 loan, lease, 303 n. 1.
Demophon, guardian of Demosthenes II, *q.v.*
Demosthenes I (orator's father), wife, *see* Kleoboule.
 μίσθωσις οἴκου, 105 n. 5.
 will, 110, 151.
Demosthenes II (orator), sister's ἐγγύη, 21, 110.
 her guardians, 8.
 her dowry, 50, 151.
 his guardians, 8, 99, 104–6.
 litigation with, 119, 121 n. 1, 128, 261, 280, 284, 292.
 mother, *see* Kleoboule.
deposit, 208, 231 n. 1, 232 n. 3, 245.
dikastery, ἐπιδικασία, 18.
 in ἀπαγωγή, 78.
 γραφὴ παρανοίας, 81.
 appeals from phratry, 90.
 wills, 90.
 adoptions, 92.
 appointment of guardians, 102.
 μίσθωσις οἴκου, 105 n. 5.
 inheritance cases, 159 n. 5.
 general, 194 n. 2.
divorce, of heiress, 11.
 general, 38, 285.
dominium, 201.
dowry, and ἐγγύη, 8.
 quasi- and παλλακή, 14.
 in ἀφαίρεσις, 31.
 return, 41, 256, 259, 279, 285.
 adoption, 87 n. 4.
 ownership, 112.
 right to, 132.
 See also interest.
Drakon, 13, 33, 36, 64 n. 1, 79.

eisagogeis, court of, 50.
Eleven, ἀπαγωγή, 78, 207.
embryo, rights, 72.
endogamy, 21.
entry, 214, 226; *see also* ἐμβατεύειν.
Ephesos, dowry law, 55.
Eretria, ἐπιγαμία with, 29.
Eumenides, altar as asylum, 172, 180.
Euripides, marriage, 16.
execution, 53, 218, 228 n. 3, 253, 254 n. 1, 260, 284, 289, 312, 313.
exposure, 71.

foreigner, *see* ξένος.
Forty, δίκη βιαίων, 34.
 δίκη ἐπιτροπῆς, 120.
 general, 194.
foundling, 71, 236 n. 3.
freedman, succession, 148.
 will, 151, 153.
 δίκη ἀποστασίου, 165.
 homicide of, 197.

gift, to women, 113.
 of slave, 176.
 acquisition by, 245.
 publicity, 305, 308.
 See also ἀνακαλυπτήρια.
Gortyn, law of inheritance, 53 n. 2.
 heiress, 309.

guardian, marriage, 24.
See also κύριος.

heiress, *see* ἐπίκληρος.
heres necessarius, 86, 95 n. 3, 125.
Hipparete, divorced, 40, 43.
dowry, 50 n. 1.
Hipponikos, divorce, 40.
hire, slaves and, 175, 176.
Homer, marriage in, 3, 5, 13, 24, 31 n. 1, 45, 46 n. 1.
adoption in, 82.
homicide, justifiable, 14, 33.
Drakon's law, 64 n. 1.
of slave, 169, 171.
by slave, 173.
metics, 196.
Hyperides, ἀποκήρυξις of son, 76.
hypothec, legal on guardian's property, 121.

incest, 22 n. 3.
interest, dowry, 47, 55, 57.
μίσθωσις οἴκου, 106, 116 n. 4.
πρᾶσις ἐπὶ λύσει, 259 n. 1, 266, 268, 275.
pledge, 260, 261, 280.
default, 282.
Isaios, credibility, 122 n. 1, 309.
ius vitae ac necis, 74.

Jokasta, incestuous marriage, 22 n. 3.

Kallias, divorce, 44.
paternity of son, 69.
Keos, export law, 182.
Kerukes, enrolment among, 69.
Kimon, 22, 25, 62.
Kleisthenes (of Sikyon), 5, 18, 24.
Kleoboule, κύριος, 8, 30 n. 1, 54.
ἐγγύη, 6, 21, 24 n. 1, 110.
dowry, 8, 54, 58, 151.
father's debts, 128 n. 3.
See also Demosthenes I *and* II.
Konon, will, 151.
Kynosarges, gymnasium for νόθοι, 65.
Kyzikos, law of sale, 291.

land, inalienable, 259 n. 2.
Laureion, mines, 203, 234, 315.
lease, to slaves, 176.
legitimacy, 12, 13, 15, 27, 42, 63, 71.
loan, ward's property, 107.
by woman, 114.
of slave, 176.
bottomry, 208, 210, 255 n. 4, 258, 272, 286, 289, 303, 316.
security, 229 n. 1, 258.
fictional, 232 n. 3.
Lykon, will, 151 n. 2, 183.
Lysias, speech *against Hippotherses*, 191.
real property, 237 n. 3.

majority, age of, males, 18, 59, 74, 99, 113.
females, 109 n. 1, 138.
males, precede in succession, 147.
manumission, 178, 182, 186.
marriage, between slaves, 177.
of freedmen, 184.
of metics, 199.
Megakles, marriage, 18, 24.
metic, marriage, 24, 29, 38 n. 1.
succession, 148.
wills, 151, 153.
and προστάτης, 165.
homicide, 170.
manumitted, 181.
land, 237.
Miletos, law of sale, 211 n. 2.
Miltiades, marriage, 24.
mines, *see* μέταλλον.
minors, disabilities, 73, 81, 95, 108, 151, 177 n. 4, 236, 248.
Mykonos, dowry register, 46 n. 3.
mysteries, slaves at, 166.

Neaira, manumission, 182.
Nikomenes, citizen decree, 26.
noxal surrender, 174.

Oianthea, seizure in, 245 n. 4.
Oidipous, incestuous marriage, 22 n. 3.
Onetor, sister marries Aphobos, 41, 43, 285.
Oreos, hypothec in, 263.
orphans, 39, 196, 247; *see also* guardian.
ownership, 52.

Palladion, 169, 197.
Pasion, wife's ἐγγύη, 21, 110.
will, 21, 46 n. 3, 47, 110, 112, 152.
appoints guardian, 99 n. 4.

estate divided, 131 n. 4, 240.
manumitted, 182.
deposit, 208.
paternity, 44, 63, 69, 74, 77, 79.
patria potestas, 70.
Peisistratos, 203 n. 2, 315.
Perikles, wife, 21, 40.
citizen law, 25, 61, 64 n. 1, 68, 88 n. 1.
guardian of Alkibiades, 104 n. 5.
guardian of Kleinias, 105.
Phaselis, defendant from, 126 n. 2.
Phormion, marriage, 21, 24 n. 1, 110.
appointed guardian, 99.
manumitted, 182.
real property, 237 n. 2, 269.
phratry, 7, 64, 69, 79, 81 n. 2, 83 n. 4, 89, 91, 242 n. 2.
Plataia, citizenship, 29.
Plato, will, 183.
pledge, of slaves, 176; *see also* ἐνέχυρον.
polemarch, 148, 151, 179, 184, 189 n. 1, 192 n. 1, 193, 273 n. 1.
poletai, 54, 203 n. 1, 244, 270, 290 n. 3.
prescription, marriage, 11.
δίκη ἐπιτροπῆς, 120 n. 6, 127.
inheritance cases, 161, 220, 233.
sale, 213.
general, 246.
primogeniture, 131.
prostitutes, 37, 182.
publicity, marriage, 10, 11.
dowry, 50.
inheritance cases, 159.
sale of slaves, 176, 291.
manumission, 183.
hypothec, 290.

ransom, 39, 165, 183.
rape, 19, 34, 36.

sale, slaves and, 175, 176, 183.
credit, 232 n. 3.
acquisition, 245.
security, 256, 291.
state, 293.
publicity, 305.
seal, of will, 154.
seduction, 19, 34, 36.
Skambonidai, law, 187 n. 2.
slavery, παλλακή and, 14.
marriage, 24.
as penalty, 26.
exposure and, 71.
homicide, 198.
sale, 211, 308.
and industry, 229.
and ownership, 236.
See also under manumission.
Sokrates, marriage, 16.
Solon, guardians' marriage, 24, 105 n. 2.
adultery, 34.
slavery for debt, 39, 73, 164.
dowry, 46.
νόθοι, 61, 65, 66.
succession, 62, 123 n. 1.
teaching son trade, 78.
idleness, 79.
testament, 82, 88 n. 4, 149.
slaves' delicts, 173 n. 2.
land, 237.
ownership, 245.
easements, 249.
ὅροι, 257.
Sophokles, γραφὴ παρανοίας, 81.
Sopolis, liabilities, 128 n. 3.
Sparta, marriage law, 19, 22 n. 3, 23.
land law, 233 n. 1.
Straton, will, 151 n. 2, 183.
surety, adultery, 33.
manumission, 179, 221.
for metic, 193.
in metics' suits, 196.
in litigation, 217, 273 n. 1.
prescription, 247.
for loan, 272.

Tenos, dowry register, 50, 114 n. 3.
joint ownership, 243.
land register, 307 n. 1.
Themistokles, daughter's marriage, 22 n. 3.
not νόθος, 25, 62, 65 n. 2.
ἀποκήρυξις of, 76.
Theophrastos, will, 151 n. 2, 154 n. 3, 183.
Therippides, guardian of Demosthenes, 8, 252.
Theseion, asylum, 172, 180.
thesmothetai, court of, 33, 34 n. 1, 195 n. 1.
Timotheos, 26.
torture, evidence under, 170.
treasure trove, 245.

usucapion, 246.
usufruct, 252.

will, appoints *κύριος*, 20, 99, 105.
  ἐγγύη by, 30, 110.
  dotal *ἀποτίμημα*, 51.
  capacity (general), 75, 82, 86, 123, 131, 139, 202.
  capacity (minors), 81.
  adopts, 90, 94, 96, 158.
  μίσθωσις οἴκου, 116.
  capacity (freedman), 149, 186.
  manumits, 183.
  document, 208.
  hypothec, 298 n. 1.
witnesses, marriage, 18.
  dowry, 49, 50.
  wills, 153.
  slaves as, 170, 176, 182.
women, disabilities, 19, 21, 32, 73 n. 3, 108, 112, 114, 151, 177 n. 4, 236.